501
MUST-VISIT ISLANDS

501
MUST-VISIT ISLANDS

Bounty
BOOKS

Publisher: Polly Manguel

Project Editor: Emma Beare

Publishing Assistant: Sarah Marling

Designer: Ron Callow/Design 23

Picture Researchers: Janet Johnson and Mel Watson

Production Manager: Neil Randles

Production Assistant: Gemma Seddon

First published in Great Britain in 2008 by
Bounty Books, a division of Octopus Publishing Group Limited
Reprinted three times

This paperback edition published in 2014 by Bounty Books,
a division of Octopus Publishing Group Limited
Endeavour House, 189 Shaftesbury Avenue, London WC2H 8JY
www.octopusbooks.co.uk

An Hachette UK Company
www.hachette.co.uk

Copyright © 2008, 2014 Octopus Publishing Group Limited

A CIP catalogue record is available from the British Library

ISBN: 978-0-753727-00-3

Printed and bound in China

Please note: We now know that political situations arise very quickly and a country that was quite safe a short time ago can suddenly become a 'no-go' area. Please check with the relevant authorities before booking tickets and travelling if you think there could be a problem.

The seasons given in this book relate to the relevant hemisphere. Be sure to check that you visit at the correct time.

Contents

Introduction

There is a magical quality about the word 'island' that sends an endorphin rush to the head and the heart. It can conjure up visions of a tiny speck of land in the midst of turquoise seas, complete with white sand and coconut palms, or perhaps of a larger island swathed in dark green forest, with neat, wooden houses and clear water washing over granite boulders. It's wonderful that there are so many islands all over this planet of ours, which is made up of 70 per cent water, that there must be one that suits you perfectly. One dictionary definition of an island is 'a mass of land that is surrounded by water and is smaller than a continent'. Some islands, like Madagascar or Borneo, are huge landmasses, home to indigenous peoples and unique flora and fauna, while others are just dots in the ocean.

Perhaps living on an island makes people feel secure – surrounded and protected by the sea as they are. Islanders tend to be proud of their homeland, and somewhat insular in nature; for example, there are people on the Isle of Wight who have never felt the need to visit mainland Britain (also an island of course), just a short boat ride away. Most people in Corfu have never set foot upon Albanian soil, despite being so close to it geographically. There are Italians in Sicily and Sardinia who have never been to the mainland of their own country. Traditionally, islanders often feel slightly superior to their nearest – and usually bigger – neighbour.

We are curious about islands and are drawn to visit them, whether they are situated in an ocean, a lake, or a river or even man-made, as in the case of Dubai's Palm Islands. For their part, islanders themselves wonder how others can bear to live in the middle of a landmass, far from the sea.

Unique cultures arise on islands, where everything – the religion, the arts, the interaction between the sexes, and even the language – may be different from the mainland. It is a real tribute to the ingenuity and variety of mankind. There are island peoples who have no desire whatever to meet foreigners or join the 21st century, and whose governments wisely leave them to get on with their lives. For example, in

2004 a group of Andaman islanders attacked a helicopter with bows and arrows when it flew over after the tsunami, to check whether or not there were survivors. On the other hand, the Dani, a tribe in the interior of New Guinea, live extremely traditionally but they accept the tourist dollar for allowing outsiders to see how they do it.

Today, some islands are becoming more politically important and find themselves at the centre of geo-political wrangles – not so much because of the land itself but because of the oil and gas that lie beneath the surrounding seas; the Antarctic islands and East Timor come instantly to mind. Often several major political heavyweights make attempts to grab these resources, and the islands' populations have to fight to keep a realistic share of the profits.

While some islands are dedicated to religion, others embrace Mammon: there are islands in the Caribbean that are such wealthy tax havens that they are almost sinking under the weight of their banks, with one per cent of the population living in luxury and the rest living on virtually nothing. The island of Manhattan is a showcase for the world's richest and most technologically advanced country, but New York City is home to some of America's most deprived and dysfunctional areas. Bali, a Hindu island with its own language, culture and local laws is located in the middle of the world's largest (in terms of population) Muslim country, Indonesia. There are islands in the world's frozen north whose inhabitants have proved incredibly ingenious at finding ways to live harmoniously with the elements despite their inhospitable nature. The world is a wonderful place, and its islands are diverse and extraordinary.

This book attempts to give you a flavour of 501 of the world's most interesting islands, but there are thousands more out there. Some are incredibly difficult to reach; others are just a short trip away from the mainland by boat or plane. Some are littered with remarkable historical ruins and echoes of ancient cultures; others are no more than sandy beaches and a few palm trees. Why not go mad and visit an island you have never been to – maybe one you had never even heard of before? If the world is your oyster, then you can surely find the island that is your pearl.

AMERICAS AND THE CARIBBEAN

The rocky coast near Cape Knud

Baffin Island

POPULATION:
11,000 (2005)
WHEN TO GO:
June to August
HOW TO GET THERE:
By air from Montreal, Ottawa or Yellowknife.
HIGHLIGHTS:
Kimmirut – famous for its aboriginal stone-carving industry.
Auyittuq National Park: a pristine wilderness within the Arctic Circle.
Pond Inlet: a stunning mix of mountains, icebergs and glaciers.
The Pangnirtung Pass – a spectacular 100 km (62 mi) hike around fjords.
YOU SHOULD KNOW:
In the summer the inhabitants of Iqaluit leave their homes to live in tents and visitors are invited too. There is no better way to plan a trip than to sit around a campfire, under the midnight sun and discuss it with the people who know the landscape best.

Baffin Island is in the eastern Canadian Arctic, lying between Greenland and the Canadian mainland. Covering 507,451 sq km (195,928 sq mi), it is the largest island in North America and the fifth largest in the world. It was named after the British explorer William Baffin but the overwhelmingly Inuit population know it as Qikiqtaaluk.

Made up of a dozen or so sparsely populated communities, Baffin lives up to its reputation for being unspoiled, untamed and undiscovered. With 60 per cent of the island lying above the Arctic Circle and summer temperatures struggling to reach even 5° C (41° F), this rugged ice-covered landscape is not for the fainthearted. However the rewards for any visitor are great, with unrivalled scenery and the chance to see the rich and diverse Arctic wildlife, including polar bears and whales in their natural environment.

Getting to Baffin Island is only feasible by air. The island has only one airport (Iqaluit) which deals with external flights and another six which handle internal transfers. Arriving at Iqaluit you will find a thriving First Nations community. This capital of the newly-formed state of Nunavut can provide all you need for a kayaking, canoeing or trekking holiday.

Most of the finest mountains are located on the Cumberland Peninsula, at the head of the South Pangnirtung Fjord. Much of the area is included within Auyuittuq National Park, and is accessible from Pangnirtung, a small coastal Inuit settlement. From here, access to the peaks is by boat, dog sled, float-plane or ski-plane, depending on ice and weather conditions.

The sheer vastness of the island is difficult to take in and any traveller should plan ahead, not be too ambitious and allow extra time for weather related delays, even in summer.

Quadra Island

At 35 km (22 mi) long and covering 310 sq km (120 sq mi), Quadra Island is the largest and most populous of the Discovery Islands, which lie between Vancouver Island and the mainland of British Columbia. A short ferry ride from Campbell River takes you through whale- and dolphin- rich waters to this island of ancient temperate rainforest.

Human activity on the island dates back over 2,000 years and is thriving. Salish and Kwagiulth First Nations communities still exist here today. A misguided search for the fabled Northwest Passage brought Spanish and British ships to these treacherous waters in the late 18th century and contact began. Today most of the descendants of the native bands live at Cape Mudge on the south of the island, where visitors can experience a flourishing artistic community. Quadra is also home to many well-known contemporary artists, writers, potters and other artisans, and a growing community of alternative health practitioners.

With its rich woodland, diverse topography, and plentiful wildlife, Quadra Island has become a huge draw for outdoor enthusiasts. There is an extensive system of lakes and rivers for kayaking and canoeing and many paths and trails for hiking and mountain biking. Guided bird watching and fishing charters run in the summer months, as do seaborne whale and bear watching trips. Its sheltered coves and inland lakes are home to an incredible variety of wildlife, including black-tailed deer, river otters, harbour seals, sea-lions, cormorants, snowy owls, the great blue heron and the rarely seen peregrine falcon.

Its relative remoteness at the top of the Strait of Georgia helps this island community retain an idyllic charm. Aboriginal and European people live side by side, and whilst tourism is growing it is not overwhelming.

POPULATION:
2,650 (2006)
WHEN TO GO:
All year round although the ferries can get crowded in the May to August period.
HOW TO GET THERE:
By ferry from Campbell River or Cortes Island.
HIGHLIGHTS:
The Kwagiulth Museum in the Village of Cape Mudge, which houses an unrivalled collection of old totem poles.
Any of the studios of the 120 or so artists who live on the island.
Nature watching and rambling.
YOU SHOULD KNOW:
Several operators offer whale and wildlife watching tours around the island. Recent research has shown the faster zodiac style boats to have an injurious effect on whale populations, so if you are booking a tour, a slow boat may seem less thrilling but you will be doing less damage to this fragile environment.

Totem poles in the village of Cape Mudge

Victoria Island

Victoria Island is part of the Canadian Arctic Archipelago that straddles the boundary between Nunavut and the Northwest Territories. Covering an area of 217,290 sq km (83,890 sq mi) it ranks as the ninth largest island in the world. Only just smaller than Britain and with a total population of little more than 2,000, it rates as one of the most sparsely populated regions on earth.

It is an island of peninsulas, craggy coastlines and innumerable inlets. Glaciers have carved the scenery into a series of moraines and glacial lakes, and though the landscape is relatively flat the Shaler Mountains in the north rise to 655 m (2,550 ft) above sea level. Though seemingly bleak, this habitat supports over two hundred species of plants and breeding populations of 50 species of bird and nine species of mammal.

This hostile environment supports only two communities of note. Located on the island's south east coast, Iqaluktuutiak (Cambridge Bay) serves as the administrative centre for Canada's Arctic region. Originally named after the Duke of Cambridge by fur trappers in 1839, the area was used by Copper Indians as a summer camp until the 1950s and given a more descriptive name, which means 'good place to fish', reflecting the local diet. Holman, situated on the island's west coast, is the best place to view the seasonal migration of caribou, musk ox and grizzly bear that use the year-round ice to move to and from the island.

This is a place where tourism feels like exploration and, whilst human activity has left some scars on the landscape, Victoria Island is still a near pristine wilderness. You will need the guidance of local experts to travel safely and to understand this magical Arctic landscape.

A snow laden church in the icy wilderness of Iqaluktuutiak (Cambridge Bay)

Manitoulin Island

The beautiful colours of the forest in autumn

Situated just off the Ontario coast in Lake Huron, Manitoulin Island, at 2,800 sq km (1,100 sq mi), is the largest freshwater island in the world. A tranquil place of small villages, gently rolling pasture, forest and lakes, its edges are fringed with long beaches and white cliffs.

The First Nations Ojibwa people, the island's original inhabitants, believed that when the Great Spirit, Gitchi Manitou, created the Earth he kept the best bits and made Manitoulin his home. In 1648 a group of French Jesuits became the first Europeans to settle on Manitoulin Island, which they named Isle de Ste. Marie. Unfortunately they brought with them new diseases that rapidly devastated the Ojibwa population. Marauding Iroquois bands then drove out those who remained, leaving the island uninhabited for over a hundred years. During the 19th century, the island's beauty attracted the attention of white settlers who, after first giving Manitoulin to other native bands, then revoked all treaties and claimed it for themselves. To this day the Ojibwa have refused to sign any treaty, and some 3,000 of them live on an 'unceded reserve' in the east of the island.

Today Manitoulin and the waters around it serve as Ontario's summer playground with boats of all kinds weaving in and out of its many bays and filling its large inland lakes. Hiking is popular and the island has a well signposted system of trails. Every August the Ojibwa Band holds one of Canada's biggest powwows (Wikwemikong or Wiky) a celebration of life through dance, storytelling and displays of arts and crafts.

POPULATION:
12,500 (2004)
WHEN TO GO:
May to October
HOW TO GET THERE:
by road-bridge from Highway 17 or by car ferry from Tobermory.
HIGHLIGHTS:
Ten Mile Point Lookout with its stunning views of Georgian Bay.
Little Current-Howland Museum – with 10,000-year-old artefacts.
Bridal Veil Falls – a popular place for a summertime swim.
Mississagi Lighthouse – now a museum celebrating the pioneer spirit.
YOU SHOULD KNOW:
Manitoulin's alkaline soil precludes the growth of North American staples like blueberries, but allows the growth of the island's trademark hawberries – celebrated in an annual festival each August and earning the islanders the epithet of Haweaters.

Sunset over St Joseph Island and Lake Huron

POPULATION:
1,960 (2005)
HOW TO GET THERE:
By road bridge via Highway 17 or by snowmobile when the river freezes in winter.
WHEN TO GO:
There is something for everyone all year round although many attractions are open only from May to October.
HIGHLIGHTS:
St Joseph Island Museum – a four building complex housing local artefacts.
Fort St Joseph – for an insight into early island life.
The view of the busy channel from Sailors Encampment.
The Artisans Gallery, Richards Landing – famous for its native craftwork.
YOU SHOULD KNOW:
The island's population swells to over 10,000 in summer so booking accommodation in advance is strongly recommended.

St Joseph Island

Many colourful stories, some legend, some historical fact, are told about St Joseph Island. It is the westernmost of the Manitoulin chain of islands, situated in the channel between Lakes Huron and Superior. It's 45 km (28 mi) long and 24 km (15 mi) wide and covers 365 sq km (141 sq mi). Originally named Anipich, the Ojibway word for 'place of the hardwood trees,' the island was given its present name by Jesuit missionaries to honour the patron saint of a new Indian church they erected. It is linked to the mainland by a toll-free bridge, opened in 1972.

St Joseph's location was of strategic importance to the British who fortified it as a bulwark against the Americans during the war of 1812. Fort St Joseph itself was abandoned when peace broke out, though it has now been restored as a National Historic Site.

Today St Joseph Island is noted for its peaceful beauty, its friendly residents and its recreational activities. It is a place of undisturbed bays, rocky inlets and the undulating hills, mixed forests, marshes and meadows that lend themselves to scenic drives, bike tours or leisurely walks. Most of the population live in the pretty villages of Richards Landing and Hilton Beach. The main industries are tourism, logging and agriculture.

Water sports are very popular here in summer and good fishing is to be found. In winter you can cross-country ski on 160 km (100 mi) of prepared trails. This is an island of festivals, from the winter Flurryfest and the Maple Syrup Festival in the spring, to Community Nights in the summer through to the Jocelyn Harvest Festival in the autumn.

Pelee Island

Pelee Island is a haven of green, encircled by the blue waters of Lake Erie. Sitting just above 42° North, it marks Canada's most southerly inhabited point (the uninhabited Middle Island, located just to the south, is the country's southernmost point). Measuring 14.5 km (9 mi) long and 5 km (3 mi) wide and located in the western half of the lake, it lies close to the Ohio boundary and on the same latitude as Northern California. Pelee's position gives it the best year-round climate in Eastern Canada.

Originally a marshland, little used by First Nations people, the island was leased by white settlers in the 19th century. Its mild climate lent Pelee to the growing of grapes, and the wine industry flourished until the Great War only to die out and then be revived again in the 1980s. The marshland was dredged in the late 19th century and tobacco was planted. Today the main crops are soybean and wheat.

Pelee Island is an important stopover for migrating birds and even non-twitchers will be impressed by the array of blue herons, cormorants, ducks and eagles on display. In 1984 the Lighthouse Point Nature Reserve was established, with trails that meander through wetland and marshes on to sandy beaches.

This is an ever-changing landscape where the coastline is easily eroded, dunes come and go, lagoons appear and new bays are formed. Its isolation makes for a gentle pace of life and the island only really springs to life during the pheasant-shooting season in autumn. It is a perfect place to walk, cycle or sail in a largely manufactured, but surprising unspoilt, nature reserve.

POPULATION:
260 (2003)
HOW TO GET THERE:
By ferry from Leamington, Ontario or from Sandusky, Ohio (USA)
WHEN TO GO:
All year round, but unless you are a pheasant shooter, it is best to avoid the autumn when the island becomes crowded and expensive.
HIGHLIGHTS:
Memorial Park, which features a giant aboriginal grinding stone.
The Pelee Island Lighthouse – built in 1833.
Birdwatching – particularly in the west of the island.
A winery tour at one of the island's vineyards.
YOU SHOULD KNOW:
Visible on a clear day, Hulda's Rock marks the spot where, according to legend, an Indian maiden jumped to her death after an ill-fated liaison with an Englishman.

An aerial view of Pelee Island

Ile d'Orléans

POPULATION:
6,860 (2006)
HOW TO GET THERE:
Across the Taschereau suspension bridge on Highway 440 from Quebec City
WHEN TO GO:
Popular all year round, but most facilities are only open from June to October.
HIGHLIGHTS:
The Maison Drouin – the oldest building on the island.
Chocolaterie de l'Ile d'Orléans – a treat for all those with a sweet tooth.
The Cidrerie Verger Bilodeau – take a guided tour and sample everything you can make with an apple.
The Île d'Orléans churches – a tour along the Chemin Royale, taking in the island's six churches.
YOU SHOULD KNOW:
During the height of winter the river freezes, allowing people to cross to and from the island on snowmobiles via an ice bridge.

Covering 193 sq km (75 sq mi), Ile d'Orléans plugs the narrowing St Lawrence River like a champagne cork, just 8 km (5 mi) east of Quebec City. Cut off from the mainland until a bridge was built in 1935, the island is a living museum of French Canadian life. This is a land of gentle terraces, rolling pasture, orchards, stone churches, quaint cottages and majestic manor houses, a place where food and wine are plentiful and café society is central.

The First Nations Algonquin people named the island Windingo, meaning 'bewitched corner,' until the French arrived in 1535 and gave it its present name, after the Duke of Orléans. The six villages of the island are connected by a perimeter road (Chemin Royale) and it is via this that most visitors explore the island and take in the wonderful mountain views across the St Lawrence.

Each village has its own church and its own atmosphere, ranging from Sainte-Pétronille, the preserve of wealthy Quebecois, to Saint-Francois, a more modest farming community where the river is widest and the views of the surrounding mountains most stunning. Sainte-Pierre boasts one of the oldest churches in Canada and is home to the island's most vibrant community. The island is home to over 600 listed buildings in all, and its close proximity to Quebec City makes it one of the most desirable places to live in Eastern Canada.

Whilst most people take their cars, the best way to absorb this wonderful island is to cycle the 67 km (42 mi) of the Chemin Royal. Any visitor to Quebec should take a day or two to sample what the island has to offer – a place where tradition is the watchword, where old farming methods combine well with fine French cuisine and the three hour lunch is king.

A traditional house overlooks a frozen St Lawrence River

Cape Breton Island

The Cabot Trail Scenic Highway

Nova Scotia's Cape Breton has an untamed beauty that makes for some of the most impressive scenery in North America. Covering 10,311 sq km (3,981 sq mi), the island is a wonderful mixture of rocky shores, rolling pasture, barren headlands, woodland, mountains and plateaux.

The Cape Breton Highlands, an extension of the Appalachian Mountain chain and a national park since 1936, dominate the north part of the island. The famous Cabot Trail Scenic Highway, one of the most spectacular scenic drives in Canada, winds through nearly 300 km (185 mi) of this ruggedly beautiful countryside.

Comprehension of the people of Cape Breton Island is not possible without some knowledge of its earliest settlers. Cape Bretoners today reflect the resolve of those pioneers – whether their roots are Mi'kmaq, Acadian, Scottish, Irish or Black Loyalist. The Island has shaped them just as they struggled to shape the island. Since then settlers have arrived from all over the world and have made their own distinct contributions.

The largest town, Sydney, still bears the scars of a failed industrial past but outside of the immediate area, the theme of the island is heritage mixed with outstanding natural beauty. Fortress Louisbourg faithfully recreates the French military might of the early 18th century, pioneer cottages line the north shore of the imposing Bras d'Or Lake and the island's most northerly point, Meat Cove offers spectacular, unspoilt ocean views.

Accommodation on Cape Breton is limited, so booking in advance is recommended, and as the public transport is poor, driving is your only real option to explore this wonderful land.

POPULATION:
150,000 (2004)

WHEN TO GO:
June to August is the best time but even then the weather is notoriously unpredictable. Though colder, September to early November offers a spectacular vista of flaming leaf colours.

HOW TO GET THERE:
By road-bridge from mainland Nova Scotia or by air to Sydney which has an international airport.

HIGHLIGHTS:
Hiking around Fortress Louisbourg.
Nature watching on Lake Ainslee.
Driving around the Cabot Trail Highway.
Fishing for salmon on the Margaree River.
Cheticamp – the largest Acadian community in Nova Scotia.
The Celtic Colours Festival in early October – a celebration of fiddle playing.

YOU SHOULD KNOW:
Much beloved by the inventor of the telephone, Alexander Graham Bell, Cape Breton was at the centre of a communications mix-up when an English couple made an online booking to go to Sydney, Australia only to find themselves flown to Sydney, Canada.

Roosevelt's cottage

Campobello and Grand Manan

Campobello and Grand Manan are the principal islands of the Fundy Archipelago, situated in the south-western corner of New Brunswick, in Passamaquoddy Bay.

Campobello, at 14 km (9 mi) long and about 5 km (3 mi) wide, is easy to see in a day. The north of the island bustles with second home owners and day trippers, while in the South the protected area of the Roosevelt Campobello International Park covers 1,135 hectares, (2,800 acres). Here you will find the famous Roosevelt Cottage, the elegant summer home of Franklin D. Roosevelt's family, along with wooded coves, mixed forests, marshes and tidal flats.

Grand Manan, 34 km (16 mi) long, with a maximum width of 18 km (11 mi), is a bird watchers' paradise, with summer nesting sites for a wide variety of sea birds. Its coastal scenery is stunning – towering cliffs up to 90 m (295 ft) high and potentially dangerous surrounding waters. Despite its three picturesque lighthouses, the island was the site of many shipwrecks during the years of sailing vessel and commercial steam traffic.

The Passamaquoddy Nation, the original inhabitants of Campobello, called it Ebaghuit, which literally means 'lying parallel with the land'. Waves of European explorers brought first French and then British rule. In 1866, a Fenian Brotherhood war party attempted to seize the island, but was dispersed by a US military force. This scare prompted New Brunswick to join with the other British North American Colonies, when the Dominion of Canada was formed. Grand Manan was also home to the Passamaquoddy Nation prior to its discovery by Europeans, who first settled on the island in the late 18th century with the arrival of Loyalist refugees from the American Revolutionary War.

The area's popularity can mean long delays for the car ferry in July and August and you are advised to book accommodation in advance in high summer.

POPULATION:
Campobello 1,195; Grand Manan 2,500 (2001)

HOW TO GET THERE:
Both islands can be reached by ferry from Blacks Harbour and Campobello is connected with Lubec in the US state of Maine by the Franklin Delano Roosevelt Bridge.

WHEN TO GO:
Bird watching in spring, summer and autumn; hiking and aquatic sports from mid-June to September.

HIGHLIGHTS:
On Campobello – the Dutch Colonial style, 34-room Roosevelt Cottage, packed with memorabilia – open to the public from late-May to mid-October.
Family-friendly gentle hikes in the Roosevelt Campobello International Park.
On Grand Manan – the thousands of puffins, gannets, guillemots, stormy petrels and kittiwakes which visit the island; best times to see them are during the spring and autumn migrations and the summer nesting season.
The Grand Manan Museum – housing the largest collections of shipwreck-recovered items in the Maritime provinces.

YOU SHOULD KNOW:
It was while on holiday with his family on Campobello in 1921 that Roosevelt contracted the polio that left him permanently paralysed from the waist down.

Newfoundland

With lofty peaks, immense landscapes and nearly 10,000 km (6,250 mi) of rocky coastline, Newfoundland is the sixteenth largest island in the world, covering 109,000 sq km (41,700 sq mi). It is an entrancing land where giant icebergs drift along the coast, whales swim in huge bays and large herds of moose graze on flat open marshes.

The rich fishing grounds off the coast first attracted the Vikings and then the British, in the form of Henry VII's agent John Cabot, in whose name the daunting Cabot Tower was built to mark the 400th anniversary of his landing in 1497. The island has a brutal history, with constant disputes largely between the British and the French. In 1713 the French gave up any claims to the island and it was run as a lawless outpost of the British Empire, which by 1829 lead to the extinction of the indiginous Beothuk people.

Newfoundland is home to two national parks. Gros Morne National Park, located on the west coast, was named a UNESCO World Heritage Site in 1987 due to its complex geology and remarkable scenery. It is the largest national park in Antlantic Canada at 1,805 sq km (697 sq mi). Terra Nova on the island's east side, preserves the rugged geography of the Bonavista Bay region and allows visitors to explore the historic interplay of land, sea and man.

The island also offers a major hiking trail running along the eastern edge of the Avalon Peninsula. The East Coast Trail extends for 220 km (137 mi), beginning near Fort Amhurst in St John's and ending in Cappahayden, with an additional 320 km (200 mi) of trail under construction. The trail winds along the coast, taking hikers through many small fishing villages and along miles of rocky, uninhabited coastline.

POPULATION:
475,000 (2004)
WHEN TO GO:
All year round but it's less cold from May to September
HOW TO GET THERE:
By air to St John's, Newfoundland's capital.
HIGHLIGHTS:
Pippy Park in the city of St John's which features an underwater lookout.
Cape Spear Lighthouse – the most easterly point in North America.
The colourful village of Trinity with a museum housing over 2,000 artefacts.
Viewing icebergs close up on a boat trip from Notre Dame Bay.
L'Anse aux Meadows National Historic Site – including a reconstruction of an early Viking settlement.
YOU SHOULD KNOW:
For an authentic depiction of life on Newfoundland read Annie Proulx's *The Shipping News,* later made into a film starring Kevin Spacey.

The village of Trinity

Fogo Island

Fogo Island, the largest of Newfoundland's offshore islands, is separated from the mainland by Hamilton Sound. The island is about 25 km long and 14 km wide and has a total area of 235 sq km (90 sq mi). Originally used by the First Nations Beothuks as a summer campground, it was taken over by Europeans in the early 16th century and given the name Fogo from the Portuguese word Fuego for fire, after the Beothuks' campfires.

Until the late 18th century Fogo Island was on an area off the coast called the 'French Shore'. However the British and the Irish came to settle here, thus ignoring various treaty obligations, and by the end of the century it had become a thriving hub for the British North Atlantic fleet. Evidence of this can be found today in the names, accents and culture of the local population. Fogo's location has long made the island a centre for transatlantic communications, with Marconi setting up a wireless station in the early 20th century.

This is an island where everything points to the sea. Red and white buildings line its craggy shoreline, while behind them muddy green pasture tells the story of the island's harsh environment, where the growing season lasts only a few months of the year. Fogo also boasts an extensive system of boardwalk trails making its North Atlantic wilderness accessible to all.

In the 1960s the islanders turned down the chance to be resettled on mainland Canada and they chose instead to preserve their unique cultural identity. Fishing still plays a central role in the islanders' day-to-day lives, but it is tourism that is increasing in importance to the area. There are now many operators offering guided nature tours to watch whales and the island's rich and varied bird life.

*One of Fogo's traditional
white buildings*

Prince Edward Island

A colourful harbour on the North Shore

The crescent-shaped Prince Edward Island (PEI) is the smallest Canadian province. Its area of 5,520 sq km (2,184 sq mi) makes it even smaller than some of Canada's National Parks, but also allows it to be explored in less than a week. The island lies in the Gulf of St Lawrence, separated from the northern coasts of the Maritime Provinces of New Brunswick and Nova Scotia by the narrow Northumberland Strait.

The Mi'kmaq people, original inhabitants of PEI called the island Abegweit, meaning 'Land Cradled on the Waves'; they believed that it was formed by the Great Spirit throwing some red clay into the sea. In 1534 the French explorer Jacques Cartier laid claim to the island but by the end of the eighteenth century the British were in control. They expelled the Acadians and named the island after Queen Victoria's father, Prince Edward. The islanders maintained a sense of independence until the Charlottetown Conference of 1864 when Canada was born, earning PEI the epithet 'Cradle of the Confederation'.

PEI is a well-known haven of peace and tranquillity for those seeking a place to get away from it all. The islanders are warm and welcoming. The nature here seems to possess a serene quality, with expansive undulating hills where rich green and ruddy farmland offer up a pleasant patchwork of colour. Dotting this gentle landscape are little hamlets, where the tempo has remained unchanged by the rigours of modern life. Like their Mi'kmaq predecessors, many of today's islanders draw their livelihood from agriculture and fishing.

This is a land of plenty with bountiful harvests from land and sea, famous for its oysters, mussels and above all lobsters. It boasts beautiful lighthouses, tree-lined streets and 19th century terraces, as well as coves, parks, rocky headlands and long sandy beaches.

POPULATION:
137,000 (2006)

WHEN TO GO:
Most attractions open from Victoria Day (in May) to Thanksgiving (early October). The island is less crowded and more spectacular in the autumn months.

HOW TO GET THERE:
Fly to Charlottetown, ferry to Wood Islands from Nova Scotia or across the Confederation Bridge.

HIGHLIGHTS:
The July Lobster Carnival in Summerside.
Green Gables House near Cavendish – the setting for the famous book.
Hiking up and down the craggy coastline in Brundenell River Provincial Park.
The view from Panmure Island Lighthouse (open May to September).
Orwell Corners Historic Village – a recreation of 19th century island life.
The visitor centre at the PEI National Park – a must for those interested in marine wildlife.

YOU SHOULD KNOW:
For that unique holiday experience check out the perennial musical adaptation of *Anne of Green Gables* during the Charlottetown Festival (June to October).

The Gulf Islands

POPULATION:
16,500 (2004)
WHEN TO GO:
All year round, although the islands
are often crowded in summer
HOW TO GET THERE:
Ferry from Vancouver (Twawwassen)
or Victoria (Swartz Bay). Float plane
from downtown Seattle
or Vancouver.
HIGHLIGHTS:
The Market in the Park (Ganges, Salt
Spring) held on Saturdays (April to
October) 'The Mother of all Markets'
Montague Harbour Park (Galiano) – a
wonderful preserve of beach
and forest.

The Gulf Islands are a group of a hundred or so mountainous islands scattered across the Strait of Georgia between Vancouver Island and the mainland of southern British Columbia. In geological terms they are part of a larger archipelago that includes the San Juan Islands just to the south in Washington State (USA). The ferry journey from Vancouver to Vancouver Island winds between this myriad of islands that boast the best climate in Canada. Of the whole group only six support any population of note.

By far the easiest to get to and therefore the most popular and populous is Saltspring Island – Canada's arts and crafts island. Its mellow pace, beautiful landscapes and isolation have drawn artists and crafts people from all over the world. It has recently become the haunt of several Hollywood film stars.

Bucolic Mayne Island is a medley of rock bays, forested hills and pasture. Once the agricultural hub of the area, it retains the rural lived-in charm of yesteryear.

Saturna Island is tucked away at the southern end of the island chain. Rural, sparsely populated and difficult to reach, it is easily the least spoilt of the group.

The Pender Islands, also known as the 'Friendly Islands' and the 'Islands of Hidden Coves', have over 20 public ocean access spots to visit along its beaches and coves. Pristine wilderness makes the Penders a hotbed for outdoor activities. Galiano Island has always enjoyed a reputation for being the most welcoming to visitors. With little land suitable for farming, the early settlers here opened their homes to tourists as a way of earning a living.

As a group the Gulf Islands are still underdeveloped and many of the best lodges and restaurants are hidden away down forest tracks. There is little in the way of organized activities – just magnificent scenery to enjoy.

The view from the grounds of Georgina Point Lighthouse (Mayne). The Brown Ridge Nature Trail (Saturna) – with great views of Washington State's Mt Baker – officially the snowiest mountain in the world.
Cycling around the unspoilt beauty of South Pender.

YOU SHOULD KNOW:
You should plan and book in advance. The BC ferry schedule can be confusing and it is not always possible to get from one island to the next. Families should also note that many resorts do not cater for children.

Boats sailing around Tumbo and Cabbage Islands

The Thousand Islands

The Thousand Islands are a network of in fact nearly 1,800 islands that span the American-Canadian border in the Saint Lawrence River. Some, like Wolfe Island, the largest at 124 sq km (48 sq mi), have significant year-round populations, while others are merely rocky outcrops visited by migrating birds. The whole area is enormously popular as a holiday destination, particularly for sailing – so much so that it's sometimes called the 'fresh water boating capital of the world'.

Around twenty of these islands form the Saint Lawrence Islands National Park, the smallest of Canada's national parks. The Thousand Islands Frontenac Arch region was designated a World Biosphere Reserve by UNESCO in 2002. The US islands include numerous New York State parks, most notably Robert Moses State Park.

The area is frequently traversed by large freighters on their way into and out of the Great Lakes shipping lanes, but is so dotted with barely concealed rocks that local navigators are hired to help the vessels travel through the hazardous waterway. Because of this it is unwise to travel the waters at night, except in the main channels and with good charts. It's a popular place for experienced divers as the waters are mostly so clear and the sea bed is littered with many shipwrecks for them to explore.

The area has long been popular with wealthy up state New Yorkers and many of the islands are privately owned. A plethora of 'No Landing' signs reminds potential visitors that they can look but not touch, so perhaps the best way to enjoy the area is from a boat.

Boldt Castle on Heart Island

Queen Charlotte Islands

Ancient Haida totems in South Moresby National Park

In the Pacific Ocean west of Prince Rupert in British Columbia, the Queen Charlotte Islands are the peaks of a submerged mountain chain. The seven largest islands of the 1,884 islands and islets in the archipelago are Langara, Graham, Moresby, Louise, Lyell, Burnaby and Kunghit. Graham Island in the north and Moresby Island in the south make up most of the landmass of the archipelago. Just 2 km (1.2 mi) into the sea, the continental shelf falls away dramatically to the immense depths of the ocean, and this is Canada's most active earthquake area.

The islands are known as Haida Gwaii (islands of the people), or Xhaaidlagha Gwaayaai (islands at the boundary of the world) to the Haida people who have lived here for at least 7,000 years. The first European contact was in 1774 when Juan Perez discovered what is perhaps one of the most beautiful landscapes in the world. Fur traders followed to exploit the extraordinarily rich fauna here, creating a major impact on the Haida. In 1787, the islands were named by the British in honour of Queen Charlotte, the wife of King George III.

Despite European interference, the islands have kept their natural tranquillity and have a rich cultural history. The Haida earn their living through mining, logging and commercial fishing, and nowadays tourism is also a good source of income. Most Haida communities can be found on Graham Island. At Skidegate there is a cultural centre with Haida artefacts and local art, at Tlell there is an artistic collective, and Old Masset is home to traditional native carvers.

Naikoon Provincial Park, in the north-east of Graham Island, covers a range of diverse environments including sandy beaches and dunes, sphagnum bogs, ancient forests and rivers. The landscape was formed during the last ice age out of the deposits left by retreating glaciers. The main attraction here are the endless stretches of broad sandy beaches. On the North Beach is Tow Hill, a 100 m outcrop of basalt columns which make a dramatic landmark. Also worth exploring is Rose Spit, an ecological reserve where you can spot migrating birds travelling over the Pacific.

The Gwaii Haanas National Park Reserve and Haida Heritage Site is in the south of the archipelago. This wilderness area of 138 islands stretching 90 km from north to south is only accessible by boat or chartered aircraft. Mountains rise steeply to the west, and the coastline is dotted with picturesque inlets, bays and islands. Rainforest and upland bog, salmon streams, estuaries and kelp beds sustain a rich diversity of life here. This is a great place to observe whales, bald eagles, nesting seabirds, black bears, river otters and sea lions.

POPULATION:
4,935 (2001)
WHEN TO GO:
April to November.
HOW TO GET THERE:
Fly from Vancouver or Prince Rupert to Sandspit, or take a ferry from Prince Rupert.
HIGHLIGHTS:
Naikoon Provincial Park – explore the gorgeous sandy beaches and dunes.
Gwaii Haanas National Park Reserve and Haida Heritage Site – this remote area is blessed with immense natural beauty. Discover the close relationship between the Haida and their natural environment.
Langara Island – in the north-west of the archipelago, this rugged island has ancient rainforests, an impressive seabird colony and an interesting lighthouse.
Port Clements – a traditional logging and fishing village where you can see the giant trees of the temperate rainforest.
Rennell Sound, bordered by the snow-capped Queen Charlotte Mountains – this is a great place for kayaking, hiking and fishing.
Louise Island – see one of the largest displays of ancient totem poles in the archipelago.
YOU SHOULD KNOW:
This is a remote area with little development, so do not expect busy resort hotels with all the tourist comforts.

St-Pierre et Miquelon

The tiny archipelago of Saint-Pierre et Miquelon sits 25 km (16 mi) off the coast of Newfoundland in the north west Atlantic Ocean, at the opening of the Gulf of St Lawrence. However it owes more to France some 6,400 km (4,000 mi) away than it does to Canada or even to Quebec. French is spoken almost exclusively, the Euro is its currency and the morning air is filled with the smell of freshly baked baguettes.

When France finally surrendered her North American colonies, she was allowed to keep these islands and they quickly became a base for French Atlantic fishing. Fiercely loyal to their motherland in spite of some shoddy treatment, particularly from De Gaulle who sent in the navy to break a dockers' strike, the islanders saw heavy losses in both World Wars.

The islands are bare and rocky, with only a thin layer of peat to alleviate the harsh landscape. The coasts are generally steep, and there is only one good harbour – in the port of St-Pierre, where over 80 per cent of the islanders live. Adding to its importance, the town of St-Pierre is also the administrative centre and the site of the principal airport. The harbour, which originally could accommodate only small vessels, has been improved with artificial breakwaters.

Once there were three main islands: St-Pierre, Miquelon and Langlade, but since the 18th century, Miquelon and Langlade have been permanently joined by a giant sand bar. Miquelon and St-Pierre are separated by a 6-km (4-mi) long strait, whose fierce currents inspired fishermen to name it the 'Mouth of Hell'.

Today the islanders rely on fishing and, increasingly, on tourism for their income. In addition, the islands receive generous grants from the French government, determined to maintain France's last remnant of its once extensive empire in North America.

The ghost village of Ile aux Marins

POPULATION:
6,400 (2005)
HOW TO GET THERE:
By air from Sydney, Nova Scotia or St John's. By ferry from Fortune.
WHEN TO GO:
The summer (June to August) is best but even then the weather can be unpredictable, with heavy fogs and cool temperatures.
HIGHLIGHTS:
A boat trip to the ghost village of Ile aux Marins, abandoned in the 1960s.
Dune of Langdale – a sweeping 10 km (6 mi) long sandbar.
The imposing 20th century Cathedral of St-Pierre.
The St-Pierre Museum – with its emphasis on the islands' nautical past.
YOU SHOULD KNOW:
The prohibition of the 1920s and 30s gave the islands a short-term economic boost when the islanders more or less abandoned fishing for a more lucrative trade in illicit alcohol. Many of the warehouses built to house this trade lie empty on the waterfront to this day.

Vancouver Island

Vancouver Island is a large island in British Columbia, just off Canada's Pacific coast, separated from the mainland by the Strait of Georgia. It is 460 km (286 mi) long and up to 80 km (50 mi) wide, a magnificent landscape of emerald forests, snow-capped mountains, flower-filled meadows, crystal-clear ice-cold lakes and rivers, and pristine coastline pounded by the Pacific Ocean. The island is paradise for outdoor pursuits enthusiasts, and it is one of the few places in the world where you can play golf and go skiing on the same day.

There are mountains down the centre of the island, the Vancouver Island Ranges, dividing it into the rugged and wet west coast and the drier east coast with a more rolling landscape. The highest point on the island is the Golden Hinde at 2,195 m (7,200 ft), lying within the Strathcona Provincial Park, and there are a few glaciers here, the largest of which is the Comox Glacier. The west coast is rocky and mountainous, characterized by fjords, bays and inlets, while the interior has many rivers and lakes, of which Kennedy Lake, northeast of Ucluelet, is the largest.

At the southern tip of the island is the elegant capital, Victoria, with its historic parliament, narrow streets dotted with cafés, pubs and colourful gardens, and boats floating lazily in the sparkling harbour. There is an abundance of sights to experience here, including the world-famous Butchart Botanical Gardens, with over a million plants. The gardens are divided into themed areas, such as Japanese or Italian, and each is a beautiful garden in its own right.

Activities available in this big outdoors include skiing, white-water rafting, caving, mountain biking, surfing, sailing, diving and snorkelling, bungy jumping and many other exciting pursuits. There are deep-sea fishing trips for halibut, salmon and chinook, whale-watching excursions or kayaking in the inlets of the Pacific Rim National Park. Trekking and hiking through the wilderness is also popular here, and can be done on horse or on foot along the trails in the fir-lined woods. Wildlife viewing is becoming more and more popular, with black bears high on the wish-list, and ecotours by boat can offer sightings of bald eagles, sea lions and sea otters.

POPULATION:
656,312 (2001)
WHEN TO GO:
April to November.
HOW TO GET THERE:
By ferry from the mainland, or by plane to Victoria International Airport.
HIGHLIGHTS:
Whale watching – visit between March and May when 21,000 whales, including the grey whale, migrate from California to Alaska.
Butchart Botanical Gardens – among the best, and most imaginatively planted in the world. Come on a summer evening to attend an outdoor concert while enjoying the gardens illuminated by coloured lights.
The fishing village of Tolfino – located on Clayoquot Sound, the village is a centre for ecotourism, with lovely sandy beaches to the south and opportunities for whale-watching and surfing.
Trekking on horseback across this magnificent landscape.
YOU SHOULD KNOW:
It is also known as 'The Island'.

Clayoquot Sound on the west coast

Isle Royale

POPULATION:
Uninhabited
HOW TO GET THERE:
By ferry from Copper Harbour,
Michigan, a journey of 90 km (56 mi)
or by floatplane from
Houghton, Michigan.
WHEN TO GO:
Only really accessible in the summer
(June to August)
HIGHLIGHTS:
The 6-hour ferry ride across
Lake Superior.
Nature watching – seeing beavers,
foxes and seabirds in their natural
environment.
Hiking across the island's well-
preserved trail system.
Just being there – cut off from the
stress of modern-day life.
YOU SHOULD KNOW:
The island is rich in mineral deposits:
US law prohibits the collection of any
materials from the area. Souvenir
hunters should satisfy themselves
with photographs and
memories alone.

At 74 km (45 mi) long and 14 km (9 mi) wide, with an area of
535 sq km (206 sq mi), Isle Royale is Lake Superior's largest natural
island, as well as being the second largest in the Great Lakes.
Although it is far closer to Canada, it was ceded to the United States
in 1843. The island's history is one of extinction and renewal, of
ventures tried and failed, leaving what is now an almost pristine
wilderness to be enjoyed by hikers and nature lovers alike. The
island, together with the surrounding smaller islands and waters,
now make up Isle Royale National Park.

For over 2000 years First Nations people visited, hunted and
fished, picked up copper nuggets, and later mined copper on the
island they knew as Isle Minong. By the mid-19th century white
settlers tried their hands at mining, logging and fishing but the
isolation of the island made this economically unviable.

On arrival at Rock Harbour, the island's only working dock, the
rudimentary welcoming sign lets you know that you are going back
to nature. There are no motorcars and only a couple of basic lodges.
A good pair of walking boots, a tent and a rucksack is all you need
to soak up this amazing landscape.

Isle Royale's animal life also expresses its island nature. In the
recent past, both wolf and moose have come in search of better
hunting and browsing grounds. Other animals found nearby, like the
black bear or the white tail dear, are missing; cut off from a good
source of food, they simply died out. This is an ever-changing
environment. Every so often, Lake Superior freezes at its northern
edges, forming an ice bridge to the mainland that allows in new
species of grazers and predators, and so another cycle begins.

Lake Superior

Aleutian Islands

A remote and sparsely populated chain of some 300 islands in the North Pacific, the Aleutians extend westwards in a 1,900 km (1,200 mi) arc from the Alaska Peninsula. By crossing longitude 180°, this rugged chain is the westernmost part of the USA and also, technically, the easternmost. The islands have 57 volcanoes and are part of the 'Pacific Ring of Fire', the area of frequent earthquakes and volcanic eruption that stretches in a huge inverted 'U' from South America to New Zealand. There are five groups within the Aleutians: The Fox Islands, nearest the mainland; Islands of Four Mountains; Andreanof Islands; Rat Islands; and the paradoxically named Near Islands, furthest from the mainland. There are few natural harbours in the chain and navigation is treacherous.

The indigenous inhabitants are the Unangan people, generally known as the Aleut. Originally exploited by Russia for the fur of seals and sea otters, the Aleutians formed part of the USA's Alaska purchase in 1867. Today, the principal commercial activity is fishing, though there is a strong (and rather secretive) US military presence.

A number of islands are inhabited, but the main centre of population is the settlement of Unalaska on the island of the same name, overlooking Dutch Harbour. Most of the rather exclusive (for which read 'expensive') tourist activity in the Aleutians is centred here, with cruise ships making it a regular port of call and the island serving as a base for tours by boat and plane.

The Aleutians are a dream destination for adventurous travellers, with a natural wilderness to explore and sensational wildlife to be found – brown bear, wolves, caribou, whales, sea lions, sea otters, porpoises, the ancient murrelet, eagles, the rare whiskered auklet, puffins and much, much more.

POPULATION:
8,200 (2000)
WHEN TO GO:
During the growing season (May to September), though winters are not always especially harsh.
HOW TO GET THERE:
With difficulty! The State Ferry operates bi-monthly from Kodiak Island to Unalaska (between May and October only), which also has regular flights from Anchorage. Beyond that, island-hopping involves custom trips with experienced guides.
HIGHLIGHTS:
The oldest Russian Orthodox cruciform church in North America, an endangered national historic monument in Unalaska.
Gently steaming Makushin Volcano, also on Unalaska Island.
The Aleutian World War II National Historic Area, Fort Schwatka on Mount Ballyhoo overlooking Dutch Harbour.
YOU SHOULD KNOW:
A small number of Aleutian Islands were occupied by Japanese forces in World War II – as close as they got to invading the USA.

Snow covered mountains along the coast of Adak Island

Kodiak Island

POPULATION:
14,000 (2000)
WHEN TO GO:
Visit in June, July or August when the salmon are running and the bears are feeding.
HOW TO GET THERE:
There is a passenger and vehicle ferry service to Kodiak and Port Lions from Seward or Homer. Commercial carriers fly into Kodiak from Anchorage.
HIGHLIGHTS:
The Baranov Museum in Kodiak, located in 200-year-old Erskine House, an old fur warehouse. It features artefacts, documents and photographs relevant to the Kodiak and Aleutian Islands.
Fort Abercrombie State Historical Park with its rugged coastline and military remains from World War II, including the Kodiak Military History Museum at Miller Point.
The Russian Orthodox Church in Kodiak, an atmospheric reminder of Alaska's Russian heritage.
YOU SHOULD KNOW:
Kodiak is home to the largest US Coastguard base in America, on the site of a US Navy air station established in 1941.

A brown Kodiak bear wades through the O'Malley River on Kodiak Island.

By far the largest of the Kodiak Archipelago's 30 islands off Alaska's south coast, Kodiak is also the second-largest island in the USA, weighing in at a hefty 160 km (100 mi) long and 16 km (10 mi) to 96 km (60 mi) in width. It is the ancestral home of the Koniag people, but the Russians arrived in the 18th century and the island was part of the USA's 19th century Alaska purchase.

Alaska's 'Emerald Isle' is aptly named for the vivid green that characterizes its summer appearance. The main town is Kodiak, with minor settlements at Akhiok, Old Harbor, Karluk, Larsen Bay, Port Lyons and Ouzinkie. The island is mountainous and heavily forested to the north, with few trees in the southern part. The main economic activity is fishing, with associated canning factories, though tourism is becoming increasingly important.

The Kodiak National Wildlife Refuge occupies a large portion of the island, and its most famous inhabitants are the huge Kodiak brown bears (estimated population 2,300). However, the Refuge is also home to native species such as red fox, river otter, ermine and tundra vole, plus incomers such as reindeer, beaver and red squirrel. Wildlife watching is a major leisure activity, as is sea kayaking. Hunting and fishing also draw many visitors in season, with amazing Pacific salmon runs up rivers like the Karluk.

Kodiak Island is one of the most unspoiled yet easily accessible wilderness areas on the planet. It's spectacular, but not for the faint-hearted. Whilst many worthwhile sights may be seen by travelling the island's relatively small number of paved roads, the truly wild experiences can only be enjoyed by employing the services of specialized guides or staying at one of many back-country lodges that offer outdoor adventures.

Little Diomede Island

Slap-bang in the middle of the Bering Strait between Alaska and Russia, the USA's Little Diomede Island and Russia's Big Diomede Island separate the former sworn adversaries by just 3 km (2 mi). The border and international dateline is equidistant from each, and the former was established to delineate the USA's Alaska purchase of 1867.

Little Diomede Island is an inhospitable, flat-topped, steep-sided rock that is just 7.4 sq km (2.8 sq mi) in size. The small Inuit population operates a subsistence economy, harvesting crab, fish, beluga whales, walrus, seals and polar bears. Almost every part of this hard-won bounty is used for some purpose. Diomede, crouching at the base of the island's western face, is actually classified as a city, proudly boasting one church, one school and a store. The entire island falls within city limits.

It is isolated by persistently rough seas and summer fog. In 1995 BBC television presenter Michael Palin arrived on Little Diomede to begin filming *Full Circle*, his epic circumnavigation of the Pacific Rim. He intended to close the circle back on the island eight months later, but unfortunately the winter seas were so rough that even the doughty US Coast Guard cutter *Munro* was unable to put Palin and his crew ashore.

Weather permitting, there is a weekly mail drop by helicopter, general supplies are landed once a year by barge and there are occasional visits by passing fishermen. Scientists are sometimes choppered in by the Alaska Air National Guard (there is an Arctic Environmental Observatory on the island).

*Ice sheets around
Little Diomede*

POPULATION:
140 (2000)
WHEN TO GO:
Wrap up well and try winter for reasons of access (see below).
HOW TO GET THERE:
Almost impossible. Try landing by chartered ski plane on sea ice in winter, but remember that a good Alaskan light plane touchdown is one you walk away from!
HIGHLIGHTS:
Seeing into the future – because the dateline runs between them, you can look across from Little Diomede and see what's happening on Big Diomede tomorrow.
The water treatment plant and newly built rubbish incinerator.
Splendid Eskimo carvings in sea ivory.
YOU SHOULD KNOW:
Be patient. One day getting there may be easy – the Diomede Islands are a certain stop on the oft-proposed 'Intercontinental Peace Bridge' across the Bering Strait.

Pribilof Islands

POPULATION:
684 (2000)
WHEN TO GO:
June to August, when the flowers are
out, birds are nesting, seals are on
shore and it's merely chilly.
HOW TO GET THERE:
Commercial carrier to Anchorage,
from whence smaller aircraft serve
the islands.
HIGHLIGHTS:
The Ridge Wall on St Paul – a
spectacular sheer cliff above the
Bering Sea that is birdwatching
heaven.
Community-owned TDX Power's
advanced wind/diesel generation
facility on St Paul, with its 37 m
(120 ft) wind turbine.
Seals, seals, seals and . . . more
seals.
YOU SHOULD KNOW:
St Paul Island is the setting for the
Rudyard Kipling tale 'The White Seal'
and poem 'Lukannon' in
The Jungle Book.

Named after a Russian navigator who visited in the 1780s, this group of four volcanic islands (five if you count Sea Lion Rock) in the Bering Sea is 320 km (200 mi) north of Unalaska Island in the Aleutians and the same distance south of Cape Newenham on the mainland. The rocky Pribilof Islands have a collective land mass of just 195 sq km (75 sq mi) and are largely covered by tundra and meadowland which produces a spectacular display of wild flowers.

The main islands are St Paul and St George, each with a settlement of the same name, whilst Otter and Walrus Islands are near St Paul. Seal hunting ended in 1966 and the main attraction is now the annual opilio (snow crab) fishery, as featured in the dramatic TV series 'Deadliest Catch'. Marine support services make an important contribution to the economy, as does US Government activity – there is a US Coast Guard base, the National Weather Service has a station and the National Oceanic and Atmospheric Administration is present.

The indigenous Alaskan Aleut people's largest community is here. They were transported from the Aleutians to the Pribilofs in the 18th century by Russian fur traders and have remained ever since. They still go subsistence hunting and are permitted to pursue their traditional quarry.

For intrepid visitors the main attraction is birdwatching, as the Pribilofs host some 240 species, including many rarities. Over two million seabirds nest annually, alongside up to one million fur seals. Various companies offer tours and this is the best way to see the islands, which are a naturalist's paradise sometimes called the 'Galapagos of the North' for their abundant wildlife, which may be observed at close quarters with the necessary permits from tribal governments.

Resting Northern fur seals

Alexander Archipelago

Pieces of iceberg from nearby South Sawyer Glacier in the Tracy Arm Fjiord

You need lots of fingers to count the islands in the rugged Alexander Archipelago, which stretches for 485 km (200 mi), hugging the southeastern coast of Alaska – there are about 1,100 of them. They are the tops of submerged mountains rising steeply from the Pacific Ocean. Deep fjords and channels separate mainland and islands, which have inhospitable, irregular coasts. The whole area is densely forested with fir woods and temperate rain forests. Much of the archipelago is protected from development and teems with wildlife.

The main economic activities are tourism, fishing and logging. The largest islands are Admiralty, Baranof, Chichagof, Dall, Kupreanof, Revillagigedo, Prince of Wales and Wrangell. Alaska's period of Russian domination is reflected in the names of several islands and the archipelago itself, which is called after Alexander Baranof, who ran the Russian-American Fur Company in the early 19th century – or Tsar Alexander II, depending on who you listen to.

People are thinly scattered throughout this vast area, with the main centres of population being Ketchikan on Revillagigedo and Sitka on Baranov, each with some 8,000 souls – the latter was once the capital of Russian America. The archipelago is traversed by heavy boat traffic along the Inside Passage, a sheltered route that follows a path between the mainland and coastal islands of British Columbia and the Alaska Panhandle.

There's no point in pretending that Alaska is a conventional tourist destination. The Alexander Archipelago perfectly illustrates this, offering both the challenges and rewards that make a visit to the 49th state an unforgettable expedition. There is no road access, so the only ways in are by sea or air, but those who make the effort will be rewarded by the ultimate wilderness experience.

POPULATION:
39,000 (2007 estimate)
WHEN TO GO:
Unless you want to risk being marooned, go between mid-May and mid-September.
HOW TO GET THERE:
Fly Alaska Airlines to the state capital of Juneau on the mainland, which offers a good ferry service to main islands. There are bush carriers who will undertake floatplane charters.
HIGHLIGHTS:
The out-of-season Alaska Day Festival in October, offering a series of events in Sitka, where the USA's Alaska purchase was signed in 1867 on the city's Castle Hill.
The Pack Creek Brown Bear Viewing Area on Admiralty Island (permit required from the US Forest Service).
A scenic ride on Prince of Wales Island's Inter-Island ferry service.
The Russian Orthodox Cathedral of St Michael (completed 1848) in Sitka.
Spectacular Glacier Bay National Park, with headquarters at Bartlett Cove, 105 km (65 m) from state capital Juneau (fly in to nearby Gustavus).
YOU SHOULD KNOW:
The entire island of Annette is a reservation, the only one in Alaska, and is home to the Tsimshian, Tlingit and Haida Native peoples.

Waves from Lake Erie break on the shore of Kelleys Island

Kelleys Island

POPULATION:
380 (2000)
WHEN TO GO:
May to August – almost everything closes in September. The island is icebound in winter.
HOW TO GET THERE:
There is a regular ferry service from Marblehead. Another runs from Sandusky to South Bass Island and Kelleys in summer only.
HIGHLIGHTS:
Inscription Rock – with (now barely visible) pictographs drawn by the Native American Eries tribe in the 16th century.
The Kelleys Island Winery, established in the 1980s at the site one of the island's oldest houses, built in 1865.
Kelleys Island Historical Association in the Old Stone Church on Division Street.
YOU SHOULD KNOW:
The Lake Erie Islands are known as the 'Vacationland of the Midwest' – so don't expect to have Kelleys all to yourself!

Though it is the largest of Ohio's Lake Erie Islands, Kelleys is still not big, with an area of just 9 sq km (4.6 sq mi). The other islands in the group are North, Middle and South Bass Islands, Sugar Island and Rattlesnake Island, located in the lake's western basin. It's not hard to read the island's history – there is evidence of lime production everywhere, and the Kelley Island Lime & Transport Company was once the world's largest producer of limestone products, operating from 1886 until the 1960s. A small quarrying operation still exists, but is a shadow of its former self. There was once one of the USA's largest wineries here, too, but it closed in the 1930s as a result of fires and Prohibition. The ruins may still be seen.

Now, however, the mainstay of the island's economy is tourism. The principal establishments are all pubs and restaurants, the most famous of which is the old Village Pump. But the real attraction is the island's natural beauty and fascinating remains of its industrial heritage, plus the fact that it's a perfect setting for outdoor pursuits.

Kelleys Island is heavily forested, with several sparsely populated residential areas that fill out in summer when the owners of vacation homes arrive. It is home to the Kelleys Island State Park, that occupies the northern third of the island and offers hiking trails, a sandy beach and campground. The adjoining Glacial Grooves State Memorial features this tiny island's second world 'first' – glacial striations containing the world's largest remains of glacial grooves. The North Shore also has a preserved limestone pavement (alvar) and a nature reserve.

Drummond Island

This is the largest island among many in St Mary's River where it ends its journey from Lake Superior by flowing into northern Lake Huron in Upper Michigan. It is also the second-largest freshwater island in the USA. Drummond Island extends to 335 sq km (130 sq mi) in area and is within touching distance of the Canadian border. The island is largely forested, with cliffs at the eastern end, and over two-thirds of the land is owned by the state of Michigan. Its economic mainstay is tourism and, whilst that has traditionally meant summer visitors, Drummond – in common with many Great Lakes islands – is trying to promote all-year-round activities to keep the tills ringing, with some success.

Drummond Island is a natural paradise, described by its proud inhabitants as the 'Gem of the Huron'. Diverse topography ranges from rocky ledges to cedar swamps, prairie meadowland to hardwood groves, rugged shores to sandy beaches. The summer wild flowers can be spectacular, as are the trees from September. It is a wildlife haven, with numerous deer the most visible animals. But there are plenty of raccoons, skunks, rabbits, squirrels, chipmunks, woodchucks and weasels. Rarer sightings include bears, moose, bobcats, coyotes and wolves. There is also a variety of reptile life, including snakes and turtles, plus many species of bird.

Vacation activities on Drummond Island include boating, camping, hunting and fishing, hiking, biking, wildlife watching, photography, stargazing (no light pollution here), off-road vehicle activity or simply exploring the island's varied terrain.

Beautiful Big Shoal Bay

POPULATION:
1,200 (2007 estimate)
WHEN TO GO:
May to September is the best time to visit, except for those interested in specialist winter pastimes like snowmobiling. Many facilities close out of season.
HOW TO GET THERE:
The M-134 highway on the mainland continues for 13 km (8 mi) on the island via the Drummond Island Ferry from DeTour Village. There is a small airport.
HIGHLIGHTS:
The new Drummond Island Museum, built after the old one (be warned!) collapsed under the weight of snow.
Big Shoal Bay, a beautiful natural enclave on the island's southern edge.
De Tour Reef Light, a preserved lighthouse in the passage between Drummond Island and the mainland.
The Heritage Trail, a hiking route created to show off the island's habitat and wildlife.
YOU SHOULD KNOW:
The British were reluctant to surrender the island, only abandoning Fort Collier in 1823, thus finally ending their military presence in the USA.

Mackinac Island

Traditional houses on the shores of Lake Huron

Showing remarkable advanced sensitivity to global warming, the inhabitants of Mackinac Island banned motorized vehicles in 1898 – a prohibition that exists to this day with limited exception for emergency and service vehicles. But there are still plenty of eco-friendly horse-drawn carriages to be seen.

The island covers 9.8 sq km (3.8 sq mi) and belongs to the US state of Michigan. It is located in Lake Huron's Straits of Mackinac, commanding the passage between Lake Michigan and Lake Huron. As such, it was of strategic importance to the Great Lakes fur trade in the 18th century and the British built a fort during the American Revolutionary War. The island, then garrisoned by the Americans, was the scene of two battles during the War of 1812. After the twice-victorious British relinquished the place in 1815, Fort Mackinac served as an outpost for the US Army.

By the end of the 19th century Mackinac Island had become a popular summer colony, and extensive preservation has ensured that much of the original character remains – to such good effect that the entire island is now a National Historic Landmark, with 80 per cent also conserved as the Mackinac Island State Park. In short, it continues to provide a civilized holiday destination for tourists generally and the people of Michigan in particular, as it has for well over a century – up to 15,000 a day now arrive in high season. They are drawn by the island's natural beauty and powerful old-fashioned charm, with little or no building in intrusive modern styles.

The island is the home of several galleries and many cultural events, including an annual show of 19th century American art from the Masco Collection. The Mackinac Arts Council organizes an outstanding programme each summer.

Beaver Island

The Great Lakes' most remote inhabited island has a great harbour, pristine woods, isolated beaches, trails for biking and trails for hiking. Beaver Island in its 14-island archipelago is the largest island in Lake Michigan, lying 51 km (32 mi) from the small mainland town of Charlevoix. It is 21 km (13 mi) long and up to 9.5 km (6 mi) wide, mostly flat with poor sandy soil. There are extensive tracts of forest.

The island has a fascinating history. It attracted white frontiersmen from the early 1800s, who made a living from trapping, fishing and, later, cutting wood for passing steamers. But the most extraordinary chapter in the island's history came when a Mormon splinter group led by James Strang evicted the previous inhabitants in the early 1850s. Strang had himself crowned king in a bizarre coronation ceremony, married several queens and encouraged his subjects to build roads, clear land and start cultivating. Unfortunately, they were not to enjoy the fruits of their labour – Strang was killed by disgruntled followers in 1856 and a land-hungry mob arrived from Mackinac Island to evict the Mormons.

The next wave of incomers was mostly Irish and Gaelic was widely spoken. The community flourished until the prolific Lake Michigan fishery declined drastically in the 1890s, after which there was a period of intense logging. When that finished the community steadily dwindled until fewer than 200 souls remained. Tourism came to the rescue from the 1970s, since when the resident population has more than doubled.

Once dependent on fishing, logging and farming, Beaver Island now relies on government services, tourism and the construction of vacation homes. It prides itself on a serene, relaxed lifestyle that attracts visitors back time and time again.

POPULATION:
600 (2007 estimate)
WHEN TO GO:
This is an open-air sort of place, which, this far north, means visiting between May and October.
HOW TO GET THERE:
There is a ferry from Charlevoix. The island may be reached by regular air taxi.
HIGHLIGHTS:
The only Mormon-era building left – their old print house, now a museum of island history.
Dr Protar's home – the simple house where a revered island character lived from 1893 to his death in 1925 (open by appointment).
Two lighthouses – Beaver Harbour Light on Whiskey Point where the island's lifesaving station was once located, and Beaver Head Light.
Guided island tours – various options, including an eco-tour.
YOU SHOULD KNOW:
Beaver Island is still known as 'America's Emerald Isle' after it was so nicknamed by the large number of islanders of Irish descent in the late 19th century.

St James Township on Beaver Island

Manitou Islands

POPULATION:
Uninhabited
WHEN TO GO:
The Sleeping Bear National
Lakeshore is open all year round, but
the islands are really a May to
September destination.
HOW TO GET THERE:
There is a ferry service from Leland,
Michigan.
HIGHLIGHTS:
Birdlife, including eagles and the
endangered piping plover that nests
on North Manitou.
A stand of northern white cedar
trees in the Valley of the Giants on
South Manitou, said to be among the
largest and oldest in the world.
The redundant lighthouse (built 1871)
that marks the deep bay harbour on
South Manitou.
Spectacular sand dunes on North
Manitou and the 'perched' dunes of
South Manitou, so called because
they sit atop limestone bluffs.
YOU SHOULD KNOW:
The Manitous are surrounded by
numerous shipwrecks, which are
popular with recreational divers.

The two Manitou Islands in Lake Michigan were once settled, but are now uninhabited. That doesn't mean they are abandoned, as both are part of the Sleeping Bear National Lakeshore. Each has a ranger station and the islands are a popular destination for day trips and adventure holidays – note that visitors who stay require park and camping permits.

North Manitou is the larger at 13 km (8 mi) long and 6.5 km (4 mi) wide, with some 32 km (20 mi) of shoreline. By the mid-1800s there were piers at which passing steamships refuelled, but the island has few exploitable resources and never had a thriving settlement. Ruined homesteads, logging roads, a few wild orchards and the old cemetery are all that remain of that era, and the principal activities are wilderness camping and deer hunting in season.

South Manitou, though just 5 km (3 mi) by 5 km (3 mi), was always more populous than its larger sibling. It had some fertile ground and the only natural harbour between the Manitous and Chicago, making the island a regular stopping-off point for lake mariners from the late 1700s into the 20th century. The hardy inhabitants have long gone, but they have left buildings and evocative ruins as evidence of their presence. This island has a system of trails and three campsites, and guided tours are available in open-top vehicles.

Chippewa Indian legend has it that a mother bear and her two cubs tried to swim across the lake to escape a fire on the Wisconsin shore. She made it and climbed a steep bluff to await her cubs. She waited and waited, but they never came. Eventually she died, and the Great Spirit Manitou marked her resting place with the Sleeping Bear Dunes and raised North and South Manitou Islands where the cubs drowned.

Sleeping Bear Dunes

Antelope Island

Utah's Great Salt Lake is the largest lake in the western United States and Antelope is the largest of ten islands in that lake. In fact, when the water level is low it ceases to be an island, becoming a peninsula. From the mainland the island appears barren and deserted, but there is abundant flora and wildlife, including the pronghorn antelope that give the island its name. Other larger species include mule deer, bobcats, coyotes, elk and bighorn sheep, whilst there is also an abundance of waterfowl. But the most striking animals are undoubtedly the American bison, a free-roaming herd of around 600 animals. They were introduced in 1893 and have played an important role in the conservation of this once-abundant species that was hunted almost to the point of extinction in the 19th century.

The island has an area of 68 sq km (42 sq mi) and is mostly flat around the outside (except on the rocky western side) with beaches and plains that stretch to the central mountains, which rise steeply to an elevation of some 760 m (2,500 ft) above the level of the lake. It was once in private ownership and included a working ranch, but was purchased by the state and Antelope Island State Park is now part of the Utah State Parks system.

This is the perfect place to see the Great Salt Lake and appreciate the vast solitude of the Great Basin it occupies. The island offers beaches, paved roads, campgrounds, a sailboat marina, hiking trails, biking, horse-riding and an excellent visitor centre.

POPULATION:
Uninhabited
WHEN TO GO:
This is an all-year-round destination, though winter activities are limited.
HOW TO GET THERE:
Via an 11 km (7 mi) causeway from West Point in Davis County. In periods when the lake is high (most recently 1981-1991) there is boat access only.
HIGHLIGHTS:
Floating effortlessly in the Great Salt Lake (nearly as buoyant as the Dead Sea!).
The buffalo corral and management facility run by the Utah Division of Parks and Recreation – annual roundup in late October.
The incredible sunsets over the western part of the Great Salt Lake.
YOU SHOULD KNOW:
Brine flies abound around the lake and are, in the local lingo, 'darn pesky'.

Antelope Island sits in the Great Salt Lake.

Boss Harbour Marsh with Western Mountain in the background

POPULATION:
Varying populations up to 10,000. Many of the islands are uninhabited.

WHEN TO GO:
Travel the Maine Marine Island Trail between July and September.

HOW TO GET THERE:
By kayak, sailboat or small motorboat only (boat hire generally available all along the coast).

HIGHLIGHTS:
A stop-off on the mainland to see Harriet Beecher Stowe's house in Brunswick, where she wrote *Uncle Tom's Cabin*.
A visit to one of the 49 islands that comprise the Maine Coastal Islands National Wildlife Refuge.
For those who prefer driving to paddling their own canoe – a visit to Georgetown Island with a wonderful shoreline and abundant wildlife.

YOU SHOULD KNOW:
As a crow flies the Maine coast is just 367 km (228 mi) long, but it has 5,597 km (3,478 mi) of shoreline – more than California.

Maine Islands

The Maine Island Trail – a member organization – organizes access to a stunning coastline. The trail runs for 565 km (350 mi) from Cape Porpoise Harbour, northeast to Machias Bay. There are over 150 designated island and mainland stops along the route, which can be travelled only by private craft. Interesting calling points are Monhegan Island, Mount Desert Island, Warren Island and Isle au Haut, though all or any part of the Trail should appeal to lovers of unspoiled places and adventurous holidays.

Tiny Monhegan is off Lincoln County. It is sustained by a winter lobster fishery and by summer visitors who come for breathtaking scenery and abundant bird life. The island has a long-established art colony that has attracted prominent painters, including Edward Hopper. Most of the island, with a resident population of less than 100, is uninhabited and may be freely explored.

Mount Desert is Maine's largest coastal island. It lies off Hancock County and is by far the most heavily populated of the Maine Islands, with some 10,000 inhabitants. It is a major tourist destination with up to four million people visiting its rugged Acadia National Park each year.

Uninhabited Warren Island is a State Park representing a typical wild stop-over on the Trail – this 70-acre spruce-covered island in Penobscot Bay offers safe mooring, campsites and fresh water for those who like to make their own way in life. A ferry goes to the neighbouring island of Islesboro, but no closer.

Isle au Haut is also in Penobscot Bay, but is inhabited by some 80 full-timers. Most of the island's 191.8 sq km (74 sq mi) area falls within the Acadia National Park, and that's what attracts visitors. It is a working island with few amenities.

Peaks Island

Once known as 'Maine's Coney Island', Peaks Island is in Casco Bay some 5 km (3 mi) from Portland. The close-knit community recently tried to secede from the city so Peaks Island could become a town in its own right, but it seems that might is right and Portland got to keep its island jewel. Peaks is one of over 200 islands in the bay and the most populous, though only 3.2 km (2 mi) long and 1.6 km (1 mi) across at the widest point. Casco Bay is where the spectacular Maine coast really begins, offering a world of rocky shorelines, wooded islands, abundant wild flowers, secluded beaches and hidden coves.

By contrast with the other bay islands, Peaks Island became a developed resort towards the end of the 19th century, with a small resident population swelled by thousands of summer visitors ever since. It was once a place of organized summer entertainment with a particularly strong theatrical tradition, its three theatres playing host to many already or subsequently famous types over the years, including D. W. Griffith and the Barrymores. Almost all the original hotels, theatres and amusement parks have been lost over the years, though the island retains many quaint cottages from the Victorian era.

As tastes changed, the island traded on its traditional small-town atmosphere and has become popular with those who like natural beauty, scrambling over a rocky seashore, bike riding, horse-riding, kayaking or simply loafing on the beach.

POPULATION:
840 (2000)
WHEN TO GO:
As with most East Coast resorts, May to September is when it all happens, but various hotels offer cosy winter breaks.
HOW TO GET THERE:
By regular ferry sailing from Portland – it's a perfect day trip.
HIGHLIGHTS:
A scenic bay cruise with Casco Bay Lines that not only takes in Peaks Island, but also Little Diamond, Great Diamond, Long, Chebeague and Cliff Islands.
The Gem Gallery on Island Avenue, featuring the work of local artists.
The annual Peaks Fest event held at the end of June to celebrate the island's unique community.
Abandoned World War II military installations including Battery Steele, whose big guns broke windows all over the island when first tested.
YOU SHOULD KNOW:
The great Portland-born Hollywood director John Ford was nicknamed 'Mayor of Peaks Island' – he worked the ferry, ushered in the Gem Theatre as a young man and vacationed on the island all his life.

The shoreline on Peaks Island shows its winter face!

Ellis Island

POPULATION:
Uninhabited
WHEN TO GO:
March to June, or September to
November
HOW TO GET THERE:
Fly to New York City, then take a
ferry from Battery Park at the
southern tip of Manhattan or from
Liberty State Park in New Jersey.
HIGHLIGHTS:
The Statue of Liberty – the ferry to
Ellis Island will take you right past.
The Ellis Island Immigration
Museum – three floors of
audio/visual displays and exhibits
detailing the history of immigration
processing on the island. The
museum attracts more than two
million visitors a year.
YOU SHOULD KNOW:
Ellis Island is part of the Statue of
Liberty National Monument.

Ellis Island has played an integral role in the shaping of America. Lying at the mouth of the Hudson River in New York Harbour, the island is an icon of America itself, a reminder of the American ideals of freedom, liberty and justice for all. In the shadow of the Statue of Liberty, this largely artificial island was the main portal for immigrants entering the United States from 1 January 1892 until 12 November 1954. Annie Moore, a 15 year-old Irish girl, was the first immigrant to be processed here, and over the next 62 years more than 12 million people followed her.

Up until 1890, the individual states regulated immigration, rather than the federal government. Castle Garden, or Castle Clinton, in the Battery served as the New York State immigration station and processed eight million immigrants between 1855 and 1890. Most of these early immigrants were from northern and western Europe, including Britain, Ireland, Germany and Scandinavia. Throughout the 19th century, political instability, famine and deteriorating economic conditions in Europe caused the largest mass migration in human history. In 1890 President Benjamin Harrison designated Ellis Island the first federal immigration station to handle the growing numbers of immigrants.

In the early years of the 20th century, officials thought the peak of immigration had passed, but it was actually on the increase and in 1907 alone around 1.25 million were processed at Ellis Island. As World War I approached, emigration to the United States slowed. During and just after the war, the island was used to detain thousands of suspected alien radicals from across the United States. Hundreds were deported simply because they were loosely associated with an organization advocating revolt against the federal government. In 1920, the immigration processing facility reopened on the island and dealt with a further 225,000 immigrants until it closed in 1954. In 1965, it was declared part of the Statue of Liberty National Monument. Today it is wholly in the possession of the federal government, but under the jurisdiction of the US National Park Service.

An aerial view of Ellis Island

Fire Island

Ocean Beach

This elongated, thin barrier island in Suffolk County, New York, protects much of the southern shoreline of Long Island from the worst excesses of the Atlantic Ocean. At the last count Fire Island was 49.5 km (31 mi) long and 0.8 km (0.5 mi) across at the widest point. But the shape is constantly changing – at one point it stretched for 95 km (60 mi) from adjacent Jones Island in the east to Southampton at the New York end and was as wide as 8 km (5 mi). In 1931 a northeasterly gale broke through to Moriches Inlet, dividing Fire Island from Southampton.

Fire Island is separated from Long Island by a series of bays – Great South Bay, Patchogue Bay, Bellport Bay, Narrow Bay and Moriches Bay. The western 7.5 km (4.5 mi) is made up of Robert Moses State Park, a hugely popular summer destination for New Yorkers. Since 1964 the rest of the island has been protected as the Fire Island National Seashore. There is no road along the island's length and vehicular traffic is banned during the summer season (June to August). Even out of season only a limited number of driving permits are available for residents.

The main resorts are Ocean Beach on the South Shore, reached by water taxi or a walk along the sand from Robert Moses Park, nearby Saltaire and Davis Park on Moriches Inlet. Among various hamlets on the island, Cherry Grove and The Pines are popular with the gay community. The year-round population is small, but thousands flock to their vacation homes or rentals in high summer, joined by many thousands more who come out from New York for the day to enjoy Fire Island's miles of boardwalk and laid-back beach life.

POPULATION:
300 (2000)
WHEN TO GO:
Join the summer crowds – this is definitely no place to be in winter.
HOW TO GET THERE:
Limited road access via Robert Moses Causeway (western end) and William Floyd Parkway (eastern end). Numerous resort ferries from Long Island in season.
HIGHLIGHTS:
The Fire Island Lighthouse, that replaced an earlier light in 1858. Now privately operated by a preservation society and open to the public.
Smith Point County Park to the east end of the island – it has a large car park with tunnel access to the seashore.
A rare survivor – the Sunken Forest on Sailor's Haven, one of the few remaining maritime forests on the eastern seaboard, featuring gnarled trees twisted by wind and salt spray.
YOU SHOULD KNOW:
In 1966, avant-garde American poet Frank O'Hara was struck by a beach buggy on the Fire Island shore. He died the next day.

Manhattan Island

At New York City's heart, Manhattan consists of Manhattan Island, a long, thin strip bounded by the Hudson River (west), East River and Harlem River (north), plus various smaller islands and a section on the mainland (Marble Hill, adjacent to The Bronx). The island is 21.6 km (13.4 mi) long and 3.7 km (2.3 mi) wide at 14th Street, the widest point, and is connected to the other four boroughs by bridges, tunnels and the (free) Staten Island Ferry. This is the commercial, financial and cultural centre of the city and therefore (New Yorkers would argue) of the world.

The frantic pace of Manhattan life generates an energy that invariably excites (but sometimes alarms) first-time visitors. A 'New York Minute' is very short, referring to the impatient character of the city in general and Manhattan in particular – once amusingly defined as 'from the lights turning green to the guy behind honking his horn'.

Manhattan Island seems familiar to people who have never been there, with a cityscape and skyline that have appeared in countless films and television series, many of which featured the twin towers of the World Trade Centre in Lower Manhattan, tragically destroyed on 9/11/2001. Manhattan is full of names that seem equally familiar – Greenwich Village, Wall Street, Broadway, the Upper East Side, Fifth Avenue, Harlem, SoHo, Times Square, Madison Square Garden… the list could go on and on. But everyone should visit Manhattan at least once for shopping and the sights, because seeing is believing.

Orientation isn't as easy as the regular grid layout of streets would suggest, partly because there are exceptions to the rule (one of the most notable is Broadway), but one of those famous yellow cabs will get you where you want to go.

POPULATION:
1,537,000 (Manhattan Borough, 2000)
WHEN TO GO:
If inclement weather bothers you, the months to avoid are December to March (often very cold, sometimes with heavy snowfall).
HOW TO GET THERE:
By air from practically anywhere in the world to one of New York's three airports (Newark, JFK and La Guardia). La Guardia is closest to Manhattan, but all have excellent links to the island.
HIGHLIGHTS:
Central Park, Manhattan's 'green lung' – the USA's first public park and the country's most-visited (currently by some 25 million people each year).

The breathtaking view from the top of the Empire State Building by day or night (buy tickets on line in advance, or be prepared to queue in line for a while).
Some of the world's finest museums – the Metropolitan Museum of Art, the Guggenheim, MoMA (Museum of Modern Art) and Whitney Museum of American Art (allow at least a day each to do them any sort of justice).
A Broadway show – there really is no business like show business, New-York style.
YOU SHOULD KNOW:
One derivation of the name 'Manhattan' is from 'Manahachtanienk' in the native Lenape language, meaning 'place of general inebriation'. Surely not!

An aerial view of Manhattan

Staten Island

The famous Staten Island Ferry

This is one of New York's five boroughs (the others being Manhattan, Brooklyn, Queens and The Bronx). It is the most geographically isolated and the least densely populated of the five. Until the 1970s Staten Island was known as the Borough of Richmond, reflecting its proximity to Richmond County, the most southerly in New York State. It is the third-largest borough at 153 sq km (59 sq mi).

The island's modern history goes back to the arrival of European settlers. Dutch attempts to settle the place in the early 17th century foundered in the face of stiff opposition from the indigenous tribes, but in 1670 they gave up their claim and English and Dutch settlers took over. It was on Staten Island in 1776 that massed British forces under William Howe learned of the Declaration of Independence, shortly before routing George Washington at the Battle of Long Island and capturing New York.

Compared to the rest of New York, the island remained relatively undeveloped until the completion of the Verrazano Narrows Bridge in 1964, which opened the place to rapid development by providing direct road access to Brooklyn. The bridge also provided a better way for traffic from New Jersey to reach the other boroughs and Long Island, and a network of new roads soon changed the island's hitherto relaxed pace of life. The North Shore is heavily urbanized, whilst the South Shore is more suburban. However, the conservationists didn't give in without a fight, and the 1960s saw the establishment of New York's largest area of parkland and preservation of large tracts of woodland for public use. Staten Island also has New York's highest (natural) point – the summit of Todt Hill at 125 m (410 ft).

Long Island

Yes, it is long – 190 km (118 mi) to be precise. And it's quite wide too – up to 37 km (23 mi) across. And populous – heading steadily towards the 8-million mark, though well over half of those live in New York. Two of the city's five boroughs – Queens and Brooklyn – occupy the western end of the island, but this is a mere geographical fact. They consider themselves part of New York City rather than Long Island and in colloquial use 'Long Island' means the suburban communities of Nassau and Suffolk Counties beyond city limits.

Long Island is a very affluent area, with enclaves of real wealth such as the Hamptons and the North Shore's cliff-top Gold Coast overlooking Long Island Sound, or South Shore communities along now-protected Atlantic beaches and wetlands. But the island's real prosperity is built on the city workers who commute into New York. Summer tourism is also important as the island has numerous parks, beaches and great scenery, tending to act as New York's playground.

The two suburban counties have roughly similar populations, but Nassau County in the centre of the island is the most heavily urbanized. By the time a determined traveller reaches the Twin Forks area in Suffolk County at the eastern extremity there is a more rural feel. It sometimes seems that the whole place is just a sprawling extension of New York, but there is more to Long Island than that. Actually, the place is something of a metaphor for the American Dream – start with nothing in the mean streets of Brooklyn, move out to an apple-pie suburb and finish up with a multi-millionaire's beach-front retreat in the Hamptons. Lots of Long Islanders have made it half way.

Beach house on East Hampton Beach

POPULATION:
7,559,000 (2006)
WHEN TO GO:
This is a summer tourist destination, with many facilities closed out of season.
HOW TO GET THERE:
From New York City by road or bus (MTA Long Island Bus) and rail (the busy Long Island Rail Road).
HIGHLIGHTS:
Coney Island in Brooklyn, that faded beachfront icon of yesteryear, now undergoing a renaissance.
Rural Long Island: Typified by the North Fork resort area with its quaint fishing villages, old-fashioned towns and famous wineries.
Unspoiled Long Island: Try the Sweetbriar Nature Centre in Central Suffolk, with hiking trails along the Nissequogue River and a summer butterfly house.
Maritime Long Island: Represented by lighthouses – lots of them, often in stunning coastal settings, many now preserved and open to the public.
YOU SHOULD KNOW:
In 1927, Charles Lindbergh's historic solo flight across the Atlantic began at Roosevelt Airfield in Nassau County.

Tangier Island

POPULATION:
600 (2000)
WHEN TO GO:
Access is easiest in the summer months and winters can be very hard.
HOW TO GET THERE:
There is a landing strip for air taxis, ferry services from the mainland (Crisfied, Maryland and two Virginia ports, Onancock and Reedville), plus island boat cruises.
HIGHLIGHTS:
Spanky's 1950s-style ice-cream parlour on Main Ridge.
Birds – thousands of pelicans, blue herons, egrets, rails, osprey, ducks and geese attracted by rich marshland.
An island speciality – Christmas decorations made from sea shells.
YOU SHOULD KNOW:
Tangier islanders only abandoned the practice of burying their dead beneath the family lawn in the early 20th century, when most of the small yards became fully occupied.

This isolated island in Chesapeake Bay is part of Accomack County, Virginia, and is separated from the Bay's eastern shore by Pocomoke Sound. It is tiny, with an area of just 0.6 sq km (0.2 sq mi). Its first known explorer was Captain John Smith of Pocahontas fame, and the island passed through various hands in the 1600s.

In fact, Tangier Island is a series of long islets divided by marsh and small tidal streams. These are all connected by narrow wooden bridges that do not permit the passage of motor vehicles, so the main modes of transport are golf cart, boat, moped, bike and foot. There are three significant ridges – Main Ridge, Canton and West Ridge. The northern part of Main Ridge is quaintly named Me at Soup. Other island districts are Black Dye, Sheep's Head and Hog Ridge.

The two words that best describe the island are 'old' and 'fashioned'. The tough and independent inhabitants speak a unique dialect thought to be unchanged since its first occupation by English colonists. There is one payphone, no ATM and the few tourist facilities have only recently started accepting credit cards. That said, the island is modernizing fast with the arrival of cable TV – a process not to everyone's liking. Tourism supplements the island's main economic activity – soft shell crabbing and oyster fishing. Men tend to focus on the latter, leaving the women to deal with tourists.

There are bed-and-breakfast establishments offering overnight stays, but most visitors come as part of an organized tour, or take a day-trip to the island by regular ferry. Upon arrival, they find a few gift shops, eateries (crab cakes a speciality), one general store... and an island with unique character.

Chesapeake Bay at sunset

Fenwick Island

A barrier island between Little Assawoman Bay and the Atlantic Ocean, Fenwick Island is part of Delaware's fast-growing beach resort area, along with Bethany Beach, South Bethany, Dewey Beach, Lewes and Rehoboth Beach. It is the southernmost of the so-called 'Quiet Resorts', though in truth the area is not always that quiet, partly because it is just across the state line from Ocean City, Maryland, which definitely is a wild place with a buzzing boardwalk and notorious nightlife. Fenwick Island, however, still claims to be a relatively peaceful enclave.

The island is named after an English planter who acquired the place in 1692, but never lived there. Until then it was known as Fishing Harbor. Its southern extremity is now marked by the Transpeninsular Line. This was surveyed in 1750-51 and runs due west to Taylor's Island and meets the 'tangent line' section of the famous Mason-Dixon line that divides the USA's old northern and southern states, the Union and Dixie. Both lines had marker stones every five miles, with the arms of Maryland's founding family (the Calverts) on one side and the arms of Pennsylvania's Penn family on the other. Many of these survive, and the marker at Fenwick is said to be 'the oldest standing man-made object on the coast between Indian River and Ocean City'.

Separated from the mainland by a narrow channel, Fenwick Island is tiny, with a landmass of just 0.9 sq km (0.3 sq mi), and is all about one of the best beaches in southern Delaware. It is partly occupied by the town of Fenwick Island, incorporated in 1953 to prevent the advance of Ocean City, with the rest considered to be part of Sussex County. The resident population is swelled by several thousand each summer, who come for the renowned fishing and the simple pleasures of a perfect beach holiday – loafing, sunbathing, swimming, sandcastle building and watching the sensational sunrises and sunsets over the sea. For the more active there is wind surfing, body surfing and jet skiing.

POPULATION:
340 (2000)
WHEN TO GO:
Although claiming to appeal to year-round visitors, out of season is reserved for those who like wild seas and deserted beaches.
HOW TO GET THERE:
Fenwick Island is reached by a bridge built in 1958 – the fourth to occupy the site.
HIGHLIGHTS:
Fenwick Island State Park, part of the larger Delaware Seashore State Park that offers an accessible expanse of beach, dunes and Atlantic scenery. Fenwick Lighthouse, completed in 1869, which sits upon the Transpeninsular Line and the Delaware-Maryland state border.
YOU SHOULD KNOW:
According to local lore, Cedar Island in Little Assawoman Bay was used to bury pirate treasure. True or false, pirates did hide out along the Delaware coast in the mid-17th century.

Fenwick Lighthouse

Traditional gingerbread houses

Martha's Vineyard

Few placenames in the USA contain a possessive apostrophe, and that says something about the exclusive character of Martha's Vineyard. In the late 19th century the US Board of Geographical Names ordered the apostrophe to be dropped, but the decision was soon reversed after high-level lobbying. This prosperous island off Cape Cod in Massachusetts is a thriving summer colony, with some 100,000 vacation homers joining year-round inhabitants and thousands more casual visitors who arrive each day.

The place was named by English explorer Bartholomew Gosnold (his daughter was called Martha), who arrived in 1602 and found a triangular-shaped island some 33 km (20.5 mi) in length. It flourished as a whaling centre in the 19th century, but when that industry declined it became a resort for tourists, especially wealthy ones, and the island still serves as a magnet for the rich and famous. It has six townships: Tisbury, including the main village of Vineyard Haven and West Chop peninsula; Edgartown, the old whaling port; Oak Bluffs with its famous 'gingerbread' cottages; agricultural West Tisbury; rural Chilmark with its hilly terrain and the fishing village of Menemsha; and Aquinnah, home to the indigenous Wampanoag tribe and spectacular Gay Cliffs.

A history of peaceful coexistence with the Wampanoags established the island's reputation for tolerance, and it has long been a place where the African-American elite has felt able to summer, mainly around Oak Bluffs. Many prominent Jewish families also have homes on the island, after being subtly discouraged from buying on nearby Nantucket Island in more prejudiced times.

Unlike Nantucket, the rapid growth of Martha's Vineyard from the 1950s was not well controlled, and some parts of the island suffered visually as a result of haphazard development.

POPULATION:
15,000 (2007 estimate)
WHEN TO GO:
June to August for the full experience, out of season to avoid crowds and explore the island's delights at leisure.
HOW TO GET THERE:
Regular ferry services from mainland ports including Woods Hole, Falmouth, New Bedford, Hyannis and Quonset Point (Rhode Island). Scheduled air services in season.
HIGHLIGHTS:
The On Time ferry trip to adjacent Chappaquiddick Island, scene of Senator Edward Kennedy's infamous plunge off Dike Bridge that killed Mary Jo Kopechne in 1969.
The USA's oldest operating Flying Horses Carousel at Oak Bluffs, built in 1876 and brought to its present site in 1886 – now a National Historic Landmark.
The Felix Neck Wildlife Sanctuary in Edgartown, principally for birdwatching.
Vineyard Haven Harbor and Marine Railway, a traditional boatyard.
YOU SHOULD KNOW:
If you go down to the sea today... Steven Spielberg filmed *Jaws* here in 1975.

Nantucket Island

The English explorer Bartholomew Gosnold was here too – putting Nantucket Island on the map in 1602 when he passed by on the Dartmouth bark *Concord*. This Massachusetts island off Cape Cod is nicknamed the 'Grey Lady' (it often rains). Nantucket was settled by the English from the 1660s, going on to become the world's leading whaling port. The industry faded throughout the 19th century and the community declined, a process hastened by a destructive whale oil fire in 1846 that destroyed much of the town.

This ultimately proved to be the island's salvation, as a hundred years of isolation and stagnation meant that very little changed on Nantucket after the Civil War era. When enterprising developers moved in after World War II, they had the vision to see that the USA's largest concentration of ante-bellum buildings was an asset to be restored rather than something to be swept away and replaced with modern development. Strict controls have maintained this policy ever since, with a result that there's little tackiness evident on this up-market summer resort island. The Nantucket Historical Association maintains six wonderful properties that represent the island's preserved heritage, including the oldest house (built 1686), the Old Gaol and Quaker Meeting house built in 1838 to serve the island's most prominent religion.

The island has an area of just 124 sq km (48 sq mi). The main settlement is also called Nantucket which lies beside the harbour at the western end. Other notable localities are Madaket, Miacomet, Polpis, Siasconset, Surfside and Wauwinet.

Much of the northeastern seaboard aims to offer the sort of idealized, laid-back beach holidays amidst traditional New England architecture that have almost become part of the American Dream (summer section). Inexorable commercial pressures have made such simple pleasures harder to find, but Nantucket delivers in spades.

Houses and dinghies in Nantucket Harbor

Rhode Island

POPULATION:
60,900 (2000)
WHEN TO GO:
September or October for
sensational foliage – the locals even
run 'leaf peeper' tours.
HOW TO GET THERE:
By road bridge. There is no scheduled
airline service to Newport State
Airport.
HIGHLIGHTS:
The Newport Cliff Walk from Easton's
Beach to Bailey's Beach – wonderful
ocean views.
Fort Adams State Park (music lovers
note that the Newport Folk and Jazz
Festivals are held here).
The amazing Green Animals Topiary
Gardens in Portsmouth.
Sachuest Point US Fish & Wildlife
Preserve in Middleton.
Wine tasting at Newport Vineyards in
Middleton or Greenvale Vineyards in
Portsmouth.
YOU SHOULD KNOW:
Polo playing has long been an island
tradition and matches can still be
seen at the Glen, Portsmouth.

Everyone knows that Rhode Island – actually the State of Rhode Island and Providence Plantations – is the smallest in the USA. But not everyone knows that the state and island that gives it a colloquially abbreviated name are not one and the same. Indeed, the Rhode Island part of the longest state name in America is unofficially called Aquidneck Island to distinguish from the state as a whole.

Now that's cleared up, what of Rhode/Aquidneck Island? It is the largest of several in Narragansett Bay, with its southern shore facing the Atlantic Ocean. The area of this well-developed island is 117 sq km (45 sq mi) and it is connected to the mainland by three bridges. The Newport Bridge goes to Jamestown on nearby Conanicut Island, and thence to the mainland on the western side of the bay. The Mount Hope Bridge in Portsmouth connects the northern side of the island with Bristol. The same area is served by the Sakonnet River Bridge over a narrow saltwater channel to Tiverton. The nearby Stone Bridge was destroyed by Hurricane Carol in 1954. The island is divided into three municipalities – Newport, Middleton and Portsmouth.

The island's population shrank by a fifth in the ten years after the US Navy reorganized its major base at Newport in 1973 but is growing again, with over half its area now built over as housing demand increases. But wetland and woodland still occupy a third of the island and there is an active preservation society trying to keep it that way.

After the naval base, the island's principal revenue generator is tourism. Narragansett Bay is a magnet for visitors and they come to Rhode/Aquidneck Island principally for the beaches and coastline, enjoying related activities like sailing, kayaking, sailboarding, diving and fishing.

Mansions dot the coast of Cliff Walk in Newport, with Newport Pell Bridge in the background.

Golden Isles

The Sea Islands are a chain of barrier islands along the coasts of South Carolina, Georgia and Florida. They were colonised by Spanish missionaries seeking to save the souls of indigenous Indians, though both groups were violently ejected by the mid-1700s. The islands featured in the American Revolution and became a haven for fleeing slaves during the Civil War, since when many have been intensively developed as resorts. The middle section of Georgia's islands is known as the Golden Isles, and consists of St Simons, Sea, Jekyll and Little St Simons Islands. Since the 1870s, all but Little St Simons have been up-market places frequented by some of the USA's wealthiest families.

The uninhabited Plum Orchard Mansion on Cumberland Island

The largest is St Simons Island (population 13,400). The resident resort community includes many well-heeled retirees and is swelled by seasonal residents and vacationers.

Sea Island is an exclusive resort created from the late 1920s. The name was changed from Long Island and a plush hotel and golf course constructed. Together, they catered for many of America's richest industrialists. Sea Island is privately owned, a gated community reserved for homeowners, club members and hotel guests. Permanent entry doesn't come cheap – a property recently sold for $12 million.

Jekyll Island (population 900) has a number of interesting buildings from the late 19th and early 20th centuries, earning a Landmark Historic District listing, and is a wildlife haven. A wide variety of mammals and reptiles may be found on the inland marshes.

In stark contrast to the other three, Little St Simons Island is virtually unchanged since it was purchased from King George III in 1760. It is the most remote of the Golden Isles, an uninhabited 10,000-acre wildlife paradise. There is public access for no more than thirty visitors at a time, who pay handsomely to explore this unique island.

POPULATION:
70,000 (2000)
WHEN TO GO:
The temperate climate allows comfortable year-round visiting.
HOW TO GET THERE:
Road access to all but Little St Simons Island (boat only).
HIGHLIGHTS:
Fort Frederica National Monument, the remains of a fort and settlement completed in 1748 by British General James Ogelthorpe on St Simons Island.
The St Simons Island Light – a lighthouse still used as a navigational aid but also a museum run by the Coastal Georgia Historical Society.
An excursion from Jekyll Island to the uninhabited Cumberland Island National Seashore, that is preserved in its natural state.
YOU SHOULD KNOW:
Before leaving the Anglican Church John Wesley, founder of the Methodist Church, was a missionary in the Golden Isles, along with his brother Charles.

Dauphin Island

Boathouses along the shore

This barrier island is 5 km (3 mi) off the mouth of Mobile Bay in the Gulf of Mexico and falls within Mobile County, Alabama. With a landmass of 16 sq km (6 sq mi), Dauphin Island is 22.5 km (14 mi) long and 2.8 km (1.75 mi) across at the widest point. The eastern end is developed, whilst the long western 'tail' is uninhabited.

The island was named after the heir to the French throne, in this case the great-grandson of the Sun King, Louis XIV, serving as a reminder that there was once considerable Gallic influence in these parts. Indeed, Dauphin Island was effectively the capital of the French Louisiana Territories for many years.

The first European visitor was Spanish explorer Alonzo Pineda in 1517. The French arrived in 1699. Pirates raided in 1711. The British captured the island in 1766, losing it to the Spanish in 1780. The Americans arrived in 1813 and built Fort Gaines, which was occupied by Confederate forces in 1861. In 1864, the island was taken by the Union during the Battle of Mobile Bay, when Admiral David Farragut entered the list of famously gung-ho naval commanders with the order 'Damn the torpedoes! Full speed ahead!' after the USS *Tecumseh* was sunk by a torpedo (then a naval mine).

Today, the town that shares the island's name is a popular resort, offering laid-back attractions like beaches, golf courses, parks, sailing and water sports. However, its main claim to fame is ornithology. The whole island is a designated bird sanctuary, and over 340 species have been recorded. There are spring and autumn migrations from the Yucatan Peninsula and South America, with Dauphin Island often the first landfall for thousands of exhausted birds.

The devastating Hurricane Katrina destroyed a third of the island's structures in 2005.

Channel Islands

This island chain lies off the coast of Southern California. Officially they are the Channel Islands of California, but are often called the Santa Barbara Islands. Indeed, the smallest in the chain is Santa Barbara which, unlike the nearby mainland metropolis bearing the same name, is uninhabited.

From north to south, the islands are: San Miguel; Santa Cruz; Santa Rosa; Anacapa; Santa Barbara; Santa Catalina; San Nicholas; San Clemente. They fall into two groups of four, the Northern and Southern Channel Islands. The archipelago extends for 258 km (160 mi) with a combined land area of 895 sq km (346 sq mi).

The only island with a significant resident population is Santa Catalina, largely developed by chewing gum heir William Wrigley II from the 1920s. It has the resort city of Avalon and small town of Two Harbours. Around one million visitors a year are attracted by a wilderness of sage, cactus and oak, plus a wonderful marine environment and genteel resort comforts.

The Channel Islands were under military control in World War II, and the US Navy retains a significant presence. In 1980 five islands (San Miguel, Santa Cruz, Santa Rosa, Anacapa and Santa Barbara) became the Channel Islands National Park. In addition, the waters six nautical miles (11 km, 7 mi) off San Miguel, Santa Cruz, Anacapa and Santa Barbara are protected as the Channel Islands Marine Sanctuary.

The National Park aims to restore and nurture an incredibly rich and diverse biosphere. No more than 250,000 people a year are encouraged to visit, protecting the Park's fragile ecology. Getting there can be an effort, with a trip by small boat or light aircraft the only options, but the effort is certainly worthwhile, allowing visitors to see what mainland California's coast was once like.

Cuylers Harbor on San Miguel Island

POPULATION:
4,000 (2007 estimate)
WHEN TO GO:
The islands have a Mediterranean climate allowing comfortable year-round visiting.
HOW TO GET THERE:
Santa Catalina can be reached by helicopter or ferry from various starting points in Orange and Los Angeles Counties.
HIGHLIGHTS:
Avalon's spectacular Art Deco Casino, a huge circular dance-hall and entertainment palace completed in 1929.
The Catalina Island Museum (in the Casino), with over 100,000 items including Native American artefacts and island-made pottery and tile.
Catalina's bison herd, descended from beasts brought to appear in the 1925 silent movie of Zane Grey's Western novel *The Vanishing American*.
The Wrigley Memorial and Botanical Garden atop Avalon Canyon on Catalina, featuring desert plants from around the world – including eight island natives found nowhere else.
YOU SHOULD KNOW:
In the early 1940s Marilyn Monroe lived on Santa Catalina with first husband James Dougherty, a Merchant Marine officer.

The Florida Keys

The Florida Keys are one of America's biggest tourist attractions. This subtropical archipelago is made up of 1,700 islands which begin at the south-eastern tip of Florida and extend in a gentle arc south-west and then west to Key West, the furthest of the inhabited islands, and on to the uninhabited Dry Tortugas, only 145km (90 mi) from Cuba.

'Key' is a corruption of the Spanish *cayo*, meaning small island. For many years, Key West was the largest town in Florida, grown wealthy on plundering the many ships wrecked on the nearby rocks and reefs. This isolated outpost was well placed for trade with Cuba, and was on the main trade route from New Orleans. Eventually, better navigation led to fewer shipwrecks, and Key West went into a decline in the late 19th century.

The Keys were long accessible only by water. This changed when Henry Flagler built his Overseas Railway in the early 20th century. Flagler extended his Florida East Coast Railway down to Key West using a series of over-sea railroad trestles, a bold and ambitious project for the time it was built. The Labor Day hurricane hit the Keys in 1935, however, with wind speeds of up to 200 miles per hour, and put paid to the Overseas Railway. The damaged tracks were never rebuilt, but the Overseas Highway (an extension of US Highway 1) replaced the railway as the main transportation route from Miami to Key West. This largely two-lane road consists mostly of bridges which connect the islands along the chain.

The Keys are known for their wildlife, with many endemic plant and animal species including the Key deer and the American crocodile. There are many different species of dolphin and porpoise in the warm water surrounding the islands, and the Keys are home to the endangered manatee (sea cow), which is always a delight to observe. The Key lime is not an endemic plant but a naturalized species introduced from Mexico. The Keys have, however, made it their own in the form of the world-famous Key Lime Pie. Each of the Keys has its own personality, but they all share a laid-back approach to life. Key West is the most popular of the islands with tourists, and from here many cruises and boat trips can be arranged to appreciate the natural beauty of this place. The island has an Old Town with charming colonial architecture, bars, cafés, restaurants and shops on its palm-fringed streets, and don't miss the Key West Botanical Forest and Garden for a relaxing stroll.

POPULATION:
79,535 (2000)
WHEN TO GO:
November to May.
HOW TO GET THERE:
Fly to Key West or Marathon airports,
or drive via the scenic
Overseas Highway.
HIGHLIGHTS:
Conch fritters followed by Key
Lime Pie.
The lovely guest houses with wrap-
around porches in Key West.
The tropical hospitality of Jimmy
Buffet's famed 'Margaritaville' –
located on Duval Street, Key West,
this laid-back bar serves fine local
food and drinks to the sound of
live music.

Relax on one of the fabulous beaches,
go sport fishing, have a romantic
seaside meal, swim with dolphins, look
for manatees.
The Ernest Hemmingway Home and
Museum – visit the house in Old Town,
Key West, where the famous author
lived and wrote for ten years. Relive
Hemmingway's lifestyle at one of his
favourite watering holes after
your visit.
PrideFest – this week-long festival
takes place in early June to
celebrate Key West's Gay and
Lesbian community.
YOU SHOULD KNOW:
Key West has long been noted as a
gay vacation destination, and is home
to the United States' first Gay and
Lesbian Chamber of Commerce.

Aerial view of Ohio Key

A rainbow and spring rain clouds at sunset

Angel Island

POPULATION:
60 (2000)
WHEN TO GO:
June to September is definitely the best time to enjoy the open-air delights of Angel Island.
HOW TO GET THERE:
By private boat or public ferry from San Francisco, Tiburon or Vallejo. Be aware that ferry services are scaled back considerably from November to mid-May.
HIGHLIGHTS:
A visitor centre and museum at Ayala Cove (formerly Hospital Cove) where there was once a quarantine station for foreign ships and immigrants suspected of carrying infectious diseases.
Island tours on a Segway, the strange self-balancing personal transportation device.
The island tram tour, an hour-long guided trip that covers all the key sights.
Spectacular views of San Francisco Bay and the Golden Gate Bridge.
YOU SHOULD KNOW:
At the end of World War II, the first thing many troops returning from the Pacific Theatre saw was a 20 m (65 ft) illuminated sign on Angel Island that read 'WELCOME HOME, WELL DONE'.

The small resident population of San Francisco Bay's largest island is regularly swelled by summer visitors who flock to Angel Island State Park, with its spectacular views of Mount Tamalpais, Marin County Headlands and the iconic San Francisco skyline. These are best enjoyed from the island's central high point, Mount Livermore which reaches 240 m (788 ft).

Angel Island has served many purposes over time. It was once a hunting and fishing ground for Miwok Indians, and used as a refuge by early Spanish explorer Juan Manuel de Ayala. The place supported cattle ranching in the 19th century, and was extensively used by the military from the Civil War until a Nike missile base was decommissioned in the early 1960s. At one point the whole island was designated as Fort McDowell. There are two lighthouses on the island, but perhaps it will be best remembered as the 'West Coast Ellis Island' – the Angel Island Immigration Station processed hundreds of thousands of Asian migrants between 1910 and 1940.

This is not a destination for sedentary visitors in search of ready-made attractions. There are good beaches for sunbathing, but swimming is dangerous, as there are no lifeguards to rescue swimmers who get into difficulty in fast-running tides. These do make beachcombing a worthwhile occupation, and there are numerous scenic waterside walks. Hiking trails and fire roads provide good walking or bicycle access to the unspoiled interior (these may be taken to the island or hired on site). Vehicles, dogs, roller skates, roller blades, skateboards, wood fires and some night travel are all banned on the island.

Alcatraz Island

If one word caused a chill to run down the collective spines of America's toughest public enemies, hoodlums, gangsters and career criminals from the 1930s to the 1960s, that word was 'Alcatraz'. Appropriately known as 'The Rock', this craggy island in San Francisco Bay was indeed a hard place, becoming the USA's most notorious federal prison.

Surrounded by strong currents, Alcatraz was considered to be escape proof. Of 34 prisoners involved in 14 attempts during the prison's 29-year life, seven were shot and killed, two drowned, five were unaccounted for and the rest were recaptured. Two made it off the island only to be returned. The most famous attempt – immortalized in the movie *Escape from Alcatraz* – saw three men vanish. They were listed 'presumed drowned', but there has been persistent speculation that they got away.

In fact, the federal prison was a short-lived if notorious part of the island's history, operating from 1934 to 1963. Alcatraz Island was first used to site a lighthouse in the 1850s, but the US Army quickly moved in to fortify the place and protect the seaward approach to San Francisco. In 1868 Alcatraz became a military prison, a role that eventually saw the completion of a huge new cell block in 1912, which was used by the military until handed over to the US Government on cost grounds.

Now a hugely popular visitor attraction dotted with buildings dating back to the Civil War era and supporting a variety of wildlife, the uninhabited island has appeared in many movies. Apart from those featuring prison life, several have used the abandoned prison as a location, including Lee Marvin's *Point Blank*, Clint Eastwood's *The Enforcer* and Sean Connery's *The Rock*. Strangely, the hundreds of tourists who visit Alcatraz every day were nowhere to be seen in any of these films!

POPULATION:
Uninhabited
WHEN TO GO:
Summer for the best weather, off season to avoid the worst of the crowds. Be prepared to book tours in advance during peak times.
HOW TO GET THERE:
There are various organized tours from San Francisco and a ferry service from Pier 33 close to Fisherman's Wharf.
HIGHLIGHTS:
The memorable audio-visual tour of the old prison – Doing Time; The Alcatraz Cellhouse Tour.
The even-more-memorable Alcatraz Night Tour, voted 'Best Tour of the Bay Area'.
Various other themed tours featuring island buildings and wildlife.
The old parade ground, now covered with rubble and an excellent wildlife haven.
Agave Path, a good walk located along a shorefront bulkhead on the south side of the island.
YOU SHOULD KNOW:
Native Americans occupied the island in 1969. Although quickly evicted, the event marked a step forward for the American Indian self-determination campaign.

Alcatraz Island and the Golden Gate Bridge

A Washington State ferry passes through the San Juan Islands.

San Juan Islands

POPULATION:
14,000 (2007 estimate)
WHEN TO GO:
Although the islands boast an average of 247 annual days of sunshine and low rainfall, winters can be windy and chilly, so they are an ideal May-September destination.
HOW TO GET THERE:
Lopez, Shaw, Orcas and San Juan (usually in that order) are reached by ferry from Anacortes. Guemes Island also has a ferry service from Anacortes. Fly to San Juan by light aircraft from Seattle.
HIGHLIGHTS:
Orca-watching from Lime Kiln Point State Park on San Juan Island (May to September).
The panorama seen from the highest point in the San Juan Islands, Mount Constitution on Orcas Island – said to be the most impressive view in Puget Sound.
Shark Reef Sanctuary on Lopez Island, a completely natural park with sensational cliff-top sea views.
Total tranquillity on Shaw Island, where the only commercial operation is the general store run by the Franciscan Sisters of the Eucharist.
YOU SHOULD KNOW:
Some lesser San Juan Islands can tell their own story – for example Barren Island, Cemetery Island, Justice Island, Picnic Island, Skull Island, South Finger Island or the Wasp Islands (named after a ship rather than the insect).

The San Juan Archipelago in the northwestern corner of the continental United States is divided. The San Juan Islands are part of Washington State, whilst a second group belonging to Canada is known as the Gulf Islands. The archipelago has more than 450 islands but fewer than one-sixth are occupied and only a handful may be reached by public ferry.

The islands were initially named by the Spanish explorer Francisco de Eliza in the 1790s, but subsequent American and British expeditions in the 19th century changed many of the original Spanish names, though not that of the archipelago itself. Most of the islands are hilly, with valleys or flat areas in between. Coastlines vary enormously, with sandy and stony beaches, inlets, coves, bays and harbours. Many shorelines are characterized by the presence of gnarled madrona trees, with pine forests often covering inland areas.

The four main San Juan Islands are San Juan itself, Orcas (the largest), Shaw and Lopez. Nearby Guemes is small, with limited facilities. The islands serve as an important tourist destination, easily reached from booming Seattle, much appreciated by those who love the sea, unspoiled nature and the great outdoors. Principal activities are hiking, sailing, kayaking and orca-watching.

But the islands are well organized to serve all the needs of visitors with numerous facilities such as museums, galleries, boutiques and restaurants to be found, especially on San Juan and Orcas. The towns are small but welcoming – historic Friday Harbor on San Juan and Eastsound on Orcas head the line-up, supported by numerous villages and hamlets full of character.

For those who can afford it, the very best way to visit the San Juan Islands is by seaplane, with views to die for all the way (be sure to get a window seat).

Bermuda & its islands

Bermuda's 180 coral islands and islets sit 1,050 km (650 mi) off Cape Hatteras, North Carolina, in the middle of the Atlantic. Effectively, they form a single island unified by the causeways, bridges, and other developments of 350 years of continuously stable history and government. First 'discovered' by the Spaniard Juan de Bermúdez in 1511, it was settled by English colonists shipwrecked on their way to Virginia in 1609 – and it remains a British Dependent Territory by local choice.

British customs and culture govern everything, though Bermuda's jacket-and-tie formality and decorum is a version of British gentility that the motherland never actually experienced outside literature and the colonies. Most visitors find afternoon tea, 'bobbies', and the manners of a bygone age quaint. They mask a steely form of rule that protects the wealth and privacy of the business institutions and many world-famous people who call tax-friendly Bermuda home.

Play the game – as you must – and you'll find one of the world's most enchanting, beautiful and historically captivating places. Bermuda's beaches are white or coral pink, a series of 30 coves and strands backed by rocky cliffs or groves of olivewood, casuarina and Bermuda cedars as well as palms. Its towns and hamlets set their white colonial and pastel neatness against the manicured green of gardens and golf courses, and huge sprays of hibiscus, oleander and morning glory mark the course of roads.

The cobbled lanes of St George, the capital until 1815, wind through a dozen military and naval fortifications preserved, like all the houses and shops, as they were built from 1615 to the mid-19th century. The authenticity of the entire area has earned it UNESCO World Heritage status. Bermuda is an island of living history, modern pleasures, and balmy climatic perfection.

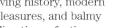

POPULATION:
66,163 (2007)
WHEN TO GO:
April to October is busier and best for watersports, people and entertainment; from November to March many boat and diving services are suspended, but it's comfortably warm, more tranquil, and 40 per cent cheaper.
HOW TO GET THERE:
By air on scheduled flights; or by private yacht or cruise liner to Hamilton or St George.
HIGHLIGHTS:
The Keep on Ireland Island North, one of Bermuda's biggest forts, and home to the Maritime Museum at the Royal Naval Dockyard.
The heavenly scent of the 14.5-hectare (36-acre) Botanical Gardens in Paget Parish, where the Double Fantasy Flower inspired John Lennon.
The sprawling underground system and tidal pools of the Crystal Caves, Hamilton Parish.
The 17th and 18th century forts around the cedar woods, the perfect cove, and rocky cliffs of Achilles Bay.
The 18th century Ducking Stool on Ordnance Island, next to the replica of the 1610 wooden sailing ship *Deliverance*.
The Confederate Museum, describes Bermuda's role in smuggling European arms and supplies in exchange for cotton from the southern States during the American Civil War.
YOU SHOULD KNOW:
Shakespeare wrote *The Tempest* after reading the original colonists' account of their 1609 shipwreck. In the play, he refers to 'the still-vex'd Bermoothes', but relocates them to Italy.

The village of Flatts

An aerial view of the Bimini Cays

North Bimini & Bimini Cays

POPULATION:
1,800 (2005)
WHEN TO GO:
Year-round. The fishing tournament season runs from March to September.
HOW TO GET THERE:
By scheduled air to S Bimini, from Nassau or Florida; by weekly mailboat to Alice Town (N) or Cat Cay (S), from Nassau.
HIGHLIGHTS:
Bottom fishing in the marshes and mangroves of South Bimini.
The dockside scales where the big game fish get publicly weighed.
Diving/snorkelling at Little Caverns.
The heritage bar-crawl known as 'Hemingway's Hideaways'.
The Bimini Museum in Alice Town, with mementos of the town's notoriety as a liquor depot for Prohibition-era rum-runners.
YOU SHOULD KNOW:
Visitors may rent only mopeds, bicycles, or golf carts – and you must drive on the left, because British rules apply.

T he Bimini Cays, 75 km (45 mi) east of Miami and Florida, mark the highest point of a submarine ridge that emerges from the turquoise water at North Bimini, and runs the length of the island along the Gulf Stream. Here, in complete contrast to the sandy slopes of the bay side where most people live, there's only a narrow coastal ledge before the ocean floor drops into a sudden deep. This is the fishing capital of the Bahamas, the site of world record catches of marlin, sailfish, giant tuna, swordfish, wahoo and bonefish.

The big game fish bring divers as well as hunters to Alice Town, the commercial centre of North Bimini and the cays. It's bisected by the King's Highway, the main drag lined by Government buildings, hotels, restaurants, stop-at-nothing bars, shops, tattoo parlours, the Straw Market, resorts and marinas. This concentration of amenities leaves Bimini's most beautiful beach empty: Queen's Highway, on the island's west, stretches past the endless sands of Radio Beach, Blister Beach and Spook Hill. Divers head for the bonanza of colourful fish on Rainbow Reef or the Bimini Barge wreck in 28 m (90 ft) of crystal-clear water; and the shallows of North Bimini's enclosed bay also provide a rare opportunity to explore the extraordinary marine life of proliferating Red Mangroves.

Bimini's reputation for fishing and adventure was cemented by the American laureate Ernest Hemingway. The combination of lush tropical mangroves and the crashing spume of the open ocean proved an irresistible lure – and inspired both 'The Old Man and The Sea' and 'Islands In The Stream'. You'll feel the same visceral attraction to Bimini's primal appeal.

Eleuthera

An idyllic beach on Eleuthera

Eleuthera is the Greek word for freedom; and it was in search of religious freedom that the island was accidentally colonised in 1648 by Captain William Sayles and a group of Puritans from Bermuda. The shipwrecked adventurers found a haven of peace, cleared of its original Lucayan Indian inhabitants by Spanish slavers, and rapidly developed their settlements along its 145 km (90 mi) of curving bays, offshore cays and natural harbours.

Here are the oldest, and still the prettiest townships in the Bahamas. Pastel green, blue, pink and yellow houses with white picket fences and gingerbread fretwork crowd stone quays; miles of pink and white sand beaches glisten into the distance; and the lush plantations of pineapple, and smallholdings of fruit and vegetable farms stretch for miles behind the fringe of coastal palms. Yet for all its length, Eleuthera is never more than 3.5 km (2 mi) wide – and at the Glass Window Bridge, which replaced an earlier natural rock archway, it narrows to less than 32 m (100 ft) between the turbulent Atlantic and Exuma Sound.

Tortuous geology has given Eleuthera some of the world's best dive sites like the Blue Hole, the Train Wreck, the Devil's Backbone and the famous Current Cut. You might prefer the bonefishing along miles of wadeable flats, or braving fishable surf for snapper, jacks and barracuda – but whatever your particular indulgence, you'll return to Eleuthera for its natural beauty and serenity. It is blessedly free of gambling, shopping and amusement parks. Even Dunmore Town, on Harbour Island off the east coast and the heart of celebrity-dripping, upscale Bahamian chic (Versace's personal architect recently re-designed what was already called 'the most luxurious beach in the world') is full of the calm and grace that form Eleuthera's greatest asset.

POPULATION:
9,000 (2005)
WHEN TO GO:
October to June. Come for the 4-day Pineapple Festival and Junkanoo party over the first weekend in June.
HOW TO GET THERE:
By air via Miami or Nassau; by excursion ferry from Fort Lauderdale; or by the weekly Out Islands mailboat service.
HIGHLIGHTS:
The fishing village of Spanish Wells off the north coast, where Spanish galleons watered, and the locals are direct descendants of the original Eleutheran colonists.
Hill Steps in Dunmore Town, an underground tunnel cut by 18th century prisoners from the cove to a nearby house; and re-used for rum-running during the US Prohibition years.
The 1.5 km (1 mi) long, vaulted magnificence of Hatchet Bay Cave.
Fishing for wahoo in 'the pocket' between Chub Cay and The Joulters.
YOU SHOULD KNOW:
The island is called 'Citagoo' in the rural patois.

Exuma Cays

Forty kilometres (25 mi) south-east of the Bahamian capital Nassau is Beacon Cay, the first of 365 cays belonging to the Exuma chain. The Exuma archipelago continues 150 km (90 mi) southwards in a gentle curve, ending with the two main islands of Great Exuma and Little Exuma. The islands are sparsely populated, mainly by conch fishermen, but offer a wonderful environment for yachting, sailing, diving, and coral reef and cave exploring.

Some of the cays are just barren chunks of reef, others are islands with densely vegetated rolling hills, caves and grottos to explore. The Exumas are famous for their pristine beauty, outstanding anchorages and breathtaking marine environment. Under the clear turquoise waters are beautiful natural gardens of coral teeming with fish and lobster. With the excellent water visibility and abundant marine life, the cays are popular with divers and underwater photographers.

Much of the area, including large tracts of offshore reefs, are protected as part of the Exuma Cays Land and Sea Park, the first national marine park in the world. There are many endemic species within the park, including the Hutia, the only terrestrial mammal native to the Bahamas. Iguanas forage unmolested and sea turtles lay their eggs on undisturbed beaches without interference. The no-fishing policy means there are plenty of species to discover in the sea, but perhaps the most intriguing are the stromatolites, blue-green, reef-forming algae. Stromatolites are the oldest living creatures on earth, with some fossil reefs dating back 3.5 billion years.

Exuma was settled in 1783 by American loyalists fleeing the Revolutionary War who established a number of cotton plantations in the cays. George Town, the biggest settlement in the chain, was named in honour of George III, to whom the settlers maintained their sovereignty. One Loyalist settler, Lord John Rolle, was a major figure in the islands' heritage. On his death in 1835, he left all of his Exuma lands to his slaves. This led to a number of towns on Great Exuma being named after him (such as Rolleville and Rolletown).

Today, George Town is a quaint village surrounding Lake Victoria, boasting a safe natural harbour. The harbour attracts boats from all round the world, and hosts the Family Island Regatta each year. The population of George Town grows from about 1,000 to more than 20,000 as teams from all over the Bahamas arrive to race around the harbour in traditional wooden boats.

An aerial view of Exuma Cays and its reefs

Cat Island

Located between Eleuthera and Long Island, Cat Island is the sixth largest island in the Bahamas at 77 km (48 mi) long and 2–7 km (1–4 mi) wide. Unlike many other islands in the chain, Cat Island is definitely low key when it comes to tourism, despite the 97 km (60 mi) of deserted pink and white sand beaches which surround it. This is one of the most beautiful and lush of the islands. From its high cliffs there's a stunning view of the densely forested foothills of Mount Alvernia. This is the highest point on Cat Island, and the highest point in the Bahamas, albeit at just 63 m (206 ft) above sea level. At the summit of Mount Alvernia is a medieval monastery called The Hermitage, hewn from the limestone cliffs by Father Jerome, a penitent hermit, as a place for meditation.

There are two theories on the naming of the island. Some believe it was named after Arthur Catt, the famous British sea captain, others that it got is name from the hordes of feral cats the English discovered when they arrived in the 17th century. The cats were said to be descendants of those left behind by early Spanish colonists as they passed through on their way to find the gold of South America.

POPULATION:
1,647 (2000)
WHEN TO GO:
Any time of year.
HOW TO GET THERE:
Fly from Fort Lauderdale or the other islands in the Bahamas, or mailboat from Nassau on New Providence Island.
HIGHLIGHTS:
The Hermitage – a medieval monastery on Mount Alvernia, the highest point in the Bahamas.
The glorious stretches of pink and white sandy beaches.
Snorkelling and diving in the clear waters.
The crumbling mansions on the old cotton plantations as a reminder of the past.
YOU SHOULD KNOW:
This is said to be Columbus' original landing site in the New World.

The first permanent settlement at Cat Island was made in 1783 by cotton planters who brought wealth to the island. Now the crumbling remains of their mansions, as well as the associated slave villages, stand among the wild tropical flowers and grasses. One such plantation is at Port Howe, a pretty village said to have been built by the intrepid Colonel Andrew Deveaux who recaptured Nassau from the Spanish in 1783. Many descendants of the original early settlers remain on the island today, including actor Sidney Poitier who spent his youth in Arthur's Town and later returned to settle here.

The island may have gained wealth from cotton plantations in the past, but slash and burn farming is now the main way of life for Cat Islanders. Many grow cascarilla bark as a cash crop, which is gathered and shipped to Italy where it becomes a main ingredient in medicines, perfumes and Campari.

Much of the folklore of the Bahamas originates on Cat Island. Traditionally, when the last remaining person of a generation dies, his or her house is left empty for the spirit to live in. The person's relatives gather stones from the site to make a new house. In the north of the island, some people still place spindles on top of their houses to ward off harm.

A pink sand beach at Conch Bay

The Cayman Islands

POPULATION:
Grand Cayman 49,792 (2006);
Cayman Brac 2,000 (2006);
Little Cayman 200 (2006)
WHEN TO GO:
Come between late April and early
December, when it's 40 per cent
cheaper, and 70 per cent less
crowded in George Town.
HOW TO GET THERE:
By air from London, Chicago, Miami
or Havana
HIGHLIGHTS:
The endangered blue iguanas and
hickatees at Queen Elizabeth II
Botanic Park on Grand Cayman.
The birds on Little Cayman –
including the Antilles grackle, ani,
snowy egret, green-backed and
yellow-crowned herons, bananaquit,
green parrot and red-footed booby.
Ten Sails Park, East End, Grand
Cayman, where ten ships were
wrecked on the reefs on the same
night in 1794.
House of Miss Lassie (Gladwyn K.
Bush, b.1914) – the artist's landmark
house is completely covered in
brilliantly coloured paintings of her
religious visions since 1984.
YOU SHOULD KNOW:
Going topless anywhere is illegal –
and don't wear a swimsuit away
from the beach! On the other hand,
there are no beach-hawkers to
annoy you.

Sunrise in the Caymans

South of Cuba in the heart of the western Caribbean, the three Cayman Islands are the visible summits of the Cayman Ridge, an underwater mountain range which drops suddenly into the 7,100 m (22,000 ft) Cayman Trench, separating them from Jamaica.

Grand Cayman is by far the largest. The 'Sister Islands' of Cayman Brac and Little Cayman are mostly a wilderness of fruit trees, orchids and cacti; where tranquility and an authentic West Indian culture are the main attractions. Just 145 km (90 mi) to the southwest, Grand Cayman at first resembles nothing so much as a transplanted American urban nightmare.

The capital, George Town, and Seven Mile Beach, its renowned local playground, are full of condos, resorts, satellite dishes and mini-malls. The streets teem with bankers and the faceless suits of the institutions that have made it the world's fifth largest financial centre. Five days a week, cruise liners decant up to 22,000 tourists, joining the millions each year whose holidays have given the Cayman Islands the eighth highest GDP per capita in the world. George Town is so busy, loud, and determinedly up for it, you feel the privateers and pirates of former times have merely put on modern dress in their eagerness to empty your wallet.

In the small towns and villages outside George Town, the atmosphere changes immediately. Grand Cayman's true self is African-European, deeply Christian, conservative and church-going (there are lots of churches); and also West Indian – openly friendly and well-mannered, laughing and hospitable. Isolated by the central mangrove wetlands – 3,440 hectares (8,500 acres) of lush forests, emerald green parrots and bright orange frogfish, the mainspring of the complex ecology that maintains both the turtle grass and shrimp mounds of North Sound Marine Reserve – Rum Point typifies Grand Cayman at its best.

The Turks & Caicos

Looking down on Parrot Cay

Just 900 km (550 mi) south east of Miami, at the very bottom of the Bahamian Archipelago, lies a British Crown Colony which uses the US Dollar as its official currency. The Turks & Caicos (TCI) – 40 islands and cays, eight of them inhabited – are full of major contradictions. They are set round the edge of two limestone plateaus, in shallow waters that merge into mangrove swamps and refresh the salt pans on which their prosperity has depended since the late 17th century. But at either end of the group, the surrounding coral reefs give way to seriously deep water channels, and the combination has given TCI the richest ecological variety of any island group in the area.

On land you can see iguanas, blue herons, osprey, pelicans, frigates, boobies and huge flocks of flamingoes. You can share the warm water, either fishing for tuna, wahoo, blue marlin or barracuda, or diving among the turtles, spotted eagle and manta rays, octopus, sharks and humpback whales for whom (from December to April) the offshore deeps are major transit points. Underwater, the reefs of Northwest Point, the historic wrecks of Salt Cay, and the waving coral formations descending the legendary 'walls' (some 2,100 m, 7,000 ft) of Grand Turk and West Caicos are as staggeringly beautiful as the onshore natural world.

The contradiction is that TCI is much more famous for its pursuit of material rather than natural wealth. Providenciales (aka Provo), at the western end, is the most developed island, with the international airport, wall-to-wall hotels, resorts, condos and 'entertainments'. To the east, Grand Turk, the TCI capital, is now a horrific service depot for the big cruise ships. Unless you come by yacht, you'll have to pass through Provo or Grand Turk. Grin and bear it – paradise lies beyond.

POPULATION:
30,000 (2007 estimate) – of which some 28,000 live in Provo and Grand Turk
WHEN TO GO:
Year round, but whale watching is only possible from December to April.
HOW TO GET THERE:
By air to Providenciales or by cruise ship to Grand Turk; then by private boat or plane charter to the other islands.
HIGHLIGHTS:
The 18th and 19th century architectural styles of TCI's original Bermudan salt merchants, along Duke St and Font St in Cockburn Town, Grand Turk.
The Molasses Reef Wreck exhibit at the TCI National Museum – it tells of the oldest European shipwreck in the western hemisphere, in 1505.
Salt Cay, proposed as a UNESCO World Heritage Site for its historic integrity.
Any of 33 protected island and marine sites totalling 842 sq km (325 sq mi).
YOU SHOULD KNOW:
Columbus first set foot on Grand Turk in 1492 – most of TCI has remained untouched since then.

The coastline of Port Anegada

Anegada

POPULATION:
200 (2001)
WHEN TO GO:
December to August
HOW TO GET THERE:
Fly to the small Auguste George
Airport, or by ferry or private boat.
HIGHLIGHTS:
Relax on a pristine white sand beach.
Flyfishing – there are good
populations of bonefish here.
See the flamingoes – they are being
reintroduced into the salt ponds at
the west end of the island.
Scuba diving – the many shipwrecks
on the reef make this an interesting
place for diving.
YOU SHOULD KNOW:
If you intend to do any fishing, you
must buy a recreational
fishing permit.

Lying in a remote corner of the Caribbean to the east of Puerto Rico, Anegada is the second largest of the British Virgin Islands (BVI). With a population of just 200, the remoteness of Anegada is one of its main attractions. Most visitors come to the island to simply unwind and relax on the beautiful but relatively deserted white sandy beaches. The clear warm waters around the island are home to a large population of bonefish, making Anegada a popular destination for flyfishing. In fact, the marine life is so plentiful here that local fishermen provide the majority of the fresh fish and lobster catch for the British Virgin Islands.

Anegada is also known for the large salt ponds that cover the west end of the island, or more particularly, the creatures that live there. In the 1830s, thousands of roseate flamingoes inhabited these ponds, but after decades of being hunted for their feathers and meat, the population had all but been wiped out by the 1950s. The flamingoes are currently being reintroduced, which offers a great draw for tourists. Too great a draw, in fact, as scientists are trying to reduce the impact of tourism on the bird population.

Anegada is the only island in the chain which has formed from coral and limestone, rather than volcanic rock. While the other islands are steeply mountainous, Anegada is flat, rising to just 8.5 m (28 ft) above sea level at its highest point; its name translates as 'the drowned land'. Extending south-east from the end of the island is the Horseshoe Reef. At 29-km (18-mi) long, it is the largest barrier reef in the Caribbean and the third largest on earth.

Many tourists hire charter boats while visiting the Virgin Islands, but some yacht-hire companies forbid clients to sail to Anegada because of the dangers of running aground on its shallow reefs. Many vessels have come unstuck here, including the HMS *Astrea* which ran aground in 1808. There are many shipwrecks on the reefs, which make this the perfect spot for scuba diving.

Virgin Gorda

The British Virgin Islands are where Caribbean dreams are made real. They are the paradigm of tropical island beach perfection, and the most popular cruising area in the Caribbean. Virgin Gorda combines the best features of all of them, packing enormous variety into its 21 sq km (8.5 sq mi). Dramatic mahogany forests crown the volcanic Gorda Peak, the island's centre and highest point. The Peak is one of several National Parks on Gorda and its neighbouring cays of Fallen Jerusalem, Prickly Pear and Saba Rock, and in its gorgeous offshore waters. They are sanctuaries for the endangered red-billed tropic bird and important sites for brown boobies, noddies, royal terns and pelicans.

On Gorda's southern tip is The Baths, the most iconic geological wonder in all the BVIs: huge granite boulders are piled haphazardly on a curving beach, some of them forming natural pools which require a ladder to reach. They have also arranged themselves into secret coves that can only be entered on all fours, and into a series of eye-popping 'caves' and chambers, where shafts of tropic sun pierce waist-deep water to create the most romantic tableaux in the West Indies. A lot of visitors come to Gorda just to see The Baths: go early or late, before or after the cruise ships land their extra clientele.

Few islands have as many secluded, luxury resorts as Virgin Gorda, and with the degree of protection offered by the Parks and marine reserves, the island doesn't even have a complete road system, so you can reach some beaches and coves only by boat. It means you can always find something idyllic and completely deserted – although there's always a bar of some kind within minutes. The area around North Sound is brilliant for getting lost among darting shoals of fish, or flocks of colourful birds, in the lap of affordable luxury rarely available to Caribbean visitors.

POPULATION:
4,100 (2002)
WHEN TO GO:
Mid-December to mid-April
HOW TO GET THERE:
Flights from Antigua via Tortola or from San Juan (Puerto Rico), St Thomas or St Croix (US Virgin Islands)
HIGHLIGHTS:
The wildlife sanctuary around the 17th century Spanish ruins at Little Fort National Park.
Diving at the BVIs most celebrated site – the wreck of the *Rhone*, a 94-m (310-ft) long Royal Mail steamer sunk in the 1867 hurricane – between Salt Island and Dead Man's Chest Island.
The exquisite beaches of Prickly Pear National Park, North Sound.
Hiking Gorda's more rugged trails, like those to the Copper Mine National Park, worked by Cornish miners between 1838 – 67.
Snorkelling or diving among the many spectacular coral reefs of the nearby Dog Islands.
YOU SHOULD KNOW:
Anchoring your boat is forbidden in most places – use the official mooring buoys or jetties instead.

The beautiful harbour of Virgin Gorda

Anguilla

POPULATION:
11,797 (2006)
WHEN TO GO:
Mid-December to mid-April (beware
Christmas & New Year, when already
high prices can more than double)
HOW TO GET THERE:
By air to Puerto Rico, Sint Maarten or
Antigua; then by boat to Blowing Point,
the ferry terminal for The Valley,
Anguilla's capital.
HIGHLIGHTS:
The magnificent cliffs and panorama of
the cays from Crocus Bay beach – from
which you can swim among the reef fish
and corals to Anguilla's hidden secret,
Little Bay.
Shoal Bay East, voted one of the
Caribbean's ten Best Beaches. It is, and
a short way offshore is a live reef of
magical colour and movement.
The stone beach 'sculptures' created by
wind and tide at Rendezvous Bay.
Swimming with turtles, and looking for
spiny lobsters on the spectacular reefs
of Anguilla's cays like Dog Island, Seal
Island, Scrub Island and Prickly
Pear Cays.
Playing dominos in a village bar. Day and
night, the loud slap of crashing dominos
is the sound track of the island.
YOU SHOULD KNOW:
Anguilla is the only former British island
in the Caribbean not to list cricket as its
national sport. Anguilla lists 'boat racing'.

*Wind-blown palms on one of
Anguilla's beautiful beaches*

Anguilla got lucky. Since the 1650s it has been more or less bypassed by major development of any kind. At 28 km (16 mi) long by 5 km (3 mi) at its widest, its scrubby hinterland was too arid for big plantations; and early efforts to export cotton, salt and tobacco faded in the early 1800s with the demise of slavery. Even the explosion of Caribbean tourism made little impact – so as the island has finally awoken to its potential, it has been able to take advantage of mistakes in other islands' development strategies.

It has kept its laid-back atmosphere and the sleepy charm of letting goats wander in the restricted traffic. Its 33 white sand beaches are free of ribbon-built hotels and amenities to cope with mass culture. Instead, Anguilla is gaining a reputation as a centre for six-star luxury, with a series of highly individual resorts designed to modify the land and seascape as little as possible. It offers visitors the dreamworld Caribbean of crystal, limpid waters and horizons merging in a hundred shades of blue – along with a degree of 21st century comfort, pampering, mouth-watering food, and the most up-to-date electronic gadgetry, that puts other places to shame. Anguilla appears to have learned that real sophistication means disguising world-class consumption behind ecological authenticity.

You might go there on business. You don't go there for shopping, or for getting raucous (unless it's to impromptu reggae beats on the beach). You go to bask in the sun in perfect conditions, to swim or snorkel or dive, or stroll or ride. You escape the rest of the world when you come. Anguilla is a purist's island, where the wind brings the scent of sea, salt, coral sand and fragrant shrubs of which it is made. Visitors are encouraged to merge with the landscape.

Barbuda

In the eastern Caribbean just north of Antigua, Barbuda is one of the Leeward Islands. On one side of the island the Atlantic Ocean ravages the wild beaches, strewing them with driftwood and shells, while on the other the calm Caribbean Sea creates endless stretches of perfect white and pink sandy beaches. The island is much less developed than many of its Caribbean neighbours, offering the perfect place to unwind. Popular activities include swimming and snorkelling, as the clear waters abound with turtles and tropical fish, as well as some interesting shipwrecks that lie undisturbed in the turquoise water.

At just 24 km (15 mi) long and 13 km (8 mi) wide, Barbuda is largely rocky and flat. Most of the island is covered in bush, home to deer and boar, land turtles and guinea fowl as well as the occasional wild cat. The island is famous for its colony of more than 5,000 frigate birds which gather on the north-western lagoon at the bird sanctuary.

There are many caves on the island. One of them, Indian Cave, contains ancient Amerindian petroglyphs carved into the rock. In others it is possible to climb right through to the top of the Highlands from where you can see for miles. Other caves go underground and underwater and should only be explored by experienced cavers.

The Ciboney were the first to inhabit the island in 2400 BC, but when Christopher Columbus landed on Barbuda in 1493, Arawak and Carib Indians were living here. Early settlements by the Spanish and French were succeeded by the English, who formed a colony in 1666. In 1685, the island was leased to brothers Christopher and John Codrington. The Codrington family produced sugar on their land in Barbuda, and also transported slaves as labour for their sugar plantations on Antigua. For much of the 18th century, the sugar plantations proved a successful and prosperous industry.

The Codrington family influence can still be seen in the street names and architectural remains on the island. The ruins of the Codringtons' Highland House stand on the highest point of the island, and on the south coast can be found the enormous Martello tower, a fort built both for defence of the island and as a vantage point from which to spot valuable shipwrecks on the outlying reefs.

A typically perfect beach in Barbuda

POPULATION:
2000 (2003)
WHEN TO GO:
November to April
HOW TO GET THERE:
Fly or take a ferry from Antigua.
HIGHLIGHTS:
Beachcombing on the Atlantic coast.
Snorkelling the shipwrecks in the shallow waters and reefs.
Indian cave – see the ancient cave carvings.
The frigate bird sanctuary at Codrington Lagoon – this is one of the best places in the world to see these birds.
YOU SHOULD KNOW:
Book accommodation in advance as there are only a few boutique-style resorts on the island.

71

A vibrant street in Speightstown

Barbados

POPULATION:
280,000 (2006)
WHEN TO GO:
November to August. Come for 'Crop Over', the festival of music competitions and traditional activities from July to the costumed parade of Kadooment Day, the first Monday of August.
HOW TO GET THERE:
By air from almost everywhere – Barbados is the international hub for the eastern Caribbean.
HIGHLIGHTS:
The underwater flora waving in the currents inside Animal Flower Cave (St Lucy).
The immaculate, blue-painted 1660 Jacobean manor of St Nicholas Abbey (St Peter).
The 'green flash' of a tropical sunset, seen from any of the fabulous west coast beaches.
The Mount Gay Rum Tour, Bridgetown – home of the 300-year-old maker (the world's oldest).
The monkeys in the tropical rain forest of Welchman Hall Gully (St Thomas).
A cricket match – on a beach or at the Kensington Oval, Bridgetown.
YOU SHOULD KNOW:
It is an offence for anyone, even a child, to wear camouflage clothing. It's not unknown for someone to arrive at the airport from, say, Antigua, trailing three or four live crayfish on a string.

Set apart in the Atlantic, Barbados sits 160 km (100 mi) east of its nearest neighbour, distanced from the brutal colonial rivalries of Caribbean history, but subject to 350 years of unbroken British rule. Even so, its nickname of 'Little England' derives from a superficial gloss of customs and mannerisms that barely disguise Barbados' West Indian core. Get past the trappings of mass tourism and you find a culture of classic calypso and soca-samba, breadfruit and flying fish, and 1,600 rum shops in which Barbadian ('Bajan') quirks and characteristics can best be appreciated. The comfortable mix of the familiar and exotic local flavour has made Barbados the most popular destination in the eastern Caribbean.

Barbados is densely populated and heavily developed. So making the most of the island requires a bit of effort – but the rewards are proportionately stupefying. Of course, you can buy your fun at any number of resorts of every standard, but strike up a conversation in a rural rum shop (usually a brightly-painted, semi-derelict shack), and you plunge into Bajan oral histories that connect you to centuries of buccaneering, colonial adventure, slavery and the sugar trade, and local predictions of the island's future in offshore banking. You might easily end by 'workin' up' (dancing). Hang out in Holetown or Speightstown, or the villages in the Scotland District, where 300 year-old mahogany woods stand on crags looking down on the rocky wilds of Bathsheba Beach, and the Atlantic thrills and terrifies surfers. You can do anything at all on Barbados, but the best thing to do is talk to the Bajans: it is they who will make you want to return.

Guadeloupe

It's called the 'Butterfly' after the shape of its two main islands, but Guadeloupe is a mini-archipelago of wide geographical contrasts. The outlying islands of Marie-Galante, La Desirade and Les Saintes are undeveloped, full of old and crumbling reminders of their historic importance as sugar plantations. Their tranquil coves are especially valued for their privacy and proximity to spectacular reefs, popularized by Jacques Cousteau himself.

Grande-Terre, the eastern wing of the 'Butterfly', is a mostly flat, dry limestone plateau perfect for the huge sugar plantations that make it so prosperous. At its extreme eastern point, St Francois, you'll come to the Pte des Chateaux, an arrangement of cliff and tumbled rock that looks like a series of castles, and carefully hides the only nudist beach in Guadeloupe. In the south, St Anne's beauty is veiled by the mind-numbing throb of salsa classes during the day. At night the beats and the action transfer to the clubs and bars of Gosier, Abymes and Pointe-à-Pitre, Guadeloupe's economic capital, and as suburban a provincial city as anything in France itself.

Guadeloupe is proud that it offers visitors a genuinely West Indian take on its metropolitan motherland, and this is most evident in Basse-Terre, the biggest island, with the administrative capital of the same name. The island's heart is a national park of mountains covered in orchid-filled tropical rainforest. The Rte de la Traversée winds through vast stands of bamboo, tall mahoganies and gums, heliconia and ginger, to the dormant summit of la Soufriere volcano. On one side you can trek your way through jungle to the Cascade des Ecrevisses, one of many waterfalls. Then go back to the terrific nightlife on the coast – if the backbeat of Zouk doesn't get you, then the Biguine, a West African/Creole form of clarinet and trombone jump-up – will. Celebrate it.

POPULATION:
453,000 (2006 estimate)
HOW TO GET THERE:
By air from Paris or Miami to Pointe-à-Pitre; or via San Juan, Martinique or Barbados. By inter-island ferry, or by private boat-taxi, from all neighbouring islands.
WHEN TO GO:
Year-round. Come for the Fete des Cuisinières in August, a culinary nirvana of French Creole celebration, with music and parades and spectacular food.
HIGHLIGHTS:
The Porte d'Enfer, an extraordinary vista of sea between coral reefs at Anse Bertrand, where the cliffs erupt with *Souffleurs* – geysers powered by sea pressure.
Snorkelling/diving in the marine Reserve Cousteau around the Ilets Pigeon.
The three Chutes du Carbet, the highest waterfalls in the Caribbean, on Basse-Terre.
The gossip, the music, and changing vistas of a local bus ride, if you have the stomach.
Guadeloupean local clubs and bars, where the combination of 'ti' punch' and salsa, meringue, RnB, and Zouk will cure all the ills of urban malaise.
YOU SHOULD KNOW:
Rum is considered an art form, and integral to Guadeloupean life. As one of France's overseas departments, Guadeloupe's currency is the euro.

Terre-de-Haut on Les Saintes

Martinique

POPULATION:
400,000 (2006)
WHEN TO GO:
Year-round. Come for a really spirited 5-day Mardi Gras in February/March.
HOW TO GET THERE:
By air from Miami, Puerto Rico or Paris; or from New York or London via Antigua, St Lucia or Barbados.
HIGHLIGHTS:
La Pagerie, (Trois-Ilets) 1763 birthplace of Josephine, Napoleon's Empress. The garden is a riot of frangipani and hibiscus. The museum includes notoriously passionate letters.
The ruins of St Pierre, once called the 'Paris of the West Indies'; the former capital holds a jazz festival each May to mark its obliteration by the eruption of Mt Pelée in 1902.
Diamond Rock, the 180 m (600 ft) high offshore pinnacle manned by the British in 1804, and for 18 months registered by the Royal Navy as an 'armed warship'.
The Musée Gauguin at Le Carbet, where the painter lived, and where Columbus landed in 1502.
Les Gorges de la Falaise – follow the floral route of 'Les Ombrages' to the waterfalls.
The perfect beach at Salines on the island's southern tip.
YOU SHOULD KNOW:
At Fonds St Jacques in 1658, Dominican priests built what is now the best-preserved plantation on Martinique. Here Pere Labat (explorer, polymath, soldier and priest) revolutionized the rum distilling process between 1693 and 1705.

Martinique's Creole chic is a Caribbean wonder. As a Department of France, the island gets all the benefits of the north European Euro-zone, allied to the technicolour brilliance of West Indian music and culture. It's a heady and glamorous mix.

The downside of the French umbilical is overdevelopment and overcrowding, which can be dismaying if you arrive from another island; but after a day or so, the infectious ambience and sheer *élan* of the island will captivate you.

Martinique is big enough to have mountains, rivers, forests and flower-filled wolds – all of which have more than 350 years of history every bit as powerful as the buccaneering tales of its reefs, coves and white sandbars. Fort de France is itself set on one of the world's loveliest bays. Head north on the Route de la Trace, a floral glory of a road rising from the central Lamentin Plain through the legendary tropical rainforest on the flanks of the dormant volcano Mt Pelée at 1,400 m (4,586 ft) and its twin Mt Carbet. Nearby at Case-Pilote is a 17th century rococo Jesuit church, the island's oldest, and the best-preserved working plantation, where the Master's House is now the Musée de la Banane, and the Creole shanties are now little craft shops. Here too, at St Marie et Macouba, perched on a cliff over the Atlantic, are some of Martinique's most famous rum distilleries – but remember local rum is often twice the strength of the other islands.

The Caravelle Peninsula is especially beautiful at Baie du Trésor and Château Dubuc. Further south, you can watch the fishing fleet come home from the hills above Le Vauclin, among the hundred secluded coves and offshore sandbars that make south Martinique so attractive to yachties.

The church of St Henri Anse d'Arlet overlooks an idyllic beach on Martinique.

St Lucia

Every inch of St Lucia tells a story. Lovely Marigot Bay in Castries is where a British Admiral ambushed the French by camouflaging his fleet with palm fronds. Forty-acre Pigeon Island, a nature reserve connected by a causeway to St Lucia's west coast, is crossed by trails linking 1,000 year-old Carib artefacts with 18th century remains like Fort Rodney and a museum highlighting Admiral Rodney's Fleet victory at the Battle of the Saintes. Incidentally, it's also where St Lucia holds its annual Jazz Festival.

One of the Caribbean's most dramatically beautiful islands, St Lucia is a mix of French and British influences, completely subsumed into a distinct West Indian culture, unique among the islands. It's a working country where tourism is just one of several industries – and although St Lucians are glad of your dollars (of course!), they welcome you primarily as visitors to their way of life.

Luckily for St Lucia, the age of big resorts is ending. The island has already recast itself, with an environmental policy designed to protect its outstanding reefs as well as a topography and ecology unmatched anywhere else. The spires of the Pitons in the south are the most famous of its volcanic mountains; the 7,689 hectares (19,000 acres) of National Rain Forest include deep valleys of giant ferns, bromeliads, birds-of-paradise and a riot of orchids, and lakes and waterfalls criss-crossed by swooping parrots, orioles, white-breasted thrashers and peewees; the Mankote Mangrove, the Bois d'Orange swamp and Boriel's Pond provide the best of many birdwatching opportunities; and from March to July you can stargaze on the beach at Grand Anse in the north, while leatherback turtles rise from the sea.

Between its natural splendour, relic-studded history, charming (and hospitable) villages, and graceful town squares, St Lucia is inexhaustibly intriguing and full of wonderful surprises.

One of St Lucia's many breathtaking scenic hideaways

POPULATION:
160,765 (2005)
WHEN TO GO:
Year-round. St Lucia's topography means that every season offers fresh novelties.
HOW TO GET THERE:
By air to Vieux Fort (international) or Castries (local/inter-island).
HIGHLIGHTS:
'Jump-up' (dancing in the streets), to soca and reggae on Friday nights at the fishing village of Gros Islet.
The colourful murals and gingerbread trim of the marketplace at Soufriere, the oldest town in St Lucia, founded by the French in 1746.
Morne Fortune (Hill of Good Luck), Castries, the 17th century French fortress completed by the British in 1796, that was the key strategic point in the wars of colonial possession.
A shower beneath the cascades of Diamond Falls, where Louis XVI built bathhouses for the French garrison troops.
A walk through Latille Gardens – a hidden treasure of tropical fruits, flowers, trees and waterfalls. Enjoy the lush colours as afternoon turns to dusk – and return by moonlight.
YOU SHOULD KNOW:
St Lucia does get a lot of visitors – but you can always find a sandy cove or a country village where you can leave the crowd behind.

The lush vegetation of Dominica's oceanic rainforest

Dominica

POPULATION:
69,625 (2001)
WHEN TO GO:
There's six times more rain in the interior than on the coast, so come for the (generally) dry season between January and June. August to October is the wettest time – but the World Creole Music Festival is from late October to November.
HOW TO GET THERE:
By air, via San Juan, Antigua, Barbados or St Lucia, to Melville Hall in the northeast (international); or to Canefield/Roseau (local islands). By boat, L'Express Des Iles ferry to/from Guadeloupe, Martinique and St Lucia.
HIGHLIGHTS:
The Roseau Museum in the old post office – and behind it the Old Market where slaves were once sold, and which is now a Carib crafts market.
The 'crushed bus' in the Botanical Gardens – testimony to the force of 1979 Hurricane David, and to nature's regenerative power (the tree is still growing on top of the bus).
Champagne – a large area near the fishing village of Pointe Michel, where volcanic activity causes thousands of bubbles to rise from beneath the sea.
The 6,880-hectare (17,000-acre) Morne Trois Pitons National Park – example of Dominica's surpassing oceanic rainforest.
The Boiling Lake: a huge 63 m (200 ft) fumarole crater, a swirling bubbling grey cauldron set high in the green mountains. The world's biggest of its kind.
YOU SHOULD KNOW:
Buying and selling coral is illegal. Please resist the temptation.

At 45 km (29 mi) long and 25 km (16 mi) wide, Dominica is the most mountainous of the volcanic Antilles. The 1,447 m (4,747 ft) Morne Diablotin and Morne Trois Pitons at 1,400 m (4,600 ft) are the highest of several peaks whose proximity attracts much more rain than most islands. The result is Dominica's famously fabulous tropical rainforest, full of rushing torrents, cascades and stepped waterfalls. It's a dark-green world slashed by ribbons of bright sunshine striking into the pretty valleys, catching the riotous colours of 18 m (60 ft) trails of orchids, bougainvillea and hibiscus, and populated by vivid blue, red and yellow signature splashes of the island's astonishing birds – including the rare sisserou parrot. Dominica's extraordinary wildlife is enhanced by its unusual geography: cool, freshwater crater lakes like the Emerald Pool, 24 km (15 mi) from Roseau, the capital, co-exist with steaming fumaroles and naturally hot-water baths.

The island is culturally different from its neighbours, too. It was French, then British, then both – but its original inhabitants, the Caribs, always tried to co-exist with their colonial overlords; and in 1903 gained title to a 1,497-hectare (3,700-acre) Territory in the northeast where 3,000 Caribs still live. They call the island Waitikubuli, and many villages still have Carib names. Away from the coast, you'll hear their Creole patois more than English, the official language.

As high as it rises, so does Dominica dive deep into the ocean. The same adventurous spirit that makes the island beloved of extreme sports enthusiasts (river-tubing, rapid-running, para-gliding off the peaks) brings divers to Dominica's reefs – great walls of colour and life, rich in great and small marine rarities. It's even a prime site for whale watching, especially in the marine reserve around Scott's Head and Soufriere at the southwestern tip. Factor in its reputation for night-life and all you need for Dominica is energy.

Grenada

With a royal flush of rainforests, rugged mountains, fragrant spice trees, rare tropical flowers, kaleidoscopes of birds, cascading rivers, waterfalls, sugar-fine white sand beaches, secluded coves, crystal-clear mountain lakes, picturesque villages, living history and unique local culture, Grenada is both the most beautiful of all Caribbean islands and the most charming. It is a cornucopia of natural wealth and human warmth – and therefore a very rare treasure.

St George's, the capital, is wrapped around a natural harbour, its traditional pastel-coloured buildings and red-tiled roofs reminiscent of a French town. It's dominated by the Gothic tower of the 1818 Cathedral, which with the Georgian public buildings (built by the British between 1780-1801) of Church Street confirm the city's rather European physical character. But its soul is in the bustle and colour and noise of Market Square, for 200 years the crucible of Grenada's post-colonial, post-slavery, Afro-Caribbean and definitively self-respecting West Indian culture of open-handed politesse. Only recently (since the USA invaded in defence of free markets [sic], in 1983), has Grenada's traditional preference for quality over quantity been threatened by new developments of the kind that have already wrecked Barbados. Grand Anse, the island's famous two-mile beach risks being over-run. Luckily, easy-going, tolerant Grenadans have a parallel tradition of repelling unwanted people and schemes – and half the island is now national park, and new schemes are to be rigorously controlled.

Don't get the idea that Grenada wants to preserve its glories in aspic. Historical chance made it the Spice Island of nutmeg, cloves, ginger, cinnamon and cocoa, instead of another giant sugar plantation. These 'industries' make aromatic additions to the sum of the island's existing perfection. Grenadans' most charming feature is the way they welcome you as an honoured guest to share their lives and lifestyle.

The ruins of Brimstone Hill Fortress overlooking the Caribbean Sea.

POPULATION:
90,000 (2007)

WHEN TO GO:
Year-round. Carnival, Grenada's biggest event, is in August; the Spice Island Billfish Tournament is in January; and the Grenada Sailing Festival is in February.

HOW TO GET THERE:
By air via Barbados, Puerto Rico or Trinidad. Or by cruise ship to St George's 300 year-old harbour of Carenage.

HIGHLIGHTS:
The panorama from the rambling fortifications of Fort George (1710), whose Napoleonic-era cannons are still used to fire salutes.
The rainbow of bird-life, tropical fauna, and rare orchids of the rainforest (ferns, mahogany and giant gommier trees) of the Grand Etang Lake Reserve.
The triple cascades of Concord Falls, near the teak groves of Fedon's Mountain, the former base of Julien Fedon, who led a slave uprising against the British in 1765.
Levera National Park – Grenada's most scenic coastal area, including coral reefs, mangrove swamp, lagoon wildfowl reserve, picture-perfect beaches, and turtle hatcheries.
The Saturday morning markets of St George's and Grenville; and any local fair, festival or market where you can talk and share a glass of rum with the islanders.

YOU SHOULD KNOW:
Undeveloped Carriacou, famous for its completely traditional West Indian villages and pristine reefs, is one of several small islands forming Grenada.

Nevis

POPULATION:
10,000 (2007)
WHEN TO GO:
Year-round. It's much, much cheaper
from May to November, outside the
northern winter 'season'.
HOW TO GET THERE:
By air, via Antigua or St Kitts; or by 6-
times a day boat ferry from St Kitts.
HIGHLIGHTS:
The pelicans and fishermen along 3-
mile Pinney's Beach, on the leeward
(west) coast.
The hot spring baths at the 1778
Bath Hotel & Spring House (recently
restored after hurricane damage and
re-opened as a hotel with public
access to the 'healing waters').
The New River Estate – the last to
produce rum commercially, and you
can see the massive machinery and
sugar boiling wall, as well as the
great house and chimneys.
The windmill tower (one of Nevis's
finest), works, kitchen and house of
the early 18th century sugar mill at
Coconut Walk Estate.
A carriage ride through the island's
historic Gingerland area. You see
authentic West Indian life from an
authentic mid-19th century, Creole,
mahogany carriage. Great cliché –
but great fun.
YOU SHOULD KNOW:
The only actual flurries of activity on
Nevis are at the Saturday market, or
when a cargo boat docks from a
neighbouring island.

Small, unhurried and serenely beautiful, dominated by a massive volcanic cone whose graceful curves slope down to luminous green flatlands fringed by ranks of tall palms, Nevis is full of old stone buildings and plantation houses that hint at the West Indies' historic grace and finery. Prettier and more difficult to reach than its sister island of St Kitts, Nevis's claim to represent the romance of the West Indies' age of elegance is quite justified.

From the 17th century, the opulent mansions of its sugar plantation owners were the haunt of high society from Europe as well as the other islands. In Charlestown you can wander among the churches, bridges, fortifications and houses with their wooden balconies and gingerbread trimmings – still much the same as when Horatio Nelson met and married Fanny Nisbet from the Montpelier Plantation, here in 1787 (their signatures are in the register at Fig Tree Church).

Nevis has everything you could dream of in the way of beaches, forests, and exuberant flora and fauna, albeit on a small scale. Follow the road that links the Golden Rock Plantation on the windward side to the northern tip. You pass a troop of African Green (Vervet) monkeys in the exotic foliage, and work your way up the ridge and ravine beds through fields of fruit and flowers set in the rainforest. A shifting panorama of nearby islands sits in a huge sea- and skyscape; inland, you realize that Nevis simply has no mass tourism. Even at the one real hotel, there are no buzzing jet skis; and visitors stay in pretty villas or the old plantations, listening to the island breathing instead of tannoy calls. But with fewer electronics and less delirium, Nevis can party just as hard as anywhere – it just does so with stress-busting charm and intensely enjoyable finesse.

*The remains of an old sugar mill
at Montpelier Plantation Inn*

Tobago

Boats moored off the beautiful island of Tobago.

Tobago is the beautiful, reserved, soul-sister of jump-jiving Trinidad, its partner in the Republic. The contrast is awesome. Tobago is small. It has no major industry to impinge on its lush fertility. It has one main town, Scarborough, and dozens of hamlets and villages with names that reflect the Spanish, French, Dutch, and English colonial powers which coveted it for centuries.

Outside the smallholdings of its sparse population, it's full of nature reserves harbouring wildlife otherwise found only on the South American mainland of which it was once part. At its highland heart, among the many waterfalls splashing down into idyllic bathing pools among the rocks and ferns, Tobago protects the oldest untouched tropical rainforest in the hemisphere. The 'rainy' season between June and December (short, sharp bursts, and a brilliant time to take a swim) freshens the landscape, which erupts into a natural carnival of colourful flowers; and this is matched underwater, where the myriad flashing shoals play lethal hide-and-seek among the cup coral in the canyons and deep caves where barracuda, dolphin and manta rays cruise. You can dig for chip-chip (a kind of shell fish) in the warm clear water of Manzanilla Bay, or hunt the big game fish like marlin, wahoo and yellow-fin tuna. You can have double fun in the knowledge that there's nothing in Tobago – in the water or on land – to kill you: no man-eating sharks, box jelly fish, bird-eating spiders, or poisonous snakes!

Undeveloped (no house, hotel or resort is allowed to build anything higher than a palm tree grows) and peaceful, Tobago does however know how to party. Carnival here is homespun, but just as colourful, rum-fuelled and demoniacally energetic as anywhere. What's more, you can practise every week throughout the year at the open air dance they call 'Sunday School'.

POPULATION:
52,000 (2006)

WHEN TO GO:
Year-round. In mid-July, the 2-week Tobago Heritage Festival is an island-wide celebration of music, dance, food and song which you follow from village to village.

HOW TO GET THERE:
By air, from London, Atlanta and Miami; or via Port of Spain.

HIGHLIGHTS:
The tiered pools of the Argyle Waterfall, one of Tobago's loveliest rainforest cascades.
Fort King George (1779), commanding the heights over Scarborough, the capital, and its harbour.
Surfing the breaks at Mt Irvine beach; then meeting the locals at next-door Buccoo Beach for 'Sunday School', Tobago's hottest weekend event, where visitors are encouraged to join in the islanders' live music, dance and beach barbecue.
The 'Nylon Pool' – way out to sea, you jump out of the boat and walk waist-deep among the fish on the sandbar just below the surface. A truly weird sensation.
The spectacular coast drive to Speyside in the north, where offshore Goat Island is home to Tobago's famous manta rays.
Goat racing and crab racing - in villages, fields, or on the beach, at any time of day.

YOU SHOULD KNOW:
Nobody is pretending it's perfect, but Tobago makes you feel good about the world again.

Trinidad

At its closest, Trinidad is just 12 km (7 mi) from Venezuela, and it has a more South American feel than any other Caribbean island. In fact, forget any Caribbean preconceptions: Trinidad is a highly developed industrial society, densely populated and cosmopolitan. It's fascinating because it's the only island wealthy enough not to depend on tourism. You will be welcomed as a visitor – but in much of the island, your visit will be permitted rather than encouraged, because of unusually strong regional influences that stem directly from Trinidad's history. Competing claims of former Spanish (still spoken in the south), sub-continental Indian, African and English interest groups still provoke political and social discord, and with the huge wealth of its oil, gas and manufacturing industries at stake, Trinidadians are apt to approach business with the same colour, flair, and violent enthusiasm that they put into carnival, music and dancing.

Port of Spain, the north-west and most of the west coast are in the grip of heavy industry. Agribusiness and crowded suburbia fills most of the central flatlands. But in every bar or roadside foodshack, you rock to irresistible Soca, Calypso, Steelpan, Indian Classical, Chutney and Limbo beats. 'Liming' – sociable talking – and laughter underpin every Trinidadian transaction. Theatre gets improvised on the street. The urge to celebrate is central to the multi-ethnic character of Trinidad, and it doesn't matter whether the inspiration is religious or secular. If you're present, you're part of the community – so join in.

Of course there are terrific beaches, too, in the northeast and southwest; tropical rainforests in the northern mountains around 940 m (3,200ft) Cerro del Aripe; and the flora and fauna of reef and swamp. But you go to Trinidad to join the dance for as long as you can keep up with the fun.

POPULATION:
1, 248,000 (2006)
WHEN TO GO:
Year-round. Come for the best Carnival in the world, two weeks in February/March.
HOW TO GET THERE:
By air to Port of Spain.
HIGHLIGHTS:
A night with the Patrol guarding the leatherback turtle breeding sites on the east coast.
Getting down with Parang (Venezuelan-influenced Christmas music), Chutney-Soca, Rapso and Pichakaree (Indo-Trinidadian fusion) – music indigenous to Trinidad.
The scarlet ibis and other exotic species of the Caroni swamp in central Trinidad.
Pointe-à-Pierre Wild Fowl Trust, near San Fernando on the west coast – a nature reserve of mango trees, myrtle and soursop, against a skyscape of flames spouting from the nearby oil refinery flare stacks!
Dunston Cave, home to a colony of the elusive nocturnal guacharo (oilbird), at the Asa Wright Nature Reserve, a former coffee plantation in the northern rainforest.
Pitch Lake, near San Fernando – the natural phenomenon of a 36-hectare (90-acre) lake of asphalt which constantly replenishes itself.
YOU SHOULD KNOW:
Trinidad still sanctions the use of the Cat o' Nine Tails to flog convicted law-breakers.

A fruit stall in the lively market at St James

St Barths

St Barths (St Barthelemy/St Barts) is very small, hilly and arid. Compared to other islands, it doesn't have a lot going for it – yet, aside from privately owned islands, it is the most chic, glamorous and swanky place in the entire Caribbean. It's where the rich, famous, and beautiful go to de-stress, gossip on their mobiles to their friends on the other side of the pool, and very, very carefully reduce the pallor of their northern skins to the lightest of sun-kissed tans.

St Barths was 'discovered' in the 1950s by Rockefellers and Rothschilds looking for privacy. Unsuitable for any kind of plantation, it had only ever been a trading post run by the French, and for 100 years the Swedes, who left only some street names in Gustavia, and a large number of descendants to intermarry with the returning French. So the island has no Creole influence, and though it has pockets of apparently Caribbean bijou prettiness, it has more of a French provincial ambience perfectly adapted to pretentious and world-class posers. In season, the really lovely stone harbour of Gustavia is literally overshadowed by the ranks of mile-high prows of superyachts. The comings-and-goings on the gangplanks during the day, and the competing buzz of ten parties taking place two inches apart at night, makes for the best 'beach TV' in the world – you'll see body language justifying not only your entire visit, but a complimentary PhD as well.

The food is legendary, like every other amenity in St Barths. Its exclusivity has attracted many of the world's great chefs, masseuses and skilled practitioners of other crafts. You can take the beaches for granted: staff will deal with whatever nature can't already provide. It is total, glorious, over-the-top fun.

POPULATION:
7,000 (2007 estimate)

WHEN TO GO:
It's packed in high season, December to April, with the Music Festival in January and Carnival in February. The islanders hold their Fêtes Patronales in August, along with Boubou's Festival and Pitea Day – in all of which the chic is authenticity.

HOW TO GET THERE:
By air via St Maarten, Antigua or Guadeloupe (NB. Owing to the short runway, pilots require a special licence to land at St Barths); by boat from St Maarten (NB. Owing to strong currents, this is a notoriously rocky crossing), or by private yacht.

HIGHLIGHTS:
Pelicans disporting on the many offshore rocks and islets; hummingbirds and yellow-breasted bananquits; frigate-birds and waders in the salt ponds and on the beaches.
Cocktails on the quay at Gustavia when the superyachts are parked up. The white sand perfection of Grande Saline, the naturists' beach where everybody goes.
The tortoises, rays and lobsters on the rich sea bed at Anse du Grand Colombier, a horseshoe cove on the 'wild' coast of the Marine Reserve, relatively undeveloped by hotels.
Next month's copy of *Vogue/Vanity Fair* before it/they go to press.

YOU SHOULD KNOW:
Traditional manners are important on St Barths, however little you are wearing. You shake hands on the first encounter of the day; kissing cheeks is customary (right cheek first) for men and women greeting women; and honking car horns to attract attention is very rude.

Gustavia Harbour

Traditional pastel coloured houses

St Vincent and the Grenadines

POPULATION:
120,519 (2005)
WHEN TO GO:
January to May. Come for the Maroon Festival on Union Island in May, when the whole island stops for the Big Drums to ring in the planting season.
HOW TO GET THERE:
By air via Barbados, Martinique, St Lucia or Trinidad to St Vincent (international); via St Vincent to Bequia, Mustique, Canouan and Union Is (local). By regular ferry to/from St Vincent around the islands to/from Grenada.
HIGHLIGHTS:
The oldest (1763) Botanic Garden in the West Indies, St Vincent – including one of Captain Bligh's original breadfruit trees, and a rare Soufriere Tree not seen in the wild since 1812. Model boatbuilding in Port Elizabeth, Bequia – in the tradition of the real schooners for which the island's whalers were famous.
The illustrations of Black Carib history in the Officers' Mess of the 18th century Fort Charlotte, with a panoramic view of Kingstown and the islands from its 201m (660 ft) ridge.
The Owia Salt Pond, St Vincent – you swim in a huge natural pool enclosed by lava peaks and ridges. The Atlantic waves pound into the rocks, and gently cascade over the edge.
YOU SHOULD KNOW:
The Grenadines are where reality beggars the most exuberant imagination.

It's easy to feel something of an intruder in the Grenadines. These islands epitomize the classic image of the West Indies – of green fertility and turquoise shallows merging into an aquamarine horizon notched by ever more dreamy coastlines, where everything appears to sparkle, and people greet each other with an open smile. You sail (you always sail in the dream) on the infectious buoyancy of easy-going happiness that characterizes the Caribbean's almost forgotten, tranquil corner. And for visitors, it's all true – with the difference that regular ferries and cheaply-available air and water-taxis mean you don't actually have to have your own boat.

Pockets of world-class luxury exist, notably in Mustique (home to Mick Jagger, David Bowie and a handful of other celebrities with a legitimate desire for privacy), Palm Island and Bequia (pronounced 'Beck-way'); but the soft trade winds will draw you south with the smell of spices from Canouan, Mayreau, and the Union Islands, and the fabulous Tobago Cays where *Pirates of the Caribbean* was filmed. You travel through a weave of French, Carib, Creole and British cultures. You find village rum shops full of animated cheer and crashing domino slates; monkeys foraging by forest lakes in the high mountains; fish markets on stone quays; 18th century cannon amid giant ferns on the walls of once-important forts or whaling stations; deserted crescents of pure-white or volcanic black sand; rocky bays that explode with the chatter of parrots – rainbows arcing across the blue. Dolphins ride your bow-wave (even in the ferry!), and at anchor, in the clear water, yellow and blue-striped sargeant-major fish flip somersaults in the passing shadow-triangle of rays.

You don't have to be rich to fall in love with St Vincent and the Grenadines, but what Grenadinians call "ri-thinkin' frame of min".

Saba

The smallest island of the Netherlands Antilles, Saba is an unspoilt island paradise in the West Indies. The rocky island is the cone of an extinct volcano rising out of the sea to 850 m (2,800 ft). The peak of the volcano, Mount Scenery, is the highest point in the Kingdom of the Netherlands. Despite being Dutch, the island's main language is English, which has been used in the school system here since 1986.

The first European to discover Saba was Christopher Columbus in 1493, though he did not go ashore due to the steep rocky cliffs which surround the island. In 1632 a group of British sailors landed on Saba after they were shipwrecked nearby. They said the island was uninhabited, but it seems likely that Carib or Arawak Indians may have been living there at the time. The island then passed variously between French, Dutch and British hands until the Netherlands finally took possession in 1816.

During the 17th century, the island was used as a hideout for local pirates. England also deported its undesirables to the area and many of them, too, became pirates taking refuge on Saba. The most famous was Hiram Breakes who coined the phrase 'Dead men tell no tales'. Through the 17th and 18th centuries, the major industries on the island were sugar, rum and lobster fishing. Legitimate trade soon became important and the islanders exported Saba lace, made by the island's women.

Today there are four charming villages on the island – Hell's Gate, Windwardside, St John's and The Bottom. The verdant forests, punctuated by the red roofs of the villages, offer a stunning contrast to the brilliant blue sea surrounding the island. The waters here are clear and the island is renowned as an excellent dive site.

Unlike many places in the world, Saba's shallow reefs are still pristine. When dive tourism began here, local fishermen agreed not to fish on the best diving reefs, so the reefs were protected before any damage could be done. The area is now more formally protected under the Saba National Marine Park. Although the shallow reefs and walls are excellent here, the island is best known for its underwater pinnacles, the rocky summit of underwater mountains. These pinnacles are home to incredible numbers of large fish and pelagics, and populations are actually increasing, making shark sightings more frequent.

POPULATION:
1,349 (2001)
WHEN TO GO:
September to February
HOW TO GET THERE:
By plane or ferry from the nearby island of St Martin.
HIGHLIGHTS:
Diving around Saba's famous pinnacles – there are numerous large fish species here, and shark sightings are becoming more frequent.
Mount Scenery – the peak of this ancient volcano can be climbed via a series of over 1,000 steps. Alternatively, take a car up the narrow roadwhich spirals to the top through the lush vegetation.
The quaint villages on the island are old-fashioned and delightful, and the local people very friendly. Take the time to look for some lovely Saba lace to take home as a souvenir.
Saba Spice – the local Saba Island rum is masterfully blended with Canadian rum to achieve a smooth, distinctive, complex taste.
YOU SHOULD KNOW:
The Saban Government has its own hyperbaric chamber to treat those suffering from decompression sickness, so you will be well looked after if you over-do it.

Red roofs of The Bottom, Saba's capital, sit in the bowl of an extinct volcanic crater.

Aruba, Bonaire & Curaçao

POPULATION:
Curaçao 133,644; Aruba 103,484;
Bonaire 14,006 (2007)
WHEN TO GO:
April to September, when it's much
quieter without the three million-plus
visitors escaping the North American
winter months.
HOW TO GET THERE:
By cruise liner – like 600,000 others
each year – or by air (international or
inter-island). There are no ferries.
HIGHLIGHTS:
The early 19th century red gold mines
at Bushiribana and the gold mill at
Balashi, Aruba.
The bone ceremonial 'vomiting stick'
and Arawak artefacts at the
Oranjestad Archaeological Museum,
Aruba.
The flamingoes, parrots, cacti and
green iguanas at Washington-Slaagbai
National Park, near Rincon, Bonaire.
The swan park at the former slave
holding camp (late 17th – early 19th
century) and lavish plantation house of
Landhuis Zuurzak, Den Dunki National
Park, Curaçao.
YOU SHOULD KNOW:
Despite their willingness to encourage
visitors, the island people take real
offence at topless sunbathing or
swimming outside hotels.

Known as the ABCs, these are the biggest of the former (disbanded Dec 1996) Netherlands Antilles, and lie off the western coast of Venezuela. They share a thriving culture evolved from their Arawak, Dutch, Spanish, West Indian, Latin and African heritage; a common geography of starkly arid, cactus-strewn interior hills, surrounded by countless bays of white sands and ridiculously opal seas where wrecks and coral reefs promise world-class diving; the prosperity of refining Venezuela's huge oil reserves and of their huge tourist industry – while still retaining the benefits of being part of the Netherlands. They are outside the hurricane belt and there's a year-round tropical climate of 28 °C (82 °F) with guaranteed sun and balmy breezes. Though each island has unique features, they are collectively distinct in every way from all other Caribbean islands.

Aruba lies closest to Venezuela, only 30 km (19 mi) away and its version of Papamiento, the polyglot patois of the Netherlands Antilles has much greater Spanish influence. You might go there for its grand, high-rise resorts, but it's the Arawak petroglyphs in Arikok National Park, which covers 20 per cent of Aruba, that will capture your imagination. So will 'socarengue', Aruba's own, super-sexy, bump'n'grind party music.

Curaçao, the nexus of Dutch Caribbean history and culture, has 'tumba', identified by its primal, undiluted African beats. Curaçao is for partying, duty-free shopping, casinos and the World Heritage capital of Willemstad, beautifully restored to its 300 year-old Dutch colonial magnificence. The northwest of the island, where former slave plantations give way to the wildlife in rugged Mt Christoffel National Park, is much less developed. Bonaire lacks the crazed sophistication of its neighbours, but it has flamingoes and a marine park of deserved world fame among divers. It also has the marvellous Simadan Festival, held between February and April just after the sorghum harvest.

The colourful harbour-front buildings of Curaçao

The coastline of Saint Maarten

Saint Maarten

Famous as the smallest island ever to have been partitioned, St Maarten/St Martin has been shared by the Dutch and French since 1630, when they united to repulse the Spanish. Until 1817 nobody bothered with boundaries, and you can still move freely about the island; but despite the inextricably mixed Dutch, French and African heritage, you can't fail to distinguish the contrasting styles of the island's French and Dutch communities.

St Maarten welcomes cruise liners, commerce, gambling, reggae, hard rock and rijsttafel restaurants. It's the only place in the Caribbean where shopping is 100 per cent duty-free, and in Philipsburg you'll find 500 of the smartest luxury shops in the world. Despite heavy tourist development, it's still a treasure-trove of old world Dutch architecture and military relics, often next to the white beaches that guarantee St Maarten's popularity. The French emphasize comfort and elegance on their side, with secluded, luxury resorts and the best food in the Caribbean. Euros will pay for your croissants in the cafés and typically Gallic, charming bistros which are as relaxed as they are cosmopolitan (though French or Dutch, you must factor in the spicy aromas of West Indian cooking). Marigot, the capital, is the most French in spirit of all Caribbean cities, a luxury colonial version of a Mediterranean market town. But on the beaches you can always tell where you are by the dress code – modest on the Dutch side, topless or nude chic on the French. Orient-Plage is officially 'clothing-optional', but on the French side no-one is looking and no-one cares. With steel bands and firelit dancing, it makes for heady beach barbecues. The combination of cultures means you can do just about anything here on some of the Caribbean's prettiest and liveliest beaches and in the towns.

POPULATION:
Sint Maarten 35,000 (2007); Saint Martin 34,800 (2007)
WHEN TO GO:
October to June. In March, the Heineken Regatta attracts world-class yachting enthusiasts.
HOW TO GET THERE:
By air from Miami, San Juan (Puerto Rico), or Caracas.
HIGHLIGHTS:
The tropic green valley of Colombier between Marigot and Grand Case.
The spectacular vista from Pic Paradis, the highest point on the island at 450 m (1,400 ft) .
Tuesday night festivities on the Blvd de Grand-Case, during high season.
The beautifully-preserved 17th century fishing village of Orléans on the east side.
The pre-Colombian and colonial treasures at the St Martin Museum in Marigot.
Fort St Louis, built in 1767 and overlooking Marigot.
YOU SHOULD KNOW:
St Maarten/St Martin operates a joint nature and marine reserve, which includes 40 km (25 mi) of trails through mountains, forests and along the shore – where you walk through groves of 200 year-old mango and mahogany trees.

The perfect volcanic cone of Mount Mazinga

Saint Eustatius

POPULATION:
3,183 (2006)
WHEN TO GO:
October to June
HOW TO GET THERE:
By air, from Miami, Antigua,
or Curaçao.
HIGHLIGHTS:
Diving with the spectacular flying
gurnards – rare in the Caribbean,
common in Statia.
Exploring the archaeological
shipwrecks, of which Statia has many.
The Historic Museum in Oranjestad,
where divers bring all their
archaeological finds.
The true Eden of The Quill crater: its
flora and fauna are pristine.
YOU SHOULD KNOW:
Peter Stuyvesant bought Nieuwe
Amsterdam (New York) from Native
Americans for 30 blue beads from
Statia. Blue beads were once used in
Statia as currency for slave wages.

Saint Eustatius is always called Statia, and pronounced 'Stay-sha'. Everything about it – history, geography, culture and amenities – defies its tiny 21 sq km (8 sq mi). Now a Dutch overseas province, it once changed hands 20 times between the Spanish, French, English and Dutch. During the English blockade of the American Revolutionary War it reached its zenith, when a population of 20,000 serviced hundreds of merchant ships at Oranjestad, the island capital. Now, after two centuries as a slumbering backwater, Statia's buccaneering past – the stone quays, ancient buildings and forts, plantation houses and offshore wrecks – is bringing it new prosperity as one of the Caribbean's most fascinating but unspoiled islands.

At its north end, a series of hills creates pockets of banana and fig groves, where overgrown lanes twist between neat, clapboard hamlets and idyllic coves. The big plantations (many now resorts), of the central plain give way in the south to the lush rainforest of the National Park, which includes the perfect volcanic cone of the 602 m (1,968 ft) Mt Mazinga. From the top, you descend 329 m (1,080 ft) into a tropical paradise called The Quill. The huge crater is filled with a magnificent array of trees, fauna and flora, most notably 17 different kinds of orchid and 55 exotic species of birds.

Underwater, Statia's volcanic origins have left fissures, pinnacles and canyons covered in corals and sponges that attract a huge variety of fish like black rip sharks, eagle rays and rarities including flying gurnards, high-hats and jack-knife fish. A single dive site consists of tangled wrecks where barracuda patrol huge schools of snappers and goat fish, and spotted morays and stingrays commonly lurk below. Statia may be small, but it has the natural wealth of a marine Serengeti.

Cuba

Cuba's history is as shocking as it is lurid. After four centuries of genocide, slavery and savage exploitation, in 1898 Spain lost control of the biggest island in the Caribbean and world's largest sugar producer to its covetous neighbour, the United States. Prevented by its own laws from annexing Cuba (as it had the Philippines, Guam and Puerto Rico), the US instead institutionalized racism, economic slavery, and tourism based on drinking, gambling and prostitution. When Castro's popular revolution stopped them, the US retaliated by wrecking Cuba's economy, but retaining 'rights' it had assigned to itself like the notorious Guantanamo naval base. For 50 years, the US blockade and trade embargos have hurt Cuba – but by delaying the island's fundamental modernization and development, they are proving to have been an even greater blessing in disguise.

Even under Castro's cyclical Puritanism, Cubans never forgot how to party, big-time. Havana, especially Old Havana, has been restored, not rebuilt as a high-rise mall – and it throbs to the happy syncopations of rumba, sound-splashed on bright colours. Havana is loaded with easy-going character that belies the true vigour and energy driving Cuban culture. You find it everywhere. As the US position becomes increasingly silly, more visitors are discovering the real thrill of vibrant beach-life, fabulous nightclubs, ecstatic rhythms, dance and laughter; plus an astounding repository of natural wealth, with all mod cons, but without the paraphernalia of dedicated consumerism that has spoiled up so much of the Caribbean. Twenty-two per cent of Cuba has recently been dedicated to protected reserves, including a 70,000 strong flamingo colony in the Río Máximo-Cagüey wetlands, winding 'mogote' caves, and the 3,000 rare Cuban crocodiles in the Zapata swamps. These, and the wrought-iron grills, dilapidated mansions, heavenly cigars and mojitos are the things others have built over or excised. Not Cuba. It's got the best of the past, and the future. Go now.

POPULATION:
11, 275,000 (2005)
WHEN TO GO:
December to March is the prime beach season but it's brilliant all year-round.
HOW TO GET THERE:
By air to Havana, from everywhere except the United States. The US also prevents all passenger ships, and most cruise ships, from calling. US visitors generally come by air, via Cancun, Nassau or Toronto.
HIGHLIGHTS:
High jinks in Old Havana – rumba/salsa/ritmo-ritmo in the winding streets of resplendent colonial buildings, an atmosphere of spiritually uplifting, world-class hedonism.
Santiago, Cuba's second city, more Caribbean than Havana, with a Creole influence in the palaces, mansions and museums that make it Cuba's historic heart.
The 1795 Tower of the Manaca Iznaga Estate, the manor of a wealthy slaver, and one of the 'ingenios' (19th century sugar mills) set among the Royal palms, waving cane and rolling hills of the Valle de los Ingenios.
UNESCO World Heritage city of Trinidad – a smuggler's backwater from 1514 to the late 18th century, when a brief sugar boom bought it the marble-floored mansions you see today.
The 235 pictographs at Cueva de Punta del Este – called 'the Sistine Chapel of Caribbean Indian art', created circa 800 AD, and the most important of their kind.

The Cathedral of Havana

Hispaniola

WHEN TO GO:
Haiti has two rainy seasons, April to
May and September to October. But
there's no peak tourist season to
raise prices, so come from November
to March. The DR is lovely from
November to July.

HOW TO GET THERE:
By air to Port-au-Prince (Haiti) or
Santo Domingo (S) or Puerto Plata (N)
(Dominican Republic).

HIGHLIGHTS:
The 19th century Marché de Fer (Iron
Market), noisy, chaotic centre of
activity in Port-au-Prince's rundown
buildings, huge coloured murals and
'taptaps' (public buses covered in
crazy art and Creole proverbs).
The Spanish architecture of Cap
Haitien, the former capital once
called the 'Paris of the Antilles',
where the aroma of orange speaks
of making Grand Marnier
and Cointreau.
The Samana Peninsula, DR, where
from January to March, 10,000
humpback whales return from the
North Atlantic to breed and nurse
their calves.
The 16th century cathedrals, fort and
cobbled streets of Santo Domingo's
Ciudad Colonial; beautifully
preserved, and now set with cafés,
lively bars and restaurants.
The lowest point on the Caribbean
(40 m, 131 ft below sea level), Lago
Enriquillo in the SW of DR – salty,
full of crocodiles, it's where tropical
rainforest meets
cactus-strewn desert.

The second-largest island in the Caribbean, claimed by Columbus in 1492, and Spain's launch pad for its South American conquests, Hispaniola has long been divided into French-speaking Haiti and Spanish-speaking Dominican Republic. Europeans brought disease to wipe out the indigenous Arawak, then imported slaves to do their bidding and work the fertile island into the most profitable 'farm' in the world – which Spain, France, Britain and the United States quarrelled over for 200 years while Hispaniola's two halves developed distinct cultures characterized by rapacious dictatorships that suppressed whole populations in the name of personal profit. Trujillo in DR used an army of bruisers; in Haiti 'Papa Doc' Duvalier had the Tonton Macoute secret police to create two-tier societies which have gone, but are not yet replaced by democratic reform.

All of which leaves visitors with a political choice. Hispaniola is geographically and ecologically astounding, in addition to having all the first-class attributes of sub-tropical hedonism demanded by northern snowbirds in search of a parasol-shaded daiquiri. The island's scale means that its flora and fauna are richer, matching higher mountains and more varied ecologies; but both Haiti and DR are poverty-stricken and over-populated, and still suffering the consequences of civil strife and exploitation. So the choice is between taking your pleasures in the confines of resorts, and taking an interest in the wildly different cultures beyond them. Hispaniolans share fantastic forms of music; vibrant colour in their art, clothes and dance; and deep spirituality expressed in every way from denominational churches to voodoo to animism. But Haiti is Afro-Caribbean, its European influences submerged since Toussaint l'Ouverture led the first slave rebellion; while DR, in just a decade or so, is on its way to becoming West Indian-American, another Puerto Rico. On Hispaniola, culture is way more intriguing than the admittedly marvellous beach life.

*Palm trees line Playa
Punta Cana on DR*

Saona

Colourful huts line Saona's beaches

Off the southeast tip of the Dominican Republic, where the Atlantic and the Caribbean go head to head, lies the incarnation of the tropical island idyll. Its curves of white sand fringed by swaying palm trees, green against the azure sea, combine in a single image celebrated by millions of Europeans as the setting for the Bounty (chocolate) Bar TV commercial. Saona is the notion of paradise made manifest – and it looks even better than on film.

There are just two tiny settlements on the 25 km (15 mi) by 5 km (3 mi) island. Punta Gorda and the picturesque fishing village of Mano Juan are sleepy relics of the trading stations established after 1493 by Colombus, who bullied the Taino chieftain Cotubanama into an unequal partnership. Cotubanama's descendants now appear to be exacting an exquisite revenge. After centuries of subsistence fishing, in just ten years they have become unofficial beachmasters to the fleet of speedboats and catamarans that each day bring over hundreds of day-trippers from every major resort on the mainland, to bear witness to the existence in fact of a television dream. But Saona is part of a National Park and Marine Reserve with no amenities except in the tiny, restricted areas allotted to each resort group – where the islanders ply the by now rum-happy tourists with trinkets, curios, 'personalized' photos or video clips and 'massages' to the thumping beats of a beach boom-box.

You can walk away along equally fabulous but empty beaches, to lagoons full of flamingoes and mangroves stirred by pelicans, red-footed boobies, and Hispaniolan lizard-cuckoos and parrots. You can snorkel or dive among giant sponges and teeming fish on the reefs where manatees float in languor and dolphins somersault. The serenity of wonderland is still there – if you want to find it.

POPULATION:
300 (2007)
WHEN TO GO:
November to June
HOW TO GET THERE:
By catamaran or speedboat from the beach at Bayahibe or Dominicus on the mainland. Most of the boats are pre-booked to resort groups, but there are some independent excursion sellers.
HIGHLIGHTS:
Getting there – with or without the rum-fuelled party boats, the speedboat/catamaran trip across the currents of the Paso de Catuano, from the limestone cliffs of the mainland to island romance on the horizon, is huge fun.
Laguna de los Flamencos near the mangroves in the southwest.
The amazing Arawak and Taino rock art in the Cueva Cotubanamá – the cave in the island's west where the Chief hid before his capture by the Spanish.
'La Piscina Natural' – underwater sandbars hundreds of metres out to sea, where you jump into waist-deep water to drink, party, and frighten the lovely fish. Or just swim.
The photo you take home showing you at the Bounty Bar beach, yes, really!
YOU SHOULD KNOW:
On the big catamarans, someone will come round putting a little hat on your head. They are not being kind – unless you reject it immediately, you will be charged at least US$4 for it on leaving the boat.

The beach at Ochio Rios

Jamaica

Jamaica is the great cultural boom-box of the Caribbean, constantly advertising an identity already so strong that it is recognized anywhere in the world. It's not at all typical of the West Indies, but by asserting itself so vigorously, this one island has come to epitomize them all.

After Columbus, who tried to make it his personal fief in 1494, Jamaica was always an English/British colony after Admiral William Penn (father of William Penn of Pennsylvania) seized it in 1655; and centuries of aggressive control by sugar oligarchs and naval and military commanders created a style still apparent in the gangs and societies that make the unofficial rules in Jamaica today. Parts of Kingston and other towns are plain dangerous for visitors, and you go warily almost everywhere outside resorts and tourist destinations. Happily, the resorts are themselves set in such beautiful places that visitors don't mind their self-imposed restrictions; but if you want to explore outside the envelope the best way is to join in one of the many festivals all over the island, in which Jamaicans celebrate their countryside, religions, planting, harvest, towns, rivers, and history, with the intense joie-de-vivre that infects the island's brilliant music, dance and theatre. On these occasions you'll see an open-hearted, deeply spiritual, carefree and generous people intent on pleasure rather than your tourist bucks, and you'll love it.

There's much to love in Jamaica, especially reggae, street markets, genteel towns like Mandeville (laid out in 1816, and still serves tea around 4 pm), Jamaican rum in its many light and dark forms, Blue Mountain coffee and the mountains themselves, the aura of elegance and celebrity inherent in Ocho Rios and Montego Bay, limpid peach sunsets silhouetting palms on Negril's 11 km (7 mi) nudist-happy beach, and – insistent and everywhere - more reggae. Grab some goat jerky and get stuck in to the fun.

Puerto Rico

Just 1,600 km (1,000 mi) southeast of Miami, the freeways, skyscrapers, malls and parking lots of the United States crash into four centuries of Spanish colonial culture. Puerto Rico sounds like the most uncomfortable kind of shotgun alliance – but being Caribbean, it gets away with it. It became American in 1898 after the Spanish-American War, and you'd think a century was enough for two fundamentally opposed cultural styles to assimilate. It isn't, even in San Juan, and even though all Puerto Ricans are US citizens. When you explore the island's mountainous interior, you feel that the infrastructure of roads and amenities is extraordinarily misplaced, like gleaming chrome set in the middle of fine old porcelain. What Puerto Rico has given so successfully to New York and other US cities, doesn't travel back the other way. The island's delights are all in its colonial history, in its Taino (Amerindian) origins, and its Caribbean present.

The best of these is Old San Juan, the island heart of the capital, and the site of its colonial government since 1509. Massive ramparts and fortifications guard its oldest sections, a maze of palatial homes, tree-shaded plazas and public buildings that demonstrate Puerto Rico's colossal wealth. The dramatic panorama from the Santa Barbara Bastion on the 42 m (140 ft) heights of Morro Fort, of towers, tunnels and 5m (16ft) thick bulwarks guarding the headland where the Atlantic is restrained by San Juan Bay, is an inspirational image of bygone power; and Old San Juan's historic splendour (now enlivened by little bars and quietly sizzling music) ranks with the world's best historical areas.

Like Honolulu, San Juan has sugar-soft white beaches; and like Hawaii generally, Puerto Rico is a unique version of the United States. Weirdly Caribbean, horribly crowded and brash, but fun.

POPULATION:
3, 927,776 (2006 estimate)
WHEN TO GO:
Puerto Rico is 'full' from December to April. Come for the Salsa Congress in July, when thousands participate in dance competitions, at Isla Verde, San Juan.
HOW TO GET THERE:
By air to San Juan, which is also the hub for domestic flights.
HIGHLIGHTS:
The trompe l'oeil painting in the cathedral dome, and the 17th century splendour of the colonial homes, plazas, fountains and churches of colourful Ponce, Puerto Rico's second city.
The stunning cavern systems, weird rock formations, world's largest underground river and blue-eyed river crabs at Parque de las Cavernas del Rio Camuy, SW of San Juan.
El Yunque, the only tropical rainforest in the US, and rich in flora and fauna
Eating 'alcapurria', a plantain fritter stuffed with seafood, from a roadside kiosk at the Balneario (public beach) de Luquillo, one of the prettiest beaches near San Juan.
YOU SHOULD KNOW:
1. There is a board game called 'Puerto Rico'. This witty game of colonial domination was ranked the No.1 Internet Game 2007. 2. Puerto Ricans who live in New York City are called 'Nuyoricans'.

The vibrant houses lining Recinto Sur Street in Old San Juan.

Isla Carmen

The Gulf of California (aka Sea of Cortez), between Baja and the Mexican mainland, is one of the world's marine marvels. Baja's 1,000 km (650 mi) spine of mountainous cactus scrub and sea pine forest guards a milk-warm oceanic playground from the violence of the Pacific. It's the southern nursery of fin, blue, sperm and orca whales, and home to countless family pods of bottlenose and common dolphins, sea lions, manta rays, and rainbow shoals of angelfish, guitarfish, redtail tigerfish and some 600 other species. Red-billed tropicbirds, blue-footed boobies, pelicans, frigatebirds and rare Heerman's gulls nesting by the thousand help to emphasize the great wildlife spectacle. And half way down the Gulf, where the temperate merges with the tropic zone, bringing together all kinds of species at their seasonal ranges in a cacophony of seabirds and harmony of underwater song, is Isla Carmen, the biggest island in Loreto Bay National Marine Park.

Carmen used to be famous for the purity of its salt deposits, discovered in the early 16th century. Now, Salinas, its only settlement, is a ghost town among the 60 m (100 ft) cliffs, sand dunes and white beaches. Shale and gravel slope sharply to high ridges veined with dry arroyos. From any of Carmen's isolated coves, you lose sight of the sea in minutes, and walk in a windswept desert of giant cacti and hummingbirds. Nobody lives here, and there are no amenities. You can camp for a few days but you need prior permission (from the park authority at Loreto on the mainland) even to be there. Since commercial and big game sport fishing were banned in 1996, the ecological chain has been fully restored both on the island and in the sea: Isla Carmen's natural wealth has never been greater than in its present, splendid isolation.

POPULATION:
Uninhabited
WHEN TO GO:
October to May; but you'll see whales by the score between January and March.
HOW TO GET THERE:
By air from San Diego or Los Angeles to Loreto on the Baja side of the Gulf; then by private yacht or boat charter (hiring a zodiac or skiff is recommended – anchoring is forbidden to prevent reef damage, and they are easier to beach and to swim from).
HIGHLIGHTS:
Getting close-up and personal to the big, barking sea lion community at Punta Lobos, a dome-shaped islet at the northern tip, connected to Carmen by a sand causeway.
Sitting low in the water in a dinghy in the company of dozens of dolphins and whales who bring their young to inspect and possibly play with you. You just laugh with happiness.
Star-gazing by the embers of your campfire; and waking to a fiery sunrise of molten bronze and gold – here, at least, nature is as it should be.
Kayaking in the caves, and between the rock formations and reefs below the cliffs.
The view of Carmen – like an offshore stegosaurus – from Loreto, itself a historical delight dating back to 1697. Loreto was the first Spanish mission in the Californias.
YOU SHOULD KNOW:
In 'The Log from the Sea of Cortez' (1951), John Steinbeck delivers a close study of marine life around Isla Carmen. He also describes breaching swordfish and 4 m (12 ft) manta rays.

A rare whale shark in the Sea of Cortez

Revillagigedo Islands

The dramatic coastline of San Benedicto Island

Most maps don't show them. Roughly 400 km (250 mi) southwest of Cabo San Lucas at the tip of Baja California, and 720-970 km (450-605 mi) west of Manzanillo on the Mexican mainland, and beyond the continental shelf, lie the four volcanic Revillagigedo Islands. Clarion, San Benedicto, Roca Partida and the biggest, Socorro, are often called 'little Galapagos', because they developed in similar isolation – to the extent that nearly half their flora, and almost all their fauna and avifauna, occur nowhere else in the world. The percentage might be higher but for the predation and damage caused by plant and animal introductions by the few travellers that ever reached the islands following their discovery in 1533, when they were uninhabited and untouched. Still, their ecology is unique. They are dominated by dry forests of cactus and sage, but in the denser and more humid areas high in the mountains (Socorro's Mt Evermann reaches 1,130 m (3,550 ft)), lichens, giant ferns and endemic ilex and bumelia are abundant. Scarred by deep ravines, the terrain has a wild beauty. It also provides cover for the invasive domestic sheep and goats who have degraded much of it, and the now feral descendants of cats, who have hunted the Socorro dove to extinction in the wild, and now threaten the Socorro mockingbird.

Walking on the islands is a weird sensation. Earth, sky, plants, birds, lizards – all familiar, but you recognize none of them. You're in someone else's version of the world, and it's a privilege, if unsettling. It makes perfect sense that the Revillagigedo Islands are one of the world's most important nesting, breeding and foraging sites for no less than four critically endangered marine turtle species – the leatherback, Pacific olive ridley, green and hawksbill. Learn from them. Turtles know a good place when they see it.

POPULATION:
250 on Socorro (staff and families at the naval station); 9 on Clarion (the naval garrison).

WHEN TO GO:
Any time you can get permission. For scuba-divers, November to May, when the weather and seas are calmer.

HOW TO GET THERE:
By boat, usually live-aboard dive vessels from Cabo San Lucas. You need permission from the Mexican Navy to land anywhere on the islands other than the naval station on Socorro. The naval airstrip at Socorro is not open to the public.

HIGHLIGHTS:
Scuba-diving with dolphins, sharks, manta rays and other pelagics.
The awesome, perpendicular cliffs – 24-183 m (75-560 ft) – of Clarion Island, broken only at Bahia Azufre (Sulphur Bay).
The lava domes, flows and cinder cones that mark Mount Evermann on Socorro as a shield volcano.

YOU SHOULD KNOW:
The islands are named after Don Juan Vicente de Guemes Padilla Horcasitas y Aguayo, 2nd Count of Revillagigedo, the 53rd Viceroy of New Spain, even though they were visited by Alexander von Humboldt, of Current fame, in 1811.

Isla Holbox

POPULATION:
1,600 (2007)
WHEN TO GO:
May to September, for the whale sharks and the breeding dolphins who like to play with them.
HOW TO GET THERE:
By air to Cancun, then by bus from Cancun City to Chiquila on the north coast of Quintana Roo, then by regular ferry or water taxi from Chiquila. There is a small air-strip for light aircraft on Holbox.
HIGHLIGHTS:
The Yalahau Cenote, a sweet water spring surrounded by the salt-water mangroves of the Yalahau Lagoon, accessible only by boat. The combination attracts crocodiles, pink flamingoes, white ibiss, spoonbills, cranes and 130 species to Isla de los Pajaros in the lagoon – and two watchtowers on stilts in the water enable you to enjoy them in safety.
Big game fishing at Cabo Catoche, where the Gulf currents meet the Caribbean.
Punta Mosquitos, where turtles come by the thousand to lay their eggs, from May to July.
Passion Island – tiny, uninhabited, and perfect.
YOU SHOULD KNOW:
Alas! In late 2007, plans for massive development (10,000 rooms in hotels, condos and villas; two golf courses; airport) on Holbox, and on the mainland facing it, were accepted. It will take some time – go before it happens.

Tucked in behind the northern tip of Mexico's Yucatan Peninsula, separated from the mainland by a shallow lagoon teeming with flamingoes, pelicans, and over 130 other rainbow-hued bird species, Holbox is the new kid on the tropical island block. It's only 12 km (7 mi) long and up to 1.5 km (1 mi) wide, but with 32 km (20 mi) of white sand beaches, and huge, endless sunsets to silhouette its ranks of nodding coconut palms, it's something of a cartoon image. Holbox (pronounced 'hole-bosh') was originally settled by pirates who intermarried with the Mayan residents, and the descendants of the original eight families still live in the island's single fishing village. Centuries of isolation have brought man and place into symbiotic tranquility, recently shared by a handful of discerning Europeans and North Americans who quietly live there. But with the neon glitz of Cancun and other high-rise resorts beginning to pall, it's inevitable that Holbox's perfection should become better known.

Its eco-credentials are impeccable, so far unthreatened even by the small hotels beginning to proliferate. The village streets are sand, bordered by quaint wooden houses in lively colours and thatched with steeply-raked palm. You can join the fishermen in pursuit of barracuda, swordfish, red snapper, speckled trout, grouper, and octopus; dive for lobster; or just wander the beaches for mother-of-pearl shells. Transport is by bicycle or golf buggy, but there are no golf courses (or cars). If you come between May and September, you can swim or snorkel within touching distance of the world's biggest fish, the whale shark. Holbox sits exactly where the turquoise Caribbean meets the nutrient-rich, emerald Gulf of Mexico, and the upwellings attract the highest concentration of the gentle, plankton-feeding monsters (typically around 14 m, 45 ft long) in the world. Holbox is a terrestrial and marine Eden.

A traditional Holbox village

Cozumel

The colourful boats of Cozumel

One of Mexico's largest islands, Cozumel lies 20 km (12 mi) from the mainland, and 60 km (36 mi) south of Cancun. It's a flat, limestone formation shaped like a holster, and pierced by dozens of *cenotes* (water-filled sinkholes), many with their own marine forms, which are an extra attraction for swimmers and snorkellers who come to explore the island's fantastic offshore reefs.

Jacques Cousteau first popularized Cozumel in 1960, when he identified Palancar at the island's southern tip as one of the world's best scuba-diving sites. He triggered an explosion of tourist development, only reined in with the establishment of the National Marine Park in 1996; but the reefs were badly damaged by the deepwater piers built for cruise ships to bring new clientele. Attitudes changed quickly. Cozumel's new islanders (the 40,000 Maya who welcomed Hernan ('Stout') Cortes in 1519 were reduced to 30 by 1570, and Cozumel became uninhabited) realized the value not just of their spectacular marine wealth, but of the island's undeveloped centre.

You'll never get a better chance to appreciate Mayan culture so close to good beaches. The biggest Mayan site, San Gervasio (named much later), was for centuries sacred to Ix Chel, the goddess of fertility, and one of the Yucatan's most important sanctuaries. There are several others, recovered from jungle and swampy mangrove lagoons now teeming with cormorants, pelicans, primary-coloured tree frogs, iguanas and crocodiles.

These days, the duty of collective care is replacing brash mistakes of the 1970s. You can see 250 species in its clear waters, including the bright blue-and-yellow queen angelfish, the toad fish (unique to Cozumel), and enormous sponges like the barrel and elephant ear, which grows to 3.6 m (12 ft) across. Cozumel is fabulously pretty and exotic, and you should go there with someone you love and watch the sunsets.

POPULATION:
73,193 (2005)
WHEN TO GO:
Year-round. Temperatures average 32 °C (90 °F) in July and August, and 24 °C (75 °F) in December and January. Come for the traditional feasting, rodeos, bullfights, music and fairs of the 5-day Festival of El Cedral in late April or May.
HOW TO GET THERE:
By air to San Miguel from Houston, New York, Miami or Mexico City; or by air to Cancun, then scheduled boat ferry from Playa del Carmen.
HIGHLIGHTS:
The Mayan lighthouse at Punta Celarain, part of the huge Punta Sur Ecological Reserve of mangrove, jungles and reefs – you can see crocodiles (safely), 220 bird species, iguanas, and from June to August, giant turtles beaching to lay their eggs.
The only inland reef formation in the world, with its own species of fish, crustaceans, and corals, at the Chankanaab Lagoon, south of San Miguel. The underwater 'Maya City' – one of dozens of attractions for children, including lots of imaginative water games, at the noisy (!) Playa Mia Grand Beach Park.
YOU SHOULD KNOW:
A plaque at the Museo Cozumel commemorates US President Lincoln's decision to buy Cozumel as a place to send freed US slaves. The Caste War of Yucatan (started 1848) forced him to change his mind.

Ambergris Caye

POPULATION:
8,000 (2007)
WHEN TO GO:
November to June
HOW TO GET THERE:
By air, via Belize City, to San Pedro; by boat (fast ferry) from Belize City to San Pedro.
HIGHLIGHTS:
The toucans, crocodiles and howler monkeys, among many marvels at the Crooked Tree Wildlife Sanctuary in the jungle.
Cave tubing, one of several adventures on jungle river expeditions on the mainland.
The major Mayan sites of Tikal, Lamanai, and Altun Ha among others near San Pedro.
Birds like the scarlet tanager, laughing falcon, white-collared seed-eater, flaming parakeet, chachalaca and green-breasted mango hummingbird. The birds are astonishing.
Swimming/snorkelling among the unique aquatic life of the Zaak Ba Ajo Lagoon – with its own, small 'blue hole', at San Juan, north of San Pedro.
YOU SHOULD KNOW:
With its abundance of first-class seafood, huge variety of seasonal tropical fruits, and combination of influences from many different cultures, the food in Ambergris Caye is justifiably famous – and it's all local.

The shallows of Ambergris Caye

In Mayan times, Ambergris Caye was a trading post supporting 10,000 people. At 40 km (25 mi) long, and up to 1.5 km (1 mi) wide, it's the largest of 200 cayes studding the coastline of Belize, and lies off the southernmost tip of Mexico's Yucatan Peninsula. In fact, the Mayans created the island by digging a channel to provide a trade route from the bay of Chetumal to the Caribbean – and it is now the border between Belize and Mexico. Then and now, there is only one major settlement, San Pedro, built over Mayan ruins and home to most of the population of Mestizos (Maya-Spanish), Creoles, Central American refugees and Americans, all of whom have merged into a one-off community with its own extraordinary 'Sanpedrano' dialect – much of which is recognizable to visitors from various languages, but usually means something quite different. It's that kind of place: quirky, fun, easy-going and very welcoming.

Visitors flock to Ambergris Caye (pronounced 'Am-BER-grease') because the 310 km (190 mi) Belize Barrier Reef, second only to Australia's Great Barrier Reef, runs parallel to the island only 370 m (0.25 mi) from the beach. It's one of the world's greatest dive sites, with every feature of caves, walls, columns, cathedrals and bridges that fantasy can dream up. Even better, the reef's proximity to shore means that swimmers and snorkellers can enjoy its delights almost as much as certified scuba-divers.

The island itself is a wildlife bonanza of white, red and black mangrove and buttonwood trees; littoral forest plants like gumbo limbo, sapodilla, fig, coco plum and palmetto; egrets, orioles, kiskadees, cinnamon hummingbirds, blue herons and rose-throated becards among some 300 species; and forests full of deer, peccaries, raccoons and occasional jaguar. And the night life in San Pedro is excellent, too – especially the 'punta', a hip-swivelling local dance.

A glorious whale shark

Bay Islands

Columbus found the Bay Islands on his fourth voyage in 1502, and Britain held them from 1643 until they were ceded to Honduras in 1860. On the three principal islands – Utila, Roatan and Guanaja – English is the first language, but the true lingua franca is scuba diving. They sit on the Bonacca Ridge, surrounded by reefs which form part of the biggest system in the world after the Great Barrier Reef. Furthermore, the Cayman Trench flanks the islands, creating spectacular drop offs from the coral walls, some just 100 m (328 ft) from the shore. Typically amazing is 'Spooky Channel', one of 50 major dive sites on Roatan's 62 km (40 mi) length – you navigate from a dock on the beach through huge coral formations that open to cathedral size before narrowing over your head in a long channel that emerges the other side of the wall. Adventurers go back and swim it at night.

Utila is smallest and flattest, wonderfully safe for children to learn watercraft. Roatan, the biggest, has a lush green mountainous backbone and the most developed infrastructure for visitors to its staggering coves (called 'bights') and beaches. Guanaja's mountains go higher still, and are covered with Caribbean pine trees; it has no roads, and its development appears to favour super-luxury resorts at odds with its largest community, Bonacca, which is a tiny, crowded cay next to the main island, criss-crossed with canals full of colourful boats and canoes and nicknamed 'Little Venice of the Caribbean'. You pay more to stay closer to Guanaja's forests, rivers and miles of unspoiled beaches, but Bonacca itself, like Roatan and Utila, is where backpackers and billionaires can meet on the equal terms of enthusiasm for crystal waters, marine menagerie and the blossoming corals of the living reefs.

POPULATION:
43,000 (2005) (Total for all 8 inhabited Bay Islands)

WHEN TO GO:
Year-round. Come for the Sun Jam, two days of music and dancing on Water Cay, the definitive deserted tropical island near Utila, in August.

HOW TO GET THERE:
By air to Coxen Hole, Roatan, from Houston or Miami, or via Tegucigalpa or San Pedro Sula; by air to Utila and Guanaja from Roatan or Ceiba; by ferry boat to all three from La Ceiba on the mainland.

HIGHLIGHTS:
Conch fritters and coconut bread at Punta Gorda, the only Garifuna settlement on Roatan, with a dynamic culture unchanged since the late 1700s.
12-18 m (39-59 ft) long whale sharks, eagle rays, Creole wrasses, groupers, octopus and reef crabs – among the pillar corals, seafans and barrel sponges on the spectacular precipice of West End Wall.
The forest waterfalls of Guanaja, 90 per cent of which is protected reserve.
Dropping in to exclusive hotels on private beaches for a drink and a dive – it's the accepted culture for meeting new people and creating parties.

YOU SHOULD KNOW:
It was from Roatan that 17th century buccaneers and pirates launched their famous collective raids on Porto Bello and Cartagena.

An aerial view of Corn Island surrounded by pristine coral reefs

Islas de Maiz

POPULATION:
8,000 (2007)

WHEN TO GO:
Any time except mid-May to mid-September, when almost daily rain creates an awful lot of mud. If you come during Semana Santa (Holy Week) at Easter, book in advance because Nicaragua heads for the beaches. Or come for the Fiesta del Cangrejo (Crab Festival) at the end of August.

HOW TO GET THERE:
By air from Managua to Big Corn; by bus from Managua to El Rama on the Escondido River, then ferry to Big Corn. Little Corn can only be reached by boat from Big Corn.

HIGHLIGHTS:
The local Sunday baseball match.
Lying in your hammock between two palm trees within finger-raising distance of a bar.
Letting yourself enjoy doing nothing much – without guilt.

YOU SHOULD KNOW:
Places like the Corn Islands are very, very rare. So rare, that a sculptural project called 'The Soul of the World' has designated the Corn Islands as one of only eight places in the world where the vertices of a giant imaginary cube emerge. Which, if you're stuck, is something to contemplate in your hammock.

Lying 70 km (45 mi) off the Caribbean coast of Nicaragua, east of Bluefields Island, Big Corn and Little Corn Islands are temples to tropical tranquility. Tourism is still in its infancy, and though there are lots of hotels and houses where rooms are for rent, local charm and generosity of spirit are a terrific substitute for electricity and other amenities associated with fluffy white towels. The only certainty is that if things temporarily don't work, you won't care, because you'll be swimming or diving or walking or lying in a hammock or drinking at one of the bars (music optional, and seldom of noxious boom-box magnitude). You might even take a book and read it while waiting for the green flash of sunset – the litmus test of tropical island perfection.

Both islands have reefs on their doorstep, and Big Corn's Sally Peaches (a beach, not a misprint) is absolutely stunning. You step off a long curve of glittering white sand, take a few strokes, and enter the first of a series of crazy-castle coral formations all of which are accessible to snorkellers. You might need scuba qualification for the furthest formations, like Blowing Rock where it feels like swimming through a model of Manhattan, but in the company of spotted eagle rays, green turtles and angelfish instead of a Hill Street squad car. Around Little Corn there are spectacular underwater caves, patrolled by barracuda, nurse sharks and scuttling lobsters among the darting rainbow shoals which no degree of familiarity could take for granted. There are several ship wrecks, including a bona fide Spanish Galleon – and if you haven't already done it, there's no better place to get PADI certification so you can get the most out of the adventure. Or indeed, a better place to regroup and recharge your natural soul.

98

Solentiname Islands

There are no roads, no cars, telephones or electricity. The Solentiname Archipelago of 36 volcanic islands is a true wilderness, uninhabited save for some 800 people spread amongst the four largest – Mancarroncito, Mancarron, San Fernando and La Venada. At the most remote, southern end of Lake Nicaragua (aka Lake Cocibolca), near the Costa Rican border where the San Juan River connects it to the Caribbean, the Solentiname are definitive tropical islands: they are covered with tropical tree species, transitional between wet and tropical dry, and attract a super-spectrum of brilliantly-coloured flora and fauna within both ranges. It's incredible that authentic natural wealth of this calibre is accessible, a couple of hours from urban catatonia.

The marks of history are faint. Museums in Mancarron and San Fernando show pre-Columbian artefacts and tell of older Chichan petroglyphs. Once, the islands protected a strategic route to the Pacific. A young Horatio Nelson lead a bloody expedition to San Carlos, built in 1527 at the San Juan River mouth, but regularly sacked by pirates like Henry Morgan. In the 19th century, until Panama did it first, the Solentiname's virgin plenty was threatened by the proposal to build a canal across the Nicaraguan isthmus. For now, the islands are held in a rhapsody of immense silence and

tranquility that heightens your every sense. The pure white of an egret is sharp against robin egg blue sky; brilliant red hibiscus deepens the green forest. A streak of yellow-and-red and a sudden shriek is a toucan; and howler monkeys send parrots clattering in a stream of firework sparks. A swirl of water is momentarily shocking – and in the hot, humid, earthy-damp air, you merge with all four elements in their fecund equilibrium. The Solentiname Islands represent eco-tourism at its classiest – a natural world you feel as well as look at.

A native Keel-billed Toucan

POPULATION:
800 (2006 estimate)
WHEN TO GO:
Year-round.
HOW TO GET THERE:
By air via Managua to San Carlos; then by slow public boat or fast private water-taxi to Mancarron or San Fernando (where you can stay in eco-friendly comfort, but don't expect resort-style amenities).
HIGHLIGHTS:
The world's only known freshwater sharks, plus tarpon, swordfish, sawfish and 40 other species in the teeming waters.
La Pajarera ('the Birdcage') and Mancarroncito Islands, especially favoured by toucans and parrots and at least 75 other species of local and migratory birds.
The swamps of Los Guatuzos Wildlife Reserve – 40,000 hectares (74,000 acres) of tropical wetlands and rainforest, home to commonly-seen caimans, crocodiles, jaguars, monkeys and feral boar; to over 389 resident bird species and thousands of migratory visitors; turtles, butterflies and extraordinary crabs; and 130 kinds of orchids – a RAMSAR-protected Wetland, and part of the Solentiname Biosphere Reserve, on the shore opposite the islands.
The lively primitivism of the wood carvings and paintings of the Solentiname artists' community, introduced by the poet-priest Ernesto Cardenal in the 1960s.
YOU SHOULD KNOW:
The canal proposal was revived in 2007, when someone realized that ships over 130,000 tons won't fit through the newly-enlarged Panama Canal – yet by 2017, there will be 3,000 ships of close to 300,000 tons all wanting to go to and from the Pacific. The threat is extremely real.

Ometepe

POPULATION:
35,000 (2006)
WHEN TO GO:
Year-round, so come for the *fiestas patronales* (patron saints' days) like Moyogalpa's Santa Ana in July, when the *Baile de las Inditas* dance celebrates both Spanish and indigenous culture; or Altagracia's all-dancing, all-drinking feast of San Diego in November. Ometepe holds more folk and religious festivals than anywhere else in Nicaragua.
HOW TO GET THERE:
By boat (car/passenger ferry or basic 'lancha' (small boat)) from San Jorge on the lake shore near Rivas; or the big boat ferry to/from Granada – San Carlos, which stops at Ometepe, and which you must book in advance.
HIGHLIGHTS:
Sunset at Punta Jesus Maria, the western tip, where a 5 m (16 ft) wide sandbar projects 1 km (0.6 mi) into the lake, with water splashing you from both sides. Magic.
The Sompopo dances at Altagracia – the line of dancers carry green leaves on their hands, and sway to the drumming like a line of red insects going to and from their nests – these insects are called Sompopos.
Troops of howler, white-faced and spider monkeys en route to swimming at the jungle San Ramon waterfall, along with the hummingbirds and urraca (blue-tailed magpies).
Staying quite still, looking at and listening to the living fairytale.
YOU SHOULD KNOW:
Ometepe is still getting used to the idea of eco-tourism. A lack of hotels means many islanders are opening their homes to (low) paying guests. The offers are genuine, and you will make new friends.

The perfect twin cones of Concepción and Maderas, two volcanoes linked by a rainforested isthmus, rise majestically from the 'sweet' (ie 'fresh') water of vast Lake Nicaragua. These are the 'two hills' of the island's Náhuatl name, Ometepe, and for many centuries they have been held in reverential awe by succeeding cultures, as the repository of myth and legend as well as an island of exceptional fertility and beauty.

Ometepe's unique, double-breasted shape was foretold in a vision to Nahuas and Chorotegas who came from Mexico and made it their sanctuary; and Chibchas came north from South America. Their petroglyphs are all over the island, greeting you on rock faces and prominent boulders, giving what is already a natural paradise another-worldly mystique. It's tempting for visitors to take cultural myths fairly lightly – but Ometepinos, though as sophisticated in modern ways as anyone, still integrate their combined history into their daily lives. The island's volcanic fertility and biodiversity is in their view a consequence of their respect for the legends associated with it. In 1957, when Concepción erupted, everyone refused a government order to evacuate: not one was killed. And Ometepe was bypassed in the revolution and the war with the Contras, which damaged so much of Nicaragua.

The friendly Ometepinos are always willing to show you some fresh delight on the island. You can sample its phenomenal riches on an easy hike on Maderas, the extinct and smaller volcano. Its crater is a slightly spooky cold lagoon, set in thick tropical jungle which really is full of howler monkeys, boas, jaguars and thousands of birds. The jungle runs down to the Charco Verde Reserve, where you find the best beaches – and an ancient witch called Chico Largo, who may offer you a life of luxury in return for transmuting your soul into one of the island's cows. It adds a dimension to eco-tourism.

Smoke drifts from the crater of Concepción.

Cocos Island

Once described as the most beautiful island in the world, Cocos lies in the eastern Pacific, 550 km (344 mi) off the coast of Costa Rica. The island formed around two million years ago from cooling lava and today the mountainous and irregular slopes are covered with misty primeval rainforest, and scored with ravines and waterfalls. Cerro Iglesias, the summit, is 671 m (2,201 ft) high and rises in the southwestern part of the island. Because the island is so remote, much of its flora and fauna is endemic, which has led it to be designated a national park and a UNESCO World Heritage Site. The only inhabitants are the park rangers.

The primeval landscape of Cocos Island

The sheer 600 m (1,970 ft) high cliffs that surround much of the island plunge deep underwater, and are riddled with secret caves. The coastline is so precipitous that there are only two safe landing places. The island was discovered in 1526, and soon became legendary as a hiding place for pirate gold.

In 1820 when the revolt of Peru seemed imminent, the Spanish Governor in Lima arranged for the Spanish treasure there to be shipped to Mexico. The loot, which included two life-sized statues in pure gold from the church, along with countless other treasures, was entrusted to a Captain Thompson of the *Mary Deare*. Thompson could not resist the temptation and, killing all the other passengers on board his ship, buried the treasure on Cocos. He died before he could return to recover it, and over the years at least 300 expeditions have been mounted to find the gold from the *Mary Deare*, or any of the other pirate treasure buried on the island. Even now people have not given up hope of stumbling across a hoard of bullion in one of the innumerable coastal caves or jungle ravines.

Nowadays most visitors come here for the diving. Cocos Island offers the perfect environment for every sort of fish, from tiny baitfish to huge whale sharks: a pollution-free, no-fishing zone at a crossing point of currents and counter-currents. The area has one of the richest concentrations of pelagic species in the world, literally hundreds of hammerhead and white-tip sharks, mantas, rays, tuna, bottlenose dolphins, green sea turtles, whale sharks and even humpback whales. Ten-day boat tours can be arranged in San José.

POPULATION:
Park rangers only.
WHEN TO GO:
Diving is best between March and December.
HOW TO GET THERE:
Fly to San José, Costa Rica, then by pre-arranged tour boat.
HIGHLIGHTS:
Diving in the waters around the island – it is literally like falling into a fish tank.
Birdwatching – despite the lack of vegetation, many species of birds visit and nest on the island.
Hire a bike and explore the many tracks that lead to the lagoon.
Atoll walking at low-tide to reach the more remote islands.
YOU SHOULD KNOW:
You can only go on an organized seasonal diving trip and with the permission of the island rangers. You are not permitted to camp or sleep on the island.

101

Isla Colon

Bocas del Toro Islands

POPULATION:
9,000 (2007)
WHEN TO GO:
The rain never entirely stops, but the islands are driest in September/October and February/March. Happily, at these times the islands are both cheaper and less crowded.
HOW TO GET THERE:
By air, from Panama City, David or Changuinola, to Bocas Town; by bus/car from Chiriqui Grande (S) or Changuinola (N) to Almirante, then by water-taxi or car ferry to Bocas Town.
HIGHLIGHTS:
Toucans in the pristine rainforest of Isla Popa – where the ancient Ngöbe culture predominates in the five main villages.
Laguna Bocatorita, on the east of Isla Cristobal, where a labyrinth of mangroves forms a giant natural aquarium 6 km (4 mi) across, drawing in fish, manatees and bottle-nose dolphins.
The only Panamanian nesting site of red-billed tropic-birds, on Swan's Cay.
Snorkelling among the mangrove channels of Cayo Crawl, en route to the magnificent coral gardens on the southeast coast of Isla Bastimentos.
The candy-coloured houses of Bocas Town, heritage of the banana boom, when 25,000 people lived here.
YOU SHOULD KNOW:
The rocks and fossils around Bocas hold the key to understanding the formation of the Isthmus of Panama, the separation of the Atlantic and the Pacific – and the triggering of the Gulf Stream.

The Caribbean coast of Costa Rica and Panama merges in a seamless sequence of barely-explored mountains and rivers, dense forests opening onto turquoise waters and pristine white beaches, mysterious mangrove channels, coral gardens and exotically-coloured wildlife. This is the Panamanian province of Bocas del Toro. Its capital, Bocas Town, is on Colon, one of the 68 Bocas del Toro Islands that fill the Laguna de Chiriqui for 100 km (60 mi). Collectively, they are one of the Caribbean's richest, unspoiled eco-surprises.

Columbus careened his boats here in 1502, on Isla Carinero, as he named it. For 300 years the Bocas Islands' remote bays were shared between the indigenous Ngöbe-Bugle people and a variety of official and unofficial pirates, until in the early 1800s the bananas and cacao business attracted immigrant Jamaicans, and turned the archipelago into an English-speaking part of a Hispanic nation.

Island culture is much more Afro-Caribbean than Latin-American. Towns and villages have a bright but dilapidated air, and the residents are perfectly matched to the young, hip crowd of international visitors. The high funk factor of thatched bars on stilts and infinite versions of incomers' fantasy tropical getaways, is driven by residents' own appreciation for the natural paradise in which they live. However hard they party, people respect the marvels of the Marine Park surrounding Isla Bastimentos, where one beach is the world's only home to the black polka-dotted, scarlet frog, and another to scores of rare sea-turtles; and to the 350 bird species, sloths, caimans, dolphins, and monkeys that you see throughout the islands.

Only on Isla Colon is uncontrolled tourist development beginning to threaten the very high diversity of marine and terrestrial ecosystems that – along with its delightful, quirky, retro-culture – has made Bocas del Toro famous.

Isla Grande

Isla Grande is where Panamanians go for the weekend to get the city out of their system. You jump in the car or bus, and in two hours you swap Panama City for snorkelling in the Caribbean, on the maze of coral reefs that mark the edge of the Portobelo National Park.

La Isla (everyone calls it just 'La Isla') is in fact only 166 m (550 ft) from the mainland. Although it's thick with tropical flowers, coconut palms and greenery, the largest of the islands in the area and the easiest and cheapest to get to, nobody went until the potholes in the road from Portobelo were repaired. By the time that happened, La Isla was safe from either ribbon development or high-end exclusivity. There are still no roads on the island – just a walkway that ambles past the bars, markets, street vendors, small restaurants, few hotels and lots of basic but comfortable, rental cabanas that have sprung up along the beachfront. Most of the island isn't even accessible, because it's carved up into half a dozen private estates, and apart from the path across its centre, you enjoy its charms from the waterline on three sides.

Isla Grande is your chance to do a full-on tropical Caribbean island, with excellent reefs, fluffy clouds and shimmering turquoise waters, at almost no expense, and with no hassle getting there. It's so lovely, and people are so happy to be there that every weekend, as you stroll, you encounter impromptu parties on the public beach and on the main walkway. You're expected to join in; and often you'll find one or more of the small community that has always lived here, fishing and growing coconuts, and now making sure you've got food, drink, music and good fellowship to help your day go well.

POPULATION:
200 (2007 estimate)
WHEN TO GO:
Any day of the week, any time of year. Weekends are obviously much more crowded, but with people who contribute to the happy, carefree atmosphere of release from quotidian stress.
HOW TO GET THERE:
By car or bus from Sabanitas or Portobelo, to La Guaira; then by water-taxi for a five-minute ride to the island.
HIGHLIGHTS:
The Spanish Forts and ruins at Portobelo, once (16th and 17th centuries) one of the world's most important cities.
La Punta, the sweeping curve of sandy beach at the island's western end.
Walking around the island on its rocky waterline: even at weekends, you can feel like Robinson Crusoe.
Climbing up to the lighthouse. The original lens was designed by Gustave Eiffel, famous for the Eiffel Tower in Paris.
The flowers, butterflies and hummingbirds everywhere.
YOU SHOULD KNOW:
When Sir Francis Drake died of dysentery in 1596 at sea, he was buried in a lead coffin near Portobelo Bay.

Part of the Spanish forts and ruins at Portobelo

Pearl Islands

POPULATION:
300 (2007) (full-time residents, but generally occupied by many more).
WHEN TO GO:
Year-round
HOW TO GET THERE:
By air, from Panama City; by sea, if you can hitch a ride on a yacht leaving the Canal, to Contadora, Del Rey, or any island en route. Inter-island services are irregular at best.
HIGHLIGHTS:
The hour-long walk round Isla Contadora, marvelling at some of the villas.
Diving the reefs off Contadora, more closely related to South Pacific corals than those of the Caribbean. Playa Larga takes you to the best place for sharks and turtles.
Sitting on a hotel terrace with a drink, enjoying the white tip sharks circling Playa Sueca.
Snorkelling at Playas Cacique, Galeon and Canoa on Contadora – but with a twice-daily tide of up to 5 m (17 ft), you need to time your plunge for low tide.
YOU SHOULD KNOW:
The Pearl Islands are (perhaps without viewers knowing) internationally famous for having featured in three seasons of the reality TV programme *Survivor*, shown in many countries.

The Pearl Islands Archipelago

Heading south from the Canal, 50 km (30 mi) into the Gulf of Panama, the first thing you see are the Pearl Islands. There are more than 200, most of them tiny, and few even inhabited. Some are hardly more than rocky islets, but most are outcrops of thick jungle fringed with sand, set in clear waters teeming with whales, dolphins, sea turtles and major game fish. By far the biggest island in the archipelago is Isla del Rey, 30,000 hectares (74,000 acres) of thickly-forested hills, natural springs, rivers and waterfalls that power lush vegetation which feels like it might at any time overwhelm the cultivated estates and fruit farms surrounding its main town San Miguel. Its charm lies in its slow pace, matched to the tranquillity of its coves and beautiful valleys.

Much smaller and of hugely greater significance is Isla Contadora, its neighbour. It got its name (it means 'book-keeper') in the era of the Spanish Conquistadors, when Spanish ships from Peru, Ecuador and Chile paused there to take inventory of their massive booty before transhipment across the isthmus, and it has never looked back. It's still a hub, if only for the Pearl Islands, but the yachts stop here to brace up before heading for the South Pacific, and because it is unquestionably the centre of island chic for the region. It's only 304 hectares (750 acres), but it is second home to many wealthy Panamanians, and to several exclusive resorts which trim the rampant orchids and vines to create the kind of Pacific terraces on which you expect to find Maurice Chevalier singing 'Some Enchanted Evening'.

Amenities on Isla Contadora include prolific reefs immediately off the beaches, and a nudist beach at Playa Sueca. It's a wonderful island.

San Blas Archipelago

A traditional bright and intricate design as seen on a mola, *a garment worn by females.*

Like so many cartoons, the majority of the 378 islands in the San Blas Archipelago are blobs of white sand with a cluster of coconut palms in the middle, strewn in an arc across the hundreds of miles between the Gulfs of San Blas and Darien, where Panama's eastern Caribbean coast meets Colombia.

Only 49 are inhabited – by the fiercely independent Kuna Indians. These islands (and the whole mainland coastal area of virgin forest opposite) are their territory, Kuna Yala, a semi-autonomous homeland that the Kuna run according to their own economics, language, dress, music and culture. Men still fish from canoes and shin up palm trees for coconuts. Picasso himself would have envied Kuna women their famous skill in creating *mola*, the rainbow-coloured fabrics crowded with geometric fish, birds and jungle animals inspired by tribal legend. You'll see it at its finest in the tidy huts of Isla Maquina, the quietest and most purely traditional settlement in the area. On many islands, the thatch roofs of the Kuna huts almost touch, so walking around is challenging, but the intimacy gives you a glimpse of the mythology and ritual of Kuna daily life, and you'll always be welcomed.

Most visitors just want to hit the tropical perfection of the islands. The most idyllic, inhabited or not, are east and north east of the busy hub, El Porvenir. Achutupu, Kagantapu and Coco Blanco are the most interesting, but the area is surrounded by some of the world's oldest reefs. In an ideal world, of course, we'd all have sleek yachts to reach the truly gorgeous *Cayos* like Holandeses, Chichime and Limones – but provided you don't expect more than a hammock and fresh fish by way of amenities, these remote, uninhabited tropical jewels are well worth the effort of getting there by lesser means.

POPULATION:
40,000 (2007 estimate)
WHEN TO GO:
Year-round, but April to June for the best snorkelling and diving.
HOW TO GET THERE:
By air from Panama City or Colon, to several of the islands; by water-bus or hired boat from Colon (you can often catch a ride with small Kuna merchant ships out of Colon – and let the crew find you your perfect Pleasure Island).
HIGHLIGHTS:
Snorkelling among the brilliant corals of the overgrown shipwreck in the shallow waters off the south side of Achutupu, a 5-star beautiful emerald island set in sapphire sea.
The thatched Kuna museum of culture (mythology, history and rituals at Carti Suitupu, where the existence of electricity from 6pm to midnight enables two dozen bars to attract more foreigners than anywhere in the archipelago, and cruise ships have begun to call.
The hypnotic charm of watching a Kuna woman sewing mola, from a swaying hammock.
YOU SHOULD KNOW:
Once you've been there and met them, you'll always call the area Kuna Yala – 'San Blas Archipelago' is for maps and tourists.

Isla Coiba National Park

Coiba

The largest – 493 sq km (310 sq mi) – island in Central America, Coiba lies 50 km (30 mi) off the Pacific coast of the Panamanian province of Veraguas. Roughly 80 per cent of it is virgin tropical rainforest, home to trees and a profusion of plants no longer found on the mainland. Throughout its hilly centre and network of rivers, thick jungle supports an unusual number of howler and white-faced capuchin monkeys, amphibians, reptiles and commonly seen, rare birds. This is where you go to see the Coiba spinetail, crested eagle, and whole flocks of gorgeous, scarlet macaws. The macaws are the most dramatic visible evidence of the island's hitherto miraculous escape from development.

From 1919 to 2004 it was a prison colony, and even now visitors' access is restricted. In fact, in the interests of protecting Coiba's pristine ecosystem, organized tours currently offer the lowest-impact form of tourism – and help to frustrate opportunities for poaching, illegal logging and other encroachments.

Although visiting Coiba isn't easy, the rewards are stupendous. The island is now the heart of a National Park covering 38 islands and a huge chunk of the Gulf of Chiriqui. Its ecological and marine importance is acknowledged by its designation (2005) as a UNESCO World Heritage Site. The Indo-Pacific current swirls its warmth through the Gulf and around Coiba, bringing with it coral, much of the Pacific tropical underwater life you just don't expect in the usually cold coastal waters of the Pacific Americas, and the larger fish/mammals like humpback whales, white tip, hammerhead, tiger and whale sharks, manta rays, barracuda, amberjack, big snappers, three kinds of marlin, and four kinds of sea turtle. The variety and numbers make for world-class diving – an obvious pedigree once you know that Coiba is the beginning of the underwater cordillera that includes both the Cocos Islands and the Galápagos.

Taboga

Established in 1524 as a deepwater harbour for Panama City, visible at night 18 km (12 mi) away on the horizon, Taboga was the very first Spanish port in the Pacific. Through it passed the gold, pearls and treasures of the Incas, in transit to Madrid, while the trinkets to buy them, and the soldiers to enforce the sale, passed the other way. In 1671 the buccaneer Henry Morgan sacked city and port, initiating Taboga's heyday as a rip-roaring pirates' lair.

The new, deep-draught steamships, and French efforts to build the canal, restored the island's prosperity in the 1870s; incidentally bringing the French painter Paul Gauguin to the area, at the start of his search for the epitome of colourful tropical exotica. He can only have been inspired – Taboga is famous as the 'Island of Flowers'.

Ever since, the island has been Panama City's favourite day or weekend out. It's so close – and so very distant in lifestyle and atmosphere. There are no cars in the maze of paths around the 300 or so houses and Spanish colonial buildings of San Pedro, and just three little trucks to carry cargo and visitors' baggage. Ruins are draped in climbing bougainvillea and hibiscus; roses and huge trumpets of morning glory fill the gardens and walkways. Around the flourishing fields of fruits such as pineapple, orange, red and yellow orchids compete for attention.

Little cafés and bars surround the plaza and beach, and you look up to where you walked, in the thickly forested wildlife reserve that covers the hills encircling the town, and the whole of the steep south shoreline. Nothing much happens these days: to do nothing, on a lovely tropical island a few minutes from the stress of the city, that's why people come.

Playa Honda

POPULATION:
850 (2006 estimate)
WHEN TO GO:
Mid-December to mid-May is the dry season – but urban Panamanians come year-round to the highly sociable festivals that take place all the time.
HOW TO GET THERE:
By boat ferry, from the left side of the pier just before the entrance to the Smithsonian Institute building, on the northern side of Isla Noas.
HIGHLIGHTS:
Game fishing – the relatively deep waters round Taboga are full of blue and black marlin, yellowfin tuna, roosterfish, cubera snapper, amberjack, wahoo and Pacific sailfish. Hanging out, playing games, or chilling over a drink in the 16th century plaza of San Pedro. The church is the second oldest in the hemisphere. The 17th century fort on El Morro, the rocky islet linked at low tide by a sandbar to the rest of Taboga. The orchids, lianas, ferns, roses, nisperos, mameyes, nance, mangoes, tamarinds and pineapples that pierce the core of your five senses, often simultaneously.
YOU SHOULD KNOW:
Pissaro used wood from Isla Taboga to build the ships he used to conquer the Incas in 1539.

Islas los Roques

POPULATION:
1,500 (2007)
WHEN TO GO:
Year-round. Between July and September the possibility of storms muddying the water makes that period less suitable for scuba-diving.
HOW TO GET THERE:
By light aircraft from Caracas to El Gran Roque (NB. Inbound flights from all points to El Gran Roque come, or remain, under flight control from Maiquetia airport on the mainland); or by boat from Isla Margarita.
HIGHLIGHTS:
Getting a close look at the complex interaction between mangrove species and the degree of water salinity – time and the conditions are on your side.
Sunset from the lighthouse (built 1870-80) on El Gran Roque – the archipelago dotted into the horizon, and on a clear day you can see Mt Avila (about 1,600 m, 5,000 ft) near Caracas.
All the marvels to be seen and done on, in and under water next to one of the biggest and best coral reefs in the Caribbean.
The archaeological remains of Amerindian activities that tell of surviving much more hostile conditions than you'll find today.
YOU SHOULD KNOW:
There are no superlatives to describe the sense of peace you get in the Los Roques Archipelago.

The Los Roques Archipelago is one of the world's biggest National Marine Parks, and lies 145 km (80 mi) due north of La Guaira, the mainland port for Caracas. About 50 coral cays and sand bars are arranged in a huge oval around a lagoon, but it's only from the air you get a true idea of its scale – it covers the same area as the whole of the Virgin Islands.

The fragility of the islands and their ecosystem is all too obvious. Luckily they are shielded from eastern currents by a 24 km (15 mi) coral reef running from north to south, and a second barrier running 32 km (20 mi) from east to west. Protected since 1972, they represent a pristine environment that attracts only the most discerning visitors, who come either in their own boats or yachts in search of solitude and untrammelled tranquillity, or in small groups by light aircraft, often just for the day, from Caracas or elsewhere on the Venezuelan mainland. The island residents, who are descendants of the 110 families who originally came from Isla Margarita in the early 19th century, to make a living as fishermen, all live on El Gran Roque ('The Big Rock').

They will welcome you as temporary family members, and you'll find that, along with the old style of manners and hospitality, they still use the old ways of fishing to catch lobsters, king conch and Spanish mackerel. If you're not staying on a boat, you'll probably eat the catch at one of the 66 posadas (small family lodges) scattered throughout the island, but all of which are within 100 m (328 ft) of the beach. Los Roques is about countless transmutations of blue and green beauty, and sharing the natural rhythms of a completely unspoiled, discrete ecosystem.

The stunning Los Roques Archipelago

Isla de Margarita

Margarita is mostly as brash as it is beautiful, Caribbean in looks and climate but completely South American by temperament. With 170 km (106 mi) of coastline, mainly endless white beaches, breathtaking coves and picturesque, rocky headlands, and a lush interior where the bromeliads, orchids, palms, bamboo and thick giant ferns have been elbowed aside for passion fruit, guava, bananas and sugar cane, it's no surprise that the island is Venezuela's top holiday destination.

It's just 60 km (40 mi) from the mainland, and big enough at 78 km (49 mi) long to get lost in, despite the highly developed agglomeration of malls, high-rise housing, traffic and colossal duty-free warehouses on the Paraguachoan (east-side) Peninsula. This intense urbanization, creeping out from the main coastal cities of Porlamar, Pampatar and Juan Griego towards the much smaller inland capital Asuncion, is made palatable by the determinedly carefree, pervading atmosphere. The casinos and night-life are really good, throbbing with 24-hour merengue and salsa in the crowded streets and on popular beaches like Parguito, Caribe and Puerto Cruz, next to huge tourist complexes. Constant balmy trade winds make Playa El Yaque in the south an international Mecca for windsurfers.

For solitude, tranquillity and romance, you go west, to the Macanao mountains and dozens of small, deep valleys blazing with hibiscus and morning glory against the jigsaw of tropic green, sky and sea. To get there, you cross Margarita's central isthmus, a 10, 000 hectare (25,000 acre) wetland maze called La Restinga National Park. Oysters cling to mangrove-roots along the canals that thread this wilderness paradise of yellow-shouldered parrots and blue-crowned parakeets, and you might see ocelots in the dappled shadows. Eventually, the dozens of lagoons lead you to a 60 km (40 mi) sandbar of crushed coral and seashells.

The impressive Isla de Margarita

POPULATION:
420,000 (2007)

WHEN TO GO:
Year-round. Venezuelans crowd the island at Christmas, Easter, and from July to September.

HOW TO GET THERE:
By air, direct from Europe and N America, or via Caracas, to Porlamar; by boat (car/passenger ferry) from Puerto La Cruz, Cumana, and La Guaira, to Punta de Piedra.

HIGHLIGHTS:
Isla Margarita's five-star history: discovered 1498 by Columbus; site of Spain's very first New World settlement 1500; seized for its pearl industry by the notorious Lope de Aguirre ('God of Wrath') 1561; first territory to fight Spain and achieve independence 1814; and the place where Simon Bolivar was confirmed as leader, and successfully launched the liberation of Venezuela, Colombia, Peru, Ecuador and Bolivia in 1818. Every fort and cannon you see on the island is a tribute to Margarita's indomitable spirit.

Diving for pearl oysters on Isla Cubagua, just offshore – its pearls were worn in the crowns and clothing of 16th century European royalty – and possibly still are.

YOU SHOULD KNOW:
Beer is cheaper than bottled water on Margarita. The island has the reputation of being 'the Caribbean on the cheap' in every way. It's true, but only because the islanders prefer to encourage visitors to enjoy themselves, rather than to fleece them.

San Andres & Providencia

POPULATION:
106,000 (2007) (San Andres 100,000;
Providencia 6,000)
WHEN TO GO:
August to May. Every couple should
spend one night of a full moon on
Providencia's Manchineel Beach – it's
the most romantic, quietly Dionysian
party of them all. Or come for San
Andres' Reina del Coco Festival
in November.
HOW TO GET THERE:
By air, from Bogota, Cartagena,
Panama City, etc to San Andres; to
Providencia, by twice-daily small
plane from San Andres. By cruise
ship from Cartagena or Panama to
San Andres; by water-taxi from San
Andres to Providencia.
HIGHLIGHTS:
Johnny Cay, just off San Andres Town
(there are water-taxis always waiting
on the beach), where you sip your
'coco loco' in the bars lining the
beach while the most lissom parade
and frolic in the perfect waves.
Eating the delicious local crab –
unlike most places, a big, black land
crab; you see them all over the
islands, where they live in burrows.
Playing Robinson Crusoe on Haynes
Cay, which has just enough
amenities (food and drink) to keep
the game comfortable.
Morgan's Cave on Providencia –
spectacular, and you might find the
pirate's treasure…
YOU SHOULD KNOW:
On Providencia, meeting people on
dive boats is the best way to make
new friends.

Only 220 km (140 mi) from the coast of Nicaragua, San Andres and Providencia are the two significant islands of a scattered Caribbean archipelago of cays that in fact belongs to Colombia, 775 km (480 mi) to the southwest.

Providencia was named by its first settlers, English Puritans who in 1627 split from their contemporaries in Massachusetts, USA, in search of somewhere warmer to practise their religion. On arrival, they turned to slavery, then piracy; and from 1670-89, the island was Henry Morgan's HQ until the Spanish regained control and lost interest. Now, the descendants of former slaves and Europeans still speak their own Creole English, and still fish and farm an island barely brushed by tourism. Blessed by copious fresh water running off its three central peaks, it's a fertile eco-paradise, part of a biosphere reserve including most of the archipelago and its 'seven-shades-of-blue' and turquoise waters.

San Andres is coral, not volcanic like Providencia, and though it's equally lovely, it's bigger and much more developed. It's where the young and energetic from the mainland go for excursions – and San Andres' 'spring break' ambience is non-stop and infectious. In between the glamorous parades, people hone their lithe forms swimming or diving in some of the fifty sites in 5,000 sq km (1,930 sq mi) of shallow reefs, wrecks, caves, tunnels, walls, multilevels and night-dive sites that surround the two islands. Their isolation has enabled the huge reef complex to grow astounding sizes of fan, finger and brain corals, with proportionately bigger and colourful shoals of fish darting among them.

In the constant excitement – either about the islands' ecology or the partying – you notice the unusual absence of Americans. It may be wise to be wary, but Colombia's mainland conflicts are pretty well ignored by the islanders. Obviously, paradise is considered neutral.

A balconied wooden building in the local Caribbean style

Islas Rosario

The 23 islands, cays and islets of the Rosario National Park are a geologically infant 5,000 years old, formed when the sea level dropped, revealing areas of coral reef, which were gradually colonized by mangroves and other accretions. Eventually, the islands consolidated into three distinct ecosystems – coastal lagoons, the mangroves surrounding them, and the very dry tropical forests of the interior. On Isla Grande, you can follow an environmental interpretation path that explains the inter-dependence of the systems and their importance to the breeding cycles of the hundreds of marine and bird species you can see all around you.

Along with the islands, the National Park protects the sea floor, and one of the most important coral reefs on the Caribbean's southern shore. Diving, snorkelling and swimming are actually encouraged, but the most beautiful underwater sites are guided, to lessen the risk of physical contact with the spectacular fans and finger-towers waving gently in the slow swirl of the currents. You see giant turtles, dolphins, sea horses and the occasional shark, and in the sea meadows, tiny shrimp hide from scuttling crabs, and fish dart from the translucent fronds to the nearest crevice of coral safety. An open-water Oceanarium gives non-divers the chance to get close to some of the 1,300 species of plants and animals native to the Islas Rosario.

The most extraordinary feature of the Rosario National Park is its proximity to Cartagena, 40 km (25 mi) away. So close to a major port, city and industrial centre, and closer still to the big merchant shipping lanes, the archipelago is a miracle of healthy productivity and abundance. You wouldn't even know it's there except for the crowds of day-trippers, for many of whom visiting a wildlife and nature park might not otherwise be possible. It's a priceless asset to Colombia and the southern Caribbean.

POPULATION:
Uninhabited
WHEN TO GO:
Year-round
HOW TO GET THERE:
By water-taxi from Muelle de la Bodeguita, across the street from the Walled City, El Centro, Cartagena.
HIGHLIGHTS:
The mangrove forests – 5 of 7 American Atlantic species of mangrove thrive in the National Park. The rarified tree species of the dry forest, like the Higuito, Majagua and Guasimo. Some, like the Matarraton and Totumo have medical significance; all shed their leaves in summer to conserve water.
Migrating birds like the tanga and barraquete duck; and residents like the gavilan pollero, crown pigeon and outrageously colourful parakeets.
The 17th century Spanish fortifications at Isla Boca Chica, built to protect Cartagena harbour from pirates and buccaneers. Now they overlook lovely beaches with great beach-shack restaurants and bars.
YOU SHOULD KNOW:
If you want to visit and/or camp on one of the smaller cays in the National Park, you need to get permission from Park authorities.

A jetty stretches out into the glorious Caribbean.

Isla de Malpelo

Around 500 km (314 mi) off Colombia's Pacific coast, a towering barren rock rises from the ocean floor with sheer precipitous cliffs. The island of Malpelo has a slightly sinister air, perhaps because it is the peak of a huge submarine ridge rising straight up from the ocean floor from depths of 4,000 m (13,120 ft). At 376 m (1,233 ft) above sea level, the island is high enough to create its own weather system and it is often wreathed in cloud, however clear the sky. At first glance, the island seems to be a barren rock without vegetation, but deposits of bird guano have helped to establish colonies of algae, lichens, mosses and a few shrubs and ferns.

However, it is not really the island but rather the waters around it that attract visitors. This is one of the most revered diving sites in the world due to its steep underwater cliffs and caves of outstanding beauty, and the amazing visibility. Powerful warm and cold ocean currents interact to create a unique habitat for a huge variety of marine life at all levels of the food chain. These deep unpolluted waters are home to important populations of large predators and pelagic species. Schools of over 200 hammerhead sharks and over a thousand silky sharks, whale sharks and tuna have been recorded here, as well as a newly discovered deepwater shark – the Short-nosed Ragged-toothed shark.

The Malpelo Nature Reserve was set up to protect the rich flora and fauna here, and covers an area with a six-mile radius around the island. In 2006, Malpelo was also declared by UNESCO as a natural World Heritage Site. The sheer granite cliffs plunge into deep water, and on one of these, known as the Altar of the Virgin, you can see countless moray eels, snappers and groupers, dolphin and mantas. At the northern end of Malpelo there is a group of three pinnacles, known as the Three Musketeers, poking out of the sea. Here there is a series of underwater tunnels, caverns and cathedrals crawling with lobsters, groupers, goat fish, silvery bait fish and white-tipped reef sharks. At La Gringa, a sheer granite wall, divers can experience hundreds of female hammerhead sharks swimming in the strong currents. This vast marine park, the largest no-fishing zone in the Eastern Tropical Pacific, provides a critical habitat for internationally threatened marine species, and a wonderful place to view them in their natural surroundings.

A school of Hammerhead sharks

Galápagos Islands

In the Pacific Ocean, some 965 km (600 mi) off the coast of Ecuador, lie the Galápagos Islands. The name comes from the Spanish *galápago*, or saddle, after the saddlebacked tortoises found on the islands. This volcanic archipelago comprises 13 main islands, six smaller islands and 107 rocks and islets. The oldest island is thought to have formed between five and ten million years ago. The youngest islands, Isabela and Fernandina, are still being formed. In 2005, an ash and water vapour cloud rose 7 km (4.4 mi) above Fernandina and lava flows descended the slopes of the volcano and into the sea.

The islands first became part of scientific history when the survey ship HMS *Beagle* under captain Robert Fitzroy visited the Galápagos on September 15, 1835 to chart the navigable waters around the islands. The captain, with his companion the young naturalist Charles Darwin, spent a month making a scientific study of geology and biology on four of the islands before they continued on their round-the-world expedition. Darwin noticed that the finches differed between the islands, and he was told by the governor of the prison colony on Charles Island that the tortoises also showed some small difference between islands. These observations were crucial in the development of Darwin's theory of natural selection which was presented in *The Origin of Species.*

Today, thousands of visitors flock to the islands each year to see the same species Darwin recorded, many of which are endemic to the islands and found only here. They include land iguanas and giant tortoises, blue- and red-footed boobies, albatrosses, flightless cormorants, Galápagos flamingoes, magnificent frigatebirds, Galápagos penguins and the buntings now better known as Darwin's finches. The islands themselves have been designated a UNESCO World Heritage Site, and even the waters around the islands have been made a marine national park to protect the marine animals here, which include Galápagos sea lions, otters and marine iguanas.

Despite these protections, the biggest threat to the islands is the rapidly increasing human population, which was estimated at around 30,000 on 2006, a massive jump from the 2001 census which recorded 18,000 inhabitants. The huge numbers of tourists are also a problem, and may end up destroying the very islands and wildlife that they come to see. In a bid to control the problem, the government is now restricting access and a tour guide certified by the national park authority must accompany each group.

POPULATION:
30,000 (2006)
WHEN TO GO:
Any time of year.
HOW TO GET THERE:
By air from Quito or Guayaquil to San Cristobal Island or Baltra.
HIGHLIGHTS:
Punta Suarez on the island of Española – see the Marine iguanas, Española Lava lizards, Hood mockingbirds, Swallow-tailed gulls, Blue-footed boobies and Nazca boobies, Galápagos hawks, a selection of finches and the Waved albatross.
Punta Espinosa on Fernandina – a narrow stretch of land where hundreds of marine iguanas gather on the black lava rocks. The famous Flightless cormorant can also be seen on this island, as well as Galápagos penguins, pelicans and sea lions.
North Seymour – an extraordinary place for breeding birds, home to a large colony of blue-footed boobies and magnificent frigatebirds.
YOU SHOULD KNOW:
Visitors to the islands must be accompanied by an accredited guide.

Red Marine Iguanas on Espanola Island in the Galápagos archipelago

The rocky coastline of Ilha Grande

Ilha Grande

South-east of Rio de Janeiro in the Agra dos Reis district of Brazil lies Ilha Grande, a long mountainous ridge emerging from the turquoise sea. There are over 360 islands in the bay, their forested slopes leading down to some of the most pristine beaches in the world. Much of the area is designated as the Ilha Grande State Park to protect its natural beauty. There was once a penal colony here, the infamous Cândido Mendes, set up to hold the country's most notorious criminals, but today people come here to enjoy themselves in the glorious natural surroundings.

Between the 16th and 18th centuries, the bay saw countless battles between corsairs, imperial invaders and pirates. This has resulted in one of the greatest concentrations of shipwrecks in the world, and a wonderful place for diving and snorkelling. Among the best sites are Lage do Guriri (Ponta de Castelhanos), Jorge Grego Island, Meros and Naufragios Islands. There is even the wreck of a helicopter 8 m (26 ft) below the surface. The ocean floor also offers a fascinating selection of caves and caverns 10–20 m (32-65 ft) high, home to a great variety of fish and corals. The excellent visibility and calm seas make diving here a memorable experience.

But if you prefer less active pursuits, take a stroll around Abraão, a pretty village with whitewashed churches and low buildings in soft hues of yellow, blue and pink. There are restaurants, cafés and craft shops here, and a lovely soft sand beach. This tropical paradise offers many other beautiful beaches, many of them acessible only by boat or kayak. Lopes Mendes is excellent for surfing, windsurfing and other water sports, as are Freguesia de Santana and Saco do Ceu. The calm, shallow, azure waters of Lagoa Azul (Blue Lagoon) on Macaco's Island are home to millions of yellow and black fish and make this a lovely place to spend the day.

Also worth a look is the cave at Acaiá. Inside the cave the intensity of the sun makes the water change from light blue to emerald green. The foam on the water catches the light and twinkles like diamonds, making this an enchanting experience.

Trekking is also a popular activity here. The forested hills are dotted with exotic, colourful blooms, and give way to coastal plains and mangroves. Wildflife includes many bird species, such as parrots and saracuras, in addition to a variety of monkeys, iguanas and snakes. Most of the trekking trails pass through tropical forest and end on a pristine beach, perfect for a picnic lunch.

POPULATION:
2000 (2007)
WHEN TO GO:
March to June
HOW TO GET THERE:
Ferry from Angra dos Reis or Mangaratiba on the mainland.
HIGHLIGHTS:
Diving and snorkelling around the many shipwrecks in the bay.
Hire a kayak to explore the beautiful coastlines and find deserted, pristine beaches for a swim.
The Praia do Sul biological reserve – explore the abundant flora and fauna of the island.
Abraão – the unofficial capital of Ilha Grande with pretty architecture and interesting churches. Here are the best bars, restaurants and hotels.
YOU SHOULD KNOW:
Most of the bay and islands are designated a State Park to preserve this tropical paradise.

Fernando de Noronha

From the warm clear waters of the Atlantic Ocean, 350 km (220 mi) off the coast of Brazil, the lush green mountains and sheer cliffs of Fernando de Noronha rise in all their tropical perfection. There are 21 islands in the archipelago, all uninhabited apart from Fernando de Noronha itself. The waters surrounding the islands are a National Marine Reserve and home to countless species of fish, rays, sharks and spinner dolphins. Considered to be one of the most important ecological sanctuaries in the world and designated a UNESCO World Heritage Site, the area attracts keen divers and wildlife enthusiasts for the trip of a lifetime.

To prevent damage to the natural landscape, only 420 visitors are allowed on the island at a time. Accommodation is in sustainable tourist lodges which are designed to have minimum impact on their surroundings. The island is nearly always fully booked, particularly in the busiest months of December and January.

First discovered by an Italian merchant and cartographer in 1503, the archipelago is 4 degrees south of the Equator. During its 500 years of history, Fernando de Noronha has been temporarily occupied by the Dutch, French, British and Portuguese, who held it from 1737 onwards and built a series of nine forts on the island to defend their territory.

Fernando de Noronha is known for its beaches, which offer crystal clear blue water perfect for swimming. The Praia do Leão and Baía do Sancho are widely considered to be the best in Brazil. With underwater visibility up to 50 metres, the island is a Mecca for divers and snorkellers, with more than two hundred species of fish, five shark species, sea turtles and dolphins. Snorkelling in the tidal pool of Praia da Atalaia is now restricted to 100 people per day, but well worth the effort for its remarkable diversity of sea life. Lobsters, octopus and numerous fish species inhabit the pool and you may even see a baby shark.

Another memorable sight is the Baia dos Golfinhos (Bay of Dolphins), where every morning more than 1,000 spinner dolphins gather to frolic and dance in the early sunshine. Sea turtles are also prolific here, using many of the wide, secluded beaches as ground on which to lay their eggs.

POPULATION:
2,100 (2000)
WHEN TO GO:
Any time of year; even in the rainy season (April–August) there are only intermittent showers.
HOW TO GET THERE:
Fly from Recife or Natal in Brazil, or take a cruise ship between October and February.
HIGHLIGHTS:
Praia do Leão and Baía do Sancho – these pristine beaches are the best on the island and widely considered to to be the best in Brazil.
Praia da Atalaia – a beautiful tidal pool just 45–60 cm (18–24 in) deep with an enormous diversity of marine life to explore with a snorkel.
Diving in the crystal clear waters to view spinner dolphins, turtles, lemon sharks and other marine life.
YOU SHOULD KNOW:
The smaller islands can only be visited with an official license from the Brazilian Environmental Institute.

Fernando de Noronha at sunset

Florianopolis

POPULATION:
406,564 (2006)
WHEN TO GO:
June to November to see Right whales migrating along the coast.
HOW TO GET THERE:
Fly to Florianopolis International Airport.
HIGHLIGHTS:
Enjoy diving, snorkelling, sailing, surfing, fishing or just relaxing by the sea on one of the many gorgeous beaches.
Catedral Metropolitana – one of the most beautiful buildings in the city, located at Praça XV de Novembro.
Ribeirã da Ilha – this pretty area is famous for its well-preserved fishing villages built by Azorean and Portuguese immigrants.
Lagoa da Conceição – try your hand at wind-surfing, then treat yourself to a seafood meal at one of the good restaurants nearby.
YOU SHOULD KNOW:
Florianopolis is known as Floripa for short.

Florianopolis, the capital city of the Brazilian state of Santa Catarina, lies mainly on the beautiful island of Santa Catarina, which is itself widely referred to as Florianopolis. This vibrant city has the best standard of living of any in Brazil, and the inhabitants know how to enjoy themselves. The island is famous for its long stretches of sugar-soft sandy beaches, excellent seafood and traditional Azorean hospitality. The tropical climate, exotic landscapes and incredibly relaxed way of life make the island a firm favourite with holidaying Brazilians, but it is also becoming more and more popular with the international crowd.

Most of the population lives on the northern end of the island. Although originally settled by the Portuguese who came from the Azores, the city has strong German and Italian influences. In the high season, from December to February, the population of the city trebles and the beaches closest to the city centre – Canasvieiras, Jururê and Praia dos Ingleses – are packed. But there are plenty more not far away.

To the east the lush green hills give way to the wide, sandy beaches of Galheta, Mole and Joaquina. Here the big, exciting waves attract surfers looking for that perfect ride. In the south-east of the island looking out into the Atlantic are the rugged, deserted beaches of Campeche, Armaçao, Lagoinha do Leste and Naufragios, which can only be reached by trail.

Ribeirão da Ilha, on the west side of the island, bears testament to Azorean immigration. The beautifully preserved Azorean and Portuguese fishing villages boast colourful architecture and friendly inhabitants. The historic centre, in Frequesia, has an attractive plaza with the Igreja Nossa Senhora da Lapa do Ribeirão church, and an interesting Ethnological Museum. The area is accessible only via a narrow, winding and picturesque seaside road affording scenic views of Baia Sul and the lush hills of the mainland across the bay.

The Lagoa da Conceição is a famous natural attraction in the centre of the island. The large lagoon is partially surrounded by sand dunes and its shallow waters and high winds make it perfect for wind-surfing. Here are also some of the best restaurants and nightlife on the island.

*Florianopolis and the Lagoa
da Conceição*

Ilha de Marajo

Bigger than Switzerland, Marajo is one of the world's great, fluvial islands. Even though it's open to the Atlantic on one side, it's completely surrounded by fresh water: the force of the Amazon outflow on its north, and the Tocantins/Para estuary on its south side, keep the salty ocean at bay.

Marajo's western half, the Regiao da Mata, is mainly thick forest and jungle. The Regiao dos Campos in the east is an area of low lying fields; and the coast is a spectacular combination of dense mangroves and lovely beaches, flanked by arcades of miritzeiros (Amazon royal palms). Despite seasonal flooding, the east is home to most of the population, and the preferred habitat of the herds of wild buffalo that provide Marajo's sustenance. In the main town of Soure, a few miles up the Rio Paracauari, buffaloes have priority rights of way, but they can still end up as food, transport, or leather goods.

During 3,000 years, Marajo nurtured successive Indian civilizations, who initiated a tradition of ceramic art, brought together at the Marajo Museum in the pretty, rustic town of Cachoeira do Arari. This area is famous for its caboclo culture, waterways and lagoons: it's where you drift in a canoe or small boat to see blue macaws and egrets, giant storks, scarlet ibis and a scandal of colourful, noisy species breaking from the green canopy. Marajo teems with caimans, sloths, monkeys, deer, turtles, boas and countless fish including pirarucus, tucunares, tambaquis and piranhas. It is an entrancing equatorial water-world, its jungle forest constantly renewed and enriched by the Amazon. If you can get past the rudimentary service culture of the island's east coast, you'll find that Marajo is as secretively different from Brazil as Switzerland is from Europe; and in its own way, just as rich.

An Amazon estuary runs through Ilha de Marajo

POPULATION:
250,000 (2007)
WHEN TO GO:
The 'dry' (less rainy) season from June to December/January. Come for the Festivals of Quadrilhas and Boi-Bumba at the end of June; September's AgroPecuária Fair of all things buffalo; or the November regional celebration in Soure of Cirio de Nazaré.
HOW TO GET THERE:
By air taxi from Belem to Soure; by passenger boat, from Pier Escadinha, Belem, to Soure; by car/bus ferry from Icoroaci 13 km (8 mi) from Belem) to Salvaterra.
HIGHLIGHTS:
Getting involved at a fazenda (working buffalo farm) in the jungle.
Witnessing the pororoca – the offshore collision between the Amazon and the incoming Atlantic tide, a phenomenon best seen at the full or new moon between January and April.
Dancing the carimbo and the lundu at rural celebrations.
Praia Pesqueiro and Praia Araruna – two of several beautiful beaches near Soure, where the tide rises and falls a mighty 3 m (10 ft).
YOU SHOULD KNOW:
Wear shoes in and around towns/villages: among the nasty parasites found here are jigger bugs that burrow into human feet.

Ilha do Papagaio

Properly speaking, Papagaio is a private island with just 20 stand-alone bungalows set in a forest of palms and fruit trees. It lies at the southern tip of Santa Caterina Island, some 30 km (18 mi) from Florianopolis, the island capital of Santa Caterina State in southern Brazil.

Two things make Papagaio really special. Firstly, most of it is a protected nature reserve, like the 145 km (90 mi) of adjoining coastline that constitutes, onshore, the Atlantic Rainforest State Park of Serra do Tabuleiro; and, offshore, Brazil's Right whale sanctuary. Less than ten years ago, Southern Right whales had been hunted almost to extinction. Now, between July and November, you can see scores of them frolicking with their calves in the area – and because they hug the shore to avoid predators, they regularly come very close to Papagaio's beaches, which protrude into their safety zone.

Secondly, besides having all the delights of a super-tranquil tropic sanctuary, including its own delicious oysters, Papagaio has its own petroglyphs. Geometric rock-carvings of some complexity found recently in and around the island's caves show that this particular paradise once belonged to a sophisticated society that extended right across Santa Caterina Island.

Papagaio also has a third attribute: its ready access to the history and the very different kind of sophistication of nearby Florianopolis, with its 17th century fishing villages, jungle-covered hills, emerald lagoons and 40 sugar-soft beaches, full of bijou clubs and glamorous people. From Papagaio, you get the best of every world laid at your feet.

A sailing boat moored in one of Papagaio's emerald lagoons.

Tinhare Archipelago

Bahia is one of the oldest regions of Brazil, settled by the first Portuguese in the early 16th century; and its atmosphere is famously laid-back. Just to the south of Salvador itself, at the heart of the Costa do Dende (named after the African oil-palms which grow everywhere) is the Tinhare Archipelago. Its small islands dot the deep blue sea, divided by rivers, lush virgin rainforests, mangroves and beautiful hidden bays with picturesque fishing villages untouched by tourism – and a handful of resorts popularized by some of the world's most famous and fashionable people.

Tinhare is the largest at 22 km (13 mi) long and 15 km (9 mi) wide, and Morro de Sao Paolo village at its northern tip is the focal point of most of what happens in the archipelago. Morro is historic – you land beneath the ruins of forts, built in 1630 to defend the bay from pirates, and the main street is a sandy path between old stone buildings now converted to little shops, restaurants and bars.

There are no cars. For transport, you use horses, donkeys or the occasional tractor for long distances, and wheelbarrows to carry your bags. It's a genuinely eco-responsible place but most people come to Morro to party, not to take in the local culture. They soak up the natural splendour, not just because it is so beautiful but also to work off the hangovers they get from the beach parties that explode spontaneously every single night of the summer. Morro is so off-the-wall that its beaches have numbers, not names. It's difficult to imagine anywhere more attractive than Tinhare Island.

WHEN TO GO:
Year-round. Go immediately after Carnival, when Tinhare is still charged with atmosphere and party-people get their second wind.

HOW TO GET THERE:
By air, via Salvador, from Rio or Recife to Morro; by boat, from Mercado Modelo in downtown Salvador or Valenca on the mainland.

HIGHLIGHTS:
The monkeys, birds and orchids you find on the Fonte do Ceu trail through Tinhare's forests.
Praia Segunda (Second Beach), for just one night of your life.
The sensational panorama from the Ruinas da Fortaleza, especially at sunset, when dolphins come out to play.
Moqueca – Bahia's signature dish, a rich stew of palm oil, coconut milk and fish or prawns, with rice, and spiced up with chilli sauce.

YOU SHOULD KNOW:
Pau Brasil (*Caesalpinia echinata*), Brazil's national tree, now an endangered species confined to Brazil's Atlantic rainforest, is still considered the only wood suitable for making violin bows.

Sao Paolo beach

One of the beautiful bays of Isla del Sol

Isla del Sol

POPULATION:
5,000 (2007 estimate)
WHEN TO GO:
October to March, when the days are warmer. Nights are always cold.
HOW TO GET THERE:
By the principal ferry boat, via several of Titicaca's islands, to/from Puno (Peru) from/to Guiaqui (Bolivia). Backpackers can reach the small Bolivian lakeside village of Copacabana by bus or car, then take an open boat for the 1-hour ride to Isla del Sol.
HIGHLIGHTS:
The settlement of Challapampa, set among Inca ruins in the 'V' of two beaches narrowing into an isthmus at the island's northern tip. Jacques Cousteau used a mini-submarine to search the offshore area for the two-ton gold chain of Inca Huascar, part of the legendary Inca treasure sunk in Titicaca when the Spanish reached Cuzco.
The imaginings triggered by the breath-sapping climb straight up 200 ancient Inca stairs, leading from the port to Yumani, the only real 'town'.
The Bolivian 'beach town' of Copacabana, site of the Fiesta de la Virgen de la Candelaria ('The Dark Virgin of the Lake'), carved by Inca Tito Yupanqui in 1592.
YOU SHOULD KNOW:
The Aymara and Quechua of Lake Titicaca, and of Isla del Sol in particular, drive hard bargains in their dealings with the urban world of their visitors – but they are not of that world; and we trespass on their sacred sites.

The biggest lake in South America, and the highest navigable lake in the world, lies at 3,810 m (12,507 ft), its 196 km (122 mi) length spanning the Andean border between Peru and Bolivia. Lake Titicaca is the cradle of Inca civilization – and Isla del Sol is the Incas' holiest site. Here, Inti's (the Sun God's) children, Manco Tupac and Mama Ocllo, burst from a prominent sandstone crag called Titikala (the Sacred Rock), banishing darkness and bathing the world in the brilliance of the re-born Sun. The Incas built a temple on the rock, later expanded by the 10th Inca Tupac, Inca Yupanqui. He also built a convent for the 'mamaconas' (chosen women) and a 'tambo' (inn) for visiting pilgrims, and these are among 180, mainly Inca, ruins on the island. But the excavations at Ch'uxuqulla, above the small Bay of Challa, also show that Isla del Sol had been a sacred place for at least 5,000 years before the Incas.

Even today, most things about Lake Titicaca are at odds with the modern, technological and political world. The Aymara people who farm Isla del Sol grow barley, quinoa wheat, potatoes and maize on the stepped terraces hacked into every available surface of the harsh, rocky terrain – just as their ancestors did for millennia, while the Incas came and went from power. Today, the island is part of Bolivia, but power and ownership simply don't matter when you are actually there. It's the resident Aymara who guard the spiritual continuum of the place. Their fishing, fields and alpaca herds allow no development of conventional tourist amenities or roads (though local families will happily rent you a cabin or room), and the way of life is utterly indifferent to visitors who pace and race. Coming from cities, take the time to pause and drink in the harsh geography, made beautiful by an innate and transcendent sense of peace.

Isla de Chiloé

Chiloé is big, 190 km (118 mi) long and 55-65 km (35-40 mi) wide, with a central spine of mountains that divides the wild, rain-swept, Pacific west coast from its warmer, drier east coast, deeply indented with natural harbours and lots of small islands.

Long before 1608, when the Spanish brought the Jesuits to drive spiritual bargains with the Huilliche, Cuncos and Chonos, the Indians settled and fished these sheltered bays; now they are full of industrial salmon pens. Colonial occupation left a highly colourful architectural mark. In towns like Castro and Chonchi, *palafitos* (stilt-houses) became fashionable in the 19th century – and they, like most other houses and buildings, are painted in a dazzling assortment of bright colours. Chiloé's truly eye-popping heritage, though, is its wooden churches. The Jesuits built hundreds in the 17th and 18th centuries, in each case incorporating local whimsy in a bid to win souls. Imaginations soared in pinnacles, towers, arches and galleries of wood, shaped by folklore and layered by mythology into hymns of colour. They marry native and Christian faiths with such unique beauty that UNESCO has listed them as World Heritage Monuments.

Meanwhile, the Pacific rages against Chiloé's west coast, and even before you reach the Chiloé National Park you'll realize that little has changed since Darwin came in 1834. Riding or hiking through pristine evergreen forest (the Valdivian temperate

rainforest is extremely rare world-wide) of myrtle, luma, coigue, tepu and larch, you'll see an unusual amount of wildlife, much of it endemic like the Chiloé fox or Patagonian woodpecker. Reach Quellon in the south and you can watch blue whales close inshore. In Ahuenco, in the Park's northern (Chepu) sector, you can walk across coastal dunes and wild beaches to the only penguin colony shared by Humboldt and Magellan penguins. Chiloé, after all, is famously friendly.

Saint-María Church in the town of Colo

POPULATION:
155,000 (2005 estimate)
WHEN TO GO:
December to March – but you can experience all four seasons within a few hours on Chiloe. In December, flowers bloom everywhere, and there are many local festivals; or come for February's Festival Costumbrista Chilote.
HOW TO GET THERE:
By air, from Santiago to the small airports of Castro or Quellon; by bus and boat, via Pargua (mainland) and Chacao (island) from Puerto Montt to Ancud (N); by boat, from Chaiten or Puerto Chacabuco to Quellon (S)
HIGHLIGHTS:
The waterfront *palafitos*, *tejuelas* (roof shingles) of Alerce wood, and other colourful architecture around the Plaza de Armas in Castro, founded in 1567.
The wildlife havens on the islands between Chiloé and the mainland – you can reach lots on foot at low tide, or with a small boat.
The winding forest trail of the Sendero El Tepual, and the traditional reed-built Chilote house and Huilliche artefacts of the Museo Artesanal at the National Park.
The 3-storey tower and multiple arches of 19th century Iglesia San Carlos de Chonchi, centrepiece of picturesque Chonchi, (aka 'the three-floored city') built into a hillside.
The ponchos, woollens, wooden crafts and basketry at the Sunday Feria Artesanal, Chiloé's best craft market, in Dalcahue.
Standing among the birds on the wilderness Pacific coast in the streaming rain, beginning to understand Darwin and much else.
YOU SHOULD KNOW:
Chiloé's Huilliche traditional culture is one of South America's most remarkable and relatively complete survival stories – including its folklore and erotic mythology.

Isla Grande de Tierra del Fuego

POPULATION:
Argentina 120,000; Chile 50,000
(2007 estimates)
WHEN TO GO:
November to March
HOW TO GET THERE:
By air, from Buenos Aires or Santiago
to Ushuaia (Argentina) (S), or from
Punta Arenas to Porvenir (Chile) (N);
by bus, via Rio Gallegos to Ushuaia.
HIGHLIGHTS:
Parakeets, condors, kingfishers, owls,
firecrown hummingbirds and hosts
of waterfowl.
World class trout fishing in the rivers
near Rio Grande, the ranching centre.
The Tierra del Fuego National Park
near Ushuaia, including the
archeological sites of 'los concheros'
and the extraordinary coastline of
Lapataia Bay.
The seals, sea lions and penguin
rookeries along the Beagle Channel.
The enormous (380 cells plus vast
workshops) 'prison at the end of the
world', built 1902-20 and closed in
1947, now the Museo del Presidio,
and the original raison d'etre
of Ushuaia.
The Museo Tierra del Fuego in
Porvenir, Chile – which tells the story
of the gold rush and other kinds of
industrial exploitation of the
indigenous people.
YOU SHOULD KNOW:
Tierra del Fuego lights up popular
imagination as 'the world's most
southerly point'. It isn't. That honour
belongs to Islote Aguila ('Aguila Islet'),
the southernmost of the Diego
Ramirez islands, and therefore of the
South American continent, about 100
km (60 mi) southwest of Cape Horn in
the Drake Passage.

The Island of Fire got its name from Magellan in 1520, inspired by the open fires that the local Yamana Indians carried in their fishing boats and in their camps to keep warm. The climate is worse than inhospitable. It snows in summer, and it's very windy, foggy, and wet as well as bitterly cold. Inland, some areas actually have a polar climate. All the rules say no trees should grow here, but Tierra del Fuego's sub-Antarctic forests are unique in the world, and tree cover (albeit so twisted and stunted by the wind that they are called 'flag trees') extends almost to the tip of South America.

Tierra del Fuego is defined by the Straits of Magellan and the Beagle Channel, both of which link the Atlantic and Pacific Oceans. It's divided politically between Chile and Argentina, who both jealously guard their rights to oil, gas and minerals. Both countries, however, have been quick to see the rising value of eco-tourism, and to appreciate the enhanced value of co-operation. On both sides, the rather shameful history of colonial depredations wreaked on the indigenous Yamana and Selk'nam by gold prospectors, whalers, and commercial hunters are now a matter of shared 'heritage' – and both in Ushuaia, by far the biggest city on the island, and Argentina's hub for most visitors, and Porvenir, Chile's main town far to the north, the museums of ethnic culture are a revelation. The ancient tribal creation mythologies add the dimension of human warmth to one of the world's most forbidding landscapes.

Tierra del Fuego is big sea-run brown trout and the great oceanic marine mammals with birds to match. You get lakes and glaciers, mountains, prairies, swamps and dense forests with the magnified beauty of wilderness on a continental scale. It is a harsh, disturbing place – and intensely rewarding to visit.

A view of the Beagle Channel

Easter Island

In the south-east Pacific more than 3,219 km (2,000 mi) from the nearest area of any significant population, coastal Chile, Easter Island is one of the world's most isolated inhabited islands. Easter Island, or Rapa Nui, is a roughly triangular island with an extinct volcano at each corner. The island and surrounding islets such as Motu Nui and Motu Iti are the uppermost peaks of a volcanic mountain which rises over 2,000 m (6,561 ft) from the sea bed below. Easter Island is a unique and starkly beautiful landscape with volcanic craters, lava formations, brilliant blue water, beaches, low rolling hills and cattle farms. However, it is not the landscape which brings visitors here but the enigmatic statues which litter the island, many of which are an imposing 9 m (30 ft) in height and very broad.

The large stone statues, or Moai, for which Easter Island is famous were carved during a short burst of creative activity in megalithic times. Nearly 900 statues have been recorded. Although often referred to as 'Easter Island Heads', the statues are generally heads and torsos. Since their discovery by Europeans in the 18th century, there has been much debate about how, why and by whom the statues were erected.

First settled by a small group of Polynesians around 400 AD, Easter Island was, for most of its history, the most isolated inhabited territory on earth. With such limited resources of food, water and wood for fuel and building, its inhabitants, the Rapanui, endured famines, epidemics and civil war, and more than once in their history the population nearly died out altogether. They also suffered slave raids and colonialism but still managed to create a cultural legacy that has brought them fame out of all proportion to their numbers. As well as the awe-inspiring statues, the Rapanui have left evidence in the Rongorongo script – the only written language in Oceania, as well as a wealth of petroglyphs, rock carvings of which Easter Island has one of the richest collections in Polynesia.

Nearly all the statues were carved out of easily worked volcanic tufa taken from a single site called Rano Raraku. The Rapanui had no metal or machinery, only simple basalt hand tools. Only about a quarter of the statues were erected on their permanent platforms – nearly half stayed at Rano Raraku and the rest elsewhere on the island, probably en route to their final locations.

POPULATION:
3,791 (2002)
WHEN TO GO:
October to November, or March to April.
HOW TO GET THERE:
Fly from Chile.
HIGHLIGHTS:
The annual cultural festival, the Tapati, celebrating Rapanui culture.
The Moai – Poike, a statue with a gaping mouth, is one of the locals' favourites. Ahu Tahai is another notable statue for its eyes and its topknot.
Don't miss the seven Moai at Akhivi, which face into the setting sun.
The island's many caves – one of them appears to be a ceremonial centre, while the other has two 'windows'.
Orongo – a ruined stone village at the south-western tip of the island. Orongo has a dramatic location on the crater lip of Rano Kau at the point where a 250 m (820 ft) sea cliff converges with the inner wall of the crater of Rano Kau.
Rano Kau, where the birdman cult flourished, south of Hanga Roa.
YOU SHOULD KNOW:
Chile first declared the island to be a National Park in 1935, and in 1996 UNESCO designated the island a World Heritage Site.

Ahu Tongariki viewed from the crater of Rano Kau

Deception Island

POPULATION:
Uninhabited (but there are 20 to 30 summer season staff at the seasonal Argentine and Spanish scientific stations on the southwest shore of the caldera, Port Foster).
WHEN TO GO:
January to March
HOW TO GET THERE:
By cruise ship from Punta Arenas, Chile, or Ushuaia, Argentina.
HIGHLIGHTS:
The chinstrap penguins at Baily Head. Working out your own strategy for maintaining the perfect temperature of your sand bath on the beach at Whalers' Bay. (Tip: you get the best results with at least three people working together). Diving on Hephaestus' Wall, a 32 m (105 ft) vertical and cinder slope covered in thousands of brittle stars, sponges, ascidians and echinoderms below the kelp – located just by Neptune's Bellows, it's one of the Antarctic Peninsula's richest underwater sites. Studying the historic graffiti of whalers, sailors and scientists who once lived on the island, scrawled on the desolate planks, rusting boilers and crushed huts left behind. Each name is the ghost of a bygone adventure.
YOU SHOULD KNOW:
Please study the code of conduct drawn up by signatories to the Antarctic Treaty and Management Plan for Protected Areas, and agreed by all tour operators. The details of where to walk, and how close to approach a penguin, etc., are really important.

For most people, the South Shetland Islands are their first sight of Antarctica. Lying 960 km (600 mi) south of Tierra del Fuego, the tip of South America, and 160 km (100 mi) north of the Antarctic Peninsula, the string of volcanic islands is a colourful break in the usual Antarctic monochrome of white, grey and blue. Deception Island lies in the middle of the chain. It's circular, a collapsed volcanic cone reduced to a ring of hills rising to 539 m (1,700 ft) around the flooded caldera, with a narrow – 230 m (754 ft) – entrance called Neptune's Bellows. It looks like one of the world's safest, natural harbours – but the volcano is still very much active.

It's been a refuge throughout Antarctic history, for explorers, naval patrols, and hunters of seals and whales. You can still see the detritus and relics of some of the 13 whaling factories operating here in 1914-15: the last of them disappeared after the 1920-21 whaling season, when the water boiled, stripping the paint off the ships. In 1963, intense fumarole activity caused a US Coast Guard icebreaker to actually run aground inside a live volcano; and a full eruption in 1969 destroyed two Chilean scientific stations and a British base. But most of the time, the thermal oddities of Deception provide a lot of fun for visitors, and sanctuary to a host of unexpected wildlife. Half the island belongs to permanent glaciers, and in the moonscape of black volcanic sand and rocks elsewhere, you don't expect to find the world's biggest colony of chinstrap penguins, hundreds of thousands of them, crammed onto Baily Head.

Eighteen species of moss or lichen grow here and nowhere else in Antarctica, and Kroner Lake is Antarctica's only geothermal lagoon. In fact Deception is one of Antarctica's greatest wonders.

A disused whaling boat

124

Tristan da Cunha Group

A Green turtle on a beach on St Helena

Lying 3,360 km (2,088 mi) from South America and 2,816 km (1,750 mi) from South Africa, Tristan da Cunha is the most remote archipelago in the world. The islands are among several volcanic stacks associated with the central and southern mid-Atlantic ridge, and governed from St Helena, 2,173 km (1,350 mi) to the north. Tristan da Cunha alone is still active, a cone with a 10 km (6 mi) base diameter, rising 2,060 m (6,760 ft) to Queen Mary's Peak. During the wet season, narrow gulches radiating from the summit become raging torrents, sweeping minerals from the steep slopes over the wall of 300 - 600 m (1,000-2,000 ft) basalt cliffs, broken only on the northwest side, where a lush coastal strip enables the Settlement (aka Edinburgh of the Seven Seas, its official name) to grow its world-famous potatoes.

The difficulty of landing on any of the Tristan Group islands has helped to preserve their ecological integrity. Since their discovery in 1506, sporadic attempts at commercial sealing, whaling or farming failed. Nobody – the Royal Navy (1873), the Royal Society (1962), nor Shackleton himself (1922) – breached the interior of Inaccessible Island until 1982, when a party of English schoolboys completed the first proper survey. The treeless mountain ridges of Gough Island are even less hospitable, but like Inaccessible, have been allowed to recover their magnificent flora and fauna as strict nature reserves. Instead, visitors can go to Nightingale Island, if accompanied by a native Tristanian. Much easier to access despite dense offshore kelpfields, Nightingale's four wetland areas are home to over a million breeding seabirds, including the yellow-nosed albatross, great shearwater and rockhopper penguin. The sight is so amazing, Tristanians go to Nightingale for their holidays, apparently unaware that Tristan da Cunha and they themselves are one of the South Atlantic's greatest attractions.

POPULATION:
Tristan da Cunha 300 (2007 estimate); St Helena 5,500 (2006 estimate); Gough Island 6 (2007), Inaccessible and Nightingale Islands are uninhabited.

WHEN TO GO:
December to March – but apart from snow on the top of the peak, Tristan's sub-tropical climate doesn't vary much throughout the year, and in the Roaring Forties, you can never take the weather for granted.

HOW TO GET THERE:
By regular service (fishing) boat from South Africa to Tristan da Cunha; by local Tristanian fishing boat to Gough, Inaccessible and Nightingale Is; by RMS *St Helena*, a dedicated service between London and South Africa calling at St Helena.

HIGHLIGHTS:
The English patois of Tristan da Cunha – a mixture of archaic Georgian-era English and early Americanisms.
Braving the extreme seas and high winds on a fishing boat to see the huge breeding colonies of Tristan albatross, fur seals, and many other marine and bird species on each of the Tristan Group islands, from offshore.
The flightless rail (*Gallinula comeri*) – one of the world's rarest birds.

YOU SHOULD KNOW:
After the 1857 famine on Tristan da Cunha, one of the few islanders who stayed was Thomas Swain – the man who caught Admiral Nelson as he fell, mortally wounded, at the Battle of Trafalgar.

The black-browed Albatross Colony in the western Falklands

Falkland Islands

POPULATION:
3,025 (2007) (about 2,100 in Stanley, and 530 at Mt Pleasant military base).
WHEN TO GO:
November to February for bird-watching; December/January and March/April for fresh-run sea-trout.
HOW TO GET THERE:
By air, from Santiago, Chile, via Punta Arenas and Rio Gallegos, Argentina; or from the UK on regular Ministry of Defence flights from RAF Brize Norton or by cruise ship.
HIGHLIGHTS:
The Maritime History Trail in Stanley – places and relics of the days of great sailing ships and early steam vessels, and including the major naval Battle of the Falklands in 1914, and the islands' role in the 1939 Battle of the River Plate.
The rockhopper penguin rookery and albatross colony on tranquil New Island in the western Falklands.
Bouncing in a Land Rover across 'the Camp' (everywhere outside Stanley, from the Spanish 'campo') with an enthusiastic islander, discovering the cattle raising traditions inherited from gauchos who worked the Falklands in the 1850s.
Battlefield sites of the 1982 war, including Wireless Ridge, Mount Tumbledown and Gypsy Cove.
YOU SHOULD KNOW:
In Stanley, a local delicacy is 'diddle dee jam' – a unique preserve made from the tiny red berries of a Falklands shrub.

Surrounded by their 200 satellite islands, the twin bulwarks of East and West Falkland stand athwart the sea lane to Cape Horn, some 450 km (300 mi) east of the South American coast. The group was the subject of desultory squabbling between Britain, Spain, France and Argentina for 200 years before Britain realized their strategic value in 1833. The islanders have vehemently asserted their preference for British rule ever since, most recently by repelling an Argentine invasion in 1982. When the dust settled, the Falklands War proved to have revived global interest in the whole group as an untouched wildlife paradise with enough amenities to make it accessible. The total population is minimal, but visitors can find hospitality even in the most remote areas.

The main islands are vast, low yellow and green tundra, ridged by hills that rise to 705 m (2,313 ft) at Mt Usborne on East Falkland. Crags and broken rockfaces loom over swamps like Lafonia on East Falkland, where peat-stained tarns and wind-rippled lakes reflect endless 2 m (6 ft 6 in) high tussac grass and huge skies, home to 600,000 sheep. Fishermen go for sea trout or mullet at Warrah in West Falkland or San Carlos or Murrel in East Falkland. The fishing season (September to March) brings five species of penguin to the islands, including rockhoppers, macaronis and magellanic (aka 'jackass'). Sea Lion Island has resident king penguins, offshore killer whales, fur and elephant seals and dolphins as well as the sea lions. The Falklands also host the world's largest colonies of the majestic, black-browed albatross, along with giant petrels and 200 other bird species.

The recent war has left its mark on the Falklands – most impressively, on the islanders' determination to show that their greatest asset, nature, has no politics.

South Georgia

The island of South Georgia, an inhospitable frozen wasteland of glaciers, snow-capped mountains and freezing winds, lies in the southern Atlantic Ocean around 2,000 km (1,243 mi) east of Tierra del Fuego. This remote Antarctic island is part of the British territory of South Georgia and the South Sandwich Islands. The British claim to sovereignty of South Georgia dates from 1775, when Captain Cook landed here and dismissed the island as not worth discovering. Argentina also claimed the island in 1927, an unresolved dispute which contributed to the 1982 Falklands war, when Argentine forces briefly occupied South Georgia.

In 1916, Ernest Shackleton became stranded on Elephant Island, 1,200 km (745 mi) to the south-west, while on his Imperial Trans-Antarctic Expedition. Shackleton and a small group of men left the rest of the party to summon help and ended up, after an arduous journey, at King Haakon Bay on the south coast of South Georgia. They then managed to make it 30 km (18 mi) overland to reach help at Stromness whaling station, which led to the rescue of the remaining men. During a later expedition in 1922, Shackleton died on board a ship off South Georgia, and he is buried on the island at Grytviken.

There is no permanent human population on South Georgia – only the British Government Officer, research scientists and museum staff at Grytviken – but there are enormous populations of penguins – the largest colonies anywhere on earth, with around 400,000 breeding pairs of king penguins, two million pairs of the macaroni penguins and large colonies of four other species. Visitors come here to watch penguin couples overcome the extreme climatic conditions and nurture their precious eggs through hatching and the vulnerable chick stage into fully fledged members of the colony. The charming creatures work tirelessly together avoiding the seals that lurk in the shallows waiting to pounce and protecting their young from ferocious skua gulls who will snatch one and tear it to shreds.

When he landed here in the 18th century, Captain Cook noted the huge seal and whale populations around the island, but just two hundred years later both had been hunted nearly to extinction. South Georgia is, however, home to 95 per cent of the world's southern fur seals, half the southern elephant seals, 250,000 albatrosses, including the massive Wandering albatross, and up to ten million other seabirds, making a trip here a totally unique experience.

POPULATION:
About 20 (2007)
WHEN TO GO:
November to March
HOW TO GET THERE:
The only access is by sea. It takes up to 10 days by organized cruise.
HIGHLIGHTS:
From November to December – this is the courting season for penguins, and seal colonies begin to establish themselves; pack ice begins to melt and the seascapes are fantastic, with pristine icebergs.
From mid-December to January – the ice has receded and the penguin chicks hatch. There is increased whale activity and seal breeding.
From February to March – there are beautiful dawns and sunsets. Whale sighting is at its best, and the fledgling penguins leave their nests.
YOU SHOULD KNOW:
South Georgia is famous for its stamps. The small numbers produced and the attractive natural scenes on the stamps make them popular with collectors.

Sunrise illuminating Grae Glacier and Cape Disappointment.

Kerguelen

POPULATION:
70 in winter, 120 in summer
(estimates)

WHEN TO GO:
November to March – but year-round
the wind speed averages 100 kph
(63 mph), the (ice-free) wave heights
are commonly 12-15 m (40-50 ft),
and it rains violently, or snows, 300
days a year including summer.

HOW TO GET THERE:
By (occasional) cruise ship; or
licensed by the French Government
in Paris or Réunion, by sea, either
accompanying a supply vessel, or
with one of the small fleet of fishing
boats from Réunion allowed to fish in
the archipelago.

HIGHLIGHTS:
Port-au-Francais – the 'capital' and
main base, with bar, gym, hospital,
library and the well-named chapel of
Notre Dame des Vents.
The partly restored 1908 whaling
station of Port Jeanne d'Arc, in the
NW corner of the Presqu'ile Jeanne
d'Arc, across the Buenos Aires
Passage from Ile Longue.
Port Christmas, one of the historic
geo-magnetic stations, at Baie de
l'Oiseau, NW Loranchet Peninsula. It's
also the place where Captain Cook
anchored on Christmas Day 1776,
and coined the nickname of
Desolation Islands.
The 'strombolic' volcano of Mt Ross –
Grande Terre's highest point at
1,850 m (6,068 ft).
Ile Foch, N of Grande Terre – the
largest island with no introduced
species (rabbits, cats, rats etc), and
used as a reference for the
archipelago's original ecosystem.
The enormous number of penguins,
seals, albatrosses, petrels, Kerguelen
terns and other magnificent
bird species.

YOU SHOULD KNOW:
Kerguelen lies on the Antarctic
Convergence, where upwelling cold
currents mix with the warmer water
from the Indian Ocean, thus
encouraging the huge number of
birds and marine mammals.

Midway between Africa, Australia and Antarctica lies the French territory of Kerguelen, also known as Desolation Island. Officially it's called the Kerguelen Archipelago, but Grande Terre, the main island, covers 6,675 sq km (2,577 sq mi), and the other 300 just 540 sq km (208 sq mi). Grande Terre looks a bit like a spiny lobster on the map, with several peninsulas and promontories, and is deeply indented with fjords, bays, and inlets. Its core is the 550 sq km (344 sq mi) Cook Glacier on the western side: the island's landscape is the result of extreme glacial and fluvial erosion, and one typical effect is the huge, flat and fertile plain of the Courbet Peninsula on the eastern side, formed by the detritus swept from the steep interior valleys.

Kerguelen is the visible part of a giant, volcanic plateau, a micro-continent that sank 10 million years ago. Today, volcanic activity is limited to a few fumaroles – but after discovering sedimentary rocks similar to ones in Australia and India, which point to Kerguelen having once been covered in tropical flora, scientists hope that the archipelago's textbook volcanic formations will explain the break-up of the once-unified super-continent of Australia, India and Antarctica.

Since its modern discovery in 1772, Kerguelen became legendary among sailors firstly for its large numbers of whales and seals, which were rapidly hunted to near-extinction, and secondly for its indigenous cabbage, rich in vitamin C, which saved countless thousands from scurvy during the 18th and 19th centuries. Now, it supports only a satellite tracking station, and a research base for earth scientists and biologists. The marine wildlife and the bird populations have recovered. Captain Cook thought it looked sterile, and named it 'Desolation'. With its restored natural wealth, and at the centre of cutting-edge geological discovery, Kerguelen confounds its nickname.

Cormorant at sunset on Kerguelen

Heard Island

Young bull elephant seals on Heard Island

Heard Island is Australia's only active volcano complex, a roughly 25 km (15.5 mi) cone thrusting 2,745 m (9,006 ft) out of the southern Indian Ocean. From Mt Mawson, the highest point, the Big Ben volcanic massif is linked by a narrow ridge to the 10 km (6 mi) long Laurens Peninsula, a mountainous headland riddled with lava tunnels. Big Ben's shape makes the already vicious weather patterns so bad that Heard Island is reputed to be the wildest place on earth. Even so, it's one of the few places in the sub-Antarctic where continuous weather observation has been possible.

Significantly, no plants or animals have ever been introduced, and since 1972 all forms of human intervention have stopped – so there's no better site to monitor the effects of climate change on permanent glaciation in an undisturbed environment. For example, there are 12 glaciers on Big Ben, contributing to the 80 per cent ice cover of the island, and forming most of the sheer, 100 m (328 ft) ice cliffs that make landing on the island so difficult. Glaciers that used to terminate only in the sea now terminate far inland.

This retreat has benefited flora and fauna. As mosses, lichens, herbs and grasses colonize greater areas, they become habitat for ever-larger colonies of indigenous birds and marine mammals. Heard is a classic example of a sub-Antarctic island with low species diversity but huge populations. There are well over a million macaroni penguins, and tens of thousands of king, emperor, and gentoo penguins; 3,000 pairs of southern giant petrels, 700 pairs of black-browed and 500 pairs of light-mantled albatross, and 31 other species. Heard Island now belongs to them and it has been declared a UNESCO World Heritage Site.

POPULATION:
Uninhabited
WHEN TO GO:
November to March – but summer is no guarantee of better weather conditions.
HOW TO GET THERE:
By arrangement with ANARE (Australian National Antarctic Research Expedition), who monitor all boat movements within the island and offshore Heritage area. NB there is no natural or built harbour or port.
HIGHLIGHTS:
Wedell, Ross and crabeater seals, at the extreme northern limit of their pelagic ranges.
The trypots (used to process seal blubber into oil), cooping iron, gun parts, hut ruins, graves and workshops, among other remnants of the sealing industry at Atlas Cove.
The Heard Island cormorant – an endemic sub-species of only 100 pairs.
The wandering albatross – reported to be breeding for the first time in 1980.
The formations of volcanic extrusion on karst along the Laurens Peninsula.
YOU SHOULD KNOW:
Before decreeing that 'artefacts should not be moved, souvenired or relocated by tourists', ANARE repatriated (to Australia) a 'blubber press and the only known carving on basalt rock from the Antarctic or sub-Antarctic'.

EUROPE

Åland Islands

*Islands in the tranquil
Åland archipelago*

In the clear blue waters of the Baltic at the mouth of the Gulf of Bothnia, Åland is an archipelago consisting of around 80 inhabited emerald islands plus 6000 smaller islets and rocks. Officially belonging to Finland, the islands were awarded a wide degree of autonomy by the League of Nations in 1921 to settle a long-running dispute between Sweden and Finland. Åland has its own government, its own flag, its own stamps and its own vehicle licence plates.

Most visitors come here for the slow pace of life and the tranquil beauty of the archipelago. The best way to explore the islands is by rowing boat. You'll soon find a beach all to yourself – perhaps even a whole island.

Fasta Åland is the largest island in the archipelago, with an area of around 1,000 sq km (600 sq mi). Here can be found Mariehamn, the only town in the archipelago, where just under half of the population of the islands live. Founded in 1861, Mariehamn is the centre of the shipping and tourist industries and home to the Landskapsregering – the local seat of government.

In the summer months, from May to August, the Åland Islands receive more sunshine than any of their Nordic neighbours, making them a popular holiday destination. In winter, visitors come for the long-distance skating or to experience ice-boating through the ice-

sheets that form around the smaller islands and skerries.

At any time of the year there are various cultural highlights to entertain visitors, including the Kastelholm. This medieval castle, mostly a ruin today, was home to many Swedish kings who ruled the combined kingdom of Sweden and Finland. The great fortress of Bomarsund was built by the Russians in 1832, but later destroyed by British and French warships in 1854 as part of the campaign in the Baltic during the Crimean War. On the other side of the channel there is a small museum with pictures and objects from the Bomarsund.

Mariehamn's Maritime Quarter is also worth a visit, where you can see traditional boat-building, a smithy and other local handicrafts. The marina accommodates small ships and traditional wooden boats. The Maritime Museum contains exhibitions of historic and contemporary boat-building.

Kvarken Archipelago

This outstanding conservation area in the Gulf of Bothnia consists of around 5,600 islands off the coast of Finland, stretching about 70 km (45 mi) east-west and 60 km (40 mi) north-south. The archipelago is continuously rising out of the sea as a result of glacio-isostatic uplift (see 'You Should Know'); islands are constantly changing and merging, peninsulas expand, reefs and rocks emerge from the sea, and bays evolve into lakes, marshes and peat fens. The rate of land rise is so fast that there are noticeable changes to the landscape within a generation.

Small clusters of low-lying wilderness islands dot the sea. Beaches of stones and boulders are bordered by alder trees, the fens abound with blueberries and rowan trees, and the open heathland merges into forests of pine and spruce. The unique charm of the Kvarken lies in its dynamic scenery, stark natural beauty, outstandingly rich bird life, and picturesque villages.

The landscape was formed under the ice sheet 10,000 – 24,000 years ago by glaciers scraping away vast amounts of clay, gravel, sand and boulders in their path. As the ice melted, this mass was deposited in various geological forms known as moraine. An unusual feature of the Kvarken Islands is the rare "de Greer" ridged moraine, as well as the more usual humps and drumlins of post Ice Age scenery.

The first written evidence of permanent villages dates from the early 15th century, but the archipelago was probably settled much earlier. The inhabitants made their living as fishermen and by small-scale sheep and cattle farming, trading fish and sealskins for grain. Today the Kvarken is sparsely populated, and its World Heritage status ensures that it will remain a protected natural region.

POPULATION:
2,500 (2005)
WHEN TO GO:
April, May, September and October for the bird migrations. June to August for boating, cycling and walking holidays. In January and February you can walk across the iced-over sea.
HOW TO GET THERE:
From Vaasa on the coast of mainland Finland, you can drive to one of the inner islands with a bridge connection, where you can either rent your own boat or take guided cruises.
HIGHLIGHTS:
Valsörarna – the 36 m (118 ft) high lighthouse built in 1885 at Eiffel's workshop in Paris.
Björköby and Raippaluoto – for canoeing through the maze of inlets and a hiking trail to Panike through incredibly varied scenery.
YOU SHOULD KNOW:
Glacio-isostasis is the reaction of a landmass that has been squashed under the massive weight of layers of ice, often kilometres thick. When the ice finally melts, the land "bounces back" as a result of the release of pressure on it and gradually rises up. At the present rate of land-rise the islands of the Kvarken archipelago will, in around 2,000 years, time form a continuous stretch of land between Finland and Sweden, turning the Bothnian Bay into a huge lake.

Stockholm Archipelago

Picturesque red huts on the Stora Nassa Island group

The Skärgården (skerry garden) stretches 60 km (40 mi) seawards from the city of Stockholm running some 150 km (95 mi) from north to south. It is an amazing labyrinth of some 24,000 forested granite islands, many of them less than 100 m (300 ft) apart. In the evening light especially, this maze of pine-covered rock floating in the sea is heartbreakingly beautiful. Here you can sail for miles, weaving your way past empty forested shores without seeing a soul. For hundreds of years the islands were sparsely populated by seafarers. Only in the 19th century did they start to become fashionable as a weekend retreat for wealthy Stockholmers.

Today, although the central archipelago is virtually a suburb of Stockholm, there are still some outstandingly beautiful places to visit. The outermost island of Sandhamn is renowned for its splendid 18th and 19th century architecture, natural landscapes, and wonderful beaches; and Grinda, one of the tiny inner islands, is a famously romantic place for an overnight stay.

In the southern part of the archipelago, Dalarö is an old customs island with a picturesque charm; the surrounding islands are brilliant for camping and kayaking. Utö, one of the outermost islands, has superb swimming while Nåttarö is noted for its fauna, fishing and pretty country lanes. Nynäshamn is a bustling port with a charming harbour from where you catch the island-hopping ferry.

To the north, Tjockö is the main island of an archipelago of about 350 islands that have a long history as a base for piracy and smuggling. Arholma, the northernmost island of the Skärgården, has a charming old fishing village and amazing views.

Although it is one of the world's largest archipelagos, the Skärgården is relatively unknown outside Sweden. Its hauntingly beautiful atmosphere, an almost spiritual quality, is an extraordinary experience.

Holmöarna

This scenically beautiful island group lies 10 km (6 mi) off the coast in the Gulf of Bothnia. It is Sweden's largest maritime nature reserve – a strange wetland of peat bog and lakes interspersed with heath, woodland and spruce forest. Holmöarna has been formed by post-glacial rebound (the reaction of land that has been weighted down by tons of ice). The islands only broke through the surface of the sea around 2,000 years ago and are still undergoing rapid topographical change: the highest point is presently only 26 m (85 ft) above sea level but Holmöarna is growing taller all the time – at a rate of about 8.5 mm (0.03 in) per year.

The islands appear to have first been settled around 1,300 and by the 16th century there were seven farms in the north of Holmön, the main island. Today this is still the only part that is inhabited – where the ferry comes in at Byviken and the nearby houses alongside a ridge of centuries old farmland, a charming patchwork of small fields that is the only area of cultivated land on the islands.

Nature lovers will be in their element exploring the magical lakes and forest and wandering along the bemusing eastern coast of inlets and skerries, peat bogs and pools, coastal birch woods and rocky shores. From Byviken you can take a boat to the islet of Stora Fjäderägg, an ancient fishing and sealing base that is now a well-known ornithology centre. The only island road runs the full length of Holmön and crosses a narrow strait, the Gäddbäckssundet, to the uninhabited island of Ängesön. To the south, the island of Grossgrunden is open heath that is difficult to access but if you do manage it there is superb fishing in the stretch of water that separates it from Holmögadd, a protected military zone famous for its old stone lighthouse.

POPULATION:
90 (estimate)
WHEN TO GO:
May to September unless you're seriously hardy.
HOW TO GET THERE:
From Stockholm, fly/drive/rail to Umeå, the largest town in northern Sweden. Take the ferry from Norrfjärden, 30 km (19 mi) NE of Umeå. It is free of charge and runs three times daily in the summer and twice daily the rest of the year. When the sea gets iced-up the ferry service is replaced with a hydrocopter service.
HIGHLIGHTS:
Boat Museum, Byviken.
Berguddens Fyr – lighthouse. An especially good spot for bird watching.
Trappudden – cliffs and post-glacial rock fields.
The beach at Jebäckssundet, 5 km (3 mi) south of Byviken.
YOU SHOULD KNOW:
Holmöarna is at the westernmost end of the Kvarken Archipelago – designated a UNESCO World Heritage Site for its extraordinary moraine scenery, formed around 10,000 years ago at the end of the Ice Age.

Lilac bushes on Grinda Island

Bohuslän Islands

Wild, rugged and bleak, some 3,000 granite islands and skerries stretch for roughly 150 km (95 mi) along the coast of the province of Bohuslän, west Sweden. They are renowned for their desolate treeless beauty. "...Huge skies, immense seas...everything so bright and shining...such a feeling of isolation" is how Ingrid Bergman described them. She holidayed here for years and her ashes were scattered off the island of Danholmen. These are islands for nature lovers, sailors and divers, with few villages, virtually no nightlife, and hardly any cars.

Although some of the settlements date back to medieval times, the islands were mostly uninhabited until the 18th century herring boom made it viable to earn a living here. Little seems to have changed, apart from the fact that tourists rather than herrings now support the local economy: picturesque fishing villages of pastel painted cottages cling to the rocks; the salt smell of the sea mingles with the scent of dill, allspice, seaweed and smokehouses; seagulls whirl and scream in the vast open sky.

Marstrand is by far the most sophisticated island. It is a popular yachting resort with superb swimming and diving, wonderful seafood restaurants and even the odd late-night bar. The Koster Islands are the other extreme. These, the westernmost islands, are a nature reserve of beautiful beaches and rocky Ice Age landscapes – a paradise of rare plants and Nordic light. The village on Gullholmen is a famously picturesque settlement of quaint wooden houses huddled together, using every inch of space. A footbridge leads to the neighbouring island of Härmanö, one of Bohuslän's largest nature reserves. Väderöarna is a cluster of windswept skerries, home to Sweden's largest seal colony; and a trip to Stora Kornö, perhaps the least touched of all by the 21st century, is a must.

Bohuslän harbour

Gotland

The whole atmosphere of this wonderful island is redolent of the Viking Age – ruins and runestones, cairns, medieval churches, windmills and trolls. According to some historians the original home of the Goths, Gotland lies 90 km (56 mi) east of the mainland and is Sweden's largest island, covering an area of 3,140 sq km (1,225 sq mi). The island is renowned for its natural beauty – a craggy limestone and shale landscape with rugged shores, mainly given over to farmland.

Gotland was once an important independent Baltic nation, eventually integrated into Sweden in 1645. The picturesque medieval city of Visby, a UNESCO World Heritage Site on the west coast, was once the main port of the Baltic with trading links as far away as Arabia. Its massive city walls are 11 m (36 ft) high and 3.4 km (over 2 mi) long; as you walk along its cobbled streets, past rose garlanded stone and wood houses, to the medieval harbour, you can't help being blown away by its Viking charm.

The bleak north coast has a peculiar Nordic beauty with its stony shoreline and breathtaking clifftop views. Most of the island is rich pastoral scenery of fields, woods and moors with drystone walls, whitewashed churches and windmills – perfect for horse riding and cycling. You can always find a secluded spot around the 800 km (500 mi) coast of rocky crags enclosing shingle and sand beaches. All along the east coast spectacular *raukar* – limestone columns up to 6 m (20 ft) high, weathered into extraordinary shapes – stick out of the sea like mysterious trolls. The most famous *rauk* is the island's landmark of Hoburgsgubben (Old Man's Rock) on the south coast which is a magnet for birds.

Part of the city wall of Visby, Gotland

POPULATION:
57,317 (2006)
WHEN TO GO:
Late May to early September
HOW TO GET THERE:
Daily flights from Stockholm. Ferry several times a day from Nynäshamn or Oskarshamn on the mainland, takes about three hours. In the summer season there is also a boat connection with the island of Oland.
HIGHLIGHTS:
Day or overnight trips to beautiful islets of Stora Karlsö and Lilla Karlsö.
Källungen's Kyrka – a 13th century church with 12th century artefacts and pictures.
Lojsta Hed – lovely moorland area.
Bunge Open Air Museum – more than 50 buildings and runestones.
YOU SHOULD KNOW:
This is an excellent place for an outdoor family holiday of biking, boating or camping. Children will be thrilled by the Viking atmosphere and the chance to visit the home of Swedish super-heroine, Pippi Longstocking.

Gotska Sandön

POPULATION:
4 (National Park staff)
WHEN TO GO:
Late May to early September unless you are a serious endurance enthusiast.
HOW TO GET THERE:
By boat from Nynäshamn on the mainland or the island of Faro.
HIGHLIGHTS:
Gamla Gården – an old farm where there are Viking artefacts.
Tarnüdden – the beach on the south coast.
Madame Souderland's homestead – the 18th century house of the first woman to live on the island.
Borgström's – a fishing cottage built out of driftwood and shipwreck in 1900.
YOU SHOULD KNOW:
Visitor numbers are strictly regulated and you have to obtain a permit. You can stay either in the camping site, a simple cottage or sleeping hut.

This giant sand dune is the most remote island in the Baltic – isolated in the middle of the sea 38 km (24 mi) to the north of Gotland. It is just 9 km (6 mi) long by 6 km (4 mi) across, part of the crest of an undersea ridge formed by glaciation, almost entirely composed of sand with a few odd areas of moraine and rocky beach. From a distance Gotska Sandon looks completely flat but when you walk around you soon realize how hilly sand dunes can be. The highest point is 42 m (138 ft) above sea level.

Despite its distance from the mainland, there are signs of human activity from the Stone Age onwards. It was used as a seal hunting and fishing base by the Faro islanders, who also grazed their sheep here, but there were no permanent inhabitants until the 18th century. From 1783-1859 the island was privately owned. It eventually became Swedish Crown territory and is now a National Park.

The island is mainly pine woods with ground cover of heather, cowberries (lingon) and moss. In places the forest is incredibly dense and contains many rare insects and plants. The entire coast is bordered by a sand ridge 10-15 m (33-50 ft) high and 100-300 m (330-985 ft) wide where there are shifting sand dunes which move up to 6 m (20 ft) a year.

There is no harbour so landing is a tricky exercise – leaping straight from the ferry onto the shore or, in bad weather, beaching by rubber dinghy. There are few concessions to the 21st century on Gotska Sandon: it is perfectly possible to be stranded for several days, the only transport on the entire island is a single tractor, there are no shops or restaurants, and hardly any inhabitants. If you want an adventure in self-sufficiency this is the place to come.

Sand dunes at Bredsand

Faro

Off the northern tip of Gotland, this magical little island is famous for its beautiful sandy beaches, moody landscapes, and dramatically beautiful raukar (limestone rock formations). For years it was a restricted military zone and has only recently been opened up to foreign tourists, although it has long been popular among the Swedes.

The island has a barren, spooky beauty. The west coast is windswept and rocky, the waves beating against the bizarre limestone monoliths, while the east is long drifts of fine white sand. At Ullahau, on the north coast, the shifting sand dunes have been planted with pine trees to stabilise the soil – a perfect children's playground that makes a brilliant winter sledging track. There are hardly any roads on the island. Dirt tracks overgrown with long grass cut through the pine forests and rocky green pastureland where sheep and cows graze. There are fields full of wildflowers, old agricultural landscapes with small fields and disused windmills, dotted with ancient farm buildings more often than not roofed with sedge.

The acclaimed film director, Ingmar Bergman lived and died here. He used the island as a location for several of his films as well as making two documentaries about its people. Visitors to Faro were never able to discover the whereabouts of his house; and the locals still remain determinedly tight-lipped. One wonders for how much longer such admirable resistance to external pressure will endure, for the day that Faro gives up this secret must surely be the day that it starts to lose its mysterious aura. Until that time comes there can be no doubt that everyone who comes here will be bewitched.

Raukar on one of Faro's beaches

POPULATION:
571 (2005)
WHEN TO GO:
The magical atmosphere of Faro is best experienced out of season. Although the weather may be a lot bleaker in April or October than in July and August, the island is at its most beautiful in terms of landscape and light, and you can be certain that it won't be packed with tourists.
HOW TO GET THERE:
From Stockholm either fly to Visby in Gotland or take a train or bus to Nynäshamn and then a ferry to Visby. From Visby go by road to Farosund where you can get the free car ferry to Faro once an hour.
HIGHLIGHTS:
The superb beaches of Sudersandsviken, Ekeviken and Norsta Auren.
Langhammars – a rocky beach with Ice Age monoliths, used as the backdrop in Bergman's film *Through a Glass Darkly*.
Faro Fyr – the 19th century island lighthouse, 30 m (98 ft) high.
Digerhuvud – a nature reserve with huge raukars (sea stacks), diving area and fishing village of Helgumannen.
Ryssnäset – a stark coastal landscape.
YOU SHOULD KNOW:
Faro has no bank, medical services or police and the natives speak their own dialect.

Oland

POPULATION:
25,000 (2005)

WHEN TO GO:
To see this beautiful island at its best, avoid the high season of July and August when it is packed with holidaymakers. It is well worth sacrificing a bit of sunshine for the sake of experiencing the Alvaret landscape in the famous Nordic light and tranquillity of April-May and September-October.

HOW TO GET THERE:
Fly/drive/train to Kalmar via Stockholm then cross over one of the longest bridges in Europe, built in the 1970s.

HIGHLIGHTS:
Borgholm Castle – 'the most beautiful ruin in Scandinavia' and one of Sweden's most famous buildings, reflecting more than 800 years of architecture and history.
The 17th century wooden windmill at Gettlinge. medieval drystone bridge, Alby. Böda Crown Park – woods in North Oland where you can see elk.
Lange Erik – the tallest lighthouse in Sweden, on the northernmost point of the island.

YOU SHOULD KNOW:
Oland is by far the best swimming spot in the whole of Sweden and a favourite place for Swedish holidaymakers. It's a great place for a family holiday with plenty to see and do.

A row of post mills on Oland

Once the private Royal Game Park of the Swedish monarchy and now one of the most popular Swedish holiday resorts, Oland is a 137 km (86 mi) long, narrow strip of land running along the southeast coast. It is renowned for its superb beaches, unique World Heritage limestone landscape, four hundred windmills, and ancient history.

Oland was first inhabited around 10,000 years ago when settlers from the mainland crossed the iced-over sea. There are traces of ancient cultures all around the island, including the remains of nineteen Iron Age ring forts, an incredibly well preserved Viking burial ground at Gettlinge, and a completely preserved fort at Eketorp dating from 400 AD. The city of Borgholm is the island's historic capital; the Swedish royal family have their summer residence at Solliden Palace nearby.

Böda Bay at the northern end of the island is 20 km (12 mi) of soft white sand, windswept dunes and pine forest. As you go south, the forest gradually gives way to fields and meadowland. Suddenly this pastoral scene comes to an abrupt end; spreading endlessly in front of you is an apparently barren steppe; you have reached the Stora Alvaret – a bizarre limestone shelf, scraped bare by glacial movement and almost bereft of soil. It covers 260 sq km (100 sq mi), more than a quarter of the island's surface. Although it appears to be treeless, if you look closely you will see a stunted forest. The trees are unable to grow any taller because they are water-starved – rain simply seeps straight through the limestone. A huge variety of rare grasses and wild flowers grows here and the ground contains thousands of fossils – an invaluable resource for botanists and the study of prehistory, and one of the strangest and most fascinating landscapes of Europe.

Tjörn

Sunrise over Tjörn

Just north of Gothenburg on the west coast, Sweden's sixth largest island covers an area of 167 sq km (65 sq mi) and is the gateway to the beautiful islands of the Bohuslän archipelago. The coastline is extraordinarily complex and varied – rocky shores, sandy stretches of beach, winding inlets and sheltered bays that are natural harbours for yachts and small boats. The island has a stark beauty and liberating sense of space about it. At its highest point, 116 m (380 ft) above sea level, you feel on top of the world as you stand on one of the craggy granite outcrops gazing across the rough treeless pasture and ancient drystone walled meadows full of wild flowers, with breathtaking views of open skies and the sea.

There are traces of human habitation on Tjörn from the Stone Age onwards and you can see Bronze Age pictures carved into the rocks and the remains of Iron Age burial cairns. For many hundreds of years the islanders have depended on the fishing and boat building industries for their livelihoods. There are pretty little villages and hamlets of red and white painted houses dotted around the coast where people still work at these traditional activities. In recent years the island has also become well known as an artists' colony; it is home to the Nordic Watercolour Museum, opened in 2000 – a centre for contemporary art, research, and training in watercolour techniques. This is the only centre of its kind in Europe, in an inspiring setting in the historic main village of Skärhamn. There are also private galleries and exhibitions all over the island.

Although Tjörn is a popular resort among the Swedes, its economy is not reliant on tourists; it is mercifully free of the rampant commercialism that is so often found at holiday destinations.

POPULATION:
15,022 (2005)
WHEN TO GO:
Mid-May to early September
HOW TO GET THERE:
Fly to Gothenburg. Tjörn is only 50 km (30 mi) away and, since 1960, has had a bridge connection to the mainland.
HIGHLIGHTS:
Sundsby – 18th century wooden stately home with a history dating from 1338.
Rörestrand beach – watch the sunset over the water.
Sandhölmen – bathing island off the pretty fishing village of Skärhamn, reached by boat.
Tjörne Huvud – wonderful view for miles across the sea.
Mjörn – a nearby island to the northeast with wild landscape and shell banks.
Walking the trail at Toftenäs through beautiful scenery.
YOU SHOULD KNOW:
Tjörn is a great place for cycling, walking, boating, and nature holidays, and an ideal base from which to explore the beautiful islands of the Bohuslän Archipelago.

Lake Mälaren Islands

POPULATION:
24, 000 (estimate)
WHEN TO GO:
late May to early September
HOW TO GET THERE:
On Stockholm's doorstep; some of
the islands are connected by bridge.
Two-hour ferry ride from Stockholm
to Bjorkö.
HIGHLIGHTS:
Lovö kyrka – a parish church dating
back to the 12th century.
Svartsö Slott, Faringsö – a rococo
castle and park.
Stenhamra, Färingsö – a beautiful
rugged area with old stone quarry.
Hantverksstallet, Gällstäo Gård –
ancient oak trees in historic grounds.
Ekebyhovs Slott, Ekerö – one of the
oldest wooden castles in Europe.
Luruddon, Helgö – ancient ruins with
dwellings dating back to 200 AD,
where a 6th century Buddha from
India has been found.
YOU SHOULD KNOW:
Although there are ferries to the
islands, the best way of visiting them
is by yacht so that you have the
freedom to explore at will. Most of
the islands have guest harbours
for mooring.

Lake Mälaren is the third largest lake in Sweden, adjoining the city of Stockholm. Its many islands contain an incredibly rich heritage, a breathtakingly lush historical landscape with palaces, old churches, runestones, forty castles, and two World Heritage Sites – the Palace of Drottningholm on the island of Lovö and the Viking sites of Birka on Bjorkö and Hovgården on Adelsö.

The Royal domain of Drottningholm with its Chinese pavilion, wooden theatre, and Baroque gardens is a stunning 17th century palace complex, modelled on Versailles and set in the pastoral landscape of Lovö. Birka, Sweden's oldest city, and one of its most famous ancient monuments, is situated on Bjorkö – an island that today has a romantic, desolate air about it. Birka was founded at the end of the 8th century and for nearly 200 years was at the centre of European trade. In the late 10th century the build up of sediment made the lake too shallow for ships to negotiate and the city was abandoned. Hovgården, the king's farm on the neighbouring island of Adelsö, remained in use until the late Middle Ages. Today these lovely islands are beautiful places in which to walk and cycle as well as see the incredibly well preserved Viking ruins.

The landscape of Lake Mälaren was formed at the end of the Ice Age when the land started to rise as a result of the gradual melting of the ice-cap lifting the tons of pressure that had been bearing down on it. Quite apart from the cultural heritage contained in these islands, the moraine ridges and lush valleys are scenically lovely – rolling farmland dotted with oak trees, pine forest on rocky hills, and trees and grasses growing right down to the waterline.

The stunning interior of Drottningholm Palace

Visingsö

Legend has it that a giant called Vist threw a lump of turf into Lake Vättern so that his wife could cross it without getting her feet wet; and so Visingsö came into being – a 14 km (9 mi) long, skinny island in the southern part of the second largest lake in Sweden. It is famous for its lovely countryside, historical sights, spotlessly clean beaches, and views of the lake from almost anywhere.

Visingsö has probably been inhabited since the Stone Age; the number of burial mounds attests to a sizeable prehistoric population. There are also a large number of graves from the Viking era.

In the 12th and 13th Centuries Näs Castle, on the southern tip of the island, was the seat of the king of Sweden. The castle was burned down in 1318 and most of it is now submerged in the lake but what remains is well worth a visit. At the turn of the 16th and 17th century the aristocratic Brahe family built the castle of Visingsborg. After 1680 it remained empty for some years, before being used to hold Russian prisoners of war who, it is said, burned it down in 1718; today one wing remains – an impressive sight. In the 1830s, a farsighted plan on the part of the Swedish navy for future ship building material led to the planting of the Elkskogen – 360 hectares (890 acres) of oak trees. However, by the time they reached maturity, their wood was no longer needed. Consequently, today you can lose yourself in a magnificent mature oak forest, the largest in Sweden.

Walking and cycling trails lead you through a rural idyll of open meadows, berry fields and, of course, the woods. Visingsö has an atmosphere pervaded with history, myth and legend in one of the most scenic regions of Sweden.

POPULATION:
800 (2007)
WHEN TO GO:
May to August
HOW TO GET THERE:
From Stockholm fly/drive/rail to Jönköping. Road to Gränna, 30 km (19 mi) to the north. Car ferry service from Gränna to Visingsö, twice hourly in the summer.
HIGHLIGHTS:
Kumlaby Church – a 12th century building with 15th century frescoes and a tower you can climb.
Tempelgården – gallery and outdoor art centre with a temple built by the theosophists, who had their European centre here in the early 20th century. A horse-drawn carriage ride around the island.
Visingsborg Örtagård – a 17th century Baroque style herb garden, with 900 species of herb and spice plants.
Erstad Kärr – nature reserve marshland in the north of the island, a breeding ground for wading birds.
YOU SHOULD KNOW:
Lake Vättern is the fifth largest lake in Europe, covering an area of 1912 sq km (746 sq mi). Its deepest point, just south of Visingsö is 128 m (420 ft). The water is so pure that it can be safely drunk untreated from almost any place in the lake.

Sheep grazing by Lake Vättern.

Ven

POPULATION:
371 (2005)
WHEN TO GO:
May to September
HOW TO GET THERE:
Ferry from Landskrona on the Swedish mainland several times a day; and from Helsingborg and Copenhagen in the summer only.
HIGHLIGHTS:
Brahe Observatory and Museum – dedicated to Tycho Brahe.
The distillery and whisky bar at Backafallsbyn – the largest collection of single malts in Sweden.
St Ibbs Church – dating back to the 13th century in a lovely spot above Kyrkbacken village.
Nämndemansgården farm – the oldest farmstead on the island; now a heritage museum.
Eating the island's pasta – a Ven speciality made from locally produced durum wheat.
YOU SHOULD KNOW:
The cliffs are heavily eroded in some places and you should be careful when walking along them. Bikes and tandems can be hired on the island so there is no need to travel with one.

The Pearl of Oresund is a tiny dot in the strait between Sweden and Denmark, 8 km (5 mi) off the Danish coast and just 4.3 km (under 3 mi) from Sweden. It is only 7.5 sq km (3 sq mi), a shelf that slopes downward south to north from its highest point at 45 m (150 ft) to just 5 m (16 ft) above sea level. The island is incredibly fertile farmland with rich clay topsoil on layers of shifting sand and clay.

Ven belonged to Denmark until 1660 when it fell into Swedish hands. During the 16th century, Tycho Brahe, a famous Danish astronomer, persuaded the king of Denmark to give him the island so that he could study the stars from here. He built a Baroque castle, now in ruins, and for the next 20 years took measurements of the night skies, incredibly precisely considering his primitive equipment.

When you go ashore from the ferry at Bäckviken, the grassy slopes of the celebrated Backafall cliffs rise straight out of the sea 40 m (130 ft) high, giving amazing views over the Oresund to the Danish and Swedish coasts. Kyrkbacken, the oldest and largest harbour with a yachting marina, is a pretty village with a fish smokery. There are sand beaches near both harbours.

Ven is a lovely island for camping and cycling holidays. Paths cut through the fields and copses so that you can wander freely everywhere. Coastal walks take you along some hair-raising cliff tops where you will see dramatic landslips and down to curious rocky shores full of marine life. Artists and craftsmen have been attracted here by the inspiring tranquillity and you can visit their studios and workshops. The bucolic surroundings, sea views, lively harbours, and sense of history make it an ideal place for anyone seeking a relaxing island break.

A marina on Ven Island

Svalbard Archipelago

Further north than Alaska and all but a few of Canada's Arctic islands, the Svalbard Archipelago is the northernmost part of the kingdom of Norway, lying about half way to the North Pole. The Gulf Stream current sinks close to the archipelago, and were it not for its moderating influence, the islands would be locked in ice throughout the year and totally uninhabitable.

There are three large islands in the Svalbard Archipelago – Spitzbergen, Nordaustlandet and Edgeøya – and many islets. The islands are barren, rugged and desolate, with around 60 per cent of the land covered with glaciation. The mountains look like steep piles of rubble, with peaks jutting out at all angles. Some are covered in snow all year round and many valleys are filled with glaciers. Vegetation is very sparse and there are no trees on the islands. However, the warm season brings many Arctic flowers into bloom, transforming parts of the islands into colourful meadows.

The islands were probably first discovered in the 12th century by the Vikings, but the earliest recorded landing here was by William Barents in 1596. Spitzbergen, the largest of the islands, became an important whaling station in the 17th and 18th centuries, and many animal trappers also arrived to exploit the archipelago's natural resources. By the 20th century, whale stocks had become so depleted that coal mining replaced whaling, an activity which still goes on today. The main settlement on the island is Longyearbyen where most of the population lives. The other islands in the archipelago are largely uninhabited, except for research scientists.

Being so far north, Svalbard gets the midnight sun from 20 April to 23 August, although the sun itself may be hidden by fog. The polar night, where the sun does not rise above the horizon at all, runs from 26 October to 15 February, and most visitors stay away during this time unless they are here to see the Northern Lights.

Most tourists come here to experience the raw climate, see the midnight sun, and try their hand at some of the exciting activities on offer here, including snowmobile trips, kayaking, ice cave exploration, dog-sleding, skiing and horse riding. The tourist board organizes many activities and tours, some of which include one or more nights of wilderness camping. Although it is possible to arrange your own activities, most visitors choose to go on an organized tour with a professional guide because of the number of polar bears on the island. Anyone straying outside the main settlement is required to carry a rifle, and know how to use it.

POPULATION:
2,400 (2005)
WHEN TO GO:
April to August
HOW TO GET THERE:
Fly from Oslo or Tromsø to Longyearbyen, or go on an organized cruise.
HIGHLIGHTS:
Try dog-sleding or driving a snowmobile.
Wildlife watching – the islands have as many polar bears as people so you are bound to see some. There are also Arctic foxes, reindeer, walruses and seals here.
Boat trips – join a boat to see whales, dolphins and seals, plus the breeding colonies of seabirds, including puffins, on the cliffs.
The intricate maze of raised stone 'doughnuts' at Kvadehuksletta on the west coast of Spitzbergen, caused by an extraordinary natural phenomenon called frost heave.
Svalbard Museum – the museum in Longyearbyen tells the story of Svalbard, from the discovery of the archipelago, 17th century whaling history, expeditions, winter trapping techniques, flora, fauna, geology and mining history.
YOU SHOULD KNOW:
In most of Svalbard's buildings, including some hotels and shops, you are expected to take off your shoes before entering.

A snow field and mountain on Spitzbergen

Lofoten Islands

POPULATION:
23,700 (2007)
WHEN TO GO:
Late May to early July for the
Midnight Sun; the best weather is
from April to September.
HOW TO GET THERE:
By ferry or air from Bodø, ferry from
Narvik or by road via Narvik.
HIGHLIGHTS:
The Midnight Sun – the sun does not
fall below the horizon for seven
weeks around midsummer.
The Maelstrom – take a boat trip out
to experience one of the world's
strongest tidal currents.
YOU SHOULD KNOW:
The sun does not rise for weeks in
midwinter.

A village on the island of Flakstadøya

Lying just inside the Arctic Circle west of Norway are the Lofoten Islands, a group of beautiful mountainous islands with wooded hillsides and lovely white sandy bays. There are five main islands in the group: Austvågøy, Gimsøya, Vestvågøy, Flakstadøya and Moskenesøya; and three smaller ones. Although the islands are so far north, they enjoy a fairly mild climate due to the Gulf Stream.

For more than a thousand years, cod fishing has been the main activity here, especially in winter when the fish migrate south from the Barents Sea and gather around the islands to spawn. Tourism is now a good source of income for the islands, their spectacular ruggedness making them ideal for hiking and cycling. Lofoten also offers unique rock climbing and mountaineering opportunities, with Alpine-style ridges, summits and glaciers, all at a height of less than 1,200 m (3,936 ft). In midsummer, this beautiful area becomes even more magical, as for more than seven weeks, the sun remains above the horizon.

The islands feature some magnificent caves, awe-inspiring to even the most well-travelled visitors. At 50 m (164 ft) high and 115 m (377 ft) deep, Refsvikhula Cave is all the more interesting because of the enigmatic characters sketched on the walls, 3,000-year-old cave paintings discovered by archaeology students in 1986. Another cave, the Storbåthallaren south of the village of Napp, has a mighty overhang, 22 m (72 ft) high and 70 m (229 ft) deep. The oldest-known Stone Age settlement in Lofoten has been discovered here. The layers of waste left on the cave floor over 5,500 years included fishing tackle, arrowheads, knives, axes, bone needles, ceramics and the remains of fish and shellfish, 16 different animals and 37 species of birds. Human bones were also found in the cave.

Visitors also come to the Lofoten Islands for off-shore activities. The rich waters support vast colonies of breeding seabirds, including puffins, kittiwakes, razorbills, red-necked phalaropes and Arctic terns, as well as white-tailed sea eagles. Sperm whales can be spotted in summer, while orca follow the herring to this area in early autumn. The infamous Maelstrom (Moskstraumen), one of the world's strongest tidal currents, lies just off the coast. First described 2,000 years ago by the Greek historian, Pytheas, the Maelstrom has been renowned and respected by seafarers for thousands of years. Nowadays boat trips and fishing expeditions pass through the area so visitors can experience the sheer thrill of it.

Iceland

The Aurora Borealis over Reykjavik

Geologically, Iceland is a hot spot caused by a mantle plume on the mid-Atlantic ridge. It's an island of 30 active volcanoes, bubbling geothermal pools, geysers (an Icelandic word), lakes, waterfalls and rivers full of the plumpest salmon and trout on earth. Much of it is barren basalt rock, glacier or icecap, and only 23 per cent supports any kind of growth. It's peopled by the descendants of Vikings who colonized it in the 9th century – and who still live by the principles of self-reliance and hard work, and by the sense of community of their forebears. Icelanders invented government by representation, with the Althing (parliament) of Thingvellir in 930; and after the vicissitudes of the Black Death and colonial strife under Denmark, and despite occupation by the World War II Allies, including the USA until 2006, reasserted their commitment to equal rights on all fronts with characteristic energy expressed both by pragmatism and cheerful exuberance. The first thing every visitor appreciates is Icelanders' sense of fun – especially at the height of the midnight sun in June, when Reykjavik becomes a 24-hour party town for young and old, and the rest of the country keeps pace, and at Christmas, when everyone celebrates the Northern Lights.

The earth's crust is very thin in Iceland. Every house gets its central heating direct from the geothermal cauldron below, and you soon get accustomed to the sulphurous smell when filling a bath. Nowhere does interactive vulcanology better than Iceland, because daily routines have been intertwined with the dominant geological behaviour of the glaciers, icefields, peaks, hot springs, lava deserts, and alternately boiling and frozen river systems. Physically, Iceland is as strange as the moon, whose surface it was chosen to represent before the moon landings – but its quality of life is considered the best in the world, and that's because of its people.

POPULATION:
313,000 (2007)

WHEN TO GO:
June to August – but Reykjavik and the coastal regions are kept ice-free by the Gulf Stream, and winter sports make Iceland a year-round destination. Come for the major festivals of June, or for Pjothatith in August, a national day of dancing, eating, drinking and singing.

HOW TO GET THERE:
By air, from Europe and the USA to Keflavik, for Reykjavik.

HIGHLIGHTS:
The world's largest colony of puffins on the Westmann Islands.
The Kverkfjoll ice caves and Hverfell Crater, near deep blue Myvatn Lake in the northeast, home to more species of breeding duck than anywhere else in Europe.
The emerald green Thingvellir glacial valley – impossibly beautiful, and the home of democracy.
Gullfoss, the 32 m (105 ft) 'golden waterfall' – in the sunshine the torrential spray creates a series of rainbows.
Bathing in the huge, milky-blue spa of the Blue Lagoon near Reykjavik; the silver towers of the local geothermal plant, rolling clouds of steam and a massage under a hot waterfall are a metaphor for Iceland's weird but alarmingly pleasant attractiveness.

YOU SHOULD KNOW:
The Arctic Open is a golf tournament played under the midnight sun.

Greenland

POPULATION:
57,100 (2006)
WHEN TO GO:
May to July for 24-hour daylight;
November to February for polar
darkness. The Northern Lights are
usually most impressive in the months
of September and March.
HOW TO GET THERE:
By air, from Copenhagen or Baltimore, to
Kangerlussuaq (W); from Reykjavik to
Nuuk (SW) or Kusuluk (E); from
Copenhagen to Narsarsuaq (S).
Kangerlussuaq is the hub for domestic
flights within Greenland. Visitors also
use scheduled ferries on the west coast,
or helicopters. Cruise ships call at
Ittoqqortoormiit.
HIGHLIGHTS:
Whale safaris from Nuuk – in summer
humpback and minke whales
congregate just offshore; and you might
also see fin, blue, sperm and pilot
whales, and narwhals.
The Viking longhouse, Tjodhilde's Church
and extensive Brattahlid ruins at
Qassiarsuk, near Narsarsuaq – from
where Leif Eriksson set sail, and
'discovered' Newfoundland.
A sailing trip among the icebergs calved
by the Ilulissat Icefjord – when the low-
lying midnight sun bathes 100 m (330 ft)
column icebergs in golden light.
A trip by zodiac or snowmobile on the
edge of the sea ice, in the National Park
that occupies the whole of northeast
Greenland – your best chance of seeing
a polar bear.
Bathing in the hot springs on Uunartoq
Island in southern Greenland – the
stone-dammed pool is surrounded by
wild flowers, and a panorama of
mountain peaks and drifting icebergs.
The white-tailed eagle, peregrine and
gerfalcon, fulmar petrel, aavooq (eider)
and aqisseq (ptarmigan) – among 60
breeding and 170 migratory
bird species.
YOU SHOULD KNOW:
The Icelandic Sagas describe the arrival
in Greenland of Norse settlers in 982.
The last word concerning the Viking
population is an account of a wedding in
Hvalsey Church, Qaqortoq (still standing)
in 1408, found in the annals of the
Vatican, in Rome.

A self-governing province of Denmark, Greenland is the world's biggest island. An ice sheet up to 3 km (1.9 mi) thick, 2,500 km (1,553 mi) long, and up to 1,000 km (600 mi) wide covers 81 per cent of it. That represents 10 per cent of the world's fresh water, and it's so heavy that it has caused the central land mass to subside more than 300 m (1,000 ft) below the surrounding sea level.

Constant movement recycles the ice sheet, and in places it's 100,000 years old at its edge. Enormous glaciers are forced outwards to the coast, where they break off into icebergs. The Sermeq Kujalleq glacier on the west coast reaches the sea through the Ilulissat Icefjord, advancing at 19 m (65 ft) per day and calving over 35 cubic km of ice per year. Now in dramatic retreat – 15 km (9 mi) in four years – the World Heritage Site of Illulissat is a spectacular demonstration of climate change.

Ice defines Greenland's culture and ecology as well as its weather. People have lived on its ice-free margins for 4,500 years, and in the south and west you can see hundreds of major ruins demonstrating the fusion of Inuit, Viking and recent Danish cultures. You can participate in modern Inuit culture in Qaanaaq in the north. Besides the traditional drum dancing, singing and kayak demonstrations, you can hunt or fish on a dog sled trip among walrus, seal, musk oxen and huge bird colonies. In season, it's one of the best places to revel in both the midnight sun and the Northern Lights (Aurora Borealis).

Ice here locks both land and sea, and culture belongs to the hunter/gatherer and the polar bear. Yet global warming means that the fate of hundreds of millions of us depends on the future of the Greenland ice sheet.

Nuuk, the snowy capital of Greenland

Clare Island

POPULATION:
150 (2005)
WHEN TO GO:
May to September
HOW TO GET THERE:
Ferries run from the mainland throughout the year, weather permitting.
HIGHLIGHTS:
The square tower, which served as Grace O'Malley's Castle, on a rocky headland at the harbour.
The ruins at Tuar Mor of a signal tower, built in 1804, as an answer to the impending threat of a Napoleonic invasion.
A visit to the neighbouring island of Inishbofin with its ruined Cromwellian castle.
YOU SHOULD KNOW:
Grace O'Malley was a notorious pirate for 50 years. At the age of 37 she gave birth on board ship whilst being attacked by Moorish pirates, and after a brief rest, joined the battle, and of course, triumphed.

Just 5 km (3 mi) from County Mayo, off the north west of Ireland, Clare Island stands guard over the entrance to Clew Bay. Only 8 km (5 mi) by 5 km (3 mi), the island is dominated by two hills, Knockaven to the east, and Knockmore to the west. Clare is fertile, green, undulating and treeless, with hundreds of sheep dotted over the landscape, their wool providing yarns which are dyed and worked into beautiful, individual scarves, bags and other woven items.

Inhabited for 5,000 years, Clare Island has many ancient sites. These include the remnants of ten promontory forts, Bronze Age cooking sites, Iron Age huts and field systems, and a megalithic tomb. The charming, white painted lighthouse on the western side has been in private hands since 1965, first as a B&B but now as a rarely used second home. Fantastic views can be enjoyed from the 19th century Napoleonic signal tower.

Clare Island is home to a 12th century Cistercian Abbey in which can be seen the remains of some of Ireland's best murals, depicting mythical figures, warriors and animals. It also contains the tomb of the island's most famous resident, Grace O'Malley, the 16th century pirate queen. During her colourful life she headed 20 pirate ships, fought – and met – Elizabeth I, and lived here in Granuaille Castle, which is due to be renovated.

Clare is also well known for the *craic*, and many wedding parties take place here as a result. There is no resident policeman here, so the opening hours of the island's bar is a moveable feast. Should a policeman be travelling from the mainland, that fact will be known in good time, since the ferry is owned by the O'Malleys, who also own the hotel...

A rain storm over Clare Island

Aranmore

Aranmore, sometimes known as Aran, lies off the indented west coast of Donegal, and is the largest of the little group of islands to be found there. At 5 km (3 mi) long by 4 km (2.5 mi) wide, and only a 5-minute, fast ferry ride away from the mainland, Aran is rapidly becoming a holiday island.

Most of the permanent population live around the southern and eastern coasts – and evidence that Aranmore has been inhabited since at least 800 BC is visible in the shell middens (mounds) found on the southern beaches. To the west, spectacular cliffs rise from the sea, and from Glen Head there are splendid views across to the mainland. Hills rise in Aranmore's centre, but most of the landscape is rocky, with many small lakes. The country roads are peaceful and the island is terrific for walking and mountain biking.

At the end of the 17th century, Aranmore was a centre of the herring fisheries, with over 1,000 people employed in the industry. However, in the mid-1800s a combination of clearance by the landowner, and famine, hit the population hard and many families left for the New World. Subsequently, the landowner's house became the island's first hotel and, where fishing was once the crux of the economy, now people fish for pleasure. Cowan's Lake, the island's reservoir, is one of the few European lakes in which rainbow trout breed naturally, while two other lakes contain brown trout.

The lighthouse at Rinawros Point was first built in 1798, but was rebuilt in 1865. The Old Coastguard Station gently decays nearby, but there are rock arches and sea caves to be seen. Enjoy the sweeping, golden, sandy beaches at Aphort and Leabgarrow, and later – perhaps best of all – visit the six or seven pubs on the island, one of which will surely tick all your boxes…

The craggy cliffs of Aranmore Island

POPULATION:
522 (2006) growing to 1,500 during summer when ex-pat families return and tourists arrive.
WHEN TO GO:
May to September
HOW TO GET THERE:
By ferry from Burtonport.
HIGHLIGHTS:
The Cave of Slaughter, where a Cromwellian captain committed a massacre in 1641.
A walk to the island's highest point at Cnoc an Iolair (hill of the eagle), where sea eagles once bred, and from which there are fine views.
YOU SHOULD KNOW:
Aranmore is twinned with Beaver Island, Lake Michigan, where many emigrants settled in the 1850s. The two communities exchange visits, and a memorial was erected at Loch an Chomhanaigh in 2000. It is rainbow trout brought from North America in 1900 that have colonized Cowan's Lake.

Aran Islands

The ruins of O'Brien's castle on the site of a ring fort near the village of Ballyhees on Inisheer Island. The 15th century castle was destroyed by Cromwell's invading army in 1652.

POPULATION:
Inishmore: 900; Inishman: 200;
Inisheer: 300 (2005)
WHEN TO GO:
At any time, but the weather is best
during summer.
HOW TO GET THERE:
By ferry from Connemara and Clare,
or by air.
HIGHLIGHTS:
Inishmore
Dun Eochla, the smallest but well
preserved fort.Arkin's Castle, built
in 1587.
Teampall Bheanain, the ruins of one of
the smallest churches in the world.
Inishman
Dun Chonchuir, a large, 5th century,
oval fort, with spectacular views.
Teach Synge, the beautifully restored
house lived in by dramatist John
Millington Synge when he was on the
island.
Inisheer
Take part in the festival at Caomhain
Caomhan's ruined church, each
14th June.
The 1934 Robert Flaherty film *Man of
Aran*, for a superb depiction of life as
it was lived on the islands.

Lying across the mouth of Galway Bay are the Aran Islands, Inishmore, Inisheer and Inishman. This popular group has inspired many artists and writers, as well as archaeologists and tourists.

First inhabited around 3,000 BC, the Arans were occupied by Stone, Bronze and Iron Age man, and they contain many early Christian monuments. Persecution of Catholics in the mid 17th century brought many more people, who, finding the islands rocky and inhospitable, devised a brilliant method of producing the topsoil needed for agriculture. Seaweed and sand spread on the rocks created fertile soil and grassland, and a totally self-sufficient way of life evolved.

Inishmore is the largest, most populated and developed island, and the good sized harbour is a hive of activity, particularly during summer, with people coming and going on ferries and yachts, and small boats busying about. Often referred to as an outdoor museum, Inishmore contains over 50 pre-Christian, Christian and Celtic monuments, as well as the extraordinary stone fort of Dun Aonghasa.

Inishman, the middle island, is the least populated and least developed of the three. There are two stone forts to visit, one of which, unusually, is square rather than circular. Inishman is also home to a collapsed Neolithic wedge tomb, Dermot and Grainne's Bed, named after the tragic lovers of Irish mythology. For more worldly interests, this is a good place to purchase some gorgeous Aran knitwear – don't confuse it with the knitwear from Scotland's Arran Islands.

Inisheer is the smallest of the Arans, but it too has a great deal to offer. Here you will find a large, 16th century castle, a 12th century church and a revered holy well. On the rocks is the wreck of the cargo ship *Plassey* which foundered here in the 1960s. The islanders rescued the entire crew safely, during storm force winds.

Valentia

Valentia Island lies at the north west end of the Iveragh Peninsula, at the entrance to Dingle Bay in County Kerry. The island is within the reach of the Gulf Stream, and has an unusually mild climate. Famous today to listeners to the BBC Shipping Forecast, Valentia was the European terminal of the first communications link with America with the laying of the transatlantic telegraph cable in 1866.

At 11 km (7 mi) long and 3 km (2 mi) wide, Valentia has a great deal to offer visitors throughout the year, including early Celtic sites, standing stones, crosses and holy wells. The lighthouse, which was once a Cromwellian fort, gives an unparalleled view over the Atlantic.

Inhabited since 6,000 BC, there are many ancient remnants of man's activities here, but signs of a much older inhabitant came to light in 1993. An undergraduate geology student discovered the fossilized footprints of a tetrapod, Acanthostega, which climbed out of the water and walked here some 365 million years ago. This is now an internationally important site, as it is the only one of its kind in Europe.

Valentia is a lovely place, with wonderful walks, beautiful views, beaches, bogs and cliffs. Knightstown, the island's hub, is a Georgian village, though the red clock tower overseeing the harbour is Victorian. In the north east of Valentia stands Glenleam House. In the 1830s its owner, the 19th Earl of Kerry, planted a unique sub-tropical garden here. Renowned amongst gardeners, it is now possible to stay in the house as well as walk amongst the gardens and woods. Valentia's climate turns the entire island into a delight. Wild flowers grow abundantly, honeysuckle tumbles over stone walls, and every road is lined with hedges bursting with brilliantly colourful monbretia and fuschia, an experience which is best enjoyed on foot or by bicycle.

POPULATION:
650 (2005)
WHEN TO GO:
Any time, though April to October is probably best.
HOW TO GET THERE:
The island is accessible via the bridge from Portmagee on the mainland. However, it's much prettier to arrive in the harbour at Knightstown by boat from Reenard Point.
HIGHLIGHTS:
Listening to traditional Irish musicians playing in the pubs in the evenings.
Deep sea angling or shore fishing.
The Skellig Experience Visitor Centre, which will fill you with enthusiasm for a trip to the nearby Skellig Islands.
Diving – there are two dive centres on Valentia.
The memorial at Foilhommerum Cliff to mark the laying of the transatlantic cable to Heart's Content, Newfoundland.
YOU SHOULD KNOW:
Valentia's famous slate quarry, opened in 1816, was an important employer here, and it is Valentia slate that you see when admiring the roof of the House of Commons in London. Above the quarry entrance is a statue of the Madonna, and just inside is a grotto, with water tumbling into pools.

Cromwell Point Lighthouse on Valentia Island

Skellig Islands

POPULATION:
Uninhabited
WHEN TO GO:
From April to late September,
weather permitting.
HOW TO GET THERE:
Only 10 boats are licensed to land on
Skellig Michael, each carrying a
maximum of 12 people, so book
ahead. Fitness is essential as there
are almost 700 steep steps to
negotiate before reaching the
monastery.
HIGHLIGHTS:
The bird life: gannets, fulmars, storm
petrels, Manx shearwaters,
kittiwakes, guillemots and many
more. Puffins – 4,000 on Skellig
Michael alone, are always popular.
In the seas around you may see grey
seals, minke whales, dolphins and
possibly even a basking shark.
The Skellig Experience Visitor Centre
on nearby Valentia Island.
YOU SHOULD KNOW:
By the end of the 18th century, the
pilgrims who came here were all
young men and women, who came
to party, not to pray. Their exploits
are documented in amusing poems
known as 'The Skelligs List'.

Situated about 13 km (8 mi) west of the coast of Kerry rise two extraordinary, rocky islands known collectively as The Skelligs, that, because of their history and ecological significance, are one of Kerry's most special attractions – though they are not for the faint-hearted.

Skellig Michael, the larger of the two rocky outcrops, rises sharply to some 212 m (700 ft), and near the summit, sited precariously on a ledge, are the remains of an early Christian monastery. Its foundation remains shrouded in mystery, but it is known that a small community of about a dozen monks and an Abbott was based here continuously between the 6th and 12th centuries before finally de-camping to an Augustinian monastery on the mainland.

The community lived an amazingly austere life. Six beehive-shaped huts and two boat-shaped oratories remain in a moving testament to the Christian faith. The huts are made of drystone, circular in shape and mortar free, with rectangular interiors having corbelled roofs, and sleeping platforms and shelves built into the structure. The island continued to be a place of pilgrimage until the 1700s and today, after all these centuries of being lashed by storms, the buildings remain intact. On visiting, one can only be astounded that people spent their lives here.

During the 1800s, George Halpin Sr – one of Ireland's greatest lighthouse designers – built two lighthouses here, manned by keepers working on a rota system. Today only one still beams out its warning, and it is fully automated.

Both islands are notable for their bird life, and Little Skellig, where there is no landing point at all, is Ireland's largest and the world's second largest Northern gannet colony, with almost 30,000 pairs. The scale and diversity of the seabird population makes The Skelligs one of Ireland's most important seabird sites.

*The monastery on
Skellig Michael*

Great Blasket

Great Blasket is the largest of six islands that lie to the west of the Dingle Peninsula. The islands are uninhabited, except during the summer months, when three people live on Great Blasket; one is a weaver and the other two run the café and the youth hostel. The island is hilly, about 6 km (4 mi) by 0.8 km (0.5 mi) wide, and is home to donkeys, rabbits and seabirds.

During the 13th century the islands were leased by the Ferriter family, who built a castle here. Sadly there are no ruins to be seen, as the stones were removed in 1840 and used to build a Protestant soup school, which closed after the Great Famine in 1879. At the same time, all but 100 of the islanders left. Until the early 1800s the islanders survived by growing crops, hunting, and fishing from the shore. The arrival of the seine boat turned them away from the land and into fishermen, catching great numbers of mackerel and pilchard. Later they took up lobster and crayfish fishing and for some years had a successful system running where they exchanged shellfish for tobacco and alcohol.

What is left of Great Blasket's village is situated on the north east of the island. In the 1920s and 30s the young people could bear the privations of life here no longer, and they began to leave for the mainland and further afield. Those who remained struggled on, growing a few vegetables and living their traditional life. By 1953/54 even these few people had to admit defeat. In the last few years, some of the stone cottages on the island have been renovated, and visitors can come to explore the place and stay here for a night or two.

A beautiful bay and the remains of an old stone dwelling on Great Blasket

POPULATION:
Uninhabited except in summer
WHEN TO GO:
April to October
HOW TO GET THERE:
Ferries run from the mainland every two hours.
HIGHLIGHTS:
The peace and tranquillity of Great Blasket can be enjoyed while exploring this lovely island. The views are superb.
Diving over the wrecks of several ships from the Spanish Armada.
YOU SHOULD KNOW:
During the 1920s and 30s some remarkable literature was produced in Great Blasket. Autobiographies describing the extraordinary every day life that was led here, all written in the Irish language, have become classics of Irish literature.

Holy Island

A place of pilgrimage for hundreds of years, Inis Cealtra – or Holy Island – has been a home to pre-Christian and Christian communities since the year dot. Covering a mere 20 hectares (50 acres), it is a repository of churches, monastic cells, and pre-1,000 AD crosses. The famous bullaun stones, (rocks or stones with deep cups carved into them), dating from the Bronze Age or earlier, lie mainly in the central and eastern part of the island, where most of the religious sites stand.

During the 6th century, St Colum founded a Benedictine monastery on Holy Island, but it was St Caimin, the 5th Abbott, whom people still revere, and many people still bear his name. After his death, the monastery continued to flourish, and was renowned for its learning. Frequent Viking raids over the next few centuries caused the monks much hardship, but in the 10th century, the warrior and chieftain, Brian Boru, who was born nearby, helped re-establish the church here, which continued to thrive until the dissolution of the monasteries and the arrival of Protestantism in the 1500s. At this point all the churches were de-roofed and left to rot – indeed today St Caimin's Church is the only one of six churches on the island that has been fully restored.

Lying at the mouth of Scarrif Bay, Lough Derg, County Clare, Holy Island is fairly hilly, with open fields grazed by animals brought over by boat. There are trees and shrubs, particularly around the edges, while the interior is covered with wild flowers during spring and summer, in particular narcissi, innumerable amounts of which cover the ground. It continues to be a place of burial, with local boat owners providing transport over to the island, where family plots in St Michael's churchyard are still used.

St Caimin's Church

Cape Clear Island

Cape Clear Island is an absolute gem, deserving of all the superlatives you can think of, the pot of gold at the end of the rainbow. Only 5 km (3 mi) long by 2 km (1.5 mi) wide, it is Ireland's most southerly inhabited point, and because of its position, its climate is more benign than that of the mainland.

Cape Clear is one of Ireland's last remaining *gaeltacht*, (Irish language speaking), islands, and during the summer months the small, permanent population swells considerably with an influx of students, anxious to brush up their language skills. This was the birthplace of St Ciaran, supposedly the earliest of Ireland's pre-Patrician saints, and the ruins of his 12th century church stands near the harbour.

The island has several ancient remains, including Megalithic standing stones and a 5,000 year-old passage grave. The ruin of the 14th century O'Driscoll Castle stills hugs its headland overlooking the harbour, which is the island's commercial centre. The castle itself is very hard to reach, a feat only to be attempted on a fine weather day.

Cape Clear's physical position off the coast of County Cork puts it firmly in the path of thousands of migrating birds – indeed it is one of the country's foremost bird watching sites. As long ago as 1959 an Observatory was established near the harbour, manned by enthusiastic and knowledgeable ornithologists.

This is a hilly, fertile place, with soaring cliffs, gentle hills, bogs, a reed swamp, a lake, lovely beaches, remote coves, heathland and farmland – just the ticket, in other words. Undeveloped and unspoilt, heather and gorse cover the hills, which in spring and summer are bright with wild flowers, while in autumn the bracken turns a deep russet red, lending a rich, mellow glow. Winter brings fierce gales, and the locals amuse themselves with storytelling and musical evenings around roaring fires.

POPULATION:
140 (2004)
WHEN TO GO:
June to September for festivities, April, May and October for tranquillity and bird watching.
HOW TO GET THERE:
By ferry from Baltimore on the mainland, all year round.
HIGHLIGHTS:
Spotting dolphins, whales, leatherback turtles, sunfish and basking shark in the surrounding waters.
The Old Lighthouse.
Learn a little more history by visiting the Cape Clear Museum.
Admire the surreally beautiful wind turbines.
Dive, windsurf, sail, canoe and fish off the island.
Enjoy the *craic* of an evening in one of the island's pubs.
YOU SHOULD KNOW:
That the first weekend of September is the time for Cape Clear's International Storytelling Festival, when professional storytellers from around the world keep you spellbound for hours.

A stone cottage overlooking Roaring Water Bay

Dursey Island and Sound

Dursey Island

POPULATION:
12 (2003)
WHEN TO GO:
April to October
HOW TO GET THERE:
By cable car from Garinish, on the
mainland.
HIGHLIGHTS:
Walk the well-signed Beara Way,
which extends onto the island.
Birdwatching – Dursey Island is
renowned amongst birders, receiving
thousands of seabirds as well as
hawks and falcons. Rare species
from America and the Arctic can be
spotted here.
Visit the island's antiquities – the
O'Sullivan Beara family vault in the
old graveyard, the ruined castle, St
Mary's Abbey, the standing stones
and the Napoleonic signal tower.
Enjoy spectacular views of the offshore islands and the West Cork
coastline.
YOU SHOULD KNOW:
In the 1970s Charles Haughey, then
Taoiseach, Prime Minister, of Eire, got
caught up in the tricky waters of the
Dursey Sound, and sailed his boat
into the rocks, requiring rescue by
the local lifeboat. Remember, if you
are visiting Dursey, there's nowhere
to stay and you must bring your own
food and water.

Off the south-western tip of the Beara Peninsula, lies the island of Dursey, separated from the mainland by the narrow Dursey Sound, a stretch of water with a very strong tidal race. The most westerly of Cork's inhabited islands, Dursey is home to only three families, although its numbers swell during the summer months with visitors looking for the tranquility that the island can guarantee.

Dursey Island has a long history, as evidenced by the bullaun stones here. The ruined church was built by the monks of Skellig Michael, and during the worst excesses of the Vikings, Irish slaves were held on the island to await ships to remove them. During the early 1600s, Queen Elizabeth's forces sacked O' Sullivan Beara's castle here, and all the captives were thrown to their deaths from the cliffs. Much more recently, a mere 30 years ago, the government decided to relocate the islanders to the mainland, following the collapse of the fishing industry, and almost everyone left.

Dursey is the only island in Europe connected to the mainland by cable car. Riding high above the swirling waters, it can carry six passengers or one cow, and takes about six minutes to complete its journey. Regulars describe it as being 'like travelling in a big biscuit tin', and locals and animals are always given precedence over tourists.

Dursey has only partial electricity, and no running water, shop or pub; its inhabitants live simple, almost spartan, lives. However, the island is beautiful, with high cliffs rising over an indented, rocky coastline, its interior a patchwork of fields divided by old, drystone walls and ditches, sheep dotted here and there. Scarlet fuchsias bloom beside small waterfalls that tumble over the rocks, and aside from various ancient remains, there are also three deserted villages waiting to be discovered.

Achill Island

Off the west coast of County Mayo lies Ireland's largest island, Achill, a picturesque place that boasts the highest sea cliffs in Europe on its northern coast. A popular tourist destination, Achill is connected to the mainland by a swing bridge that enables cars to cross as well as boats to pass. Two large, bleak mountains, Slievemore and Croughan, both rising over 650 m (2,100 ft), loom impressively over the island, 87 per cent of which is formed of peat bog, home to unique communities of plants.

Believed to have been inhabited since 3,000 BC, Achill's megalithic tombs and promontory forts are evidence of its long history. Kildamhnait Castle, built during the 15th century, is also known as Grace O'Malley's Castle, as it once belonged to Achill's ruling family, the O'Malley clan, of whom Grace was the most famous, or infamous, member.

There are several pretty villages on the island, and plenty of choice as to where to stay. Most of the island's architecture is modern, and less attractive than the traditional whitewashed, raised gable cottages of yore, but the building boom of the last 30 years gave much needed work to the islanders, as well as providing many holiday homes. At the base of Slievemore mountain lies the fascinating Deserted Village, thought to have been abandoned during the Great Famine. Almost 100 roofless stone houses stretch out along the road, a strange, slightly eerie sight.

Around the southern tip of Achill runs a 40 km (25 mi) stretch of road, Atlantic Drive. Best travelled by bicycle, this takes you past a ruined 18th century church, a holy well and provides spectacular coastal views. The island boasts five Blue Flag beaches, including the lovely Keem Bay in the west, and Annagh, only accessible on foot or by sea.

POPULATION:
2,700 (2004)
WHEN TO GO:
Accessible all year round, Achill is at its best during the summer months.
HOW TO GET THERE:
By air to Knock, train to Westport, and then bus or car.
HIGHLIGHTS:
Achill Mission at Dugort. Known as The Colony and founded in 1831, this Protestant mission and surrounding buildings is an important historical site.
The Valley House near Dugort, where a notorious attack on an English female landowner occurred in 1894.
The lovely villages of Dooagh and Dooega.
The Achill Seafood Festival, held each July.
YOU SHOULD KNOW:
An ancient prophecy by Brian Rua O'Cearbhain foretold that 'carts on iron wheels' would carry bodies into Achill on both their first and last journeys. In 1894, the Westport – Newport railway was extended to Achill Sound. Amazingly, on its first journey, the train carried the victims of the Clew Bay Drowning and on its last, in 1937, it carried the victims of the Kirkintilloch Burning disaster.

The beautiful sandy beach of Keem Bay

Tory Island

POPULATION:
170 (2001)
WHEN TO GO:
June to September for the best weather.
HOW TO GET THERE:
Ferries run from four ports on mainland
Donegal from June to September,
weather permitting.
HIGHLIGHTS:
An Cloigtheach, the Bell Tower, built in
the 6th or 7th century and the last
remnant of the monastery that
dominated the island until the
16th century.
Leac an Leannan, the Wishing Stone. This
is a flat-topped rock that visitors are
advised not to try to stand on – instead
you can still make a wish if you manage
to throw three stones onto it.
The Tory Lighthouse, built in 1828 by
George Halpin Sr, a famous designer of
Irish lighthouses.
YOU SHOULD KNOW:
During the 1970s, conditions were so
poor that it was thought the population
would have to move to the mainland.
However, with the help of a semi-retired
priest from Dublin, who lobbied
relentlessly on their behalf, that plan was
dropped and help was forthcoming.

*The prehistoric Balor's Fort
looks out over Tory Island*

Tory Island is tiny, only 5 km (3 mi) long and 1 km (0.75 mi) wide, but with four towns and a number of historical sites, it remains a strong community. Rugged, treeless, bleak and buffeted by wind, Tory Island is also remarkably beautiful in its way. Both mystical and remote, this granite rock rises from the sea off the north-west coast of Donegal.

In the past, the island's economy relied on fishing and farming, but today it is reliant on governmental support. Few people visit Tory Island, and most of those who do, come to see the group of artists who work here. In 1956 the painter Derek Hill arrived on the island. A local man, James Dixon, looked at Hill's painting and said he thought he could do better himself. This led to the birth of the Tory Island school of painting, and today not only does the island have its own gallery, but its artists have been shown internationally. Patsy Dan Rodgers, one of the artists, has been designated Tory's 'King' and representative. He is an honorary member of New York University where an exhibition of these depictions of a fast disappearing way of life was shown to great acclaim.

The islanders are very traditional, Gaelic-speaking, and they live simply. Tory Island is an extraordinary place to visit and to enjoy the various sights, such as the 12th century Tau Cross, one of only two in Ireland, or Dun Bhaloir, Balor's Fort, situated on a peninsula with high cliffs on three sides, it is reached by crossing a narrow isthmus. Otherwise why not just watch the seabirds, marvel at the shifting light on the cliffs and sea, and socialize with the locals?

Rathlin

The island of Rathlin lies about 9 km (6 mi) off the north east coast of County Antrim in Northern Ireland and less than 25 km (16 mi) from Scotland's Mull of Kintyre. Only 7 km (4 mi) long by 1.6 km (1 mi) wide, and shaped like a boot with its toe pointing towards Ballycastle Bay, it's a small island with a big history.

First inhabited in 6,000 BC, Rathlin became a source of flint implements. St Columba is said to have stayed here en route to Scotland in the 6th century and in 735 AD the island suffered the first of the many Viking raids on Ireland. Robert the Bruce is said to have stayed in Bruce's Cave, gaining inspiration from a spider weaving its web across the entrance, although this is one of several places said to own that distinction. In 1575 hundreds of women and children, refugees of the MacDonnell Clan, were slaughtered here by men led by Francis Drake. Rathlin was fought over by both Scotland and Ireland, and was finally agreed to be Irish in 1617.

These days Rathlin is one of Northern Ireland's Special Areas of Conservation, and is an RSPB Reserve. A viewing platform has been spectacularly sited over two great basalt crags named the 'Stags of Bull Point', where thousands of sea birds, over 30 species, wheel and fly. Rathlin is, most importantly, home to the largest colony of Atlantic puffins in Europe. Thousands of birders visit each year, though its permanent population is tiny.

Around the island, the waters are treacherous and rough, and despite the presence of three lighthouses rising amongst impressive cliffs, forty shipwrecks lie beneath them. In 1898 Marconi transmitted the first commercial radio signals from the East Lighthouse to Ballycastle. In spite of – or perhaps because of – the dangerous seas, Rathlin has always been known as a smuggler's haven.

Rathlin Island

POPULATION:
75 (2001)
HOW TO GET THERE:
By ferry from Ballycastle to Church Bay.
WHEN TO GO:
April to August for the puffin breeding season.
HIGHLIGHTS:
The West Lighthouse.
Exploring the sea caves and watching the seal population.
Diving over some of the 40 shipwrecks.
The standing stones, Iron Age fort and the remains of Bruce's Castle.
YOU SHOULD KNOW:
In 1987 Richard Branson crashed his hot air balloon into the sea a few kilometres off Bull Point after a record-breaking flight from Maine, USA. He and fellow balloonist Per Lindstrom were rescued by a fishing boat; they later returned to the island with a £25,000 cheque for the Rathlin Island Trust, towards the renovation of the old Manor House.

Isle of Man

POPULATION:
80,058 (2006)
WHEN TO GO:
Any time of year, but June to early
October for beach holidays.
HOW TO GET THERE:
By air or sea from the UK
and Ireland.
HIGHLIGHTS:
The Laxey Wheel, the largest working
water wheel in the world.
The House of Manannan, with its
replica Norse longship.
Castle Rushen in Castletown and
nearby Rushen Abbey.
Ballaheannagh Gardens.
Moore's Traditional Museum, with its
working demonstrations of Manx
kipper curing.
The inscribed Celtic and Viking stone
crosses in the churchyards of
Maughold and Brannan.
YOU SHOULD KNOW:
One of the island's main attractions
is the annual TT race, an international
motorcycle race run over the
mountain course at Snaefell, the
highest peak on the island at
621 m (2,036 ft).

A British Crown dependency, though not actually part of the UK, the Isle of Man lies smack in the middle of the Irish Sea, in the centre of the British Isles. Relying on the UK for its foreign policy, defence and trade, the islanders are fiercely independent and proud of their heritage. Its parliament, Tynwald, is widely considered to be the world's oldest continuous parliament.

Inhabited since Neolithic times, settled by Celts and Vikings, the island only came under the control of the Crown in 1765. Ferries from England brought tourism during the Victorian era, an industry of continuing importance, but the island's success story has been its low taxation economy, and the development of off-shore banking and other financial services.

A central valley bisects hills to the north and south of the island and much of the interior is moorland, with deep valleys and pockets of woodland. Most of the towns and villages are set in protected bays around the coast. Douglas, the capital, has a marvellous Victorian promenade. Peel, in the west, is the island's only city, its harbour busy with fishing boats, once the mainstay of the economy. Linked to Peel by a causeway is St Patrick's Isle, with its 14th century castle walls enclosing ruins that encompass the island's ancient history. In the 1980s the burial site of an important Viking woman was found here, and her jewellery and other effects reside in the Manx Museum.

The Isle of Man is a treasure trove – here you will find endless prehistoric and early Christian sites, stone crosses and promontory forts. Take a trip to Cregneash in the southwest where traditional village life continues as it has for hundreds of years. If history is not for you, hike through the beautiful countryside, get around by steam or electric train, or enjoy a simple seaside holiday.

Rows of bay-fronted hotels and guesthouses line the Victorian promenade in Douglas.

The Isle of Wight

Possibly the best known of England's islands, the Isle of Wight lies in the English Channel, separated from the mainland by the Solent. A ridge of chalk, one of the thickest in the British Isles, runs across the centre of the island, ending dramatically in the three white sea stacks known as the Needles, from the last of which rises a red and white banded lighthouse that was built in 1859.

The island's history goes back 10,000 years – and before that, dinosaurs roamed the countryside. The Romans called it Vectis; they arrived here in 50 AD, stayed for 400 years and left a legacy of two well-preserved Roman villas for us to enjoy today. The Normans built Carisbrooke Castle and further fortifications were built by the Tudors. By the 19th century, the island had become a tourist destination, and Queen Victoria bought Osborne House in Cowes as a summertime retreat, returning there to die in 1901.

About half of the island is designated as an Area of Outstanding Natural Beauty, and there are some 40 Sites of Special Scientific Interest, with habitats supporting the now rare red squirrel, and the Glanville fritillary, an endemic orangey-red butterfly. The coastal path and seven long distance trails enable the visitor to enjoy the island's downs and woodlands as well as its long sandy beaches, dramatic cliffs and coastline.

Sandown, Shanklin, Ryde, Ventnor and Yarmouth are all family holiday destinations, but it is Cowes that is internationally known as a yachting centre, and Cowes Week brings thousands of visitors for its highly competitive races. Another draw is the unexpected annual Garlic Festival, and, for the young, the music festival. First organized in 1968, and featuring stars such as Bob Dylan and Jimi Hendrix, the Isle of Wight Festival was revived in 2002 to instant, enormous success.

The sweeping bays of the Isle of Wight

POPULATION:
132,731 (2001)
WHEN TO GO:
Any time, but May to early October for summer holidays.
HOW TO GET THERE:
By sea from the mainland.
HIGHLIGHTS:
The Needles Battery.
Brading Roman Villa.
Mottistone Manor.
Tennyson Down and monument.
Appuldurcombe House, near Wroxhall. Ryde Pier.
YOU SHOULD KNOW:
A number of famous people have loved and lived on the Isle of Wight. These include the painter J.M.W. Turner, the poets Keats and Tennyson – who wrote 'The Charge of the Light Brigade' in his house at Farringford: the architect John Nash, the author J.B. Priestly and the film-maker Anthony Minghella.

The Abbey Gardens in Tresco

The Isles of Scilly

POPULATION:
2,153 (2001)
WHEN TO GO:
Anytime but best between April and November.
HOW TO GET THERE:
By plane, helicopter or boat from the mainland.
HIGHLIGHTS:
St Warna's Well, St Agnes.
Turks's Head, the most south-westerly pub in the land, St Agnes.
Cromwell's Castle, Tresco.
Valhalla Museum, Tresco.
Megaliths on the island of Gugh, connected to St Agnes at low tide.
The chambered tomb in Samson Hill, Bryher.
YOU SHOULD KNOW:
Myths and legends are integral to the Scillies' heritage, and the islands are said to be the last visible areas of the drowned land of Lyonnesse, the birthplace of the Arthurian knight, Tristram, and the site of King Arthur's final showdown with Mordred.

The Isles of Scilly are the most westerly part of Britain. An archipelago of 140 islands, with nothing between them and the USA, they are blessed with a benign climate, despite receiving gale force winds during winter.

There are five main inhabited islands; St Mary's being the most developed. Although tourism accounts for 85 per cent of their economy, St Mary's is intensively cultivated. Clement weather produces early flowers, and flower growing remains a considerable industry. The Scillies were designated an Area of Outstanding Natural Beauty in 1975.

Tresco, the second largest island, is also much visited, thanks in large part to the fabulous Abbey Gardens. Acquired in 1834 by Augustus Smith, a keen botanist and Lord Proprietor of the Scillies, the gardens, full of exotic tropical and sub-tropical plants, were designed and terraced around the ruins of the 10th century Abbey.

St Martin's, the third largest island, is very unspoilt. Here you can find Bronze Age burial chambers and the remains of a 5th century chapel. Daffodils and Amaryllis Belladonna are grown commercially, but it's the gorgeous beaches and crystalline waters that most people come for.

St Agnes, the most southwesterly island, is known for its lovely coastline, white sand beaches, coves and rock pools. Granite boulders are strewn over parts of the interior and great granite outcrops guard the western shore. Famed for its wildlife, twitchers arrive en masse each October hoping to spot rare birds blown off course during their migration.

Small and quiet, Bryher is peppered with pre-historic sites. Covered in a blaze of gorse and wild flowers in spring and summer, it's another twitcher's paradise. Bryher makes a perfect getaway from the stresses of modern life, its coastal path offering fabulous views of the rocky shoreline and across the water to Tresco. All in all, the Scilly Isles offer something for everyone.

Jersey

Just 22.5 km (12 mi) north of France's Cotentin Peninsula, in the English Channel, lies Jersey, a self governing British Crown Dependency. A well-populated and attractive island, its low taxation has transformed the economy into a centre for off-shore banking and other financial services. Despite this side of island life, tourism and agriculture remain the backbone for most of the inhabitants.

Occupied since the Stone Age, Jersey has had a turbulent history, with Romans, early Christians, Vikings and Normans all making their mark here, the island came under English rule in 1204. Six hundred years of French attacks followed, but peace finally reigned following the defeat of France in 1815. Invaded and occupied by Germany in 1940, Jersey was forced to reinvent itself, which it did successfully, at the end of World War II.

St Helier, the administrative capital, is an attractive town set around a large bay, but its pretty, narrow streets and prosperous atmosphere hide Jersey's bitter past. During World War II an enormous underground hospital was hacked and tunnelled into a rocky hill, mainly by Russian and Polish slave labour, at the cost of many lives. The complex, at St Lawrence, has been restored as a reminder of what might have been, and the hardship suffered by the islanders during those years may explain their desire for financial success.

Jersey's landscape is delightful and very varied. St Ouen's Bay, in the west, is a magnificent expanse of sandy beach, protected by headlands at either end. The north coast is quite different, its rugged cliffs and sheltered coves attracting thousands of nesting seabirds. Four of the island's coastal wetlands have been designated Ramsar Wetland Sites. The interior contains freshwater ponds and reservoirs, lovely wooded valleys, and agricultural land. This is the home of a favourite British delicacy, Jersey potatoes, and Jersey cattle provide superb dairy produce and beef.

POPULATION:
91,321 (2007 estimate)
WHEN TO GO:
Jersey's climate is mild, but visit between April and November for the best weather.
HOW TO GET THERE:
By air or sea from England and France.
HIGHLIGHTS:
L'Islet and Elizabeth Castle, accessible by causeway at low tide.
The Durrell Wildlife Conservation Trust.
Grosnez Castle.
Samares Manor.
Corbiere Lighthouse.
The annual Battle of Flowers carnival, held during the second week of August.
YOU SHOULD KNOW:
Like the rest of the Channel Islands and the Isle of Man, Jersey is not part of the United Kingdom or the European Union.

Mont Orgueil Castle overlooks the small town of Gorey.

Guernsey

POPULATION:
65,031 (2004)
WHEN TO GO:
Any time of year, but April to October
for the best of the weather.
HOW TO GET THERE:
By air or sea from England
and Europe.
HIGHLIGHTS:
Sausmarez Manor.
The German Occupation Museum.
The Little Chapel.
Rousse Headland and the Napoleonic
Loopholed Tower.
La Claire Mare, including Colin Best
Nature Reserve and Les Anguillieres
Marine Nature Reserve.
Lihou Island, an uninhabited bird
sanctuary, reached by a tidal
causeway and containing the ruins of
a 12th century abbey.
YOU SHOULD KNOW:
Victor Hugo lived in exile on
Guernsey for 14 years from 1855,
writing *Les Misérables* and other
works here. His house, owned by the
city of Paris and in which the French
Consulate is based, is now a
fascinating museum of his life
and work.

Guernsey lies in the English Channel, and at about 48 km (30 mi) west of the Normandy coast it is considerably closer to France than to England. It is a self-governing British Crown Dependency, with several other islands in its bailiwick. It has a successful economy based on tourism, off-shore banking, insurance and agriculture, and thanks to low taxation is known as a refuge for the wealthy.

Inhabited since around 6,000 BC, Guernsey became part of England in 1066, and gained its self-governance as a reward for loyalty from King John in 1204. Used by pirates in the Middle Ages, Guernsey became prosperous during the 19th century, and apart from suffering severely during World War II, during its 5-year occupation by Germany, it remains so today. If the island has a problem, it is that too many people want to settle here.

Mainly flat and low-lying, Guernsey is cultivated intensively, and much of its 63 sq km (25 sq mi) is covered with greenhouses sheltering tomatoes and flowers. It is also home to the island's icon, the Guernsey cow, today being raised for beef as well as milk. However, there's still enough room for several nature reserves, and the variety of habitat is extensive, ranging from wooded valleys, marshland and reed beds to heathland and dunes. The southern coastal path offers 44 km (28 mi) of coastal scenery, and broad sandy bays provide happy seaside summer holidays.

If beach holidays are not your thing, or you hit a spell of poor weather, Guernsey has plenty of other attractions on offer. Castle Cornet, which guards St Peter Port harbour, dates from the 13th century and was built by King John. Connected by causeway to mainland Guernsey in 1860, the castle contains six museums. Another fascinating part of the island's history, the Nazi occupation, is well observed and documented in a number of different locations.

Sailboats moored by Castle Cornet.

Sark

Sark is the smallest of the four main Channel Islands. It lies in the English Channel, about 128 km (80 mi) from England and about 32 km (20 mi) from the coast of Normandy. It is as well that it is small, as there are no cars on the island, and transport other than on foot consists of horse-drawn carriages, tractors and bicycles.

Sark's history is long, and complex. Until the mid 16th century it was a place of pirates, frequently invaded by the French. In 1563, Helier de Carteret, the Seigneur of St Ouen in Jersey, received a charter from Elizabeth I to settle on Sark. Many of the island's laws date back to this period, and the feudal head of Sark is still known as the Seigneur.

The island is formed of steep, rocky cliffs, averaging about 90 m (330 ft) above sea level, rising to a central plateau. At its highest point a windmill can be found, dated 1571. In order to reach this plateau, passengers disembarking in the miniscule harbour must travel upwards through a rock-hewn tunnel made in 1866.

Greater Sark is connected to Little Sark by a narrow, paved isthmus known as La Coupée. Just 2.7 m (9 ft) wide, it has dizzying 90 m (300 ft) drops to either side. La Seigneurie, de Carteret's manor house built in 1565, is believed to stand on the site of an early Christian monastery. Although privately owned, its gardens, some of the finest in the Channel Islands, are open to the public.

This is a delightful island, with gorgeous sandy beaches and coves around the coast, ensuring shelter from winds of any direction. There are woods filled with springtime bluebells, and over 600 different plants and wildflowers grow here. Seabirds nest on the cliffs, and birds of prey, songbirds and migrants enjoy its unspoilt landscape.

POPULATION:
610 (2002)
WHEN TO GO:
Any time, but April to October may provide the best weather.
HOW TO GET THERE:
By ferry from Guernsey, Jersey and Normandy.
HIGHLIGHTS:
St Peter's Church (1820).
Sark Prison – built in 1856 and capable of accommodating only two people, this is the smallest prison in the world.
La Grande Greve, perhaps Sark's most special bay.
A walk through Dixcart valley to the ancient cannon at Hogs Back.
The Boutique and Gouliot Caves.
Swimming at low tide in the Venus Pool on Little Sark.
YOU SHOULD KNOW:
Amongst the curious laws on Sark – no income tax; 'Clameur de Haro', whereby the immediate cessation of any action seen to be an infringement of one's rights can be claimed and gained and then heard at Sark's court; the Seigneur is the only person on the island with the right to own doves, as well as the only one allowed to have an unspayed female dog!

La Coupée connects Sark with Little Sark.

Eel Pie Island is one of London's most sought-after locations.

Eel Pie Island

Lying in the River Thames, opposite Twickenham – one of London's more sought after locations, is Eel Pie Island. Tiny in size but huge in reputation, Eel Pie is a legend in the lifetime of the baby boom generation. A mere 181 m (600 ft) from end to end, the island is mainly residential, with a few small businesses and a miniscule nature reserve at each end.

As long ago as the early 1600s, Eel Pie was somewhere to have fun – a map from 1635 shows a bowling green, and there were public houses here by the 1700s. One of these, rebuilt in the 1830s, became a much grander establishment called the Eel Pie Island Hotel, which soon became extremely popular. The Twickenham Rowing Club, one of the Thames's oldest, built its headquarters here in 1880, and today the Richmond Yacht Club is also located on the island.

The hotel contained a sprung dance floor. Used first for ballroom dancing, the 1920s and 30s saw well attended tea dances. However, during the 1950s its owner turned it into a major British jazz venue and by the 1960s jazz was overtaken by rhythm and blues music. All the seminal bands of the era played the Eel Pie Hotel: Long John Baldry, John Mayall's Bluesbreakers, Pink Floyd, The Who, and most famously, The Rolling Stones. It was party time, and hundreds of young Londoners made their way here to make merry. Closed in 1967, briefly re-opened in 1969, the hotel became a hippie commune. In 1971, it was mysteriously burnt to the ground whilst being demolished.

In 1996 another fire damaged Eel Pie, and today boat building is in decline, and new developments loom. However, the inhabitants remain a wonderfully eclectic mix of rich and poor, all brought together by the lure of art, music and a bohemian lifestyle, and all determined to keep the island's unique atmosphere intact.

POPULATION:
120 (2007)
WHEN TO GO:
Any time
HOW TO GET THERE:
By footbridge or boat.
HIGHLIGHTS:
Exploring the island and, for some, remembering times past.
Boating on the River Thames.
A trip to Hampton Court.
YOU SHOULD KNOW:
Eel Pie Island was named for its famous eel pies. King Henry VIII loved them and insisted that the first pie of the season was delivered to Hampton Court by the Waterman of Twickenham. Sadly, pollution has put paid to the eels, and the pies are no longer made here.

The Farne Islands and Lindisfarne

Just off the coast of Northumberland, lies a group of some 20 tidal islands. Divided into inner and outer groups, these are colloquially known as the 'Farnes'. Apart from a few seasonal National Trust bird wardens, they are uninhabited. Rugged and bleak, the smallest islands are just bare, rocky peaks, while the largest support vegetation on peaty soil.

Inner Farne is closely connected to St Cuthbert, who lived alone here for some years. Further hermits followed the saint, who died in 687, many of whom came from the monastery at Durham. In 1255 a small Benedictine monastery was established here, with two separate chapels.

Always dangerous to shipping because of hidden rocks and sea stacks, a warning beacon was first lit in 1673, since when the islands have seen the construction and destruction of many lighthouses. Two fully automated lighthouses stand today on Inner Farne and Longstone and lighthouses ruins can be seen. The islands are known as one of Britain's major seabird sanctuaries as well as being home to several thousand Atlantic grey seals.

To the north of the Farnes lies mystical Lindisfarne, or Holy Island. Connected by a tidal causeway to the mainland, much of both it and its surrounding tidal area is a National Nature Reserve, protecting internationally important winter populations and rare migrant birds.

Lindisfarne's famous monastery was founded by St Aidan in 635 AD, and St Cuthbert was both Abbott and Bishop here for two years. This is one of the most important early Christian sites in England. The remarkable illuminated manuscript, the Lindisfarne Gospels, was made on the island in the early 700s, and is now protected in the British Library. Also on the island is a Tudor castle. Owned by the National Trust, it was built in the 1570s and restored by Edwin Lutyens in 1901, with a garden designed by Gertrude Jekyll.

Lindisfarne monastery

POPULATION:
The Farne Islands are uninhabited; Lindisfarne 162 (2007)
WHEN TO GO:
The best time for birds is during autumn and winter, but Lindisfarne is at its best during spring and summer.
HOW TO GET THERE:
By boat to the Farnes, foot or car to Lindisfarne, depending on the tides.
HIGHLIGHTS:
Scuba diving over the many wrecks surrounding the Farne Islands.
St Cuthbert's Chapel, Inner Farne.
The Pele tower, a small 16th century defensive fort, Inner Farne.
The ruined Lindisfarne monastery, its museum and visitor centre.
The old lime kilns on Lindisfarne.
Lindisfarne Mead – its recipe passed down from medieval times is still a closely guarded secret of the family who still produce it at St Aidan's Winery.
YOU SHOULD KNOW:
Longstone Lighthouse was the home of keeper William Darling. In 1838 his 22 year-old daughter, Grace, saw a shipwreck on a nearby rock. In their rowing boat, she and her father achieved the extraordinarily courageous rescue of nine people in terrible weather conditions, and she became a national heroine.

Foulness

POPULATION:
212 (2001)
HOW TO GET THERE:
By road bridge from Shoebury, having first obtained permission.
WHEN TO GO:
Any time of year, but it is best on a hot summer's day.
HIGHLIGHTS:
The villages of Churchend and Courtsend.
Birdwatching.
YOU SHOULD KNOW:
Bridges to the island were only built in 1926; prior to that access was by boat or on foot. No-one knows when the sea walls were first built, but several of the marshes had sea walls by the beginning of the 13th century. Foulness has been flooded on a number of occasions, the last in 1953, during the Great Tide, when two people lost their lives.

Foulness is the largest of the Essex islands, indeed it is the fourth largest island off England's coast, and yet because of its unique situation, it is one of the least known. There are only three freeholders on Foulness – the Parish Council, the Church of England and, by far the most important, the Ministry of Defence, who bought these 2,550 hectares (6,300 acres) in 1915. It is here that the MoD tests military ordnance.

Physically, Foulness is in the Thames delta, bounded by the rivers Crouch in the north, the Roach and Shelford Creek in the west, with the River Thames to the south and east. The island is made of fertile alluvial marshland, and almost all of it is below high tide level, necessitating its enclosure by a sea wall. Some of the land is farmed, cattle and sheep can be seen grazing and the surrounding Foulness and Maplin Sands are a haven for wading birds, including the second largest population of avocets in the country. Herons can frequently be seen in the many creeks and backwaters. No wonder this was once a favourite destination of smugglers.

You need to make an effort to visit Foulness – by invitation by a resident, or by booking lunch at the 17th century George and Dragon, the island's only pub. Either way, a pass has to be obtained, or you will find yourself turned away from the MoD checkpoint at the start of the series of bridges that connect Foulness to the mainland. Once on the island, you'll find most of the residents living in two villages at the northern end. The atmosphere of Foulness is of a place apart, and for the visitor it is quite an experience, if you can cope with occasional loud explosions.

Brownsea Island

POPULATION:
No permanent population.
WHEN TO GO:
Any time, but booked groups only between November and April.
HOW TO GET THERE:
By boat from Sandbanks or North Haven and Poole Quay, or on a day trip from local resorts, or by privately owned boat.
HIGHLIGHTS:
The mid-19th century St Mary's Church.
The site of Baden-Powell's first Scout camp.
The annual Brownsea open air Shakespeare theatre.

In the mouth of Poole harbour, opposite the town of Poole in Dorset, lies Brownsea Island. The largest of a group of small islands, Brownsea is wholly owned by the National Trust, and as such may be visited by the public. All of Brownsea is designated a Site of Special Scientific Interest, and the northern end of this small, 2.4 km (1.5 mi) long by 1.2 km (0.75 mi) wide, island is leased to the Dorset Wildlife Trust as a Nature Reserve.

Brownsea's lengthy history includes early Christianity, the Vikings, and Henry VIIIth's fortification programme, designed to protect Poole harbour. The island passed through many hands. During World War II it was used as a decoy for the port – so successfully that it received several bombs. In 1961 the owner, who was reclusive and had allowed Brownsea to revert to nature, died,

Brownsea Castle

and the National Trust was able to acquire it.

However, Brownsea is best known as the seat of the Scouting movement. At the turn of the 20th century, Robert Baden-Powell was a guest on the island, and in 1907 he hosted the first Scout Camp for twenty Dorset boys, and thus began a worldwide movement. Brownsea castle and its grounds are now leased by the John Lewis Partnership as a summer holiday destination for its staff.

Brownsea is a place of many habitats, and is home to a wealth of wildlife and plants. It contains saltmarsh, reed beds, freshwater lakes, heathland, peaceful pinewoods and a brackish lagoon. It is one of the last havens of the indigenous red squirrel – probably due to having no competition from the grey variety – and there are many non-native sika deer and rabbits. The island has wonderful birds: herons, little egrets, terns in summer and avocets in winter.

YOU SHOULD KNOW:
2007 was the Scouts' 100th anniversary, and several events were held. The highlight was the Sunrise Camp, which brought together 310 young people from 155 countries to celebrate the occasion. At the exact moment that Scouting had begun 100 years previously, every Scout in the world, all 28 million of them, renewed their Scouting promise.

Mersea Island

POPULATION:
6,500 (2007)
WHEN TO GO:
At its best between April and October.
HOW TO GET THERE:
Via The Strood, the main Colchester to Mersea road (B1025)
HIGHLIGHTS:
Cudmore Grove Country Park.
The Mersea Island Museum.
Colchester Oyster Fishery.
West Mersea Barrow.
Mersea Week and Regatta, annually in August.
Mersea Seafood Festival, annually in September.
YOU SHOULD KNOW:
The author Sabine Baring-Gould (1834-1924) was the rector of East Mersea's St Edmunds Church for a decade. He is best known for the hymn 'Onward Christian Soldiers'.

A row of colourful beach huts on West Mersea Beach

Derived from the Old English *meresig*, meaning island of the pool, Mersea Island lies just off the Essex coast in the estuary of the Blackwater and Colne rivers. At 14 km (9 mi) southeast of Colchester, Mersea is Britain's most easterly inhabited island. It is small at 8 sq km (3 sq mi), but despite its sizeable population it still has salt marshes and plenty of space for farmland. Here too are beaches, beach huts, and restaurants at the water's edge where you can eat locally caught fish and even drink wine from the local vineyard.

Inhabited since about 3,000 BC, it was under Roman rule when a causeway was first built, connecting Mersea to the mainland. Known as The Strood, the causeway floods whenever the tide is particularly high. Mersea has been a holiday retreat since Roman soldiers first retired here, and once Britain had been pacified, wealthy Romans settled here too. In 1898 archaeologists uncovered the foundations of a villa, together with mosaic flooring and pavement. The Romans left a legacy that is still valuable today – oyster farming, and Mersea Native oysters are still an important (and seriously delicious) part of the local economy.

Most people live in the small town of West Mersea, others in the village of East Mersea with a scattering elsewhere. Farming, fishing, boat making and the tourism industry are the major occupations of this tightly knit community, which has two newspapers and every facility needed in terms of shops, schools and so on. During the summer the population swells dramatically, and the waters are full of colourful sailing boats, wind and kite surfers. The harbour at West Mersea is a bustling mass of boats and boatyards, and is home to the West Mersea Yacht Club, making Mersea one of the east coast's main sailing centres.

Lundy

Some 19 km (12 mi) out in the Bristol Channel, where the Atlantic Ocean meets the Severn River, lies the island of Lundy. Protected by its high, granite cliffs and remote location, the island has a colourful past. Today it belongs to the National Trust, is leased to the Landmark Trust, and its solitary and beautiful nature brings visitors back here over and over again.

Lundy has been inhabited since pre-historic times, and has suffered endless disputes over its ownership. In 1242, Henry III built a castle here to consolidate his control – instead Lundy became anarchic and chaos reigned until William Hudson Heaven bought the island in 1834. He erected many of the buildings, including St Helena's Church but sold the island to Martin Harman, a naturalist, in 1925. Harman transformed Lundy, and the National Trust acquired the island from his children in 1969.

The island consists of open moorland in the north, some farmland and a village to the south. Some 20,000 visitors come here each year, for the day or to stay in one of the 23 beautifully restored buildings that include a lighthouse and the castle. Those spending longer here can walk the glorious 11 km (7 mi) coastal path, admiring the surrounding waters that form Britain's first Marine Nature Reserve. Marine life is exceedingly rich – in particular there are rare species of seaweed, corals and fans. Grey seals are much in evidence, and basking sharks can also be spotted.

Much of Lundy is an area of Special Scientific Interest, and the flora and fauna are rich and varied. It has its own endemic species of cabbage, and its own, distinct breed of Lundy pony. It is also, naturally, bliss for birders. Although puffins are now few, the cliffs are home to thousands of seabirds, and in spring and autumn rare visitors occasionally appear, having been blown off course during migration.

POPULATION:
18 (2007 estimate)
WHEN TO GO:
Any time, but April to November is probably best.
HOW TO GET THERE:
By ferry from Bideford or Ilfracombe, or (November to March) helicopter from Hartland Point.
HIGHLIGHTS:
The disused granite quarries.
The Devil's Slide – great for rock climbing.
The three lighthouses – one of which you can stay in, the other two are functioning.
Diving over the wrecks and enjoying other water sports such as surfing.
The Soay sheep and feral goats.
YOU SHOULD KNOW:
In 1929 Martin Harman issued his own Lundy postage stamps, their value expressed in 'puffins'. These stamps are still printed today, but must be stuck on an envelope's left hand corner, their cost including Royal Mail's charges. Known as 'local carriage labels' in the world of philately, some of Lundy's stamps are now highly prized.

The ferry calls at Lundy Island.

Anglesey

The famous sign outside the railway station in the village that boasts the longest name in Britain.

Separated from the north west coast of Wales by the Menai Strait, lies the island of Anglesey, the largest of the English and Welsh islands. Low lying – the highest point, Holyhead Mountain is only 218 m (720 ft) – the island is mainly agricultural. Its coastline, however, is superb, with sandy beaches, caves, rocky coves and sheer cliff faces, and 95 per cent of which is a designated an Area of Outstanding Natural Beauty.

This is an ancient island, inhabited for some 9,000 years. Its history dates back to the Mesolithic era, and it was home to Druids, Romans, Celts, Vikings, Saxons and Normans before being conquered by Edward I in the 13th century. All these peoples left their mark here, and Anglesey contains a treasure trove of ancient monuments, from standing stones and Stone Age burial sites to historic churches and castles.

Beaumaris Castle, a 13th century masterpiece, is a UNESCO World Heritage Site. Unfinished, it was the last of Edward I's 'iron ring' of castles built around the Welsh coast. This magnificent moated fortress is widely regarded as the finest of Edward's castles. Overlooking the Menai Strait, it commands fabulous views.

Anglesey is connected to the mainland by two bridges. The first, the Menai Suspension Bridge was designed by Thomas Telford in 1826, and the second, newer bridge, is a reconstruction of Robert Stephenson's original. There are many small towns on the island, and 70 per cent of the population here are Welsh speakers.

Most of Anglesey's two million visitors each year come for the coastline, enjoying the beaches, sailing, wind surfing and other outdoor activities. These include the splendid Coastal Path, the circular route of which connects 36 villages and passes through glorious scenery, including Newborough Forest on the south-eastern tip of the island.

Caldey Island

Caldey Island, which lies 5 km (3 mi) off the south coast of Pembrokeshire, is one of Britain's holy islands. Only 2.4 km (1.5 mi) long and 1.6 km (1 mi) wide, it has been inhabited since the Stone Age, and since Celtic times it has been inhabited by monks.

A Celtic monastery was founded here by Pyro, in the 6th century, and the Old Priory is believed to have been built on that original site. During the 10th century, Viking raids are thought to have put an end to the monastic settlement, but 200 years later Benedictines from St Dogmaels in Pembrokeshire built a Priory here, where they remained until the Dissolution of the Monasteries in 1536. In 1906 Anglican Benedictines bought Caldey and the Abbott, Aelred Carlyle, commissioned the beautiful Italianate Abbey from architect John Coates-Carter. Unable to make ends meet, the Benedictines sold the Abbey to Cistercian monks, Trappists, in 1926, where they remain peacefully ensconced in what is now a Grade II* listed building.

Although Caldey is best known for its monastery, it has a pretty village, too. Here one can buy a number of things made on the island, which provide an income for the monks. Farming produces milk, butter and cream and the monks produce yoghurt, ice-cream, shortbread and chocolate, which are on sale in the village. Their most famous product, however, is a range of perfumes and skin creams, made from Caldey's flowers, herbs and gorse.

This is a wonderful place to visit, with a uniquely serene and tranquil atmosphere. Quiet and unpolluted, with no traffic to disturb the peace, Caldey can be explored on foot. From the gorgeous Priory Beach to the lighthouse at the summit of the island, magnificent views over the south coast of Pembrokeshire can be enjoyed.

A view out to the Atlantic Ocean from the shores of the serene Caldey Island.

POPULATION:
50 (2003 estimate)
WHEN TO GO:
From Easter to the end of October.
HOW TO GET THERE:
Boats run from Tenby Harbour at high tide, and Castle Beach landing stage at low tide. Boats don't sail on Sundays.
HIGHLIGHTS:
St Illtyd's Church and the Old Priory.
Attending Mass in the Abbott's Chapel and touring the monastery (men only).
A guided walk to discover more about Caldey.
The Caldey Stone, inscribed in both Celtic and Latin.
St Margarets, Caldey's sister island (joined at low tide) – a seal and bird sanctuary.
Visiting the Post Office and Museum, and having a postcard franked with Caldey's unique imprint.
YOU SHOULD KNOW:
The Caldey Island monastery provides spiritual retreats throughout the year for both men and women (though only men are permitted to enter the main building), and it is possible to stay on the island.

Bardsey Island

POPULATION:
8-13 including ornithologists (2007)
WHEN TO GO:
April to October
HOW TO GET THERE:
By ferry from Porth Meudwy or
Pwllheli.
HIGHLIGHTS:
Celtic crosses.
The 13th century bell tower.
The Bardsey Bird and Field
Observatory.
Bardsey lighthouse – 30 m (99 ft)
high, this is the only square
lighthouse maintained by Trinity
House.
The ancient Bardsey Apple Tree, a
descendant of apple trees tended by
monks 1,000 years ago, and declared
'unique' by experts at the National
Fruit Collection in Brogdale, Kent.
Cuttings have been planted in order
to raise money for the Bardsey Trust.
YOU SHOULD KNOW:
Both Merlin and King Arthur are said
to be buried in a glass coffin in a
cave within Mynydd Enlii. A 12th
century historian claimed that Avalon
was an island of apples, and its name
was derived from the Welsh word,
afal. Perhaps the Round Table will be
discovered here one day…

*Bardsey Island seen through
the morning mist*

About 3.2 km (2 mi) off the tip of the Llyen Peninsula in north Wales lies another holy island. Bardsey, or Ynys Enlli in Welsh, meaning 'island of the great current' is only 2.5 km (1.5 mi) long, but traces of hut circles attest to it having been inhabited since Neolithic times.

During the 5th century, persecuted Christians began to take refuge here, and by the next century a monastery had been built by St Cadfan. Bardsey soon became a major place of pilgrimage, as well known as Iona or Lindisfarne, and it was said that three pilgrimages to Bardsey equalled one to Rome. Many of the faithful remained on Bardsey until they died, and yet more were brought for burial. This led to it becoming known as 'the isle of 20,000 saints'. The ruins that can be seen today are those of the 13th century Augustinian Abbey of St Mary, which was deserted during the Dissolution of the Monasteries in 1537. Bardsey then became a refuge of pirates and ne'er-do-wells until the owner, Lord Newborough, established a farming and fishing community during the 19th century. In 1979 the island was bought by the Bardsey Island Trust, and it is now an Area of Outstanding Natural Beauty, attracting both Christians and those interested in natural history and archaeology.

Most of Bardsey is flat and low lying, and from the slopes of Mynydd Enlli, which rises to 167 m (551 ft), a pattern of fields, divided by old stone walls, can be seen. The coastal margins are home to many rare plants, including over 350 species of lichen, and during spring and autumn many rare and migratory birds can be seen, including a large colony of Manx shearwaters, and, recently, puffins.

Lewis and Harris

Lewis and Harris, curiously, is one single island, the largest and most northerly of the Western Isles, otherwise known as the Outer Hebrides. By far the largest portion is Lewis, in the north, which becomes Harris at the point where two sea lochs, Resort and Seaforth, cut deeply into the land, itself a natural barrier of bleak, treeless mountains and moorland. Harris, in turn, is also split between north and south by a narrow isthmus, again formed by two sea lochs.

This is an ancient place, with fabulously dramatic landscapes, and a fascinating history and culture. Unlike many of the Scottish islands, it is not dependant in any way on tourism. If you are interested in Gaelic culture, this is its heartland: the majority of the population speak Gaelic as their first language, and keep to their traditional way of life. One third of Scotland's crofts are found here, and a string of settlements run up the west coast from Calanais to the Butt of Lewis in the far north. This is, of course, the home of the world famous Harris tweed, although today most of the weaving is done in Lewis, as that is where most of the island's population live.

The main town, Stornaway, in the east, lies on an impressive harbour, but its main point of architectural interest is the grandiose Lews Castle, built in the 1850s. The interior of the northern part of Lewis is rich in peat moors, while the south and Harris have spectacular mountain scenery, and stunningly beautiful beaches. All the most notable sites are on the west coast of Lewis, while the south, and Harris, offer stunning views over lochs, rivers, and the sea. The Uig peninsula has some of the most spectacular coastal scenery imaginable.

POPULATION:
20,000 (2006)
WHEN TO GO:
May to October
HOW TO GET THERE:
By air from Glasgow, Edinburgh and Inverness, or by ferry from Ullapool or Skye.
HIGHLIGHTS:
The 5,000-year-old Calanais (or Callanish) standing stones.
The village of Garenin with its restored thatched 'blackhouses' and museum.
The Butt of Lewis and its lighthouse overlooking the wild, crashing sea.
The Hebridean Celtic Festival at Lews Castle – a fabulous Celtic music festival held each July.
YOU SHOULD KNOW:
This is the heartland of the 'Wee Frees', the Free Presbyterian Church of Scotland, who rule with an iron hand. Almost everything closes on Sundays, which are reserved for church going and bible reading. Devotees observe many strange religious decrees, most of which appear to have been made to keep women in their place – they are forbidden to attend burials, for example, even that of their husbands or children.

The 5,000-year-old Calanais standing stones

North and South Uist, and Benbecula

POPULATION:
North Uist: 1,386; Benbecula: 1,883;
South Uist: 2,064.
WHEN TO GO:
May to September for the machair in
flower. Brown trout fishing: 15th
March to 30th September; salmon:
25th February to 15th October; sea
trout: 15th February to 31st. October.
HOW TO GET THERE:
By car over Scalpay Bridge or car
ferry from Harris or Skye, or by air to
Benbecula from Glasgow, Barra and
Stornaway.
HIGHLIGHTS:
Buy and enjoy lobsters and other
seafood at Grimsay, North Uist.
Taigh Chearsabhagh arts centre and
museum in Lochmaddy, North Uist.
Try your hand at deerstalking on the
North Uist Estate.
Visit the lovely islands of Eriskay
and Barra.
Explore the important and ancient
religious site at Howmore, South Uist.
Loch Druidibeg Nature Reserve,
South Uist.
YOU SHOULD KNOW:
Flora MacDonald was born on South
Uist. In 1746 she helped Bonnie
Prince Charlie, dressed up as her
maid, to escape to Skye where she
lived with her husband. This romantic
episode lives on in the well-known
song that begins 'Speed bonnie boat
like a bird on the wing'…

Loch Olavat on Benbecula

North Uist lies just across the sound from Harris. In sharp contrast, however, it is flat and low-lying. The eastern half of the island, which is 27 km (17 mi) long and 21 km (13 mi) wide, is covered with freshwater and sea water lochs – sheer heaven for trout and salmon fishermen. The Balranald RSPB reserve is a sanctuary for rare corncrakes, and has an extraordinary concentration of breeding waders, as well as raptors, songbirds and terns.

Lochmaddy, the ferry port, makes a good base from which to explore, being close to various curious prehistoric sites, such as the stone circle of Pobull Fhinn. The north and west coasts consist of vast, empty sandy beaches.

Between North and South Uist, and joined by a causeway, lies Benbecula, an unimpressive island of small lochs and peat bogs, and home to an army base. It does, however, have an airport, and its main claim to fame is a cave on its only hill, in which Bonnie Prince Charlie hid whilst waiting to escape to Skye.

South Uist is something of a gem. Its west coast has some of the finest beaches and swathes of machair (sandy, coastal grasslands), covered in heavenly wildflowers during the spring in the Western Isles. A ridge of mountains, broken by lochs, runs down the eastern side, while the crofting settlements are in the west. Rueval is home to a missile tracking station which, juxtaposed with the hundreds of archaeological sites in the area, looks completely surreal. Another nature reserve here is also worth a visit – made up of several types of habitat, you might even get to see a glorious golden eagle.

If you are keen on the great outdoors, North and South Uist are terrific for angling, bird watching or simply enjoying beaches and moorland that you seem to have all to yourself.

St Kilda Archipelago

Way out in the Atlantic Ocean, some 66 km (41 mi) to the west of the Outer Hebrides, rises the St Kilda Archipelago, with the exception of Rockall, the westernmost of British islands. St Kilda belongs to the National Trust for Scotland, and is a UNESCO World Heritage Site.

The archipelago consists of four main islands – Hirta, Soay, Boreray and Dun, which is almost an extension of Hirta, and several magnificent sea stacks. Hirta has the highest sea cliff in the British Isles, and Stac an Armin, just north of Boreray, is Britain's highest sea stack. In 2,000, marine scientists found that they are all peaks of the same, drowned mountain. Hirta was inhabited from about 5,000 years ago until 1930, when the last 36 inhabitants asked to be evacuated as conditions there had become untenable. In 1957 a missile tracking station was set up which today is manned by a civilian.

Hirta's sheer cliffs jut starkly from the sea on three sides, while the fourth has Village Bay, the only possible landing place and the site of the main settlement. Here there are Victorian cottages and many *cleits* – turf roofed, drystone structures – that were used to store the smoked or wind-dried seabirds, the basis of the islanders' diet. Nearby are numerous archaeological sites from which Neolithic stone tools, Iron Age pottery and Viking artefacts have been recovered.

But it's the birds of St Kilda that are the thing: these are the largest colonies of fulmars, gannets and puffins in Britain. Visually enthralling, the islands are green but treeless, having no plants growing higher than grass level. Great clouds of birds, unbelievable numbers of them, wheel and shriek in the sky, and clownish puffins whizz up and down the cliffs and grassy slopes like clockwork toys.

The rocky islands of Dun and Hirta, part of the St Kilda group

POPULATION:
There are small numbers of civilians working on the MOD base, otherwise just a few National Trust volunteers work on Hirta during the summer.
WHEN TO GO:
Mid-May to mid-August
HOW TO GET THERE:
Unless you have your own boat, the best way is to join a National Trust for Scotland working party. Contact the NTS first whichever way you want to visit.
HIGHLIGHTS:
Spot the petrels, Manx shearwaters, kittiwakes, guillemots, razorbills, gulls and great skuas that also breed here.
Watch for grey seals, basking sharks, killer and minke whales in the waters nearby.
See primitive Soay sheep, which look rather like goats and which may have been here since Neolithic times.
Visit the excellent museum in Cottage No. 3.
YOU SHOULD KNOW:
Stac an Armin was regularly climbed by the St Kildans in order to collect eggs and catch birds to eat. Unfortunately, in 1840, the last great auk in Britain was beaten to death at the top of the stack by two men who believed it to be a witch.

*Portree – the pretty main town
of the island*

Skye

POPULATION:
8,847 (2007)
WHEN TO GO:
The summer months are likely to
have the best weather, but the spring
and autumn will be less busy.
HOW TO GET THERE:
By road, or ferry from the mainland.
HIGHLIGHTS:
The extraordinary peaks of Quiraing,
near Staffin.
The haunted ruin of Duntulm Castle.
The 13th century Dunvegan Castle,
stronghold of the MacLeods.
Armadale Castle and the Museum of
the Isles.
The Bright Water Visitor Centre, once
the home of naturalist Gavin Maxwell,
at Kyleakin, and the Forestry
Commission otter hide at
nearby Kylerhea.
YOU SHOULD KNOW:
In 1891 Sir Hugh Munro published his
famous book, *Table of Heights over
3,000 Feet*, giving his name to all
Scottish peaks over 914 m (3,016 ft),
of which there are 284. In 1901, the
Reverend Robertson invented a sport
which becomes ever more popular –
that of 'bagging the Munroes'. He
bagged, or climbed, them all except
for the Inaccessible Pinnacle in the
Cuillins, which are home to 12 of
the Munroes.

No doubt the best known of all the Scottish islands, Skye, which is about 80 km (50 mi) from top to bottom, has a great many things going for it, not least the most achingly beautiful scenery. Ever since the Victorians discovered the joys of climbing the spectacular Cuillin Ridge, the island has attracted more and more tourists, and this, in the summer months, together with its notoriously changeable climate, is its only downside.

Visited by St Columba in 585 AD, Skye was in the hands of the Norsemen for 300 years before being divided by three Scots clans, who fought over it constantly. Its most famous resident, Flora MacDonald, achieved lasting fame for her help in the escape to France of Bonnie Prince Charlie in 1745, and her grave can be visited at Kilmuir. During the 1800s many families were forced to leave the island due to the disastrous Jacobite rebellion and the clearances. Today, tourism is the backbone of the economy, and a bridge has been built to link the island to the mainland.

The biggest draw is the Cuillin Ridge, which is a fantastic area for climbing and hill-walking, but the northern Trotternish Peninsula is equally inspiring, with amazing coastal views and weird and wonderful rock formations such as Kilt Rock and the 50 m (165 ft) high rock needle, the Old Man of Storr. This last is only a few miles from Skye's main town, Portree – a pretty little place on a deep sea loch.

On the west coast, the Minginish Peninsula is worthy of a visit. If the weather is inclement, or you have had enough walking, drop into the famous Talisker Distillery. Founded in 1830, its single malt whisky was a favourite of Robert Louis Stevenson, and since then it has become the favourite of a great many more people too!

Iona

The island of Iona lies just to the southwest of Mull and is small at 5 km (3 mi) long and about 1.6 km (1 mi) wide. Known as the 'Cradle of Christianity', this may have been a Druidic centre even before the arrival, in 563 AD, of St Columba, an Irish prince, who landed with 12 disciples at what is known today as St Columba's Bay. Until his death in 597 AD, he converted the Scots to Christianity, founding a monastery here and forming a centre of Christian learning and pilgrimage. Centuries later, in 1203, a Benedictine abbey and an Augustinian convent were built, followed by another abbey in the 1500s. During the Reformation Iona was ransacked, and 357 of 360 Celtic crosses were smashed to smithereens. Today, the abbey complex is restored and the National Trust of Scotland maintains the rest.

The main village and ferry port, Baile Mor, is a moment away from the pink granite ruins of the convent, while a little further on stands the 15th century Maclean's Cross. The Street of the Dead, leading to the abbey itself, is a 13th century, red granite street, along which Scottish kings were carried for burial. Here stands the 9th century St Martin's Cross, the finest example of a Celtic cross in the British Isles.

Despite the hordes of visitors – 250,000 annually – Iona is worth exploring. With its fantastic white shell beaches to the north and east, the machair and shingle containing semi-precious stones to the west, and the cliffs and bays of the south with their rounded rocks and green pebbled beaches, there's a particular quality about it, an inexplicable atmosphere. Treeless and austere, the pin sharp light picks out the subtle colours of the rocks, the sands and the sea, which varies from brilliant turquoise to deep purple. Stay for a day or two and let Iona's magic capture you.

POPULATION:
85 (2007)
WHEN TO GO:
At its best from May to September
HOW TO GET THERE:
By ferry from Mull.
HIGHLIGHTS:
The Iona Heritage Centre.
Iona abbey, and the related monastic buildings.
St Oran's Chapel.
Oran's Cemetery, containing the graves of 48 Scottish kings, eight Norwegian kings and four Irish kings.
The views of Mull from the top of Dun I.
YOU SHOULD KNOW:
The former Labour Party leader, John Smith, is buried in Oran's Cemetery. He loved Iona, and his favourite walk was to the Bay at the Back of the Ocean, one of Scotland's loveliest beaches.

Iona Abbey

Islay

POPULATION:
3,700 (2007)
WHEN TO GO:
Any time
HOW TO GET THERE:
By ferry from Kennacraig in West Loch Tarbert, or by air from Glasgow.
HIGHLIGHTS:
The National Nature Reserve at Duich Moss.
The Islay Festival of Malt and Music, held each late May/early June.
The Museum of Islay Life at Port Charlotte.
The ancient burial grounds at Nerabus, containing wonderful medieval gravestones.
The island of Jura, a five-minute ferry journey from Islay, this wild, mountainous island is fantastic for hill walking.
YOU SHOULD KNOW:
Portnahaven, a charming fishing village 11 km (7 mi) south of Port Charlotte, is home to the world's first commercial wave-powered generating station. Known as 'Limpet', it powers 200 homes on the island.

The green, hilly island of Islay was, in medieval times, the capital of the Western Isles. Today, Islay is synonymous with its unique, peaty, single malt whisky, and the island is home to eight separate distilleries. Between them they produce some four million gallons of whisky per year, much of which is exported. Most visitors come for the whiskey trail, leaving the rest of the island relatively unknown. The remainder come for the birds because, between October and April, Islay is a destination on the migration route of thousands of white fronted and barnacle geese, flying south from Greenland for the winter.

Islay is always windy, but fairly mild, and the land is fertile. There is moorland, woods, machair, sea lochs and a rugged coastline with great expanses of beach. Inhabited since Neolithic times, there is much here to interest archaeologists, for example the Kildalton

High Cross, often considered to be the finest in Scotland, which was carved from bluestone in 800 AD. Close to the cross are some remarkably carved, 15th century gravestones, and further on, at Trudernish Point are standing stones.

The island's main centre of population and ferry port is Port Ellen, which was planned and laid out in the 1820s. An attractive town, its own distillery dominates the skyline, though it is no longer operational. Nearby, however, are three very well-known distilleries: Laphroig, Lagavulin and Ardbeg, beautifully situated and fun to visit. At Laphroig you not only see the malting but also the peat kilns. Bowmore, on the east side of Loch Indaal, is Islay's current 'capital,' and home to its eponymous oldest distillery, started in 1779. Port Charlotte, on the west of Loch Indaal is probably Islay's prettiest village, and makes a good base for a few days.

The Paps of Jura mountains seen from a cottage on the north coast of Islay.

Mull

POPULATION:
Just under 3,000 (2007)
WHEN TO GO:
The best months are May to October
HOW TO GET THERE:
By ferry from Oban, Lochaline or Kilchoan.
HIGHLIGHTS:
Duart Castle, one of the oldest inhabited castles in Scotland.
Mackinnon's Cave, the largest in the Hebrides.
MacCullock's Tree – a 50 million-year-old fossilized tree.
Go whale watching.
Visit the Tobermory Distillery for a guided tour and a wee dram.
Walk the white sands of Calgary Bay, an area of outstanding natural beauty.
YOU SHOULD KNOW:
Only 11 km (7 mi) west of Mull, and easy to visit, is the island of Staffa, formed from extraordinary hexagonal basalt columns, and the renowned Fingal's Cave. Visited by endless notables – Queen Victoria, Wordswoth, Keats, Turner, Sir Walter Scott and many more – Mendelssohn was so inspired that he began composing 'Die Fingalshohle' the moment he got back to the mainland after hearing the waves crashing inside it.

Duart Castle, one of the oldest inhabited castles in Scotland

Mull is a remarkable island. Mountainous, but with good agricultural land, it has a mainly rocky coastline indented with sea lochs, one of which, Loch na Keal, cuts in deeply enough to give the island a 'waist'. Mull is the second largest of the Inner Hebrides islands, and the most accessible. It has a long history: mentioned by Ptolemy in the 2nd century AD, fought over against Irish Celts and later, Vikings, it contains dozens of ancient remains, including standing stones and stone circles.

Mull receives many visitors, drawn to the multiple attractions of fabulous mountains, pretty villages, impressive castles and peaceful beaches. The capital, Tobermory, is situated on a lovely bay, lined with gaily-painted stone houses built in the 1780s. Wooded hills, sheltering more homes, rise steeply behind it. In 1588 a ship from the Spanish Armada anchored in the port to stock up on provisions. The story has it that one Donald MacLean boarded the ship to receive his payment but was instead imprisoned in the magazine. He escaped, blowing up the ship as he went, and sinking both it and its treasure. Many attempts to retrieve the treasure have been made, but little ever found.

There is a great deal to do here. You can climb Ben More, 966 m (3,169 ft), go hill walking, caving, hunting, shooting and fishing. You can look for red and fallow deer, otters and the extremely rare Scotch burnet moth. If you haven't seen enough wild hen harriers, buzzards and golden eagles, you can see all these and more at Wings Over Mull, where demonstrations by trained birds are given. If it's raining – which it might well be – take the short trip on the miniature steam train that trundles from the ferry port of Craignure to the Victorian Torosay Castle with its terraced gardens and walkway bordered by Venetian statues.

The Small Isles

Collectively known as the Small Isles, Eigg, Rhum, Muck, Canna and Sanday are tranquil gems, situated to the south of Skye. The dominant feature of Eigg, (pronounced egg) the Sgurr of Eigg, is a basalt peak formed from columnar lava, which rises to 393 m (1,297 ft) from the plateau which makes up most of the rest of the island. In 1997 the islanders managed to buy Eigg from its owner, having launched an appeal and formed a partnership with the Highland Council and the Scottish Wildlife Trust.

Rhum is the largest and most mountainous of the islands, and is a Scottish Natural Heritage nature reserve. Permission has to be sought before visiting, but once there, you can trek the nature trails and enjoy glorious scenery. The flora and fauna here are special – the spotted orchid is an endemic sub-species. Rhum has its own herd of ponies, as well as Highland cattle, feral goats and red deer, and it is twitcher heaven, especially since the SNH have successfully reintroduced the magnificent white-tailed sea eagle, its wingspan exceeding even that of the golden eagle, which can also, occasionally be seen.

Muck is a miniscule – just 3 km (2 mi) by 1.6 km (1 mi) – privately owned, gorgeous island. In spring the machair is a blanket of wild flowers, and the beaches glitter with white shell sand. At Gallanach Bay, such bliss, you can watch otters and porpoises play.

Canna and Sanday are joined by a footbridge, and the area between them forms the best harbour in the Small Isles. Owned by the National Trust for Scotland, Canna is run both as a bird sanctuary and a farm, and visitors to the island come to walk. Originally wooded with rowan and hazel, spruce, pine, oak, larch and other trees have been introduced. Puffins and Manx shearwater breed on the western cliffs, and altogether 157 bird species have been recorded here.

POPULATION:
Eigg: 78; Rhum: 30; Muck: 34; Canna and Sanday: 16
WHEN TO GO:
Any time, but May to September is possibly best.
HOW TO GET THERE:
By ferry from Mallaig
HIGHLIGHTS:
Massacre Cave and Cathedral Cave (especially if a Mass is being said) on Eigg.
Kinloch Castle and the Bullugh Mausoleum on Rhum.
The views over the Small Isles from the top of Ben Airean on Muck.
The Celtic Cross and ruins of St Columba's Chapel on Canna.
YOU SHOULD KNOW:
Ferries to the Small Isles do not operate on Sundays.

The Sgurr from Galmisdale on Eigg

Coll and Tiree

Coll and Tiree are situated out in the Atlantic Ocean, to the west of Mull. Low lying and pretty remote, they were once one. Both much the same size, about 19 km (12 mi) by 5 km (3 mi), treeless and windswept, they boast the record number of sunny days in Scotland. These days Tiree attracts numerous windsurfers each October for the Tiree Wave Classic event.

If Coll is shaped like a fish, its village, Arinagour, is situated on the west of the gill that is Loch Eatharna, a sheltered anchorage. A village of little, whitewashed cottages, this is where half the island's population lives, and where the shops and post office are. Two 'castles' both called Breachacha, stand on the southwest coast, one dates from the 15th century, while the other is from 1750. To the west of the castles is a huge area of vast sand dunes, and two golden sandy bays. Coll's highest point is Ben Hogh, on the summit of which is an enormous boulder, balanced precipitously on three small boulders, and said to have been placed there by a giant.

Tiree's expanse of fertile machair was once known as 'the breadbasket of the Inner Hebrides'. Today the population survive on crofting and tourism. The island is known for its 'black' and 'white' houses – the black ones have drystone walls, rounded corners and thatched roofs set with the walls for wind protection. The white houses have had their walls cemented and whitewashed and the thatch replaced with corrugated iron. There are also 'spotty' houses, where only the mortar has been painted white.

The Ringing Stone, to the west of Vaul Bay on the north coast, is a large boulder covered with ancient markings. When struck by a stone, it produces a strange, metallic tone. Legend has it that if it ever breaks in two, Tiree will disappear forever beneath the waves.

POPULATION:
Coll: 172; Tiree: 750 (2002)
WHEN TO GO:
Best between April and November
HOW TO GET THERE:
By ferry from Oban, or by air from
Glasgow to Tiree.
HIGHLIGHTS:
The RSPB Reserve at Calgary
Point, Coll.
Walk the beach at Crossapol Bay, Coll.
Visit Dun an Achaidh an ancient fort,
and see the standing stones and cairns
near the road running west from
Arinagour, Coll.
Dun Mor Vaul, the remains of an ancient
broch (a circular stone fort) near Vaul
Bay, Tiree.
The Island Life museum at
Sandaig, Tiree.
The Skerryvore Lighthouse Museum –
tribute to the building of the
magnificent Skerryvore Rock lighthouse
that stands in the ocean some 16 km
(10 mi) southwest of Tiree.

Stones hold the thatched roof in place on this Tiree cottage.

Arran

Cosily nestled in the Firth of Clyde between Ayrshire and Kintyre, is the island of Arran. This is the largest, (at roughly 32 km (20 mi) long by 16 km (10 mi) wide) and southernmost island in Scotland, and the most accessible of them all. People have been holidaying here since the early 1700s, and tourism is still Arran's most important source of income.

Arran, however, is not just a convenient holiday island - it also mimics Scotland as a whole. The north has harsh, high mountains, deep, lonely glens and a small, scattered population, like the Highlands, whilst the warmer, gentler south has moors, forests, some agricultural land and several sandy beaches. The island contains a wealth of archaeological remains, not surprisingly since people have lived here for thousands of years – Britons, Romans, Norsemen, they all left their mark.

Situated on the east coast, on a broad bay backed by hills is Brodrick, Arran's main town and ferry port. To the north of the bay, beneath the highest hill, Goat Fell, stands Brodrick Castle, with notable gardens that include one of Europe's finest collections of rhododendrons. At the northern tip of the island is Lochranza, a charming village with the ruins of a 13th century castle standing on a promontory. The northern half of Arran is visually stunning golden eagle territory. The bare granite peaks and fabulous, wild scenery provide terrific hill walks and climbing.

In the west, Machrie Moor is known for its neolithic sites – there are six stone circles on Arran. Lamlash and Whiting Bay on the south east coast are both resorts, but the best beaches are further south and quite difficult to reach. Arran has many outdoor attractions, not least a road that runs all around it – a siren's call to cyclists.

A mountain stream flows through North Glen Sannox.

POPULATION:
5,000 (2007)
WHEN TO GO:
Any time, but it's probably best from April to October
HOW TO GET THERE:
By ferry from Ardrossan.
HIGHLIGHTS:
The week-long Arran Folk Festival, held every June.
The Machrie Moor Standing Stones and Fingal's Cauldron.
Torrylinn Cairn, a 4,000-year-old tomb.
Torrylinn Creamery, where you can see the cheese-making process and buy Arran cheese.
YOU SHOULD KNOW:
Just north of Whiting Bay, a ten-minute boat trip away, is Holy Island, the 7th century home of St Molias. Bought by the Samye Ling Tibetan Buddhist order in 1991, the plan is to create Europe's largest spiritual sanctuary on the island. Visitors are welcome but are asked to abide by the Five Golden Rules of Buddhism.

The Orkneys

The Orkneys consist of some 70 islands and islets lying a hop, skip and a jump to the north of John o' Groats, where the North Sea and the Atlantic meet and clash in the Pentland Firth. Apart from Hoy, the islands are low, fertile and surprisingly green, with barely a tree to be seen, and the coastal scenery is spectacular. Despite benefiting from the Gulf Stream's warming influence the islands are windy, and in autumn and winter suffer from incredibly violent storms.

Splitting naturally into the North Isles, the South Isles and, between them the major island, known as Mainland, only 16 islands are inhabited. Historically, the Orkneys have been inhabited since the Stone Age, as the many fascinating relics clearly show. Closely linked with Norway for centuries, they only became part of Scotland in 1471.

Mainland has two main towns, Kirkwall, the capital, which stands at the narrowest point of the island, and Stromness, on the south-western shore. This is a truly picturesque port, its many sandstone jetties a visible reminder of the time when it was a base for first the Hudson Bay Company ships and then the Davies Strait whaling fleet. Kirkwall is both larger and less immediately attractive, though it does have a spectacular medieval, sandstone cathedral.

To the southeast, Mainland is joined by causeway to several smaller islands, including Burray and South Ronaldsay. To the southwest, Hoy juts from the sea, its famous sea stack, the Old Man of Hoy, a draw for rock climbers from around the world.

Orkneys' North Isles include Shapinsay, Rousay and Westray, each with its own attractions. North Ronaldsay is the most northerly and isolated of all, and has a unique, almost pioneering atmosphere. On the migration route of many rare birds, a permanent Bird Observatory was established here in 1987.

POPULATION:
Just under 20,000, with 85 per cent living on Mainland (2006)
WHEN TO GO:
Spring and summer, when the islands are carpeted with wild flowers and the moors and cliffs are alive with birds.
HOW TO GET THERE:
By ferry from the mainland, or by air.
HIGHLIGHTS:
Mainland's Maes Howe, Europe's most impressive Neolithic burial chambers.
Mainland's Skara Brae, the extensive remains of a Neolithic village.
Dive the shipwrecks at Scapa Flow, Mainland.
North Ronaldsay's New Lighthouse – designed by Alan Stevenson in 1854, this is the tallest land based lighthouse in Britain.
The remarkable and moving Italian Chapel on Lamb Holm, built out of Nissan huts, scrap metal and driftwood by Italian prisoners of war during World War II. Masses are still regularly held here.
Mainland's Standing Stones of Stenness and the extraordinary Ring of Brodgar.
YOU SHOULD KNOW:
Scapa Flow is a great natural harbour with an extraordinary naval history. For the first half of the 20th century it was the Royal Navy's main base, with up to 100 warships at anchor at any one time. At the end of World War I the entire German fleet was interned here, and scuttled by its commanding officer. Between the wars the largest salvage operation in history took place, but there are still 15 German ships and one U-boat on the seabed.

Waves crash against Yesnaby Castle Stack.

Fair Isle

Skroo Lighthouse

Lying halfway between the Orkneys and The Shetlands, Fair Isle is a tiny, isolated island, with a population of about 70 souls. Just 4.8 km (3 mi) long and 2.4 km (1.5 mi) wide, it is probably the windiest of the British Isles.

In the first half of the 20th century, evacuation of the island was considered, but the ornithologist, George Waterson managed to buy it and founded the Bird Observatory there in 1948, effectively saving it. In 1954, he passed Fair Isle to the National Trust for Scotland. This is a paradise for birds, ornithologists and twitchers, and each year hundreds of birders flock here when some particularly rare species makes an appearance.

The majority of the population inhabit the southern end of the island, as this is where the only crofting land is available. Fair Isle Crafts, an island cooperative, produces the famous Fair Isle knitwear, the profits from which have funded the island's wind and diesel electricity generators. Other crafts such as ship building and fiddle making are thriving.

The north and west of the island have the finest and most dramatic of scenery. Steep, red sandstone cliffs rising from the water have been pounded by the waves and battered by the wind into convoluted shapes cut by narrow inlets and caves, while rock arches and sea stacks litter the coastline. On the east coast, the 135 m (446 ft) promontory of Sheep Rock thrusts its way into the sea.

As for the birds, some 345 different species have been recorded here, the highest number in Britain. Any number of sea birds can be seen, great colonies of them, including puffins and skuas, and the sound of thousands of birds communicating with each other is just amazing. Fair Isle is on several migration routes, and the Bird Observatory is one of Europe's most important ornithological centres.

POPULATION:
About 70 (2004)
WHEN TO GO:
April, late June to early September and late October for bird watching, and late October for rare migrating birds.
HOW TO GET THERE:
By air or by ferry from May to September.
HIGHLIGHTS:
The George Waterson Memorial Centre, May to mid-September. The North and South lighthouses.
YOU SHOULD KNOW:
The two lighthouses were built in 1892 by the Stevensons. Both were automated in 1998; the South Lighthouse was the last manned lighthouse in Scotland.

Mainland

POPULATION:
17,550 (2001)
WHEN TO GO:
The best months are probably April to September – and don't forget that during the summer months the Shetlands never really get dark.
HOW TO GET THERE:
By air or ferry
HIGHLIGHTS:
The Folk Festival, every April/May.
The Fiddle and Accordion Festival, every October.
Stanydale Temple, an impressive Neolithic roundhouse.
The island of Mousa and the wonderfully preserved Mousa Broch, a 2,000-year-old defensive tower.
The Shetland Library and Museum in Lerwick.
YOU SHOULD KNOW:
The festival of Up-Helly-Aa is held on the last Tuesday in January, and a version of it has been held since Norse times. Celebrating the rebirth of the sun, this is a fire festival, and hundreds of people in fancy dress ritually burn a replica Viking longship.

Physically closer to Norway than to the Scottish mainland, and reflected in the history and many of the place names, Mainland is the largest of the Shetland Islands, and is connected by bridges to the small, narrow fingers of Trondra, West Burra and East Burra. The Shetlands have been inhabited since forever, and were an essential base for the Vikings from which to strike at Ireland, Scotland or the Isle of Man. Mentioned in many Icelandic sagas, they were first mortgaged to King James III of Scotland, then annexed by him in 1472.

Lerwick, the Shetlands' capital, is a thriving, grey stone town, set on a protected natural harbour. At one time the largest herring port in northern Europe, Lerwick languished for decades during the 20th century, until the discovery of off-shore oil during the 1970s raised its profile once again. Nearby, a mile west of town, is the ancient, fortified site of Clickimin Broch, a Bronze Age settlement that was occupied from the 7th century BC to the 6th century AD.

The former capital, Scalloway, only 10 km (6 mi) from Lerwick, is dominated by Scalloway Castle, built in 1600. The town's museum tells the story of the Shetland Bus, the name given to the Norwegian resistance operation of World War II that brought refugees to safety and returned with weapons and fighters.

Mainland has some spectacular scenery, wild moorland ending in dramatic cliffs that plunge into the sea beneath, beautiful lochs and inlets – this is a great place for walking or cycling. The far southwest is close to the RSPB Reserve and an unusual shell and sand isthmus, the largest in Britain and popular with land-yachters. The southern tip of the island has another bird reserve, another Stevenson lighthouse and Jarlshof, the most impressive archaeological site in the archipelago, inhabited continuously from the Bronze Age to the 17th century.

Waves break against the rocky coastline around Sumburgh Head.

Foula

If you find yourself tipping up at Foula, then you are probably either the owner of a boat, or an island 'collector', for this wee speck in the ocean is the most remote of inhabited British islands. Foula rises 22 km (14 mi) west of Mainland, in the midst of the turbulent waters of the Atlantic.

Foula has long been inhabited – recently, the remains of a stone circle was found at Da Heights, in the north, with an alignment to the midwinter sunrise. Conquered by Norsemen in 800 AD, they settled on the reasonably fertile, eastern coastal strip. People here are proud of their Norse heritage, as their culture and traditions bear witness. The last person here who spoke Norn, the old Norse dialect, died in 1926 and a local tradition is the observance of the Julian calendar, meaning that Christmas is on January 6th and New Year on January 13th.

To the west of the two main settlements, Ham, where the ferry docks, and Hametoun, further south, moorland rises to five great peaks, running most of the length of the island. In the west, the Kame is a magnificent cliff, the second highest in Britain, which rears straight up from the waves beneath, and from which, on a good day, you can see all the way from Unst to Fair Isle. Further south is the sinister vertical chimney, Sneck o'da Smallie, that drops right down into the sea – some say all the way down to Hell.

Foula is a great place for birds – 250,000 of them, including the largest colony of great skuas in Britain. Artic terns wheel and screech in the sky, and the cliffs are alive with puffins, guillemots, razorbills and fulmars. Red-throated divers inhabit every small loch on the island, and many rare birds have been spotted here, especially during the spring and autumn migrations.

POPULATION:
31 (2007)
WHEN TO GO:
The summer months are best, but spring and autumn bring migratory birds. Travel to Foula depends on the weather – and even if you arrive on the right day, you might not be able to leave as planned.
HOW TO GET THERE:
By air or sea from Mainland.
HIGHLIGHTS:
The panoramic view from the top of The Sneug.
Spot pods of killer whales, porpoises and seals.
YOU SHOULD KNOW:
There are fearful reefs around Foula, and many ships have foundered here, including *Titanic*'s sister ship, *Oceanic*, which was stranded in 1914, and disappeared completely within 14 days. The 'smiddy' at Ham sells objects made from copper salvaged from her.

Wild Shetland ponies

Unst

POPULATION:
1,067 (2007)
WHEN TO GO:
April to September
HOW TO GET THERE:
By ferry from Mainland via Yell.
HIGHLIGHTS:
The ruins of Muness Castle.
Unst Boat Haven and Heritage Centre
The Valhalla Brewery.
Bobby's bus shelter – a most eccentric,
fully furnished bus shelter on the
outskirts of Baltasound.
YOU SHOULD KNOW:
In 1700 a sea eagle stole a baby girl
from her home on the hill above Nor
Wick Bay, and took her to the island of
Fetlar. A young boy saw her being
deposited in the eagle's nest and was
able to rescue and return her to her
family. They later married and lived on
Yell. This is believed to be a true story.

Unst is the most northerly inhabited British island and third largest of the Shetlands. At 19 km (12 mi) long and 8 km (5 mi) wide it contains diverse terrain due largely to its complex geology. Large swathes of serpentine and metagabbro broken with schists form the eastern side, while the west is gneiss, studded with occasional garnets, underlying the peat moorland. To the south there is limestone and to the north east talc – the only talc mine in Britain.

Unst, like others of the northern islands, has spectacular cliffs, cut by inlets and guarded by sea stacks and sea arches, and beautiful, lonely sandy beaches. It also has rolling, grassy, heather-clad hills, peat moors, freshwater lochs and fertile land, and has been inhabited since the Iron Age, as can be seen in the many ancient archaeological sites. One of its two standing stones, Bordastubble, is the highest in the Shetlands.

There are two National Nature Reserves here. The most unusual, Keen of Havar, is a sub-Arctic stony desert, composed of serpentine scree, a greeny-greyish blue stone that is home to a number of minute rare plants, including frog orchids and mouse-eared Edmondston's chickweed, which grows nowhere else the world.

To the west of Burra Firth, a deep inlet on the north coast, is Hermaness, a bleak, rugged headland that is home to about 140,000 nesting seabirds – huge colonies of fumars, guillemots, kittiwakes, gannets and even great skuas. From the headland you can see the amazing rock lighthouse of Mukkle Flugga, a heroic feat of construction performed by David Stevenson in 1858. Here too is Britain's most northerly golf course. In Baltasound, the main town on Unst, you can send postcards from the most northerly post office as well as enjoy the beer from the most northerly brewery.

The bleak, rugged headland of Hermaness

Zealand

POPULATION:
1,950,000 (2006)
WHEN TO GO:
May to September
HOW TO GET THERE:
The easiest way is to fly direct to Copenhagen.
HIGHLIGHTS:
UNESCO World Heritage Cathedral, Roskilde.
Tivoli Gardens, Copenhagen – world famous funfair.
Kronborg Castle, Helsingør (Elsinore) – one of northern Europe's most important Renaissance castles, where Shakespeare's *Hamlet* was set.
The old port town of Koge.
The castle of Vordingborg.
Louisiana Museum of Modern Art, Humlebaek – a renowned collection.
YOU SHOULD KNOW:
You can easily take a trip into Sweden while you are in Zealand by simply crossing the Öresund – ferries run round the clock or you can drive across the recently built bridge, inaugurated in 2000.

According to Norse mythology, Zealand was originally a piece of Swedish mainland that the goddess Gefjun stole from the king and transported out to sea to give to the Danes. At 7,031 sq km (2,715 sq mi) Zealand is the largest island of Denmark, separated from Sweden by the narrow strait of the Öresund.

The north of the island is known as 'Royal North Zealand' because of its associations with the Danish monarchy. In July every year the Royal Palace at Fredensborg on Lake Esrom is thrown open to the public. The main cities of Copenhagen, Helsingor and Roskilde (the former capital) are all in the north of the island; this is where you will find most of the major historical sights and urban thrills. In complete contrast, South Zealand is countryside – virgin forest and farming land with small sleepy towns, narrow lanes, medieval churches and white sandy beaches.

Copenhagen, on the eastern shore, spilling over onto the neighbouring island of Amager, is one of Europe's most delightful capitals with its palaces, historic squares, Frederiksberg Park, and the vibrant port of Nyhavn where Hans Christian Andersen once lived. In the harbour sits the Little Mermaid, the national symbol of Denmark.

Glaciation has left its traces all over the island in the form of a gentle landscape of fertile moraine valleys and pebble ridges, lakes, fjords and peninsulas, all carved out during the Ice Age meltdown. You are never far from a sandy seashore or a picturesque fishing village and there are charming towns like Hundested with its bustling port or Frederiksvaerk with its canals.

Zealand is an island of many aspects with a strangely compelling Viking charm about it. Just when you think you've seen it all, you realize that you've barely skimmed the surface and that there is always something more to be discovered here.

The Castle of Frederiksberg

Lolland

Known as Denmark's 'South Seas Island', Lolland is 1,243 sq km (280 sq mi), the third largest island in the Danish archipelago. It has an irregular coastline indented by fjords and a picturesque rural landscape rich in cultural monuments. Winding country roads lead through the finest farmland in Denmark, passing small villages and glorious beechwoods, manor houses and medieval churches to a coast of white sandy beaches. At the heart of the island is the Maribo Lakes bird sanctuary – one of the most important nature reserves in Denmark, where sea eagles breed.

This is an island for sports and nature lovers. As well as golf courses and riding schools, there are miles of lanes for cycling and superb swimming, fishing and boating facilities. The Navskov Fjord in the east of the island, covering more than 50 sq km (30 sq mi) and dotted with islets, is a favourite yachting area, while the best bathing beaches are to be found along the south coast – long stretches of clean white sand with a shingle sealine and safe shallow water.

The largest town on the island is the east coast port of Navskov at the head of the fjord. It still exudes a charming 16th century ambience with narrow cobble-stoned lanes leading down to the harbour, an old apothecary shop in the market square, half-timbered houses and the Gothic Church of St Nikolai. There are several other atmospheric old market and port towns such as Maribo, Bandholm and Rodby. There is an extraordinarily beautiful, strange late-summer light in Lolland which has always attracted artists to the island. It is celebrated in an annual autumn cultural event – 'Lys over Lolland' – well worth an out of season visit.

Farmland in Saeland on Lolland

POPULATION:
68,224 (2006)
WHEN TO GO:
April to October
HOW TO GET THERE:
Ferry to Rodbyhavn from Puttgarden, Germany or
to Tars from Langeland, Denmark; or by road – through the tunnel under the Guldborgsund, route E47 from Copenhagen via Falster.
HIGHLIGHTS:
Storstroms Art Gallery, Maribo.
Boat trip to the nearby small islands of Asko, Fejo and Femo.
Nakskov – see the Russian submarine U-359 and find out about the Cold War years.
Oreby Mill.
Knuthenborg Safari Park – the largest in Europe.
Engelsborg – the early 16th century castle and shipyard.
YOU SHOULD KNOW:
Thanks to a huge drive by the local community, with central government support, more green energy per inhabitant is generated here than anywhere else in the world. All electricity and 75 per cent of heating needs on the island are provided by local renewable resources.

Fejø

POPULATION:
611 (2005)

WHEN TO GO:
May to September – particularly beautiful in mid-May when the island erupts into a huge cloud of scented blossom.

HOW TO GET THERE:
The hourly ferry service from Kragenas on Lolland takes 15 minutes.

HIGHLIGHTS:
Fejø kirke – late 12th century church, one of the oldest in Denmark.
Dybvig Vavn – harbour and boatyard where you can see traditional fishing boats being built.
Østerby forge – old blacksmith's, looking just as it has done for hundreds of years.
Fejø Museum – to find out more about the island history.
A plate of local lamb salami washed down with a glass of Fejø cider.
Ferry trip to the neighbouring islands – you will find yourself charmed by the swallows. Every spring they migrate from Africa to travel to and fro with the island ferry, making a living by begging titbits from the passengers.

YOU SHOULD KNOW:
There is not much accommodation on Fejø – a village inn, a farmhouse B&B, and six rental cottages; or you can camp.

The harbour at Fejø

One of several tiny islands off the north coast of Lolland, Fejø is an idyllic rural backwater of fruit trees, sand and sea that has, so far, managed to escape the scars of mass tourism. The island is just 16 sq km (6 sq mi) of low-lying, rich clay with a 30 km (19 mi) coastline of gently sloping sand beaches – perfect for swimming, kayaking and windsurfing. It is inhabited by warm-hearted people who live from the produce of their smallholdings and the proceeds of their apple and pear orchards. Fejø apples are the best in Denmark and every year boxes from the latest harvest are sent to the Danish Royal Family.

The first written records of Fejø's history are 13th century, although there is plenty of archeological evidence of human habitation from 10,000 BC onwards. In the 17th century, while under Swedish occupation, the last bit of forest was cleared to make way for agricultural land. The islanders eventually acquired their own freehold, liberating themselves from the dominance of the large landowners of Lolland, and by the early 19th century the island population had reached its height of 1,500 inhabitants – sufficiently large to maintain a doctor and midwife.

Although most of the island is given over to fruit farming, there is some lovely wild walking and riding country at Skobnakken, on the north coast, and Skalo, a 100 hectare (250 acre) salt-meadow islet approached by a causeway where wading birds roost and cattle roam free. There are two charming villages of traditional thatched cottages – Vesterby, where the ferry comes in, and Østerby with its old boatyard – each with a picturesque harbour and jetty. Despite its tiny size, Fejø is a wonderful place for farm and beach holidays, with plenty of activities to suit children and adults alike.

Funen

The third largest Danish island, lying between Jutland and Zealand, Funen has 1,125 km (700 mi) of varied coast – broad, sandy beaches interspersed with grassland reaching to the sea line and stretches of steep cliff with magnificent views over the Baltic. The low-lying, undulating countryside is dotted with more than a hundred fairytale castles, sumptuous manor houses, historic churches and windmills. It is one of the loveliest regions of Denmark.

The island's cultural centre is Odense – a city with a thousand years of history, nowadays best known for being the birthplace of Hans Christian Andersen. Wandering around the ancient town centre, you can easily conjure yourself into a fairytale. In the summer, the city buzzes with lively, round-the-clock street life and a warm, friendly atmosphere emanates from the many bars, cafés and music venues round the main square.

The historic coastal towns are well worth seeing. The east coast port of Nyborg, one of the oldest towns in Denmark and former capital, has a magnificent medieval castle near the marketplace. Faaborg, on the south coast, is particularly beautiful with its 17th century half-timbered, pastel coloured merchants' houses. There is also a wonderful art museum and some of the island's best beaches. The southern port of Svendborg is the gateway to the cluster of small islands off the coast. Just to the west is Skovsbo Strand where the famous playwright, Bertolt Brecht lived and worked for some years.

Funen is a relaxed rural paradise where the pace of life is slow and nothing seems to have changed for centuries. It is little wonder that it is called the 'Garden of Denmark'.

POPULATION:
447,000 (2006)
WHEN TO GO:
May to September
HOW TO GET THERE:
From Copenhagen – the Great Belt Bridge, a combination bridge and tunnel, connects Funen with Zealand by road and rail. A staggering feat of engineering, it is worth crossing just for the sake of it.
HIGHLIGHTS:
Egeskov Castle and Gardens – a Renaissance castle built on oak pillars in the middle of a lake.
Valdemars Slot – a 17th century Baroque castle.
Mads Lerches Gard, Nyborg – built in 1601, this mayor's house gives a wonderful insight into 17th century life.
H.C. Andersen's Hus – a museum dedicated to the fairytale writer's life and works.
Odense City Museum – a genuinely interesting city museum tracing Odense's history back to its Viking past.
YOU SHOULD KNOW:
The famous 'time warp' island of Aero is just off the south coast of Funen and is well worth a visit. Its capital Aeroskobing is an 18th century town preserved intact and the entire island is a picture-book cliché – but none the less charming for that.

Egeskov Castle

Bornholm

POPULATION:
43,040 (2006)
WHEN TO GO:
May to September
HOW TO GET THERE:
Fly or take the overnight ferry from Copenhagen. Alternatively, take a ferry or catamaran from Ystad (Sweden).
HIGHLIGHTS:
Rundkirkes – four medieval round churches.
Ertholmene (Christiansoe) – Denmark's easternmost point, a 17th century island fortress with fewer than 100 inhabitants, 20 km (13 mi) to the northeast.
Bornholm Art Museum, near Gudhjem.
Gronbechs Gard, Hasle – historic merchant's house transformed into an exhibition and cultural centre.
NaturBornholm, Aakirkeby – cultural and natural history centre designed by visionary Danish architect, Henning Larsen.
Eating warm smoked herring from the fish smokehouses of Aarsdale or Hasle.
YOU SHOULD KNOW:
If you want to visit Bornholm in June or July be sure to book accommodation well in advance. Although the island is a little-known international tourist destination, it is extremely popular among the Danes.

In the middle of the Baltic, some 100 km (60 mi) off the coast of Zealand, a solitary granite outcrop suddenly rises out of the sea. Bornholm is one of the oldest visible rocks in the world, formed by volcanic activity more than a thousand million years ago.

This idyllic little island is 588 sq km (227 sq mi) of rolling hills covered in a patchwork of farms, forests and heathland crisscrossed by more than 200 km (125 mi) of paths – a paradise for cyclists and hikers. Sandy beaches stretch all along the southern shore while towards the north the coastline grows increasingly rugged with small sheltered coves nestling between dramatic rock formations.

Bornholm appears to have been inhabited since at least 3600 BC and everywhere on the island there are reminders from the past – traces of Neolithic and Bronze Age settlements, strategically placed medieval runic stones and churches, picturesque old fishing villages and hamlets. The island's history is a turbulent one, attested to by the fact that the largest fortress in Northern Europe has been standing here since the 13th century. The massive Hammerhus was erected on the northern tip of the island, affording a sweeping view of the surrounding seas and Swedish coast whilst protected from a land attack by a deep wooded valley.

The unusual quality of light here, with only four hours of darkness in summer, has long attracted Danish artists to the island. There is also a thriving music scene – in the summer months the island comes alive with village fêtes and a jazz festival.

The main town of Ronne, on the west coast, is a lively 700-year-old port with cobbled streets and a beautiful church. Whether you are seeking natural beauty, culture or entertainment, this beautiful island provides them all.

One of four medieval round churches to be found on Bornholm. These churches were also used as fortresses – probably to ward off Slavic pirates.

Samsø

Once a Viking assembly ground and site of a legendary battle against the 'Berserkers', a terrifying warrior cult, Samsø lies 15 km (9mi) off the east coast of Jutland. It is only 28 km (18 mi) long with a complex, indented coastline linking its two distinct parts, North Island and South Island. These ancient islands were joined at the end of the Ice Age, when the melting glacier waters washed up deposits that created the landscape around Stavns Fjord – a strikingly beautiful conservation area of more than 1,500 hectares (3,700 acres) of low-lying heathland, meadows and reefs. The highest point at 64 m (210 ft) is Ballebjerg in North Island, a region of rolling countryside ideal for cycling and walking, while South Island is open farming land gently sloping to the coast, dotted with picturesque villages, manor houses, and harbours with lovely views over the Baltic.

Samsø is renowned as an ecological 'green dream' island. The entire community has pulled together to demonstrate that it is perfectly possible to be carbon neutral. Electricity is produced by the island's windmills and an offshore wind farm, which between them are able to generate more than enough energy to supply the inhabitants and offset the fuel used by the island ferry service; any excess is sent to the mainland. The islanders heat their water by means of solar panels at community heating plants as well as individual straw-burning central heating systems. All the island's vehicles are run on home-grown biofuel.

Apart from a few days every July, when visitors pour in for the annual Music Festival, Samsø is a remarkably uncrowded, eco-tourist haven in which to unwind, admire the scenery, and experience the hospitable tranquillity and relaxed pace of Danish island life.

Timber-frame houses on Samsø

POPULATION:
4,124 (2006)
WHEN TO GO:
Early May to early September
HOW TO GET THERE:
Ferry from Hov, near Aarhus, Jutland to Saelvig, Samsø or from Kalundborg, Zealand to Kolby Kaas, Samsø.
HIGHLIGHTS:
The Samsø Labyrinth – officially the biggest maze in the world with a path 5,130 m (16,830 ft) long, was opened here in 2000.
Ballen fishing village.
Nordby – the prettiest village on the island with timbered houses and distinctive church belfry.
The harbour at Langor.
YOU SHOULD KNOW:
The island is famous for its early new potato and strawberry crops. In June and July young people come from all over the EU for strawberry-picking holidays.

The Faroes

Battered by the North Atlantic seas between Iceland and Norway, the Faroes are a group of 18 hauntingly beautiful islands. The archipelago covers a total area of 1,399 sq km (545 sq mi) and has a relatively benign climate, warmed by the Gulf Stream. The scenery is breathtaking: rugged basalt mountains up to 880 m (2,880 ft) high are thickly carpeted with impossibly green grass, incised everywhere by waterfalls, rivers and fjords. Sheer cliffs soar upward, ledges teeming with colonies of puffins, gannets and storm petrels. Extraordinary skies constantly transform the landscape, playing kaleidoscopic tricks of light and shade; sea mists descend suddenly, only to give way moments later to streams of sunshine.

Little is known of the islands' early history. Irish hermits settled in the 7th century, introducing sheep and oats, and by the 9th century Vikings had landed. The islands fell under Norwegian control but, from the 14th century, increasingly fell under the sway of Denmark. Today, although still Danish territory, the islanders take pride in their independence of spirit and inimitable forms of Viking language, singing and dance.

The Faroes are still mercifully tourist-free. Many of the inhabitants still live by sheep farming and fishing, in isolated crofts and old fishing villages of brightly painted houses with turf roofs. The charming port of Torshavn, Europe's smallest capital, is on Streymoy, the largest island. A bridge and tunnel connect Streymoy to nearby Eysturoy and regular ferries ply between all the islands. The westernmost island of Vágar has the best tourist facilities and Sudoroy, two hours to the far south, is perhaps the most beautiful of all.

It is impossible not to succumb to the eerie enchantment of these captivating islands, where the only sounds are of birds calling, water trickling over rocks, wind lashing across the headlands, and the breakers dashing the cliffs at the outer edges of the world.

POPULATION:
48,317 (2006)
WHEN TO GO:
May to September, unless you're an exceptionally hardy type.
HOW TO GET THERE:
Regular year-round car ferries from Denmark, Norway, Scotland and the Shetlands. Alternatively, fly to Vágar – the only island flat enough for an airport.
HIGHLIGHTS:
Historic villages – Sandavágur on Vágar and Gjógv on Eysturoy.
Rinkusteinar – 'rocking stones' near village of Oyndarfjordur on Eysturoy.
Lakes of Vágar – Fjallavatn and Hviltkinnavatn.
14th century Magnus Cathedral and the oldest inhabited wooden house in Europe, both to be found at the lovely village of Kirkjubøur on Streymoy.
Vestmanna on Streymoy – Boat trip through gorges to spectacular bird cliffs.
Beinisvøro Mountain on Sudoroy.
YOU SHOULD KNOW:
Although the Faroes are part of the Kingdom of Denmark, they are moving towards full self-government – they already have their own parliament, flag and language, and are not part of the EU.

A typical fjord village on the Faroe Islands

Terschelling

POPULATION:
4,702 (2007)
WHEN TO GO:
June to September
HOW TO GET THERE:
Ferry from Harlingen (The Netherlands) to West-Terschelling.
HIGHLIGHTS:
Oerol Festival – 10 days every June when around 50,000 people suddenly descend on the island for this incredible cultural event. The whole island becomes an open-air venue for inspired drama, music, art and dance. The villages, dunes, woods, barns and boathouses are used as improvised stages and galleries.
The 16th and 17th century Commodore Houses built for the commanders of the whaling fleets, near Brandaris lighthouse – a 16th century firehouse, 54 m (177 ft) high – in West Terschelling.
The historic village of Midsland.
De Boschplaat Nature Reserve – though there is restricted access during breeding season, from mid-March to mid-August.
YOU SHOULD KNOW:
Don't bother to bring a car here. There are plenty of buses and taxis but the best way of getting around is by bike.

*One of Terschelling's
superb beaches*

The Dutch island of Terschelling snakes its way along the Dutch coast for 29 km (18 mi) creating a barrier between the North and Wadden Seas. It is the most accessible of the West Frisian Islands, with miles of unspoiled shoreline and a wonderfully varied landscape for its size – only 4 km (2.5 mi) across at its broadest point.

The north coast is a white-sand beach, up to 1 km (over 0.5 mi) wide, backed by windswept dunes with a hinterland of pine forest. To the south is salt marsh – lush meadowland where cattle graze and cranberries grow. The entire eastern end of the island is a nature reserve for migratory birds. From all over the island there are beautiful views – southwards across the mottled earthy shades of the marshes and light-reflecting shallows, northwards over the seemingly endless expanse of the North Sea to a distant horizon.

The main town, West-Terschelling, is a charming port on the south coast, steeped in maritime history. The islanders are renowned for their seamanship, resilience and resourcefulness, and for hundreds of years made fortunes in the whaling industry as well as playing a major role in the 17th century Anglo-Dutch naval trade wars. Only in the 19th century, with the re-routing of shipping, did they turn to farming and, more recently, tourism for their livelihood.

There are walks, cycle paths and bridleways that take you all over the island, superb beaches for sand yachting and surfing, and plenty of opportunities for sailing or just mucking around on a boat. Although Terschelling can be busy in the summer, the island rarely feels crowded. There is a real sense of being at one with nature here – a wonderful sense of freedom and space under vast, ever-changing skies.

Heligoland

The tiny island of Heligoland, 70 km (44 mi) off the German coast, towers up unexpectedly, its dramatic rust-coloured cliffs rising up to 61 m (200 ft) high out of the grey emptiness of the North Sea. It is a geological mystery – although its bedrock is limestone, like the White Cliffs of Dover, the island itself is composed of layers of sandstone, unlike any other rock form in the region.

In the 19th century, this 1 sq km (0.4 sq mi) wedge of land was considered the healthiest place in Germany and attracted the attention of artists and writers, Kafka and Goethe among them. The invigorating sea air has an exceptionally low pollen count and the climate is mild, with more sunshine than the mainland and long balmy autumns. Even in winter the weather is rarely cold – fig and mulberry trees flourish here. A ten-minute boat ride to the north-west is a low-lying islet known as The Düne, part of the main island until 1720, when a violent storm caused a huge surge that permanently separated it. It is uninhabited apart from a seal colony, and there are two idyllic, long sandy beaches for bathing and camping.

Amazingly, considering its remoteness, there are signs of prehistoric habitation here. From the 7th century it was populated by Frisians, who named it "Helgyeland" (Holy Land). Although the islanders were semi-autonomous, surviving by fishing, smuggling and wrecking ships, sovereignty alternated between Denmark, Britain and Germany. In 1890, the British swapped it with Germany in return for Zanzibar, but after World War II, the Royal Navy evicted all the inhabitants and tried to bomb it to bits. Although they failed, the force of the explosions left a huge dent in the landscape – a permanent reminder of Heligoland's turbulent past.

POPULATION:
1,650 (2006)

WHEN TO GO:
The best weather is from May to October but the island is interesting at any time of year.

HOW TO GET THERE:
The ferry from Cuxhaven takes two hours. Passengers are met by fishing boats which take them to land.

HIGHLIGHTS:
Lange Anna – a freestanding rock stack 47 m (135 ft) high, Heligoland's symbol.
Lummenfelsen (Guillemots' Rock) – the smallest nature conservation area in the world, where you can watch seabirds and seals.
Unterland heated open-air seawater swimming pool.
Heligoland Historical Museum – to find out more about the history, culture and traditions of this island.
Marine Biology Institute Aquarium – for a close-up look at plants and creatures lurking in the North Sea.
Eating Heligoland lobster – expensive but worth every penny.

YOU SHOULD KNOW:
Heligoland is a tax-free zone so all goods you buy there are at bargain prices, but check your allowances – you may be stopped at customs on re-entering mainland Europe.

An aerial view of Heligoland

A narrow guage railway runs from Hallig Langeness to Oland.

Wadden Sea Hallig Islands

POPULATION:
About 290 (Langeness 100, Hooge 120)
(2004)

WHEN TO GO:
The tourist season is May to September but nature lovers and endurance enthusiasts will find the Halligen fascinating at any time of year.

HOW TO GET THERE:
Ferry from Schlüttsiel or Dagebüll, or from the North Frisian Islands of Amrum, Föhr or Sylt.

HIGHLIGHTS:
The lighthouse on Hallig Oland – the only lighthouse in Europe with a thatched roof has a lantern painted red on one side and green on the other to show ships at which point they must change course.

The Königspesel, Hooge – a richly ornamented room with all its original fixtures and fittings in a traditional house showing how people lived on the Halligs.

View from Nordemarsch Lighthouse, Langeness.

Museums, Langeness.

YOU SHOULD KNOW:
The seasonal migrations (spring and autumn) in this globally significant birding region are amazing to experience – the skies are choked with wild duck, crane and geese – more than 3 million birds whirling overhead. Be warned – the tides are notoriously tricky and you should never wander around the mudflats without local guidance.

The Halligen (salt lands) are not strictly islands; they are patches of raised saltmarsh created by tides and floods, without any sea defences. There is huge tidal variation in this part of the North Sea and in winter, at high tide, the islands virtually disappear, while at low tide you can walk across the mudflats to adjacent Halligen. Of the hundreds that once existed only ten remain, scattered over an area 20 x 30 km (12 x 19 sq mi) in the Waddenmeer National Park of Schleswig-Holstein. They are part of the same extraordinary tidal ecosystem that has effected the creation of the North Frisian Islands.

The surreal scenery of these 'dreams floating on the sea' is unforgettable – eerie mirages often appear to be hanging in thin air as land, sea and sky all merge. It is a testament to human ingenuity that the islanders have found a way of inhabiting the continually shifting marshlands. For centuries, they have protected their buildings and livestock against the ravages of the *landunder* (storm tides) by building their houses on *warften* (raised dwelling mounds). Throughout the 17th and 18th centuries they grew enormously wealthy through seafaring, whaling and cattle-rearing. However, the region never recovered after a devastating flood in 1825 destroyed 90 per cent of the old farmsteads and drowned hundreds of the islanders.

Hallig Langeness is the largest at 9.5 sq km (3.7 sq mi) but Hooge at 5.7 sq km (2.2 sq mi) with its church and ten *warften*, is considered the 'Queen of the Halligen'. The other Halligen are bird sanctuaries. The solitude and tranquillity you will find on these strange islands confronts you with a stunning sense of the forces of nature as you immerse yourself in the power of the sea and revel in the scarcely believable sunrises and sunsets.

North Frisian Islands

The North Frisian Islands were once part of the mainland 'geest' – a sandy heathland ridge stretching along the North Sea coast of Germany. Centuries of battering by powerful tides have created the islands of Sylt, Amrum and Föhr, all still in a continual process of changing size and shape. They are part of the unique ecosystem of tidal flats, beaches, sandbanks and saltmarsh along the low-lying coastal region of Schleswig-Holstein.

Sylt is still linked to the mainland by a causeway at low tide. This 'island with a thousand faces' is the largest at 100 sq km (62 sq mi) and most sophisticated of the North Frisians. The west coast is a dramatic landscape of cliffs, dunes and crashing waves, renowned for its 40 km (25 mi) of sandy beaches; to the east, open heathland gives way to stark, wild saltmarsh. There are excellent sports facilities, beautiful walks and cycle paths here and the island is a fashionable holiday retreat for German celebrities.

The least populated island is Amrum – only 20 sq km (12 sq mi) – a remote paradise to immerse yourself in nature. You will find the widest sandy beach in Europe here, with spectacular dunes up to 32 m (105 ft) high. Föhr at 82 sq km (50 sq mi) is the greenest of the three islands, a mecca for birdwatchers, with a single seaside resort, the town of Wyk, and sixteen tiny hamlets.

A visit to the North Frisians is a step into another world with its own distinctive folk culture. The inhabitants still speak their own Frisian dialect, wear traditional costume, and live in picturesque villages of neatly thatched houses with immaculate, brightly coloured cottage gardens. The islands are a fascinating, relatively little-known region of Northern Europe resonating with the unique history of these hardy but hospitable, seafaring people.

POPULATION:
Amrum 2,300; Sylt 21,000; Föhr 8,800 (2005)

WHEN TO GO:
The tourist season is May to September but nature lovers and hardy souls will find the islands interesting throughout the year.

HOW TO GET THERE:
Ferry from Schlüttsiel or Dagebüll and ferries running between the islands.

HIGHLIGHTS:
Bronze monument to poet Heinrich Heine by Arno Breker – City Hall, Sylt.
Historic houses in Westerland, Sylt.
Frisian Cathedral of St Johannis and 12th and 13th century churches, Föhr.
Frisian Museum, Föhr.
Frisian village of Nevel, Amrum.

YOU SHOULD KNOW:
Only walk across the mudflats if accompanied by a local expert guide. The tides are notoriously tricky and on even the sunniest day sea mist can descend without warning.

Rügen

POPULATION:
73,000 (2001)
WHEN TO GO:
Rügen is beautiful at any time of year. The tourist season is April to October.
HOW TO GET THERE:
By boat – either across the Strelasund on the car ferry from Stahlbrode to Glewitz, or across the Baltic from Scandinavia (Sweden, Bornholm or Lithuania) to Sassnitz. By car – drive across the Rügendamm drawbridge (built by the Nazis in 1936); though the bridge is not always down and there are often tailbacks. By plane or train.
HIGHLIGHTS:
Chalk Coast Boat Trip – sets off from Binz pier along the coast and to the neighbouring islands. See Wissower Klinken – the bizarre chalk promontory, subject of a famous painting by Caspar David Friedrich.
Castle Raiswiek – a neo-Renaissance castle now a hotel. Well worth taking a peek inside and enjoying its beautiful gardens, a horticultural masterpiece.
Königsstuhl National Park Centre – on top of the cliff – gives you an overview of the island and has some s tunning exhibits.
Jagdschloss Granitz – a historic hunting lodge in the Granitz woods, more like a palace. From its tower roof you have a panoramic view over the island.
Kap Arcona – the northernmost point of Germany, painted by Manet. Here is the picturesque fishing village of Vitt, a watchtower, and two lighthouses.
YOU SHOULD KNOW:
The Nazis built a huge spa complex 3km (2 mi) long on the coast near Binz as part of their *Kraft durch Freude* (Strength through Joy) plan of controlled leisure time for the nation. Eight identical buildings were erected to provide holiday accommodation for 20,000 German workers. The plan never came to fruition but these chilling buildings (used later by the Soviets as an army barracks and now listed as a striking example of Third Reich brutalist architecture) are a spooky tourist curiosity known as the 'Kolossus of Prora'.

Until 1990, the enchanting Baltic Sea island of Rügen was behind the Iron Curtain, inaccessible to Westerners. It is the largest of Germany's islands, nearly 1,000 sq km (385 sq mi) with a 570 km (356 mi) long, wiggling coastline of steep cliffs and broad, shallow inlets. It is a picture-book paradise of white cliffs, wide sandy beaches, woods and moorland with romantic castles, old brick churches, reed-thatched fishermen's huts and old-fashioned towns of *fin de siècle* villas.

The main town of Sassnitz, the 'Gateway to Scandinavia', is a bustling, colourful port with the longest seawall in Europe, a 1,450 m (4,750 ft) long mole where you can spend hours watching the boats come in – from passenger liners to fishing skiffs. Nearby is Jasmund National Park where the sheer chalk cliffs, renowned for their extraordinary peaks and chasms, plunge dramatically into the sea. Behind the steeply sloping hinterland of dense beech forest, there is unusually diverse woodland, including wild apples and pears. There are several idyllic resorts dotted around the coast in the south east – old spa towns with impeccably clean, safe beaches that still preserve their 19th century charm, offering health cures ranging from fasting to medicinal chalk meals.

In complete contrast to the woods and hills of the eastern side, the scenery of the West Coast National Park is a low-lying area of saltmarsh wetlands, tidal flats and peat bog with an incredible variety of flora and fauna. The lagoons here are a haven for thousands of migrating cranes and geese – a birdwatcher's paradise.

You get around the island along the 'green tunnels' – ancient avenues where the trees meet overhead. Cycling down these leafy country alleys, hemmed in by greenery, you begin to believe the islanders' pagan tales of dwarves and giants. Rügen is undoubtedly magic.

The white cliffs of Rügen

Hiddensee

This sliver of land, clinging to the west coast of the island of Rügen on Germany's Baltic coast, has preserved all the charm that attracted so many famous early 20th century artists, writers and intellectuals to its shores, including Einstein, Freud, Brecht and Thomas Mann.

Hiddensee is less than 17 km (11 mi) long and just 250 m (820 ft) wide at its narrowest point. The landscape is exceptionally beautiful with incredibly varied scenery – precipitous rocks contrasting with the wide sandy beaches, meadows and saltmarshes, huge dunes, sandflats and undulating heathland. Large parts of the island are only just above sea level while the highest point is 72 m (236 ft). The broad white sands along the western and north coasts, stretching for some 16 km (10 mi), are some of the finest anywhere in the world; only the chilly Baltic wind reminds you that you are not in the Caribbean.

No cars are allowed here. Transport is provided by horse-drawn carriages or bicycles. The main town, Vitte, is a small port on the east coast just to the north of the Dünenheide, a beautiful area of heathland which in August is a blazing purple carpet of heather. The only other sizeable settlement is the unspoilt little village of Kloster on the north coast, which grew from a Cistercian monastery established in 1296.

Hiddensee has a faintly bohemian atmosphere – a retreat for individualists seeking peace from the madding crowd. It is still known as an artists' haunt and you will stumble across small galleries and roadside exhibitions wherever you go. Although there are loads of day-trippers in the summer months, it is not hard to escape by walking just that little bit further to find yourself surrounded by a seemingly unending expanse of sea and sky with a feeling of unbounded space.

Lighthouse on Hiddensee

POPULATION:
About 1,300 (2006)

WHEN TO GO:
The high season runs from May to September but the island caters for tourists throughout the year and hardy types will enjoy the bleak winter landscapes just as much as, if not more than, the summer ones.

HOW TO GET THERE:
Ferry from Stralsund on the mainland (2 hours) or Schaprode on the island of Rügen (45 mins) several times a day.

HIGHLIGHTS:
Inselkirche – the island church and graveyard in Kloster.
Schluckwieck – the highest point on the Dombusch cliff. Brilliant panoramic view from the lighthouse.
Gellen sandbank – shifting sand dunes in the south of island for bird watching, part of the Boddenlandschaft National Park, which has Europe's biggest crane roost – around 30,000 fly in every August.
Neuendorf – a charming village of whitewashed houses and the most southerly settlement on the island.

YOU SHOULD KNOW:
You must book months in advance to get a hotel room between June and August; camping is not permitted anywhere on the island. There is a daily 'spa tax', collected by your landlord or, for day-trippers, by the ferry company.

Reichenau

Reichenau Island lies in Lake Constance in southern Germany. For more than 1,000 years, the Benedictine complex here was one of the most important religious centres in Europe. It has been listed by UNESCO as a World Heritage Site because it is the best-preserved ancient monastery north of the Alps and played an influential role in the development of Christian art.

The monastery was founded by St Pirmin in 724, who settled there with 40 of his followers. The abbey soon became a flourishing concern, one of the most important religious and cultural centres in Europe. It was here that the famous monastery plan of St Gall was drafted, an influential set of rules for monastery construction and one of the most important documents of Western monasticism. The monastery's abbots were government officials at the Court, educators of the royal princes, diplomats and envoys of the Emperor.

In the 10th and 11th centuries, the Abbey was home to a famous scriptorium, where the monks produced magnificent illuminated manuscripts for influential customers such as Emperor Otto III and Heinrich II. They used gold, silver and purple inks, and precious metals and ivory for the bindings. Many of these beautiful works can still be found in some of the most revered libraries in the world.

During its heyday, the Reichenau abbey collected many precious relics which remain to this day in their splendid shrines in the treasure vault. On certain holy days they are carried across the island in festive processions. The most important relics include those of the evangelist Mark, the jug from the wedding at Cana, and the relic of the Holy Blood.

The abbey's bailiff lived in a two-storey stone building which was raised by two more storeys of half-timbered construction in the 14th century. Today housing the island's museum, this is one of the oldest half-timbered buildings in southern Germany. As well as telling the story of the monastery, it has exhibits about life on this tranquil island and the surrounding area.

The religious sites on Reichenau

Island are not just limited to the monastery. In the 9th century, Abbot Hatto built a church devoted to St George on the island. The nave still displays some beautiful Ottonian murals showing the miracles of Christ, the only remaining murals of their kind painted before the year 1,000 north of the Alps. Above the entrance to the crypt lies a tomb in which the relics of St George are kept.

The church of St Peter and Paul, a three-nave basilica, was built in the 12th century in Reichenau-Niederzell. Its east towers were added in the 15th century, and the western porch in the 16th or 17th century. The semi-circular apse features a painting from the 12th century, depicting Christ with the Apostles. Other murals were added over the following years, and today there remain scenes from the Passion in the southern side chapel and the porch, and scenes of St Peter in the chancel. In 1756 the church of St Peter and Paul was renovated in the Baroque style, with flat ceilings and Rococco stucco, a style which is still evident today.

Vineyards on Reichenau

Traditional deckchairs on the beach at Usedom

Usedom

POPULATION:
76,500 (2005)
WHEN TO GO:
May to September
HOW TO GET THERE:
Fly to Usedom. Road/rail from Szczecin, Poland or Zussöw, Germany.
HIGHLIGHTS:
Wasserschloss, Mellenthin – Renaissance castle.
medieval churches in the villages of Benz, Morgenitz, Zirchow and Liepe.
Kamminke – a small fishing port.
Coastal views from the villages of Ziemitz and Neeberg.
Stolpe Castle.
Swinemünde outdoor market in the Polish part of the island.
YOU SHOULD KNOW:
In World War II the island was used as a forced labour and prisoner of war camp. The small village of Peenemünde, renowned as the 'cradle of space travel', was the centre for the V2 missile tests that formed the basis of all modern rocket technology.

Germany's second largest island, Usedom is a picturesque, low-lying landscape of rolling meadows, woods and lakes dotted with thatched cottages, windmills and medieval churches. The island, 445 sq km (175 sq mi) in area, lies to the northeast of the lagoon of Stettin at the mouth of the River Oder, the border between Germany and Poland. Inhabited since the Stone Age, first by Slavic tribes then Viking pirates, Usedom was German territory until 1945, when Poland was granted sovereignty over the eastern end and the entire German population were expelled to the west of the island.

The sunniest spot on the North German coast, Usedom is perfect for seaside holidays, with over 100 km (60 mi) of cycle paths, 400 km (250 mi) of walking trails and 40 km (25 mi) of flawless sandy beaches. The northwestern hinterland is one of the most beautiful parts, where the woodland descends steeply to the coast and you are likely to spot sea eagles circling overhead. In the south east of the island there are some lovely stretches of gently undulating scenery enclosing lakes and sleepy villages.

The island's historic spa towns exude an unmistakeable air of culture and luxury. There are rows of magnificent 19th century mansions, elegant Art Nouveau villas, and stately piers more than 300 m (985 ft) long. Ahlbeck, Heringsdorf and Bansin, three former fishing villages on the north coast, are amongst the oldest of the Baltic 'bathtub of Berlin' seaside holiday resorts. They are popularly known as The Dreikaiserbäder (The Emperor's Three Baths), the haunt of the cream of 19th century society and international names like Johann Strauss, Tolstoy and Maxim Gorki. Today, strolling along the promenades, it takes little imagination to transport oneself back into the glamour of the past, retracing the footsteps of European nobility.

Mainau

Emerald water and snowy mountain peaks provide a scenic backdrop to this glorious 45 hectare (111 acre) 'island of flowers', one of three very different but equally interesting islands in Lake Constance. The lake, which is Central Europe's third largest, lies on the Rhine between Germany, Switzerland and Austria.

Visitors to Mainau invariably have all their expectations surpassed when they find themselves landing in one of the most beautiful parks of Europe with a fairytale Baroque palace at its heart. The island gardens are an implausible jungle of exotic vegetation, citrus trees and orchids, made possible by the mild microclimate of the lake. The overwhelming variety of different species, colours and fragrances is an incredible sensory experience – you can relax under palm and sequoia trees, explore winding side paths, catch the scent of orange blossom in the air mingled with all sorts of less familiar fragrances, and dazzle your eye with a kaleidoscope of colour before wandering through parkland to an incredible view over the lake itself.

For 500 years Mainau belonged to the Order of the Teutonic Knights, a Roman Catholic military religious order formed at the end of the 12th century to fight in the Crusades. In 1853 it was bought by the Grand Duke of Baden, who built the palace as a summer holiday residence. The island passed through his heirs until 1932, when it was inherited by Count Lennart Bernadotte, a philanthropist who had a philosophy of environmentally friendly gardening for the benefit of humanity. He initiated the idea of the garden in its present form, set up the Bernadotte Foundation to run it, and opened Mainau to the public.

Count Bernadotte died in 2004, but the island is still run by the Countess on behalf of the Foundation according to his principles; the garden of Mainau is not only breathtakingly beautiful but a model of sound ecological practice.

POPULATION:
Family and retainers
WHEN TO GO:
April to September
HOW TO GET THERE:
Regular boat services from Konstanz or the island of Lindau.
HIGHLIGHTS:
Butterfly House – the largest in Germany.
Palm tree glasshouse.
Schlosskirche.
Mainau Children's Land – Waterworld.
Lake Constance Natural History Museum.
Rhine Falls, Neuhausen – the largest waterfall in Europe, 60 km (38 mi) away.
YOU SHOULD KNOW:
The head gardener or one of his team is always available to dispense gardening tips and ecology advice to visitors.

Tulips on Mainau Island

Hiiumaa

POPULATION:
11,900 (2003)

WHEN TO GO:
May to September, although hardy
eco-tourists will be prepared to
brave the icy Russian winds for the
sake of the winter scenery and
wildlife.

HOW TO GET THERE:
Ferry from Rohuküla, mainland
Estonia, takes 90 minutes; or from
Triigi, on the neighbouring island of
Saaremaa, takes 60 minutes. (No
boats in winter when the sea is iced
up). Twice-daily flights from Tallin to
Kärdla airport, takes 45 minutes.

HIGHLIGHTS:
Kopu lighthouse – more than 500
years old, this is the third oldest
working lighthouse in the world;
36 m (120 ft) high, it was built as a
seamark to prevent the local
wreckers and pirates from leading
ships aground on the reefs.
Sääre Tirp – a 3 km (2 mi) long
tongue of land stretching into the
sea, one of the most beautiful places
on the island.
Pühalepa Church – one of the oldest
on the island, with a stone pulpit
dating from the 13th century.
Rebastemäe Nature Trail – passes
through highest point of Hiiumaa.
Ristimägi – Hill of Crosses – a sandy
hillock where traditionally any
passer-by leaves a cross made out of
any material at hand.
Kassari Peninsula – wooded
landscape with secluded beaches,
thatched chapel, windmill
and orchard.

YOU SHOULD KNOW:
Estonians regard the island as a sort
of national nirvana. Many artists and
musicians have retreats here.

Hiiumaa is a bleak but breathtakingly beautiful island in the Eastern Baltic, a nature reserve that covers an area of just under 1,000 sq km (390 sq mi). It is Estonia's second largest island, separated from the mainland by a 22 km (14 mi) wide strait and surrounded by some 200 deserted islets and reefs where, over the centuries, hundreds of ships have come to grief; today there are seal colonies, a rarity in the Baltic.

More than half the island is covered in pine, birch, and spruce forest with many rare plant species – a haven for wildlife; elks, deer, wild boar, and even lynxes may be spotted. The 320 km (200 mi) coastline of meadowland, peat moor, juniper shrubbery, and dunes is highly indented with long stretches of isolated sandy beach. Amongst the hundreds of bird species that nest and migrate here are black storks, golden eagles, cranes and avocets. Less than a quarter of the island is farmland and there is only one sizeable settlement, the town of Kärdla.

Kopu lighthouse is the third oldest working lighthouse in the world.

Human settlement on Hiiumaa dates back to around 4000 BC. It was inhabited by nomadic Germanic tribes until the Swedes discovered it around 1300 AD. Eventually the island became Swedish territory until, at the beginning of the 18th century, it was integrated into the Russian Empire. After enduring turmoil in both World Wars, it became part of independent Estonia in 1991. Although little of the island's history has been recorded, there is a strong sense of its seafaring tradition that continues to be handed down from one generation to the next.

For eco-tourists, Hiiumaa is as unspoiled as it gets – a perfect place to commune with nature, explore unusual scenery and escape from the mainstream tourist routes.

Kihnu

Kihnu lies 12 km (7 mi) off the coast of Estonia and is the largest of more than a dozen islands in the reefs and shallows of the Gulf of Riga. It is 16 sq km (6 sq mi) in area with a low ridge running down the middle and only 9 m (30 ft) above sea level at its highest point. The island farmsteads are enclosed by forest, which prevents soil erosion as well as protecting the islanders from the bitter northeast winds. Huge broadleaf trees stand like sentinels in the coastal meadowlands that lead to a 36 km (22 mi) long shoreline of dunes and shifting sands where the scent of juniper is everywhere in the air. The island is a nesting place for hundreds of bird species and the coastal reef is home to the last grey seal colony in the Baltic.

The first historical documents relating to Kihnu date from the late 14th century but excavations show that the island was inhabited – at least, during the summer months – from around 1500 BC. It has at various times been under Danish, Swedish, Estonian, Polish and Russian rule, reflecting the turbulent history of the Baltic. Since time immemorial the men here have been seafarers and fishermen, skilled at woodwork and shipbuilding, while the women are wholly responsible for working the land and keeping alive the rich island culture of music, dance and poetry.

A trip to Kihnu transports you back in time into a fascinating folk culture. The inhabitants speak their own language and wear traditional homespun costume. Each woman makes her family's clothes with intricately knitted, woven and embroidered patterns symbolizing ancient legends. The islanders are symbiotically bound up with their harsh environment, their survival entirely dependent upon cultural loyalty and community sharing. Against all odds, they have managed to hang onto their heritage at the same time as welcoming strangers to their shores.

POPULATION:
639 (2004)
WHEN TO GO:
May to September unless you want a cold weather experience. In winter the island is ice-bound and covered in snow.
HOW TO GET THERE:
Fly or ferry from Parnü on the Estonian coast; in winter, drive across the iced-up sea for an unusual experience.
HIGHLIGHTS:
Lemsi – a fishing village and port.
Kihnu Local Lore Museum – Kihnu's history and cultural centre with an art collection including paintings by acclaimed Estonian artist, Jaan Oad.
Kihnu Orthodox Church – containing the grave of legendary seafarer, Kihnu Jonn.
Kihnu lighthouse.
Juanipäe – St John's Day, summer solstice ritual celebrations on the shortest night of the year, 23 June, with dancing and singing until sunrise.
A trip to the nearby island of Manija to see the huge Kokakivi boulder.
YOU SHOULD KNOW:
The rich cultural heritage and fragile eco-structure of Kihnu are incredibly vulnerable. The island has been declared a UNESCO Masterpiece of the Oral & Intangible Heritage of Humanity in an attempt to minimize the negative impact of mass tourism and assist the islanders in preserving their way of life without selling out to the tourist trade.

Ruhnu

A beautiful, isolated island in the deep-water central part of the Gulf of Riga, 37 km (23 mi) from the mainland, with just one village on it, Ruhnu is a hidden corner of Europe. It is the perfect summer retreat for a backwoods holiday – just over 11 sq km (4 sq mi) of wild pine forest and windswept beaches where you are free to roam in an environment that feels almost untouched by man.

Estonia's only non-coastal island, Ruhnu is the protruding part of an undersea ridge. In the east, the dunes and ridges rise up to 30 m (98 ft) above sea level, while the western shore is low-lying meadowland. Not much is known about the island's early history. Artefacts found here, dating back to 5000 BC, indicate that it was a prehistoric seal-hunting base; so far, traces of six Stone Age settlements have been unearthed. At some point, probably around the 13th century, Swedish settlers arrived and Ruhnu fell under the control of the Swedish Crown. In 1721, like the other islands of the Eastern Baltic, it became Imperial Russian territory. During World War II almost all the islanders were evacuated to Sweden, leaving Ruhnu virtually uninhabited. After the war, it was repopulated by Estonians but a devastating storm in the 1970s led to most of the 400 new residents leaving again. Since 1991, when Estonia gained independence, the island's population has remained small, increasingly boosted in the summer months by western tourists with an eye for adventure.

Ruhnu is an all too rare oasis of tranquillity, an idyllic escape from the rat race. You are surrounded by natural beauty, and as the islanders have not yet become jaded from the effects of mass tourism they are genuinely welcoming to visitors.

POPULATION:
60 (2004)
WHEN TO GO:
May to September
HOW TO GET THERE:
Regular ferry from Kuressaare on the island of Saaremaa, or try finding a boat leaving from one of the mainland ports. Once-weekly flights from Pärnü.
HIGHLIGHTS:
Churches – a remarkable 17th century wooden church standing perfectly intact next to a replacement 19th century stone one.
Ruhnu lighthouse – designed by Eiffel and transported in pieces from France.
Limo beach with singing sands.
Estonian Ruhnu sheep – a distinct breed used mainly for wool.
Ruhnu Museum – to find out more about the island's history and nature.
YOU SHOULD KNOW:
There was until recently a brown bear lurking in the forest, thought to have made its way from the mainland on an ice-floe. It is believed to have returned the way it came since it hasn't been spotted since late 2006, but nobody is quite sure.

A wooden church on Ruhnu Island

Kuril Islands

This chain of 56 volcanic islands stretches for almost 1,300 km (700 mi) like stepping-stones all the way from the Kamatchka Peninsula to Hokkaido, Japan. They form the boundary between the Sea of Okhotsk and the Pacific Ocean and are the summits of undersea stratovolcanoes, part of the Pacific Ring of Fire. Offshore is the Kuril trench, one of the deepest ocean regions of the world, 10.5 km (6.4 mi) deep.

The Kurils are astoundingly beautiful with dense vegetation except at the highest elevations and an amazing variety of spectacular scenery ranging from dramatic volcanic ridges and craters to alpine tundra, meadows and wetland. There are broadleaf woods, coniferous forests, crater lakes enclosed by trees, lush narrow valleys and fast running streams with coasts of steep cliffs, volcanic sand beaches and rocky shores. Many millions of seabirds congregate on every available hummock and cliff ledge during the breeding season, and the seas are rich in marine life including shoals of orcas, Baird's whales, fin and sperm whales, sea otters, sealions and fur seals.

Forty of the islands are volcanically active, with fumaroles, hot springs and frequent eruptions. The remainder are sparsely inhabited, mainly by fishermen scraping a subsistence living in a severe climate of blistering winter winds and summer fogs with the ever-present possibility of earthquakes, tsunamis and sulphurous eruptions. A combination of distance from the mainland, the depth of the ocean and strong currents have been major barriers to plant and animal dispersal so that each island has it own self-contained ecosystem and natural history. The Kurils are in one of the least scientifically explored regions of the world – an eco-adventurer's paradise, full of unique biological and geological wonders.

POPULATION:
16,800 (2003)
WHEN TO GO:
June to October
HOW TO GET THERE:
You need a lot of determination to get to the Kuril Islands. By boat to Kunashir (the southernmost island) from Kushiro, north Japan. Irregular ferry services to the other inhabited islands and a once monthly boat from Korsakov, the southern port of Sakhalin Island, Eastern Russia. To explore the Kurils thoroughly you must charter a boat or join an eco-expedition.
HIGHLIGHTS:
Alaid Volcano – the highest point of the Kurils at 2,339 m (7,672 ft) on Atlasov Island, a near perfect symmetrical cone rising straight out of the sea, considered to be even more beautiful than Mount Fuji.
Tao-Rusyr Caldera, Onekotan – 7.5 km (nearly 5 mi) diameter with lake and dome.
Golovnin Volcano, Kunashir – crater of 4 km (2.5 mi) diameter with boiling lake.
YOU SHOULD KNOW:
The Kurils were discovered in 1634 and first charted in 1739. They were seized by Japan in the 19th century and only returned to Russia at the end of World War II.

An aerial view of the dramatic volcano ridges of the Kuril Islands

Komandorskiye Islands

POPULATION:
750 (estimate)
WHEN TO GO:
May to October – the autumn colour
in September is especially beautiful.
HOW TO GET THERE:
Either as part of a Kamchatka or
Arctic cruise; or, from the city of
Petropavlovsk-Kamchatskiy in Far
Eastern Russia, take a plane or
helicopter to Nikolskoye Airport on
Bering Island.
HIGHLIGHTS:
Commander Vitus Bering's grave –
with bronze bust and tombstone.
Northern fur seal colonies.
Arctic foxes – exquisite but impudent
scavengers who show little fear
of humans.
The deposits of semi-precious stones
in Buyan Bay.
Mushroom and berry picking on
the tundra.
YOU SHOULD KNOW:
The tundra is an extremely fragile
environment where, below the
topsoil, there is a permanently frozen
layer of earth. During the short
summers the melting snow cannot
sink into the ground so it runs off to
form marshy wetlands. The tundra is
a major carbon-dioxide sink – it
absorbs more carbon-dioxide than it
releases. The Komandorskiye Islands
were designated as a Biosphere
Reserve by UNESCO in 2002.

A windswept, treeless archipelago off the coast of the Kamchatka Peninsula in far eastern Russia, the Komandorskiye Islands are the crowns of a huge volcanic ridge under the Bering Sea, connected to the Ring of Fire Aleutian Islands several hundred miles away. These desolate tundra islands are a scientific nature reserve, a land area of some 2,000 sq km (780 sq mi) consisting of Bering and Medniy Islands and thirteen islets. They have a unique ecosystem that supports a staggering amount of rare marine and bird life in terms of both diversity and density.

The islands are named after Commander Vitus Bering, an heroic Danish explorer in the service of Peter the Great. On the homeward journey from Alaska in 1741, he managed to land his damaged ship on what is now Bering Island before dying. The islands were uninhabited until 1825 when the Russian-American Company transported an Aleut workforce to exploit the seal trade. Today a small community of Russians and Aleuts make their living by fishing and ecotourism.

A dark, frozen wasteland in winter, as the days lengthen the tundra gushes into life. Rivers of melting snow stream down the mountainsides, waterfalls tumble over the sheer cliff faces, and the frozen coast is transformed into a magical wetland where a myriad of colours is reflected in watery pools. A grey-green carpet of lichen spreads across the mountain peaks while the lower slopes sprout yellow rhododendrons and long green grasses. Mushrooms of mythic proportions erupt out of the earth and berry bushes drip with fruit. The coastal waters literally teem with whales, porpoises, seals and sea otters, the cliff ledges shelter millions of birds, thousands of salmon spawn in the rivers – an ecotourist dream.

A Northern fur seal

216

Wrangel Island

Wrangel Island is the northernmost World Heritage Site in the world, a bleak and desolate rocky outcrop between the Chukchi and East Siberian Seas north of the Arctic Circle. Ravaged by howling icy winds, snow-covered for eight months of the year and in complete blackout from November to January, this Russian island is nevertheless one of the most valued wildlife habitats on earth.

Unlike the other islands in the Russian Arctic, Wrangel was not extensively glaciated during the last ice age, so its ecosystems are among the richest in the entire Arctic. The island is home to 417 species of plant, and boasts a whole range of different habitats, from Arctic desert and tundra to rich grasslands, marshes and meadows of dwarf species, to mosses and lichens.

The island's coastlines feature high cliffs, swamps and coastal lagoons, and sand or rocky beaches. In the north, the low, tundra plain is punctuated by lakes and rivers, while the south of the island is more mountainous, with the highest peak – Sovetskaya – at 1,096 m (3,595 ft).

The island is almost uninhabitable for humans, but it is paradise for other animals. Here is the largest populations of polar bears in the Russian Arctic, and the world's largest population of Pacific walruses with up to 100,000 in the warmest years. The island is also home to Arctic foxes, the Wrangel lemming and the Siberian lemming, and the waters around the island are feeding grounds for Beluga and Grey polar whales.

Wrangel Island is also a great place to observe colonies of nesting seabirds, with over 100 species coming here to breed. It is the only place in Europe that the Snow goose can be seen nesting.

During the Arctic winter, the island is still and dark with a constantly howling wind. As spring arrives, so do tens of thousands of birds to begin breeding and nesting in the cliffs around the coast. Walruses lie around on the ice floes and rocky spits, and polar bears appear from their dens, complete with newborn cubs. This is a magical time to visit the islands as the tundra is transformed into a kaleidoscope of colour with beautiful flowers bobbing their heads in the breeze.

Ice-filled Arctic waters around Wrangel Island

POPULATION:
Fewer than 100
WHEN TO GO:
July and August
HOW TO GET THERE:
From Anchorage (Alaska) via Provideniya (Russia) on an organized tour.
HIGHLIGHTS:
The polar bears – the island has the highest concentration of polar bear dens in Arctic Russia.
Whale watching.
The nesting seabirds, including the Snow goose – this is a great place to observe the bustling and squabbling colonies raising their young from egg to chick to fledgling.
YOU SHOULD KNOW:
In the first half of the 20th century, human activity and uncontrolled hunting nearly wiped out the wildlife on the island. It is entirely due to the persistence of conservationists that this unique island is now protected.

Franz Josef Land

POPULATION:
Uninhabited
WHEN TO GO:
July to August
HOW TO GET THERE:
On a cruise boat from Spitzbergen
(Svaalbard)
HIGHLIGHTS:
Cape Flora, Nordbrook Island – sea
bird colony and remains of
settlement built by 19th century
Arctic explorers.
Rubini Rock, Hooker Island – home to
thousands of seabirds.
Cape Norway, Jackson Island –
remains of Norwegian explorers
Johansen and Nansen's hut.
Stolichky and Appolonov Islands –
walrus rookeries.
Alger and Wilczek Islands – polar
bears.
YOU SHOULD KNOW:
A trip to Franz Josef Land is an
extreme adventure. It is a Russian
military zone and you can only go
there on an escorted expedition.
Landing on the islands is entirely
dependent on weather conditions.

A strangely compelling world of icebergs, glaciers and the midnight sun, Franz Josef Land is one of the few remaining truly wild places on the planet. It is an archipelago of 191 volcanic islands, indented with dramatic bays and fjords, covering an area of 16,130 sq km (6,290 sq mi) in the Barents Sea, almost entirely within the Arctic Circle. Here is the most northerly point of Europe, only 911 km (569 mi) from the North Pole, at Cape Fligely on Rudolph Island.

A pair of Austrian explorers, Julius Payer and Karl Weyprecht landed here in 1873 and named the archipelago Franz Joseph Land in honour of their Emperor. But Austria never claimed the territory and in 1926 the Soviet Union won a race against Norway to gain sovereignty; it now belongs to Russia. Apart from a meteorological station on Zemlya Aleksandri (Alexandra Land), the westernmost island, the islands are uninhabited. Over a fifty-year period, the highest temperature recorded is 13 °C (55.4 °F) and the lowest -54 °C (-65.2 °F).

In the summer months the icy sea takes on a crazy mosaic appearance. Almost 85 per cent of the land surface is permanently glaciated with an ice layer averaging 180 m (590 ft) thick. The only colour to be seen in this blinding ice-white wilderness is in the extraordinary reds and greens of the lichens and mosses that cling to the stark rocky outcrops. The dramatic scenery is at its most majestic on Champ Island in the centre of the archipelago. Here are the highest cliffs and mountains of the archipelago and extraordinary boulders – perfectly spherical and up to 3 m (10 ft) in diameter. The unforgiving climate supports arctic foxes, walruses, polar bears and beluga whales, and 37 bird species including kittiwakes and fulmars. A trip to Franz Josef Land is a unique and unforgettable experience.

A mountain and glacier in Franz Josef Land

Sakhalin Island

This narrow strip of land only 6 km (4 mi) off the far eastern coast of Russia is 1,000 km (625 mi) long. It lies in some of the most productive fishing waters of the world. The countryside is wild and untouched – it has not even been fully geographically explored. The northern third is a swampy taiga plain but the remainder is a savagely beautiful volcanic landscape with miles of beautiful broadleaf forest where an estimated 3,500 brown bears roam. There are two mud volcanoes, more than 16,000 lakes and some 60,000 rivers and streams teeming with wild salmon.

Sakhalin was already inhabited when Japanese settlers came across from Hokkaido in the early 19th century, attracted by the seas full of fish, whales and seals. They proclaimed sovereignty in 1845, to the chagrin of Russia which negotiated a treaty ten years later dividing the island in half. The Tsar then immediately established a penal colony in the northern swamp and eventually got back the southern part in 1875 by swapping it for the Kuril Islands. The writer and doctor, Anton Chekov spent three months here in 1890 researching the plight of the prison population. He pronounced the prison to be 'hell' and his report into the terrible conditions led to its closure.

The island's capital, Yuzhno-Sakhalinsk is a quirky town, an incongruous mix of quaint wooden houses, concrete blocks and sparkling new office buildings, all within a few moments stroll of untamed woods. The island was only opened up to foreigners in 1990 so the tourist industry here is still very much in its infancy, although growing rapidly. If you have a pioneer spirit and are prepared to rough it a bit, Sakhalin is a dream place for a backwoods nature adventure.

POPULATION:
673,000 (2005)
WHEN TO GO:
June to October when there's a chance of seeing whales. The scenic views are breathtaking in September to October.
HOW TO GET THERE:
Domestic flights from Khabarovsk, Vladivostock, Moscow and Irkutsk. Direct international flights from Seoul or Tokyo to Yuzhno-Sakhalinsk; or ferry, April-mid December, from Wakkanai, northern tip of Japan to the port of Korsakov.
HIGHLIGHTS:
Zhdanko Ridge, Buruny Bay – volcanic rock formations, hardened lava streams, and waterfalls.
Vaidinskaya Cave – karst cave, considered the most beautiful in the Russian Far East.
Velikan Cape – amazing cliffs and rock formations.
A steam train tour of the island.
YOU SHOULD KNOW:
Sakhalin is still a difficult part of the world to get to and to live in, with a harsh climate of bitter winters and sea fog in the short summer months.

Traditional Russian dachas in the Sakhalin countryside

Severnaya Zemlya

POPULATION:
Uninhabited apart from scientific observatories.
WHEN TO GO:
June to August
HOW TO GET THERE:
On an icebreaker ship as part of an Arctic North-East Passage adventure cruise.
HIGHLIGHTS:
Polar bears on Golomyanny Island – where two families of polar scientists have been living and working for the past 16 years.Icebergs in the Red Army Strait. Weird ice formations of the Arctic desert.
YOU SHOULD KNOW:
Global warming is causing the Arctic Sea ice to melt at an extraordinary rate. Over the past two winters the total amount of ice has shrunk by 6 per cent compared to 1.5 per cent over the entire previous decade.

This Arctic archipelago covers a total land area of some 38,000 sq km (15,000 sq mi) nearly half of which is permanently iced over – a frozen wonderland of 17 distinct glacier systems containing ice domes, ice shelves, ice flows and the largest ice cap of the Russian Arctic, 819 m (2,686 ft) thick.

There are four major islands and some 70 small ones with dramatic mountainous scenery, rising to a height of 965 m (3,165 ft) containing lowland areas of arctic desert, tundra and coastal plains. Despite the severe conditions – a mean annual temperature of -16 °C (3.2°F) and six months of the year in total darkness – there is a remarkable variety of plant and animal life. In the short summers the ice-free areas suddenly sprout a strange patchwork of red and green lichens, velvety mosses and bright purple saxifrage. Polar bears trek across the ice floes, and wolves, reindeer, arctic foxes, collared lemmings and arctic hares all manage to survive here, as well as 32 bird species including snowy owls, little auks, and kittiwakes.

The existence of Severnaya Zemlya (North Land) was unknown until 1913. It was the last archipelago in the world to be discovered and is the least accessible group of islands in the Arctic, surrounded by iced-up seas. Boris Vilkitsky, a Russian surveyor exploring the region in an ice-breaker, unexpectedly found himself in the 55 km (34 mi) wide strait (later named after him) that separates the islands from mainland Siberia. This was a momentous discovery: ever since the 16th century explorers had been attempting to shorten the trade route to Asia by finding a North-East Passage from the Barents Sea to the Bering Strait. Today, the journey into one of the least explored and most extreme regions on earth is still an arduous one – a once in a lifetime adventure.

Solovetsky Islands

Less than 160 km (100 mi) from the Arctic Circle in the western part of the White Sea, the Solovetsky archipelago is an ancient place of pilgrimage with a historic UNESCO World Heritage fortified monastery. There are six large islands and countless skerries covering a total land area of 300 sq km (120 sq mi). The climate is relatively mild, benefiting from the Gulf Stream current, and the scenery is extraordinarily varied – hills and pine forests, fens, lakes and birch trees, sandbanks covered in boulders, rocky ridges and sand dunes – a haven for an abundance of flora and fauna.

Solovetsky has a memorable history of both intense spirituality and indescribable suffering. The first permanent settlers were two hermits, Sabbatius and Herman, who arrived on Greater Solovetsky, the largest of the islands, around 1430. They were soon joined by like-minded searchers after solitude and a monastery was founded in 1436. The island gradually grew into an influential religious and political centre, attracting the attention of the Tsar who gave orders for fortifications to be built and a garrison to be stationed here.

The hermits' spiritual dream was beginning to turn into a worldly nightmare. Their monastery became one of the largest and most powerful of the Russian kremlins (fortresses) and by the end of the 17th century it was one of the largest monasteries in the world. Later, as its strategic importance declined, the island became a place of exile and death for political and religious troublemakers, a practice that grew to apocalyptic proportions under Stalin.

Despite the bleakness of its past, there is a hypnotic spiritual quality in the atmosphere of Solovetsky. There are spectacular natural as well as manmade wonders and you cannot help but fall under the spell of the Russian north.

POPULATION:
1,000 (2002)
WHEN TO GO:
June to September
HOW TO GET THERE:
Sea boats from Karelian towns of Kem and Belomorsk. Cruise ship from Moscow and Arkhangelsk. By helicopter from Petrozavodsk or Arkhangelsk, twice weekly plane from Arkhangelsk.
HIGHLIGHTS:
Solovetsky Kremlin – massive walls up to 6 m (20 ft) thick – built of boulders from the beaches, complete with monastic buildings and churches.
The Botanical Garden – wide variety of plants.
Zayatsky Islands – prehistoric sacred labyrinths, burial mounds, medieval church, and bird colonies.
Exploring the intricate canal and lake system in a rowing boat – the canals were dug out by the monks over the centuries.
Belugas Cape – where you can see whales. Muksalma Island Dam – 19th century monks used Muksalma to graze their cattle; to make transportation easier they erected a huge boulder dam about 1 km (0.62 mi) long and 6.5 m (21 ft) wide, an incredible feat of engineering.
YOU SHOULD KNOW:
Under Stalin, the island was made into a gulag (forced labour camp) and hundreds of thousands of prisoners died here. In 1980, when the Orthodox Church was re-established, Solovetsky instantly became a place of pilgrimage. At the 19th century Church of Ascension on Sekirnaya Hill, you can see the Commemoration Cross erected to honour the people executed here.

A view of Solovetsky monastery

Kizhi Island

POPULATION:
300 museum employees (estimate)
WHEN TO GO:
Any time of year
HOW TO GET THERE:
Train from Moscow or St Petersburg
to Petrozavodsk, the capital of
Karelia. Take a hydrofoil (1¼ hours) or
helicopter (25 mins) from
Petrozavodsk. In winter you can take
a snowmobile across the ice. Or take
a cruise ship from St Petersburg
or Moscow.
HIGHLIGHTS:
The iconostasis – mainly 17th and
18th century, stunning display of 104
icons in four tiers surrounded by gilt.
Yamka and Vasilyevo – 18th
century villages.
Church of Lazar – 14th century, the
oldest wooden church in Russia,
transplanted from its original position
on the south shore of Lake Onega in
1960. Chapel of Veronica's Veil – on
the highest point of the island.
YOU SHOULD KNOW:
You cannot stay overnight on Kizhi.
The maximum amount of time you
can spend on the island is 11 hours
(in summertime). There are lovely
places to stay in traditional rustic
guesthouses on neighbouring islands.

*The Church of the
Transfiguration with its
ornate wooden cupolas*

Lake Onega in the wilds of Karelia is the second largest lake in
Europe. It has a surface area of around 9,800 sq km (3,820 sq mi)
and is dotted with more than 1,500 islands and skerries. The Pearl
of Onega is a tiny island of 3 sq km (1 sq mi) in the north of the
lake renowned for its World Heritage Site – an iconic masterpiece of
folk architecture known as the Khizhi Pogost.

The Pogost consists of three buildings made entirely of wood,
without any nails or metal ties. The architectural jewel is the
Church of the Transfiguration – 37 m (120 ft) high with 22 cupolas,
built in 1714 as a spiritual beacon for the Russian colonizers of the
lakeside wilderness. On completion, the master carpenter is said to
have hurled his axe into the lake in triumph exclaiming: 'There has
not been, nowhere is and never will be a church like this!' The
church was designed to be used only in the summer months and, in
1764, the winter Church of the Intercession was erected nearby.
The two churches are joined by a 19th century bell tower, a
replacement for an earlier one. Both individually and together these
three buildings are utterly awe-inspiring. Whatever the angle, their
sublimely beautiful shapes are in perfect harmony with each other,
blending into the surrounding landscape with such sensitivity that it
barely seems possible that they were not all the work of one
visionary genius but were built at separate times by the rustic skills
of the simple peasants of the region.

In all, there are 87 wooden buildings on Kizhi, including 18th
century farmsteads, windmills and chapels, set in centuries old
agricultural land. The whole island is a delightful historical,
architectural and ethnographic monument to the traditional folk
culture of Lake Onega.

Nilov Monastery

Stolbny Island

The island of Stolbny is one of some 160 islands on Lake Seliger in western Russia, about 360 km (225 mi) from Moscow. The lake is a complex system of 212 sq km (83 sq mi) of interconnected lakes, channels and islands, a protected nature reserve surrounded by spectacular wild countryside of hills, fens, pine forest and birch woods, inhabited by moose, brown bears, lynxes and wolves.

In this outstandingly beautiful natural setting, Stolbny, a tiny island 10 km (6 mi) from the southern lakeshore, is remarkable for its enormous monastery, a breathtaking edifice that emerges majestically out of the waters of the lake. Built between the late 16th and early 19th centuries, the Nilova Pustyn Monastery, better known as Nil's Hermitage, is one of the most impressive ensembles of neoclassical architecture in Europe with four 18th century domed churches and an early 19th century cathedral, set in gardens enclosed by an elegant stone embankment.

The origins of the monastery are not altogether clear but according to one story in the summer of 1528, a holy man known for his healing powers and gift of prophecy heard a heavenly voice commanding him to settle on the uninhabited island of Stolbny. He died in 1555 having lived here as a hermit for 27 years. His fame spread and the Tsar agreed to erect a monastery for the glory of God and the service of the people. By 1594 a church and the monks' quarters had been built. The monastery became renowned for its miraculous healings and was once one of the most visited Christian religious centres in the world attracting tens of thousands of pilgrims every year. It is one of the greatest cultural monuments of the Orthodox era.

POPULATION:
A small community of monks.
WHEN TO GO:
May to September, or December to January for breathtaking winter views and New Year Festival.
HOW TO GET THERE:
From Moscow or St Petersburg by train or car to Ostashkov via Tver. From Ostashkov quay take a boat to Stolbny, or drive 25 km (16 mi) beside the lake from where you can reach Stolbny by walking across a narrow wooden bridge and over a small dyke.
HIGHLIGHTS:
The immense Cathedral bell tower – panoramic view over the woods and lake.
Vosdvizhenskaya Church – pure white 18th century church.
A boat trip to explore the other islands.
Ostashkov – one of Russia's prettiest provincial towns.
YOU SHOULD KNOW:
At the outbreak of World War II, when Russia and Germany still had a peace pact, the Bolsheviks murdered all the monks and used the monastery to hold Polish prisoners, almost all of whom were executed in 1940. After this terrible massacre the island was deserted; only in recent years have monks returned to renovate the buildings and re-establish Stolbny as a religious centre.

Olkhon is one of the largest lake islands in the world.

Olkhon Island

POPULATION:
1,500 (2006)
WHEN TO GO:
The peak of the tourist season is from mid-June to mid-August when the weather is warm and dry. The end of May to the beginning of June is cooler but less crowded. For a winter experience, the best month is March. The weather is terrible in October, November and April – to be avoided!
HOW TO GET THERE:
A bus runs five days a week between Irkutsk and Kuzhir, Olkhon, an 8-hour trip including the ferry crossing.
HIGHLIGHTS:
Cape Burkhan – Shamanka Rock, the most sacred site on Lake Baikal with Buddhist inscriptions.
Peschanaya Bay – moving trees in shifting sand dunes.
Museum of Nature and History, Kuzhir.
Lake Khankhoy – the largest of Olkhon's salt lakes, where you can swin and fish.
Cape Sagan Khushun – a dramatic white marble promontory covered in red lichen.
YOU SHOULD KNOW:
Lake Baikal is a UNESCO World Heritage Site. The lake contains as much water as all the Great Lakes of North America combined. Despite its great depth, the water is well-oxygenated providing a unique biological habitat. It is one of the deepest active rifts on earth with sediment on the lake floor more than 7 km (4 mi) thick.

The great watery abyss of Lake Baikal is a huge rift valley in the heart of Siberia formed some 25 million years ago. It is both the oldest and the deepest lake in the world, containing around 20 per cent of the planet's fresh surface water. Olkhon, one of the largest lake islands in the world, is the geographical, historical and spiritual heart of Baikal, separated from the southwestern shore by a treacherous narrow strait near the lake's deepest point of 1,637 m (5,370 ft).

There are plentiful traces of human habitation on Olkhon from as long as 13,000 years ago; 143 archaeological sites have been discovered – rock paintings, burial mounds, settlements, defensive walls and sacred places. The Buryat inhabitants of the island are an indigenous people of Mongolian descent, yurt (tent) dwellers with a rich oral tradition and shamanic religious practices. The island is steeped in native myth and legend.

This beautiful island is 730 sq km (285 sq mi) in area and 72 km (45 mi) long, a wild prehistoric landscape of taiga (primeval fir forest), steppe, salt lakes and sand dunes, formed by the earth's shifting tectonic plates. All along the east coast, craggy mountains rear straight out of the lake up to 818 m (2,680 ft) high, in striking contrast to the rolling southern plain carpeted in wild grasses and aromatic herbs that seems to stretch forever – perfect for horse-riding and cycling. There is one proper village, Kuzhir, and a single main road run the length of the island. The rocky promontories along the western shore enclose deep bays with sandy beaches where you can camp in a yurt and go kayaking and fishing. You really are in the wilderness here: there are no power or telephone lines, no cell-phone reception, and the only electricity is from domestic generators.

Vasilyevsky

When Peter the Great decided to build his capital city at the mouth of the River Neva in 1703 he chose the largest and westernmost of the islands at the river's delta to be at its heart – the 'window by which the Russians might look out into a civilized Europe'. Vasilyevsky was a marshy uninhabited wasteland which the Tsar was determined to transform into his administrative centre, with streets of grand houses running alongside broad canals, modelled on Amsterdam. However, it proved impossible to transport materials, drive piles into the boggy ground and erect buildings at the speed required; the city continued to develop on the mainland and the canal plan was eventually scrapped.

Today, Vasilyevsky forms the northwestern corner of central St Petersburg, just across the river from the Winter Palace. The island is saturated in the city's past, containing many of the oldest buildings, dating from the early 18th century. The southern part is built on a grid with 30 'lines' going from south to north across three main avenues – the only traces that remain of Peter's grandiose canal scheme.

The eastern point where the Neva divides, known as the Strelka (Arrow), is a grassy crescent that was engineered by raising and lengthening the ragged, marshy end of the island and re-shaping it into a perfect semi-circle. Here are some of the grandest historical buildings, including the majestic Stock Exchange, reminiscent of a Greek temple. The Strelka is dominated by the Rostral Columns, 30 m (100 ft) tall red pillars decorated with ships' rostra, built in the early 19th century as a symbol of the naval supremacy of the Russian Empire.

From the Strelka there is a superb vista across the arc of the River Neva to the centre of one of the most beautiful cities in the world.

POPULATION:
1 million (2006)
WHEN TO GO:
Any time.
HOW TO GET THERE:
Fly to St Petersburg.
HIGHLIGHTS:
The historic buildings along the quay, including the Academy of Arts – late 18th century waterfront buildings.
Picturesque cobblestone lanes of terraced cottages washed in pale yellows and ochres.
The Institute of Russian Literature (Pushkin House) and Museum of Literature with manuscripts dating back to the 13th century – originally the Customs House.
Twelve Colleges – a long narrow early 18th century building originally intended to house government offices but taken over by the University.
Lieutenant Schmidt Bridge – the first bridge across the Neva.
The interior of Andreyevsky Cathedral
YOU SHOULD KNOW:
Vasilyevsky is traditionally a student and workers district – a convenient area of the city in which to find relatively cheap accommodation.

The Neva River divides at the Strelka into two channels.

Margaret Island

Lying in the Danube anchored to the mainland by the Arpad and Margaret Bridges, Margaret Island is a wonderful green space between Buda and Pest. This tiny island – 2.5 km (1.4 mi) by 500 m (1,640 ft) has been used for various purposes over the years – a place of religious retreat, stabling for the horses of the Turks (and a home for their women of ill repute), a landscape garden for the royal family of Buda and, since 1869, a public park.

King Bela IV had a convent built here on what then was called Rabbit Island; his 11-year-old daughter Margit became a resident in 1251 (she was canonized in 1943) and now the island is named after her. The north of Margaret Island still has several old religious buildings – the cloister and church of the Dominican nuns, a 13 to 14th century Franciscan church, and the reconstructed Premonstratensian chapel whose tower houses the oldest bell in Hungary. Cast in the 15th century, it was found in 1914 in the roots of a storm-damaged tree, having been hidden from the Turks.

As in mainland Budapest, therapeutic springs make bathing here

a popular activity. The modern Hotel Thermal offers medical treatment facilities, and the Platinus Outdoor Baths in their lovely garden setting are filled with spa water. The Alfred Hajos sports swimming complex was designed by and named after the Olympic gold medalist. An open-air theatre and cinema occupy the south of the island.

Margaret Island is a peaceful, green place; it is car-free, though cycles and horse drawn vehicles are available. It also offers tennis, roller-skating and there are plenty of cafés.

The National Parliament on the Danube, looking towards Margaret Island.

Donauinsel

Donauinsel, which lies within the city area of Vienna, is a man-made island that divides the Danube from the New Danube. It stretches 21 km (13 mi) along the river, but has a maximum width of only 210 m (689 ft). It is used nowadays as a recreational area, but its main purpose is as a part of Vienna's sophisticated flood prevention scheme.

The enormous flow of water down the Danube had always resulted in serious flooding and, in 1870 to 75, work was undertaken to create a managed flood plain. A century later, a revised plan resulted in the dredging of a new river bed; the scheme included plans for the strip of land produced from the material excavated by digging out the 'New Danube' to be used as a leisure facility. This

Fireworks during Donauinselfest

ambitious project was carried out from 1972 to 88 and city dwellers are now able to enjoy sunbathing and swimming on their own beaches – including nudist areas to the north and south of the island.

There is provision for various other forms of exercise including cycling, canoeing and rollerblading, as well as a range of bars, restaurants and nightclubs. There is, in addition, an important ecological aspect to Donauinsel. The northern and southern extremities resemble a wilderness, whilst small areas of water meadow and a mature poplar forest enable a variety of plants, birds and animals to survive in the heart of the city.

HOW TO GET THERE:
U-Bahn station; weekend night buses.
WHEN TO GO:
All year
HIGHLIGHTS:
Copa Kagrana – The Viennese found the beach opptsite the district of Kagran so exotic they nicknamed it after its Brazilian counterpart. Donauinselfest – the annual June party, the largest of its kind in Europe, with up to 3 million visitors.
YOU SHOULD KNOW:
Donauinsel has the world's longest waterslide.

Zitny Ostrov

Extending from Bratislava to Kormano – 84 km (52 mi) – Zitny Ostrov (Rye Island) is Europe's largest river island – so large that most visitors are unaware of being on one. It lies between the Danube and its slower flowing tributary the Little Danube, in the Danubian Plain. Several rivers flow across it and the rich alluvial deposits make it the most fertile land in Slovakia. The island also contains central Europe's largest reservoir of high quality drinking water and it has the warmest and driest climate in Slovakia. A beautiful area of marshes, natural and man-made lakes and rich farmland, the south has been designated a Protected Landscape. The calm waters of the Little Danube provide excellent boating through the alluvial forests; the controversial hydroelectric dam at Gabcikovo may be visited.

Zitny Ostrov has two main towns, both of which have strong Hungarian influences. Dunajská Streda has a majority Hungarian population, though the only reminder of a significant Jewish minority is a 1991 memorial. There is evidence of Bronze Age settlement here. In the late 1990s the town centre was rebuilt with distinctive white buildings topped by towers and elaborate tiled roofs. A large thermal park offers year-round bathing in naturally heated water. Komarno, Slovakia's principal port, lies on the Hungarian border – a bridge leads into Hungarian Komarom, which used to be part of Komarno. Here two thirds of the population speak Hungarian and the street signs are bi-lingual. Europe Place is a large shopping and leisure centre built in a variety of European architectural styles. A native son of Komarno, Franz Lehar is honoured with a biennial music festival, whilst the annual Komarno Days Festival celebrates Slovak and Hungarian culture.

HOW TO GET THERE:
From the capital Bratislava there is a good transport network.
WHEN TO GO:
May to September
HIGHLIGHTS:
The museum of Zitny Ostrov in Dunajská Streda, housed in an 18th century mansion. The exhibits include an excellent presentation of island life.
The fort at Komarno (still in military occupation) offers occasional tours.
Komarno Orthodox Church is the legacy of Serbs who fled the Turks and settled here in the early 18th century.
The watermills on the Little Danube – these wooden pan mills along the riverside have been used for centuries.
YOU SHOULD KNOW:
The former Romantic Officers Casino in Komarno is now the Public Library.

Ile de Ré

POPULATION:
16,000 (winter), 160,000 (summer)
(2004)
HOW TO GET THERE:
Across the toll bridge (near
La Rochelle).
WHEN TO GO:
All year round but it can get very
crowded in high summer.
HIGHLIGHTS:
The 15th century Eglise St-Martin – a
fine Gothic church.
Hotel de Clerjotte – a naval and art
museum.
The Ars-en-Ré Market – for a fine
selection of local produce.
The Phare des Baleines – the views
from the top of this lighthouse are
stunning.
Lileau des Nigres – a maze of
marshes and one of Europe's top
bird-watching sites.
YOU SHOULD KNOW:
From the mid-19th century until
World War II the citadel at St-Martin
was used to house prisoners on their
way to be transported to the
colonies. Most met a swift end; one
resident who didn't was Henri
Charriére, aka Papillon, who
managed to escape on a sack of
coconuts after 13 years of enforced
exile and later went on to write a
bestseller about it.

Just 3 km (2 mi) off France's Atlantic coast, facing La Rochelle, lies the 30 km (19 mi) long Ile de Ré. It is an island of fine sandy beaches, whitewashed cottages, wild hollyhocks, salt marshes and it has a luminosity so delicate it begs to be photographed. Centuries of human activity, principally salt extraction, have shaped the land, turning what was four islands into one. Wine and oysters are now the island's mainstays, its vineyards belonging to the same appellation controlée as Cognac.

Ile de Ré is one of the sunniest parts of France. Its climate is mild and the vegetation has an almost Mediterranean feel. Palm trees grow readily, and the contrast of white houses against the deep blue sky evokes some Greek village adrift on the Atlantic. A toll bridge from the mainland was completed in 1987, which was to change the character of the island irrevocably. However even the heavy flow of summer visitors and second-homeowners has not been able to dent Ré's charm and in the winter the island is lived in and tranquil. Once across the bridge you have a choice of two routes. The north road goes to the pretty harbour of St-Martin-de-Ré; the south road leads you through farm villages and onto long beaches. Eventually both roads merge, leading to the more rugged western cape of the island.

The island can easily be toured in a weekend, but you will need more time to explore the proper way, by bicycle. Long before the bridge brought carloads of tourists, Rétias, as the islanders are known, conducted their lives on bikes, and they still do. A remarkable system of narrow lanes connecting villages, vineyards and beaches takes you where cars can't.

Just a baguette in the basket is all that is needed to complete this typical view of island life.

Ile d'Ouessant

From the old Breton Enez Eusa meaning Island of Terror, Ile d'Ouessant is an untamed, craggy, hauntingly beautiful island in the English Channel. The most westerly point of European France and roughly 7 km (4.4 mi) long and 4 km (2.5 mi) wide, it has long been a beacon for ships entering the Channel and is home to the world's brightest lighthouse.

Ouessant, or Ushant in English, is a flat-topped island with spectacular cliffs all round. Its central plateau, averaging up to 60 m (195 ft) above sea level, offers easy walking and cycling. For walkers, there are few paths and you will have to navigate your own way through beds of heather and mossy grassland, but the bouncy turf is guaranteed to put a spring in your step.

Traditionally the sea provided the islanders with both employment and resources, and with the men folk away for extended periods it was left to the women to tend the fields and harvest the seaweed. The insides of houses are richly adorned with wooden panels and much of the furniture is made from driftwood. The sea is also crucial to the climate of the island, it is warm in winter, (February can be warmer than on the Riviera) and cool in summer because of its exposure to the prevailing westerly winds.

The island is a convenient stopping-off point for migrating birds, although nesting places on the cliffs are restricted by high waves. The wild weather also throws many birds off course and over 300 species have been identified by the local ornithological centre.

Although no longer isolated, as testified by the thousands who arrive by ferry in high summer, a few local traditions continue. Women still make intricate lace crosses in memory of men lost at sea and the local sheep are free to wander as they please. However when they are caught they are often made into the mouth-watering local dish *ragout de mouton*!

Créac'h lighthouse

POPULATION:
1,000 (2005)
HOW TO GET THERE:
By ferry from either Port de Commerce (Brest) or Le Conquet; or by air from the international airport of Brest-Guipavas.
WHEN TO GO:
All year round but beware of windy weather.
HIGHLIGHTS:
The Phare du Créac'h – a lighthouse visible from over 50 km (32 mi) away.
Ecomusée d'Ouessant – two houses that recreate traditional island life.
Musée des Phares et Balises – a nautical museum.
Calèches du Ponant – a leisurely horse drawn carriage ride.
YOU SHOULD KNOW:
The local ferries allow very few cars on board, which is just as well as there are only 6 km (3.75 mi) of roads on the island – far better then to rent a bicycle and enjoy the island at a leisurely pace.

The lighthouse and fort

Chausey Archipelago

In the sea there lies a giant elephant, you can stroke him, he is very quiet and not dangerous at all, because he is made of stone – a local fable

Due to their French jurisdiction, the Chausey Islands, located in the English Channel south of Jersey are not generally included in the geographical definition of the Channel Islands, though geologically they join with them to form a larger archipelago. The islands are popular with French tourists but are almost ignored by the English – there is no ferry link between Chausey and the other islands.

Myth and legend surround this island chain, which in spite of being Europe's largest archipelago, is little more than a cluster of grey granite lumps just above the surface of the sea. Subject to one of the highest tidal variation in the world (14 m, 46 ft), it is said that there are 365 islands at low tide and 52 when the tide is in. Fierce sea currents create a multitude of rocky inlets linked by vast sandy stretches. The stark beauty of the area has attracted the attention of marine artists from around the world.

Only one island, Grande Ile, supports any population. Cars and even bicycles are banned, so the pace of life is pedestrian in the best sense of the word. Even in summertime the facilities on the island are limited, so the best way to enjoy the ever-changing landscape is with the aid of a good pair of walking boots and an ample packed lunch. A coastal path encircles the island and affords good beach access.

This is a fragile environment and there are restrictions on landing boats during the bird-nesting season (April to July). It has few permanent residents, save for a lighthouse keeper and a handful of fishermen and there is even talk of banning tourism altogether.

POPULATION:
Winter 10, Summer 100 (2005)
HOW TO GET THERE:
By ferry (summer only) from Saint-Malo or Granville.
WHEN TO GO:
June to September, although accessible by private boat all year round – weather permitting.
HIGHLIGHTS:
The Chausey Regatta every August.
The local seafood – lobster, mussels and oysters.
Watching the ebb and flow of the spectacular tides.
Sailing in and out of the islands' many inlets.
YOU SHOULD KNOW:
Granite from the Chausey Islands was shipped to Paris, sculpted and then used in the building of the nearby Mont Saint Michel.

Ile de Noirmoutier

Immortalized in a painting by Renoir, Ile de Noirmoutier, which is located off the west coast of France, has long been a summer playground. Stretching 20 km (12 mi) out into the Bay of Biscay, the island caters well for visitors, although tourism does not dominate. Salt marshes continue to be worked and there are still thriving farming and fishing communities.

The island can be accessed by bridge but it's more romantic to approach it via the Passage de Gois, a causeway passable only at low tides. The island town of Noirmoutier-en-l'Ile, located to the north east, is an unassuming place. It houses a 12th century castle, a church with a Romanesque crypt and an excellent market. To the north of the town the Chaize Forest of oaks and mimosas is also worth exploring.

In high summer the west coast is a magnet for sunbathers, with its long sandy beaches resembling those of the mainland. Inland, were it not for the presence of a system of Dutch polders and saltwater dykes, you could be forgiven for thinking that you were far from the sea. In the south of the island the winding roads take you through traditional villages of whitewashed cottages.

Today the theme of the island is recreation, far removed from its monastic origins. The island's restaurants are plentiful and of high quality. There are eight sailing clubs and a well laid out cycling route. For younger visitors there is Sealand, a well-stocked aquarium and Oceanile, a swimming pool complex complete with waterslides and the like. It is an island for the French day-tripper who first checks the weather forecast and then decides to go out and have some fun.

POPULATION:
10,000 (2005)
HOW TO GET THERE:
Across the bridge from Fromentine or via the Passage de Gois.
WHEN TO GO:
Spring to autumn – although a thriving mosquito population in the summer makes wearing insect repellent essential.
HIGHLIGHTS:
The castle at Noirmoutier-en-l'Ile, complete with its 11th century dungeon.
A tour of any of the island's world famous salt works.
The village of Barbatre – as pretty a settlement as you will see in all Atlantic France.
The food – the island is famous for its oysters, lobster and potatoes.
Any of the three regattas that take place each August.
YOU SHOULD KNOW:
Highly prized throughout Europe, a kilo (2.2 lb) of Noirmoutier potatoes once fetched over 200 euros at auction.

Salt pans on the island

Belle Ile

POPULATION:
5,250 (2005)
HOW TO GET THERE:
By ferry from Quiberon (year round) or from Vannes (summer only).
WHEN TO GO:
Spring and autumn are less busy.
HIGHLIGHTS:
Musée Historique – housed in the citadel at Le Palais, it records the island's often turbulent history.
Grotte de l'Apothicairerie – a spectacular coastal cavern.
Storm-watching at Pointe des Poulains – the island's most northerly point.
The cave system at Aiguilles de Port-Coton
YOU SHOULD KNOW:
The British navy captured Belle Ile in 1761, but two years later swapped it for the Mediterranean island of Menorca.

As the name suggests this is a truly beautiful island. A combination of a rugged coastline, attractive fishing villages and white sandy beaches, has made it a magnet for summer tourists. In July and August the population can increase ten-fold, all crammed into 84 sq km (36 sq mi). However, even in peak times, it is possible to lose oneself on this island of contrasts. The deeply eroded south-west is a true Côte Sauvage (wild coast), while the sheltered eastern side can feel positively Mediterranean in spite of its Atlantic location.

Belle Ile's history is closely linked both to the English, who occupied the island for two years, from 1761 to 1763, during the Seven Years War, and the Acadians, who took refuge on the island when the English got the upper hand in France's Canadian colonies.

Now the island is known for the more traditional pleasures of any vacation on the Brittany coast: swimming, boating, fishing, cycling and hiking. It also houses a collection of attractive lighthouses, most notably Le Grand Phare on the west coast, and La Citadelle Vauban, one of a series of substantial 17th century military fortresses built for Louis XIV by Marshal Vauban and now turned into a historical museum.

The island has long attracted the attentions of the world's best artists. Inspired by its natural splendour, Monet, Van Gogh and Henri Matisse amongst others produced some of their finest work here. The island is also said to have inspired the Op Art movement of the 1950s when the Hungarian-born artist Victor Vasarely visited and was inspired by the shapes of the pebbles on the beach at Sauzon.

Belle Ile boasts one of the best hiking routes in Europe. The spectacular 95 km (60 mi) coastal path takes about a week to complete and there are ample *gites d'ètape* (walkers' hostels) and campsites en route.

The picturesque port of Sauzon

Iles de Lérins

Boats moored by the tranquil island of Ste-Marguerite

These two tiny islands, a 20-minute ferry ride from the hustle of Cannes, offer respite for jaded souls and depleted credit cards. Ste-Marguerite is 3.25 km (2 mi) long by 1 km (0.6 mi) wide and St-Honorat even smaller, at just 1.5 km (0.9 mi) by 0.4 km (0.25 mi). Ste-Marguerite is more touristy than its monastic neighbour, but outside its busy port, well-kept trails lead through one of Europe's oldest eucalyptus and evergreen oak forests. St-Honorat's pine and eucalyptus forests are edged with the colour and fragrance of wild flowers and herbs.

Both are blessed with unspoilt beaches, decorated by nature with driftwood and said to be the least crowded on the French Riviera. Neither island allows cars, bicycles or camping, though a forest of motorized yachts clogs the narrow channel between them.

Ste-Marguerite is dominated by its fort and has been occupied at different times in its history by waves of invaders – Barbary pirates, Genoan pirates and the Spanish, twice.

St-Honorat was owned by Benedictine monks from the founding of its first monastery in 410 AD, and was taken over by Cistercian monks in 1869. Remnants of the original abbey remain, but the majority of the building dates from the nineteenth century. The monastery itself is open to the public for spiritual retreat only, but the church and small chapels dotted about the island welcome a more worldly appreciation. The conversion of Ireland to Christianity owes much to St-Honorat, as it was here that St Patrick studied before embarking on his most famous project.

Carrying along a picnic is recommended, as St-Honorat has only one small restaurant, while the few restaurants on Ste-Marguerite keep pace in price with the glitzy mainland.

POPULATION:
Ste-Marguerite 20 (permanent winter population); St-Honorat 28 Cistercian monks.

HOW TO GET THERE:
Ferry from Cannes.

WHEN TO GO:
April to October, but best to avoid the fortnight of the Cannes Film Festival in May.

HIGHLIGHTS:
Forte Ste-Marguerite – which dates from the early 17th century.
Ste-Marguerite's Musée de la Mer – with local Roman artefacts and the remains of a 10th century Arab ship.
Cuvée St-Honorat – in time-honoured tradition of monastic communities, the Cistercian brothers produce a highly prized wine from the island's vines. The monks also produce beer and essential oils, which they sell along with CDs of their chants.
Son et Lumière show – in summer; this portrays the history of the islands and includes an after-dark ferry trip.

YOU SHOULD KNOW:
The cell in which Dumas' Man in the Iron Mask was incarcerated is one of a number that can be explored in the Forte Ste-Marguerite.

Ile de Bréhat

Not so much an island as a small archipelago composed of two main islands, Ile de Bréhat, just 3.5 km (2.2 mi) long and 1.5 km (0.9 mi) wide, is surrounded by a wash of reefs and islets stretched across Paimpol Bay off the coast of Brittany. This car-free island with its mild microclimate is a haven for flora and fauna. In summer the smell of ripening figs, eucalyptus, honeysuckle and mimosa fills the air, while the local ornithological survey has noted over 300 species of marine birds.

All boats to the island arrive at the tiny harbour of Port-Clos. From there it is a ten-minute walk to the pretty village of Le Bourg, full of character with a plane tree-shaded square. Be warned though that at low tide the ferries dock some distance from the harbour, requiring a five-minute hike up the beach. Now deemed a conservation area, no new building is allowed on the island and existing buildings are subject to very strict planning regulations. Civic pride is central to the islanders' way of life.

The Pont ar Prat bridge takes you to the wilder north of the island which has the feel of the open sea, with its tiny, whitewashed lighthouse overlooking craggy pink rocks and tidal races at the tip of the island. A network of well signposted, paved roads and dirt paths meander amongst large granite houses concealed by high walls and gardens awash with geraniums, agapanthus and maritime pines.

In the past, Bréhat's vivid colours and tranquil pace drew artists such as Henri Matisse and JD Fergusson – today, the idyllic island is a smart resort drawing in young, trendy Parisians.

POPULATION:
420 (2005)
HOW TO GET THERE:
By ferry from Pointe de l'Arcoust (year round) or from Erquy (summer only).
WHEN TO GO:
May, June and late September to early November are the less busy times.
HIGHLIGHTS:
Verreries de Bréhat – a glass works housed in the citadel in the southwest of the island.
La Chapelle Saint-Michel.
Le Phare du Paon – the lighthouse of the 'Peacock'.
Le Moulin à Marée du Birlot – the recently restored tidal grain mill.
YOU SHOULD KNOW:
Most day-trippers miss the island's most spectacular feature by leaving too early. The sunset over the Atlantic combined with the pink colour of the island's bedrock makes for a truly wonderful sight.

Les Iles d'Or

POPULATION:
450 (excluding military personnel)
(2006)
HOW TO GET THERE:
By ferry from Hyères (year round) or
from Toulon (summer only).
WHEN TO GO:
April to June, late September to
early November.
HIGHLIGHTS:
La Hameau – a Mediterranean
botanical garden (Porquerolles).
14th century Fort Ste Agathe,
housing an underwater
archaeological exhibition
(Porquerolles).
Fort Napoléon – built in 1813 and
now faithfully restored (Levant). The
Eminence and Estissac Forts – with
free exhibitions in the
summer (Port-Cros).
Aquascope boat – a glass-bottomed
boat tour of the local
seascape (Port-Cros).
YOU SHOULD KNOW:
In order to protect this fragile
environment visitor numbers are
limited to 5,000 per day on
Porquerolles and 1,500 on Port-Cros.

Situated off the Cote d'Azur in southern France, the three islands that make up les Iles d'Or, also known as Les Îles d'Hyères, have a history littered with destruction and lifted by preservation. Forts have been successively destroyed and rebuilt from the time of Francis I through to the present day, with both Porquerolles and Levant still having a strong military presence. The island group is blessed with an exceptionally mild climate, which makes it popular – some would say over-popular – with tourists. The heat of summer is usually tempered by a delightfully cool sea breeze.

Porquerolles is the most accessible of the trio. Formerly in private hands, most of the island was acquired by the state in 1971 and the land is now protected and conserved. The port, which shares the island's name, is a hive of activity. As soon as you arrive, you will be captivated. Behind the boats tied up to the quay, the first houses can be seen, surrounded by lush vegetation. After leaving the port you arrive in the village with its large square and beautiful church, a cluster of shops and alfresco eateries.

Port-Cros, the middle of the three islands, was afforded National Park status in 1963. Uniquely for Europe this park extends some 600 m (2,000 ft) in to the remarkably clear waters that surround the island, providing an underwater haven for both marine life and divers alike. Inland, Port-Cros is the hilliest and wildest of the three islands, with a well-marked nature trail system.

Levant is an oddity: similarly covered in lush vegetation and blessed with fine sandy beaches, 90 per cent of the island is given over to the French military. The remaining 10 per cent has become a Mecca for naturists.

A view down to the crystal clear waters at Porquerolles

Elegant mansions line the streets of Ile Saint-Louis.

Ile Saint-Louis

POPULATION:
Permanent winter population 1,750
(2003)

WHEN TO GO:
Though less crowded than Ile de la
Cité, it can be busy in the summer
months, June to August. Be prepared
for some shops and cafés to be
closed in August.

HIGHLIGHTS:
St-Louis en l'Ile Church – first built in
1622, with a magnificent wooden
door decorated with angels.
The island's main street, rue de Saint
Louis-en-l'Ile, with wonderful
speciality boutiques and shops.
The performers at Pont Saint-Louis
Dining at one of the island's many
fine restaurants.
Walking from Ile St-Louis to Notre
Dame Cathedral, where an ascent of
the spiral staircase affords a
wonderful view of the city.

YOU SHOULD KNOW:
The Haschischins Club used to meet
monthly at Hôtel Lauzun (17 quai
d'Anjou); hashish jelly was consumed
there by such notable club members
as Manet and Baudelaire.

As you enter the Island, past the street entertainers on Pont St-Louis you leave behind the hustle and bustle of its more illustrious sister, Ile de la Cité. With Notre Dame behind you, you could be forgiven for thinking that someone had transported a village and placed it in the centre of Paris. For centuries the Ile St-Louis was nothing more than a swamp, until in the 17th century the developer, Christophe Marie, filled it with elegant mansions along narrow streets, so that by 1660 the island was completely transformed.

In the 1840s the Ile gained popularity as a Bohemian hangout. Residents of this small boat-shaped island have always included wealthy intellectuals, artists and politicians. Voltaire, Cézanne, Baudelaire and Chagall, as well as Racine, Marie Curie, Ernest Hemingway and President Pompidou all lived there at one time.

As you travel eastwards along rue St-Louis-en-l'Ile you enter the heart of the island where Louisiens, as the locals are known, enjoy cafés, art galleries and unique shops. It is a great place to grab a famous Berthillon sorbet and people watch, although anything more than window-shopping could prove expensive. Quai D'Orleans is home to the area's most imposing buildings – of particular note are the 17th century Moorish influenced Hotel Rolland and the former Polish Library, now home to a museum.

Since the island is at the very centre of Paris, views of the River Seine are stunning and particularly atmospheric in the evening. If you're looking for absolute seclusion, head for the southern quais and you'll reach the finest sunbathing spot in Paris.

Corsica

'Get away from here before you are completely bewitched and enslaved'; such was the advice given to Dorothy Carrington by a fisherman in her classic 1971 portrait of Corsica, *Granite Island*.

Corsica is essentially a mountain range that rises from the sea bed. Its craggy coastline is washed on all sides by the Mediterranean Sea. It is 184 km (115 mi) long and 83 km (52 mi) wide covering an area of 8,772 sq km (5,980 sq mi), with Monte Cinto as its highest point at 2,707m (8,798 ft). The mountains are divided by deep valleys carved out by fast flowing rivers – which makes for spectacular scenery, reminiscent of the Dolomites.

The earliest known settlements on Corsica can be traced back over 10,000 years, and traditionally most inhabitants lived in the rugged mountain interior to avoid attack. The shoreline was the preserve of fishermen though much of this is now given over to the tourist trade. At various times through history the island has been governed by Vandals, Romans, Greeks, Genoese and even briefly by the British. Though it became part of France in 1768, the island with its Baroque churches, Genoese fortresses and Tuscan based indigenous language (Corsu) feels more Italian than French.

Aside from the spectacular countryside the towns of Corsica also merit exploration. Often described as 'little Marseilles', Bastia has a vast seafront esplanade and an old quarter of haphazard streets, striking Baroque churches and lofty tenements. The true Corsican experience can be found at Corte, the spiritual and cultural heart of the island situated at the confluence of two rivers; it's a good base for the best hiking on the island. For a more villagey feel head for Piana, which offers spectacular views of Les Calanques without the crowds of Porto.

Be prepared to be bewitched if not enslaved.

POPULATION:
280,000 (2005)
WHEN TO GO:
During the summer months (June-August) the island can get crowded, whilst off-season some facilities close down so check before travelling.
HOW TO GET THERE:
By air from Paris or Nice to Bastia, Calvi or Ajaccio, or by boat from Marseilles, Nice or Toulon to Ajaccio or Bastia.
HIGHLIGHTS:
The megaliths and menhirs at Filitosa – the island's greatest archaeological treasure.
The GR20 – a clumsily named but spectacular 16-stage hike (allow 12 days to complete, but only attempt it if you are fit).
Museu di a Corsica in the Genoese citadel at Corte – explore the island's history from ancient times to the present.
Les Calanques de Piana – weird and wonderful cliff formations; the best way to see them is from a boat.
The town of Sartène – a reminder of what Corsica used to be like, perpetuating traditions that go back to the Middle Ages.
The clifftop citadel at Bonifacio, with marvellous views of Sardinia.
YOU SHOULD KNOW:
Wild herbs grow almost everywhere on Corsica and greatly influence the local diet. *Stufatu*, a fragrant mutton stew, is a must for anyone dining out.

The town of Calvi

Ibiza

POPULATION:
113,908 (2006)

WHEN TO GO:
June to September for the most riotous club scene in Europe; October to May if you want a calmer but rainier experience.

HOW TO GET THERE:
Direct flights to Ibiza. Boat from Palma, Majorca.

HIGHLIGHTS:
Portal de Ses Taules – a massive gateway in the city wall, entrance to Dalt Vila.
Santa Eularia des Riu – a 16th century hilltop church.
Santa Agnes de Corona – inland from the east coast, a picturesque village on top of a hill surrounded by almond trees.
Cala Mastella – a peaceful cove with tiny beach on the east coast.
Es Vedra – a mystical rock off the west coast, said to be one of the earth's most magnetic points.
Benirras Beach – to watch the ageing hippie islanders drumming in the sunset every Sunday.

YOU SHOULD KNOW:
If you are not interested in the club scene, you still should not rule out Ibiza as a holiday destination. It is an amazingly beautiful place with some wonderful historic sites and traditional rural culture. Increasingly on offer are agrotourist holidays in the beautiful inland regions of the island, well away from the clubs and developments.

A view of the harbour and picturesque old town

Renowned as the clubbing capital of the world, hedonists have been flocking to Ibiza in droves ever since the 1960s, when the first hippies, in pursuit of nirvana, were drawn to the island's Mediterranean beauty. The islanders were incredibly poor and welcomed strangers to their shores with open arms, absorbing newcomers into the local culture with such ease that they soon became part of Ibiza's intrinsic character. Despite half a century of particularly boisterous mass tourism and the inevitable charmless coastal developments that accompany it, the island has still somehow managed to retain much of its original attraction.

Ibiza is part of the Balearic archipelago, about 100 km (60 mi) southwest of Majorca. It is scenically incredibly beautiful – 571 sq km (222 sq mi) of pine forested hills and terraced fields, dotted with whitewashed hamlets and solitary churches. The coastline is rugged with stretches of sandy beach and sheltered coves. From the cliffs there are beautiful views of the sea, and you can walk inland through untouched Mediterranean countryside where the scent of pine trees lingers in the air.

The historic Balearic port of Ibiza is a UNESCO World Heritage Site. The old town, Dalt Vila is exceptionally picturesque, built on the side of a cliff with medieval city walls and a maze of narrow streets winding uphill to the 14th century cathedral and the castle. There are two beautiful beaches nearby – Ses Salines and Es Cavallet.

Sant Antoni de Portmany on the west coast is the most developed part of the island, where clubbers congregate for a non-stop party. If the Bacchanalian atmosphere here gets too much, you can head for the unspoilt north coast where you can always find a quiet *cala* (cove) to relax in with only the sea, the cliffs and the sky for company.

Formentera

Less than 6 km (4 miles) south of the party island of Ibiza, Formentera is its complete antithesis – an island with very little coastal development, and not a club in sight. Its relative inaccessibility and lack of water has protected it from the ravages of tourism and it is one of the least spoilt spots in the Mediterranean with only one proper tourist resort, Es Pujols.

The smallest and southernmost of the Balearics, as well as the hottest and driest, Formentera is famous for its peaceful, laid-back atmosphere and incredible stretches of white sand beach, often deserted, where nobody turns a hair at nudity. The scenery is dramatic – an arid, windswept landscape, wild and wooded, with a varied, indented 80 km (50 mi) long coastline which includes dunes, salt flats and innumerable sandy coves. The 19 km (12 mi) long, relatively flat island is best explored by bike. Country lanes lead past *fincas* (farmhouses) festooned with bougainvillea, stone-walled vineyards, and small pastures where sheep and goats shelter in the shade of contorted fig trees. Wherever you are, the sea air is heady with the scent of rosemary, wild thyme, juniper and pine.

Life has always been hard on Formentera. Although there are signs of human habitation from more than 4,000 years ago, it was deserted for nearly 300 years between the early 16th and late 18th centuries for fear of pirates, until a few resourceful farmers resettled here, determined to eke out a living despite the lack of water. The island's fortune changed dramatically in the 1960s when hippies who had had their fill of Ibiza started to move here. It only took Bob Dylan to stay in a windmill on the island for it to acquire a reputation as the hippest spot in Europe – a reputation that has stuck fast and still stands today.

The town square at Sant Francesca

POPULATION:
7,461 (2002)
WHEN TO GO:
May to September for the perfect dream Mediterranean holiday experience.
HOW TO GET THERE:
A high-speed ferry departs from Ibiza approximately every hour.
HIGHLIGHTS:
The Blue Bar – one of the best beach cafés in the Balearics, in the middle of the famous Platja de Migjorn, a beautiful 5 km (3 mi) stretch of beach that runs along the south coast.
Faro de La Mola – a lighthouse standing on the highest point of the island, described by Jules Verne as a magical place in his novel *Hector Servadac*. The nearby town of El Pilar de la Mola has a beautiful church and Sunday hippie market.
Es Cap de Barbaria – walk along the cape to the lighthouse to watch the sun go down.
Estany des Peix – a lagoon with a narrow opening to the sea.
YOU SHOULD KNOW:
The strip of water between Formentera and Ibiza is a marine reserve dotted with islets, part of which is a UNESCO World Heritage Site. In order to dive in the reserve area, you must obtain a permit.

Majorca

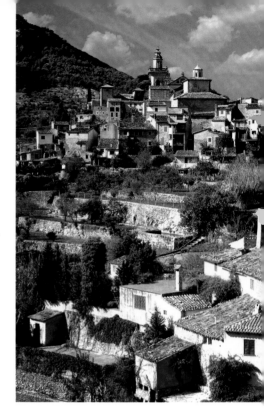

WHEN TO GO:
April, May, September and October
are lovely times of year for walking,
cycling, climbing and sightseeing –
the weather is not too hot and the
island is far less crowded than in the
high season of June to August when
tourists flock to the island for its
beaches by day and club scene
by night.

HOW TO GET THERE:
Fly to Palma or take a ferry from the
ports of Barcelona or Valencia in
mainland Spain.

HIGHLIGHTS:
Cathedral, Palma – a masterpiece of
13th and 14th century Gothic
architecture.
Deia – a charming village where the
English writer Robert Graves lived,
with spectacular sea views.
Narrow gauge railway from Palma to
the picturesque mountain town of
Soller – an unforgettable train ride
through incredible scenery and a
scarily long tunnel.
The huge market at Inca.
Jardins d'Alfàbia – Arabic gardens.
Alcudia – a walled medieval city, with
remains of Roman houses.

YOU SHOULD KNOW:
The first 'tourist' to visit Majorca was
Chopin. He came to stay here in
1838, accompanied by his French
mistress, Amantine Dudevant (better
known as the feminist writer George
Sand) in a vain attempt to escape the
gossip about their relationship and
restore his health, broken by
tuberculosis. They rented a monk's
cell at the Carthusian Monastery –
one of the great historical sights of
the island, set in the lovely mountain
town of Valldemossa.

*The unspoilt mountain town
of Valldemossa*

Package holidays to Majorca started in 1952 so it is unsurprising that this island is practically synonymous with mass tourism. Do not let this put you off – despite the ugly blot made by the holiday industry, parts of Majorca are still amongst the loveliest places in the world. The historic sights, mountain villages, perfect Mediterranean climate, wonderful beaches, and sublime scenery are what originally attracted tourists here. No less today than then, a holiday here lifts the spirits of even the most jaded traveller.

Majorca is the largest – 3,640 sq km, (1,405 sq mi) – of the Balearic Islands, 88 km (55 mi) off the southeastern coast of Spain. The island's turbulent history had, by the 19th century, led to a bleak existence for its inhabitants many of whom were forced to emigrate – little wonder that they grabbed the opportunity to turn their island into a holiday resort. Amazingly, although Palma Bay has been sadly disfigured by high-rise hotels, nightclubs and overcrowded beaches, Palma itself is an outstandingly beautiful, atmospheric capital city with a historic town centre and wonderful local market, the Mercat Olivar.

To reach the island's northernmost point, Cap Formentor, you take perilous, winding roads through breathtaking mountain scenery, soaring 1,445 m (4,740 ft) to the northwest of a fertile central plain of vineyards, orange and almond groves, windmills and sleepy market towns. The headland is a sheer cliff 384 m (1,260 ft) high, known as the 'meeting point of the winds'. The sight of the beach way below as you are buffeted from all directions is enough to make the strongest head spin.

It is not hard to escape from the tourist trap parts of the island. As soon as you do, Majorca shows you her other face – the idyllic Mediterranean island she still is at heart.

Menorca

The smaller sister island of Majorca, Menorca is only a fifth of the size – 700 sq km (270 sq mi) in area, and less than 50 km (32 mi) long. The island has a beautiful hilly landscape and pine-fringed coast with more beaches than all the other Balearic Islands combined – ranging from long stretches of silver or golden sand to tiny *calas* (sandy coves). It is blissfully free of tourist development and was designated a UNESCO Biosphere Reserve in 1993.

Menorca is renowned for its stone megaliths, some 1,600 of them dotted all over the island, attesting to a prehistoric civilization dating from 2000 BC. From Monte Toro – the highest point at 355 m (1164 ft) – there are panoramic views of the rolling countryside, increasingly wild and rugged to the north and carpeted with a patchwork of fields to the south. The isolated *calas* around the coast are best explored by renting a boat. Many of them are only accessible by sea and even in high season you can always find one to yourself to while away an idyllic day of sand and sea.

Mahón, the island's capital on the east coast is a sleepy, elegant city of Georgian architecture built during a period of British colonial rule in the 18th century. It has one of the world's largest natural harbours, cause of a centuries-long squabble between the English, French and Spanish, and is surrounded by breathtaking scenery. But the architectural jewel in the island's crown is the medieval Moorish town of Ciutadella, with its narrow maze of streets, old walls and beautiful Baroque 17th century palaces – a cultural gem.

POPULATION:
88,434 (2006)
WHEN TO GO:
May to early July and September to October if you want to avoid the worst of the holiday season yet still take advantage of the Mediterranean climate.
HOW TO GET THERE:
Boat from Palma, Majorca, Barcelona or Valencia; direct international flights to Mahón.
HIGHLIGHTS:
Church of Santa Maria, Mahón – with one of Europe's most famous pipe organs on which daily concerts are performed.
Plaça d'es Born, Ciutadella – one of the finest squares in Europe.
Caves at Cala Morell – incredible prehistoric caves.
Naveta des Tudons – the most famous megalithic monument in the Balearics 4 km (2.5 mi) from Ciutadella Fornells – an attractive former fishing village famous for its lobster, set in a lovely bay close to the northernmost tip of the island – Cap de Cavalleria – from where there are stunning views. There is a wonderful beach nearby – Platja Binimella.
YOU SHOULD KNOW:
The British introduced the art of gin distilling to Menorca in the 18th century and it is still produced here today in more or less the original manner. You can take a tour round the Xoriguer Distillery in Mahón.

Boats moored alongside the restaurants in Ciutadella.

The Canaries

POPULATION:
1,995,833 (2006)

WHEN TO GO:
All year. The Canaries have a sub-tropical climate with very little variation in temperature and warm seas whatever the season.

HOW TO GET THERE:
International flights to Tenerife, Lanzarote and Gran Canaria. Ferry to any of the five larger islands from Cadiz, mainland Spain. Local flights or ferries between the islands.

HIGHLIGHTS:
Barrio de la Vegueta, Las Palmas – the historic district of Las Palmas with beautiful colonial architecture, a UNESCO World Heritage Site.
Telde, Gran Canaria – a village in a beautiful setting with traces of the Guanches, the original inhabitants of the Canaries.
Betancuria, Fuerteventura – the oldest village of the Canaries with a cathedral dating from 1410.
Montaña de Fuego, National Park of Timanfaya, Lanzarote – active craters in sensational volcanic moonscape.
Valle de la Orotava, Tenerife – a beautiful valley with the lovely town of Orotava where you can see the Casas de los Balcones, traditional 17th century buildings.
Santa Cruz de la Palma – an incredibly picturesque port town with steep alleys, backed by a huge volcanic crater, the Caldereta.

YOU SHOULD KNOW:
The Canaries are a self-governing region of Spain. Although they were one of the original package tour destinations, the tourist developments are generally well-contained and do not interfere with the enjoyment of the islands' rich heritage and sublime scenery. The fact that four of Spain's National Parks are to be found here – on the islands of La Palma, La Gomera, Tenerife and Lanzarote – and no less than five UNESCO sites gives some indication of the staggering natural and cultural beauty of the Canaries.

The stunning volcanic landscape of Montaña de Fuego, National Park of Timanfaya

The Canaries are a group of seven volcanic islands off the Atlantic coast of North Africa. They cover a total area of 7,450 sq km (2,900 sq mi) containing some of the world's most dramatic scenery. Each island has its own unique landscape and endemic flora and fauna, ranging from the desert of Fuerteventura to the lush mountainous forest of La Gomera. Las Palmas de Gran Canaria is the cosmopolitan capital of the archipelago, reputed to have the best climate in the world.

The Spanish first invaded the Canaries in 1402 but it took the better part of a century to gain complete control of this strategic point on the Atlantic trade route. For the next 300 years, the islands grew increasingly wealthy from trading profits until, in the 19th century, a recession led to mass emigration to America. The development of the tourist industry eventually turned the tide and today, around 10 million tourists visit every year.

Tenerife, the largest island, has the most varied scenery – a landscape of fertile valleys, steep cliffs and wide sandy beaches dominated by the towering outline of El Teide, the third largest volcano on earth at 3,718 m (12,195 ft) high. La Palma, the 'green island', has the world's largest volcanic crater, La Caldera del Taburiente with a diameter of 9 km (6 mi) and a depth of 770 m (2,525 ft).

The smallest island, Hierro is also the rockiest with a dramatic coastline plunging straight into the sea. Lanzarote is the most extraordinary of all – a surreal volcanic landscape of petrified lava from 18th and 19th century eruptions. The stark beauty of its eerily empty scenery, dotted with ancient vineyards, brilliant coloured flowers and sparkling white houses is unlike anywhere else on the planet – a truly memorable experience.

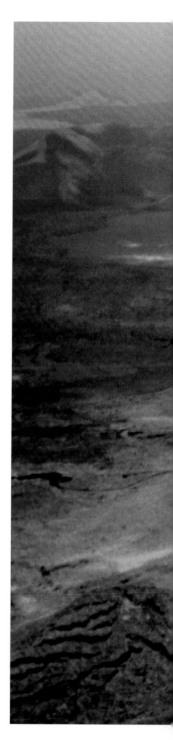

The Azores

POPULATION:
238,767 (2002)
WHEN TO GO:
June to October are the warmest and
driest months. November to January
is pleasant but rather cooler.
February to May tends to be rainy
but the azaleas are in bloom in April,
which more than makes up for
the showers.
HOW TO GET THERE:
International flights from Portugal to
São Miguel, Terceira, Faial, or Pico.
HIGHLIGHTS:
Furna do Exofre – sulphur grotto with
underground crater lake (Graciosa)
Convento de Esperança – with
magnificent statue of Christ
(Sao Miguel).
Fajazinha – picturesque village and
waterfall of Ribeira Grande (Flores).
Horta – important 19th century
whaling port with historic sights
(Faial)
Maia and Sao Lourenço – most
beautiful bays in the Azores
(Santa Maria)
Angra do Heroisme – historic city,
UNESCO World Patrimony (Terceira).
YOU SHOULD KNOW:
The Azores are an ideal place for
whale watching and swimming with
dolphins. The seas around the islands
are a natural sanctuary with more
than 20 species of marine mammals.

An archipelago of nine volcanic islands approximately 1,500 km
(940 mi) from mainland Portugal, the Azores are the remote western
tip of Europe. They are the tops of some of the biggest mountains on
the planet, mostly hidden under the Atlantic Ocean but rising to a
spectacular 2,351 m (7,711 ft) above sea level.

All the islands are wildly beautiful with coastlines of cavernous
cliffs, rocky outcrops, black sand beaches and sheltered bays. Traces
of massive volcanic eruptions can be seen everywhere in the incredible
scenery. Rugged mountains with deep ravines, crater lakes and curious
rock formations contrast with verdant plains – the 'terras do pão'
(lands of bread) – where fields are bordered with thousands of wild
flowers and boundaries are marked with hedging of hydrangeas,
azaleas and camellias. The islands vary in size from Corvo, just 17 sq
km (7 sq mi) to São Miguel, 759 sq km (295 sq mi), each with its own
unique characteristics, history and old island architecture.

The Azores were uninhabited when the Portuguese arrived in
1439. São Miguel and Santa Maria, the most easterly islands, were the
first to be settled and there are some magnificent period buildings in
Ponta Delgada, the largest city of the islands. During the 16th and
17th Centuries, Terceira, the third island to be colonized, became an
important port for the Spanish galleons raiding Mexico and Peru.
Later, in the 1820s, it became the base for the liberal struggle against
absolutist rule in the Portuguese civil war.

Rural life in the Azores is much as it must have been for centuries
and there is a calm, unhurried atmosphere even in the main towns. As
you explore the different islands, you become increasingly aware of
the striking individuality and unique charms of each one – the pearls
of the Atlantic.

The town of Terceira

Madeira

Best known for its cake and wine, Madeira is a sub-tropical island of prolific beauty. The wild volcanic scenery of mountains, forest, streams and waterfalls provides a spectacular backdrop to luxuriant, terraced slopes where vines are cultivated, tropical fruits drip from the trees and roses grow as big as your fist – a truly breathtaking co-operation between nature and man.

This 740 sq km (290 sq mi) island is the top of a 5 million-year-old mid-Atlantic volcano that last erupted 6,500 years ago. A 1,220 m (4,000 ft) high mountain ridge, incised with deep ravines, runs east-west and one of the tallest cliffs in Europe, Cabo Girão, soars up to 589 m (1,932 ft) on the south coast. Ponta de São Lourenço, a 9 km (6 mi) long peninsula of weird rock formations, juts out at the eastern end of the island, attracting hundreds of seabirds.

Originally known to the Romans as the Purple Island, a chance landing by the navigator, João Gonçalves Zarco at the nearby island of Santo Porto in 1418 led to the arrival of the Portuguese. The capital city, Funchal was founded in 1421 and became an important stopping point between Europe and the New World. Today it is a bustling, historic town with old architecture and beautiful views.

The name Ihla da Madeira (Island of Wood) derives from the island's dense primeval laurisilva forest. What remains of it, still covering a fifth of the land, is now under UNESCO World Heritage protection. There are more than 2,150 km (1,350 mi) of *levadas* (irrigation channels) criss-crossing the mountains to divert water from the northwest to the dry south-eastern slopes; they serve a secondary purpose as footpaths for accessing the interior – a great way to explore the incredible scenery of this 'floating garden'.

POPULATION:
241,400 (2006 estimate)
WHEN TO GO:
All year – very pleasant sub-tropical climate, warmed by the Gulf Stream.
HOW TO GET THERE:
Direct flights to Madeira from most cities in Europe.
HIGHLIGHTS:
Monte Palace Tropical Gardens – contains one of the most important tile collections in Portugal; the beautiful town of Monte is often compared to Sintra in mainland Portugal.
São Vicente Caves and Volcano Centre – on north coast; take a trip into the earth following the lava channels.
São João do Pico Fortress – worth the steep climb to get a magnificent view.
Sé Cathedral – early 16th century Gothic/Moorish design with ten arches.
Capela das Almas Pobres – small chapel dug out of the mountainside.
Markets of Porto Moniz, Ponta Delgada and Santo da Serra.
YOU SHOULD KNOW:
The Madeira Mardi Gras Carnival and Spring Flower Festival are both major tourist attractions; New Year celebrations feature a spectacular firework display.

The view from Lombo do Mouro

An aerial view of Porto Santo

Porto Santo

POPULATION:
4,474 (2001)
WHEN TO GO:
February to October but unless you
are taking children avoid July and
August when the island is invaded by
families.
HOW TO GET THERE:
Daily car ferry or fly from Madeira.
HIGHLIGHTS:
Taking a taxi, minibus or bike tour
round the island.
Christopher Columbus's house
and museum.
Pico do Castelo – island fortress.
Portela – lookout point with
spectacular views of the ocean and
over the island.
Nossa Senhora da Piedade –
town church.
Camacha – village on the north coast
with fig trees and windmills.
YOU SHOULD KNOW:
The golden sand of Porto Santo is
said to have therapeutic properties.

In the sunshine, as you approach Porto Santo by air, the whole island seems to glow a glorious golden-yellow against the glistening cobalt blue sea, broken only by odd strips of green pine trees and purple mountain folds. Known to locals as a 'painting made by god', this idyllic island, 46 km (29 mi) to the northeast of Madeira in the Atlantic Ocean, is more reminiscent of North Africa than Europe – a starkly beautiful desert landscape of palm trees and cacti, dotted with pine groves, stone-walled vineyards, and small wheatfields. Porto Santo is only 14 km (9 mi) long and 5 km (3 mi) wide with an incredible golden sand beach stretching 9 km (5 mi) along the south coast; to the north there are mountains, rising to the Pico do Facho at 500 m (1670 ft), with a steep, rocky coastline.

Porto Santo was the first island of the Madeira archipelago to be discovered. In 1418 the Portuguese navigator, João Gonçalves Zarco was blown off course from the African coast and found a safe harbour here; he named it Porto Santo (Holy Port) in gratitude. Christopher Columbus came here in 1486 and married the governor's daughter before moving to Madeira to study navigation. The harsh existence and frequent pirate attacks persuaded many of the settlers here to decamp for an easier life in Madeira.

The islanders survive largely by fishing, subsistence farming and goat-herding, using donkeys for transport and oxen to thresh the grain. The main town, Vila Baleira on the south coast is a picturesque cluster of whitewashed houses with a cobbled square, medieval monuments, and small cafés where you can dawdle in the shade of palm trees watching the fishing boats. This is one of the least developed beach resorts in Europe – an unspoilt island paradise.

Capraia

Capraia, covered in pristine Mediterranean flora and fauna.

Wild, hilly and barely inhabited, Capraia is the only volcanic island in the Tuscan Archipelago. A 300 to 400 m (984 to 1,312 ft) ridge divides it into two unequal slopes. On the west, sheer walls of rock are cracked into ravines and riddled with caves; to the east the terrain slopes in a series of shallow valleys down to the sea.

People live either in the port, round a little bay, or in the village that sits on top of the nearby promontory. The rest of the 19 sq km (7.7 sq mi) island is covered in brush, with a few small villas and old farm buildings used briefly in summer. Humming insects follow the scent of wild herbs and flowers, but the ragged shrubs and trees can't hide the many poignant reminders of Capraia's turbulent past. A Roman fortress overlooks the town, crumbling watchtowers dot the landscape, and ruined villas recall the Romans' long romance with the island. The network of trails that hikers use today are 2,000 year-old Etruscan logging trails that often peter out in some rocky outcrop. For centuries after they left, Capraia was a sanctuary for hermits and anchorites – their peace interrupted (bizarrely) in 1796 when the island was seized by England's Admiral Nelson. Otherwise, the anchovy fishermen stayed near the port, and the island became an agricultural penal colony, closed in 1986.

Nature has largely reclaimed Capraia, and most of the island, and the sea for miles around it, is part of a huge National Park and Marine Reserve. There's no nightlife, no neon and no marketing scam to exploit the pristine Mediterranean flora and fauna. For visitors, the symbiosis of land, sea and people is like stumbling on a blueprint of how you want the Mediterranean to be: itself.

POPULATION:
366 (2004)
WHEN TO GO:
April to October – but July and August are both the hottest months and the most (relatively) crowded.
HOW TO GET THERE:
By ferry from Livorno, or by private yacht.
HIGHLIGHTS:
The spectacular, fire-red rock of Cala Rossa (Red Cove), at the southern tip of the island; it used to be one of the craters of the volcano.
Il Laghetto, once the volcano's main crater and now a *stagnone* (small pond), where migratory birds rest on their flight to Africa.
The Roman fort overlooking the port and torre al Bagno, the tower standing on the naturally levelled rocks where islanders come to sunbathe and swim.
Snorkelling or diving in the protected waters of the Marine Reserve at Cala della Mortola, Capraia's only real beach and approachable only by water.
YOU SHOULD KNOW:
If you come by boat, make sure you don't land within the environmental reserve, or use a drag anchor.

Elba

POPULATION:
30,000 (2007)
WHEN TO GO:
Year-round
HOW TO GET THERE:
By ferry/car ferry from Piombino on
the west coast of Italy.
HIGHLIGHTS:
The stunning views from Napoleon's
principal house, the Palazzo Mulini,
above Portoferraio.
The castle at Volterraio.
The ancient hilltop village
of Marciana.
The pebbled strand of Capo Branco,
where Jason is said to have paused
in his quest for the Golden Fleece.
The museum at Napoleon's summer
house, Villa San Martino.
The panorama from Mt. Capanne,
1,019 m (3,343 ft), Elba's
highest point.
YOU SHOULD KNOW:
The most famous palindrome in the
English language runs: 'Able was I ere
I saw Elba'!

On the map Elba looks like a fish, swimming placidly some 20 km
(12 mi) off the Italian mainland at Piombino. It's the biggest of the
volcanic Tuscan islands, easily accessible, and one of the favourite
destinations of Italians themselves. Phoenicians and Greeks traded
with the Etruscans who first brought it prosperity; and the Romans
built a naval base there to defend the original iron mines lying below
Elba's characteristic green cloak of holm oak and chestnut forests.
The combination of mountains, meadows and woods was irresistible
to the ruling Florentines of the Renaissance, and the Medici took it
as a family fief from 1548. The Medici fortified Portoferraio, Elba's
principal town, against the corsairs of North Africa's Barbary Coast;
and established the culture that still makes the island so
enchantingly different. It's even why Napoleon chose Elba for his
retirement in exile in 1814 – and as its sovereign (for just ten
months!), he created the system of government that is still in
use today.

There are dozens of secluded coves, backed by rocky cliffs and
topped by lavender and perfumed grass along the lanes between
olive groves and vineyards. Etruscan hamlets top the hills, and
elegant villas sit among cypress gardens. The cafés in every cobbled
square and the flag fringed harbour still share their sophisticated
glamour. Elba is often busy, but it's still a place to laze. The longest
of many beaches lies on the Gulf of Lancona at the island's
southernmost point; and you can see the day's catch of anchovies,
tuna and sardines at fishing villages like centuries-old Cotone. Elba
remains as seductive today as it was 2,000 years ago.

Portoferraio at sunset

Porto Isola del Giglio

Isola del Giglio

Only 16 km (9.5 mi) off the Argentario promontory, Giglio's granite hills rise 496 m (1,634 ft) to their central peak above the Tyrhennian Sea. From Poggio della Pagana you can see almost the entire 28 km- (17 mi-) coastline of the 8 km- (5 mi-) long island. To the west, steep slopes drop to majestic cliffs sheer above the sea; but to the east is a slightly gentler landscape, shelving to long sandy bays divided by rocky headlands. Aleppo pinewoods crown its higher ridges, and the lower slopes are vineyards; the rest is a characteristic Mediterranean mixture of scrub, wild flowers and herbs, broom, thorn trees, chestnuts and cypresses.

Giglio's history is written in its three small towns. The oldest is Giglio Castello, a walled and turreted medieval hilltop maze of arches, dark under-passages and steep alleys of stone houses. Its 13th century appearance hides a much older occupation. First the Etruscans, then the Romans made Giglio a significant military base; and the Romans built Giglio Porto on the east coast as a commercial junction for its maritime trade. Both Pliny and Julius Caesar wrote about it, and numerous Roman wrecks offshore show how busy it was. Visitors still arrive here, and stroll among the colourful restaurants and bars that line the quay between the two piers. The Torre Saraceno, built by Ferdinand I in 1596, stands by the south pier, a reminder of the terrible raids by Barbary corsairs from the 16th century until 1799. On Giglio's opposite side, in what is now the chief tourist resort of Campese, the early 18th century Medici built another imposing watchtower for the same reason. Since those days, Giglio has thrived on its wine production and its granite quarries; they were closed in 1962 to allow the island to revert as much as possible to nature.

POPULATION:
1,406 (2007)
WHEN TO GO:
April to September. Go in spring when the island explodes with colourful wild flowers.
HOW TO GET THERE:
By ferry from Porto Santo Stéfano on Argentario, or by private yacht.
HIGHLIGHTS:
The ruins of the sumptuous patrician Roman villa at Giglio Porto, built by the Domizi Enobarbi family in the 1st and 2nd centuries.
The early 14th century gate and fortifications of the Rocca Pisana at Giglio Castello.
The ivory crucifix (by Giambologna) and other relics in the church of S. Pietro Apostolo in Giglio Castello.
Diving in the many caves below the sheer cliffs on the west coast of the island – Giglio has at least 12 major dive sites.
The birds – cormorants, red partridges, shags, kestrels, hawks, blackcaps, goldcrests, nightingales, redpolls and rare Corsican seagulls are among many resident and migratory species.
YOU SHOULD KNOW:
Giglio granite forms the columns that support many churches and basilicas all over Italy.

*Ruins of Villa Domizia
on Giannutri*

Giannutri

The smallest and most southerly inhabited island of the Tuscan Archipelago, Giannutri is a half moon of just 3 sq km (1.16 sq mi). From the sea it appears inaccessible, even forbidding; but the black volcanic boulders that form an unbroken barrier around it are more blessing than bane. Centuries of shifting rock falls have made it one of the finest diving sites in the Mediterranean, with no sand to cloud the lapis waters; and since there are no beaches at all to attract conventional tourism, the circlet of rocks has preserved the island's wild beauty from all modern depredations.

Patrician Romans loved it. They built the small port, and dotted their villas among the vines, olive trees and myriad wild flowers of the interior. Long abandoned, one of them was restored in the late 19th century by one of Garibaldi's naval captains, Gualtiero Adami. He cultivated some of the land, becoming known as Giannutri's own Robinson Crusoe. Local legend has it that the wind is the howling of his lover, Marietta, perpetually desolate after his death in 1922.

There are no cars, and few people. You walk in the cacophonous 'silence' of the purely natural world, senses sharpened by intense colours and heady perfumes of herb and flower. Offshore it gets even better. Dolphins, turtles and sea horses patrol huge meadows of ravishing underwater Poseidonia, set with waving sea fans of coral and sea roses. Ghosts of 2,000 year-old wrecks are shrouded in fronds and guarded by darting fish. Large areas of the Marine Park are set aside for swimming and diving, to the exclusion of boats either in transit or moored, and of fishing. You can do those in many other places. Giannutri's utopian charm provides an opportunity to escape all forms of modern hurly-burly, on land or underwater.

POPULATION:
102 (2005)
WHEN TO GO:
May to September
HOW TO GET THERE:
By ferry from Porto Santo Stéfano
on Argentario.
HIGHLIGHTS:
The Roman seaside Villa Domizia.
The lighthouse at Punto Rosso, built
in 1861.
The rare Mediterranean corals and
underwater meadows of the
Marine Park.
YOU SHOULD KNOW:
The exact zoning of the Marine Park;
there are heavy fines for breaking
the rules.

Ischia

Ischia is the largest of the islands in the Bay of Naples, and many people consider it to be more beautiful even than Capri to its southeast. Ischia is a volcanic island 10 km (6 mi) long and 7 km (4.5 mi) wide that rises to 788 m (2,500 ft) at Monte Epomeo, which divides the island into two zones. The south and west takes the brunt of hot dry winds from Africa, and cacti, agave and palms thrive in the sub-tropical landscape. In the northern shadow of Monte Epomeo, chestnuts flourish among typical Mediterranean trees like holm oak, cypress, cork, almond and olive as well as the vines that fill the terraces. Citrus groves scent the whole island, and flowers run riot in the richly fertile volcanic soil. Even more extraordinary is that despite its high population and millions of visitors, Ischia still has dozens of deserted beaches and coves, and much of its interior is an empty pastoral idyll.

People come for its thermal springs and volcanic mud treatments – Ischia's prime attraction (alongside its excellent strategic position) for a succession of historical overlords from the Greeks in 800 BC, via the Romans, Saracens, Normans, Sicilians, Aragonese, Austrians, pirates, Bourbons, Britons and French, to the wealthy Europeans who now make its coastal strip a sophisticated playground and magnet for the young and beautiful.

Ischia has lost its jet-set exclusivity since the 1960s when it epitomized the fashionable notion of 'La Dolce Vita', but that has been replaced by a new kind of participatory glamour that draws in visitors. Just as it matches thermal springs and hot muds to different therapeutic treatments, Ischia matches its towns and resorts to a wide variety of visitors' expectations. Tranquil countryside walks, café-crawling, beach promenading, or 24-hour fashionable clubbing co-exist without tears. Ischia really is a holiday paradise.

POPULATION:
60,335 (2007) (and six million visitors each year)

WHEN TO GO:
March to November. Come at the end of summer for the Settembre Sul Sagarato in the village of Piazzale Battistessa – two weeks of parades, concerts and general carousing.

HOW TO GET THERE:
By hydrofoil from Naples Beverello or Sorrento to Ischia Porto (E), Casamicciola (N) and Forio (W); or by ferry from Naples Beverello or Pozzuoli, to Ischia Porto.

HIGHLIGHTS:
San Montano bay near Lacco Ameno – where the thermal activity makes the shallow seawater very hot for swimming on Negombo beach.
The spectacular Castello Aragonese, high on a rock connected to Ischia Porto by a stone bridge, rebuilt in 1441 on fortifications begun in 474 BC, along with the Guevara Tower.
Il Torrione, the watchtower at Forio built in 1480, and restored as part museum and part artist's studio.
The stunning southern Mediterranean gardens of Villa la Mortella in Forio, planned by the English composer William Walton in 1946 to include only authentic local flora, and now reaching magnificent maturity.
Concerts at Villa la Colombaia, Forio – formerly the home of film director Luchino Visconti, with a lovely park.
The white façade, decorated with 700 majolicas of saints and scenes from the Passion, of Santa Maria della Neve at Forio (aka the Church of the Soccorso, because of its world-famous location on the promontory square), and its unique and harmonious blend of Greek-Byzantine, Moorish and Mediterranean architecture.
Cooking dinner in the thermally heated sand of Fumarole beach near Sant' Angelo, Ischia's most chic resort.

YOU SHOULD KNOW:
The most ancient springs on Ischia were consecrated to Apollo (Casamicciola), Hercules (Lacco Ameno), Venus Citaerea (Citara in Forio) and the Nitrodi Nymphs (Barano).

The spectacular Castello Aragonese, connected to Ischia Porto by a long stone bridge.

Capri

POPULATION:
13,100 (2001)
WHEN TO GO:
May, June, September or October.
HOW TO GET THERE:
By ferry or hydrofoil from Naples, Sorrento, Salerno, Positano or Amalfi.
HIGHLIGHTS:
Villa San Michele – built by Swedish doctor Axel Munthe, the villa has stunning gardens with views across the sea.
Villa Jovis – Tiberius' magnificent villa, one of the best-preserved Roman villas in Italy.
Grotta Azzurra – the Blue Grotto on Capri's north-west corner is accessible by boat. Book a trip with one of the many operators in the area.
The chairlift from Anacapri up to Monte Solaro takes 12 minutes and provides you with breathtaking views of the island.
YOU SHOULD KNOW:
Book accommodation before you go in the busy summer months.

On the south side of the Gulf of Naples, the beautiful island of Capri has been a celebrated beauty spot for centuries. Today this small island is a popular resort catering for well-heeled Italians and international celebrities, as well as day trippers from nearby Sorrento and the Amalfi Coast. The island rises sharply from the sea and is a beautiful jumble of tumbling purple, pink and white bougainvillea, lemon trees, narrow, winding lanes and pastel houses.

Capri's natural beauty was appreciated as far back as Roman times. The emperor Augustus came here to unwind, supposedly creating the world's first paleontological museum in the Villa Augustus, to display the Stone-Age artefacts found by his builders. Augustus' successor Tiberius built a series of villas on Capri, the most famous of which is the Villa Jovis, one of the best preserved Roman villas in Italy. The eight levels of walls and staircases which remain today only hint at the grandeur the villa must have had in its heyday. Recent reconstructions have shown the building to be a remarkable testament to 1st-century Roman architecture. In 27 AD, Tiberius permanently moved to Capri, running the Roman Empire from here until his death in 37 AD. Both Tiberius and his grand-nephew Caligula were reported to indulge in orgies and torture, even to throw women off the cliff next to the villa, although these may be rumours put about by their detractors.

Today Capri town and Anacapri, the two towns on the island, are crowded with tourists, but the rest of the island is hilly, beautiful and much quieter. Visit the gardens of Caesar Augustus and admire the astonishing views across to the Faraglioni, impressive rock stacks in the sea. At Anacapri don't miss the wonderful gardens of Villa San Michele, built by Axel Munthe on the ruins of one of Tiberius' villas.

Perhaps the most enchanting sight on the island is the Grotta Azzurra, or Blue Grotto, a magnificent sea cave on the rocky coast. Roman emperors reportedly used the Blue Grotto as a private bath. In modern times, it has become a popular tourist attraction visited by boat. Passengers lie down while the guides pull the boat through the low entrance into the cave. Inside, the sea seems to be lit from underwater, making it an astonishing, iridescent blue.

The beautiful island of Capri

Sardinia

Like Sicily, Sardinia belongs to Italy, but has its own distinct history, culture and language. Today it may be famous for its beautiful beaches and mysterious hinterland, but over 3,500 years Sardinia has survived countless invasions by Greeks, Phoenicians, Carthaginians, Romans, Arabs, Byzantine Turks and even Catalans. All these communities still exist in some form, and hundreds of local festivals reflect their indomitable cultural impact. You can see prehistoric castles, villages, temples and tombs all over the countryside – staging posts in the fascinating evolution of one of the Mediterranean's least-known people.

The island has two faces. Its coastline is unequalled in Europe for dramatic beauty coupled with prodigious fertility. Mimosa, oleander and the butterscotch scent of St John's wort waft past the discreet villas of the Costa Smeralda. Elsewhere you'll find huge rock formations eroded into fantastic animal shapes, ancient fishing villages and huge sand dunes concealing colonies of flamingoes. From the coastal plains you ascend a series of green valleys rising to Punta la Marmora at 1,834 m, (6,017 ft) on the mountainous plateau of the Barbagia region. It's an imposing wilderness of oak forests and spectacular canyons, and prehistoric rock villages are the only human habitations.

To the north, around Nuoro, each valley, and each traditional hill town like Desulo or Sorgono, seems to be the province of a different clan. A world away from the sophistication of some of Sardinia's cities and resorts, these places are the collective soul of the island. Their dialects and daily routines provide a direct link with the earliest Sardinians, who built the 7,000 (of 30,000) surviving circular fortifications and dwellings called *nuraghe*. Big and complex, these megalithic structures are spread across the island, and are found nowhere else in the world. Just like all the rest of Sardinia's potent attractions.

POPULATION:
1.66 million (2006 estimate)

WHEN TO GO:
Year-round – but Sardinia can be a place of extreme summer heat and vicious winter winds. Come in early May for the Festival of Sant' Efisio in the ancient town of Nora; since 1656, the guilds and confraternities of all the island's villages wear traditional costume, sing and dance in the most colourful and important of events.

HOW TO GET THERE:
By air to Cagliari (S), Alghero (W) or Olbia (N & E); by ferry from Naples or Civitavecchia to Cagliari (S) or Porto Torres (N).

HIGHLIGHTS:
The best and most complete of Sardinia's prehistoric structures, the Nuraghe Su Naraxi complex in Barumini – with the others, a UNESCO World Heritage Site. The 12th century battlements and medieval town of Alghero, where Catalan is still spoken.
The Maddalena archipelago opposite the Costa Smeralda in the north – especially the rose-coloured beaches of Budelli. The Nuragic village, and Roman and Carthaginian ruins of Nora, where the amphitheatre, forum, baths, temple and casbah are set picturesquely by the sea.
La Pelosa, one of Sardinia's finest beaches, at the small fishing village of Stintino on the northwestern tip. The 'palios' (horse races) and votive-candle racing, typical of the many village festivals around the middle of August.

YOU SHOULD KNOW:
'Fil'e ferru' ('iron wire') is an alcoholic local speciality. In the 19th century its distillation was illegal; when the bottles were buried, a small iron wire was stuck in the earth to mark the spot.

The picturesque harbour at Alghero

The town of Lipari at dusk

The Aeolian Islands

Named after Aeolus, god of the winds, the Aeolian Islands are a volcanic archipelago not far from Sicily's northern coast in the Tyrrhenian Sea. Also known as the Lipari Islands and Isole Eolie, the principal islands of this chain are Lipari, Salina, Filicudi, Alicudi, Stromboli, Panarea and Vulcano. Between them, the islands boast some beautiful scenery, great beaches, castles, thermal resorts, water sports, good fishing and, of course, some live volcanic activity.

These beautiful islands are quite rugged, with deep caverns, extraordinary rock formations, steep cliffs and splendid views. The volcanoes of Stromboli erupt fairly frequently. Rossellini's 1950 film,

Stromboli, was inspired by this volcano, which still regularly sends molten lava down its scarred rocks. This, however, hasn't prevented these islands from becoming popular smart resorts for well-heeled Italians, so expect crowds in summer.

Lipari is perhaps the most interesting of the islands from a historical point of view, with its citadel and archaeological remains. It is from here that most of the boat trips to the beaches and the other islands start out. Buoyant pumice and smooth black obsidian litter the beaches, and Lipari is well-served by restaurants and cafés. Filicudi, with its basalt shoreline, is much less developed as a tourist resort – the water is magnificently clear, you can hire a boat or scuba dive, and the beaches are often empty.

Panarea offers a lovely scene of rocky hills, ancient settlements, green slopes and pretty buildings characterized by columns and arches. Here can be found the Hotel Raya, opened in the 1960s by artist Paolo Tilche, which has given Panarea the reputation as a party island.

The garden island of Salina offers tranquillity, perfect if you are looking for a hideaway. It is one of the greenest of the islands, producing capers, delicious fish and octopus and a golden dessert wine, Malvasia. It was here that the film *Il Postino* was shot in the 1990s. There is a museum in Lingua, an interesting church in the port town of Santa Marina and spectacular rock formations at Pollara. The stone beaches are clean and rarely crowded, and the views over to Lipari and Stromboli are beautiful.

Stromboli has become the island of choice for a select fashionable crowd. The vulcano is still the main attraction, and is best viewed from an evening boat trip from where you can see the fiery show. Vulcano is fast becoming the most visited of the Aeolians. Volcanic activity ceased long ago but you can still climb the vulcano and peer down into the plugged core and appreciate the views to Lipari and Filicudi. Vulcano's other great attraction is the open-air pool of volcanic mud, which attracts bathers looking for a cure for skin complaints and other ailments.

POPULATION:
13,431 (2002)
WHEN TO GO:
May, June or September.
HOW TO GET THERE:
By boat, ferry or hydrofoil from Milazzo, Palermo or Naples.
HIGHLIGHTS:
The archeological museum in Lipari – artefacts from archaeological sites on the islands and shipwrecks.
The lighthouse with the horses's head on Strombolicchio.
Stromboli at night from a boat trip in the bay.
The ancient citadel (castello) of Lipari, with its acropolis.
The extraordinary red, ochre and yellow shoreline of Vulcano.
Laghetto di Fanghi – the volcanic mud baths on Vulcano are reputed to have therapeutic properties. Wash off the mud in the sea, warmed by the hot springs.
YOU SHOULD KNOW:
The archipelago is a UNESCO World Heritage Site due to its geology and vulcanology.

San Pietro

POPULATION:
6,500 (2007 estimate)
WHEN TO GO:
April to October. Come for the couscous festival in April, or the 4-day 'Girotonno' in early June celebrating the end of the 6-week spawning run of red tuna, for which San Pietro's fishermen are famous.
HOW TO GET THERE:
By ferry, from Porto Vesme (a tiny harbour south of Portoscuro) or Calasetta (on the neighbouring island of Sant' Antioco, which is connected by a Roman causeway to Sardinia itself), to Carloforte.
HIGHLIGHTS:
The dramatic cliffs of Mezzaluna in the south, and the amazing 'Colonne' ('Columns') – offshore pinnacle stacks formed from the same deep rose-coloured trachyte.
The wooden statue of the Black Madonna, symbol of the islanders' release from slavery, in the 19th century Chiesa della Madonna dello Schiavo in Carloforte. The lighthouse on the crags of Capo Sandolo, where enticing grottoes are cut into the cliffs, and you can see individual pebbles on the sea floor 20 m (66 ft) underwater.
The Festival 'Dall' isola dell' isola una penisola' ('The island [San Pietro] of a promontory of an island [Sardinia]) which celebrates San Pietro's Ligurian 'apartness' in street theatre, dance, music, stilt-walking, and communal feasting, at the end of summer.
Freshly caught red tuna, prepared with an extraordinary blend of Genoese (Ligurian) and North African influences.
YOU SHOULD KNOW:
San Pietro is unashamedly introverted, and much more likely to welcome the smaller number of visitors who come in May or September, than the August crowds.

Just 7 km (4.3 mi) from its southwest coast, San Pietro typifies the amalgamation of cultures so characteristic of Sardinia. Though sparsely inhabited for centuries, it was only fully settled in 1736, when King Charles Emmanuel III of Savoy granted it to the descendants of Ligurian coral fishermen from the Genoese suburb of Pegli, who had been enslaved by corsairs and held on the Tunisian island of Tabarka. In gratitude, they named their new town in the King's honour, and today the island itself is often known as Carloforte. Dominated by the belltower of San Carlo, Carloforte is one of the most characteristic fishing villages on the 53 sq km (32 sq mi) island. Its bastions, defense walls and ramparts recall the ever-present pirate threat of the time – though they have been replaced on the seaward side by the lovely 'Lungomare', an elegant, late 19th century promenade. With the smell of pesto – a Genoese speciality – everywhere and the heavily Ligurian local accent, San Pietro feels weirdly dislocated from the normal world.

Its geography helps. Inland it's mountainous and green, full of pine groves, junipers and strawberry trees. In one remote valley near the west coast, lush with wild rosemary, orchids and succulents unique to the island, there's a sanctuary for a very rare breed of (notoriously stubborn) miniature donkey, the 'asinello sardo'. Resident on San Pietro for 5,000 years, they faced extinction by road-kill and human appetite. Now they, and all the island's wildlife, are protected and recovering in numbers – especially the birds. Once, Phoenicians called it 'sparrow hawk island', and with their prey (hares and small animals) again thriving, the sparrow hawks are back. Like the flamingoes which have chosen it as their refuge, they demonstrate San Pietro's unspoiled environmental purity.

The crystal clear waters around San Pietro

Ponza Harbour

Ponza

The largest of the Pontine Islands between Rome and Naples, Ponza is a volcanic remnant lying 33 km (20 mi) south of Cape Circeo, in the Tyrrhenian Sea. It's an irregular crescent of vividly coloured cliffs and crags 12 km (7 mi) long and never more than 2 km (1.4 mi) wide. The kaolin and tufa rock has eroded into fantastic shapes, inspiring names like 'the monk' and 'the giant pair of pants'; and there are giant 'faraglioni' – rock stacks that appear to march out of the sea and across the beach. Long ago, the Etruscans enhanced Ponza's natural charms by hollowing out luminescent sea-grottoes in the cliffs, and the Romans dug through solid rock to create galleries that gave access to the best beaches. In that era, Ponza was covered by primeval forest – and on Monte Guardia, its highest hill, you can still see the rotting stumps of giant trees with a diameter of 2.5 m (8 ft). Now you look down on stepped terraces of vines, cactus pears and fig trees, engulfing the wealth of ruins, ancient and modern, left by a dozen occupying powers.

Ponza was once a Roman penal colony for unwanted Christians. Its isolation also served for the Roman Emperor Nero's exile, and again for Mussolini in 1943. Today the clusters of domed pastel cubes that are the hallmark of Ponsese architecture are exclusive in a different way. What little room there is on the island to expand is protected from development, and existing residents have curtailed neon bars and discos. You don't have to be rich to enjoy its tranquillity, beauty, and terrific diving, but Ponza's style certainly favours the wealthy Italians who holiday here. It's a discreet, clubby kind of place – but most visitors agree that it's a club they would be only too happy to join.

POPULATION:
3,315 (2000)
WHEN TO GO:
April to October. Come for the Festival of San Silverio, Ponza's patron saint, around 20 June.
HOW TO GET THERE:
By hydrofoil from Anzio or Naples; by ferry from Formia, Anzio and Terracina, to Ponza.
HIGHLIGHTS:
The long crescent of dark volcanic sand under the high cliffs of Chiaia di Luna, accessible on foot from the port via a gallery drilled through the rock by the Romans.
The Grotte di Pilato, three caves near Le Forna where the Romans dug out fishponds to harvest their favourite muranea fish.
Swimming among the arches and grottoes of the Piscine Naturali at Le Forna, an enchanting place to relax.
Hiring a boat to explore the dramatic coastline of Ponza, and to dive among the shoals of colourful fish that congregate in its exotic underwater rock formations.
The nature reserve and ruins of the 1213 Benedictine monastery on the nearby island of Zannone.
YOU SHOULD KNOW:
Lucia Rosa is a local heroine who threw herself into the sea rather than marry against her wishes. To many people round the world, she is a martyr for women's rights, and a symbol of human rights.

The Valley of the Temples at Agrigento

Sicily

The largest island in the Mediterranean, and the first multicultural society in the world, Sicily is the eye of the needle of European history. Strategically placed at the tip of Italy, it has served as the clearing house for occupying powers from the Middle East, Central Asia, Africa, Greece, the Balkans, Iberia, northern Europe, and even (recently, briefly, but with equally profound influence) America. It's big enough to absorb, and small enough to transform by osmosis every culture imposed on it, and with a sense of identity strong enough to influence other cultures in turn. Blessed with a near-perfect climate and fertile, volcanic soil, the island promises the best kind of Mediterranean beach holiday, then subverts its own hedonism with the competing magnet of cultural riches.

Sicily is a triangle with a 1,000 km (600 mi) coastline, mainly rocky in the north, and sandy in the south. In the east Mount Etna, Europe's most active volcano, rises to 3,330 m (10,800 ft) above a plateau of lava and limestone scarred by ravines and dramatic gorges. Mountain forests give way to great plains of wheat, and whole ranges of terraced vines, oranges, lemons, olives and almond trees; a rural culture as ancient as the ruins they surround. But history is very much alive in Sicily: in the palaces of Palermo, the Baroque fantasia of Noto, Agrigento's spectacular temples, medieval Monreale or Greek Taormina you feel the continuum of the Sicilian character – explosive, indulgent, amused and amusing. In these places, and even in the dusty, traditional farming villages of the interior uplands, Sicily is glamorous. It's a glamour earned by millennia of hard graft, recycling what history has left there for the benefit of new visitors.

The Borromean Islands

Lake Maggiore is the westernmost of Italy's three major pre-alpine lakes. The Borromean Islands lie in Maggiore's western arm between Stresa and Verbinia. They are tiny. The three islands and two islets together cover only 20 hectares (50 acres), and only one of them is inhabited throughout the year. Their name comes from the illustrious Borromeo clan, whose family fiefdom they have been (and still partially are) since the 14th century. Over the years, the Borromei developed the three islands as summer palaces and gardens, both of which they stocked with treasures and opulent rarities that properly reflected their exalted status in politics, the Church, and the highest social echelons of Europe. Now the islands and their enchanting location are a major local tourist attraction.

Isola dei Pescatori, the most northerly of the three, is no longer in the Borromeo family. Only 350 m (1,100 ft) long and 100 m (320 ft) wide, it is home to an ancient fishing village of a single main street with cobbled alleys leading off it to the stone promenade running round its edge – a bulwark against the erosion of frequent flooding. The fishing still pays: the island is popular with day-trippers, and it's the only one you can stay on. As a community, the village long preceded the Borromei. The old houses have granite portals and wooden balconies of rustic simplicity, and the Church of San Vittore il Moro contains the remains of a 9th century chapel. The island's charm is a total contrast to the magnificence of Isola Bella, once a barren rock, then from 1632 the huge summer palazzo of the House of Borromeo. Between 1751 and 1837, guests like Edward Gibbon, Napoleon and Josephine de Beauharnais, and Stendhal enjoyed its grandeur. They also enjoyed the exquisite gardens of the Borromeo's minor palace on Isola Madre, built by the family to escape their own social whirl, and still full of the rare plantings and exotic birds they brought there.

POPULATION:
Isola dei Pescatori 50; (the other islands are uninhabited except for caretakers/custodians).

WHEN TO GO:
Year-round. The climate of Lake Maggiore is famously mild in winter and summer. Come in June/July when Isola Bella hosts the Stresa Music Festival.

HOW TO GET THERE:
By ferry (a single route serves each of the three islands in turn), or water-taxi, from Stresa, Baveno, Pallanza and Intra.

HIGHLIGHTS:
The 17th century Flemish tapestries in the Palazzo on Isola Bella.
The 17th and 18th century furniture and collections of china and livery in the house on Isola Madre – reflecting the private, more human side of the grand family Borromeo.
The grottoes at the Palazzo of Isola Bella, decorated with scenes of marine flora and fauna by some of Italy's greatest artists.
Taking a picnic and bathing in the tranquil isolation of Malghera (between I. Bella and I. dei Pescatori) or Isolino di San Giovanni, just off Pallanza.

YOU SHOULD KNOW:
The Borromeo family has included counts, dukes and cardinals – but its most illustrious ancestor is the family saint, St Charles Borromeo.

Isola Bella sits in Lake Maggiore.

San Giulio

Close to Lake Maggiore in the foothills of the Alps, Lake Orta is a
tranquil, often misty vision of scenic charm. Of the villages and tiny
market towns that sit comfortably on its green, wooded hillside
banks, Orta town is the prettiest and one of the oldest. It lies on the
end of a promontory opposite the intriguing island 400 m (1,300 ft)
offshore on which much of its reputation rests.

Isola San Giulio is tiny – only 275m (825 ft) long and 140m
(420 ft) wide, but crowded with buildings, towers and terraces
positioned with casual elegance among lofty trees. Dominating them
all is the great cruciform of the Benedictine monastery and seminary
that in 1842 replaced the castle and Bishop's Palace that had stood
there for over 1,000 years. But the largest building on the island is in
fact the Basilica of St Giulio, founded in 390 by Julius of Novara,
whose remains still lie in its crypt. Not much was left after Otto I
destroyed the original in 962; but Otto deeded the land to the
Basilica's canons and the present Romanesque building, begun at
that time, has been extended ever since.

When you actually step onto the island, San Giulio's haunting
beauty is magnified by the unexpected quiet. The short circular lane
between the monastery and the sumptuous 18th century private
villas lining the shore is even called 'The Way of Silence', and dotted
with signs admonishing you to 'Listen to the water, the wind, your
steps' or advising 'If you can be yourself, you are everything'.
Perhaps in reaction to the self-conscious spirituality, one of the
private villas carries a Venetian proverb instead – 'Protect this house;
so never may a lawyer or a doctor set foot here'.

Isola San Giulio in Lake Orta

POPULATION:
1 (officially – the resident priest of St Bartholomew's)

WHEN TO GO:
Year-round. Come for the All Souls' Day (November 2) procession of Sacconi Rossi (Red Hoods), when the Devoti di Gesu Crocifisso al Calvario e di SS Maria Addolorata, for centuries specialists in hauling bodies out of the river for Christian burial, commemorate the dead by walking the island perimeter in costume and with a service at the Church of S Giovanni Calibita. It's not a tourist ceremony – it is linked directly to fundamental Roman mythology and belief.

HOW TO GET THERE:
By car, from Trastevere (left bank), via the restored 46 BC Ponte Cestio, to one of about 30 parking spaces near the piazza; or on foot, from the Piazza Monte Savello near the Ghetto, via Ponte Fabricio.

HIGHLIGHTS:
The view from the downstream end of the Ponte Rotto (Broken Bridge), the only remaining arch of the 179 BC Ponte Aemilius. To one side you can see the circular hole in the embankment of the Cloaca Maxima, Rome's main sewer since 300 BC.
The carved stone wellhead in the Basilica of St Bartholomew, according to legend on the same spot that Aesculepius' snake nested by a freshwater spring.
The 17th century church of S Giovani Calibata. The spire, commissioned in 1867 by Pope Pius IX to replace the destroyed ancient Roman obelisk that made the island look more like a ship, and designed by Ignazio Giacometti with the statues of SS Bartholomew, Paulinus of Nola, Francis and John.
The 11th century tower and fortress of the Pierleoni, the only Jewish family to produce a Pope (Anacletus II 1130-38). Now the HQ of the Sacconi Rossi.

YOU SHOULD KNOW:
Rahere, medieval playboy and court jester to King Henry I of England, was cured of malaria at the hospital of St Bartholomew. He reformed, became a monk, and in 1123 founded the world famous hospital of St Bartholomew ('Bart's') in London.

Tiber Island

Where the Tiber flows through Rome, there is a single island in its southern bend. Technically, Tiber Island is an eyot, measuring a mere 270 km (900 ft) long and 66 m (205 ft) wide it is an agglomeration of ancient fluvial silt and detritus. To Romans, it is the site of the oldest human settlement in the area, only abandoned by their city fathers in the 9th-8th centuries BC when improved archery techniques forced them to move to the Capitoline Hill for safety.

As Rome grew across its seven hills, the island became first an isolation ward for the chronically sick, and then a place of healing and even cure. As early as 290 BC, it was associated with the cult of Aesculepius, the Greek god of healing; remains of the temple dedicated to him, and artefacts of the cult, were discovered at the downstream end in the 19th century underneath the 10th century church of St Adalbert. Today this church is called St Bartholomew's after its primary relics, and is enclosed by a massive basilica. The island's medical traditions are continued at the upstream (eastern) end, where since 1548 hospitaller monks have run one of Rome's most significant hospitals.

The more you investigate tiny Tiber Island, the more you will be intrigued by small details. The pedestrian Ponte Fabricio, Rome's oldest (62 BC) surviving bridge, connects it to the Campo Martio. Two four-faced Janus herms are mounted on its parapet – Janus is usually two-faced, looking both ways, and four-faced images guarded only the most important intersections. Look under the perimeter stairway at the downstream end to see the 1st century travertine marble decoration of the island as a trireme warship, with Aesculepius' snake visibly slithering aboard. We take the snake-entwined Caduceus for granted as the symbol of medicine – Tiber Island reminds us of once widespread commitment to its real meaning.

Colourful boats and homes line one of Burano's canals.

Burano

POPULATION:
3,000 (2007)
WHEN TO GO:
Year-round. The sound of lapping water, and the colours of the houses reflected in the canals, are just as striking in winter mists as in the intensity of the sun.
HOW TO GET THERE:
By vaporetto (water-bus) No. LN (Laguna Norte) from the Fondamento Nuove on Venice's north shore; or by water-taxi from Marco Polo airport.
HIGHLIGHTS:
The impressive tilt of the 53 m (170 ft) high Campanile Storto ('Drunken Tower'), built in Renaissance style in the 17th century and restored with neo-classical elements between 1703-14. You can see it best from the Ponte di Terranova.
The wonderful paintwork – amazing even by Burano's rainbow standard – of Casa Bepi Sua, the archetype of Buranese buildings.
The Wednesday morning market.
Tiepolo's 'Crucifixion', painted in 1725, in the Chiesa di San Martino Vescovo.
The Museo del Merletto, the lacemaking museum of masterpieces including wedding dresses and parasols, some as old as the 15th century.
YOU SHOULD KNOW:
Philippe Starck, the interior designer known for his minimalist work, owns three houses on Burano.

One of the few islands in the Venetian lagoon with sufficient character to emerge from the shadow of its illustrious neighbour, Burano lies 7 km (4 mi) north of Venice. It was settled by people from the Altino region on the mainland, escaping from the carnage of barbarian invasion in the 5-6th centuries. Like Venice, the flimsy wattle-and-daub houses were gradually replaced by stone houses for the fishing community that evolved there; and the tradition of brightly-painted houses for which it is now famous grew with the community.

Burano's isolation was reinforced by Venice's power: the Doges used it as a dumping-ground for victims of plague, malaria and madness. It became, and still is, self-sufficient, with a strong sense of workaday identity that makes it an authentic link in the fabric of Venetian social history. It has no airs or graces, and its ambience is the opposite of that inspired by the grandeur of the Grand Canal. It contains no major 'sights', and there's no space to facilitate a tourist industry, though the Buranese welcome visitors.

Burano is world-famous for its lace. Lacemaking developed over the centuries in the nimble fingers of the fishermen's wives, waiting for the boats to return, and from the 16th century to the end of the Venetian Republic in 1797 it enjoyed royal patronage. It was revived in the desperate winter of 1872, when ice prevented fishing, and Burano faced starvation. The ancient patterns and the delicacy of execution were immediately successful; but now there are no new apprentices to learn, and 'Burano' lace on sale is invariably machine-made and imported. Otherwise, Burano is physically unchanged, except for the covering of one canal to make its only piazza. If Venice demands a series of superlatives, Burano is superlatively ordinary – and that is its beauty.

Torcello

Lying at the northern end of the Venetian Lagoon, Torcello is a quiet, haunting, deserted place, with a handful of old buildings and just a few dozen inhabitants, who grow vegetables. A thousand years ago it was more important than Venice and had a population of over ten thousand.

The islands in the lagoon were first settled in the 5th and 6th centuries. In 452 AD, Attila the Hun destroyed the beautiful coastal city of Altinum and its inhabitants sought refuge in this marshy region using rafts of wooden posts as foundations. Germanic attacks continued on this isolated corner of Byzantium, and in 638 Torcello became the see of the Bishop of Altinum. It became a very important centre of trade and was more or less autonomous. However the lagoon around the island gradually became a swamp; navigation became impossible and malaria was a serious danger. Most of the island's population departed and Venice began its ascendancy.

In its heyday, Torcello had palaces, monasteries and churches, but with its decline, nearly all of its buildings were dismantled and used in the construction of Venice. The Cathedral of Santa Maria Assunta, founded in 639, still stands however – its 11th century campanile can be seen right across the lagoon. There are a few cafés, a museum and another church on the island, as well as the Locanda Cipriani inn and restaurant, where famous figures from the arts and European royalty have enjoyed the peace and the captivating views. From the landing stage you reach the centre of Torcello by following a brick path and crossing the old stone bridge.

POPULATION:
60 (2005)
WHEN TO GO:
All year
HOW TO GET THERE:
Ferry from Venice
HIGHLIGHTS:
The Cathedral, which has many untouched Veneto-Byzantine features.
The Madonna and Child mosaic with its stunning gold background – one of the great works of Byzantine art.
The mosaic of the Last Judgment, covering the whole of the Cathedral's west wall. Santa Fosca – 11th century church in the form of a Greek cross.
The museum – housing art, archaeology and historical exhibits in the 13th century Palazzo del Consiglio.
Attila's Throne – an ancient stone seat outside Santa Fosca.
YOU SHOULD KNOW:
The Locanda Cipriani has works produced by Chagall and Max Ernst during their visits to the island.

The pretty houses of Torcello

Malta

POPULATION:
401,880 (2007 estimate)
WHEN TO GO:
March to December
HOW TO GET THERE:
Direct flights from many European cities; ferries from Sicily.
HIGHLIGHTS:
Valletta, the capital – a glorious city with important buildings and museums, steep streets, sea views and, even in summer, sea breezes. The Archaeological Museum, which puts the Neolithic sites in context.
St John's Co-Cathedral – awe-inspiring and opulent: the works of art include a fine painting by Caravaggio
Mdina Rabat – high above central Malta, Mdina, the Arab capital, is now a beautiful, silent Baroque town. Lively Rabat has Roman remains and a cave where St Paul is said to have preached.
The Neolithic temples of Hagar Qim and Mnajdra – two large complexes set on a beautiful clifftop on the south coast.
The temples of Hypogeum and Tarxien – of great archaeological importance, these are located in a suburb of Valletta; visits are limited.
YOU SHOULD KNOW:
The Knights of the Order of St John paid a token of a falcon to the Holy Roman Emperor for the island.

Malta lies in the middle of the Mediterranean; its closest neighbour is Sicily but it looks very North African. The landscape is sun-bleached, rocky and waterless; where the thin soil can be farmed it is intensively worked. The tawny fields are criss-crossed by dry-stone walls – the soft golden limestone is used for all construction here. Though relatively small, Malta is one of the most densely populated places in Europe; yet somehow does not feel it.

Civilization came very early – the Neolithic temples date to 3500 BC. Later Malta's strategic position made it very important and it was colonized by a succession of powers from the Phoenicians to the British. Christianity arrived during Roman rule with St Paul, who was shipwrecked here and then sheltered by the islanders. The Arabs had impact on the language – Malti has Arabic grammar but uses words from many languages and is written in the Roman alphabet. The Knights of St John arrived in 1530, held the fortified island against the Turks and handed it to Napoleon in 1789; they left the greatest architectural legacy. In 1942 Malta endured five months of intensive German bombing. It became independent in 1964 and is now part of the E.U. English is universally spoken.

This is a holiday island, with a good climate and excellent swimming and diving, but the unique historical sights are the real highlights. The Knights' fortified cities that surround the magnificent Grand Harbour are unforgettable. Ancient temples and

other fascinating archaeological sites dot the island. Hundreds of churches, many flamboyant, domed Baroque structures, dominate town, village and landscape. Despite mass tourism, Malta retains the feel of an older world. The people are well mannered, friendly and devout – though they enjoy the summer-long fiestas, when the night explodes with fireworks.

A narrow street in the beautiful Baroque town of Mdina

Gozo

Tiny Gozo – 14 km (9 mi) at its widest, lies close to north-west Malta, but it has a strong identity of its own. The island is much more fertile than its neighbour, producing grapes, fruit and vegetables on its terraced slopes. There are flat-topped hills, steep green valleys and some lovely undeveloped beaches ranging from rocky coves to long sandy sweeps. More conservative than Malta, Gozo has a relaxed, rural atmosphere. It was settled around 5000 BC, and it was here that the earliest of the great temples was built. Its fortified city, high in the centre of the island, was not proof against the Arabs or later Turkish invaders who almost depopulated the island, but it remained self-reliant and during World War II could offer refuge to evacuees from Valletta and provisions for beleaguered Malta.

There are only two real resorts – busy Marsalform on its wide bay, and popular Xlendi, squeezed into a narrow fjord. Inland Gozo is sprinkled with sleepy villages and little towns, all with their huge domed churches – like the Maltese, Gozitans are very devout.

Rabat, the principal town, was renamed Victoria for the British Queen's Jubilee. It is built on a cluster of steep conical hills which feature on the coat of arms. It is a handsome town of shady squares, churches and Baroque buildings, two splendid theatres and quiet lanes where women sit making lace. Day-trippers flood over from Malta, but, with its slow pace and peaceful walks and its reserved but friendly natives, Gozo is a rewarding place to stay.

POPULATION:
31,053 (2005)
WHEN TO GO:
April to November
HOW TO GET THERE:
Ferry from Malta.
HIGHLIGHTS:
Ggantija Temples, in Xaghra – the most impressive temples in the Maltese islands, and the oldest, dating from around 3600 BC.
Calypso's Cave and Ramla Bay. Gozo is said to be the isle of Calypso and the cave above the glorious red-sand bay is where she supposedly kept Odysseus prisoner.
The Citadel in Rabat, built high above the town. The fortifications offer fine views over the whole island.
The Cathedral – with a trompe l'oeil painted ceiling; money ran out before the dome could be built but the painting is very effective!
The modern church at Xewkija, with one of the largest domes in the world.
The salt pans along the coast from Marsalforn – a web of old rock pans where seawater evaporates into crystals.
YOU SHOULD KNOW:
In the 1970s, a bridge was begun from Malta to Gozo, but work was halted after Gozitan protests.

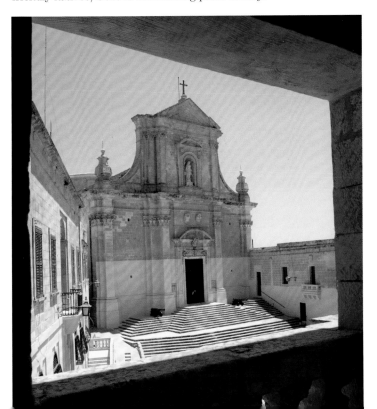

Gozo Cathedral

Some of the 147 islands of the Kornati Archipelego

POPULATION:
No permanent inhabitants.
WHEN TO GO:
May to September
HOW TO GET THERE:
There are no ferries between the islands. Rent a boat, sail your own, or take an excursion from the island of Murter (headquarters of the National Park and connected to the mainland by bridge at Tisno). The nearest sizeable town is Sibenik, within 50 km (30 mi) of both Split and Zadar airports.
HIGHLIGHTS:
Island of Mana – longest 'crown', 1,350 m (4,428 ft).
Klobucar – the islet with the highest 'crown', 82 m (269 ft).
The geological phenomenon of magazinova skrila, a peculiar limestone rockslide at Kravjacica, Striznja, or Vruje on Kornat.
The breathtaking view of the archipelago from Otocevak on the island of Piskera.
YOU SHOULD KNOW:
You must buy entrance, fishing and scuba diving passes at the National Park Office in Murter or at one of the reception centres in the Park. Apart from a few areas prohibited for conservation purposes, you can sail freely throughout the archipelago.
Camping on the islands is not allowed but you can moor your boat for an overnight stay in any of the sixteen specifically designated coves. It is also possible to rent a cottage.

Kornati Archipelago

According to Irish playwright George Bernard Shaw, the Kornati Islands were made by God as his final act of Creation out of 'his tears, the stars, and his breath. The sublime beauty of this labyrinth of 147 islands, islets and reefs is overwhelming: dazzling white limestone cones punctuated by daubs of deep green erupt like magic from the contrasting blues of sea and sky. In the evening light the white rock is suffused in rosy pink and orange hues, and at night there is so little light pollution that an infinity of stars is visible, awe-inspiring in number and intensity.

The geomorphology of the region is extraordinary. The Kornati are the 'crowns' of a tectonic rift that runs underwater from Istria, partially emerging above sea level along a 35 km (22 mi) stretch of the central Croatian coast. The white limestone terrain is largely barren, apart from sparse patches of aromatic shrubs and scattered vineyards or small citrus groves. The islands end abruptly at their south-west faces where jagged cliffs, indented with caves, crevices, and inlets, plunge into a sea trench that is the richest fishing ground in the Adriatic.

Eighty-nine of the islands and their surrounding waters are a National Park covering an area of 220 sq km (86 sq mi). Less than a quarter of the ark is land, the largest island being Kornat at 33 sq km (13 sq mi). Day excursions can be made to the islands but it is worth trying to spend at least one night. 'Robinson Crusoe' holidays can be arranged: a weekly boat drops you off to stay in a hut without electricity or running water – until the next boat passes by to 'rescue' you from this magical otherworld.

Dugi Otok

This curious island in the northern Dalmatian Archipelago gets its name (Long Island) from its distinctive skinny shape, 43 km (27 mi) long and under 5 km (3 mi) wide. The karst limestone rock here has formed into an extraordinarily varied morphology with a height range of more than 300 m (1,000 ft). The landscape is dry and rugged, with regions of completely bare rock giving way to sparse grazing pastures of thorny shrubs and aromatic herbs, interspersed with copses of maritime pine and olive trees.

On the northern tip of the island, Saharun is an immaculate beach of pure white sand – a breathtaking contrast to the intense blue of the Adriatic. The west coast has steep cliffs rising to 338 m (1,109 ft), while the east coast is a low-lying intricate shoreline of rocky coves and shingle beaches culminating in the fantastic Telascica Bay at its south-eastern tip – one of the largest bays in the Adriatic, protected by steep cliffs up to 166 m (545 ft) high. It is a 10 km (6 mi) long conservation area of complex inlets, an extraordinary salt lake, and offshore islets that seem to hover surreally on the still waters of the bay. To its northeast you find yourself in a parched, barren moonscape – turn to the southwest and you are suddenly surrounded by pine, fig and olive trees.

Dugi Otok is a fascinating place to explore on foot, with traces of Illyrian and Roman settlements as well as early Croatian remains, picturesque old villages and the attractive fishing town of Sali. The island is all the more charming for being one of the less frequented of the Croatian coast with a slow pace of life and relaxed, friendly atmosphere.

POPULATION:
1,772 (2001)
WHEN TO GO:
April to October
HOW TO GET THERE:
From Zagreb, fly or drive to Zadar. The ferry from Zadar to Dugi Otok takes 1½ hours.
HIGHLIGHTS:
Strasna Pec – a cave with amazing stalactites and stalagmites.
Saljsko Polje – 'Olive forest' with olive trees up to 700 years old.
The lighthouse of Veli Rat – climb to the top for an amazing view.
National Park of Kornati – 147 islets off the south east coast.
The village of Dragove – with a 15th century church and fine views.
Snorkelling in Pantera Bay – sunken boat wrecks.
YOU SHOULD KNOW:
The underwater caves and offshore waters of Dugi Otok are among the best places for scuba diving in the region.

The tranquil bay around Luka

The beautiful medieval walled town of Korcula

Korcula Island

In Central Dalmatia rising out of the Adriatic off the southern coast of Croatia is the island of Korcula, with its low mountains, pine forests, olive groves and scent of wild herbs. At 47 km (29 mi) long and 6 to 7 km (3.7 to 4.3 mi) wide, it is one of the larger of Croatia's thousand islands. The island is hilly, the highest peak being Klupca just above village of Pupnat at 568 m (1,864 ft). The southern coast of the island is steep and eroded, while the northern shores, facing the mainland, are tamer and boast little pebble beaches. In the far north-east of Korcula, near the village of Lumbarda, there are some lovely sandy beaches.

The main draw on this enchanting island is the town of Korcula, a beautiful medieval walled town on a promontory of land protruding out into the Peljesac Channel. The city was surrounded in the 14th century by thick defensive stone walls punctuated by 12 imposing towers, many of which remain today. The island has changed hands several times over the centuries, but the architectural legacy left by the Venetians between 1420 and 1779 is second to none, and is most apparent in the town. Inside the walls the narrow lanes branch off the main street like the bones of a fish, planned in this way to reduce the effects of wind and sun and make life more comfortble for the inabitants.

Built in the 15th century, Revelin Tower forms the present-day Land Gate which is the main entrance into the Old Town. There was once a drawbridge here, but it was replaced by stairs when the threat of invasion was reduced. The symbol of Venice, the winged lion of St Mark, can be seen above the arch. The view from the top of the tower is lovely, and offers a 360° panorama of the town and its attractive rooftops.

Probably the most important building in the Old Town, the Sveti Marko Cathedral (Cathedral of St Mark) was built in the 15th century in the Gothic-Renaissance style. The main portal, built by Bonino of Milan in 1412, features Adam and Eve on either side, and St Mark above. There is a beautiful fluted rose window in the centre of the façade. The Renaissance interior was carved by a famous local stonemason, Marko Andijic, and contains treasures such as an early Tintoretto.

The Venetian architecture is most obvious in the streets around the Cathedral of St Mark, where there are various Gothic, Renaissance and Baroque palaces built for Korcula aristocrats. Opposite the cathedral is Arneri Palace, with its lovely Gothic facade and Renaissance-Baroque cloister. Next to it is Ismaeli Gabrielli's Palace, built in the Renaissance style in the 16th century, currently housing an art gallery and the Town Museum with exhibits relating to shipbuilding, seafaring and stone-masonry. Also close-by is the 17th-century Bishop's Palace, which holds the town's treasury with a collection of paintings including works by Raphael, Leonardo da Vinci, Carpaccio, Bassano and Tiepolo.

The town of Korcula is famous for Moreska, a traditional sword dance which was common throughout the Mediterranean in the 12th and 13th centuries and became popular in Korcula in the 16th century. The dance probably originated in Spain, inspired by the conflict between Moors and Christians. In Korcula its popularity was probably linked with the struggles against the Ottoman Empire. Through the centuries Moreska vanished from the Mediterranean and now it is only performed in Korcula.

POPULATION:
16,182 (2001)
WHEN TO GO:
April to July, or September to October.
HOW TO GET THERE:
Fly to Dubrovnik or Split, then take a ferry to the island.
HIGHLIGHTS:
Views from the top of Revelin Tower (the Land Gate) over the rooftops of the town to the sea.
The Venetian Palaces in the Old Town – the Baroque, Gothic and Renaissance architecture is beautiful. Some of the palaces now house museums and galleries, which offer a great way for visitors to see inside.
The Cathedral of St Mark – a lovely Gothic-Renaissance cathedral with lots of art treasures.
Moreska – a medieval sword dance performed only in the town of Korcula. Performances take place close to the Land Gate in the summer months.
YOU SHOULD KNOW:
There is only a handful of hotels on the island so make sure you book before you go.

Ciovo

The island of Ciovo is an extension of the magnificent medieval UNESCO World Heritage coastal town of Trogir to which it is connected by a drawbridge. In the past Ciovo was known as 'the barn of Trogir' because so much of the town's food was grown in the island's fertile soil. Today, it has become a popular summer retreat for residents of the nearby city of Split as well as being Trogir's beach.

The island has a hilly landscape, just less than 30 sq km (12 sq mi) in area, with lush and varied scenery. The northern coast is covered in a profusion of pine and cypress forest and, along the south, there are cliffs up to 150 m (490 ft) high. Here, near the church of Prizidnice, there is a famous 460 year-old hermit's sanctuary built into the rocky cliffside. It is an extraordinarily atmospheric pilgrimage site with wonderful views over the startlingly blue waters of the Adriatic. The inland scenery is a picturesque cultivated landscape of olives, figs, almonds and vines, dotted with villages and hamlets. There are innumerable secluded coves along the coasts, with sand or shingle beaches.

There are signs of habitation on the island dating from prehistoric times. In the Middle Ages it was used only as a leper colony but in the 15th century, when the Dalmatian coast was menaced by attacks from Turkish pirates, the citizens of Trogir retreated here for safety and eventually the island became an integral part of the town.

Ciovo is a rare combination of unspoilt seashore side by side with stunning historic urban architecture, with the added bonus that the island has not yet been overrun by mass tourism.

A view of Ciovo from the Adriatic

*The village of Baska on
Krk Island in the Kvarner Gulf*

Krk

Krk vies with neighbouring Cres as the largest island of the Adriatic, covering an area of 409 sq km (160 sq mi). The island is famous for its beaches and ancient cultural heritage as well as its olive oil, white wine and honey. Known as the 'golden island', it is a lively tourist destination with excellent entertainment, sports and sailing facilities in a beautiful natural setting.

The limestone terrain is varied with more vegetation than many of the Croatian islands. The rugged north-west is wild and barren with a high point of 569 m (1,866 ft). The terrain here is difficult and can be dangerous when the fierce Bora north wind is blowing. Towards the south the landscape grows gentler with fertile cultivated valleys and wooded hills. About a third of the island is forested and there are two lakes that provide the fresh water supply. The coastline is ragged with numerous sand or shingle coves reached by steep paths down the cliffs, often sheltered by pine trees.

Krk is rich in animal and bird life and there are wonderful walks and cycle paths that meander through the woods, between picturesque villages, and along the rocky shores. The old towns and villages have some outstanding historic sights including the magnificent 12th century cathedral, medieval city walls and castle of Krk town. In the south, Punat, a picturesque coastal resort of narrow streets and old stone houses, has the largest marina in Croatia, and Baska Bay is renowned for its magnificent beach, nearly 2 km (over 1 mi) long. Despite the popularity of Krk, you can still find traditional folk culture amongst the trendy tourist attractions. There is something for everyone here – sports, sightseeing, drinking, dancing or simply lounging around by the sea.

POPULATION:
17,860 (2001)
WHEN TO GO:
May to September
HOW TO GET THERE:
Krk has an international airport, which serves as the airport for Rijeka, the nearest mainland town, only 30 km (20 mi) away and linked to the island by a 1,400 m (4,590 ft) long causeway. There is a regular bus service between Krk and Rijeka. Ferries from the islands of Rab or Cres.
HIGHLIGHTS:
Vbrnik – a picturesque village, clinging to the cliffside, that produces Vbrnicka zlahtina, a golden white wine known as the island's best.
Soline Bay – a former salt pan with water at a maximum depth of 1 m (3 ft), rich in mineral deposits and known for its health-giving properties.
Omisalj – the oldest settlement on the island on a 90 m (295 ft) high cliff on the north-west coast.
YOU SHOULD KNOW:
Krk is an important Croatian heritage centre. The Baska Tablet (now in the Croatian Academy in Zagreb) was found here. It is a stone slab dating from 1100 on which the name 'Croatia' appears for the first time. It is considered the 'birth certificate' of Croatian culture.

Hvar Town – one of the best-loved resorts on the Dalmatian coast

Hvar

POPULATION:
11,459 (2001)
WHEN TO GO:
April to June, or September to October
HOW TO GET THERE:
By ferry from Split.
HIGHLIGHTS:
The church of St Lawrence at Vrboska – the church houses some valuable works of art and cultural treasures.
Stari Grad – ancient Greek Pharos set in a deep bay on the coast.
Jelsa – a small town and important port in the north of the island known for the wonderful red wine produced there.
The vineyard of Zlatan Otok at Sveta Nedjelja – sample the wines.
The islets of Paklenski Otoci and Scedro – these lovely islets offer great opportunities for walking, swimming and sailing, with wonderful views of Hvar.
YOU SHOULD KNOW:
Hvar was voted one of the ten most beautiful islands in the world in 1997 by *Traveller* magazine.

Just off the Dalmatian coast rising out of the clear waters of the Adriatic Sea lies the Croatian island of Hvar. Around 80 km (50 mi) long, this narrow island is a gentle tapestry of lavender fields, vineyards, olive groves and pretty Venetian villages. The main centre of population on the island is the town of Hvar, one of the best-loved resorts on the Dalmatian coast. The Venetians based their Adriatic fleet here in the 15th and 16th centuries, which brought great prosperity to the island. In 1571, however, the Turks invaded and laid waste to Hvar, so the buildings which make up the town today were built from the late 16th century onwards. The medieval walls and fort in such a beautiful setting by the sea make Hvar well worth exploring.

At the heart of the town is St Stephen's Square, with the magnificent 16th century cathedral at one end and the harbour at the other. Also close by is the theatre of Hvar, the oldest communal theatre in Europe built in 1612. South of the square, there is an impressive 15th-century Franciscan monastery, now a museum, where concerts are performed during summer.

One of the prettiest villages on the island is Vrboska, lying in a picturesque cove at the end of a long bay, surrounded by pine forests and lovely beaches. Its compact stone buildings line the waterways, crossed by charming bridges. The churches in Vrboska house a number of very valuable works of art, some of the greatest cultural treasures of the island.

Along the southern coast of the island are several smaller islands, including Paklenski Otoci in the west and Scedro in the south. Paklenski Otoci is known for its beautiful beaches, clear sea and natural beauty. The island of Scedro offers a safe anchorage for boats and a pleasant place for swimming and walking. The western side of the island offers lovely views of Hvar's mountain ridge, particularly memorable at sunset.

Lastovo

One of the remotest islands of the Adriatic, Lastovo is the largest island in a nature reserve archipelago of 46 islands and islets. It is 56 sq km (22 sq mi) in area, a lush limestone karst landscape of wooded hill slopes pitted with caves and fertile cultivated valleys. The highest point at Hum is 417 m (1,368 ft) and there are three hills that are over 400 m (1,300 ft) high. The island has a dramatic coastline of craggy cliffs with unusually picturesque coves on the west coast.

Inhabited by the Illyrians and then the Romans, who named it Augusta Insula (Emperor's Island), the islanders have always had an independent spirit. For a long time Lastovo was a pirate haven – the Venetians eventually tired of having their ships raided and they razed the port to the ground. As a result, the inhabitants, unbowed, took the precaution of re-building on the slopes of a hill facing inland, which is where Lastovo's main town (Lastovo Town) still stands today. It is a picturesque village of stone houses with narrow stepped streets and a Renaissance church. The island is noted for its 15th and 16th century architecture with more than thirty churches and chapels dotted around.

Lastovo is a peculiarly enticing destination for travellers who want to head off the beaten track. There are no hotels on the island and it is a five-hour ferry ride from the mainland, which means that despite its outstanding natural beauty, all but the most determined tourists will find themselves landing on Korkula or Hvar, equally beautiful but a lot more frequented. On Lastovo you can find a solitary paradise with only the sounds of the sea and the birds as you bask in the warm sunshine and immerse yourself in the breathtaking scenery of green forest and deep blue sea.

POPULATION:
835 (2001)
WHEN TO GO:
May to September or February to see the Poklad, a 3-day traditional carnival that has been celebrated every year from at least the 16th century.
HOW TO GET THERE:
Ferry or high-speed boat from Split via Korkula and Hvar.
HIGHLIGHTS:
Zaklopatika Bay.
Skrivena Luka (Hidden Harbour) – a low sandy bay completely invisible from the sea.
The Church of Saint Cosmos and Damien.
Exploring the island's coastline and surrounding islets by boat.
The lagoons of Malo Lago and Velo Lago.
YOU SHOULD KNOW:
The last recorded outbreak of vampirism occurred on Lastovo. A diarrhoea epidemic that caused many deaths on the island in 1737 was blamed on vampires and led to a court case.

One of the many churches and chapels on the island

Brac

Supetar is the largest town on Brac.

The third largest island in the Adriatic at 396 sq km (144 sq mi), Brac is also the highest of the central Dalmatian islands, rising to 778 m (2,552 ft). Rugged, pine-forested hills are interspersed with scenic green valleys of vineyards, olive groves and cherry and almond orchards. Brac is famous for its beautiful white limestone and dolomite rock, quarried here for centuries and used in decorative stonework since Roman times.

The greatest tourist draw of the island is undoubtedly Zlatni Rat (Golden Horn), arguably the most beautiful beach in the Adriatic, and certainly the most unusual. It is a 0.5 km (0.3 mi) long tongue of pristine golden sand that juts straight out into the translucent blue water of the Adriatic. A parasol of pine trees runs down its spine and its tip visibly shifts with the tide. This is by far the largest and best-known beach of the island, but all around the coast there are small rocky coves and sandy beaches sheltered by pine trees.

Brac is steeped in history. Inhabited since Neolithic times, the island was first colonized by the Illyrians of the Balkan Peninsula, before becoming part of the Roman and Byzantine Empires. It was annexed to Croatia in the 9th century then fell under Venetian control from 1420 to 1797. Throughout the 19th century it was mainly under Austro-Hungarian rule. This motley heritage is richly reflected in its architecture. All over the island there are beautiful sacral and secular buildings dating as far back as the 10th century. There are also several quaint villages where the old terracotta-tiled stone houses are huddled in narrow cobbled lanes. The combination of natural beauty, superb beaches and cultural heritage in a wonderful Mediterranean climate makes Brac a perfect holiday island.

Cres

One of the largest of the 1,200 islands along the Croatian coast, Cres is situated in the Gulf of Kvarner to the east of Istria. It is long, narrow and mountainous, stretching 68 km (43 mi) from north to south and 12 km (8 mi) across at its widest point. The inaccessible sheer rock face of the spectacular east coast cliffs are a habitat for the griffon vulture, the largest bird in Europe. The northern hills are cloaked in woodland of oak, hornbeam, elm and chestnut, in stunning contrast to the grazing pastures, olive groves and pine thickets further south. In the middle of the island there is the mysterious natural phenomenon of Lake Vrana. It is the main source of fresh water for both Cres and the neighbouring islands, but geologists cannot explain where its 220 million cu m (7,766 million cu ft) of water comes from.

There is evidence of Neolithic habitation: traces of cave dwellings and Bronze and Iron Age hill-forts and tumuli. The Romans conquered the island during the reign of the Emperor Augustus and later it became part of the Byzantine Empire. For several hundred years it was ruled by Venice before falling under the sway of the Austro-Hungarian Empire, eventually becoming integrated into Croatia in 1945. The island's cultural heritage can be seen in the picturesque villages and the charming main town of Cres where there are plenty of remnants of the island's Venetian era.

Surrounded by a tranquil, clear blue sea, with isolated bays and rocky coves, this wild, sparsely populated island is scenically dotted with old ruins, cemeteries and chapels; crumbling dry-stone walls follow the contours of hills on which a huge diversity of native plants can be found. Cres is an ecotourist delight.

POPULATION:
3,184 (2001)
WHEN TO GO:
April to October.
HOW TO GET THERE:
The nearest international airports are Trieste, Pula and Zagreb. Cres can only be reached by boat, either directly on the 12 times daily ferry from Brestova, on the Istrian peninsula, or via the islands of Losinj or Krk.
HIGHLIGHTS:
The 16th century Venetian clock tower in Cres town.
Valun – with a picturesque harbour and 11th century Valun Tablet.
The walk from Stivan to Ustrine – takes 2½ hours, or turn it into a full day.
Lubenice – an ancient village with a beautiful view.
Beli – one of the oldest settlements on the island with an Eco-Centre.
The view from Gorice – the highest point of the island at 650 m (2,130 ft).
YOU SHOULD KNOW:
The shores of Cres are pebble, which is probably the reason why the island has managed to avoid the full glare of the holiday industry and to retain its pristine natural environment. Don't let the lack of sand put you off. The beaches are clean, uncrowded and excellent for swimming and scuba diving.
A view of Cres and other islands in the Predoscica and Kvarner Gulf

*Neo-classical buildings line the
elegant port of Vis.*

Vis

POPULATION:
5,000 (2004 estimate)
WHEN TO GO:
Mid-June to mid-September
HOW TO GET THERE:
Fly to Split, then ferry or hydrofoil
from Split or the islands of Korcula or
Hvar.
HIGHLIGHTS:
The Archaeological Museum.
Zelena Spilja – an emerald cave near
Rukavak Bay.
The 16th century St Cyprian Church.
Uvala Stoncica and Uvala Stiniva –
delightful small coves.
Blue Cave on the islet of Bisevo.
Gradac Cliff.
YOU SHOULD KNOW:
For centuries Vis has been famous
for its viticulture, producing both red
and white wines. Opol is an
outstandingly good light red wine.

The furthest out to sea of the inhabited Dalmatian islands, 45 km
(28 mi) from the mainland and separated from Hvar by an 8 km (5 mi)
wide channel, Vis is an island of wild, windswept beauty. It is just over
90 sq km (35 sq mi) in area with a landscape of rugged cliffs and hidden
caves, limestone hills and fertile valleys. After World War II, when it was
a partisan hideout, the island became a Yugoslav army base, closed to
tourists until 1989. It is therefore refreshingly undeveloped in
comparison with the better-known holiday islands in the area and has
preserved a genuine island culture dependent on fishing and agriculture.

The town of Vis (Issa) on the north-eastern coast of the island is the
oldest urban settlement on the Adriatic. Inhabited since 3000 BC, the
island was colonized by Greeks from Sicily who established a *polis*
(democratic city-state). It is estimated that the city had 12,000 to
14,000 inhabitants and was therefore a place of enormous significance.
You can still see Greek and Roman ruins here as well as some lovely
16th and 17th century churches and villas. On the west coast, the 17th
century fishing village of Komiza, with its Renaissance citadel and
monastery is in a huge sandy-bottomed bay. This picturesque village is a
motley jumble of houses huddled round a harbour at the foot of Hum,
the highest hill on the island at 587 m (1,925 ft).

As well as its beautiful wild mountain scenery and unspoiled cultural
heritage there are some beautiful beaches, the best known being Zaglav,
10 km (6 mi) south of Vis Town. There is also superb paragliding here
and some great diving sites, with six sunken wrecks dating from ancient
times to World War II.

Ilovik

The 'island of flowers' is the southernmost inhabited island of the Losinj archipelago. It is 5.8 sq km (2 sq mi) of gentle hills with a high point of only 91 m (298 ft). There are underground wells all over the island that sustain a lush tangle of Mediterranean thickets and vineyards as well as oleanders and roses, palms and eucalyptus trees. The 15.4 km (9.5 mi) long shoreline is easily accessible with lots of secluded bays. The largest is Parzine on the southeast coast, popular for its sandy beach.

The tiny uninhabited islet of Sv. Petras lies just to the north. It is covered in olive trees with the remains of a Benedictine Abbey and the island cemetery. The monks who once lived here used to graze their sheep and grow vines on Ilovik, which was their property for centuries. Sv. Petras protects Ilovik from the harsh northerly winds and the narrow 1.5 km (1 mi) long channel between the islands has served as a safe anchorage since ancient times. It is used by local fishermen and in recent years has become a popular central stopping point for yachts touring the Adriatic.

Ilovik's tiny village, with two shops, a post office and a bar, has only existed since the 18th century when farmers from the nearby island of Losinj made a deal with the church to buy the island and started to settle here. Around almost every house there are colourful flowers and the islanders are justly proud of their carefully tended vegetable patches. Ilovik is an island where you can enjoy uncrowded beaches and a peaceful atmosphere as you immerse yourself in a profusion of unspoilt nature.

POPULATION:
100 (2006 estimate)
WHEN TO GO:
May to September
HOW TO GET THERE:
By boat from Losinj or Rijecka.
HIGHLIGHTS:
Sicadriga – an archaeological site with ruins of a medieval church.
Straza Hill – prehistoric and Byzantine remains.
The ruins of a Venetian castle and the 11th century Abbey walls on the islet of Sveti Petar.
The Golubinka Cave and rock formation on Sveti Petar.
Eating freshly caught fish on the waterfront.
The underwater shipwreck, with a cargo of amphorae.
YOU SHOULD KNOW:
The Ilovik islanders have one of the highest life expectancies – 95 years!

A fisherman returns to Ilovik at dawn.

Losinj

POPULATION:
7,771 (2001)
WHEN TO GO:
May to September
HOW TO GET THERE:
Direct flights to Losinj from major airports in Croatia, Italy, Germany and Austria; or ferry from Venice or Zadar to Mali Losinj; or drive to Losinj from the island of Cres by crossing the road bridge at Osor.
HIGHLIGHTS:
In Mali Losinj – The graveyard around St Martin's Church, where the tombstones give a rundown of the island's history.
In Mali Losinj – the Church of the Nativity of the Virgin, with some fine art works. In Veli Losinj – the 15th century Venetian tower, built to protect the town from pirates.
In Veli Losinj – St Anthony's Church.
Losinj Dolphin Reserve – a trip on a boat to watch the dolphins.
YOU SHOULD KNOW:
In classical mythology the islands of Losinj and Cres were known as The Apsyrtides and were joined together at the bottleneck of Osor. The Romans dug a narrow canal, only 11 m (36 ft) wide to separate them for navigational purposes. A bridge at Osor now connects the two islands.

In the Gulf of Kvarner, nestling alongside the southwest coast of the neighbouring island of Cres, Losinj is a 31 km (19 mi) long narrow island of dolomite covered in lush greenery. The east coast is low-lying, with coves and islets towards the south, while the steep rocky hills of the northwest rise to a high point of 588 m (1,930 ft). Most of the island's 75 sq km (29 sq mi) is evergreen woodland of holm oak, myrtle and laurel.

The heart of the island is Mali Losinj on the southwest coast. This charming amphitheatre of a town is built in tiers around the concave curve of a hill called the Umpiljak and has a harbour said to be the most beautiful in the whole of the Adriatic. There is a wonderful view northwards across the blue waters of Cikat Bay, a long stretch of beach enclosed by sweet scented Aleppo pinewoods. On the opposite coast, only 4 km (2.5 mi) away, the picturesque former fishing town of Veli Losinj is notable for its narrow cobbled streets, fine Baroque houses and beautiful gardens full of exotic plants.

Under Venetian rule, Losinj developed into an important centre for trade, seafaring and the shipbuilding industry, reaching its height in the 18th century. In 1797 the island was subsumed into the Austro-Hungarian Empire and during the 19th century it grew increasingly popular as a health resort. The clear blue sea and uplifting pine-scented air imparts a sense of wellbeing and energy that will appeal to anyone wanting a recuperative holiday of walking, water and sport. There is great windsurfing and scuba diving, cycle tracks through the woods, hill climbs with superb views, and interesting towns where you can stroll past sumptuous 18th and 19th century villas soaking up the island's history.

Boats alongside the harbour restaurants in Veli Losinj

Krapanj

It is worth taking a detour off the conventional tourist route to visit this quaint island just 300 m (330 yd) offshore from the mainland town of Brodarica. Krapanj is the smallest and lowest inhabited island of the Adriatic at 36 hectares (89 acres) and only 7 m (23 ft) above sea level at its highest point.

A nobleman by the name of Juric purchased the uninhabited island in 1436 and donated it to the Franciscans who built a monastery here. When the Turks started plundering the coastline, the monks sheltered refugees from the mainland and eventually allowed them to build a settlement. The settlers were originally farmers who had to turn to fishing to scrape a living. Their fortune changed at the beginning of the 18th century when a visiting friar from Crete taught them the art of sponge harvesting and processing. Individual sponges were painstakingly harpooned from a boat and a skilled operator could spear one at a depth of 15 m (50 ft). The market for sponges proved a highly lucrative one – the Venetians couldn't get enough of them and by the mid 19th century there were 40 boats operating from Krapanj exporting sponges to Venice. In 1893 the first diving equipment was introduced, which enabled the spongers to harvest at much greater depths and soon earned them a reputation as skilled divers.

Krapanj has an utterly unspoilt, authentic atmosphere – you can dawdle in one of the waterside coffee houses chatting to the locals, visit a monastery stuffed with antiquities and works of art or wander through the picturesque streets of the town. Above all, this is a terrific little place to learn about the underwater world and improve your diving skills under the guidance of friendly locals who are happy to share their generations of experience.

Krapanj is the smallest and lowest of the inhabited Adriatic islands.

POPULATION:
2,500 (2004 estimate)
WHEN TO GO:
May to September
HOW TO GET THERE:
Boat from Brodarica, 8 km (5 mi) south of Sibenik, which is well connected by bus or train with Split, Zagreb and Zadar.
HIGHLIGHTS:
The sponge museum.
The 16th century painting 'The Last Supper' by Francesco da Santecroce.
The Renaissance cloister of the monastery.
Tasting the locally produced rakia and eating fresh fish.
YOU SHOULD KNOW:
Of all the Croatian islands, Krapanj is the most densely populated. Almost all the islanders live in the town and no cars are allowed.

Mljet

POPULATION:
1,111 (2001)
WHEN TO GO:
May to September
HOW TO GET THERE:
Ferries from Dubrovnik or Peljesac peninsula.
HIGHLIGHTS:
Odysseus' Cave – accessed by a 30 m (100 ft) long tunnel and used as a harbour by local fishermen, supposedly where Odysseus fell in love with Calypso and stayed for seven years.
Govedari – a hill village dating from the early 18th century.
The sandy beaches and pinewoods at Saplunara on the east coast.
Polace – the 5th century Roman palace and other ancient ruins.
Swimming in the salt lakes.
YOU SHOULD KNOW:
There is a wide diversity of flora and fauna (including the monk seal – an endangered species) but no snakes on Mljet. The Benedictines introduced mongooses to the island to get rid of them, which upset the natural ecological balance of the island but did do the trick.

Arguably the most beautiful and greenest of all the Croatian islands, Mljet is situated some 30 km (19 mi) from Dubrovnik. The island is a 37 km (23 mi) long sliver of limestone with a gorge splitting its entire length from north to south and a landscape of dramatic, heavily forested peaks and chasms. An area of about 30 sq km (12 sq mi) to the west of the island is a National Park with two salt lakes interconnected by a narrow channel set in idyllic scenery of mountain and forest. In the larger lake there is a tiny island with a picturesque 12th century Benedictine monastery.

Legend has it that St Paul the Apostle landed at Mljet after his ship was wrecked on his way to Rome in 61 AD. In the 12th century the Benedictines acquired the island and built their monastery. Eventually, in the early 15th century, they handed control to Dubrovnik but the monastery still retained its material and spiritual influence, gradually sliding into decline in the 18th century; it finally collapsed under the rule of Napoleon in 1809. Today, Mljet is justly famous for not only its astounding natural beauty but also its distinctive cultural heritage. Village life continues much as it has done for hundreds of years with traditional folk costume, music and dance.

For nature lovers and ecotourists, Mljet is a paradise. You can cycle, walk and climb without restriction throughout the breathtaking scenery of the National Park, swim in the lakes, or take a kayak out onto the calm Adriatic to explore the complexities of the coastline and watch the marine life in the crystal clear sea. There are charming villages, medieval churches, and historic ruins to wander around, beautiful beaches to relax on, and wonderful local wine and goat cheese to sample. A perfect island dream?

Rab

Renowned for its mountains, pine forests, sandy beaches and fairytale main town, Rab is one of the most bewitching islands of the Adriatic. It is situated just off the coast between the islands of Krk and Pag, only 2 km (1.25 mi) from the mainland at its south-eastern tip. It is 22 km (14 mi) long and about half as wide, covering an area of 93.6 sq km (36.5 sq mi) and surrounded by islets and rocky reefs. It is well known for being one of the sunniest places in Europe with a gentle climate, sheltered by its mountains from the effects of the Bora (the harsh north wind of this region).

The island's scenery is outstandingly beautiful: from the dramatic cliffs of the windswept east coast, a progression of hills and plateaux rises to a 400 m (1,300 ft) mountain ridge that runs down the middle of the island, providing shelter for the verdant slopes of vineyards and forests to the west. Paradise Beach, one of the most famous beaches in Croatia, is on the north-eastern Lopar peninsula. It is nearly 2 km (1 mi) long in a setting of pinewoods with fine golden sand and crystal clear shallow water – perfect for children.

Plenty of traces of Rab's stormy past and rich cultural heritage can be found in the island's magnificent architecture. Rab Town is a picture-book fantasy – built on a steep west coast promontory overlooking a deep blue sea, it is an enchanting Venetian extravaganza of bell towers, palaces, squares and churches in a maze of quaint twisting lanes.

This magical island has become famous for its summer concerts, art exhibitions, and tolerant attitude to naturism. If you want to absorb some culture at the same time as acquiring an all-over tan, Rab is definitely where it's at.

POPULATION:
9,480 (2001)
WHEN TO GO:
End of May to September. The island is really bustling in July and August – with a great holiday atmosphere for those who enjoy the buzz. June and September are much quieter.
HOW TO GET THERE:
12-minute ferry ride from Jablanac on the mainland to Misnjak on Rab throughout the year; or ferry from Krk or Pag to Lopar or catamaran from Rijeka. There is a bus from Zagreb to Rijeka. By plane – the easiest way is to fly to Rijeka airport (on Krk) with pre-booked ferry transfer to Rab.
HIGHLIGHTS:
Belfry of St Mary's Church – an extraordinarily impressive 12th to 13th century bell tower 26 m (85 ft) high.
The Monastery of St Euphemia – with two churches, a beautiful sarcophagus and art works.
Dominis-Nimira Palace – a 15th century Venetian palace.
The 13th century Duke's Palace.
Komrcar Park – an area of pasture turned into a beautiful parkland about 80 years ago.
Kampor – an old fishing village with a peaceful atmosphere and lovely walks nearby.
YOU SHOULD KNOW:
Tourism on Rab started at the end of the 19th century but it made its mark on the international tourist map when Edward VIII and Wallis Simpson had a holiday here. Supposedly, it was they who started the habit of naturism here by swimming in the nude.

The view from St John the Baptist Church in Rab Town

Elaphiti Islands

POPULATION:
850 (2006)
WHEN TO GO:
May to September
HOW TO GET THERE:
Ferry from Dubrovnik to each of the
three major islands, or you can take a
day-excursion boat trip visiting
all three.
HIGHLIGHTS:
The late Gothic Rector's Palace –
Sipan.
The remains of the 11th century
Church of St Peter – Sipan.
The 16th century Holy Trinity Church –
Lopud.
The 15th century Monasteries – Lopud.
The ruins of old basilicas and
summerhouses – Kolocep.
The Witches Cave and Blue Cave –
Kolocep
YOU SHOULD KNOW:
There are naturist beach areas on all
the islands.

*The pretty harbour on
Lopud Island*

These thirteen tiny islands stand out like enticing green jewels in
the brilliant blue sea off the coast of Dubrovnik. They have
breathtakingly beautiful scenery – outstanding seashore landscapes,
verdant wooded hills, and lush valleys of citrus and olive groves.
Villages of traditional pantiled stone cottages nestle in the
picturesque bays where the inhabitants maintain their traditional
way of life as farmers and fishermen.

The Elaphiti cover a land area of less than 30 sq km (12 sq mi)
and only three of the islands are inhabited. Kolocep, a favourite
local swimming spot, is the closest to Dubrovnik – a mere 20-minute
boat ride. The island is only 2.5 sq km (1 sq mi), covered in lush
vegetation with paths through fragrant pine woods and olive groves.
There are two charming hamlets where exotic flowers, palm trees,
aloe and cacti grow in the islanders' gardens. Lopud is the most
popular of the islands, renowned for its magnificent fine white sand
beach backed by green-forested hills. Sipan, the largest island at
16.5 sq km (6 sq mi), is famous for its wine.

The islands are first mentioned by the Ancient Greek historian
Pliny the Elder and their name is derived from the Greek for 'deer'.
During the 10th century they became part of the territory of the city
of Dubrovnik and churches and monasteries began to spring up. By
the 15th century, Sipan had become a favourite summer retreat for

the local aristocracy and you can still see the remains of magnificent mansions secreted among the woods of the coastal bays. Today, the Elaphiti are a favourite getaway from the summer heat of the city – an idyllic place to swim, sunbathe, walk and relax.

Silba

One of the smaller northern Dalmatian islands, only 15 sq km (6 sq mi) in area, Silba has a gentle terrain of low hills covered in richly varied Mediterranean vegetation of trees, shrubs and flowers interspersed with vineyards. Country footpaths lead through wooded valleys to the shore, where there are a number of lovely secluded coves and small harbours. There are no cars on this delightful island – the locals use two-wheeled handcarts as transport. There is a single village at the island's narrowest point – only 700 m (2,295 ft) wide – by the beautiful beach of Sotorisce, renowned for its exceptionally clear turquoise water and shallow sandy seabed.

Silba was colonized by Croatians as early as the 8th century and became church property in 1091– the religiosity of the inhabitants is attested to by the six island churches. Over the centuries the islanders developed an extremely profitable trade transporting cattle from the mainland town of Zadar to Venice and established themselves as the leading seafarers and shipbuilders of the region. The island became known as the 'door to Dalmatia' and reached a height of prosperity during the 18th century when it had a fleet of almost 100 ships. For many years the island was privately owned by a Venetian noble family who extracted a hefty tithe on all the inhabitants' earnings. Eventually, after a lengthy land dispute, the Silbans acquired the rights to their island on St Joseph's Day, 19 March 1852, a date that is still the most important holiday of the year here.

One of the sunniest of the Adriatic islands, with a gentle westerly breeze in the summer that prevents the heat from ever becoming oppressive, Silba is a charming island for peaceful beach, boating and fishing holidays.

POPULATION:
265 (2001)
WHEN TO GO:
Late May to early September
HOW TO GET THERE:
Boats daily from Zadar and twice weekly from Rijeka or Pula on the mainland, or the island of Losinj.
HIGHLIGHTS:
The 17th century Church of St Mark and its cemetery.
Dobre Verde and Nozdre – small secluded bays backed by woods.
Pernastica – one of the ten most beautiful sand bays in Croatia.
Toreta – a 15 m (50 ft) hexagonal tower with amazing view from the top.
Vele Stene – the only place on the island where the shore is steep. Varh – the highest point of the island at 80 m (260 ft).
YOU SHOULD KNOW:
There are no hotels on Silba but there are plenty of rooms and apartments to rent.

The only village on Susak

Susak

POPULATION:
Under 200
WHEN TO GO:
May to September
HOW TO GET THERE:
Daily boat connection from Losinj.
Losinj can be reached by air or boat
from the mainland.
HIGHLIGHTS:
Merina Chapel of the Mournful
Lady graveyard.
The lighthouse on the Garba, highest
point of the island.
The village church with a 12th
century cross.
Bok Bay naturist beach.
Tasting the island wine.
YOU SHOULD KNOW:
Susak is famous for diving – it's
considered to be one of the best
spots in Croatia for the less
experienced with an underwater
reef, canyon and wreck.

This tiny island of only 3.8 sq km (1.5 sq mi), in the open sea to the west of Losinj, is one of the lowest islands in the Gulf of Kvarner with a high point of 98 m (320 ft). Susak is geologically unique in the region: its terrain is entirely composed of sand, in thick layers up to 100 m (330 ft) deep resting on a bedrock of limestone. This is one of the few places in Croatia where you will have no problem at all finding a proper sandy beach. There is a coastal path around the entire 11 km (7 mi) shore, all of which is fine golden sand with safe swimming.

Like so many of the Dalmatian islands, Susak has a tumultuous history of plunder and conquest. The island was an important western navigational point on the sea route from Istria to Dalmatia and it is marked on nautical charts dating from the 13th century. The islanders have lived in such isolation that even today they have preserved their own centuries-old dialect, customs and wedding rites as well as an extraordinary female folk costume featuring a very full, very short, brightly patterned skirt reminiscent of a ballet tutu.

Susak has always been renowned for the exceptional quality of its wine, considered the best in Croatia. Sadly, after World War II the political and economic climate precipitated a mass exodus to the USA leading to the abandonment of most of the land. However, the fifteen vineyards that are still under cultivation continue to produce superb wine. Today Susak is still a peculiarly quaint place with just one village, built round a small sheltered bay used for mooring yachts. It is the perfect place for a relaxed beach holiday far from the madding tourist crowds.

Brijuni Archipelago

Once a pestilential hellhole, turned into a folly for the aristocracy, commandeered as Communist leader Marshall Tito's summer retreat, and now a National Park, these tiny islands have a bizarre fairytale quality to them – a surreal juxtaposition of verdant woodland, landscaped meadows, wild animals and Roman ruins, surrounded by the intense blue of the Adriatic Sea.

This tiny low-lying archipelago of two islands and 12 islets, only 7.42 sq km (3 sq mi) of land altogether, lies 3 km (2 mi) off the west coast of the Istrian peninsula. The bedrock is white limestone with a topsoil of exceptionally fertile red clay that supports a wide variety of lush vegetation. The islands' shores are indented with secluded coves and the surrounding waters are a conservation area rich in sponges and crustaceans as well as all sorts of fish, and even turtles and dolphins.

Veliki Brijun and Mali Brijun have been inhabited since prehistoric times and there are valuable historical remains, particularly from the Roman and Byzantine eras. Over the centuries the islands were ravaged by piracy and war but it was a malaria epidemic that caused their eventual depopulation. In 1893 an Austrian industrialist, Paul Kupelweiser acquired them to develop an exclusive summer playground for European aristocracy. He drained the fetid pools that were a breeding ground for mosquitoes, imported exotic tropical plants, and transformed the overgrown thickets of Veliki Brijun into a sublime parkland. After World War II Marshall Tito commandeered the islands. He established a safari park and made it known that he expected his guests to donate an animal to his collection – hence the zebras, camels, elephant, ostriches and deer that still roam freely.

The curious history, amazing scenery, and unexpected wildlife of the Brijuni Islands are an experience not to be missed – one of the most extraordinary and romantic places along the Croatian coast.

POPULATION:
Uninhabited – apart from park and hotel staff
WHEN TO GO:
May to September
HOW TO GET THERE:
Daily ferry from Fazana, a town on the Istrian coast, to Veliki Brijun. To get to Fazana, fly to Venice, Trieste or Pula. From Venice there is a boat/bus connection to Fazana and from Trieste or Pula there are buses. Fazana is only 8 km (5 mi) from Pula.
HIGHLIGHTS:
Gradina Hill – a prehistoric settlement. Verige Gulf – a Roman palace with temples and outbuildings, an outstanding example of Roman architecture.
The 15th century Church of St Germain with a collection of frescoes. Dobrik Bay – Byzantine Castrum and 5th century basilica and 6th century church.
Mali Brijun – 19th century fort. A ride round Veliki Brijun on the tourist train.
YOU SHOULD KNOW:
Tito entertained an eclectic selection of celebrity guests on the Brijuni islands, including Elizabeth Taylor and Fidel Castro.

The ruins of the Byzantine Castrum in Dobrik Bay

Crete

POPULATION:
540,045 (2001)
WHEN TO GO:
April, May, June, September
and October
HOW TO GET THERE:
Direct and domestic flights to Iraklion
and Hania; domestic flights to Sitia.
Ferries from the mainland and inter-
island ferries.
HIGHLIGHTS:
Knossos – Arthur Evans's
reconstruction is unmissable; Malia,
Phaestos and Zakros are fascinating;
they have not been rebuilt.
The Archaeological Museum in
Iraklion – for an overview of
Minoan civilization.
The Samaria Gorge – Europe's largest
gorge, home to golden eagles and
Cretan ibexes.
Rethymnon – the back streets of the
old town with wooden Ottoman
houses, leaning balconies and
old mosques.
The Lasithi Plateau – the windmills
may not be working but this is a
lovely green plateau with pretty
villages and the birthplace of Zeus.
YOU SHOULD KNOW:
A real escapist spot, the small island
of Gavdos, some 50 km (31 mi), off
Crete's south coast, is the most
southerly landmass in Europe. A few
fishermen live there, and it is possible
to stay.

The harbour at Rethymnon

The largest – over 250 km (160 mi) long – and most southerly of the Greek islands, Crete joined independent Greece in the early 20th century, and it retains strong cultural traditions. Its spine of impressive mountains – the highest, Psiloritis, is 2,456 m (8,060 ft) – is snow-covered in winter. The south-west is barren and impenetrably rocky, though the east and south are very fertile – Crete exports a range of agricultural produce to mainland Greece.

The extraordinary Minoan civilization which flourished from 2800 until 1450 BC, was followed by a succession of great powers including Greece, Rome, Byzantium, Venice and the Ottoman Empire. Now the island's archaeological and architectural heritage sums up its history, for here are Minoan sites – Knossos is one of many – and villas and towns, churches and forts, mosques, ghost villages, ancient harbours and cities with fascinating old quarters. Modern invasions too have left their mark – atmospheric spots redolent of the German occupation during World War II and the almost continuous resort development of the north coast which mass tourism has brought.

But Crete offers more than package holidays and archaeology. Inland, for the serious walker there are the challenging mountains and gorges, for the rambler, marked tracks through verdant valleys and spacious uplands, passing a less-visited site or a traditional hill village. In spring the island blazes with wildflowers and hundreds of migrating bird species pass through.

Beaches are not all packed. The far west has remote, empty sands, the south coast small resorts often reached by a spectacular road journey, sometimes by boat.

Crete's cities, Iraklion, Rethymnon and Hania, provide museums, markets, nightlife; they buzz with life and character.

Egina

Egina's geographical position at the mouth of the Saronic Gulf made it an important maritime power in classical times. Athens, concerned by its strength and the huge fortunes amassed from trade with Egypt and Phoenicia, attacked. After two sea battles the islanders were forced to pull down the city walls, destroy the fleet and leave. Egina achieved importance again in 1827-9 as temporary capital of partly-liberated Greece. Now its fame is as Greece's leading pistachio producer, and a weekend beach resort for Athenians.

Egina Town is a bustling, attractive place, with coloured fishing boats bobbing alongside yachts in a harbour that is lined with handsome buildings, cafés and restaurants, an ideal place to sit for a while and soak up the atmosphere. A single column marks the site of the Temple of Apollo, and there is a well-presented archaeological museum.

The island's major resort, busy Ayia Marina, lies, with several smaller resorts, on the east coast. Inland, the pleasant countryside is mountainous. There are several isolated monasteries and churches, including the enormous church dedicated to the first Greek Orthodox saint of the 20th century, Saint Sophia. On the road to Mount Ormos lies the Hellenic Wildlife Rehabilitation centre, which welcomes visits

and help with its work for injured birds and animals. Central and western Egina is green and rolling, carpeted with pistachio orchards. Along the west coast lie further beaches, including the pretty harbour village of Perdhika. From here it is a short boat trip to the uninhabited islet of Moni with its lovely beach and excellent swimming.

The Temple of Aphaea

POPULATION:
13,552 (2001)
WHEN TO GO:
May and June, September and October
HOW TO GET THERE:
Ferry/hydrofoil from Piraeus.
HIGHLIGHTS:
The Temple of Aphaea, 112 km (70 mi) east of Egina Town. Built in the 5th century BC, at the height of Egina's power, this beautiful and complex Doric temple is the major ancient site in the Saronic Gulf islands.
Paleohora – a fascinating 'ghost town' which was built as the island's capital in the 9th century. It was abandoned in 1827. Deserted, scattered with ruined churches and homes, it has a melancholy attraction.
Fish supper - the tavernas along the waterfront at Perdhika are considered to offer the best seafood in the area.
YOU SHOULD KNOW:
Minted on the island in its heyday, the silver 'turtle' coins were the first in Greece.

Fully-laden mules come to market.

Idhra

POPULATION:
2,719 (2001)
WHEN TO GO:
May and June, September and October
HOW TO GET THERE:
Ferry/hydrofoil from Piraeus.
HIGHLIGHTS:
The Koundouriotis Historical Mansion – a splendid 18th century building, home of a hero of the Greek independence struggle and later a president of republican Greece, which has been restored to its former glory, and is now a museum. The mansions in Idhra town – the homes of the merchant families, many designed by Venetian or Genoese architects. A map of the mansions is available.
Profiti Ilias Monastery, which lies in the hills above Idhra town; the stiff climb rewards with marvellous views.
YOU SHOULD KNOW:
The Miaoulia Festival in June celebrates Idhra's contribution to the independence struggle with feasting, fireworks and a mock battle in the harbour.

Tiny, rocky Idhra lies close to the Peloponnese in the Gulf of Hydra. Its only town, and port, rises in tiers of fine buildings from a horseshoe harbour. Its beauty has made it a favourite with artists and film-makers – and with tourists, who come in hordes: cruise-ships, day-trippers and Athenian weekenders. Despite the visitors, Idhra remains alluring. Greek law protects the island from over-development, and from the blight of traffic – everything except building materials and garbage is carried by donkeys.

Because of its infertility, the island was not much settled in ancient times. When Greeks and Albanians arrived from the Ottoman-controlled mainland, they perforce took up ship-building, and by the 18th century, Idhra was extremely wealthy and possessed a large merchant fleet. Nineteenth century Idhra had a population approaching 20,000; its ships formed a large part of the fleet that fought the Greek War of Independence, and the town became a fashionable resort for Greek socialites.

Now the lovely town with its superb grey stone mansions continues to charm. Away from the waterfront bars, shops and tourists, the streets are quieter; higher up, smaller white houses with brightly painted doorways, steps and balconies crowd the steep deserted lanes. Away from the town on the way-marked tracks or the paved path to the town beaches the walker will find peace and solitude.

Spetses

The most distant of the Argo-Saronic islands from Piraeus, Spetses offers a coastline dotted with pine shaded coves and beaches and a hilly interior which, despite forest fires, is still well wooded. It has long been a favourite with holidaymakers, although responsible planning has allowed the island to retain its charm.

Like Idhra, Spetses was largely settled by refugees from the mainland, and became wealthy through ship-building. Spetses' most colourful character was Laskarina Bouboulina, heroine of the War of Independence. Twice widowed and very wealthy, she commissioned her own fighting ship and led the blockade of Nauplion in 1821. She died at home – shot in a family dispute. Her mansion has been made into a museum by her descendents. A later son of the island, philanthropist Sotirios Anargyrios, replanted the pines and financed roads and several buildings, including a boarding-school based on the English pattern. Writer John Fowles taught here – he later used the island as a setting for his novel *The Magus*.

Dapia harbour is lined with old Venetian houses. Ship-building still flourishes on Spetses, and the walk along the shore passes boatyards with traditionally constructed wooden craft.

Cars are restricted on the island; the more distant coves and seasonal tavernas may be reached by bus, scooter, bicycle – or even horse-drawn carriage.

POPULATION:
3,916 (2001)
WHEN TO GO:
May and June, September and early October
HOW TO GET THERE:
Ferry/hydrofoil from Piraeus.
HIGHLIGHTS:
The old fortified harbour, where bright fishing boats jostle with luxury yachts; the harbour wall still bristles with cannons.
The Museum – housed in the splendid Mexis mansion, home of the island's first governor. It contains paintings, relics of the War of Independence and a collection of ships' figureheads.
YOU SHOULD KNOW:
Boubalina, heroically directing cannon fire, featured on the old 50-Drachma note.

Agia Paraskevi beach

Hios

POPULATION:
51,936 (2001)
WHEN TO GO:
June and early July, September.
HOW TO GET THERE:
Domestic flight or charter flight to Lesvos or Samos and ferry connections. Ferry from Piraeus. International ferry from Cesme, Turkey.
HIGHLIGHTS:
Pyrgi - one of the mastic villages. Its houses are decorated by cutting geometric patterns through the whitewash to the black volcanic sand. This striking and ancient technique is called xista.
Mesta – the best preserved of the mastihohoria, it retains its defensive towers. A dark, labyrinthine place with massive walls, it is a fine example of 14th century defence architecture.
Nea Moni – in the centre of Hios, this 11th century Byzantine monastery is one of the most beautiful and important monuments in the Greek islands. It has extraordinary mosaics and a memorable setting.
Mastic gum – before the petro-chemical industry, mastic gum was used in various cosmetic and pharmaceutical products. Two products still available in Hios are the sweetened gum for chewing and a liqueur called Mastiha.
YOU SHOULD KNOW:
The mastihohria were the only towns spared in the massacre of 1822. The Ottoman court relied heavily on mastic jelly beans to please the ladies of the harem.

Homer described Hios as craggy, and the north is mountainous, but the rolling shrubby hills of the south are very fertile and the Ottoman name – 'Resin Island' – may seem more appropriate. Lying a few miles off Cesme on the Turkish coast, this is an island of fine beaches, fascinating villages – and mastic trees.

Hios was important and prosperous in antiquity – only here does the mastic bush produce a commercially viable amount of the highly prized mastic gum. After the Genoese seized control of this lucrative trade in 1346, Hios became one of the most cultured and wealthy islands in the Mediterranean. The Ottomans took the island in 1566; when the islanders rebelled in 1822 the reprisals were brutal; thousands died, and many more were exiled. In 1881 an earthquake destroyed much of what remained.

Hios Town is a big, modern city, but it has interesting museums, authentic tavernas and a lively bazaar. The north is an area of difficult roads and deserted villages, though Hiots returning from overseas are now restoring family homes in the 'ghost towns'. The south is dominated by the mastihohoria, the architecturally unique mastic villages. Built by the Genoese to be pirate-proof, they have a rather oriental feel, with arches spanning the narrow streets to minimize earthquake damage. Around the island the visitor will discover Byzantine monuments, fertile plains, the remains of Genoese mansions and good, isolated beaches. Because of its continued prosperity, Hios has not courted mass-tourism and is still largely, delightfully untouched.

Balconies on decorated houses in the old mastic village of Pyrgi

Ikaria and Fourni

Ikaria is a narrow, windswept island lying between Samos and Mykonos; it is rugged but fertile, with a wealth of vineyards, olive and fruit trees. Much of the south coast is rather desolate, with steep cliffs, while the north and west offer several fishing villages with small beaches and the only real resort, Armenistis.

Named after the legendary Icarus who fell into the sea just off the coast when the sun melted the wax on his wings, Ikaria is reputed to be the birthplace of Dionysus, the god of wine. The island was used for years as a place of exile for dissidents and has a strong tradition of left-wing ideals and inhabitants who are self-sufficient and idiosyncratic. Its other claim to fame, the radioactive springs, are still in operation – though the highly toxic ones have been closed.

Because of its odd past, relative inaccessibility and its lack of photogenic architecture or spectacular scenery, Ikaria has been neglected by mass-tourism. The main port, Ayios Kirykos, has little for the visitor. Armenistis lies on the north coast in a glorious setting; it has two beautiful long beaches with, unusually for Greece, good surf. This is great walking country – maps are available with well-marked tracks and trails.

Fourni is the only one of a tiny archipelago of islands that has tourist facilities. In its only town the traveller will find waterfront tavernas with fine seafood – Fourni has a huge fishing fleet, and a thriving boatyard – and a surprisingly lively nightlife. There are a handful of good, secluded beaches a pleasant walk away.

POPULATION:
Ikaria 8,312; Fourni 1,469 (2001)
WHEN TO GO:
June, early July and September. For surfing – July to September.
HOW TO GET THERE:
Ferry/hydrofoil from Samos. Inter-island ferry from Piraeus.
HIGHLIGHTS:
Ikaria: Kambos, a village on the north coast with the island's oldest church, the ruins of a Byzantine palace, a small museum and some good walks.
Khristos Rahon, one of a group of villages known collectively as Rahes. Here, the villagers speak a Homeric dialect, and they all keep very strange hours, rising in the late morning and spending their nights chatting, eating, shopping – and drinking the local home-made wine.
Fourni: the wonderful fresh fish in the tavernas.
YOU SHOULD KNOW:
For three months in 1912, Ikaria was an independent republic, with its own money and stamps.

A church at Armenistis on Ikaria

Waterfront view of Mytilini harbour and Agios Therapon Church

Lesvos

POPULATION:
93,428 (2001)
WHEN TO GO:
May, June and September
HOW TO GET THERE:
Direct charter flights. Domestic flights from Athens and Thessaloniki. Ferry from Piraeus and inter-island ferries.
HIGHLIGHTS:
Molyvos (Mithymna) is 61 km (38 mi) north west of Mytilini. Solid, red-tiled stone houses rise from the pretty harbour to a Byzantine-Genoese castle, which gives a view across the straits to Turkey. Molyvos teems with tourists, but remains a beautiful little town with its flowery lanes and lovely old Turkish mansions.
Plomari – a sizeable settlement on the south coast. It is home to several ouzo distilleries, and is in the heart of the olive-growing area. The villages in this region are linked by restored paths which cross not only olive groves but also well-watered, fertile countryside, forest and woodland. These paths are well-signed and are a delightful way to see the landscape and untouched villages of Lesvos.
YOU SHOULD KNOW:
There are about 11 million olive trees on Lesvos, some of which may be over 500 years old. For three centuries of Ottoman rule, olive-oil production was the monopoly of the Pasha.

Remote and fertile Lesvos is large enough to maintain its traditional industries – ship-building, breeding livestock, distilling ouzo and, most importantly, growing olives (the oil is some of the best in Greece). The landscape ranges from rich and green to rocky and volcanic; it is dotted with hot springs, many dating from antiquity. The water in the marble baths at Effalou is reputedly efficacious for a variety of ailments. All around the coast are good beaches with calm, clean water.

In classical times, Lesvos was home to artists, writers and philosophers, most famously the lyric poet Sappho. The Romans considered it an ideal holiday destination, the Byzantines employed it as 'humane' exile, the Genoese held court here and for the Ottomans it was 'the Garden of the Aegean'. More recently there followed a period of Socialism – it became known as 'Red Island'. Greece's best-known naive painter was born here, as well as a Nobel-laureate poet, thus continuing the cultural tradition of antiquity.

Though Lesvos receives a good number of package tourists, the attractive resorts retain character. North-west from Mytillini, the sprawling port and capital, lie seaside towns, wooded valleys and frescoed monasteries. In the west is the 'Petrified Forest' of prehistoric sequoias. Skala Eressou on the west coast has a good, long, sand beach. It is built on the site of ancient Eressos, birthplace in 630 BC of Sappho, and is a sort of pilgrimage destination for gay women. Skala Kallonis has a bird-watching centre – Lesvos is home or transit point to more than 200 species of bird. The south, lying between two huge inlets, is verdant, and thick with olive groves. The coast has several small beach resorts.

*Themistokleous Sofuli Street
in Samos town*

Samos

Lying very close to the Turkish coast, lush Samos was, until recent wildfires destroyed much of its dense forests, one of the most beautiful islands of the Aegean. Fortunately the west and north-west remain largely untouched by fire – or by mass-tourism.

Samos was once the wealthiest island in the Aegean. In the 6th century BC under the rule of the tyrannical but brilliant Polykratis, it was home to an intellectual group that included Pythagoras and Aesop, though with the ascendancy of Athens the island went into decline. It was ruled by the Romans, Venetians and Genoese, but by 1562, when the Ottomans arrived, it was almost deserted. It was re-populated with Orthodox settlers from all over Greece and Asia Minor. Fortunes picked up after the granting of semi-autonomous statehood in the 19th century, but occupation during World War II and emigration afterwards left it sadly desolate once again. Today the tourist market is of vital importance to Samos.

Vathy on the north-east coast is the island's capital, but Pythagorio in the south has more to interest the visitor. Built on the site of Polykratis' capital, the busy town and the surrounding area is rich in reminders of ancient glories, and subsequent history.

The north and south coast beaches are numerous, good, but mostly developed. Kokkari, west of Vathy, is a successful windsurfing resort. The energetic will discover lovely beaches in the far west, accessible only by foot. Two of these are designated refuges for the rare monk seal. Inland Samos is ideal for the walker, bird-watcher and botanist: here are thick, well-watered woodlands loud with songbirds, mountains, pretty hill-villages and monasteries. Early spring brings wildflowers and migratory birds.

POPULATION:
32,814 (2001)
WHEN TO GO:
May and June, September and early October. For birdwatchers – March and April.
HOW TO GET THERE:
Direct charter flights. Domestic flights. Ferries from Piraeus. Inter-island ferries, inter-island hydrofoil (summer only).
HIGHLIGHTS:
The Archaeological Museum in Vathy is one of the best provincial collections in Greece.
The Heraion, shrine to Hera the mother goddess is just outside Pythagorio. Little remains of what was one of the Seven Wonders of the ancient world, but the foundations give an idea of the scale and grandeur of this huge temple.
The Efpalliniio tunnel - just north of Pythagorio, this1,040-m (3,412-ft) long aqueduct was built in the 6th century BC but it remains a technological marvel - the two rock-cutting teams met with no vertical error.
Mykali – this small south coast resort east of Pythagorio is a must for bird watchers. Its winter-filled salt-marsh provides a stopover for migrating flamingoes from December till April.
YOU SHOULD KNOW:
Samian ware, the fine pottery of Samos, was highly prized in the ancient world. Pottery is still made in hill villages today.

Thassos

POPULATION:
13,675 (2006)
WHEN TO GO:
June and September
HOW TO GET THERE:
Charter flights to Kavala and
hydrofoil/ferry connection.
HIGHLIGHTS:
The ancient acropolis in Limenas.
Above the theatre near the start of
the walls lie the foundations of the
acropolis and of later fortification.
The views down across the town and
out to sea are wonderful.
Alyki – a hamlet towards the south of
the island. A few traditional
whitewashed buildings, fishing boats,
a small pebble beach and a headland
covered in pines and archaeological
excavations (which have prevented
development of the village). The
tavernas and beach get busy; the
swimming off the marble foundations
is delicious.
Theologus – the only inland village
with a bus service, this was the
island's capital under the Ottomans.
A stroll around this spacious
traditional village in the mountains is
enjoyable and refreshing.
YOU SHOULD KNOW:
There is a story that the governor of
ancient Limena kept his mistress at
Alyki. Visitors agree that the
atmosphere there is happy and
peaceful – perhaps the site is
haunted by happy spirits.

Thassos lies close to Kavala on the coast of north-east mainland Greece. It is a small, more or less round island, circled by fine sand beaches and a convenient coast road. The interior, despite disastrous fires in the 1980s and 90s, is wooded, watered by many streams, clothed in vineyards and orchards, and dotted with handsome villages. It is very popular with tourists – not only the package variety, but also visitors from mainland Greece and from south-east Europe. Rare pure-white marble has been quarried here since ancient times and still brings large revenues to the island, as do olives, honey, fruit and nuts.

Drawn by reserves of gold, the Parians settled here in the 7th century BC and developed a powerful city state. A succession of foreign powers settled, and taxed, this wealthy little island.

The capital and main port, Limenas, is largely modern, but has an attractive harbour and many easily-visited archaeological sites, including the ancient agora, a theatre and the massive 5th century city walls. South from Limenas, the first public beach is spectacular – long, fine sand, it enjoys a backdrop of impressive mountains. Mount Ipsarion, at 1,204 m (3,950 ft) high, can by climbed by a marked path. Small resorts with excellent beaches continue the circuit, though some of the west coast is rather exposed and windswept.

The mountain villages with their thick-walled slate-roofed houses, pretty gardens, and tree-shaded squares make a lovely excursion. Each is reached up a valley road, but no roads link them cross-country. Take a seat under a plane tree outside a taverna and try the local spirit, tsipouro – but get someone else to drive back down the winding road!

*The view down to the harbour
from the amphitheatre*

Hozoviotissas Monastery

Amorgos

The most easterly of the Cyclades, Amorgos is rugged and mountainous, often battered by wind and wave. It is hospitable and unspoilt – visitors come for excellent walking and the relaxed, uncommercialized atmosphere, or to see the location of Luc Besson's film, *The Big Blue*. The south coast is sheer, steep and unpopulated but for one monastery built into the cliffs. The north coast is sheltered by the mountains and has two harbours and a scattering of hill villages.

In antiquity Amorgos boasted three cities, Egiali, Minos and Arkessini. For the Romans, it was a place of lenient exile. Pillaging by pirates in the 7th century forced the islanders into the hills. After Venetian occupation, Barbarossa the Turk seized it in 1537 and the island remained Turkish till 1822.

The principal port, Katapola, straggles round a large bay backed by a coastal plain in the south-west. There are several small beaches in the area. Katapola means 'Below the Town', and a steep road leads up to Hora, a delightful white cube town with a car-free main street winding along a ridge topped by ruined windmills. A path climbs down to the popular south-facing beaches at Ayia Anna.

The eastern port, Egiali, is quieter, with a long sandy beach and a scatter of accommodation built on the site of the ancient city. In the hills above the town lie the lovely traditional villages of Tholaria and Langada. A good road now links the two ports – until recently the easiest connection was by water.

POPULATION:
1,869 (2001)
WHEN TO GO:
May, June and September
HOW TO GET THERE:
Inter-island ferries; some come from the mainland (Rafina).
HIGHLIGHTS:
Walking – a network of paths between Katapola and Hora, a strenuous loop into the hills around the villages, or from Katapola to Egiali along the dramatic windswept spine.
Hozoviotissas Monastery – plastered into the side of a cliff high above the sea.
The ancient cities: partially excavated, Minos is in the hills above Katapola; Arkessini in the south-west has tombs and massive walls.
YOU SHOULD KNOW:
The miraculous icon of the Virgin in the monastery came from Hozova in the Middle East, where monks committed it to the sea.

The Terrace of the Lions

Delos

POPULATION:
14 (2001)
WHEN TO GO:
April to June, September and October
HOW TO GET THERE:
Day trips from Mykonos; trips from
more distant Naxos, Paros and Tinos
may allow less time ashore.
HIGHLIGHTS:
The Museum – with some fascinating
exhibits, though the significant finds
are in Athens.
The Terrace of the Lions: sculpted
and given by the Naxians. Five of the
nine remain, one is in Venice and the
others disappeared.
The outstanding mosaics in the
House of the Tridents and the House
of the Masks.
The Sanctuary of the Foreign Gods –
this area contains temples and
shrines built by resident merchants.
Mount Kynthos – the walk to the top
is rewarded with fabulous views of
the site and the surrounding islands.
YOU SHOULD KNOW:
The island is home to ruins from as
far back as 3 BC.

Just south of Mykonos, tiny Delos is a site of great archaeological importance. This was, in legend, the birthplace of Apollo and his sister Artemis, and in the 8th century BC a four-yearly festival in his honour was established, followed in the early 7th century BC by the building of the Sanctuary of Apollo. The island grew in religious and commercial importance. Athens formed the Delian League against the Persian threat, and its treasury was sited here. In Hellenistic times Delos was one of the most important religious centres in Greece, with pilgrims from all over the Mediterranean. Merchants, bankers and mariners also settled here. Rome declared Delos a free port in 167 BC and trade overtook religion – Delos was the largest slave market in the Mediterranean.

But the island was sacked in 88 and 69 BC and stripped of its treasure; ancient religions lost significance and trade routes changed. Delos's long decline began. Almost deserted, it was part of the Ottoman Empire, then a pirate base.

Now, visitors are not allowed to stay on Delos. The Romans decreed that no-one should die or be born here; the only hotel has been ruined for 1600 years. Starting from two separate harbours, the Sacred and Commercial, the site divides into two corresponding areas. In the huge expanse of rubble that is the Sanctuary, there are temples to Apollo and Artemis, a sanctuary of Dionysus, the dry Sacred Lake and much more. In the Theatre Quarter are streets of the remains of artisans' houses and merchants' mansions and a large but fragmentary theatre. The Slave Market lay in the partly excavated Maritime Quarter.

A visit should be carefully planned; many of the day-trips allow too little time in this extraordinary place.

Paros and Antiparos

Central to the Cycladic group, these islands are separated by a shallow channel, which was formed by an earthquake around 550 BC. Paros was important in antiquity; it is large, fertile and produced the famous marble beloved by sculptors and used to make Early Cycladic figures, the Venus de Milo and Napoleon's tomb. Like its neighbours it was part of the Duchy of Naxos and later the Ottoman Empire – though the Russians held it briefly in the 18th century.

Paros is an attractive island with gentle landscapes, peaceful beaches, and, outside a very busy tourist season, an unspoilt feel. Parikia is a bright, bustling port, the hub of inter-island ferry traffic. Away from the waterfront the old town is a tangle of narrow white lanes. It has several museums and a handful of archaeological sites, and the town beaches are reasonable.

Naoussa still has its pretty harbour full of bright fishing boats and its whitewashed old quarter, though now tourist development encircles the village. Around the large bay are some lovely beaches.

The east coast too has excellent beaches and a few attractive villages, though south and westwards small settlements have been swamped by concrete. Inland, traditional white villages and timeless monasteries are scattered around the slopes of Mount Profitis Ilias.

Antiparos, though so close, has its own identity. The delightful little harbour settlement with its lively waterfront and old quarter now spreads into newly built accommodation. Around the coast lie beaches of fine gold sand and, away from the town, some peaceful walks.

POPULATION:
Paros, 12,853; Antiparos, 1,057 (2001)
WHEN TO GO:
May, June, September and October
HOW TO GET THERE:
Domestic flights. Ferry from mainland – Piraeus and Thessaloniki. Inter-island ferry.
HIGHLIGHTS:
The One Hundred Gated Church in Parikia – designed by Isidore of Miletus in the 6th century and still essentially Byzantine.
The Valley of the Butterflies – a cool, refreshing spot. Jersey tiger moths arrive in early summer.
Lefkes – this beautiful old capital with its handsome buildings is a popular spot.
The Cave of Antiparos – now with concrete steps and lighting, but it remains mysterious and awe inspiring.
Watersports – windsurfing, kiteboarding, sailing and diving can be found at various beaches.
YOU SHOULD KNOW:
The cave of Antiparos has long attracted vandals – Russian sailors broke off stalagmites and took them home and Lord Byron apparently left graffiti.

A typical stone-paved street in Parikia

Naxos

POPULATION:
18,188 (2001)
WHEN TO GO:
May to early July, September and
October
HOW TO GET THERE:
Domestic flights; flights to Mykonos
and connecting ferry. Ferry from
Piraeus, Crete or Thessaloniki. Inter-
island ferries.
HIGHLIGHTS:
The portera – a huge stone
doorframe to a never-completed
temple to Apollo on an islet just by
the harbour.
The Temple to Demeter, south of
Sangri – fascinating ruins on a hilltop
location.
Flerio – the marble quarry here is
home to two large and very finely
detailed 6th century BC Kouroi left
lying unfinished because of faults in
the stone.
The Domus Della-Rocca-Barozzi in
Naxos Town – a home of the old
Venetian nobility.
YOU SHOULD KNOW:
After Ariadne died, Dionysus threw
her wedding crown of seven stars
into the night sky where it became
the Corona Borealis.

*Bustling and enjoyable
Naxos Town*

Largest and most fertile of the Cyclades, and often described as the most beautiful, Naxos is green and mountainous with distinctive architecture and sandy beaches. It is a prosperous agricultural area, growing olives, potatoes, fruit and the citrus – a large fruit used to make preserves and a sweet liqueur, which Naxos exported worldwide in the 19th century. Recently, tourism has become important.

Legendary Theseus abandoned Ariadne here, despite her aid in the Cretan Labyrinth. Dionysus was on hand to comfort her – the god of wine and ecstasy belongs to Naxos and many boys are still named after him. The island has been inhabited since Neolithic times. During the Classical era, its fine white marble was famously used for sculpture and architecture. In 1207 Marco Sanudi founded the Venetian Duchy of Naxos (towers and mansions all over the island date from this period). Later, Cretan refugees colonized the east.

Naxos Town is the bustling and enjoyable port capital. Up from the waterfront, steep alleys wind under archways to the Kastro, the Venetian capital. Many houses still bear the insignia of the original residents; during siesta the atmosphere is hushed, timeless.

The town beach is pleasant but busy; further south, resorts are smaller and the sands emptier. Inland Naxos is scenic and fascinating. The Tragea, the central high plain around Mount Zeus, is a lovely region of olive groves, little churches and traditional villages. Apiranthos, a hilly collection of fine stone houses, is an excellent base for walkers. It has several small museums. The villagers are descendants of the Cretans.

Milos and Kimolos

The most westerly of the Cyclades, Milos is a joy for the geologist. It is volcanic, with a dramatic coast, strange rock formations, hot springs and fertile lowlands. However, much of the landscape is disfigured by mining – it produces bentonite, perlite and china clay. But industry has brought prosperity; tourism is low-key here, despite some lovely beaches.

Ancient Milos was important for obsidian (used to make sharp tools) and for its sheltered harbour; it was settled by Minoans and Mycenaeans. In 416 BC, Milos paid dearly for refusing to join the alliance against Sparta – Athens executed the men and enslaved the women and children. Under Venetian and Turkish rule, Milos remained undistinguished.

Adhamas, the main port, is a pleasant, lively place. The north-west, inhabited since early times, has a cluster of pretty villages. Plaka, the island capital, an unspoilt whitewashed maze, has the remains of a Venetian kastro and glorious views. Tripity is built downhill near early Christian catacombs. At the bottom of the green valley the fishing village of Klima was the port for ancient Milos, whose remains straggle down the hill.

There are good beaches on the south coast, some with accommodation, others difficult to reach. Most of the south-west around Mount Profitis Ilias is bleak and deserted. The windswept north has hamlets and beaches; Pollonia in the far north-east has a diving centre and is popular with windsurfers.

Kimolos used to export chalk (*kimolia*) and still extracts Fullers earth. The craggy interior is barren, the south fertile, with a string of fishing villages and beaches. In the centre, the ruins of Venetian Paleokastro crown a cliff. This is a peaceful and friendly place.

The fishing village of Firopotamus on Milos

POPULATION:
Milos 4,771, Kimolos 769 (2001)
WHEN TO GO:
May, June, early July and September
HOW TO GET THERE:
Milos: domestic flights; ferry from Piraeus and Crete. Inter-island ferries.
Kimolos: boats from Pollonia on Milos; inter-island ferries.
HIGHLIGHTS:
Boat trips round the island visit the inaccessible beaches and view the geological oddities.
Tiny, photogenic Klima, with brightly painted boathouses lining the shore.
The museum in Plaka – containing a copy of the 'Venus de Milo'.
Dazzling white Hora above the bay in Kimolos – with a well-preserved 16th century stockade-type Kastro.
YOU SHOULD KNOW:
The 'Venus de Milo' now in the Louvre Museum in Paris was found by a farmer in 1820; her arms were knocked off in the scramble of her hand-over to the French for 'safe keeping' from the Turks.

Mykonos

POPULATION:
9,306 (2001)
WHEN TO GO:
May and October
HOW TO GET THERE:
Charter and domestic flights; ferries from Piraeus
HIGHLIGHTS:
Little Venice, where multi-coloured balconies hang over the sea facing the setting sun.
The windmills – one working mill is also a museum.
The museums – there are several interesting museums including a folklore collection in an 18th century mansion.
Scuba diving – legal here, and most beaches have a dive centre.
The nightlife – there are plenty of stylish and romantic places to eat and drink.
YOU SHOULD KNOW:
Le Corbusier is thought to have exclaimed about Mykonos: 'Whatever architecture has to say, it is said here'.

This small, rocky island has no ancient sites – it was eclipsed by its tiny neighbour Delos – and little history. It is battered all summer by the Meltemi (winds from the north). It is the most popular and most expensive of the Cyclades. Long before *Shirley Valentine*, Mykonos was an international favourite – with bohemians in the 1960s, then the European jet setters and latterly its beaches have become a destination for gay travellers. With its square white houses, blue domed churches and golden sands, it is, for many, the image of Greece; outside the long season, when sun beds cram the beaches and the town throbs with music, the magic is still strong.

Mykonos Town demands a photo at every turn. Sugar-cube houses are heaped around the harbour where tourists feed the pelican. (The original, christened Petros, arrived in a storm in 1956 and soon became a star.) The old town was designed as a maze to confuse marauding pirates; the little alleyways still bewilder visitors. The whitewashed houses, highlighted with blue painted woodwork, are wreathed with scarlet and magenta flowers.

Inland, the only sizeable town is Ano Maro, a pleasant place, rather self-consciously traditional, and a good base for walks in the rolling countryside. Here the bare brown hills are sprinkled with hundreds of little churches and the snowy cubes of farms.

Mykonos's beaches are justly famed. The tourist industry works to keep them clean, and has banned over-large development. The most popular sands run along the south coast; overcrowded, noisy stretches are interspersed with quieter nudist areas and, for those prepared to walk, there are still some relatively uncommercialized spots. The north is very windy, though Panormos Bay provides shelter.

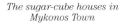

The sugar-cube houses in Mykonos Town

The Minor Cyclades

This chain of tiny islands lies between Naxos and Amorgos. Only four of the islands are inhabited year-round. In antiquity, all were populated – large numbers of ancient graves have been found. For centuries simply the haunts of pirates, they now attract Greeks in search of their roots and travellers looking for an uncommercialized spot to get away from it all.

Dhonoussa is the least accessible of the islands, lying off Naxos's empty east coast, while the others form a group to the south, en route to Amorgos. Stavros, the port settlement, is backed by low hills. A walk through cultivated land reaches dramatic scenery, remote beaches and pleasant hamlets. Only Kalotaritsas on the north coast has amenities.

Ano Koufonissi is tiny, though more populous, with a sizeable fishing fleet. (Larger Kato Koufonissi is almost uninhabited). The main settlement, Hora, spreads around the harbour. The beaches here are outstanding; some of the golden crescents along the south coast have tavernas and rooms. This island is becoming popular and is busy in season.

The ferry for Skhinoussa docks at Mersini; Hora, the town, in the hills above the minute harbour, has fine views; trails lead from here through low hills and pastures to numerous beaches. Only two, Tsigouri and Almyros, have facilities.

Iraklia, the first stop for the boat from Naxos, gets its fair share of visitors, though, with few amenities, it retains its unspoilt atmosphere. Ayios Yeorgios straggles behind the harbour and a shaded beach. A pleasant walk leads to Panayia, an unspoilt village at the foot of Mount Papas.

POPULATION:
Dhonoussa 110; Koufonissi 366; Skhinoussa 206; Iraklia 151 (2001)
WHEN TO GO:
May to early July and September
HOW TO GET THERE:
Inter-island ferries from Amorgos or Naxos.
HIGHLIGHTS:
Koufonissi – noted for its good fish tavernas.
Keros – a day-trip from Koufonissia, there is the site of an important Neolithic village on uninhabited Keros.
Livadhi – the best beach on Iraklia: among the remains of the deserted villages are remnants of Hellenistic and Venetian architecture.
The Cave of Ayios Ioannis on Iraklia – in this large cave an icon of the saint was found by a shepherd in the 19th century.
YOU SHOULD KNOW:
Over 100 Early Cycladic (3000-2000 BC) figures have been found on Keros; the finest are on display in Athens.

A church in Panayia

The church of Panayia Evangelistria

Tinos

POPULATION:
8,574 (2001)
WHEN TO GO:
May to early July and September
HOW TO GET THERE:
Ferry from mainland (Rafina and Thessaloniki); inter-island ferries.
HIGHLIGHTS:
The dovecotes – these sturdy structures are surmounted by symbolic patterns of open work slate. They are fine examples of vernacular architecture.
Pyrgos – a marble-working village with a museum and school of sculpture.
In pretty Volax, elderly Catholics weave beautiful baskets.
Kolymbithra, a double bay on the north coast – the wilder half is home to visiting flamingoes in spring.
YOU SHOULD KNOW:
Doves were introduced to Tinos by the Venetians; they provided meat, feathers for bedding and droppings for fertilizer.

A large island in the north-eastern Cyclades, Tinos is lovely. It is mountainous, with terraced hillsides, unspoilt remote hill villages and a coastline dotted with good, largely undeveloped beaches. Its landscape is characterized by hundreds of ornate, whitewashed dovecotes, and tall belfries. The Venetians controlled Tinos for 500 years, holding out against the Turks longer than anywhere else in the Aegean. During this time, Catholic and Orthodox churches competed in building these belfries. Several of its many villages are still Catholic.

Although Tinos receives few foreign visitors, thousands of Greeks come as pilgrims, particularly on 25 March and 15 August. Since the 19th century, when a nun had a vision directing her to a miraculous icon of the Virgin, Tinos has been the Lourdes of Greece. Tinos Town, which is modern and functional but relaxed, is packed with shops selling religious paraphernalia; the icon, in the church of Panayia Evangelistria is almost invisible beneath gold, silver and jewels. A thick pad running up the processional street is for pilgrims approaching the church on their knees.

At Kionia, a beach resort outside town, the Sanctuary of Poseidon and Amphitrite has the remains of hostels for ancient pilgrims – Poseidon delivered the island from a plague of snakes. On a rocky crag inland are the ruins of the Venetian capital, Exobourgo. Clustered around the foothills lie dozens of lovely villages and hamlets, each distinctive, and well worth exploring. Tinos enjoys a strong tradition of crafts.

The islanders are open and welcoming – pay them a visit!

Santorini

In the southern Aegean Sea, about 200 km south of mainland Greece, lies Santorini, a spectacular volcanic island in the Cyclades group known for its dramatic views, brilliant sunsets and fine beaches. The beauty of the island and its dynamic nightlife have made this a popular tourist destination.

From above it is obvious that the island, shaped like a ring with a huge bay of sea in the centre, is what remains of a giant volcano which erupted in around 1650 BC, one of the biggest volcanic explosions the earth has ever seen. The walls of the caldera surrounding the bay in the centre rise a sheer 300 m out of the sea. The traces of previous eruptions can be seen in the coloured bands of rock on the island's cliffs: each one is a layer of compressed ash ejected in one eruption. The small island in the middle of the bay is another volcanic cone forming.

Evidence suggests that the massive eruption caused a tsunami which led indirectly to the decline of the Minoan civilization centred on nearby Crete. The Minoan settlement on Santorini itself was engulfed in lava and the stunning remains, at Akrotiri, make a fascinating day out. There are three-storey houses with magnificent frescos, ceramics and staircases, and the hot and cold running water system suggests this was a prosperous and refined town.

Thira is the island's capital, perched high up on the cliffs 300 m above its port below. Its architecture is an attractive mix of Venetian and traditional Cycladic and the white cobblestone streets are lined with shops and cafés. Thira can get busy in summer as cruise ships dock here while the passengers explore the town. There are three main means of getting from the port up to the town – by cablecar, by donkey, or by walking up the 300-odd zigzagging steps.

The town of Ia (sometimes spelled Oia), with its pretty whitewashed buildings and blue domes, is one of the most charming places on the island, albeit rather busy with tourists. The town offers views of the open sea to the east, as well as the bay to the west, and many people congregate here in the late afternoon to watch the sunset over the bay, a really memorable experience.

POPULATION:
13,670 (2001)
WHEN TO GO:
April to October
HOW TO GET THERE:
By ferry from the Greek mainland or other Greek islands, or by plane from Athens, Thessaloniki and a few other European cities.
HIGHLIGHTS:
The excavations at Akrotiri – this Minoan town was buried by lava during the volcanic eruption, and the excavations have revealed multi-level buildings and beautiful frescoes.
The Archaeological Museum at Thira – the story of Akrotiri and other ancient settlements on the island is told through Neolithic and Bronze Age artefacts.
The beaches – the best beach is probably that at Perissa, but the black sand beach in the charming town of Kamari also makes a nice day out.
Mesa Gonia – a small village with lovely traditional architecture, some ruins from the 1956 earthquake, restored villas and a winery.
Pyrgos – an inland village with some grand houses, a ruined Venetian castle and some Byzantine churches.
YOU SHOULD KNOW:
The island is also sometimes referred to as Thira.

The pretty town of Ia overlooks the Aegean Sea.

Alonissos

POPULATION:
2,700 (2001)
WHEN TO GO:
June and early July, September and
early October
HOW TO GET THERE:
Charter/domestic flights to Skiathos
and hydrofoil connections.
Ferry/hydrofoil from Thessaloniki and
Volos via Skiathos.
HIGHLIGHTS:
Old Alonissos – otherwise known as
Hora – this beautiful old town is being
sensitively renovated by returning
islanders and foreigners and has
several good tavernas, perfect spots
to recover from the energetic walk
up the hill and watch the sunset.
A boat trip excursion takes in the
numerous small islands, landing
on some.
The Monk seal information centre in
Patitiri and the Monk seal
rehabilitation centre in Steni Vala
provide insight into these
rare mammals.
YOU SHOULD KNOW:
Evidence has been unearthed of the
oldest prehistoric habitation in the
Aegean – near the site of ancient Ikos
at Kokkinokastro.

*One of the secluded bays
on Alonissos*

The furthest of the Sporades from mainland Greece, Alonissos has not been overwhelmed by tourism. It is a serene place, heavily wooded with pine and oak, an island whose numerous good beaches are reached by rocky donkey paths, whose residents are careful of the area's ecology. In 1992 the seas around the island were designated a National Marine Park and several of the many small islets are off limits. The park is for the protection not only of the endangered European Monk seal, but also of rare sea birds and a unique species of wild goat. Here all homes have cesspit drainage; no sewage enters the brilliantly clean sea. Many islanders fetch fine drinking water from mountain springs, using the piped variety only for washing. Visitors who come to Alonissos are attracted by the tranquility and beauty and by the charmingly hospitable islanders.

Alonissos has rebuilt itself from disaster. In 1950, phylloxera wiped out the flourishing wine-making industry, after which many islanders left for the mainland to make a living. In 1965 Hora, the old capital, was destroyed by earthquake. The residents were re-housed down by the harbour in rapidly constructed accommodation. Patitiri still has a rather thrown-together look, though the waterfront is undergoing a facelift and the port has a lively and friendly atmosphere.

Little traffic on the one real road makes it a perfect place for walkers. Tracks lead into the woods and hills from which paths run down to one of the many small shingle beaches. Swim in the crystalline water and enjoy a lazy meal of freshly caught fish in one of the beachside tavernas.

Skyros

The largest and most sparsely populated of the group, Skyros lies far south of the other Sporades, closer to Evvia than to mainland Thessaly. The north of the island is rolling, cultivated and forested, while the barren, mountainous south is home to an ancient breed of half-wild ponies. Skyros has many beaches, some only accessible on foot; the finest lie on the north-east coast. Until quite recently, few tourists made the journey apart from those attending courses at a long-established centre for alternative lifestyles. Now, more independent travellers visit Skyros.

In mythology, Theseus met his death here, and the young Achilles, disguised as a girl, was hidden. In Byzantine times the island was again a hiding place – for wrongdoers exiled from the mainland. The trade and collaboration by these men with seafarers and pirates resulted in a wealthy élite who filled their mansions with treasures – some looted. The Skyrians' extraordinary traditional homes, like tiny family museums, have their roots in this period. On display among skilful modern needlework and painted pottery are old embroideries, copperware and porcelain. The furniture may have been intricately carved 200 years ago – or last week.

In the far south, at Tris Boukes, is the grave of poet Rupert Brooke, who died offshore en route to Gallipoli in 1915.

Skyros Town is a glorious tumble of Cycladic-style white cube houses on a rocky bluff, high above the lovely, long sand beaches of Magazia and Molos. The maze of little lanes is a real joy; you may see old Skyrians in traditional dress – the men wearing heavy, laced sandals which resemble medieval footwear – sitting outside doors, open to reveal their precious inheritance.

POPULATION:
2,602 (2001)
WHEN TO GO:
June, early July and September
HOW TO GET THERE:
Domestic flight from Athens or Thessaloniki, or ferry from Kymi on Evvia and connecting bus from Athens.
HIGHLIGHTS:
The Faltaits Museum - housed in the family's mansion in Skyros Town, this is an outstanding collection of Skyrian folk art, rare books and photographs and treasures.
The Kastro - this mainly Byzantine fortress above Skyros Town is reached through a tunnel in the walls and a monastery courtyard. The views are outstanding and the walk up through the quieter back lanes enjoyable.
The Brooke monument – a classical bronze, 'Immortal Poetry' faces the sea at the edge of Skyros Town. When it was unveiled in the 1930s its nakedness caused a stir.
YOU SHOULD KNOW:
The pre-Lenten Carnival surely has its roots in pre-Christian ritual – transvestite 'maidens' dance around town with young men in goat costumes, garlands and sheep bells.

Skyros Town

Skopelos

Picturesque Skopelos Town

Skopelos lies off the coast of mainland Thessaly and like the neighbouring Pelion Peninsula it is mountainous and densely wooded. The north-east, with its high cliffs, is deserted and exposed; a few coves are accessible by boat. The south and west provide sheltered harbours, small villages, pebble beaches and wonderfully clear water. Possibly the lack of long sand beaches has protected the island from mass-tourism and preserved its traditions. Development is low-key, and many visitors come from the mainland. This fertile island produces olives and grapes, but its specialities are plums and almonds. Walkers will find farms, olive groves and orchards, cool pine forests and hills, perhaps one of the many isolated churches. A signed track from Skopelos Town passes several monasteries and affords some stunning views.

Archaeological evidence suggests that Skopelos was a Minoan outpost. Legend has it that the governor was the son of Ariadne and Dionysus, the god of wine, and that this Staphylos (the name means 'grape') introduced wine-making. After living under a succession of nationalities over the centuries, the whole population of the island was slaughtered by the Ottoman pirate-admiral Barbarossa in the sixteenth century. Recovery is evidenced by the exceptionally fine houses in Skopelos Town – the island escaped earthquake damage and World War II devastation.

Built around a sheltered bay, the harbour-front is packed with bars, shops and tavernas. As the buildings climb the amphitheatre of hills, the roads narrow to stepped lanes, with small houses squeezed between tiny churches. Everything is dazzlingly whitewashed, highlighted by bright shutters and trails of vivid flowers. The strenuous climb ends at a ruined fortress, which offers a marvellous panorama of the town, and nearby bars for refreshment.

POPULATION:
4,696 (2001)
WHEN TO GO:
June and early July, September and early October
HOW TO GET THERE:
Charter/domestic flights to Skiathos and hydrofoil connections. Ferry/hydrofoil from Thessaloniki and Volos via Skiathos.
HIGHLIGHTS:
Glossa - the island's other major settlement. Built high above the north-west coast, it's a very traditional Greek hill town – white-washed, tranquil and beautiful, it seems untouched by time.
A meal in one of the tamarisk-shaded fish tavernas overlooking the tiny harbour at Agnondas.
YOU SHOULD KNOW:
The inhabitants of Glossa may have immigrated from Thessaly; their architecture is distinctive from the rest of the island, as is their dialect.

Karpathos

A long, narrow, rocky island midway between Rhodes and Crete, Karpathos has always been sparsely inhabited. There is evidence of Minoan and Mycenaean trade and Classical settlement, but the Knights of St John built no castles, and the Ottomans installed a single judge. Later, ethnologists came to study the age-old customs and unique dialect of the northern village, Olymbos.

In the more populous south, Pigadhia is a busy, pleasant modern port town set at one end of a fine long beach. The main attraction of the desolate and windswept south is top-class windsurfing. North of Pigadhia, where the eastern shore drops steeply into exceptionally clear water, lie beautiful, isolated beaches, best reached by boat. The west coast offers a few more resorts: developed Arkasa, small fishing villages and coves, remote Paralia Lefkou with its good beaches and hill walks.

Inland, a group of lovely hill villages with cool climates and glorious views are inhabited by returned islanders. Karpathos is, surprisingly, a very wealthy place: many of its men emigrate to the USA, send money back, and eventually return home with their fortunes.

The north has always been cut off from the south by mountains; now there is a road, but no buses. A ferry or excursion boat is the easiest way to reach Diafani, a small port with a relaxed atmosphere, good beaches and walks. Day-trippers visit Olymbos to see the women (very few men live here) in their elaborate costumes, which only the older ones now wear all year round. They still bake bread in communal ovens and their homes are decorated inside with embroideries, outside with painted carved plasterwork. Traditions are vanishing with exposure to the 'modern' world, but it remains a wonderful place.

POPULATION:
16,441 (2001)
WHEN TO GO:
May, June and September
HOW TO GET THERE:
Direct charter and domestic flights. Inter-island ferry from Crete or Rhodes or Piraeus.
HIGHLIGHTS:
Stay in Olymbos and enjoy the life of the village after the day-trippers depart.
Walking in north Karpathos on old trails to traditional villages and deserted shores.
Music – the lucky may hear live music played on ancient instruments; the songs and scales have their roots in Byzantium.
YOU SHOULD KNOW:
The double-headed eagle seen on many of the plasterwork balconies in Olymbos is the symbol of the Byzantine Empire.

Chapels on Karpathos

311

Kalymnos

POPULATION:
16,441 (2001)
WHEN TO GO:
May, June and September
HOW TO GET THERE:
Flight to Kos and ferry transfer from Mastihari; ferry and inter-island boats from Piraeus and Rhodes.
HIGHLIGHTS:
The Nautical and Folklore Museum in Pothia – for an insight into the history of sponge diving.
Vathys, the cool green valley behind Rina, where citrus groves lie below tawny hills.
Khristos tis Ierousalim, an early Byzantine basilica close to Hora.
Telendos – this tranquil island just off the west coast has beaches, tavernas and a few places to stay.
YOU SHOULD KNOW:
Pale yellow sponges are bleached with nitric acid, which weakens the fibres. The brown ones last longer.

Kalymnos is arid and mountainous, though in history its good harbours gave it some importance and it is dotted with the ruins of early Byzantine basilicas. Its fame though was as 'the sponge fishing island'. In its heyday, a huge fleet left each year after Easter, returning in the autumn. Half the divers never came home. Decompression chambers arrived only in the 1950s; now a few elderly disabled survivors are reminders of the effects of 'the bends'. In 1986 local sponges were almost completely wiped out by a virus and the government turned to tourism to bolster the economy. The string of resorts along the good beaches of the greener west coast became a popular package destination.

The main port, Pothia, lines a big and very busy harbour, backed by tawny hills. It is brash, noisy, photogenic, unpretentious and very Greek. Old warehouses still process imported sponges.

On the road to the resorts lie Khryssoherias, a castle of the Knights of St John, and Hora, the medieval capital. From here steps climb to the Byzantine citadel. South-west of Pothia, Vlyhadia is one of a small number of legal diving areas in Greece. It has a Museum of Submarine Finds.

The east coast is harsh and uninhabited but for Rina, a tiny port and yacht anchorage at the mouth of a fertile valley. Here there is swimming in the narrow turquoise inlet and a spring where islanders fill containers with fine drinking water from the mountains.

In recent years, resort tourism has declined, but visitors come now to trek the long and sometimes challenging paths, to climb the almost sheer cliffs of northern Kalymnos and to enjoy the island's traditional atmosphere.

The town of Pothia

Leros

Tourism has never been large-scale in Leros. Its economy was based on prisons and asylums and the Junta's dissidents were housed here. More recently, bad publicity resulted in reorganization and Leros has emerged from its 'institutional' image. Lying just north of Kalymnos, it is a friendly, prosperous, off-the-track island, its rolling hills interspersed by fertile valleys and a coastline indented by huge, almost landlocked bays. These provided anchorage not only for fishing boats but for whole fleets. During World War II, the English landed after the Italian capitulation but were displaced by overwhelming German forces in the Battle of Leros, 12-16 November 1943.

The Italians had established an important naval base here in 1923 and in 1935 built Lakki as a showpiece of Fascist Art Deco. Its scale is too grand for its current inhabitants – towering palm trees, over-wide boulevards lined with monumental grey mansions. Many of these buildings have been allowed to deteriorate, but a phased restoration is under way. The town still has the ghostly feel of a deserted film set.

Leros is a compact island and its principal low-key resorts are within walking distance of each other. North of Lakki, the lively working port of Pandelli and adjacent Vromolithos with its sand and gravel beach form a pleasant whole. Platanos, the island's picturesque capital, is crowned by a dramatic Knights' castle, and merges with Ayia Marina, an attractive port village on a fine bay. Alinda, the longest established resort, and neighbouring Krithoni lie further along the bay. Behind the beach is a very well maintained and peaceful Allied War Graves cemetery. Around the coastline are further tamarisk shaded beaches and villages.

The attractive port village of Ayia Marina

POPULATION:
8,207 (2001)
WHEN TO GO:
May, June, early July and September
HOW TO GET THERE:
Domestic flights. Charter flight to Kos and ferry connection. Inter-island ferries.
HIGHLIGHTS:
Food – as well as good fresh fish, Leros' cuisine is rich in tradition and still offers delicious local specialities.
Ayia Kioura, north of the airport. This little chapel was painted with striking murals by Junta-era political prisoners.
Diving – from Xirokambos, south of Lakki. First class dives around reef and shipwrecks.
YOU SHOULD KNOW:
Brightly-painted garden ornaments seen around the islands are made from bomb nose-cones and shell casings.

313

The harbour village is the only settlement on Kastellorizo.

Kastellorizo

POPULATION:
430 (2001)
WHEN TO GO:
May, June, early July and September
HOW TO GET THERE:
Flights from Rhodes. Ferry from Rhodes and inter-island ferries.
HIGHLIGHTS:
The Museum in Kastellorizo's ruined castle is interesting and friendly. The Grotto of Perasta. This enormous cave with stalactites and strange blue light may be visited by boat.
YOU SHOULD KNOW:
The Lady of Rho, Dhespina Akhladhiotis, lived till 1982 on the tiny islet of Rho; she hoisted the Greek flag each day in defiance of the Turks.

Named for the red stone castle that once dominated the port, Kastellorizo is the smallest of the Dodecanese – and the largest of an archipelago of tiny islets, which gives it its other name, Megisti. It is more than seventy nautical miles east of Rhodes, just a stone's throw from Kas on the Turkish coast. It is a barren and rocky place, with a tiny permanent population. Supplies are shipped from Rhodes – or brought in unofficially from Turkey.

In the nineteenth century the population of this thriving community with its fine natural harbour and merchant fleet was over 10,000. After power shifts in the Eastern Mediterranean, evacuation and occupation in two World Wars and a huge explosion which destroyed many homes and prompted further migration, it was left almost deserted. Now the harbour resounds in the summer to Australian accents: many migrants are returning to find their roots, reclaim and rebuild their family homes. Another boost to visitor numbers has been the Oscar-winning Italian film, *Mediterraneo*, which was filmed on the island.

The only settlement is the harbour village and its little 'suburb' over the hill. The waterfront is lined with graceful neo-classical houses, and the path round the headland passes Greece's only Lycian house-tomb. Peaceful walks around the island pass monasteries and ruins. On the zigzag stepped path to the top of the crag above the town you may see flocks of bee-eaters – the migration route of these colourful birds touches the island.

There are no beaches, but very enjoyable swimming is possible from rocks, and from the 'lido' platform at the mouth of the harbour. The water here is glass-clear and peacock-hued.

Patmos

The most northerly of the Greek Dodecanese Islands, lying not far off the west coast of Turkey, Patmos is just 12 km (7.4 mi) in length. Graced with secluded bays, pretty offshore islets and a good deal of peace and quiet, this is a great place to unwind away from the crowds. However, this is not usually why visitors come to Patmos. Known as the 'Jerusalem of the Aegean', Patmos is where St John the Divine wrote the Book of Revelation. The island has a mystical, otherworldly atmosphere, and many visitors report having extraordinarily vivid dreams here.

Patmos and Christianity have been closely linked since the 1st century AD when the Emperor Dometian drove the Apostle St John the Divine to exile here. It is said he experienced terrible visions of the Apocalypse while on the island. A small cave, midway between the port of Skala and the capital of Chora, is allegedly the scene of God's revelations. St John stayed in the cave during his exile and dictated the Book of Revelation to his disciple, Prochoros, around 95 AD.

The cave is now a small monastic complex known as the Cave of the Apocalypse; 43 steep steps lead down into the cave, which still consists of the original living rock. Pilgrims come from all over the world to see the stone where St John laid his head and the stand where Prochoros wrote. At the mouth of the cave is the late 11th-century chapel of St Anne. The nearby Patmian School was first established in 1713 as a seminary, and its students have risen to the highest ranks of the Greek Orthodox Church.

In 1088, the Emperor Alexius I Comnenus ceded Patmos to St Christodoulos, so he could found a monastery here in honour of St John. He chose a spectacular site that dominates the whole island, and the Greek Orthodox rituals still practised here are virtually unchanged since the 11th century. The fortified monastery consists of a complex of buildings. Apart from the main church, in which Christodoulos' sarcophagus can be found, the Chapel of the Theotokos contains Byzantine frescos of the Virgin Mary which were only discovered in 1958 as the result of an earthquake. Other treasures are in the Library and the Treasury, which house a wealth of important works, some dating back to the early 6th century, and some beautiful illuminated manuscripts.

POPULATION:
3,044 (2001)
WHEN TO GO:
April to October.
HOW TO GET THERE:
By hydrofoil from Samos or ferry from Kos to Skala port.
HIGHLIGHTS:
The Monastery of St John – built by St Christodoulos in the 11th century, the monastery has some wonderful frescos and works of art, as well as a fantastic view of the island.
The Cave of the Apocalypse – this is where St John had his visions of the Apocalypse and dictated the Book of Revelation to Prochoros.
YOU SHOULD KNOW:
Patmos is an important pilgrimage site.

A mosaic of St John the Theologian in the Patmos monastery

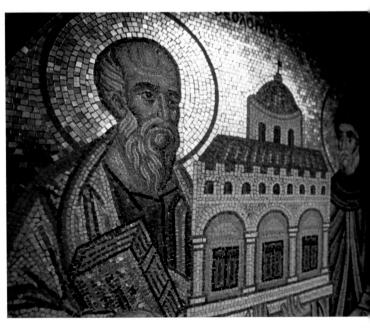

Nyssiros

POPULATION:
948 (2001)
WHEN TO GO:
May, June, early July and September
HOW TO GET THERE:
Flight to Kos and ferry. Inter-island ferries from Rhodes and Piraeus.
HIGHLIGHTS:
The crater – the air stinks of sulphur, blow-holes emit jets of steam, brilliant yellow sulphur crystals. The ground is spongy and hot. From under it comes hissing and bubbling. Paleokastro is a fine 7th century BC Doric defensive bastion south of Mandhraki.
YOU SHOULD KNOW:
Poseidon was annoyed by a Titan, and crushed him under a huge rock, which became Nyssiros. Poor Polyvotis still struggles to escape, and groans. His name is used by the locals for the volcano.

Compared with its large northerly neighbour Kos, Nyssiros is surprisingly green, although its scant water is sulphur-tainted. Its slopes are covered in volcanic-soil-loving oaks. This is not just a small, round island with volcanic soil – it is a volcano. The craggy hill-tops form a circle round a volcanic caldera created by an eruption in 1422. The first great eruptions happened thirty or forty thousand years ago; the most recent in 1933. Contented livestock wander in the woods, though the fertile terraces are largely uncultivated, for the islanders now derive much of their income from pumice extraction – another legacy of early volcanic activity.

The port and island capital, Mandhraki, is a cheerful, charming place with its Knights' castle, closely packed, brightly-painted houses, narrow lanes and sea views. Pali, a pleasant fishing village to the east, has accommodation and a good beach, with long walks to more isolated spots. A trek through the hills reaches the volcano via Emborios, an almost deserted village, which offers sustenance and a public steam bath (volcano heated!) in a grotto. Nikea, a lovely, lively village further round the rim, has a pretty pebble-mosaic square and views over the sea and volcano. A bus stops here and a steep path down into the caldera starts.

From mid-morning till early afternoon, day-trippers from Kos pour into the blighted lunar landscape of the caldera, where there are five craters, with a path into the largest. Few visitors stay on Nyssiros; after the boats depart, a somnolent peace descends.

The lovely village of Nikea with the volcanic crater in the background

Symi

Lying just 41 km (25 mi) north-west of Rhodes close the the Turkish mainland, the little island of Symi is part of the Dodecanese Islands. The interior of this lovely mountainous island is divided by beautiful valleys and its coast is characterized by rocky outcrops and lovely bays, many only accessible by boat.

The island belonged to the Roman Empire, then the Byzantines, until its conquest in 1373 by the Knights of St John whose skills in shipping and commerce brought several centuries of wealth, mainly through boat-building and sponge-diving. The Ottoman Empire took Symi in 1522 but its prosperity continued and its export of sponges still provided much of its wealth. The island's heyday was in the mid-19th century when its population numbered around 30,000, and many of the neoclassical mansions on the island date from that period. Symi was passed between the Turks, Italians, Nazis and British until it finally joined Greece in 1948.

The main settlement, in the north-east of the island, is also called Symi, but locals usually refer to it as Yialos. The town is divided into an upper and lower part. The upper part is known as Chorio and is dominated by the fortress of the Knights of St John. The castle was built in the early 15th century on the site of a much older fortification. It survived until World War II when it was used as a munitions store. This was blown up, destroying the castle and the church within its walls. Parts of the walls remain and there are lovely views from the site. The lower part of town around the port area is stunning, surrounded as it is by green hills making a natural amphitheatre. The two halves of the town are linked by the Kali Strata, 350 steps lined with pastel-coloured neoclassical houses with flower-filled courtyards.

There are many lovely churches and monasteries on the island, some of which can be explored on foot, others that are only accessible by boat. The church of Constantinos and Eleni on the southern slopes of Vigla has lovely gardens and terraces. Set in a bay to the south-west of the island is the monastery of the Archangel Michael at Panormitis, an important pilgrimage site visited by people from all over Greece. Built in the early eighteenth century on the site of a much older monastery, it contains a wonderful iconostasis, fine Byzantine frescoes and two museums with a fascinating library.

Every year from July to September, the famous Symi Festival takes place on the island. The festival features dance and theatre events, as well as a host of open-air concerts by many leading Greek musicians.

POPULATION:
2,606 (2001)
WHEN TO GO:
May to October.
HOW TO GET THERE:
By boat or hydrofoil from Rhodes or Piraeus.
HIGHLIGHTS:
Hire a boat and explore the lovely coastline to find a secluded beach for a picnic.
Hiking – the island lends itself to exploration on foot, and the beautiful countryside is peppered with isolated chapels and wonderful views.
The monastery of Megalos Sotiris – a picturesque monastery with spectacular views. A lovely walk to an old vineyard and the ruins of old wine presses is sign-posted from here.
The Archaeological and Folklore Museum in Chorio – open mornings only, the museum has some interesting exhibits and artefacts.
Chatziagapitos Mansion in Chorio – a restored 18th-century mansion open to the public.
YOU SHOULD KNOW:
Although the island used to be famous for its sponges, those now on sale on the island are imported.

The beautiful harbour at Symi

Rhodes

POPULATION:
117,007 (2001)
WHEN TO GO:
April to June, September and October
HOW TO GET THERE:
Charter and domestic flights. Ferry
from Piraeus. Inter-island ferries,
catamarans and hydrofoils.
International ferry from Marmaris,
Turkey.
HIGHLIGHTS:
The Palace of the Grandmasters –
heavily reconstructed by the Italians,
it is attached to two fascinating
collections, the medieval Exhibit and
Ancient Rhodes.
The Acropolis of Lindhos – gloriously
photogenic Hellenistic and Doric
remains in a spectacular setting high
above the town.
Thermes Kallitheas, south of Rhodes
town. A partly restored orientalized
Art Deco complex of pools and
domes set in a palm grove.
YOU SHOULD KNOW:
The Colossus of Rhodes, one of the
Seven Wonders of the World, was
built after the siege in 305 BC; it
collapsed after an earthquake in
227 BC. The story has it that it was
sold as scrap hundreds of years later,
only to return in the form of
Ottoman cannonballs.

Large, beautiful and fertile, lying on trade routes close to Asia Minor, Rhodes is now one of the major tourist destinations in the Mediterranean. It has a long history of invasion. The first Siege of Rhodes was laid in 305 BC, a century after the city-states of Lindos, Kameiros and Ialyssos united. After almost a year Demetrius Poliorketes and his superior forces sailed, leaving a powerful and wealthy independent city-state which eclipsed even Athens in the arts. The Knights of St John held it as their main base from 1309 till Suleyman the Magnificent laid the second Siege of Rhodes in 1522, and the whole Dodecanese became part of the Ottoman Empire. The Italians seized the island in 1912, the Germans in 1943; after British administration it joined unified Greece in 1948.

Lindos and the Acropolis

The Old Town of Rhodes, which seethes with tourists all day, is a remarkably preserved and exquisite medieval city. The massive walls, the bustling squares, the palaces and the rather stern, straight streets, all built of glowing golden stone, are a legacy of the crusading Knights. The Ottomans left mosques, Turkish baths and a very oriental-feeling bazaar area. In Mandhraki, the ancient harbour, the Colossos of Rhodes once stood. Some fine Italian Art Deco buildings remain in the New Town. There are several museums and a rousing Sound and Light presentation.

South of the city, big resorts have swallowed most of the coastal area. Heavily commercialized Lindos with its steep lanes, frescoed church and sheltered harbour (supposedly St Paul's landing place) is still beautiful. The wooded, hilly countryside, unspoilt villages and lonely churches of the interior are best explored by car. Tour buses visit the Valley of the Butterflies. The far south is almost undeveloped, though the southernmost point, Prassonissi, is a Mecca for windsurfers.

Corfu

The most northerly and, with Greece's highest rainfall, the greenest of the Ionian Islands, Corfu lies close to the mainland and the Albanian coast. Described by Homer as 'beautiful and rich', it is mountainous, lushly fertile and fringed by fine beaches with lovely aquamarine waters.

From the 8th century BC, Corfu was subject to a succession of powers, though it never became part of the Ottoman Empire. Venice held it for 200 years, then Napoleon seized it, and for some years it was a British Protectorate. Long a favourite with travellers, its quiet, idiosyncratic life is lovingly recorded in the books of Lawrence and Gerald Durrell. Now, despite some indiscriminate tourist development, it remains bewitching.

Corfu Town is a lovely place, a blend of splendid Italianate buildings, narrow alleyways and grand, French-influenced arcades. There are museums and fine churches, including the Church of Ayios Spyridhon, where the mummified body of the island's patron saint lies in a glass-fronted coffin. (It is paraded through the town several times a year.) A popular excursion is to the photogenic islets of Vlaherna and Pondikonissi.

North from Corfu Town, brash or prestigious resorts are interspersed with fishing harbours and backed by magnificent scenery. Southwards lie the site of the ancient capital, Corcyra, and some large resorts. Then a winding coastal road reaches some quieter beaches. The west coast boasts long stretches of glorious sand, a backdrop of green mountains – and some of the largest hotel conglomerations. Even here, more peaceful coves can be reached by boat, or a scramble on foot.

Inland, traditional villages offer shade and good food. Corfiot cuisine, unusually, has no Turkish influence, and often seems more Italian than Greek. A stroll and a climb in scented mountain air amid ancient olive trees rewards with views over ethereal greenness towards the heavenly blue sea.

The Vlacherna Monastery in Kanoni

POPULATION:
109,540 (2001)
WHEN TO GO:
May, June, September and October
HOW TO GET THERE:
Direct charter flights; domestic flights. Ferry from the mainland (Igoumenitsa); international ferry from Italy.
HIGHLIGHTS:
The excellent Archaeological Museum in Corfu Town.
The Asiatic Museum, housed in the former residence of the British High Commissioner.
Mon Repos, the birthplace of Prince Philip, now an interesting museum with lovely grounds, south of Corfu Town.
Watching the sunset from Kaiser's Throne, an observation tower above Pelekas village on the west coast.
The 'ghost village' of Ano Perithia in the north of the island with its several thriving tavernas.
YOU SHOULD KNOW:
A wide green esplanade, the Spianada, in Corfu Town, is home to Greece's only cricket pitch.

Paxi and Andipaxi

Paxi is a tiny island, and has no spectacular sandy beaches or historical sites; its limited accommodation is block-booked in season, and its popularity with yacht flotillas has pushed prices up. However, visitors fall in love with it. Largely unspoilt – its tourism is run by small, discriminating companies – it is beautiful, friendly and charming.

The east coast is characterized by low hills and shingly coves, the west by precipitous cliffs above inaccessible caves and beaches. There are three coastal settlements. Gaios, the capital and main port, is a pleasant, attractive town of old, red-roofed, pastel-washed buildings around a seafront square, with views of two islets. Longos to the northwest is a pretty fishing village and a quieter resort. Picturesque Lakka sits on a beautiful horseshoe bay at the north of the island. It has a couple of beaches and some good walks. Inland Paxi, with its ancient olives and scattering of farms and villages, is perfect walking country. The one main road runs down the spine of the island.

Andipaxi, with its gorgeous sandy coves and dazzlingly blue water, can be reached by excursion boat from any of the resorts. The beaches do get busy, but it is possible to walk across the islet (it is covered in vines, and produces good wine) to quieter bays.

POPULATION:
2,500 (2001)
WHEN TO GO:
May, June, September and October
HOW TO GET THERE:
Ferry from the mainland (Igoumenitsa); hydrofoil from Corfu.
HIGHLIGHTS:
Walking is the best way to get to know the island; good maps and guides are available.
Boat trips – the boat from Paxi to Andipaxi may visit some of the most dramatic caves in the region.
YOU SHOULD KNOW:
The statue on Gaios waterfront commemorates a Paxiot sailor who tried to set fire to the Turkish fleet.

The Trypitos Arch on the south coast of Paxi

Ithaki

POPULATION:
3,080 (2001)
WHEN TO GO:
May, June and September.
HOW TO GET THERE:
Ferry from the mainland (Astakos
and Patras); inter-island ferry.
HIGHLIGHTS:
Walking – with its small scale, quiet
lanes, paths over gorse covered hills
and wonderful views, this is a
walkers' island.
Anoyi – once an important
settlement, this sleepy village has
some fine old buildings.
Afales Bay – a little-visited sweep of
pebble and sand below the supposed
School of Homer at Platrithies.
YOU SHOULD KNOW:
Ithaca (Ithaki) has long been the
symbolic image for the end of
a journey.

Two narrowly connected mountain tops rising from the sea, little Ithaki nestles close to north-eastern Kefallonia. With its wooded valleys, vineyards, forested hills and small pebble beaches, it is an excellent place for a quiet stay. Though day-trippers do visit, tourism is low-key here.

Legendary Odysseus returned to his home on Ithaca after years of wandering and much of the detailed geographical description of his island matches features on modern Ithaki. Various sites have been linked to those in the Odyssey, but there is little real evidence. Historically, Ithaki was almost uninhabited till the Venetians re-settled it, and it is hard to imagine this peaceful place the splendid hub of a maritime kingdom.

The harbour town of Vathy, set on a deep bay within a bay, was sympathetically restored after the 1953 earthquake; it has a lovely waterfront and provides a taste of old island life. Within walking distances are a couple of small beaches and the Odysseus' sites of the Arethoussa Spring and the Cave of the Nymphs. Alalkomenae, the site Schliemann claimed as the castle of Odysseus, consists of foundations – the artefacts found are in the museum. There is a good beach at Pisaetos, below the site.

A spectacular bus ride across the isthmus to northern Ithaki reaches Stavros, a busy little town set in fine hilly countryside. An alternative location for the castle is at Pelikata Hill. On the east coast, the tiny harbour settlements of Frikes and Kioni are popular with visitors. Kioni has pretty old buildings and a busy yacht anchorage; Frikes, hidden in a deep wooded valley, is, with its sheltered mooring, a year-round port. It has some pleasant waterfront tavernas.

The pretty harbour at Kioni

Lefkada

Lefkada was attached to the mainland until a canal was cut in the 7th century BC. Now it is reached by road over a pontoon swivel bridge. The heavy Venetian fortification of the north coast, some of which remains, was not enough to prevent the Ottomans taking it in 1479; their tenure lasted about two centuries.

The island is mountainous and very fertile, lush with olive groves and vineyards and traditional villages. The west coast is rugged, the east sheltered, with calm beaches. Some of the low-lying areas are marshy.

The main town, Lefkada, in the far north, was badly hit by earthquakes. Now it is an attractive working town, rebuilt with low-rise buildings, narrow lanes and arcaded streets. Southwards, past a few small fishing ports and pebble beaches, lies Nydhri, the most highly developed resort town. It has good beaches and a lovely setting overlooking small satellite islands. Boat trips tour these – some are privately owned. Further south, several fine bays enclose quieter resorts or fishing villages. Vassiliki is situated on a huge, windy bay: the charming little harbour is lined with shade trees and tavernas. The breezy beach at Pondi, a little west, is visited by vast numbers of windsurfers.

The rocky west coast is dotted with lovely beaches. Most accommodation here is in village rooms or campsites. The southernmost point, Cape Lefkatas, is also known as Sappho's Leap – here the lovelorn lyric poet reputedly threw herself into the sea.

POPULATION:
22,500 (2001)
WHEN TO GO:
May, June and September
HOW TO GET THERE:
By road from the mainland; inter-island ferries.
HIGHLIGHTS:
Meganissi, the largest of the satellite islands. Green and peaceful with pretty beaches and deep bays, it has accommodation.
Windsurfing – Vassiliki is home to some of Europe's best windsurfing.
The beaches – the most southerly beaches on the west coast are, with their dramatic white cliffs and turquoise water, among the loveliest in the Ionian.
YOU SHOULD KNOW:
The German archaeologist Wilhelm Dorpfeld believed that Nydhri, not Ithaki, was Odysseus' capital. He lived there and is honoured by a statue on the quay.

The stunning beach at Port Katsiki

Kefalonia

Like other Ionian islands, Kefalonia was never taken by the Ottomans – it was too important to the Venetian maritime empire. Also like its neighbours, it was occupied by Italian and then by German forces during World War II; during the Italian 'capitulation', over 5,000 troops were massacred. Louis de Berniere's book *Captain Corelli's Mandolin* covers this tragedy. A flood of tourists came to the island after the film in 2000, though they found none of the elegant Venetian architecture; this was destroyed in the 1953 earthquake.

The largest of the Ionian Islands, with a mountainous interior and magnificent beaches, it absorbs the crowds, and its towns and villages retain traditional independence. After the earthquake, Kefalonia re-housed rather than re-constructed; Argostoli, the capital, is a beautifully situated, functional concrete town. The south of the island is rugged and barren; along the coast are the biggest package resorts and the best beaches. Poros and Skala on the south-east coast are older resorts.

Sami, a large working port built and rebuilt on the site of the ancient capital offers a couple of decent beaches and tavernas which, after the location filming, have now been appropriately re-named. Ayia Efimia, north of Sami, is a friendly fishing village and low-key resort. On the northernmost point of the island stands Fiskardho, the only town to survive the earthquake. Its pretty harbour front curls round a bay bobbing with yachts. Crowded but charming, it has pleasant walks to pebble beaches. The west coast is spectacular – the road runs along dizzying cliffs above dramatic beaches. The landscape of the rather remote Lixouri peninsula has been strangely moulded by the earthquakes; it has some good, quieter, red-sand beaches.

The stunning view down to the sea from a coastal road between Skala and Poros

Zakynthos

The most southern of the Ionian chain, Zakynthos, also called Zante, shares the history of invasion, freedom from Ottoman rule, and devastation by earthquakes. Much of the island is still green and unspoilt. The north and west is barren and mountainous, the centre very fertile, with farms, vineyards and lovely old villages set in beautiful countryside where life is more or less untouched by tourism.

Zakynthos Town was rebuilt on the old plan, an attempt to recreate the atmosphere of the pre-earthquake 'Flower of the Levant'. It is a handsome place, with arcaded streets, grand public buildings, museums and a busy working port. Round-the-island boat trips to sea caves and beaches start here. The ruined Venetian Kastro high above the town makes a pleasant walk.

On the east coast, the resorts close to Zakynthos Town are overcrowded. However, the Vassilikos Peninsula to the south still has small resorts and beaches, and travelling northwards the parade of fishing villages and beach resorts become less developed. The north coast is rocky and inaccessible, with dizzying views. There are one or two spots along the wild and remote west coast where the sea can be reached.

Major package tourism has taken over the south. Kalamaki and Laganas offer round-the-clock entertainment, English pubs and water sports on a fine but over-subscribed beach, which was once a major breeding ground of the loggerhead turtle. Marine biologists are in dispute with tourist bosses over the protection of this endangered creature.

Smugglers Cove – the most famous beach on Zakynthos

POPULATION:
38,600 (2001)
WHEN TO GO:
May, June, September and October
HOW TO GET THERE:
Direct charter and domestic flights. Ferry from the mainland (Kylini); inter-island ferries.
HIGHLIGHTS:
Yerakas – this splendid beach at the tip of the Vassilikos Peninsula is a protected breeding ground for the loggerhead turtle. There is a Turtle Information Centre here.
Boat trips – shorter, less crowded trips to the Blue Cave and Shipwreck Beach run from Ayios Nikolaos in the north-east.
The Byzantine Museum, Zakynthos Town, with artwork and treasures from pre-earthquake buildings.
YOU SHOULD KNOW:
The Virgin of the church in Keri, a village in the south-west, is said to have saved the island from marauding pirates by wrapping it in sea mist.

Kekova

In one of the most attractive spots on Turkey's Turquoise Coast is the lovely Mediterranean island of Kekova. At just 4.5 sq km (1.7 sq mi), the island is uninhabited but lies in a bay close to the mainland. On the north shore of the island are the ruins of ancient Apollonia, dating back to the 5th century BC. The reason these unassuming ruins attract so many visitors is that they lie partially submerged beneath the waves, an amazing sunken city in the clear blue waters of the bay.

The city was submerged by a series of earthquakes over the centuries. Today, marble columns and aches rise into the water, and stone steps lead down into the ocean floor. You can explore the sunken ruins by kayak, or take a ferry trip to view them as swimming is no longer allowed here. Further west on the shore of the Bay of Tersane, where the remains of a frescoed Byzantine church lie, swimming is permitted and this is an evocative and lovely place for a picnic.

Apollonia was part of Lycia, an important kingdom in this region. The Lycian capital was at Xanthos, west of Kekova, where King Sarpedon was born before he went on to fight in the Trojan Wars. The Lycians traded with the Ancient Greeks and as trade increased, so did piracy. For this reason, many harbours and ports, including Kekova, were fortified. As you glide over the calm waters, you can see the remains of buildings and walls beneath your boat, a rather unsettling experience!

On the mainland close to Kekova are some more beautiful ruins, those of ancient Simena, dating back to the 4th century BC. Today the fishing village of Kale stands on the site. A medieval castle sits atop the little hill and from here you get a good view of the ruins, once a thriving city which did not begin to decline until the 9th century AD, when an earthquake damaged the city. The ruined fortress, Simena Castle, features the pointed arches of the Lycian

The ancient city of Lycia

POPULATION:
Uninhabited
WHEN TO GO:
April to November.
HOW TO GET THERE:
By boat from Kas or Kalkan.
HIGHLIGHTS:
Kayaking above the ruins of ancient Apollonia.
The village of Kale with its lovely fish restaurants.
The Lycian tombs in the water below ancient Simena, an enchanting place for a barbecue on the beach and a swim in the turquoise bay.
The amphitheatre at Simena, the smallest in Lycia with seats for just 400 in the audience.
YOU SHOULD KNOW:
Due to visitors taking home souvenirs from the ruins, it is no longer permitted to swim among the ruins of Apollonia. However, there are other ruins close by which can be explored from the water.

period and the walls show signs of having been repaired during the Byzantine era. Look out for the unusual ogival-shaped Lycian tombs which rise from the shallow bay below. Just inside the castle is the smallest amphitheatre in all Lycia, with just seven rows of seats, an orchestra pit and a changing room for the performers.

Outside the castle are the ruins of the Temple of Poseidon, from where you get a wonderful view across the sea of the whole area and its bays, islands and inlets. Farther down towards the sea there are the remains of houses, tombs and a bath house, all of which are well worth exploring.

Gökçeada

The westernmost point of Turkey and its largest island, Gökçeada lies at the entrance to the Bay of Saros in the northern Aegean, 53 km (33 mi) from Çannakale on the Dardanelles Strait. It is one of the least frequented islands of the Aegean despite being renowned for its outstanding natural beauty – nearly 290 sq km (113 sq mi) of volcanic landscape clothed in pine, olives and vineyards, steep hilly sheep pastures dotted with whitewashed houses, a ragged coastline of strange rock formations and sandy beaches surrounded by the intense blue waters of the Aegean.

The reason for Gökçeada's relative lack of tourism is historical. In classical times the island was a colony of Athens known as Imbros, established around 450 BC and lasting for the next six centuries. After the collapse of Athens as a major power, the island was at the mercy of every Mediterranean empire builder and constantly threatened by pirates. At various times it has been Persian, Roman, Byzantine, Venetian, Ottoman and Greek. Throughout the 20th century, tensions between Greece and Turkey eventually led to most of the ethnic Greeks leaving the island and, until recently, kept it out of bounds for tourists.

Gökçeada's inhabitants survive much as they always have done – from fishing, olive oil, wine and honey production and sheep rearing. As well as the main town of Çinarli (Panayia), there are nine villages, mostly up steep hills reached with some difficulty along the notoriously treacherous island roads. The island has some superb beaches, although you need some determination to access the best ones along the south coast.

There is no doubt that the holiday industry will soon ensure that Gökçeada becomes as well known as the rest of the Aegean. Now is the time to visit this undiscovered, distinctive island before the inevitable happens and it turns into a tourist trap.

POPULATION:
8,875 (2000)
WHEN TO GO:
April to October
HOW TO GET THERE:
Fly or drive to Çannakale and take the ferry, which sails past the dramatic coastline of the Gallipoli National Park. You can take a shorter route from Kabatepe on the Gallipoli Peninsula, but you will miss the spectacular views.
HIGHLIGHTS:
Aydincik (Kefalos) Beach – a brilliant spot for windsurfing with a nearby sulphur salt lake spa to wallow in.
Kaleköy Kastro – old castle ruins on a hill with spectacular views.
Zeytinli and Tepeköy – atmospheric villages.
The beautiful valley near the village of Sahinkaya where there is a crater pool.
National Underwater Park – the coastline between Kaleköy and Kuzulimam, where among the marine life there are old wrecks, artefacts and ancient ruins.
The historic village of Derekoyu – a fascinating abandoned village, said to have once been the largest and wealthiest in the whole of Turkey.
YOU SHOULD KNOW:
Of all the islands in the world, Gökçeada has the fourth largest number of natural fresh water sources.

327

Avsa

POPULATION:
2,000 (estimate)
WHEN TO GO:
May to October
HOW TO GET THERE:
By ferry from Istanbul.
HIGHLIGHTS:
The Byzantine monastery.
Eating freshly caught fish of every
conceivable variety.
Walking up into the vineyards to
taste the wine.
Taking a boat trip to the
neighbouring islands of Ekinlik and
Marmara.
YOU SHOULD KNOW:
Turkey is a conservative country and
although the island's nightlife may
appear liberal, there are much
stricter boundaries than the average
westerner is used to. It is worth
remembering that excessively sexual
or drunken behaviour is likely to
shock and won't do wonders for
your reputation.

Only 40 years ago Avsa was a quiet backwater known only to a privileged few. Although its clean air, sparkling sea, golden sand, island wine and fresh fish has made it ever more popular as a Turkish holiday resort it is still relatively unknown among foreign tourists and remains off the beaten track.

The island lies in the Sea of Marmara, the small inland sea between the Black Sea and the Mediterranean. It joins the Black Sea at the Bosphorus, the strait along which the city of Istanbul is built, so it is no surprise that the lovely islands of Marmara should be holiday resorts for stressed Turkish city-dwellers desperate to escape the stifling summer heat of Istanbul.

Avsa is in one of the main wine-producing regions of Turkey. It is 21 sq km (8 sq mi) of gentle granite hills covered with olives and vineyards that in places run all the way down to the sandy beach. Oleander trees and flowers grow all around the coast and long bays of gloriously soft sand alternate with stone outcrops where the granite has been worn smooth by the sea to create extraordinary shapes. These rocky areas are wonderful for clambering among, or just finding a quiet spot to sit with a bottle of local wine gazing out across the sparkling sea.

The island's town, Avsa, is a typical Turkish seaside resort with holiday homes, restaurants, and scrawny cats hanging around the harbour hoping to snatch a morsel from the fishing boats as they unload their catch. In the summer months the island is a hive of activity and has a vibrant nightlife. In the evenings the air is filled with music and laughter from the bars and clubs as well as the scent of flowers and the smell of the sea.

Bozcaada

There are so many idyllic islands in the Aegean – more than 3,000 of them – that it can be hard to distinguish between them. But Bozcaada really is different – it is one of the only two islands in the region that is Turkish. In Greek mythology it was called Tenedos and because of its strategic position, just south of the Dardanelles Strait, it has been occupied and fought over since time immemorial. For centuries the population was ethnically Greek; today, although it is almost entirely Turkish, the island's distinctive culture bears many traces of its Greek inheritance.

Bozcaada is a roughly triangular shape of just under 38 sq km (15 sq mi) and has relatively flat terrain. From the highest point, Göztepe at 192 m (630 ft) there is a panoramic view across the whole island and on a clear day you can see as far as Levkos. About a third of the land is covered in vineyards, the remainder being scattered trees and scrubland containing an unusually diverse range of plants – 437 species in all. The sea is remarkably clear and seaweed-free, so Bozcaada's waters are superb for diving. There are plenty of pure sand beaches; Ayazma Bay is the longest and most accessible stretch, consequently the most crowded, but there are eleven other sizeable bays, as well as innumerable coves and inlets for anyone seeking solitude.

An impressive Venetian fortress that attests to Bozcaada's turbulent past guards the island's harbour. The stone and wood town architecture is a charming mixture of Turkish and Greek houses – stylistically quite different from each other. The food, too, is a fusion between both cultures, giving it a distinct edge over the usual fare of the Aegean Islands. Red poppy syrup, a local speciality, is an interesting alternative to the island wine.

POPULATION:
2,427 (2000)
WHEN TO GO:
May to September
HOW TO GET THERE:
There are four main ways to get to Yükyeri wharf at Geyikli to catch the ferry for the half-hour trip to Bozcaada:
Fly to Çanakkale from where there are frequent bus connections to take you to Geyikli, 56 km (35 mi) away.
Bus from Istanbul, an 8-hour journey to Geyikli.
By car from Istanbul a) drive either to Gelibolu or Eceabat and take the car ferry across the Dardanelles to Lapseki or Çanakkale then drive down the coast to Geyikli; or b) take the express car ferry from Istanbul to Bandirma and drive a further 3 hours to Geyikli.
HIGHLIGHTS:
Aleybey Mosque probably built in 1700.
Aya Paraskevi Ayazma – a monastery with a small chapel shaded by eight old plane trees where a traditional saint's day festival is held every July.
A tour of one of the island's four wineries.
The wind farm – wind turbines behind the old lighthouse in the west of the island are an impressive sight.
A boat tour of the island – enabling you to explore coves inaccessible from land.
YOU SHOULD KNOW:
The sea is substantially colder here than in other parts of the Aegean because of the cold water springs around Bozcaada. In the sweltering months of July and August it is a welcome, refreshing contrast to the beach.

Fishing boats line Tenedos harbour at dusk.

Büyükada

POPULATION:
6,000 (estimate); the population of the Princes' Islands is 17,738 (2000)
WHEN TO GO:
April to October. The Princes' Islands do get very crowded with Istanbullu holidaymakers at the peak of the season but it is still well worth making a day trip if you are in Istanbul in July or August to get some respite from the heat and see the magnificent architecture.
HOW TO GET THERE:
Regular ferry service from all Istanbul's main docks or high-speed sea bus from Kabatas docks.
HIGHLIGHTS:
Ayios Nikolaos Monastery – a romantically rundown old building. Splendid Palace Hotel – built in 1911 and visited by Edward VIII and Wallis Simpson.
Ayia Yorgi Church – dating back to the 6th century.
YOU SHOULD KNOW:
Leon Trotsky lived on Büyükada for four years after he was banished from the Soviet Union by Stalin in 1929. He wrote most of his *History of the Russian Revolution* during his stay here.

A short ferry ride from the centre of Istanbul transports you into another world – of pine trees, monasteries, and 19th century grandeur. Büyükada (Big Island) is, at just 5.4 sq km (2 sq mi), the largest of the Princes' Islands, an archipelago of nine islands in the Sea of Marmara, on Istanbul's doorstep.

As soon as you step off the ferry at the ornate Ottoman terminal building, you are greeted by the sound of horses' hooves, the sight of contented island dogs lazing on doorsteps in the sun, and the mouth-watering smells of freshly cooked fish and grilled meat wafting from the harbour restaurants. The town's cobbled streets are lined with magnificent 19th century wooden houses whose elaborate balconies and shutters are wreathed in honeysuckle, jasmine and mimosa. In the summer, the lively town is heaving with crowds but you can easily retreat into the hills and woods or to one of the innumerable sandy coves around the coast.

The Emperor Justinian II built a palace here in AD 569 and the islands were later used as a place of exile for unruly Byzantine princes (hence the name). For hundreds of years Büyükada was inhabited only by a few monks and nuns, farmers and fishermen. The 19th century development of a ferry service enabled wealthy city dwellers to travel here with relative ease and, attracted by the Princes' pastoral charm, they began to build summer houses on the islands. Today, in the summer months Istanbullus flock here to escape from the stifling heat and clamour of the city.

Mercifully, cars are banned here. You can go everywhere in a phaeton (horse and carriage), by bike, or on foot. The silence, fresh sea breeze, wonderful swimming, and heart stopping views are in blissful contrast to the stressed-out streets of Istanbul.

The Monastery of St George is nestled between Büyükada's highest hills.

Akdamar

Lake Van is a salt lake – a mysterious inland sea 1,670 m (5,480 ft) above sea level in the heart of the Anatolian Mountains. Nobody can explain the salinity of the water, nor the fresh-water spring on the island of Akdamar. On this tiny island, less than 1 sq km (0.25 sq mi) in area, there is an incredible monument – the Cathedral Church of the Holy Cross, an extraordinarily beautiful example of Armenian architecture.

The Church was built in the 10th century and was the seat of the Armenian Catholicos (prelate) for nearly 700 years, from 1116 until 1895. It is the only remaining building of the Palace of Aght'Amar, built for the Armenian king between 915 and 922 – a magnificent complex of buildings, complete with streets and gardens, entirely built out of a lovely pinkish-red tufa (volcanic rock) which must have been transported from miles away. The Church, which contains 34 rooms, is set in an almond grove. Its exterior walls are carved with exquisitely fine reliefs of biblical, harvesting and hunting scenes that are unique – nothing remotely comparable has been found anywhere else in the world.

The overwhelming beauty of the scene is awe-inspiring. Reddish stone contrasts with blue water against the backdrop of the snow capped Anatolian Mountains towering over the lake. Of all the islands in Lake Van, Akdamar becomes green earliest in the spring, and when the almond trees come into blossom the island is a truly sublime experience. There is a wonderful swimming spot where you can plunge off the rocks into the deep salty water of the lake or just gaze around you absorbing the serene beauty of your surroundings.

The Cathedral Church of the Holy Cross

POPULATION:
Maybe a museum keeper or two.
WHEN TO GO:
March to April, to catch the almond blossom in full bloom.
HOW TO GET THERE:
Fly/train/bus from Ankara to Van. From Van by road to Gevas 45 km (28 mi) to the southwest. Boats leave from Gevas wharf and take about 20 minutes to get to Akdamar.
HIGHLIGHTS:
Çarpanak – a nearby island with a 12th century church.
The medieval citadel at Van.
Muradiye Waterfalls.
Look out for Van cats – famous for having one blue and one yellow eye.
YOU SHOULD KNOW:
The church was extensively restored by the Turkish government and only re-opened for viewing in April 2007. It has caused some controversy between Turks and Armenians, between whom feeling historically runs extremely high. Many Armenians still regard the island as a holy site and they not only object to the name change of the island from Agh'tamar but to the secularisation of this important religious building.

Cyprus

POPULATION:
762,900 (2001)
WHEN TO GO:
April to June and September
to November
HOW TO GET THERE:
Direct flights to South Cyprus.
Flights to North Cyprus via Turkey.
Ferries from Turkey to North Cyprus.
HIGHLIGHTS:
Ancient Kourion, near Limassol –
performances take place in the
huge amphitheatre.
The frescoed churches in the
Troodos – a World Heritage Site.
The Tombs of the Kings in Pafos –
these unique tombs show
Egyptian influence.
Bellapais, North Cyprus – the lovely
mountain village, home to Lawrence
Durrell, with its impressive
Augustinian monastery.
Ancient Salamis, north of Famagusta
– the extensive site of a city first
mentioned in 709 BC.
The Karpas Peninsula, North Cyprus.
A nature reserve protects the
island's best beaches and the green
and loggerhead turtles that
nest here.
YOU SHOULD KNOW:
Cyprus's national cocktail the Brandy
Sour was invented in the 1930s for
young King Farouk of Egypt. He
asked for a drink that looked like
iced tea!

Cyprus, probably named for its copper, smelted since Neolithic times, is the legendary birthplace of Aphrodite. Two impressive mountain ranges surround a huge fertile plain and lovely beaches circle the coastline. Its climate has long attracted visitors – it is now renowned as a place for retirement – or partying.

Lying close to the Middle East and always strategically important, it was taken by many great powers including Greece, Rome and Egypt. The long reign of the French Lusignan dynasty brought prosperity and Roman Catholicism. In 1570 the Turks took the island. It became a UK Crown Colony after World War I. Independence came in 1960, but intercommunal strife increased and in 1974 an unsuccessful Greek coup prompted a Turkish invasion. The island was divided. It is now possible to cross the border, but violence and negotiation alternate and rules can change overnight.

However, north or south, the islanders are warmly welcoming and Cyprus has many attractions. The southeast with its raucous resorts also has archaeological sites and sunsets from Aphrodite's 'birthplace' at the Rock of Remios. Pafos, though surrounded by development, remains a charming town. To the northwest is the remote Akanas Peninsula, with further isolated regions along the coast. Inland, the magnificent Troodos region has forested mountains, lost villages, painted churches, unique wildlife and winegrowing.

In the North, small resorts cluster around the beautiful harbour town of Kyrenia. Famagusta is full of ruined Gothic churches inside

its golden stone walls; outside lies a haunted, wired-off modern town. The rocky coast and bristling Kyrenia range hold unspoilt beaches and villages, classical sites, monasteries and Crusader castles.

Lefkosia (Nicosia) is the world's only divided capital. Inside the massive Venetian fortifications, both sides – the cosmopolitan south and the north with its dusty lanes – are fascinating. Both have streets which end in a wall fluttering with defiant flags.

The Makheras Monastery
in the Troodos

AFRICA &
ARABIAN
GULF

Palm Jumeirah

POPULATION:
Dubai 1,241,000 (2006). Palm Jumeirah yet to be assessed (8,000 residential units are planned).

WHEN TO GO:
The weather is more manageable and cooler from November to April. In the Muslim month of Ramadan hotel prices may drop, but it's illegal to eat, drink or smoke in public between sunrise and sunset.

HOW TO GET THERE:
Flights to Dubai.

HIGHLIGHTS:
Wandering the island – the sheer scale and glamour of the development, and some of its celebrity-type residents (including David Beckham).
Al-Ahmadiya School – Dubai's oldest school and stunning courtyard house.
Dubai's skyscrapers and souks – the gold souk, perfume souk and spice souk.
The old Bastakiya Quarter.
The world's only seven-star hotel – Burj Al Arab in Dubai. Shaped like a sail and with its own helipad. Jumeirah Beach Park – walkways, barbeque pits, clean sands and a women-only day.

YOU SHOULD KNOW:
Camel racing is a major spectator sport in the United Arab Emirates, and Dubai.

Self-declared 'eighth wonder of the world', Palm Jumeirah is an audacious feat of human engineering. Fashioned on the date palm, with its roots on the Dubai coastline and its 17 fronds fanning out into blue waters, this is the first of the planned 'Palm' islands and, though it's the smallest of the three, it is already the world's largest man-made island.

Extravagant boutique hotels and villas are built and residents moving in, with the project aiming for completion in 2009. Measuring 5 x 5 km (3 x 3 mi), the crown is connected to the mainland by a 300 m (98 ft) bridge, and the very top of the palm is reached by a sub-sea tunnel. Ninety four million cubic metres of sand and seven million tons of rock have gone into the formation of this premier resort. Beaches, marinas, cafés and restaurants of every conceivable nature are planned.

Dubai is purported to be the fastest growing city in the world, and the shortage of beaches and hotels seems to have given rise to the three Palm Island resorts which will together increase Dubai's coastline by 520 km (323 mi). Created using land reclamation by the government-owned Al Nakheel Properties, this striking palm blueprint allows for far more beach, and residences, than a plain old circular island. In 2007, the Cunard Line sold the *Queen Elizabeth II* liner to Dubai World – to be permanently anchored at Palm Jumeirah as a hotel and tourist destination.

Once a peaceful town frequented by Bedouin fishermen and pearl divers, Dubai is now rich and racy, and somewhat surreal. Shiny skyscrapers overshadow the surviving and still buzzing souks, and shopping is the major pastime.

Here you are not escaping from people but maybe from reality, and in terms of sheer scale and daring there really is nowhere like it on earth.

*An aerial view of
Palm Jumeirah*

Socotra

In the Indian Ocean off the Horn of Africa lies a small archipelago of four islands and islets. Although closer to Africa, the islands are part of the Republic of Yemen. The archipelago consists of the main island of Socotra and three smaller islands known collectively as The Brothers – Abd al Kuri, Samhah and Darsa. The islands were separated from the mainland so long ago that much of their flora and fauna has evolved here, making the islands of great ecological importance. Due to their geographical isolation, the islanders have also had little outside influence, and arriving on Socotra is like stepping back in time.

The culture on Socotra is very different from the ways of the modern world. Until the airport was built in 1999, the only way to get here was by boat, and during the monsoon season the strong winds and high seas made the island inaccessible. Most Socotris still live without electricity, running water or a paved road. Until 1990 the island still had a barter economy, and even today most people in the mountainous areas still live in caves.

The main island is a little over 130 km (80 mi) long and around 35 km (21 mi) wide. Socotra is a place of contrasting landscapes, with the turquoise lagoon at Qalansiya and the white sand dunes at Ras Momi, the flower-filled alpine meadows of the Haghier Mountains and the desolate cave-riddled plateaux of the interior. Rising to over 1,500 m (4,921 ft), the Haghier Mountains loom over Hadibo, the island's capital, and dominate the skyline. The red granite peaks are peppered with silver lichens which grow thickly on the bare rocks above the tree line. Streams bubble down from the misty heights, teeming with lively fish and freshwater crabs. Limestone plateaux spread east and west, providing alkaline soils for the iconic Dragon's Blood Tree for which the islands are famous. The locals collect the blood-red resin, known as cinnabar, from the tree by making incisions in the bark. In the ancient world, it was used to enhance the colour of precious stones and glass, and as a pigment in paints, and had various medicinal qualities.

The long isolation of the Socotra archipelago and its fierce heat and drought have combined to create a unique endemic flora and fauna. There are no fewer than 300 plant species, 113 insect species, 24 reptile species and six bird species that can be found nowhere else in the world. Botanists rank the flora of Socotra among the ten most endangered island flora in the world, and steps are being taken by the government to protect this unique and spectacular habitat.

The blue lagoon of Qalansiya

POPULATION:
43,000 (2004)
WHEN TO GO:
October to February.
HOW TO GET THERE:
Fly from Sana'a or Al-Mukalla.
HIGHLIGHTS:
The enormous cave at Huq – the eastern end of the island has a vast system of caves and underground pools lying below the Momi plateau. Huq cave, particularly, has wonderful stalactites and stalagmites.
The souq in Hadibo – look out for the local pottery, made by women on the islands, particularly *gisfa*, large ornamental water pots.
Birdwatching – the island group has a rich bird fauna, including endemic species such as the Socotra Starling, the Socotra Sunbird, the Socotra Sparrow and the Socotra Golden-winged Grosbeak.
The white sandy beaches – the best are probably at Ras Ersel and Ras Momi.
YOU SHOULD KNOW:
The island's tourist infrastructure is a pioneering example of ecotourism and In order to protect the island's unique heritage, visitor numbers are limited.

337

Elephantine Island

POPULATION:
2,000 (2006 estimate)
WHEN TO GO:
Very hot between June and August
(daytime temperatures around 40ºC
(104ºF). So December to February is
great if you hate the heat, but March
to May and September to November
gives warm days and fewer crowds.
HOW TO GET THERE:
Motor launch or felucca from Aswan:
plane, train or boat from Cairo or
further afield.
HIGHLIGHTS:
The Aswan Museum at the southern
end of the island.
The botanical garden on nearby
Kitchener Island.
The Aswan High Dam and
Lake Nasser.
Afternoon tea at the Old Cataract
Hotel, Aswan.
A trip on a felucca on the Nile
at sunset.
A short flight to Abu Simbel, the
stunning temple of Ramses II.
YOU SHOULD KNOW:
A rare calendar, known as the
Elephantine Calendar, dating to the
reign of Thutmose III, was found here
in fragments. The island is equally
famous because the Well of
Eratosthenes is located here, and
was where Eratosthenes made the
first measurement of the
circumference of the earth in around
240 BC.

*A boat cruises along the Nile
alongside Elephantine Island.*

Known to the Ancient Egyptians as Abu or Yabu – meaning elephant – Elephantine Island is a truly ancient site resting as it does at the First Cataract of the Nile, and creating a natural boundary between Egypt and Nubia. Being the largest island at Aswan, it was easily defensible and at one time was thought to be a major ivory trading centre – possibly giving rise to its name. But rumour has it the name may also arise from the elephant-shaped granite boulders lying around its shores.

It is said that Khnum, the ram-headed god of the cataracts, dwelled in caves beneath the island and controlled the waters of the Nile. Nowadays, the southern tip of the island holds the ruins of the Temple of Khnum, which was rebuilt in the 30th dynasty. Up until 1822, there were also temples to Thutmose III and Amenhotep III here, but the Ottoman government in their 'wisdom' destroyed them.

Elephantine is an exquisite island, steeped in ancient history and blessed with significant artefacts. Transported instantly back in time, you wander under banana trees and date palms through colourful Nubian villages with narrow, dusty alleyways and mud houses painted or carved with crocodiles and fish.

On the edge of the island is one of the oldest Nilometers in Egypt – a stone 'yardstick' used to measure the height of the River Nile. It was last reconstructed in Roman times and was still in use as late as the 19th century. Its 90 steps, leading down to the river, are marked with Hindu-Arabic, Roman and hieroglyphic numerals, and inscriptions carved deep into the rock during the 17th century can be seen at the water's edge.

Elephantine Island is a green, flower-festooned oasis of calm – lapped by the turquoise waters of the Nile and clinging quietly to its exotic past.

Jerba Island

Located in the Gulf of Gabès off the coast of
Tunisia, the island of Jerba is a simple place
with palm-fringed beaches, olive groves, date
plantations and white-washed buildings, but it
is said to have an enchanting history. Jerbans
claim that the Land of the Lotus Eaters Homer
described in *The Odyssey* is theirs. The local
legend goes that after Odysseus' ship had been
blown off course around Greece, he and his
men found themselves in a strange land in the
south of the Mediterranean where the
islanders ate the honeyed fruit of the lotus
flower. Odysseus and his crew stayed here
enjoying the soothingly narcotic fruits as they
recovered from battle.

Today the beautiful island is noted as a
centre for the Islamic sect al-Ibadhiyah, and
also for its Jewish population which has lived
on the island since 586 BC, just after the
destruction of King Solomon's temple in
Jerusalem. Populations have declined in recent
years due to emigration to Israel and France, but the present
synagogue, El Ghriba, is a place of pilgrimage for Jewish people
worldwide and tourists of all religions. This is thought to be the oldest
synagogue in Africa and one of the oldest in the world, built by Jewish
priests who came to Jerba after the destruction of the temple in
Jerusalem. The present building dates from the 19th century, and
inside is a rich mix of blue tiles and coloured glass windows.

One of the nicest ways to explore Jerba is by bicycle. The island is
characterized by pretty, but busy, beaches lined with palms, and a
gentle rural interior. Here farmers grow olives and dates in the brilliant
sunshine. The architecture is clean and simple, with white-washed
fortified mosques which are unusual in Tunisia. Fishing is a major
industry here but it is still done by traditional methods. See the
terracotta pots stacked on the dockside at Houmt Souk which are used
to catch octopus, a method perfected by the Phoenicians 3,000
years ago.

If you get the chance, stay in one of the *funduqs* in Houmt Souk.
Usually set around a leafy courtyard with a trickling fountain and
colourful tiles, these evocative buildings have been receiving guests for
hundreds of years. The accommodation is sometimes basic, but the
atmosphere is fantastic. The souk on Jerba is a great place to buy
souvenirs including rugs, tiles, lamps, leatherwork, hands of Fatima,
sculptures made of crystallized desert gypsum and carved pipes. Just
be sure to haggle.

*Traditional rugs and pottery for
sale at Midoun*

POPULATION:
116,300 (2004)
WHEN TO GO:
April to June.
HOW TO GET THERE:
Mellita International Airport has daily
services from Tunis and
western Europe.
HIGHLIGHTS:
Boukha – the locally brewed fermented
drink made from figs or dates is said to
mimic the fabled response to imbibing
lotus juice.
El Ghriba synagogue – in the village of
Er Riadh, this is said to be the oldest
synagogue in Africa and has
biblical significance.
Er Riadh – a charming village steeped
in history, with its winding cobbled
streets and courtyards full of
bougainvillea and cacti.
Guellala – this village is renowned for
its pottery. Many white-washed shops
line the streets selling local,
handmade wares.
YOU SHOULD KNOW:
Book accommodation well in advance
in the summer months as the island
can be very busy.

São Tomé and Principe

POPULATION:
137,500 (2005)
WHEN TO GO:
Avoid the rainy season from October to May. The driest and coolest months are from June to September. The rest of the year is hot and muggy.
HOW TO GET THERE:
Flights from Lisbon.
HIGHLIGHTS:
Manta rays and sea turtles.
A picnic at Boca do Inferno – a blowhole south of the capital.
Ascent of ancient Pico São Tomé (2 days with overnight stop).
The rare birdlife.
The family-run chocolate factory on Principe.
YOU SHOULD KNOW:
Divers are in their element here – it is sometimes possible to become a member of the 'Equator Diving Club'.

Part of an extinct volcanic mountain range, São Tome was named after Saint Thomas by Portuguese explorers, who discovered the island on his feast day. Together with neighbouring Principe, it forms an island nation in the Gulf of Guinea, 250 km (155 mi) off the coast of Gabon that is the smallest Portuguese-speaking country in the world.

For centuries both São Tomé and Principe were important centres for the organized slave trade. Fronted by the Portuguese colonialists, in the 1500s the sugar cane trade here once led the world, and later large-scale coffee and cocoa plantations emerged and engulfed the island. Then in 1975 a national freedom movement led to the collapse of the Portuguese empire and finally brought independence to the islands. With this came the decline of plantations and the mass exodus of Europeans.

On this seriously undiscovered island just above the equator, you can sip some of the best coffee in the world – and, caffeine-charged – sway to the rhythms of *ússua* and *socopé*. Culturally, the people of São Tomé are African but they have been hugely influenced by the Portuguese rulers of their land.

The rich diving in these crystalline waters is yet to be fully appreciated and inland, deep in tropical forests, are some of the rarest birds in Africa. After years of unrest only now is this tiny island state recovering and beginning to feel stable. For the dedicated traveller it's an untapped, untouched haven – life here is sweet and waiting to be shared.

The monument that marks the Equator passing through the Ilhéu das Rolhos at the southern tip of São Tomé and Principe.

Bioko

Lying in the Gulf of Guinea, Bioko is an acutely mountainous, volcanic island still inhabited by the indigenous Bubi people, who speak a Bantu language brought over from mainland Africa. Swathed in tropical rainforest, this boot-shaped island is 70 km (43 mi) long and 32 km (20 mi) off the coast of Cameroon. Bioko has more species of rare monkeys than any other place in Africa; of the seven monkey species living on the island, four are among the continent's most-endangered. This is the place for the adventurous at heart, happy to head well off the beaten track and into deep mud.

Tropical rainforest covers the island of Bioko.

The Bubi clans still account for most of the human population, but given Bioko's colourful past this is now mixed with Spaniards, Fernandinos and immigrants from Rio Muni, Nigeria and Cameroon. First named 'Formosa Flora' – Beautiful Flower – by the Portuguese navigator Fernão do Pó in 1472, it then fell into the hands of the Dutch India Company who quickly established trade bases on the island in the 1600s without Portuguese consent – centralizing the trade of slaves in the Gulf of Guinea.

In colonial times it was known as Fernando Pó, and under the Africanization policy of dictator Masie Nguema Biyogo it was renamed Masie Ngueme Biyogo Island. When he was overthrown in 1979 it was renamed Bioko.

Rare primates once thrived in the deep rainforests – the Bioko drill, black and red colobus monkeys – but the luxury bushmeat market in the capital city of Malabo is taking a dangerously heavy toll. Malabo sits at the northern end of the island on the rim of a sunken volcano. Despite being the capital of Equatorial Guinea, this is a pretty poorly developed place with limited paved roads. There are few tourist attractions, but on the densely forested slopes a new world awaits.

POPULATION:
130,000 (2007)
WHEN TO GO:
Average temperatures of 25ºC (77ºF) and annual rainfall of 2,900 mm (75 in) make this an onerous climate. To avoid the rainy season go between November and April.
HOW TO GET THERE:
Flights to Malabo. Ferries to Malabo from Douala and Bata.
HIGHLIGHTS:
Trekking through the rainforest, searching for primates.
Hiring a boat out of Bata (on the mainland) to spot migrating whales.
The neighbouring paradise island of Corisco.
Malabo Cathedral.
The Moka Valley with its crater lake, between Malabo and Riaba.
YOU SHOULD KNOW:
Travel on any internal carriers should be considered carefully as air traffic control in Equatorial Guinea is marginal at best.

341

Cape Verde Islands

POPULATION:
420,979 (2006)
WHEN TO GO:
October and November when the land is green after the rains, and before the winds pick up in December.
HOW TO GET THERE:
International flights to Sal and Santiago.
Sporadic ferry services from Dakar and Las Palmas.
HIGHLIGHTS:
Mindelo Carnaval on São Vicente in February – with Rio-style floats and costumes.
Taking in the lively port city of Mindelo on São Vicente.
The lovely town of Vila Nova Sintra on Brava.
Vila de Ribeira Grande on Santo Antao – the first European town in the tropics.
Breakfast on *cachupa* – a delicious bean dish.
Island hopping by ferry – discovering the islands' delights for yourself.
YOU SHOULD KNOW:
The easiest place to get a visa is in Lisbon, or by going through a specialist travel company. In West Africa, the only consulate is in Dakar, Senegal – once you have found it, getting a visa should be easy.

The beach and village of Tarrafal on Santiago Island

Tipping off the African map, the Cape Verde islands would appear to sit more happily with the Azores, or even the Canary Islands. Composed of nine main islands in two groups – the Windwards and the Leewards – six are volcanic and shapely, while three are sandy and flat. This is no tropical paradise, yet despite the hassle of getting here the islands are well worth the trek.

The Portuguese arrived here in 1460 and made the islands part of the Portuguese empire. Cape Verde became an important watering station for passing ships, then a sugar cane plantation site, and later a major hub of the transatlantic slave trade. In 1975, Cape Verde gained independence from Portugal.

With jumbled African and Portuguese roots, Cape Verdeans certainly know how to make music and dance – samba and salsa sprinkled with African tribal sounds. The soft *morna* lament gives way to the sensual, upbeat *coladeira* and *batuque* dance, and love songs unfurl in Cape Verdean Creole. The official language may be Portuguese, but Creole is favoured colloquially.

The first port of call is often Praia on Santiago Island – Cape Verde's capital. The beaches are fine and white and the mountains impressive, but more importantly it forms the perfect springboard for island hopping. Brava is the smallest inhabited island, the hardest to reach but also the most beautiful. On brooding Fogo there is fine walking, and hikes up into the old volcano crater. There is a good deal of rivalry and many cultural differences between islands – right down to the way the women tie their headscarves.

This small nation lacks resources and has suffered severe droughts. Over the centuries, disastrous famines have continually rocked the lives of the islanders, yet their spirit remains alive and contagious.

Saint-Louis

In the north-west of Senegal, near the mouth of the Senegal River, lies the town of Saint-Louis, capital of French Senegal from 1673 until independence in 1960. The centre of the old colonial city lies on a narrow island in the river, measuring just 2 km (1.2 mi) long by about 400 m (1,312 ft) wide, although the modern city now sprawls on the mainland either side.

The first permanent French settlement in Senegal, Saint-Louis was founded in 1659 by French traders on an uninhabited island. Named after the French king Louis XIV, the town commanded trade along the Senegal River, exporting slaves, animal hides, beeswax and gum arabic. Between 1659 and 1779, the city was administered by nine different chartered companies. A Métis (Franco-African Creole) community soon developed, characterized by the famous *signares*. These bourgeois women entrepreneurs dominated the economic, social, cultural and political life of the city, creating an elegant urban culture with time for refined entertainments. They controlled most of the river trade and financed the principal Catholic institutions.

Louis Faidherbe became the Governor of French Senegal in 1854, and spent a great deal of money modernizing the town, including bridge building, setting up a drinking water supply, and providing an overland telegraph line to Dakar. The fortunes of the town began to dwindle as Dakar became an ever more important city. Saint-Louis' port proved difficult for steam ships to access, and a railway between Saint-Louis and Dakar, opened in 1855, took most of its up-country trade.

Today Saint-Louis is a sleepy backwater which retains its lovely colonial architecture. In 2000 it was added to the World Heritage List, and many of its beautiful buildings are being renovated. Among the sites and monuments to see on the island are the Governor's Palace, a fortress built in the 18th century across from Place Faidherbe, the Gouvernance which comprises the town's administrative offices and Parc Faidherbe in the centre of town, named for the French governor. The museum at the southern end of the island tells the story of Senegal's history and peoples, with displays of traditional clothes and musical instruments, and there are various mosques and catholic churches to visit.

The heritage of the *signares* lives on in Saint-Louis today, with the festivals for which the town is famous. *Fanals*, a night-time procession of giant paper lanterns, takes place at Christmas, usually coinciding with the Saint-Louis Jazz Festival, the most important jazz festival in Africa. The annual pirogue race, organized by teams of fishermen from Guet-Ndar, takes place on the river and makes a vibrant spectacle.

A fisherman passes by Saint-Louis at dawn.

POPULATION:
176,000 (2005)
WHEN TO GO:
November to May
HOW TO GET THERE:
Fly to Dakar-Bango airport.
HIGHLIGHTS:
Pont Faidherbe – designed by Gustav Eiffel and originally built to cross the Danube, the bridge was brought to St-Louis in 1897. It is 507 m (1,663 ft) long and offers wonderful views of the town.
The wonderful colonial architecture – stroll around the island and appreciate the lovely buildings, many now with a faded elegance.
National Park of the Langue de Barbarie – in the estuary of the Senegal River, the park is home to thousands of water birds, including cormorants, brushes, pink flamingos, pelicans, herons and ducks.
Fauna Reserve of Guembeul – around 12 km (7.5 mi) south of the city, the reserve shelters birds and endangered species including the Dama gazelle, the Patas monkey and the African spurred tortoise.
YOU SHOULD KNOW:
The town is known as Ndar in the local Wolof language.

343

The island lies in the River Gambia.

James Island

POPULATION:
Uninhabited
WHEN TO GO:
Best time to visit is between November and February when it's dry and relatively cool. During the wet season (June to October) it's less crowded and cheaper but roads may be inaccessible and malaria is more widespread.
Migratory birds visit between October and April – peak tourist season.
HOW TO GET THERE:
Pirogue (dugout wooden canoe) from the shore.
HIGHLIGHTS:
The history of the island and the River Gambia, and their part in the slave trade.
River fishing.
Bird watching.
Gambia's unspoilt beaches.
Abuko Nature Reserve and Bijilo Forest Park.
Fort Bullen in Barra, at the mouth of the river.
YOU SHOULD KNOW:
Around November to February dry, dusty 'harmattan' winds do blow off the Sahara.

Gambia is a mere sliver of a country with a generous heart, and James Island is a constant reminder of its more turbulent past. This minute island bears witness to the dark days of the slave trade, and sitting as it does in the middle of the River Gambia, about 2 km (1.2 mi) south of Jufureh and Albreda, it was once at the centre of struggles between Africa and Europe. As the river formed the first trade route into the African interior, it also became an early corridor for the slave trade.

On the island are the remains of Fort James – a Dutch nobleman, Jacob Duke of Courland, built the fort in about 1651. The English captured it in 1661 and the island became known as Fort James or James Island, after James, Duke of York. The fort was used as a trading base, first for gold and ivory then for slaves such as Kunta Kinte, who was portrayed in the film *Roots*. The English and French fought over the fort for more than a century.

The fort remained a slave collection point right up until slaving was abolished. Over time it was completely destroyed, then rebuilt at least three times. Now only ruins remain. The island was so small that it had to be 'extended' to accommodate other buildings, which was achieved by creating embankments supported by stakes. Even these are being slowly eroded – and the river is encroaching on the ruins. Now only groves of hefty baobab trees stand to attention beside the old walls.

James Island is a stop-off for enthusiasts. Continuing up-river by boat you are drawn into mangrove creeks and mud-hut villages. The Gambia is a vivid, laidback country and James Island is a small yet stark reminder of another life and times.

Isle of Gorée

The Isle of Gorée lies just 4 km (2.5 mi) from Dakar on the Senegalese coast in the middle of the natural harbour formed by the Cap Vert Peninsula. The protection of the bay explains why the island has been ruled over the years by the Portuguese, Dutch, English and French, each of whom wanted to profit from the safe anchorage there and use the island as a stopover point for ships sailing the trade route between the Gold Coast of Ghana and the West Indies.

At first sight, the island is a peaceful, beautiful place with its imposing forts and pretty pink houses, in harmony with the blue of the sea and the green of the lush gardens. Yet this tranquillity masks a darker past as many of these lovely buildings played an important role in the slave trade. Between the 15th and 19th centuries, Gorée served as the largest centre of the slave trade on the African coast. An estimated 40 million Africans were held for weeks in the houses' dark and dank basements, waiting for ships to take them to the Americas. There were even torture chambers for the slaves who rebelled.

By the end of the 18th century, Gorée was a wealthy place where tradesmen, soldiers and officials lived in sumptuous luxury amid the beautiful scenery. Yet it was also a gateway to hell for thousands of African slaves. Among the most poignant sights on the island is the Slave House, or Maison des Esclaves, built by the Dutch in 1776. It has been preserved in its original state and is now a UNESCO World Heritage Site. The 'door of no return' is an emotional shrine and continues to serve as a reminder of human exploitation. Some believe Gorée was not the site of transportation of such immense numbers of slaves, but no one can disagree with the awe and contemplation that the imposing, silent walls of the Slave House inspire.

Also worth visiting on the island are the Church of Saint Charles on the Place de l'Eglise, with its French provincial architecture, the picturesque ruins of Fort Nassau, the Castle of Saint Michel, which was originally built on the steep basalt hill by the Dutch in the 17th century, and the Historical Museum in the old Fort d'Estrées.

POPULATION:
1,056 (2005)
WHEN TO GO:
March to June, or September to November
HOW TO GET THERE:
By ferry from Dakar.
HIGHLIGHTS:
Visit the Maison des Esclaves, or Slave House, with its 'door of no return'.
The Botanical Gardens on rue du Port – see the famous baobab trees which are prevalent here. The scientific name of the baobab (*Adansonia*) comes from French botanist Michel Adanson, who visited Gorée in the mid-1700s. The gardens are dedicated to Adanson.
The small swimming beach near the ferry slip, perfect for a quick dip.
YOU SHOULD KNOW:
The name Gorée comes from the Dutch *Goeree* meaning island or possibly *Goode Reede* meaning 'good harbour' for its sheltered bay.

Colourful pirogues – dugout canoes – on the beach

Dahlak Kebir

POPULATION:
1,500-2,000 (2007)
WHEN TO GO:
Best between October and March
HOW TO GET THERE:
Ferries from Massawa, Eritrea – also linking with other islands.
HIGHLIGHTS:
Snorkelling and diving.
The pre-historic Islamic ruins at Adel.
The Afar fishing villages.
On the mainland – travelling on the steam train from Asmara down to Nefasit.
YOU SHOULD KNOW:
On the island there are 365 cisterns carved from coral limestone, used to collect rainwater – one for each day of the year to accommodate the arid climate, and providing the inhabitants of Dahlak Kebir with a reliable source of drinking water.

Clustered in the Red Sea, off the Eritrean coast, only four islands in the Dahlak Archipelago are inhabited – Dahlak Kebir being the largest. Charter a yacht out of Massawa and cruise the islands – snorkelling, diving and fishing along the way. The waters here have been nicknamed 'fish-soup', as a thousand or so species of fish dart around the reefs.

The Dahlak people still converse in Dahlak and follow a traditional way of life, fishing and herding goats and camels. Off the white sands, around submerged coral reefs, lurks an underwater wonderland of dolphins and dugongs, turtles and hermit crabs, shipwrecks and pumice stones spewed from submarine volcanoes.

The village of Dahlak Kebir lies on the west of the island and is renowned for its ancient cisterns and necropolis, dating from at least AD 912 and holding 800 tombs with coral gravestones that carry Kufic (ancient Arabic) inscriptions. In Roman times there were pearl fisheries here, and even today the occasional pearl is still found.

Under past Ethiopian rule, the archipelago was designated as a national park, and now you can't go there alone and without permission. During the war of independence a group of Eritrean freedom fighters carried out diving operations against the Ethiopian armed forces. Now these same freedom fighters make up the core of Eritrean diving tourism.

In a bizarre twist of fate, the war-torn years have made this a very different sort of diving spot from the rest of the Red Sea. During the fighting, fishing came to a halt and this led to a spectacular increase in the numbers of fish. Another advantage of this forced isolation is their relative lack of shyness. Here the fish swim right up to you.

Lake Tana Islands

Here lies the source of the famous Blue Nile. From Lake Tana, this mega-river sets out on its endless journey via Khartoum to the Mediterranean. Cradled in the Ethiopian highlands, this is the country's largest and most important lake. It holds many scattered islands and their actual numbers depends entirely on the level of the lake at any given time – the water has fallen by about 1.8 m (6 ft) in the last 400 years, and currently there seem to be 37 islands – of which 19 have, or have had, monasteries on them.

The joy of these mysterious and isolated islands is that they shelter well-hidden churches and monasteries of immense historical and cultural interest – decorated with ludicrously beautiful paintings and housing innumerable treasures. Hire a boat from the enchanting town of Bahir Dar to the south of the lake and chug out to the monasteries, where monks proudly display their treasures.

Remains of ancient Ethiopian emperors and treasures of the Ethiopian Church are stowed away here. On the island of Tana Qirqos is a rock on which the monks believe the Virgin Mary rested on her journey back from Egypt. The body of Emperor Yekuno Amlak is interred in the monastery of St Stephen on Daga, and others are also entombed here. The monasteries are believed to rest on even earlier religious sites and include Tana Qirqos, which is said to have housed the Ark of the Covenant before it was moved to Axum.

On a more practical level, Lake Tana is a vital source of water and hydroelectricity for Ethiopia, and supports a massive fishing industry. Attracted by both the water and wild food, local and migrating birds flock to the shoreline – as do many less brightly plumed birdwatchers. Lake Tana and its extraordinary islands are a lure for both their wildlife and rich, forgotten treasures.

POPULATION:
15,000 (2005 estimate)
WHEN TO GO:
Avoid the rainy season, especially in October and November
HOW TO GET THERE:
Boat trips from Bahir Dar. A ferry service links Bahir Dar with Gorgora, via Dek Island.
HIGHLIGHTS:
The monasteries and their treasures. Eating fish from the lake in one of Bahir Dar's restaurants.
Boat trips on the lake.
Tis Issat, the Blue Nile Falls – about 30 km (19 mi) downstream from Bahir Dar. Birdwatching around the lake.
YOU SHOULD KNOW:
Some of the island monasteries, particularly in the central part of the lake, do not allow women – it's worth checking before you make the trip.

The calm waters of Lake Tana

Lamu Island

Part of the Lamu Archipelago in the Indian Ocean close to the northern coast of Kenya, Lamu Island is surrounded by long, white sandy beaches framed by rolling dunes, as unspoiled today as they were when the island was first settled in the 14th century.

A port was founded on the island by Arab traders, who built the Pwani Mosque. The port prospered on the export of timber, ivory and amber, and soon became a major centre for the slave trade. After defeating nearby Pate Island in the 19th century, Lamu became a major local power. After the abolition of slavery in 1873, however, the island's economy suffered and has never made a come back. Today, tourism is an important source of income here.

Lamu town, the largest settlement on the island, was founded in the 14th century and contains many fine examples of Swahili architecture. The old town is designated a World Heritage Site as the oldest and best-preserved Swahili settlement in East Africa. With the simple lines of its architecture, built in coral and mangrove wood and featuring porches and rooftop patios, the town has managed to retain its distinctive character and charm. Donkeys wander through the narrow labyrinthine streets as there are no motorized vehicles on this idyllic island.

There are several museums in town, including the Lamu Museum which displays the island's ceremonial horn, and another museum dedicated to Swahili culture. Also worth a visit is Lamu Fort, built on the seafront by the Sultan of Pate in the early 17th century to protect members of his unpopular government. The Riyadha Mosque was built in 1900 and soon became one of the most prestigious centres for Islamic studies in Eastern Africa. The mosque is the centre for the annual Maulidi Festival which attracts pilgrims from all over Africa.

The most spectacular beaches on the island are those around Shela, a village about 3.2 km (2 mi) from Lamu town, with their clean white sand and traditional dhows. The area was unfortunately damaged in 2004 during the tsunami caused by the Indian Ocean earthquake, but it is still a lovely place to while away the day.

The Riyadha Mosque, built in 1900, is an important centre for Islamic studies.

POPULATION:
75,106 (1999)
WHEN TO GO:
December to January.
HOW TO GET THERE:
Fly from Mombasa or Nairobi, or take a ferry from Mokowe on the mainland or Manda Island.
HIGHLIGHTS:
Just chilling out – as there are no cars, this is a very peaceful place with just the sound of braying donkeys and palm trees rustling in the breeze. Leave the mobile phone and laptop at home and enjoy the tranquillity.
The Lamu Museum – housed in a building once occupied by Jack Haggard, Queen Victoria's consul. There are displays on Swahili culture, including a reconstructed Swahili house and relics from Takwa. Here the ceremonial horn of the island is on display.
The seafront restaurants in Lamu town – enjoy very fresh seafood at reasonable prices.
The donkey sanctuary in northern Lamu – set up to protect the 2,200 working donkeys on the island and ensure their well-being.
YOU SHOULD KNOW:
Lamu is strictly Islamic so be sensitive as to how you dress.

Mombasa

In south-eastern Kenya, on an island separated from the mainland by two rivers, Mombasa is the largest port in Eastern Africa. It is Kenya's second largest city and plays an important role in the country's economy, both as a major hub for imports and exports, and as a draw for tourism.

In 1498, Vasco da Gama visited the then-Arab city on his crusade to spread the Christian faith and to improve Portugal's trade links. Although he met with much hostility, he made an alliance with the King of Malindi. When the Portuguese forces arrived two years later, they appointed the King to be the Sultan of Mombasa and he used his influence to tame the local population and rule on behalf of the Portuguese. Mombasa became an important trading station for the Portuguese, and in the 1590s they built a great stronghold, Fort Jesus, to protect themselves against attack and act as a trading centre. The main goods which passed through the port were spices, coffee, cotton and slaves, who were imprisoned in the fort before they were sent away on ships.

The Portuguese ruled Mombasa for around 200 years until they were overthrown by the Omani Arabs, who themselves gave up the city to the British in 1888. In 1963, Mombasa became part of the newly independent Kenya.

Apart from the excellent beaches to the north and south of the city, Mombasa's greatest attraction is its lovely Old Town, with its narrow alleyways and Arabic architecture, featuring carved doorways and fretworked balconies. Bright colours and exotic scents abound, making this a real sensory experience. Don't miss the Old Harbour where traditional dhows come and go delivering fish and other goods from along the coast. The hot, steamy climate dictates the pace of life in Mombasa – slow and easy going. The overall atmosphere is friendly and vibrant, and the nightlife good – bars and restaurants are lively and stay open late.

POPULATION:
700,000 (2004)
WHEN TO GO:
June to March
HOW TO GET THERE:
Fly to Moi International Airport
HIGHLIGHTS:
A dhow cruise around the harbour – no trip is complete without a magical cruise on a traditional Mombasan boat.
Fort Jesus – this stronghold overlooking the sea, built by the Portuguese in the 1590s, now houses a museum displaying artefacts from the time the fort was built. It was here that slaves were imprisoned before being shipped abroad and you can visit the torture chambers and holding rooms.
The beaches to the north and south of the city are lovely, with white sand and coral reefs, and make a great day out.
The famous elephant tusks on Moi Avenue – the arches made out of intersecting tusks form a letter 'M' for Mombasa. They were built to commemorate the visit of Queen Elizabeth II in 1952.
Wandering around the labyrinth of narrow lanes and quaint shops in the Old Town.
YOU SHOULD KNOW:
Mombasa Island is joined to the mainland to the north by the Nyali Bridge, to the south by the Likoni Ferry and to the west by the Makupa Causeway and the railway line.

The varied rooftops of the Old Town

Kiwayu

POPULATION:
800 (2004 estimate)
WHEN TO GO:
January and February are hot and dry
and the most popular. From June to
September the weather is still dry.
March to May are much quieter and
cheaper, but wetter.
HOW TO GET THERE:
Flights from Nairobi or Mombasa to
Kiwayu (via Lamu). From Lamu by
motor boat (2 hrs) or dhow (7 hrs).
HIGHLIGHTS:
Picnics at Turtle Bay.
Canoeing up mangrove channels.
Fishing for your supper.
Hiring a dhow and crew to explore
the islands.
On neighbouring Lamu Island – the
centuries-old Maulidl Festival.
YOU SHOULD KNOW:
Crews from local villages may look
slightly scruffier but are better sailors
than most, and they know these
somewhat tricky waters well.

Step barefoot from the boat and sink into the warm, soft sands of this pencil-thin paradise island in the Indian Ocean, just off the Kenyan coast. Just 48 km (30 mi) south of Kiwayu sits Lamu – that equally other-worldly yet thoroughly discovered island, packed with visitors and hotels. Fortunately, this 'honeypot' destination manages to steer the crowds away from its less known sister island and only the more intrepid travellers, including the odd mega-celebrity, are tempted to the secluded shores of Kiwayu.

Kiwayu may be remote and undiscovered but for those in the know it's relatively easy to reach. Hiring a dhow out of Lamu is the most pleasurable, slow way to arrive. You can spend days just kicking up the sand and patrolling the shores. On the east side of the island are tidal pools for snorkelling and dipping; and if you can drag yourself away from the beach there are game drives into the bush – alive with lions, giraffes, buffaloes and elephants.

The sea provides the main exercise of the day – snorkelling, diving off coral cliffs, water-skiing or just dipping a toe in the cooling, crystal waters. Offshore, manatees and dugongs float by and for keen fishermen it is apparently easy to land marlin, barracuda and swordfish.

Accommodation runs from plush safari lodges to cheaper guest-houses and camping areas. Wherever you stay, the simple pleasures remain the best. At the end of the day walk to Kiwayu's highest point and watch the crimson sun sinking over the sea.

Local fisherman carry their catch ashore.

Ssese Islands

A dusty road on Bugala Island

In the northwest corner of Lake Victoria, on the Ugandan side, are the 84 Ssese Islands. Just over half of these islands are inhabited and the largest of these, at 40 km (25 mi) long, is Bugala on which is located the islands' main town of Kalangala. Other islands to visit include Bubeke, Bukasa, Banda and Bufumira. The Bantu-speaking Bassese tribe inhabit the islands, and in ancient times this was one of the most important spiritual centres in the region.

Lake Victoria itself was once a huge swamp, but is now the largest lake in Africa, the world's third largest freshwater lake and the source of the White Nile. The huge Nile perch is one of the key catches in the lake, but its over-fishing is at last beginning to sound alarm bells.

These islands have empty, palm-fringed white beaches and virgin rainforest.

People tend to come to the Ssese Islands either to fish or to chill out, read books, relax and hang about the camps on the beach. Walking is one of the main activities, and for birding enthusiasts, the islands are home to a huge diversity of colourful birdlife – turacos and native paradise flycatchers are common. People do swim in the calm waters of the lake but be warned, there is a bilharzia risk.

POPULATION:
35,000 (2006)

WHEN TO GO:
Late December to late February – dry and hot. June through to September is a pleasant alternative.

HOW TO GET THERE:
Ferries from Bukakata on the mainland to Luku on Bugala Island, and from Kampala to Banda and Bukasa. Also there is now a large ferry from Entebbe and Kalangala. Fishing boats take slightly longer.

HIGHLIGHTS:
Camping in a patch of tropical rainforest.
Sun-seeking in the Bay of Lutobaka, on Bugala.
Sailing tours on Lake Victoria.
Island hopping by canoe.
Fishing for Nile perch and tilapia.

YOU SHOULD KNOW:
There are very few vehicles on Bugala Island, so do not expect garage facilities, although there is a fuel station in Kalangala where fishermen come to purchase petrol.

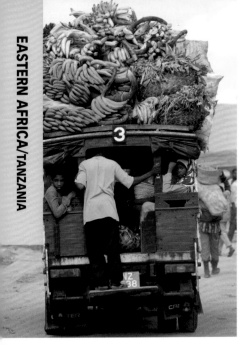

Zanzibar

Located 35 km (22 miles) from the coast of Tanzania in the Indian Ocean is Zanzibar, boasting white sand beaches lined with palm trees, native forests and an abundance of coral reefs perfect for snorkelling and diving. Today it offers a tropical paradise for holidaymakers, but this low-lying coral island has a chequered history of foreign occupation, intensive commerce and slavery.

The island was first inhabited by the Hadimu and Tumbatu tribes who came here from Africa. In the 10th century, Persian merchants arrived, brought to the island by monsoon winds as they sailed through the Indian Ocean. As they needed the monsoon winds to take them home again, they had to stay on the island for months at a time. They eventually decided to build permanent settlements on Zanzibar, and it soon became a centre for trade in its own right. This busy hub was influenced by the merchants who passed through, with Arabs, Indians, Chinese, Portuguese, Dutch and British leaving their mark here and blending together to create a unique culture.

Shirazi Persians and Omani Arabs settled on the island and ruled the Sultanate, which is why there is such a strong Arab influence evident today. Stone Town, the centre of the old city, has changed little in the last 200 years with its mosques, busy bazaars and grand Arab houses with their ornamental carved wooden doors studded with brass. The Indian influence can be found in the coloured glasswork and decorative balconies of many of the buildings, while the British left some staid colonial houses in the wealthier parts of town.

Today the economy is based on tourism, although fishing is still a major occupation. The island also exports many different types of spices, as well as cocoa and coconuts.

As well as the beaches and beautiful architecture, the island is also home to abundant wildlife, including red colobus and blue monkeys, which can be observed in Jozani Park, a large area of mature native forest which is now protected. There are also many other types of mammals here, including red-bellied squirrels and sun squirrels, and over 200 species of birds. Zanzibar is also a good place to see turtles, including the green turtle and the hawksbill turtle, which can be seen laying their eggs on the beaches near the lighthouse at Ras Ngunwi. Whale watching is also popular here, with humpback whales migrating through the channel in spring and then again in September. Long-snouted spinner dolphins and bottlenose dolphins are also favourites in these waters and it is possible to swim with them if you join an organized tour.

POPULATION:
1,070,000 (2004)
WHEN TO GO:
June to October.
HOW TO GET THERE:
Fly to Zanzibar International Airport or by ferry from Dar es Salaam.
HIGHLIGHTS:
The beaches – the island has many lovely beaches for sunbathing and swimming. The East Beaches are popular as the sand is brilliant white, and the warm waters are deep blue. The scuba diving is good here, with plentiful corals and rich marine life. Swim with the dolphins or arrange a ride in a local's dhow.
Stone Town – explore the lovely buildings, like the House of Wonders and the Arab Fort. Arrange a walking tour with a local guide who can explain some of the fascinating history.
Jozani Park – this beautiful forest has excellent nature trails, featuring some very exotic (and large) trees. See the Red Colobus Monkeys which are native to the island but now nearly extinct. They are curious and playful and will pose for a photograph.
Spice tours – these enjoyable organized tours explain how the different spices grow, allowing you to tour the beautiful plantations of cardamom, ginger, cloves, nutmeg and saffron, and sample some luscious tropical fruits.
YOU SHOULD KNOW:
Zanzibar was the last place to abolish the slave trade.

A van loaded with bananas leaves Stone Town market.

Mafia

Mafia is a sleepy, untouched retreat from the real world, and a slice of the old Swahili Coast where people go about their lives simply and traditionally. It may be part of the Spice Islands, alongside Zanzibar and Pemba, but is governed from the mainland. In reality it's a cluster of one main island – 48 km (30 mi) long – and numerous tiny ones, and is now the site of the largest marine park in the Indian Ocean, supporting fine unbleached corals.

For a small island such as this the sea rules. Every conceivable form of boat is crafted locally – from large ocean-going dhows to smaller *masha* or fishing boats and canoes. Crabs are scooped up from the shoreline and seaweed cultivated for sale. The main way of life is fishing, and the waters are rich for both fishermen and divers. Coconuts and cashews are key cash crops, but the price of coconuts on the world markets has fallen in recent years and fishing has become more commercially viable. Mafia is also famous for the striking raffia mats that the women of the island weave, often plaiting as they stroll along. This is an under-developed place, and the infrastructure is poor – there is only electricity around the main tourist areas and very few houses have running water. Most locals get around on foot or bicycle on bumpy tracks.

Mafia's rich history dates back to the 8th century when it was a regular stop-off for Persian boats, and trade routes stretched between the Far East and mainland Tanzania. Mafia has seen Portuguese, German and British occupation and this chequered history has resulted in a shifting, mixed population.

POPULATION:
40,801 (2002)
WHEN TO GO:
July to October and December to March
HOW TO GET THERE:
Small aircraft from Dar es Salaam or by road from Dar es Salaam to Kisiju and then boat to Mafia.
HIGHLIGHTS:
The ruins of 10th/11th century mosques at Kisimani Mafia near the capital Kilindoni.
Diving and snorkelling.
Exploring the deserted beaches.
The world-class deep-sea fishing.
A trip round the island on a traditional sailing dhow.
YOU SHOULD KNOW:
The name Mafia derives from the Kiswahili *mahali pa afya* meaning 'a healthy dwelling-place'.

The crystal-clear waters between Mafia Island and Chole Island

Pemba

POPULATION:
265,000 (2004)
WHEN TO GO:
Tropical climate with high humidity. December to March is the hottest – 25-29ºC (77-84ºF). Avoid the longer rains of mid-March to May/June and shorter rains (showers) in November to January. Diving is good throughout the year, except May to June.
HOW TO GET THERE:
Flights from Zanzibar Island or from Dar es Salaam or Tanga on the mainland. Dhows from Tanga – erratic service.
HIGHLIGHTS:
Mtambwe Mkuu – by dhow or canoe out of Wete harbour.
Ras Mkumbuu ruins – the site of a Swahili settlement dating back to the 11th century.
Ngezi Forest – home to Pemba flying foxes.
Ras Kiuyu Forest Reserve. Fishing for striped marlin and sailfish.
YOU SHOULD KNOW:
The Portuguese introduced bullfighting here in the 16th century – and they are still held in a few places such as Pujini between August and February.

The pungent aroma of cloves pervades the air. One of the legendary Spice Islands, Pemba has more cloves growing on it than its big sister Zanzibar, just 50 km (31 mi) to the south. On this verdant, hilly island there are over three million clove trees, and this valuable spice is the main export of the Zanzibar Archipelago. Pemba is also renowned for its voodoo and traditional healers, and many are still drawn here to seek cures and learn ancient skills.

In the past political unrest kept visitors away, but now more adventurous spirits are making their way here and avoiding the growing crowds on Zanzibar. Many come to dive – the reefs are unspoilt and for experienced divers the drop-offs are vertiginous. Overhangs, caverns and coral gardens litter the sheer walls and reefs; titan triggerfish, wrasse and Spanish dancers ride the currents. The diving on Pemba is some of the best in the world.

Tourism is still in its infancy and accommodation a little sparse, but resorts are springing up and life is changing. The main town of Chake-Chake sits high on a hill overlooking the bay and Misali Island, and about 10 km (6 mi) southeast stand the ruins of a fortified palace dating back to the 15th century. This was the seat of the infamous Mohammed bin Abdul Rahman who ruled Pemba before the arrival of the Portuguese. These are the only known early fortifications along the whole coast of Eastern Africa.

Chake-Chake is the administrative centre of Pemba.

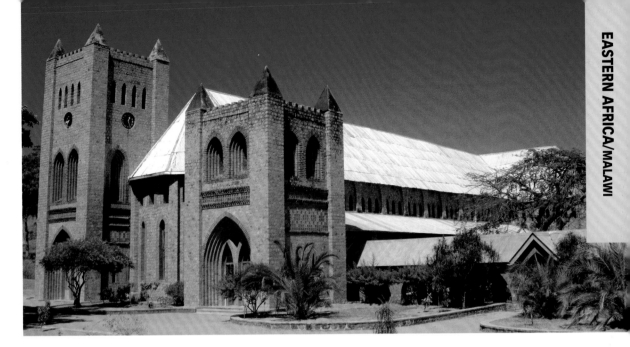

St Peter's Anglican Cathedral

Likoma

Off the eastern shores of Lake Malawi lies Likoma Island and its smaller neighbour Chizumulu, making up a tiny piece of Malawian territory in Mozambican waters. Likoma has remained largely untouched since Scottish missionaries discovered it in the 1880s and it became the headquarters of the University Mission to Central Africa – Livingstone's mission. This led to the islands being retained by Malawi when the lake was divided politically after World War II.

North Malawi as a whole has been long forgotten. Here the massive undulating Nyika plateau collides with the very edge of the Great Rift Valley. In perfect isolation, Likoma commands breathtaking views of the mountains and wilderness of Mozambique, just kilometres away.

Likoma's main town is overshadowed by the mighty Cathedral of St Peter, built in 1903 with elegant stained glass and carved soapstone. The rest of the island is simpler – mainly grassland scattered with mango and baobab trees.

Lake Malawi covers a fifth of the country's total area – about 590 km (365 mi) long and 85 km (52 mi) wide – hence its popular name of 'Calendar Island'. Usually gentle by nature, winds from the north or south can whip the lake up into a frenzy. Below the surface, the lake bubbles with fish and fishing villages along its shores reap the benefits.

The best and easiest way to get around Likoma is on foot. At the southern tip of the island, beyond the baobab plains, lies a crescent-shaped beach of the finest golden sand, framed by mango trees. This island is rich in history and also in silence.

POPULATION:
9,000 (2007)
WHEN TO GO:
Best to visit in the dry season from late April to November. May to August are cooler and dry, but September and October can get hot and humid.
HOW TO GET THERE:
Flights from Lilongwe or boats from the port of Nkhata Bay. Dhows cross between the two islands.
HIGHLIGHTS:
The Anglican cathedral in the main town.
Boat safaris to Mozambique and to other islands.
Snorkelling and scuba diving.
YOU SHOULD KNOW:
Electricity on the island is usually switched off after 10 pm to save generator fuel.

355

Bazaruto Archipelago

POPULATION:
3,500 (2007)
WHEN TO GO:
Year round, but avoid the cyclone
season in February. Little rainfall
between April and November.
HOW TO GET THERE:
Flights into Viklankulo (sometimes
via Maputo) with connections on to
the archipelago.
HIGHLIGHTS:
Marlin fishing from mid-September
to the end of December. Sailfish
fishing from April to August, and
fishing for smaller game fish such as
king mackerel, bonito and travelli all
year round.

Halfway up the Mozambique coast lies a chain of five islands making up the Bazaruto Archipelago. Formed from sand deposited by the Limpopo River, fine beaches and coral reefs come naturally; and having long been a national park, so does the wildlife. Bazaruto, Benguerra and Magaruque are the largest islands, with Santa Carolina and finally Bangué coming in on the small side.

Thanks to their protected status and relative isolation from the ravages of war, nature has been free to flourish here; and bizarre yet endearing dugongs or sea cows spend their days grazing among sea-grass meadows offshore. Bazurato Island itself is 37 km (23 mi) long, and here gaudy pink flamingoes strut the tidal flats, while large Nile crocodiles lurk in the inland freshwater lakes. The west is cloaked in grassland and thicket while the east coast is built entirely of impressive sand dunes. Benguerra is about 11 km (7 mi) long and its blend of forest, savannah and wetlands provides rich pickings for local wildlife. Cashew nuts are native to the island and grow mainly on the seaward side.

Wild orange trees and sisal trees abound, as do mlala palms – the leaves of which are used in the weaving of mats, baskets and hats. Nature lovers, sun worshippers and water sports enthusiasts alike are drawn here. It may be said of other places, but this is as close as it gets to a true tropical paradise. With clear turquoise waters and endless palm-dotted beaches, this is the place to escape from the pressures of everyday life – to snorkel and surf, and run coral pink sand through your fingers. There are no roads, no shops and no tourist attractions to divert you from the serious business of relaxing.

Birdwatching – sunbirds, bee-eaters, paradise flycatchers and crab plovers.
Shell-seeking for the famous 'Pansy Shells' at North Point, Pansy Island and various sand dunes.
Dining out on freshly caught fish, cooked in the Portuguese style.
YOU SHOULD KNOW:
The locals use the husks from the harvested cashews to make very intoxicating liquor.

The Island of Mozambique

POPULATION:
14,000 (2006)
WHEN TO GO:
May to October
HOW TO GET THERE:
Fly from Nampula. By traditional dhow from the mainland, or cross the bridge by car.
HIGHLIGHTS:
The port area and its fascinating mixture of architectural styles.
The Chapel of Nossa Senhora de Baluarte – this church was built by the Portuguese in 1522 and is believed to be the oldest European building in the southern hemisphere. Other churches worth a visit include the Church of Santo Antonio and the Church of Misericordia.
YOU SHOULD KNOW:
A 3-km bridge connects the island to the mainland.

The tiny coral island of Mozambique lies in the Nampula Province of Northern Mozambique and has a unique historical heritage unmatched in the rest of Mozambique, and perhaps the rest of Africa. It was the capital of Mozambique for nearly four centuries under Portuguese rule, and had been used as a major base for Arab traders long before that. Today much of the island has been designated a UNESCO World Heritage Site.

The island was a major Arab port and centre of boat building when Vasco da Gama arrived in 1498. By 1507, the Portuguese had established a port and naval base on the island, and went on to build the Fort of São Sebastião. The settlement, now known as Stone Town, became the capital of Portuguese East Africa. It withstood Dutch attacks in 1607 and 1608 and remained a major trading post for the Portuguese on the sea route from Europe to the East Indies, trading in slaves, spices and gold. With the opening of the Suez Canal in 1869, however, the island's fortunes waned.

A study in architectural contrasts, the island's port is resplendent in Arab, Indian and Portuguese influences, a reminder of its glory days. The limestone houses around the port lie on winding, tangled streets surrounding a central square, their facades featuring cornices, high rectangular windows and rows of pilasters. The Chapel of Nossa Senhora de Baluarte, built in 1522, is thought to be the oldest European building in the southern hemisphere, and the finest example of Manueline vaulted architecture in Mozambique.

Other interesting buildings on the island include the Palace and Chapel of São Paulo, which was built in 1610 and is now a museum; and the Museum of Sacred Art with an excellent example of a Makonde crucifix, housed in the former hospital of the Holy House of Mercy.

Mozambique Castle

Quirimbas Archipelago National Park

This sprawling, stunning archipelago is made up of 32 coral islands peppered along the Mozambique coast from Pemba to the Rovuma River – which forms a natural barrier with Tanzania. The southern-most eleven islands and a vast area of mainland forest now make up the Quirimbas National Park. Here elephants pluck mangoes off the trees just metres from the Indian Ocean, and inland four of Africa's 'Big Five' animals still roam.

The archipelago has some of the finest coral reefs in East Africa. The fish here are big – parrotfish, angelfish, cave bass and morays all seem to be oversized. Kingfish will come for a snorkel along the shores, and manta rays and hammerhead sharks can also make an appearance. Matemo Island has countless coves and beaches and is brilliant for diving. On the other hand Medjumbe is a tiny castaway of an island and an idyllic romantic retreat. Quilalea is uninhabited and it feels like you have the whole place to yourself – along with the teeming marine life, of course. Vimizi is rated one of the world's top ten dive sites, and along the shoreline are tracks made by turtles as they scoop and heave their hefty frames up the beach.

In contrast and for a little culture, Ibo Island has beautiful old buildings and a long, dark history dating from well before the arrival of the Portuguese. Once a fashionable town, many of the 18th and 19th century Portuguese-built homes have been abandoned and are now crumbling. Given its history, Ibo is also one of the most visited islands.

When it emerged from a bloody civil war in 1992 no-one expected Mozambique to become Africa's hidden jewel and conservation champion – a safe haven for dugongs, sea turtles and for those fortunate enough to visit its multi-faceted shores.

POPULATION:
Ibo 5,000; Vimizi 1,000; Matemo 500 (2005 estimate). Many of the islands are uninhabited.

WHEN TO GO:
Tropical climate – the rainy season is from December to April, but most days are sunny and the rain is usually in short, sharp showers. It's a little cooler from May to September, and diving is fine all year round.

HOW TO GET THERE:
Flights from Dar es Salaam or Johannesburg to Pemba Island, then on to islands such as Ibo or Matemo. Boats between islands.

HIGHLIGHTS:
Humpback whale watch from June to September.
Going fishing with the locals in their dhows.
Tracking elephants at night.
The island of Ibo – once a trading port for slaves and ivory, and with a magnificent old fortress.

YOU SHOULD KNOW:
Mozambique is a malaria zone so take care and cover up. Quilalea Island is the only malaria-free island in the whole archipelago.

Portuguese colonial buildings line the harbour of Ibo Island.

INDIAN OCEAN

Madagascar Island

The Republic of Madagascar occupies the island of the same name, the world's fourth largest, located in the Indian Ocean off the southeast coast of Africa. Madagascar has a mountainous heart and central plateaux, with rain forests to the east and dry forests and deserts to the west and south. The capital is Antananarivo (Tana for short), and the other major cities are Antsirabe, Mahajanga and Toamasina. The island was violently annexed by France in the late 19th century, attaining independence in 1960. A period of political instability seems to be over and this intriguing nation is at last finding its feet.

Madagascar's long isolation from outside influences has resulted in unique flora and fauna, with many plants and animals that are found nowhere else. Unfortunately, this special ecosystem is under threat from extensive logging and slash-and-burn agriculture. Belated realization of the irreversible damage this is doing has seen a new emphasis on conservation, so there is hope for the island's ecological future. This also has an important economic dimension, with ecotourism a growing trend and Madagascar possessing more potential than most. Unique attractions include lemurs, the mongoose-like fossa and three endemic bird families, but there's plenty more to look at – the island is home to five per cent of the world's plant and animal species.

Tourism has not been a priority in a country that largely depends on agriculture, fishing and forestry. The infrastructure is poor, with only one main road from Tana to the south-west coast. Adventurous visitors tour by bicycle, or charter a yacht with local guide for a memorable exploration of the coastline. Otherwise it's a case of taking an internal flight to the town or city of your choice, finding a hotel and sallying forth from there by bus or taxi.

Village houses in the morning mist near Perinet

Nosy Boraha Island

Local boys walking cattle along a pristine beach.

Also known, rather more romantically, by its French name of Ile Sainte Marie, Nosy Boraha is situated off Madagascar's north-east coast and is a former haunt of pirates, who lived on an island in the bay of Nosy Boraha's main town, Ambodifotatra. Their cemetery still exists and a number of sunken wooden ships from the 17th and 18th centuries, said to be pirate vessels, may be seen below the surface. The island is 60 km (38 mi) long by less than 10 km (6 mi) wide, surrounded by sandy beaches that are fringed with palm trees and protected by coral reefs. The island has a verdant, hilly interior.

These attributes have made Nosy Boraha Madagascar's leading holiday destination, though happily it has yet to be spoiled by excessive commercialism. Holidaymakers can enjoy the essential ingredients of any Indian Ocean resort holiday – sultry tropical weather, low-profile waterside accommodation, wonderful beaches and the usual water sports – swimming, snorkelling and diving within the reef are excellent. But here there is the added bonus of an accessible interior where the rainforest offers fascinating opportunities to observe the rich variety of local flora and fauna. Best of all, this is one of the best places in the world to whale-watch, with humpback whales cavorting in the channel between the Nosy Boraha and the Malagasy mainland during the busy breeding season (July to September).

Those who hire cycles can not only enjoy Nosy Boraha's natural beauty, but can also see how the relaxed islanders enrich their lives with traditional family and social events that invoke the revered spirits of their ancestors – it's the authentic Madagascar experience!

POPULATION:
60,000 (2007 estimate)
WHEN TO GO:
Outside high summer (December to February), when it's uncomfortably hot and very humid.
HOW TO GET THERE:
Internal flights serve the island from most Malagasy cities. By boat from Manompana or Soanierana-Ivongo on the mainland.
HIGHLIGHTS:
Ambodena Forest, alive with wildlife – including lemurs, a huge variety of birds, geckos, chameleons and arboreal frogs.
Marine turtles nesting on the beach at Cocoteraie, where villagers now make an income from guarding the nests and showing them to visitors, rather than eating the turtles and their eggs.
The primeval forest at Ikalalao, remarkable for its many orchid species including the large variety known as the 'Queen of Madagascar'.
A stay in one of the lodges in wildlife sanctuaries, where the focus is on guided animal viewing activities.
YOU SHOULD KNOW:
Nosy Boraha's nickname is 'the scented island', because aromatic coffee, cocoa, cinnamon and vanilla grow in profusion.

*Waves break against the outer
sandbars of Aldabra Atoll.*

Aldabra Atoll

POPULATION:
Uninhabited
WHEN TO GO:
May to September
HOW TO GET THERE:
Virtually the only way is to join a
cruise ship, embarking at Victoria, on
Mahé Island.
HIGHLIGHTS:
The Aldabran giant tortoises – there
are ten times the number of giant
tortoises on Aldabra than
on Galápagos.
The colonies of breeding birds on the
islets in the lagoon – see frigate
birds, red-tailed tropic birds and
boobies.
The Aldabra flightless rail – the only
flightless bird left on any Indian
Ocean island.
YOU SHOULD KNOW:
Aldabra Atoll is uninhabited and very
isolated. Astove Atoll, part of the
Aldabra Atoll, used to be occupied by
African slaves who escaped from a
Portuguese ship in 1760.

Aldabra Atoll is part of the Aldabra Group, one of the archipelagos of the Outer Islands of the Seychelles. The second largest atoll in the world after Kiritimati, Aldabra is the coraline tip of a volcanic seamount, rising from depths of 4,000 to 4,500m (13,120 to 14,760 ft). At 34 km (21 mi) long, 14.5 km (9 mi) wide and just 8 m (26 ft) above sea level, the atoll consists of four coral limestone islands forming a circle around a lagoon of 224 sq km (86 sq mi). The lagoon is tidal and loses two-thirds of its waters at low tide. Aldabra was given World Heritage status in 1982 to protect its delicate natural environment.

Because the atoll is so remote, many of its species of flora and fauna are found only here. The islets and rocky outcrops in the lagoon provide nesting areas for thousands of birds. It has possibly the largest population of red-tailed tropic birds and the second largest colony of frigate birds in the world. Many other birds are found here too, including the Aldabra flightless rail, the only flightless bird found on any Indian Ocean island.

The Aldabran giant tortoises are, however, the atoll's most renowned residents, being the last of the giant tortoises which were once spread across the entire region. Commercial exploitation is believed to have rendered all other giant tortoises in the area extinct by the mid-19th century, and very nearly exterminated the Aldabran population. Two species of marine turtle also nest on beaches on Aldabra: the green turtle and hawksbill turtle.

Unlike the nearby Seychelles, the atoll is inhospitable to humans as the limestone has been eroded into sharp spikes and water-filled pits. However, the mangroves support fish nurseries, and the lagoon is home to a wealth of marine life, from black-tipped reef sharks to eagle rays and parrot fish. For almost a century, scientists have been studying the flora and fauna of the atoll, which is uninhabited other than by those working at the scientific research station.

Mahé Island

Africa's least-populous sovereign state is the Republic of Seychelles, another of the Indian Ocean's fairly numerous island nations. Officially, there are over 150 islands in the Seychelles, consisting of a mix of granite and coral islands located 1,500 km (930 mi) to the east of the African mainland and 1,600 km (994 mi) to the north east of Madagascar. Other neighbours include Mauritius, Réunion, Zanzibar, Comoros, Mayotte and the Maldives. The Seychellois make good neighbours – they are often described as the world's friendliest people.

Mahé is the largest island, in the north of the archipelago. It contains the capital city of Victoria (no prizes for guessing that this was once a British colony) and has 90 per cent of the country's population. Settlement is concentrated in the north and east, while the south and west are largely occupied by the Baie Ternay Marine National Park and Port Launay Marine National Park. The island's high point, Morne Seychellois, is also a National Park that offers striking scenery and rewarding hiking opportunities. Visitors who merely pass through Mahé on the way to resort islands are missing something – the place is spectacular, with towering mountains, abundant tropical vegetation and beautiful beaches, mostly uncrowded...or, better still, empty.

Victoria is the world's smallest capital city, and its quaint streets and old harbour can easily be explored on foot. The clock tower is a replica of that housing Big Ben at London's Houses of Parliament. The market is open six days a week (excluding Sunday) and local crafts are on sale alongside a wide range of fruit, vegetables and fish. It's possible to take a boat tour of the St Anne Marine Park from Victoria Harbour, covering six offshore islands that include an important nesting site for hawksbill turtles.

POPULATION:
72,000 (2005 estimate)
WHEN TO GO:
All year round – the climate is evenly hot and humid. Even during the rainy season (January and February) there is plenty of sunshine.
HOW TO GET THERE:
Various international carriers fly to Mahé, including Air Seychelles – which also operates internal inter-island services.
HIGHLIGHTS:
The National Botanical Gardens on the outskirts of Victoria – a shady green oasis with a lovely orchid display.
Beau Vallon beach, the most popular on the island, where the action continues with good nightlife after dark.
The annual Creole Festival – a colourful (and noisy) event that takes place during the last week of October.
Victoria's Museum of History, full of exhibits and historic artefacts relating to the cultural and natural history of the Seychelles.
YOU SHOULD KNOW:
Although predominately Catholic, the Seychellois are a superstitious lot and many believe in old magic known as *gris*. But don't worry if you forget to tip – sorcery was officially outlawed in 1958!

Local children playing in the sea.

Praslin Island

Despite being the second-largest island in the Seychelles, Praslin still isn't all that big, with an area of just 38 sq km (15 sq mi). It is 45 km (28 mi) north of Mahé, and in the 18th century was the haunt of Arab merchants and a notorious pirate hideaway. There is obviously some modern development, but those old-time visitors would still recognize the place.

Nowadays the incomers are mostly holidaymakers, honeymooners or cruise passengers. They are all drawn by fabulous beaches, sculptural granite rocks, coral reefs swarming with colourful fish and the lush interior vegetation of the archipelago's most popular tourist destination. There are numerous hotels, resorts and self-catering units, though the island never seems overcrowded. Its two villages are Baie St Anne in the east and Grand Anse in the south and both are worth visiting. Bicycles may be hired, and provide an excellent way of exploring the island.

This is the ultra-tranquil place that thinks Mahé's slow way of doing things is a touch hectic, so life on Praslin is virtually laid back to the horizontal. But those who do stir themselves and leave the beach can visit the fabulous Vallée de Mai, a primeval forest complete with the soaring Coco de Mer palm trees that produce the world's largest nut – just one example of flora unique to Praslin – and also rare endemic bird species like the Seychelles bulbul, fruit pigeon and black parrot. This fascinating place is a UNESCO World Heritage Site, and well deserves the accolade.

POPULATION:
6,500 (2007 estimate)
WHEN TO GO:
Any time – the hot climate hardly varies and the sea remains warm all year round.
HOW TO GET THERE:
By air taxi or fast catamaran from Mahé.
HIGHLIGHTS:
A souvenir that can be obtained nowhere else – an expensive, rare, numbered Coco de Mer nut, once reserved for sultans and said to have magical sexual powers (you'll know why when you see one).
One of the world's most beautiful beaches – Anse Lazio on the east coast, which must be seen to be believed.
The black pearl farm – cultured black pearls at the Indian Ocean's only oyster farm, and also giant clams.
YOU SHOULD KNOW:
General Gordon of Khartoum was convinced that the Biblical Garden of Eden was on Praslin.

Sunrise over Praslin Island

La Digue Island

If it were for sale, La Digue would attract keen competition from the world's billionaires – this is an enchanting tropical paradise. The fourth-largest island in the Seychelles, La Digue extends to an area of 10 sq km (6 sq mi) and lies to the east of Praslin Island. It supports a population that used to survive on fishing, copra and vanilla production but nowadays tourism is the name of the game and the whole island is geared to providing a memorable holiday experience. There are several hotels and guest-houses that offer simpler accommodation and it's also possible to see this magical place by making a day trip from nearby Praslin.

The beaches – especially Anse Source d'Argent and Anse Pierrot – are fabulous, often set off by tumbled rock formations that seem like dramatic granite sculptures. There are plenty of hidden coves to discover, too. Getting around is a matter of foot or pedal power, as there are few vehicles and the locals use ox-drawn carts, which perfectly match the unchanging pace of island life. Focal points are the harbour at La Passe on the west coast and L'Union Estate where traditional activities like copra production and boat building are still practised. A working vanilla plantation welcomes visitors.

La Digue's interior rises to Eagle's Nest Mountain (also known as Belle Vue), a peak that is 300 m (985 ft) above sea level and rewards the active visitor with wonderful views. The densely forested Veuve Nature Reserve occupies much of the interior, and there are picturesque swamps, pools and inlets.

POPULATION:
2,100 (2007 estimate)
WHEN TO GO:
This is a year-round destination, with the hot, humid climate tempered by cooling winds.
HOW TO GET THERE:
By fast ferry from Praslin or Mahé. An expensive helicopter transfer is also available.
HIGHLIGHTS:
A day trip to Praslin's small offshore islands – Félicité, Ile Cocos, Grand Soeur and Petite Soeur.
A famous island sight – giant tortoises in their rocky enclosure.
The lovingly maintained church of Our Lady of Assumption, with an impressive stone-built calvaire by the entrance.
YOU SHOULD KNOW:
La Digue is home to the critically endangered Black Paradise Flycatcher, known locally as 'the widow' – a bird thought to be extinct but now rediscovered.

The striking coastline of La Digue

Silhouette Island

POPULATION:
135 (2007)
WHEN TO GO:
May to September
HOW TO GET THERE:
By helicopter or boat from Mahé.
HIGHLIGHTS:
The deserted sandy beaches set in
scenic coves.
The giant tortoises – visit the breeding
centre out near the Dauban Coconut
Plantation.
Snorkelling above the undamaged
coral reefs.
They have a cast-iron neoclassical
mausoleum here that is supposedly
the most remarkable piece of
eccentricity in all of the Seychelles
islands.
YOU SHOULD KNOW:
The island is situated within a Marine
National Park.

The island of Silhouette lies 20 km (12 mi) north-west of Mahé and with an area of 20 sq km (7 sq mi), it is the third largest island in the Seychelles. Unlike many of the other islands in the chain, Silhouette is formed of granite, but the rocks are softened by the dense, lush rainforest which covers this round island. With a tiny population, and just one small hotel on the island, this untouched paradise is the ultimate get-away.

Named after Etienne de Silhouette (1709–1767), the French minister of finances under Louis XV, the island has five peaks over 500 m (1,640 ft), making the scenery rather dramatic. The summit of Mount Dauban at 740 m (2,428 ft), the highest point on the island, looms above the idyllic, unexplored rainforest thick with rare hardwoods, incense trees and pitcher-plant orchids endemic to Silhouette.

The island supports one of the richest biodiversities in the western Indian Ocean, with many endemic and endangered plants and animals. The large areas of primeval forest are untouched by modern man and are home to, among other species, the last known Seychelles sheath-tailed bats in the wild.

Among the more famous inhabitants are the giant tortoises. The Seychelles tortoise was almost completely eradicated by sailors who used them for food as they were able to survive aboard ships for up to six months without food and water. This activity lasted until 1840 when the last of the animals was taken into captivity. A handful of them were found in captivity in the 1990s, as were a few Arnold's giant tortoises, also previously thought to be extinct. The Seychelles Giant Tortoise Conservation Project aims to keep these two species from extinction. You can see giant tortoises at the breeding centre near the old Dauban Coconut Plantation.

Silhouette Island at sunrise

The island's marine environment is just as rich as that on land, and there are coral reefs and granite cliffs to explore. The huge, colourful coral reefs are home to exotic fish of all shapes and sizes, making the island appealing to snorkelling and diving fans. The coral habitats are exceptionally healthy, though the strong currents can be a problem for swimmers. There are also some pristine beaches on the island, set in pretty coves and secluded bays, and it is likely you can find one all to yourself. This island is heaven for honeymooners, or those who simply want to unwind in an island paradise.

Mauritius

Part of the Mascarene Islands, the Republic of Mauritius is off the coast of Africa in the Indian Ocean, 900 km (560 mi) east of Madagascar. The republic consists of five islands – St Brandon, Rodrigues, two Agalegas Islands and Mauritius itself. The latter was originally uninhabited, but the Dutch named the island and established a colony that was seized by the French in 1715. They renamed the place Ile de France and built a prosperous economy based on sugar. But the British took the island in 1810 and it reverted to the original name.

Independence was granted in 1968 and this Commonwealth country is a stable democracy with one of Africa's highest per capita incomes. This might be guessed by a visitor to Port Louis, who finds a sophisticated place with a cluster of high- and medium-rise buildings that might be mistaken from afar as the downtown area of a small American city…were it not for its location beside the azure Indian Ocean, surrounded by lush tropical vegetation. Tourism has become an increasingly important sector of the economy, which had hitherto been based on sugar plantations and off-shore financial services.

The effort to attract visitors is proving successful, and might not even need the boost of a move to duty-free status. Mauritius is the most accessible island in the Indian Ocean, with wonderful beaches and crystal-clear waters. Important though these essential ingredients of every tropical holiday destination may be, Mauritius has something extra – friendly people and a vibrant cultural mix that will leave an indelible impression. There is a festival or fiesta practically every week and a tempting variety of ethnic cuisines. The place must be good – author Mark Twain remarked that Mauritius was made before heaven, and heaven modelled on Mauritius.

POPULATION:
1,157,000 (2000)
WHEN TO GO:
Temperature is high all year round, though trade winds keep down humidity. May to November are peak months, January and February are cyclone-prone.
HOW TO GET THERE:
By air from several departure points in Europe (especially France) and Africa.
HIGHLIGHTS:
Black River Gorges National Park – an area of outstanding natural beauty reached by the island's only mountain road.
Curepipe – in the centre of a lovely upland area, the place resembles an old English market town.
The Grand Bay Resort, for those who like some lively nightlife after a day on the beach.
The colourful Flacq Market in the east of the island for the best local produce and handicrafts.
Dutch ruins at Vieux Grand Port, the oldest settlement on the island, dating from the 17th century.
Chamarel – an extraordinary multi-coloured landscape made up of different volcanic ashes, culminating in a waterfall complex.
YOU SHOULD KNOW:
Mauritius was the only known habitat of that famous non-flying bird immortalized in the oh-so-sadly-true phrase 'dead as a dodo'.

An aerial view of Blue Bay and its sandbanks

Rodrigues Island

POPULATION:
38,000 (2006 estimate)
WHEN TO GO:
Any time – the temperature is pretty even all year round.
HOW TO GET THERE:
Fly in from Mauritius or Réunion. By boat from Mauritius (36 hours).
HIGHLIGHTS:
The Grand Montagne Nature Reserve, where restoration of indigenous forest is taking place.
A visit to the delightful stone-built, Gothic-style St Gabriel Cathedral.
The bustling Saturday market in Port Mathurin.
A selection of caves with amazing stalactites and stalagmites.
YOU SHOULD KNOW:
Arabs visited Rodrigues as long ago as the 10th century – their name for the island was Dina Moraze.

The smallest of the Mascarene Islands, Rodrigues is an autonomous region of the Republic of Mauritius, though it aspires to independence. It is 560 km (350 mi) east of the main island, extends to 110 sq km (42 sq mi) and is surrounded by a coral reef and various islets. This isolated volcanic island has developed an environment that contains many unique species of flora and fauna. Originally a stopping point for passing mariners, who used to restock their larders with endemic Rodrigues giant tortoises (to such an extent that they soon became extinct), the island was a French possession until the British captured it in 1809. The capital is Port Mathurin on the north coast.

The landscape is a memorable mix of towering central massif, craggy hillsides, windswept pastures, a rocky shoreline punctuated by white beaches and an extensive lagoon that comes complete with tiny 'desert islands'. For more active visitors, this is a haven for hikers and nature lovers, whilst those who simply want to laze around in the sun or enjoy water sports will not be disappointed.

However, the true strength of Rodrigues is that the island is a tranquil place where time seems to have stood still. Residents live an unhurried traditional life, far from the pressures of the modern world, cultivating fruit and vegetables, raising animals, fishing in the lagoon (especially for octopus) and creating wonderful handicrafts. Their friendly character and warm welcome will be long remembered by visitors. Those who want to get away from it all and experience the magic of Rodrigues will find a selection of accommodation ranging from 5-star hotels through to comfortable cottages. It's a long way from anywhere, but the necessary effort is definitely worthwhile.

The windswept pastures of Rodrigues Island

Réunion Island

Not everyone knows this, but Réunion is part of the European Union, being one of France's fully incorporated overseas *départements*. As such, it is one of the French Republic's 26 regions, with the same status as those on the European mainland. Because Réunion is in a time zone to the east of Europe, the first-ever purchase with the EU's new currency was made here in 2002 – a 1-euro bag of lichees in Saint-Denis market.

This tropical island is in the Indian Ocean, 200 km (130 mi) to the south west of Mauritius. The British seized the Mascarene Islands early in the 19th century, but Réunion was later returned to France. It was uninhabited when the first Europeans visited – Portuguese explorers in 1513 – but the Réunion of today is well populated and economically successful. It is 63 km (39 mi) long by 45 km (28 mi) wide.

Réunion's claim to vulcanological fame is that – like Hawaii – it is located on a hotspot above the earth's crust. The Piton de la Fournaise is a shield volcano that has erupted more than one hundred times since the 17th century and is still erupting, most recently in 2007. The higher Piton de Neige is an extinct volcano. The island has a great variety of landscapes – volcanic peaks and lava beds, heavily forested slopes, coastal lowlands, rocky shores and a few sandy beaches (black and white).

Tourism is an important economic activity and a typically French range of accommodation may be found – hotels, pensions, gîtes and the occasional resort. Getting around isn't hard – there is a good public bus service on paved roads, though traffic can jam up at peak times – and Réunion offers a really excellent and varied range of interesting visitor attractions.

A waterfall in the Marsouins River plunges down a heavily forested slope.

POPULATION:
785,000 (2007 estimate)
WHEN TO GO:
The very rainy season (December to March) is best avoided.
HOW TO GET THERE:
By air, ideally (for cost reasons) from Paris or Mauritius. By boat from Mauritius.
HIGHLIGHTS:
The Aquarium de la Réunion, for a wonderful presentation of the island's marine life.
Three impressive volcanic calderas – Cirque de Salazie, Cirque de Cilaos and Cirque de Mafate.
Croc Park – over 150 snappy crocodiles occupying pools in a forest setting.
In the beautiful old Colonial Council building at Saint-Denis – the island's Natural History Museum.
The Cooperative de Vanille de Bras-Panon, for a fascinating insight into the traditional production of vanilla.
YOU SHOULD KNOW:
Back in 1952, the greatest 24-hour precipitation ever recorded took place on Réunion – 1,869.9 mm (73.6 in). And 3,929 mm (154.7 in) once fell in 72 hours.

The Comoro Islands

This archipelago lies in the Mozambique Channel between Madagascar and the African mainland. The former French possession divided into two entities in 1976 – the Union of the Comoros and Mayotte, which chose to remain a French overseas collective. Both have a largely Muslim population. The political situation remains unstable – each of the Union's smaller islands has made a unilateral declaration of independence (since rescinded) and there have been numerous coup attempts in the Union, which claims Mayotte.

Be that as it may, the Union (population 798,000 in 2005) and Mayotte (population 186,000 in 2007) have a lot to offer the intrepid traveller who does, however, have to get used to the variety of alternative names used to describe these fascinating islands. The Union is made up of Grand Comore (Ngazidja), Anjouan (Nzwani) and Mohéli (Mwali). Mayotte consists of the two islands of Grand-Terre (Mahoré) and Petite-Terre (Pamanzi).

Grand Comore is the largest island, an irregular plateau anchored by two volcanoes and shaped by lava flow. Anjouan is a similar lava plateau with three mountain chains. Mohéli is the smallest, with valleys and forests running down from the central mountain chain. Together, they extend to 2,235 sq km (863 sq mi). Mayotte has an area of 375 sq km (145 sq mi) and the gently rolling land rises to volcanic mountains.

The economy of the Comeros is based on small-scale farming, animal husbandry and fishing, augmented by financial support from France. Tourism is not highly developed in the islands, but those who make the journey find good accommodation and an unspoiled place whose colourful and friendly people live as they always have. The beaches rank alongside the world's best – there are splendid reefs, beautiful lagoons, lush forests, volcanic lakes, tumbling waterfalls and picturesque former colonial towns.

POPULATION:
985,000 (estimate)

WHEN TO GO:
Choose your preferred weather – hot, wet and humid from November to April; hot, dry, windy, cool at night between May and October.

HOW TO GET THERE:
The Union is served by Hahaya Airport at Moroni on Grand Comore, which accepts international flights and is also the base for island-hoppers. Fly to Mayotte from Paris via Réunion or Moroni.

HIGHLIGHTS:
The capital of Anjouan, with its bustling streets and alleys, old Sultan's Palace and Friday Mosque.
An area of outstanding natural beauty on Anjouan – the Dziancoundre Waterfall.
An expedition to Karthala, an active volcano on Grand Comore.
Mohéli Marine Park off the island's south coast, where humpback whales breed and green turtles nest.
The bustling market at Dzaoudzi on Mayotte's Petite-Terre for an authentic slice of island life.

YOU SHOULD KNOW:
Two-thirds of the world's natural perfume essence comes from the Comoros, after being processed from orange, jasmine and ylang-ylang blossoms.

Local boys take the plunge!

The Maldives

The Republic of Maldives is an island nation that consists of 26 main atolls encompassing some 1,200 islets, 200 of which are inhabited. They are scattered in the Indian Ocean 700 km (435 mi) to the south-west of Sri Lanka. With a maximum natural height of 2.6 m (7.5 ft), the Maldives are threatened by global warming, as a comparatively modest rise in sea level would make them uninhabitable. Havoc caused by the tsunami in 2004 serves as a stark reminder of the sea's destructive power.

Tourism is the major money-spinner. Visitors are wooed with the slogan 'the last paradise on earth' and they do indeed enjoy relaxed resort holidays in an idyllic setting, with a pleasant climate that encourages water sports such as fishing, swimming, snorkelling, scuba diving, water skiing and windsurfing. A typical resort in the Maldives will consist of an island occupied only by the workforce and visitors, with no local inhabitants, which will be up to 1,000 m (3,300 ft) by 250 m (800 ft) in size. There will be swaying palm trees and a beautiful beach encircling the island, protected by a house reef that encloses a safe lagoon. They come in three varieties – luxury for honeymooners and the jet set, family resorts and dive resorts.

The capital is Malé, an extraordinary city that occupies an entire island – a place of contrasts where high-rise buildings rub shoulders with the narrow streets, lanes and alleys of the old bazaar area. This crowded place houses a quarter of the country's population and is about as close as tourists get to the 'real life' of the Maldives – most of the other islands with local communities are off the tourist map. But if sun, sea and sand are your idea of bliss, the Maldives will delight.

POPULATION:
299,000 (2006)
WHEN TO GO:
High season (December to April) gets the best weather but is expensive (if you fancy Christmas, start entering the nearest lottery now). Low season has higher humidity and occasional squalls.
HOW TO GET THERE:
Fly in to Malé International Airport on Hulhulé Island right next to the capital. Onward transfer to resorts by float plane or boat.
HIGHLIGHTS:
A stay on Seenu (Addu Atoll) for a chance to meet and mix with local people in traditional island communities.
The 450-year-old Friday Mosque (Hukuru Miskiiy) in Malé – it has a superb interior. The nearby minaret dates from 1675.
For divers – the internationally famous Banana Reef dive site, against a backdrop of dramatic cliffs and caves.
The National Museum in Malé, containing many treasures once owned by local sultans, together with pre-Islamic stone carvings.
YOU SHOULD KNOW:
Don't expect a bargain – there is no budget accommodation or travel, resorts are expensive and innumerable 'extras' are charged.

An aerial view of a breathtaking island and lagoon

Sri Lanka

The Pearl of the Indian Ocean lies only 31 km (19 mi) off India's south coast. Its modern name is taken from the Sanskrit ancient Indian epics *Mahabharata* and the *Ramayana*, and means 'resplendent land'.

Sri Lanka's chief characteristic is intensity – of colour, of beauty, of religious belief, of sectarian commitment, and of affection it inspires in everyone who goes there. The first to stay became the stuff of legend: the 2,500 year-old *Mahawamsa* chronicle describes the arrival of the 'Sinhala' ('lion race'), and the island's history since has been a series of shifting kingdoms, each leaving a treasury of ruins and literature, and a tangle of relationships that are still being decoded in its modern political life. When you go to Sri Lanka's cultural triangle of Anuradhapura, Polonnaruwa and Dambulla/Sigiriya, you see the architectural glories of the past, but they are living history. They are active religious sites, not floodlit movie sets.

The island has the perfect set-up. At any time of year you can lounge on immaculate beaches, and cool off in the hills when you get hot. Colombo, the capital, is a chaotic modern city, and an appropriate synthesis both of Sri Lanka's indigenous cultures and its Portuguese, Dutch and British influences. Tropical beaches stretch north to the bustle of Negambo, a characteristic fishing community; and south in a chain of pink and white arcs, past turtle hatcheries (Indurwa), masked carvers (Ambalangoda), and the coral reefs of Hikkaduwa. Go to Yala West National Park, a teeming rainforest of elephants, leopards, buffaloes, monkeys, crocodiles, deer, sloth bears and a galaxy of birds, on your way to the lush, lakeside hill resort of Kandy. It's Sri Lanka's exotic spiritual centre, and its spectacular parades of frenetic dancers, firewalkers and pounding drummers are, in fact, often a signal to prayer.

POPULATION:
20,000,000 (2003)
WHEN TO GO:
December to March on the S and W coasts, and the hill-country; May to September on the E coast. But any other time, the rain isn't constant, and there's always a beach fit for purpose.
Come for August's Kandy Esala Perahera, a brilliant 10-day festival in honour of the sacred tooth relic of the Buddha, or the Kataragama Festival.
HOW TO GET THERE:
By air, to Colombo.
HIGHLIGHTS:
The Festival of Kataragama in the SE hills during August, when tens of thousands of Hindus, Buddhists and Muslims unite in pilgrimage to one of Sri Lanka's most important and holiest sites.
The water gardens and royal palace of the 5th century rock fortress of Sigiriya – and the nearby 19 km (12 mi) 1st century, 200 m (560 ft) high cave temple of Dambulla, where the gilded caves shelter 6,000 sq m (20,000 sq ft) of Buddhist murals.
Sunrise at World's End, a 700 m (2,400 ft) vertical drop at the edge of Horton Plains National Park, a 2,000 m (6,500ft) high grassland plateau full of birds and wildlife.
The Pinnewala Elephant Orphanage and Hakgala Natural Reserve, set among the dense forests and oceans of tea in the plantations around Nuwara Eliya, famous as a hill station favoured by the colonial British.
Anuradhapura, Sri Lanka's capital for 1,300 years until the 10th century, and home to the world's oldest authenticated tree – the 2,000 year-old sacred Bodhi tree brought by the sister of Mahinda, who brought Buddhism to the island. One of seven UNESCO World Heritage Sites on the island.
YOU SHOULD KNOW:
The Rabana is a huge circular drum used (usually by women in the villages) on holidays and during festivals for long-distance gossip – it's fundamental to the blazing colour and sound characteristic of Sri Lanka's ancient folk culture.

Buddhist monks watch elephants in the river at the Pinnewala Sanctuary

Cocos Islands

Stick a pin in a globe through the Cocos (Keeling) Islands, and it emerges almost exactly through the Cocos in Costa Rica! Discovered in 1609, they were settled and owned by a single family from 1827 until the Australian Government acquired them in 1978.

Lying 2,770 km (1,732 mi) northwest of Perth, the 27 coral islands are formed into two large, heavily vegetated atolls. Not only are they the only atolls that Darwin ever visited, but the coral ecosystem remains intact – and you can still see in their pristine condition exactly why they played such an important part in his theory of evolution. North Keeling, set apart from the other islands, isn't even inhabited; but you can see extreme rarities like the Cocos buff-banded rail, robber land crabs, and both green and hawksbill turtles among other wonders, under its protection as Pulu Keeling National Park, covering both North Keeling and its surrounding waters.

The Cocos (Keeling) islanders live on Home and West Islands, both given over to copra and coconut plantations that only add to their tropical glamour. There is no tourist industry at all. Instead, there are facilities for visitors, sponsored by islanders who take an almost personal interest in everyone who comes. If you happen to be there, you're genuinely welcome to participate in the school fête, sports day, or concert night; and you'd be an idiot not to join in quiz night at the Cocos Club, or not to watch the annual Ardmona Cup Aussie Rules football match. The tradition of hospitality is both Australian and Malay, representing the origins of the tight-knit community. The islanders, as much as the islands themselves, have retained a form of unpolluted innocence, and share a mutual respect that visitors immediately respond to. These islands are a dreamscape worthy of Gauguin.

A pristine white beach – so typical of the beautiful Cocos Islands

POPULATION:
546 (2007)
WHEN TO GO:
Year-round. The trade winds last from April to September, and the calmer doldrum season from November to April. Rain is more intense between March and July, but it usually falls in the evening after long, sunny days.
HOW TO GET THERE:
By air, from Perth, to West Island, Cocos (Keeling) Islands
HIGHLIGHTS:
Swimming and snorkelling among the wrasse, parrotfish and reef sharks of the 'Rip' on Direction Island.
The details of Australia's first naval victory, the sinking of the SMS *Emden*, the World War I German raider, among many unusual documents and exhibits at the Museum on Home Island.
Cycling the tracks through the exuberant hibiscus and foliage to the majestic Alexandrian laurels (*Calophyllum* trees) of Bob's Folly, on your way to Trannies Beach, West Island.
Heading up to Northpoint or the West Island jetty at the full moon – when hundreds of land crabs make their way to the water to spawn.
YOU SHOULD KNOW:
Unless the front door of a house is wide open, it is considered more polite to go around to the back door than to knock on the front.

375

Majuli Island

POPULATION:
140,000 (2001)
WHEN TO GO:
November to April
HOW TO GET THERE:
Ferry from Jorhat
HIGHLIGHTS:
Visiting the *satras* – some of the specializations are dance and arts at Bengenaati, jewellery and handicrafts at Auniati and mask making at Shamaguri. Ras Purnima, the three-day festival that takes place in October/November.
Angammi Tribal Museum at Auniati – containing old manuscripts and artefacts.
Bird watching.
Studying neo-Vaishavite philosophy at one of the satras. You might be able to stay there if you show real interest.
The spectacular sunsets over the Brahmaputra River.
YOU SHOULD KNOW:
As many as a hundred varieties of rice are grown on Majuli Island.

Majuli Island lies in the Brahmaputra River in Assam. Once it was the largest riverine island in the world, but every year the monsoon erodes more of its shore, and though it is still large – about 1,440 sq km (555 sq mi) – the island is shrinking at an alarming rate. Formed after a flood in 1750 when the river divided, it is a tranquil, flat, watery area, mostly consisting of paddy fields, water meadows, rivers and lakes and it's home to many rare and migratory birds.

Traditionally, the islanders – who comprise several tribal groups – cheerfully rebuild their bamboo and mud houses after each monsoon season, but recently several villages have been entirely lost. It is to be hoped that the government honour its undertakings to prevent this unique location from disappearing completely.

Majuli is famous for its *satras* – Hindu monasteries set up in the 15th century by the philosopher Srimanta Sankardeva, who frowned on the caste system and idolatry. Now villagers meet in the large prayer halls to praise Vishnu in music, dance and poetry. Around 20 of the original 65 *satras* survive; as well as serving as places of worship, they are important as treasuries of the area's culture, each one specializing in a different branch of the arts. The main settlements and *satras* are Kamalabari, with its centre for learning, and Garamur, which specialises in ancient weaponry.

The hospitable islanders tend dairy herds, fish and build boats. The women are famous for their exquisite weaving and their fine pottery. Majuli itself is renowned for the many different types of rice that are grown there.

Waiting for the ferry on the banks of the Brahmaputra River.

Diu Island

Diu is a former Portuguese possession that was taken over by India in 1961 and is now governed from Delhi. It is a small island – only 42 sq km (18 sq mi) – lying off the southern coast of Gujarat's Kathiawar Peninsula and it's joined to the mainland by two bridges.

Diu has preserved a distinctive Portuguese atmosphere and within the Old Town are narrow streets and many public and private buildings in Lusitanian style. Of the churches only one, St Paul's is still used for daily mass, whilst that of St Francis is now a hospital and St Thomas doubles as a museum and guest-house.

The Muslim, Hindu and Christian populations manage to co-exist with few problems, but as cheap alcohol is readily available and Gujarat is a dry state, Diu has something of a reputation for being a rather lively destination for Indian tourists.

The north and south coasts are very different with the former mainly comprising marshland and saltpans (flamingo and other water birds may be seen here in early spring) whilst the latter has limestone cliffs, inlets and sandy beaches. The most popular beach is at Nagoa, which is a favourite venue for Indian day-trippers and those interested in water sports, whilst further west lies the more western orientated resort of Sunset Point. For those interested in the more traditional aspects of Indian life the small fishing village of Vanakbori at the western end of the island has much to offer.

In general Diu is a laid-back and leisurely kind of spot and consequently walking, cycling and swimming tend to be the most popular activities for the tourist.

POPULATION:
21,576 (2001)
WHEN TO GO:
May to September
HOW TO GET THERE:
Flights from Mumbai to Diu airport or via road and rail links nearby on the mainland.
HIGHLIGHTS:
The Shell Museum near Nagoa beach – with over 2,500 shells collected by Captain Fulbaria over a period of 42 years.
The Portuguese fort – mostly dating from 1546-1650, this is now derelict but there is a good collection of cannons, cannonballs and parrots.
Fortim-do-Mar – a former jail just off the island. It's off limits to tourists, but you can circumnavigate it by hiring a fishing boat.
YOU SHOULD KNOW:
The spiky palm-like trees around Nagoa beach are Hoka trees imported from Africa 400 years ago; they don't exist anywhere else in India.

The bustling marketplace in the fishing village of Vanakbori

Kochi

POPULATION:
596,473 (2001)
WHEN TO GO:
March to October.
HOW TO GET THERE:
Fly to Kochi International Airport.
HIGHLIGHTS:
Kalady – on the banks of the River
Periyar, this is the birthplace of Sri Adi
Sankaracharya, the Hindu philosopher.
The Adi Sankara shrine and eight-storey
painted Adi Sankara Keerthi Sthambam.
The elephant sanctuary – just
north of Guruvayur at Punnathur Kotta,
this former rajahs' palace is home to
50 elephants.
Mattancherry Palace – built by the
Portuguese, then modified by the
Dutch in the 17th century and
presented to the Rajah of Cochin. It has
fine murals depicting scenes from the
Mahabharatha and Ramayana.
Jew Town – the rajah gave the
area known as 'Jew Town' to the
Jewish community to protect them
from persecution. The Paradisi
Synagogue, built in 1568, is
magnificently decorated with Chinese
tiles and Belgian chandeliers.
YOU SHOULD KNOW:
The city is also known as Cochin.

Fishermen at Fort Kochi

Built on a series of islands and peninsulas, between the western ghats in the east and the Arabian Sea in the west, Kochi is the capital city of the enchanting southern Indian state of Kerala. During its long and fascinating history, the city has been occupied by the Arabs, British, Chinese, Dutch and Portuguese, all of whom have left their mark on the culture and architecture of this vibrant place. When you see fishermen plying the coastal waters with massive Chinese fishing nets as you stroll down Fort Kochi beach against a backdrop of European-style residences, you will realize what a mixture of cultures exists here.

The city became a major player in world trade when Kodungallur (Cranganore) was destroyed by flooding in 1341 and a natural harbour formed at Kochi. Kochi became a prosperous port trading in pepper, cardamom, cinnamon, cloves and other products native to the area's lush soils.

Kochi is still an important trading port today. The modern port is sited on Willingdon Island, a man-made island created from the materials dredged while deepening Kochi Port. The island is named after Lord Willingdon, a former governor of Madras who was involved in the project. Willingdon Island soon became the commercial heart of the city. It is connected to the mainland by Venduruthy Bridge and today houses some of the district's best hotels.

Bolghatty Island, also known as Ponjikara, is popular with tourists and houses the Bolghatty palace. The palace was built by the Dutch during their occupation and is today a heritage hotel. The island also

has a golf course. Vypin Island was formed after the flood in 1341. Today it has one of the highest population densities in the world. It is connected to Kochi by a bridge and ferry.

Kochi boasts plenty of historical and cultural gems for the visitor. These include St Francis' Church, the oldest European church in India and burial place of Vasco da Gama. Vasco House, on Rose Street, with its glass paned windows and sweeping verandahs, is one of the oldest Portuguese homes in the country.

Sited on a pretty island on Vembanad Lake, Vallarpadam Church has a serene and calm atmosphere. The church was built by Portuguese missionaries in 1524. It is said that the missionaries discovered a painting of the Lady of Ransom and, later in a dream, were asked to establish a church in Vallarpadam. Mattancherry Palace was built by the Portuguese, then later modified by the Dutch and presented to the Rajah of Cochin. The beautiful palace has served as the location for many coronations throughout history.

Chorao Island

Up-river from Panaji and close to historic Old Goa, Chorao lies between the wide, slow Mandovi and Mapusa rivers. Its Sanskrit name, Chuddamani, means 'Most Beautiful Diamond'. It is a peaceful, lush area of mangroves and fertile fields, with navigable waterways and some protective banking. The Mandovi River is partly tidal and the mixture of fresh and salt water makes the island a prime site for water birds, some migratory, and the southwest region is an important bird sanctuary. Sadly, river traffic is eroding the fragile shores. To some extent, Chorao has been protected by the stop-go construction work on a hugely expensive bridge project – while the island had only its ferry links it was shielded from destructive development. It is to be hoped that awareness of the delicate ecological balance will continue to keep this place unspoilt.

It is said that centuries before the Portuguese arrived, this was a place of learning, with a university of Sanskrit. In the 16th century, the Portuguese re-named the island, and Christianized it. It was such a pleasant place to live that many fine mansions with lovely gardens were built for the gentlemen who were ferried down river to work in crowded Panaji and it became known as the 'Island of Noblemen'. But, like Old Goa, it was depopulated by epidemics, and now all that remains of the Portuguese are a couple of churches and views of the skyline of Old Goa over the river.

Hindu temples were rebuilt in the 20th century and Hindus are now the majority here. The islanders fish, grow cashews and produce a liquor called Fenny. Most of the colonial buildings lie in moss and creeper-covered ruins.

POPULATION:
18,500 (2004)
WHEN TO GO:
November to March
HOW TO GET THERE:
Ferry from Ribander or Pomburpa.
By bridge from Bicholim.
HIGHLIGHTS:
Dr Salim Ali Bird Sanctuary – many species, including grey and purple herons and the migrating Siberian crane, may be spotted from a boat trip through the mangroves.
The 16th century church of St Bartholemew.
The adjoining island, Divar – an important place of Hindu pilgrimage.
YOU SHOULD KNOW:
A large Jesuit seminary, now in ruins, was once the home of the Patriarch of Ethiopia.

Lakshadweep Archipelago

POPULATION:
60,595 (2001)
WHEN TO GO:
October to April
HOW TO GET THERE:
Flights from Kochi and Bangalore to Agatti or ferryboat from Kochi.
HIGHLIGHTS:
Seeing India's only true coral atolls, often barely 1.83 m (6 ft) above sea level.
Diving – there are packages for beginners and experienced divers (health certificate required).
Minicoy Island's lighthouse, dating from 1885.
The aquarium on Kavaratti Island.
The unusual walking sticks made of tortoise shells and coconut shells by craftsmen on Amini Island.
YOU SHOULD KNOW:
Marco Polo referred to Minicoy as 'the island of females'.

Though the name means 'hundred thousand islands', there are about 36 islands and islets in this archipelago, which is the smallest union territory of India. Eleven of the group, which lies 200-300 km (125-186 mi) off the coast of Kerala in the Arabian Sea, are inhabited. The total land area is just 32 sq km (12 sq mi) and none of the islands exceeds 1.6 km (1 mi) in width. The islands are coral atolls and reefs, inhabited on the eastern sides and protected by lagoons on the west. Like all 'coral islands', they offer superlative swimming and diving.

The islanders are related to the people of Kerala and the language is Malayalam, except on Minicoy, where both the ethnicity and the language (Mahl) are related to the Maldives. Almost the whole population is Muslim; in the 7th century missionary work and contact with Arab traders persuaded the islanders to convert. From the 12th to the 18th century, when the British took control, the islands were ruled by successive *bibis* ('female rulers') and their husbands, and now it is a matrilinear society where women enjoy unusual economic independence.

The islanders cultivate bananas and vegetables in the rich coral soil, but the mainstay is the coconut. The fibre products, coir and copra, have always been in great demand. Fishing is important, and Minicoy has a tuna-processing plant. The government is now promoting tourism to bolster the economy and Lakshadweep is becoming a popular destination for Indians. Though western visitors – notably Vasco da Gama and Ibn Batuta – explored extensively in the past, today there are very strict limits for foreign tourists and alcohol is prohibited. The easiest way to see Lakshadweep is by organized tour.

An aerial view of the islands and reefs

Andaman and Nicobar Islands

This large group of over 570 islands – of which around 30 are inhabited – lies in the Bay of Bengal quite close to the Indonesian island of Sumatra, but more than 1,000 km (625 mi) from India, of which it is part. It is thought that the name Andaman derives from the name of the Hindu monkey god Hanuman, as most of the islands' inhabitants are Hindu, though there is a sizeable Christian minority. At present the Nicobars may not be visited and access to some of the Andamans is restricted.

The penal colony at the capital Port Blair on South Andaman became notorious in 1872 after the murder of the Viceroy. It lasted until Independence in 1947. Since then, mass immigration from India and developing tourism have effected change. Though the high rainfall and humidity make malaria a risk, and the best beaches are on islands remote from Port Blair, the crystal clear waters and abundance of natural life make a visit worthwhile. A high percentage of the hundreds of bird, animal and plant species are unique to the islands and the butterflies and moths are among the most spectacular in the world. Beaches are rich in shells and corals.

Some of the many islands that can be visited from Port Blair are Interview Isle with its population of feral elephants (left there by loggers), Havelock Isle, settled by Bengalis after Partition, with mangrove swamps and superb snorkelling and Viper Isle, which was once home to several prominent political prisoners, including Subhar Chandra Bose. India's only active volcano can be seen on Barren Isle. On Ross Island the buildings and gardens of the old British administration are deserted.

POPULATION:
356,265 (2005)
WHEN TO GO:
November to May
HOW TO GET THERE:
Flights or ferry boats from Kolkata and Chennai to Port Blair.
HIGHLIGHTS:
The Cellular Jail National Memorial at Port Blair, which now has a museum and a Sound and Light show describing its grim history.
Samudrika Naval Maritime Museum – with displays of marine biology and of the flora and fauna as well as information on tribal communities.
Viewing the marine life from glass bottomed boats.
Scuba diving and snorkelling in the Mahatma Gandhi National Maritime Park, which covers 15 islands.
The Mount Harriet nature trail – for the birds, animals, butterflies.
The Island Tourism Festival in January – with lots of music and dancing.
YOU SHOULD KNOW:
Part of the Sherlock Holmes story 'The Sign of Four' is set in the British penal colony; later in the story, an islander, complete with blowpipe and poisoned darts, appears in London.

Elephants enjoying the cooling effects of the sea.

ASIA

Tioman Island

Verdant rainforest covers the interior of the island.

Tioman Island (Pulau Tioman) is a small island around 32 km (19 mi) from Malaysia, one of about 60 volcanic islands situated off the southern shores of Malaysia's east coast. The island, 39 km (24 mi) long and 12 km (7 mi) wide, is densely forested and surrounded by some spectacular beaches and coral reefs, making it a great place for rainforest treks, relaxing on the beach and snorkelling. The island is sparsely inhabited, with eight main villages, the largest being Kampung Tekek in the north.

The island was used by Arabian merchants in the 10th century, as well as merchants from India, Persia and China who came to export betelnut, sandalwood and camphor. In 1830, pirates landed here and took 70 of its inhabitants away as slaves, leaving the island deserted for 15 years. In the 1920s the island was again deserted after a devastating outbreak of malaria swept through the population.

The most popular activity for visitors to Tioman Island today is snorkelling, and some of the best sites include Paya, which offers a variety of colourful corals and fish, Pulau Tulai (Coral Island) and Renggis Island where the water is pristine. At Air Batang there is a vast garden of yellow coral, and turtles can be spotted here.

Already the most developed of Malaysia's eastern islands, Tioman is the site of a $10 million marina project, complete with cargo jetty extending 175 m (574 ft) into the sea at Kampung Tekek. The Malaysian Nature Society and WWF Malaysia have described the project as a disaster for the environment. Construction has already caused the widespread death of corals and much of the marine life around the site, so be sure to choose one of the other beaches for snorkelling and diving.

At Juara, a lovely quiet beach on the east coast of Tioman, three rivers flow down from the mountains and onto the beach, offering a refreshing alternative to swimming in the sea. A path leads from the beach to a series of waterfalls in the jungle where you can swim and climb over the large rocks.

The interior of the island, around 12,000 hectares (29,652 acres) of dense verdant rainforest, is a strictly enforced nature reserve. There are many endemic species here, and among the protected species of mammals are the mouse deer, binturong, black giant squirrel, long-tailed macaque, slow loris, brush-tailed porcupine, red giant flying squirrel and common palm civet. If you are lucky you may spot a soft-shelled turtle or a Tioman walking catfish while in the rainforest.

The beach at Pantai Cenang

Langkawi

Langkawi is the collective name for an archipelago of around 100 islands in the Andaman Sea, close to the north Malaysian coast. Only two are inhabited – Pulau Langkawi, the main island, and Pulau Tuba, and these are islands of rocky mountains, lush jungle and white sandy beaches lapped by green water.

'Langkawi' is sometimes translated as 'Land of Eagles', and you can still see white-bellied fish eagles here. However, the group is more popularly known as the 'Isles of Legends', and the best known of these is of Mahshiri, a beautiful woman falsely accused of adultery. It is said that when executed for this crime, she bled white blood, and cursed the islands for seven generations. Her tomb remains a major tourist attraction.

Curses notwithstanding, Langkawi has seen dramatic economic development in recent years: in 1987 it was designated a tax-free zone and later gained recognition as a UNESCO World Geopark. This combination has resulted in over two million visitors every year. Some of the best hotels in Malaysia are now situated here (this is not a budget destination!), mostly on the western side at Pantai Tenghah and Pantai Cenang, though the north coast is also developed. Despite this growth in tourism, the main town of Kuah retains its fishing heritage and relaxed lifestyle.

Government policy prohibiting beachfront development over coconut-tree-height is both commendable and in keeping with the up-market approach. Tax-free shopping aside, water sports are the major attraction here. Scuba diving and snorkelling are best within the Pulau Payar Marine Park. The interior of the island offers jungle trekking in one of the world's oldest rainforests, which is home to more than 200 bird species.

POPULATION:
60,000 (2005 estimate)
WHEN TO GO:
Year round
HOW TO GET THERE:
Boats from Penang, Kuala Perlis, Kuala Kedah and south Thailand. Flights from Kuala Lumpur, Georgetown, Ipoh, Singapore and Japan.
HIGHLIGHTS:
The cable car ride to the top of Gunung Mat Cinang.
Lagend Lankawi Dalan Taman in Kuah – a 20-hectare (49-acre) theme park with giant sculptures illustrating some of the islands' many legends.
Crocodile Adventure on the north coast – Malaysia's largest crocodile farm, with over 1,500 saltwater crocs.
Telaga Tujuh – the 'Seven Pools' which you can slide down over the moss, preferably stopping before the water cascades over a cliff to form a 90 m (295 ft) waterfall.
The palace built in 1999 for the film *Anna and the King* which you may visit whilst it still stands.
YOU SHOULD KNOW:
The Galeria Perdaria contains a strange collection of over 10,000 items presented to the former Malaysian Prime Minister Dr Mahathir, who has been very influential in promoting Langkawi.

385

Penang

Situated on the north-western coast of the Malay Peninsula at the entrance to the Straits of Malacca, Penang Island covers an area of 292 sq km (112 sq mi). The island is separated from mainland Malaysia by a channel of sea varying between 3 km (1.9 mi) and 13 km (8 mi) wide, and they are linked by the 13.5 km (8.4 mi) Penang Bridge, one of the longest bridges in the world.

The island has the oldest British settlement in Malaysia, which was founded by Captain Francis Light in 1786 while he was searching for a docking place for ships of the East India Company. Captain Light made a treaty with the Sultan of Kedah who gave him permission to colonize the sparsely populated island.

Penang today is a fine mixture of old and new: bustling, industrial port meets historic Old Town. In the capital, Georgetown, modern skyscrapers tower above one of the largest collections of pre-war buildings in south-east Asia. Colourful produce markets compete for space with high-tech electronics manufacturers. There is also a fascinating mixture of cultures here. Hundred-year-old churches, Chinese temples, Indian temples and mosques stand side by side.

In the middle of the bustling modern city is Penang Hill (Bukit Bendera), at almost 900 m (2,953 ft) high, with its cool, clean air. From its summit there are amazing views of the town, the island, and even the mountains on the mainland when the sky is clear. There is a Swiss-built funicular railway to take visitors to the summit, which creaks its way up through the beautiful tropical forest. At the top of the hill there is a café, a Hindu temple and a mosque.

If you want to escape the busy city, there are other attractions on the island, including plenty of lovely beaches, some quaint fishing villages, beautiful stretches of forest and cascading waterfalls. Among the less crowded beaches are Muka Head, Pantai Keracut, Monkey Beach, Pantai Acheh and Gertak Sanggul.

Penang Island is enriched by its numerous ethnic communities, among them Malays, Chinese and Indians, which live side by side in harmony to create a multi-faceted culture. Each community maintains its cultural identity through religious festivals and cultural shows, including angsawan, Boria, flag processions, the Chingay Parade, the Nine Emperor Gods Festival, the Hungry Ghosts Festival and Thaipusam. This succession of colourful festivals unravels throughout the year and when one big celebration is finished, another begins.

A street trader in Penang

POPULATION:
678,000 (2000)
WHEN TO GO:
December to July
HOW TO GET THERE:
Fly to Penang International Airport, or cross the bridge from the mainland.
HIGHLIGHTS:
Penang Hill – trek up the hill or take the funicular railway to experience amazing views of the whole island.
Beaches – among the nicest beaches are Muka Head, Monkey Beach and Pantai Acheh.
Pantai Acheh Forest Reserve – this lowland forest covers most of the north-western tip of Penang Island and hosts a diverse eco-system of forest vegetation, mangrove swamps, rock coast and sandy beaches.
Snake Temple – built in 1850 to commemorate the Chinese monk Chor Soo Kong, the temple is situated in the small town of Bayan Lepas and is famous for the pit vipers which live in the temple.
YOU SHOULD KNOW:
The official religion is Islam, so avoid revealing clothing or displays of affection in public.

Labuan

Labuan consists of a main island and six smaller islands 8 km (5 mi) off the northwest coast of Borneo, north of Brunei Bay. Its name derives from the Malay for 'anchorage' and it is in fact Malaysia's only deep-water port. Once a part of the Sultanate of Brunei, it was ceded to Britain in 1846. During World War II it was occupied by the Japanese, and was finally handed to the Federal Government of Malaysia in 1984.

The ethnic composition is predominantly Malay, with a sizeable Chinese minority and some Indian immigrants and it feels quite cosmopolitan, especially in Bandar Labuan, the main town and port. Its position in the middle of the Asia-Pacific region and close to shipping routes and offshore gas and oil fields prompted the Government to encourage foreign investment, and today Labuan is a free port and International Offshore Financial Centre. As a result, duty free shopping is a great attraction for the many tourists who come from Brunei – there is even a month-long, end of year 'shopping carnival'.

The main island covers 75 sq km (50 sq m) and is essentially flat – the highest point is just 85 m (280 ft) above sea level – and mostly covered in vegetation. There is little agriculture – the best land is used for residential or tourist development or, in the southwest, shipbuilding, manufacturing and oil and gas production.

In addition to shopping, Labuan has some good beaches, notably Pohon Batu and Pancur Hitam. The clear blue waters around the islands are perfect for diving, and also offer marvellous fishing, both deep-sea and around the coasts.

POPULATION:
78,000 (2000 estimate)
WHEN TO GO:
January to March, July and August
HOW TO GET THERE:
By air from Kuala Lumpur and Brunei or by ferry from Sabah, Sarawak and Brunei.
HIGHLIGHTS:
The War Memorial, Allied Landing Point and Japanese Surrender Park. The landscaped cemetery for 3,900 Allied soldiers, maintained by the Commonwealth War Commission, with a special section for the Punjab Regiment.
An Nur Jamek Mosque – an exciting work of modern architecture that cost US $11 million.
Wreck diving – one of the best sites in Asia, with World War II (including USS *Salute*) and post-war wrecks.
Sea sports – each May, the International Sea Challenge comprises an underwater treasure hunt, cross-channel swim, jet sport challenge and big-game fishing tournament.
YOU SHOULD KNOW:
The first Labuan postage stamps (1879) have the usual profile of Queen Victoria, but are highly unusual in incorporating Chinese and Arabic scripts.

Perhentian Islands

POPULATION:
1,100 (2000 estimate)
WHEN TO GO:
March to mid-November
HOW TO GET THERE:
Boats from two fishing villages on the northern Terenggam coast (Air-Kota Bharu airport has taxi desks where transport to the above and boat tickets are available).
HIGHLIGHTS:
Sunbathing, snorkelling, scuba diving and sea kayaking.
Shark and turtle watching (turtles nest on both islands).
Walking the jungle trails that cross both islands.
YOU SHOULD KNOW:
Accommodation is limited and advance booking strongly advised.

This small group of islands lying just 20 km (12.5 mi) off the northeastern Malaysian peninsula, consists of two inhabited islands, Perhentian Besar and Perhentian Kecil (large and small Perhentian), separated by a fast flowing channel, and a few uninhabited ones. The name in Malay means 'stopping point', though British translation had them marked on maps as 'Station Islands'. Sparsely populated by fishermen in the past, tourism is now the islands' mainstay.

These days the local government is keen to preserve the natural beauty of the area – the coral round the islands is some of the best on the east coast and the fine sandy beaches plus crystal clear water have proved a major attraction. In consequence, strict planning restrictions are enforced and a marine park conservation charge levied on all visitors. The three main beaches on the west coast of Perhentian Besar are divided by rocky outcrops. Perhentian Kecil, rapidly losing its previous backpacker image, has prime resorts at Long Beach and Coral Bay.

Apart from the village of Pasir Hantu ('Sand of Ghosts') on Kecil, where medical and police aid may be sought, the only island buildings are resorts. There is no mains electricity or main telephone network connection and the water is from local wells. The wearing of revealing clothing and the consumption of alcohol are not encouraged and the only available means of transport, other than walking, is by boat. The interiors reach a maximum of 100 m (328 ft) above sea level and are covered in dense tropical jungle with no roads and few footpaths. However, intrepid walkers may see flying foxes, macaques and monitor lizards.

The fine sandy beach at Pulauin

Pangkor Island

Pangkor is situated off the west coast of peninsular Malaysia, about halfway between Kuala Lumpur and Penang and only 7 km (4.4 mi) across from Lumut. It is a small island being only 8 sq km (3.2 sq mi) but it has an interesting history, having been a major tin producer in the 19th century. Problems within the local Malay/Chinese communities led to the 1874 Pankor Treaty, which ushered in British control in Malaya.

The island has some of the best beaches on this side of the Malay Peninsula and these are situated on the west coast. The east coast mainly consists of fishing villages, whilst apart from a few trails, the interior is largely inaccessible, despite there being a coast-to-coast road.

Fishing, boatbuilding and allied industries employ the majority of the population, with cuttlefish and anchovy being the most common type of catch – their early morning landing at Pangkor town is a bustling, colourful sight. The island is one of Malaysia's largest dry fish suppliers and in addition it is credited with the invention of 'Fish Satay'.

The main beaches are at Teluk Nipah, Pasir Bogak and Teluk Belanga, whilst at Teluk Ketapang ('Turtle Bay') if you are lucky, you might spot the increasingly rare giant leatherback turtles, which lay their eggs here from May to July. Jungle trekking in the interior offers the opportunity to see many rare orchids and butterflies – there is a four-hour trail that crosses the island. For the less energetic, it is possible to follow the road around the island in a day.

The main cultural event is the two-day Hindu festival of Thaipusam, which takes place between mid-February and early March. This begins on the west coast beach of Pasir Bogak and ends at the Pathirakaliaman Temple on the east coast and is worth catching if you can.

POPULATION:
25,000 (2005 estimate)
WHEN TO GO:
Year round
HOW TO GET THERE:
Direct flights from Kuala Lumpur or ferries from Lumut on the mainland.
HIGHLIGHTS:
The remains of the 17th century Dutch fort – situated in a pretty village, which still retains traditional stilted wooden houses.
Batu Bersrat – the Tiger or Written Rock – scene of an old legend, with the symbol of the Dutch East India Company and a depiction of a tiger stealing a child carved upon it.
Foo Lin Kong Temple – containing not only a shrine with shrunken heads but also a mini version of the Great Wall of China behind it.
YOU SHOULD KNOW:
The private island of Pangkor Laut just off the main island is Malaysia's most exclusive hotel, and a favourite with the late Luciano Pavarotti, after whom a suite is named.

The remains of the 17th century Dutch fort

Redang Islands

POPULATION:
2,500 (2006 estimate)
WHEN TO GO:
March to October
HOW TO GET THERE:
Flights from Kuala Lumpur or
Singapore or ferries from Merang.
HIGHLIGHTS:
Learning to dive – Redang offers
diving courses as well as dives for
the experienced.
Turtles – the island is a conservation
site for sea turtles; both the green
and hawksbill nest here.
Forest geckoes – the large spotted
Tokay gecko can grow to over
0.3 m (1 ft) long.
YOU SHOULD KNOW:
The festival of Candat Sotong in April
involves using hand-held lines to
catch squid.

There are nine islands in the Redang Archipelago, which is close to Merang on the coast of Terengganu State. Pulau Redang is popular with Malaysian tourists and those from further afield, and much of the east coast is now taken up with tourist development – even the forest has been cleared to make way for a golf course. Kampung Air ('Water Village') was built by the government in 1976 to rehouse the fishing families displaced by hotel building. Like the old village, it is built on stilts over the water; it houses around 1,200 people. Most of the east coast is now lined with up-market resorts.

The coral reefs around Redang and its satellite islands make up one of Malaysia's marine parks, whose management involves the protection of sensitive ecosystems from the impact of human activity.

Tourists are required to pay a conservation fee on arrival. Jet-skiing and water-skiing are banned to protect the coral, and the only fishing allowed in the park area is by the residents, but Redang offers exceptional diving and snorkelling. Outside the monsoon season, diving visibility is at least 20 m (66 ft) though corals and fish can be clearly seen a few metres from the beach. The reefs, composed of corals of a variety of colours and formations, teem with an extraordinary diversity of marine life, including angelfish, reef shark, squid, lionfish, butterflyfish and batfish. Most diving sites lie off the eastern shore, but it is also possible to snorkel off the southern coast and around the islets of Pulau Piriang and Pulau Ekor Tibu.

Banggi

Malaysia's largest island, with an area of 440 sq km (264 sq mi), Pulau Banggi is off the northeast coast of Sabah. It was finally recognized as belonging to Malaysia, after years of dispute with the Philippine Government. The inhabitants are comprised of Bonngi, who speak a unique form of Bornean dialect, and the Orang Sama, or Sea Gypsies.

Banggi is sparsely populated – there are just fifteen villages, renowned for their traditional tribal tree houses. Visitors may stay at a small Government Rest House, but in other respects there are few concessions to tourism here – there are no shops, TV or Internet access, and travel around the island is difficult.

Banggi is positioned where the Pacific and Indian Ocean biospheres meet and its great ecological significance is enhanced by the fact that the reefs are still undamaged by the destructive fishing methods that have despoiled many other southeast Asian sites. Fortunately, this is recognized, and Banngi is now part of a conservation area that covers a rich mix of habitat – reefs, sea grass, open sea and mangroves – where endangered species such as sea turtle and dugongs live.

Diving from these reefs is particularly rewarding – the water is warm and clear and, as well as many coral-dwelling fish, octopus, giant clams, sponges, crinoids and marine algae can be seen. Projects to improve the living standards of the islanders are also underway; the establishment of a commercial rubber plantation, and 'seaplant farming', an initiative by the University of Malaysia at Sabah for seaweed cultivation, will offer alternative livelihoods to the people of Banggi.

POPULATION:
20,000 (2003 estimate)
WHEN TO GO:
Year round
HOW TO GET THERE:
Ferries from Kudat – but departures are unpredictable
HIGHLIGHTS:
Tun Mustapha Marine Park – the site of the second largest coral reef in Malaysia.
Banggi Environmental Awareness Centre – an educational and information resource situated in the largest settlement at Karakit.

Singapore

POPULATION:
4,550,000 (2007)
WHEN TO GO:
January to May.
HOW TO GET THERE:
Fly to Changi Airport.
HIGHLIGHTS:
The Singapore Art Museum – located on Bras Basah Road in a renovated school house, the museum has 13 galleries and is home to the national art collection of Singapore. It was opened in 1996 and holds over 4,000 works of art.
Walking along the waterfront to Merlion Park – the park offers great views of the city's skyline, and an opportunity to see the famous merlion sculpture, a landmark of the city.
The Jurong Bird Park – one of the biggest bird parks in the world, with over 8,000 birds. See the parrot

On the southern tip of the Malay Peninsula, Singapore is one of the few city-states left in the world. The nation comprises one main island and 62 smaller islands in the mouth of the Singapore River. Since independence in 1965, it has become one of the world's wealthiest countries. Combining skyscrapers and subways, with traditional Chinese, Indian and Malay influences, it is a fascinating melting pot of different cultures, all adding their own distinct character to this bustling city. Add in a tropical climate, world-class food, excellent shopping and vibrant nightlife, and you have a very attractive destination.

In 1819, Sir Thomas Stamford Raffles landed on the island, at the time inhabited by just a few fishermen. He recognized its potential as a strategic trading post on the Spice Route and signed a treaty with Sultan Hussein Shah on behalf of the British East India Company to develop the island. Raffles declared Singapore a free port, with no duties or taxes, so the trading post soon grew into one of Asia's busiest, drawing traders from far and wide. It quickly became a great economic success and a jewel in the British colonial crown. William Farquhar, Raffles' deputy, oversaw a time of rapid growth and immigration, fuelled by a no-restrictions immigration policy. Singapore was made a British crown colony in 1867, answering directly to the Crown. Just 50 years after Raffles arrived on the island, Singapore had a population of 100,000.

The island was taken by the Japanese during World War II but reverted back to British rule in 1945. In 1963 it joined with Malaya, Sabah and Sarawak to form Malaysia, but split again after two years to be an independent republic. Since then the state has seen a dramatic economic boom, owing to both foreign investment and government-led industrialization, which has created a modern economy based on electronics and manufacturing.

Shopping is a national pastime in Singapore, and there is an abundance of shopping malls in the city, particularly around Orchard Road. The low taxes on imports make prices competitive here. With its clean streets and anonymous architecture, Singapore can at first feel blandly modern. But beneath the glitzy surface there is a wealth of multi-cultural diversity as a walk around Chinatown, Little India or Geylang Serai will demonstrate.

circus, the penguin parade and demonstrations with birds of prey. The bird shows are great fun and a perfect way to entertain children.
Sri Mariamman Temple – the oldest Hindu temple in Singapore, the current structure was built in 1862. This colourful and decorative temple has been designated a National Monument by the government.
The food stalls in the hawker centres – here prices are low, hygiene standards are high and the food can be excellent.
The Botanic Gardens – the gardens cover 67 hectares (166 acres) and include the National Orchid Garden, with a collection of more than 3,000 species of orchid.

YOU SHOULD KNOW:
Singlish is commonly spoken on the streets of Singapore, a local dialect which mixes English, Chinese, Malay and Indian words and grammar.

Phuket

POPULATION:
313,835 (2007)
WHEN TO GO:
All year round, but best between
November and May.
HOW TO GET THERE:
By air, bus or rail to Surat Thani and
then bus, or by sea. Phuket is
attached to the mainland by a bridge.
HIGHLIGHTS:
Diving and snorkelling off Phuket.
Yachting and sea canoeing around
the island.
The Sino-Portuguese architecture in
Phuket City.
Ko Sire with its sea gypsy village and
reclining Buddha.
Sirinath National Park.
YOU SHOULD KNOW:
In 1785 Phuket was attacked by
Burmese troops, in part of an
attempt to take control of the
country. The governor died and the
island would have been taken but for
his widow and her sister, who
disguised Phuket's women as men
and attacked the Burmese. Thinking
that Phuket had received
reinforcements, the Burmese
withdrew. King Rama 1 bestowed
royal titles on the sisters and their
action is remembered by the
Heroine's Monument, located at a
roundabout on the main highway.

Thailand's largest and arguably most popular island, Phuket, lies in the Andaman Sea, off the west coast of southern Thailand, and is a province in its own right. In December 2004 the island was devastated by the tsunami that hit so much of Asia, and many coastal resorts and villages suffered terribly. Fortunately, Phuket is a wealthy province, and today, thanks to a major re-building programme, the island is back in business, and visitors are unlikely to see any noticeable damage.

Phuket is largely mountainous, its highest point being Mai Thao Sip Song at 529 m (1,745 ft), and much of it is forested. From the 16th century until relatively recently, tin mining was important to the economy, and the culture of the Chinese workers has informed that of Phuket. Other influences include Portuguese and Islam – some 35 per cent of the population are Muslims.

Phuket has been known as a holiday island since the 1980s, and its beaches sprout new resorts, restaurants and dive operations with every passing year. Most of the best beaches – huge swathes of white sand, or little sheltered coves – are on the west coast, but those towards the northern tip are much less visited. Patong, the most popular, is very highly developed, and Phuket City is awash with tourists shopping and partying the night away.

The island's interior is worth exploring, with rubber plantations, rice fields and fruit groves providing employment for islanders who live traditionally, a world away from the international tourism scene. Khao Phra Thaeo National Park, just 20 km (12.5 mi) from Phuket City, is a must – its hills and valleys are covered with tropical rainforest, and it contains a Lar gibbon rehabilitation centre. These charming creatures are endangered, and this project is important to their survival.

One of the many fabulous beaches on Phuket

Ko Phi Phi

Some 40 km (25 mi) from Krabi, off Thailand's south western coast, Ko Phi Phi is a group of limestone islands that jut sharply from the surrounding turquoise sea. Phi Phi Don is both the largest and the only one with a permanent population. Phi Phi Leh is much visited but uninhabited. The remaining islets are little more than limestone rocks.

Phi Phi Don divides into two sections joined by a narrow isthmus, on either side of which are two superb sweeps of white sand. It is startlingly beautiful with green hills culminating in astonishing cliffs plunging down to the water, many glorious beaches and unparalleled views. The islands are part of a National Marine Park, which should, though does not, protect them from the worst excesses of the developers.

During the 1940s, Phi Phi Don was populated by Muslim fishermen, and even now a good 80 per cent of the inhabitants are Muslims. Later, coconut plantations were introduced, but by the 1970s travellers had got wind of this remote and delicious paradise, and a fledgling tourist industry grew up. The good news is that as diving and snorkelling are so popular, the fishermen no longer use dynamite, and the surrounding coral is in better shape than it might be. Conversely, attempts to limit the numbers of tourists and tourist facilities, to better preserve the nature of the place, have failed due to greed.

Phi Phi Leh is all towering cliffs, caves and a sea lake. Tourists visit for the day to swim, but it is also famed as a centre of the birds' nest soup industry. Swiftlets nest high up in rocky hollows, and licenced collectors climb rickety-looking scaffolding three times a year to harvest these nests, made of saliva, which are as desirable and valuable to the Chinese as white truffles are to Europeans.

A beach on Ko Phi Phi Don

POPULATION:
1,500 (2006)
WHEN TO GO:
November to April
HOW TO GET THERE:
By boat from Phuket or Krabi.
HIGHLIGHTS:
On Phi Phi Don: Rock climbing. Sea kayaking. Game fishing. Snorkelling with sharks.
Viking Bird Nest Cave, with prehistoric wall paintings and nests on Phi Phi Leh.
The Beach – the actual beach made famous by the eponymous film starring Leonardo di Caprio.
YOU SHOULD KNOW:
Phi Phi Don was shattered by the 2004 tsunami. Over 70 per cent of the buildings were destroyed, about 4,000 people were drowned, survivors were evacuated and the island was closed. Help International Phi Phi was set up by a former (Dutch) resident and with the help of both Thais and back-packing volunteers cleared 23,000 tons of debris, 7,000 tons of it by hand. A second organization cleared debris from the bays and reefs and one year later 1,500 hotel rooms were back in action.

Ang Thong Archipelago

POPULATION:
100,000 (2004) over the 6 inhabited islands
WHEN TO GO:
December to February, August and September
HOW TO GET THERE:
Boat from Ko Samui
HIGHLIGHTS:
Ko Pha-Ngan and Ko Tao are two of the most beautiful islands. Take a sea-kayaking trip or snorkel around the coral reefs.
The salt water lake on Ko Mae Ko – its well worth the walk up to view the lake.
The views from the top of Wua Talap Island of the whole archipelago and across the mainland.
YOU SHOULD KNOW:
Access to the National Park is controlled. Several boat rental companies in Ko Samui are licenced to hire boats to visit the islands.

Bathed in the aquamarine waters of the Gulf of Thailand about 30 km (20 mi) from Ko Samui, the Ang Thong Archipelago is a collection of 42 uninhabited islands famed for their natural beauty. The islands have been designated a National Marine Park to save them from development and excessive tourism, making them a pleasant and relaxing place to visit. The best way to explore is by boat as most of the islands are close together. Each island is different, but they are characterized by limestone cliffs, tropical forest, caves and secret lagoons, pristine white sand beaches, coral reefs and aquamarine waters.

Ko Mae Ko (Mother Island) is a must-see. Encircled on all sides by limestone cliffs, the emerald lake in the middle of the island is linked to the sea by an underground tunnel. It's a strenuous climb to view the lake but well worth the effort as you gaze down on the stunningly beautiful water and are rewarded by a spectacular view across the whole park.

Other popular islands are Ko Sam Sao (Tripod Island) with its extensive coral reef and Wua Talap Island (Sleeping Cow Island), the summit of which offers magnificent views across the entire archipelago and the mainland. The headquarters of the national park are situated here, and there is bungalow-style accommodation for visitors. There are caves in many of the islands with intriguing rock formations to discover. The lovely white sandy beaches, many of them deserted, are surrounded by coral reefs and the warm shallow waters are ideal for swimming. Other popular island activities include sea-kayaking and snorkelling around the coral reefs.

Ang Thong National Marine Park

Ko Lanta Yai

Situated off the coast of south-west Thailand, between the mainland and the Phi Phi islands, is another, less well known archipelago, Ko Lanta. Made up of 52 islands, 12 of which are inhabited, with only three of them easily accessible. Of these, Ko Lanta Yai is the largest, at 30 km (19 mi) long by 6 km (4 mi) wide. There are two main towns – Ban Sala Dan on the northern tip and Ban Ko Lanta, the district capital, in the east. This has bars, restaurants and shops, but remains a laid back, friendly place. Situated around the coast are several other villages and small resorts linked by a cement road.

Some of the archipelago is part of a National Marine Park; however Ko Lanta Yai is only partially protected, as much of the island belongs to the Chao Naam (sea gypsies) who settled here long ago. Fishing and tourism are mainstays of the economy and in the hilly interior, rubber trees, cashews and bananas are grown. Towards the south, pockets of forest still exist, though not for long if the developers have their way. For now, though, tourism is still less developed than it might be.

Visitors come for sun and sea, and the best beaches run all the way down the west coast of the island, virtually uninterrupted. Offshore there are coral reefs to marvel at and there is good diving just a boat ride away. The atmosphere on Ko Lanta Yai is less frenetic than that of Ko Phi Phi or Phuket, and development is slower. The joys of this place are simple – long walks on the beach, lazy days spent swimming, eating delicious seafood, reading, or snoozing in a comfortable hammock.

POPULATION:
20,000 over the 12 inhabited islands (2006)
WHEN TO GO:
November to March to avoid the monsoon.
HOW TO GET THERE:
By ferry from the mainland, Phuket or Ko Phi Phi.
HIGHLIGHTS:
Ban Sangka-U, a traditional Muslim fishing village.
Tham Mai Kaew, a series of limestone caverns.
A boat trip to Ko Rok Nok and Ko Rok Nai.
A night on tiny Ko Bubu.
YOU SHOULD KNOW:
Ko Lanta Yai escaped relatively lightly from the 2004 tsunami, losing 11 people. Tourists on the island at the time set about helping with the clean up, and most businesses were fully operational within just a few days.

A plantation of coconut palms alongside Klong Khong Beach

The Full Moon Party

Ko Pha Ngan

The now notorious Ko Pha Ngan is an island in the Gulf of Thailand, about halfway between Ko Samui, to the south, and Ko Tao, to the north. Twenty years ago the island received just a tiny trickle of backpackers looking for escape from Ko Samui, which already appeared overcooked from a hippy point of view. Today the island is the home of the Full Moon Party, a monthly event that brings thousands of young travellers here to dance the night away.

The island's economy is almost entirely based on tourism, and almost all its beaches are home to little groups of inexpensive bungalows, and ever more trendy resorts, but it is the Hat Rin peninsula at the southeast of Ko Pha Ngan, with beaches to either side, that draws the crowds. The eastern side, Hat Rin Nok, is a long stretch of golden sand beach, backed by coconut trees. Once the site of a few cheap bamboo huts, a couple of cafés and no electricity, it is now lined with restaurants, shops and travel agents, as well as accommodation, and it's become 'traveller town'.

On full moon night everyone takes to the beach, many decorated in UV body paint, to drink and dance to sound systems playing booming house and trance music. And then there are the drugs – despite the heavy penalties that can be incurred, not to mention potential danger to health, drugs are still ubiquitous at this party, as the hospitals can attest.

Ko Pha Ngan is pretty, its hilly, forested interior includes a National Park. Trek up to great look-out points, or cool off under waterfalls if you need a rest. The main town, Thong Sala, is on the west of the island. However, you can choose to stay on a distant, secluded beach, accessible only by boat, and there you may still find a little peace.

Chalok Baan Kao Beach

Ko Tao

Ko Tao is situated a couple of hours boat ride from the mainland, in the Gulf of Thailand. Twenty years ago only the most intrepid of backpackers made it to the island, due to its relative remoteness. Today all that has changed, and Ko Tao has become a major dive centre.

This is a lovely place, all 21 sq km (8 sq mi) of it, and its rocky green interior is bursting with coconut groves. Those not involved with coconuts are either fishermen or in the rapidly expanding tourist trade. There are gorgeous little coves and beaches around the island, some of which are only accessible by boat, but it is the surrounding shallow coral reefs and marine life that are the main attraction here.

Of course you don't have to be a diver to enjoy Ko Tao, but if you are, or have ever wanted to be, this is a great place, and still reasonable, price-wise. The water is clear, the visibility excellent, and you will see a wealth of multi-hued fish and coral even if you stick to snorkelling. Less developed than neighbouring islands, there is still a variety of places in which to stay – everything from basic bamboo beach huts to boutique resorts.

One of the best dive sites is Sail Rock. Shaped like an iceberg, it rises from the sea floor at 40 m (132 ft) and reaches 15 m (50 ft) above the surface, providing fabulous dives for all levels of experience. At certain times of year, you might even get to see a whale shark…

Back on land, there are other activities to occupy your time – elephant rides, rock climbing, yoga, massage and cookery courses. Rent a bike and tour the island using the single existing road, walk, or just find a peaceful spot and laze the days away.

POPULATION:
5,000 (2006)
WHEN TO GO:
December to May
HOW TO GET THERE:
By boat from the mainland, Ko Samui or Ko Pha-Ngan.
HIGHLIGHTS:
Snorkelling at the Japanese Gardens.
Diving at Shark Island.
Diving at Southwest Pinnacle.
Spa treatments at one of the spa resorts.
Learning the martial art of qi gong.
YOU SHOULD KNOW:
Ko Tao literally means Turtle Island – it is thought that the island is shaped like a turtle diving south towards Ko Pha-Ngan.

Ko Samui

Ko Samui, in the Gulf of Thailand, lies some 80 km (50 mi) from the mainland town of Surat Thani. This was the first of the Gulf's islands to receive tourists – backpackers began arriving here about 30 years ago, moving on to Ko Pha Ngan and Ko Tao as the island became more developed. The building of an airport placed Samui firmly into the package holiday niche, leaving Pha Ngan to the partygoers and Tao to the divers.

Apart from tourism, the island is a huge coconut producer, harvesting some three million nuts per month, and palm trees and golden, sandy beaches are the hallmark of the place. At 15 km (9 mi) long and about the same in width, it's impossible not to notice that some of the development back from the beach is pretty nasty. Fortunately new construction cannot be higher than a coconut tree, although large hotel groups seem to get away with it.

Samui tries to cater for everyone, and the individual beaches that lie off the main coastal road do have their different atmospheres. Chaweng and Lamai are the most developed – some would say ruined! Maenam and Bophut are quieter while Choeng Mon, in the north east, is really the classiest, with a few smart hotels round a pretty, tranquil bay.

This is a classic Thai holiday island. People come to swim, snorkel, and wander along the beaches in the daytime, stopping for a bite to eat, a massage, or to have beads braided into their hair. At night there are endless restaurants, bars and clubs to visit, some of which are home to Thai sex trade workers. Ko Samui really does go out of its way to provide tourists with whatever they fancy.

POPULATION:
48,000 (2007)
WHEN TO GO:
Anytime, but it rains most in November.
HOW TO GET THERE:
By ferry from Surat Thani, Ko Pha Ngan or Ko Tao, or by plane from Bangkok, Phuket, Pattaya, Singapore, Hong Kong or Kuala Lumpur.
HIGHLIGHTS:
Bungy jumping at Chaweng beach.
Buffalo fighting.
Thai boxing.
The Butterfly Garden.
A day trip (at least) to the exquisite Ang Thong National Marine Park.
YOU SHOULD KNOW:
The first people to settle here were Chinese from Hainan Island, a mere 150 years ago. They were responsible for setting up the first coconut palm plantations.

Wat Plai Leam

The Islands of Phang-Nga Bay

Phang-Nga Bay is one of Thailand's most jaw-droppingly beautiful seascapes. Covering some 400 sq km (154 sq mi) tucked in between Phuket and Krabi, the bay, edged with mangrove forests, is home to hundreds of limestone karst formations. Some of these are tiny spires, some are large and bizarrely shaped, reaching up to 300 m (1,000 ft) in height, and all covered in tangled rain forest vegetation.

Formed some 12,000 years ago when the sea rose dramatically, flooding a limestone range that had already been eroded, some of the islands have been hollowed out by the forces of nature, leaving hidden, magical lagoons known as *hongs* in their centres. Invisible from the outside, the *hongs* are accessible by sea canoe, but it's only during certain tides that the channels beneath the seemingly impenetrable rock face are navigable. These secret lagoons are tidal, supporting their own ecosystems, while the enclosing circle of cliff walls are covered with extraordinary vegetation, reminiscent of a prehistoric world.

The central area of the bay boasts fantastically sculpted karst islands, including the famous 'James Bond' island, where *The Man with the Golden Gun* was filmed. A stop here, of course, is part of every itinerary and the souvenir sellers are all there, waiting to pounce. Very few of these islands are inhabited, and even fewer have anywhere to stay.

Ko Panyi is an exception – a Muslim fishing village, mainly built on stilts, it teems with visitors during the daytime, but after they have gone it reverts to relative normality. Here you can rent your own sea canoe, and explore the bay at your leisure. It really is quite something – the cliffs are coloured with red and orange sponges close to the water line, and the scenery is awe-inspiring. Apart from rock climbing, most people come here for water-based activities – sea kayaking, sailing and, above all, fishing.

POPULATION:
700 (2006 estimate)
WHEN TO GO:
December to May for the best weather.
HOW TO GET THERE:
By boat from Phang-Nga town, Phuket or Krabi.
HIGHLIGHTS:
Ko Panak, with its five hidden *hongs*.
Khao Kien, with its ancient rock paintings.
Ban Bor Tor, a long tunnel filled with stalactites and stalagmites.
YOU SHOULD KNOW:
These karst islands are the perfect environment for reptiles, in particular water snakes. Watch out for the water monitor, up to 2.2 m (7 ft) long – they look like crocodiles and haunt the mangrove swamps.

Some of the limestone spires of the islands of Phang-Nga Bay

Ko Chang

POPULATION:
5,000 (2007)
WHEN TO GO:
November to May for the best
weather.
HOW TO GET THERE:
By boat from Laem Ngop, usually via
Trat, which also has a small airport
with flights from Bangkok and
Ko Samui.
HIGHLIGHTS:
The waterfall at Klong Nueng.
The hornbills, sunbirds, parrots and
other birds among the 61 resident
species.
Visit Ko Kut, Ko Maak and Ko Wai,
islands accessible from Ko Chang.
Travel to Cambodia, only 91 km
(57 mi) north west of Trat.
YOU SHOULD KNOW:
Ko Chang was the site of a naval
battle between the Royal Thai Navy
and the Vichy French in January
1941, during which the Thais were
trounced. There is a memorial on Hat
Sai Yao (Long beach) marking this
battle that gave rise to today's naval
presence on Ko Chang.

Ko Chang is the largest of the 52-island archipelago that makes up the Mu Ko Chang National Marine Park. It is also Thailand's second largest island, after Phuket. At 30 km (19 mi) long and 14 km (9 mi) wide, it is no surprise that it is developing into a premier tourist destination, drawing both Thais and foreigners.

Less than a decade ago the island was well off the beaten track, but all that has changed, and today the west coast, strung with sandy beaches, is also strung with beach resorts and bungalows. A coastal road runs around the island, which is mountainous and densely forested in the interior – the highest point, Khao Salak Phet, reaches 743 m (2,500 ft) in height. Treks can be arranged, on foot or by elephant (Ko Chang means Elephant Island), and there are waterfalls in which to swim and magnificent scenery to enjoy.

The island's east coast has been saved from development by its lack of sandy beaches, and here life goes on in its traditional form, with tiny fishing villages, rubber and palm plantations, and fruit orchards. The National Park office can be found at Than Mayom, and the villages of Bang Bao and Salak Phet, on the south coast are both reasonably calm spots in which to stay – the former being the jumping off point for the archipelago's other islands.

Many visitors come to Ko Chang for diving and snorkelling, both of which are very rewarding here, although not as spectacular as the dive sites in the Andaman Sea. If you're looking for a fun, active, beach holiday, with plenty of nightlife, you needn't look further than Hat Sai Khao (White Sand Beach). Fringed by palms and casuarinas, this is Ko Chang's longest and most commercialized beach. For the other extreme, try Hat Sai Yao in the far south.

Hat Sai Khao

Ko Samet

Ko Samet, in the Gulf of Thailand, some 200 km (125 mi) south east of Bangkok, is a favourite holiday island for both Thais and foreigners alike. A mere 30-minute boat trip from the mainland, Ko Samet is quite easily reached from Bangkok, and its famous, white powder sand beaches have made it popular with everyone – families, backpackers, package holiday tourists, even working girls from Pattaya in need of a rest.

Declared a National Park in 1981, the island should have been protected from development, but in reality all the accessible beaches around this 6 km (4 mi) long island have resorts, beach bungalow operations, restaurants and bars lining the sand. Most of the development is on the east and north eastern side, while the most up-market resorts are at the northern tip, the west and the south. Outside the park, the only village, Na Dan, where the boats arrive, is where most of the population live.

The island's interior is quite different – mountainous and covered with dense rainforest, it shelters gibbons, long tailed macaques, monitor lizards, fruit bats, hornbills and many gorgeous butterflies. There are a few tracks cross the central ridge from east to west, but otherwise this at least is left in its natural state. It's worth trekking across though, for great cliff-top views and, of course, magnificent sunsets.

Hat Sai Kaew, or Diamond Beach, is the closest beach to the ferry pier, and at 780 m (2,600 ft) long, is an amazing swathe of sand. Soft and white, its high silicon content makes it squeak underfoot and obviously, it is extremely popular. If you walk south you'll find a mermaid statue, placed here in recognition of the 19th century epic poem written by one of Thailand's greatest poets, Sunthorn Phu, and partly set on Ko Samet.

POPULATION:
1,000 (2005 estimate)
WHEN TO GO:
Pleasant at almost any time of year, September and October bring the most rain.
HOW TO GET THERE:
By road to Ban Phe, then boat to Ko Samet.
HIGHLIGHTS:
Swimming, snorkelling and fishing off the island.
Watch a fire show at Ao Phai beach.
YOU SHOULD KNOW:
Don't buy anything from the touts at Ban Phe pier. Buy single ferry tickets to the beach you're aiming for and find accommodation once you have arrived – easiest on a weekday. Beware mosquitoes and petty theft.

Hat Sai Kaew

Ko Tarutao

Ko Tarutao is the largest of the 51 mainly uninhabited islands of Ko Tarutao National Marine Park. One of the least visited or developed of Thailand's islands, it is also one of the most glorious, if tranquillity and utter simplicity are what you are after. You won't find beach bars and boom-boxes here.

Rising just north of the marine border with Malaysia, Ko Tarutao, which means old, mysterious and primitive in the Malay language, is about 24 km (15 mi) long and 11 km (7 mi) wide. Mountainous and covered in primary, semi-evergreen rainforest, its highest point reaches 708 m (2,300 ft). While the west coast has pristine beaches stretching along almost its entire length, the rest of the coastline consists of mangrove swamps, and the limestone rock that forms the north and south east of the island is riddled with caves gouged out over millennia by the tumultuous force of the sea.

The park's headquarters are at Ao Pante, in the north west of the island, and it is here that you land. This is the main hive of activity, with a few bungalows run by the park authorities, a small shop, library and restaurant, as well as a visitor centre. There are three or four other beaches on the island where you can stay, and camping on the beach is also possible, for a small fee.

A 12 km (7.5 mi) road connects Ao Pante to Ao Taloh Wow in the east, built by prisoners during the 1930s and 40s. This and other trails weave through the forest, a marvellous experience enabling you to see quantities of birds, including three types of hornbill. Wildlife thrives here, and in the surrounding seas there are dugong, dolphins and sea turtles as well as about 25 per cent of the world's fish species.

Tranquil Ko Taruto is covered in primary semi-evergreen rainforest.

Ko Si Chang

Situated in the north of the Gulf of Thailand lies the small, rocky island of Ko Si Chang. While it may not be the best of the Thai islands, it has two huge advantages. It is little known, even by Thais, and it is the closest place you can reach from Bangkok if you need sea and sand, but have only a couple of days.

A 45-minute ferry journey from the coastal town of Sri Racha brings you to the island's one small town, dominated by a brightly painted, multi-tiered Chinese temple, reached by a long flight of steep steps. The best way to see the island is to take a motor bike *samlor*. Your driver will tour the island with you, waiting while you visit the various sights, and even allow you a few hours at the island's best beach.

The main sight here is Rama V's palace and grounds, built in the late 19th century for the recuperation of sickly members of the royal family. Just a few of the buildings still stand, and only the foundations of the actual palace remain – the King moved the golden teak building to Bangkok, where it is now the much visited Vimanmek Palace. The gardens are lovely: linked ponds are shaded by ancient frangipani trees, and stone steps lead to balustraded terraces. Four wooden villas, fronting the sea, house various displays and historic photographs.

There are several places in which to stay, and plenty of places in which to eat scrumptious fresh seafood. The main beach is rather small, but the water is turquoise in colour, clear as glass and fabulous for swimming. Tourists are surprisingly few, most just come for the day, and the island is calm and quiet – just what you need if you've been in Bangkok for a while.

Wat Atsadangnimit, Rama V's meditation chamber

POPULATION:
4,500 (2006)
WHEN TO GO:
November to April for the least rain.
HOW TO GET THERE:
By ferry from Sri Racha.
HIGHLIGHTS:
Tham Saowapha, a large, limestone cave.
Visakha Puja festival each May.
King Chulalongkorn's Birthday festival, each 20 September.
The panorama from the Khao Khat headland at sunset.
Sri Racha town for its excellent markets, delicious food, curiously charming exercise park and its lack of westerners.
Wat Tham Yai Prik meditation centre, a wonderful experience for Buddhists and non-believers alike.
YOU SHOULD KNOW:
Ko Si Chang and Sri Racha are close to a deep-sea port and you will see huge numbers of barges waiting to unload as you sit on the ferry. Don't be put off; they don't affect the island or the water around it.

Surin Islands

POPULATION:
150 (2007 estimate)
WHEN TO GO:
The Park is only open from
November to April, due to the
difficult seas.
HOW TO GET THERE:
By pre-booked, live-aboard boat trip
from Phuket or Ranong, or ferry from
Khuraburi. Don't forget there is a fee
to enter all of Thailand's
National Parks.
HIGHLIGHTS:
The Visitor Centre and
interpretive trail.
The turtle hatchery.
The Chao Leh village.
YOU SHOULD KNOW:
The Andaman Sea Chao Leh number
about 5,000 altogether, divided into
five groups with different dialects
and customs. They have been around
for hundreds of years, possibly
originating in the Nicobar Islands.
The Surin group are Moken,
extremely traditional people who live
mainly in houseboats called *kabang*,
and collect shells and sea slugs,
which they trade for food staples.
Animist and musical, the Surin
Moken are suffering horribly since
the 2004 tsunami ruined their boats,
and interference from outsiders has
hindered more than it helped.

The Surin Islands are one of Thailand's least visited destinations. A group of five islands, both they and the surrounding waters form the Mu Ko Surin National Marine Park. Situated in the Andaman Sea, they lie some 55 km (34 mi) from the mainland, just south of the marine border with Myanmar.

The two main islands, Ko Surin Nua and Ko Surin Tai are separated by a narrow – 200 m (660 ft) – strait, which you can walk across at low tide. The other islands are simply rocky crags, with sparse vegetation. Until World War II they were uninhabited, and by 1981, when they became a national park, only a few hundred people lived here and therefore easy to relocate. Today, a few officials man the park office on Surin Nua, and a small community of Chao Leh (sea gypsies) live semi-permanently on Surin Tai.

The Surins are almost completely unspoilt. There are a few places to stay, (or you can hire a tent) and one, park-operated restaurant which rents out diving and snorkelling gear. There are glorious bays, full of marine life and pristine corals, and the islands themselves are spectacular, their summits rising from the sea, several hundred metres high. There are areas of mangrove, beach forest and dense tropical rainforest, all of which provide habitat for some 80 different species, including flying foxes, lesser mousedeer, reticulated pythons and the rare Nicobar pigeon.

Most visitors come on 'live-aboard' boat trips – the Surin Islands are marvellous for snorkelling and diving, and the coral-covered pinnacle of Richelieu Rock is a big draw, with whale sharks occasionally in evidence. If you can cope with the lack of five star facilities, arrange to stay on Surin Nua and relish the sense of remoteness, closeness to nature, and perfect peace broken only by the sound of the sea, the wind, bird and animal calls.

The Surin Moken are a nomadic tribe of sea gypsies who live in huts built on stilts.

Similan Archipelago

Around 70 km from Phang Nga in southern Thailand, an archipelago of nine granite islands rises out of the Andaman Sea. The reefs around the islands, with some of the most stunning underwater scenery in the world, constitute one of the most famous dive sites in Thailand. The Similan Islands – Ko Bon, Ko Bayu, Ko Similan, Ko Payu, Ko Miang (two adjoining islands), Ko Payan, Ko Payang, and Ko Huyong – all fall within the Similan Islands National Park which was created in 1982. The park was recently expanded to include the two more remote islands of Ko Bon and Ko Tachai. Similan is a Malay word meaning nine.

The islands themselves are virtually uninhabited, apart from park rangers and tourists coming here for the diving. In fact, it is forbidden for tourists to land on several of them due to reef conservation efforts, and to protect the beaches where turtles come to lay their eggs. The island of Ko Pa Yan is owned by HM the Thai Princess who has a house there.

The islands offer two sorts of diving. On the eastern sides, which are protected from the monsoon storms, the white sandy beaches and gently sloping reefs provide safe and enjoyable snorkelling territory. The western shores of the islands get the full force of the waves, and here there are craggy granite boulders in amongst the reefs, with lots of swim-throughs, arches and caves up to 30 m (98 ft) deep. Probably the most famous dive site on the western side is Elephant Head rock, a maze of swim-throughs and sudden strong currents running in all directions.

The beautiful corals, sea fans and anemones make this an underwater paradise, which is teeming with marine life in all shapes and sizes. Shoals of vividly coloured fish such as angel fish, butterfly fish and many more swirl around the submerged landscape. The relatively strong currents around the islands keep the reefs clear of sand, making the water clear and visibilty good.

The islands are also an interesting place for keen birdwatchers. pied imperial pigeons, Nicobar pigeons, forest wagtails and white sea eagles are commonly sighted here, and as few species have been officially recorded on the islands, there is potential to add to the list. All the accommodation is on Ko Miang, and consists of small beach-side bungalows and ready-pitched tents, so expect basic facilities in this glorious location.

The reefs around the island contain some of the most stunning underwater scenery in the world.

POPULATION:
Uninhabited
WHEN TO GO:
December to May
HOW TO GET THERE:
By boat from Phuket, Thap Lamu or Hat Khao Lak.
HIGHLIGHTS:
Diving and snorkelling the clear waters around the islands in one of Thailand's most glorious natural landscapes.
Hiking to the top of Ko Similan for breathtaking panoramic views across the archipelago.
The sea turtles at Ko Huyong – they come here to lay their eggs between January and July.
YOU SHOULD KNOW:
An entry fee is payable in cash when you enter the park.

Koh Kong

POPULATION:
No permanent population yet.
WHEN TO GO:
November to April for the least rain.
HOW TO GET THERE:
By road from Phnom Penh,
Sihanoukville, or Thailand to Koh
Kong town, then by boat to Koh
Kong island.
HIGHLIGHTS:
Take a boat trip around the
other islands.
Take a boat trip up the Ta Tai River.
See if you can spot a rare dugong,
once reasonably abundant near
Prek Ksach.
YOU SHOULD KNOW:
There are several other islands near
the town, and some of the best
beaches can be found on nearby Koh
Kapi, where camping is a possibility.

Koh Kong is a confusing destination – it is the name of the province which encompasses both part of mainland Cambodia and many offshore islands; of the provincial capital, also known as Dong Tong or even Krong Koh Kong; and also of the country's largest island, from which the province took its name. Just 80 km (50 mi) south of Thailand's Ko Chang, this once wild region is seeing many more visitors, now that the border crossing with Thailand is open.

Arriving from Thailand, a boat trip across the river to the town of Koh Kong had many people thinking they were on an island already – the new connecting bridge may prevent this misapprehension. Koh Kong island itself, a boat ride away, is 22 km (14 mi) long and 7 km (4 mi) wide, and as yet remains undeveloped. Unsurprisingly, the Cambodian government plans to make it an international tourist resort, but at present it is a peaceful paradise of empty beaches, coconut palms, forested hills and waterfalls that vary between 6 m (20 ft) and 25 m (82.5 ft) high. Dolphins regularly visit the island's six beaches, both morning and afternoon. If you come prepared, it is possible to camp here, and soon there will be bungalow operations and simple mod cons to make life easier.

Arrange a trip to the island from Koh Kong town, where you will probably be based. A reasonably large town with a population of 22,000, there are plenty of places to stay here, and some lovely country nearby. This close to Thailand, the Thai Baht is common currency, and most people drink Thai beer rather than Cambodian. If you are travelling in either direction, try to allocate a few days here – one day you'll be able to say you knew Koh Kong Island in all its natural glory.

Koh Sdach

POPULATION:
2,500 (estimate)
WHEN TO GO:
November to April
HOW TO GET THERE:
By ferry en route to or from
Koh Kong or Sihanoukville.
HIGHLIGHTS:
The simple delights of staying on an
unspoilt island.
YOU SHOULD KNOW:
Koh Sdach means King's Island.
Legend has it that a king and his
army took refuge here after battling
with foreign invaders. Finding no
source of fresh water, the king
summoned the powers of the gods
and a spring magically appeared. It
can still be seen, near the dock.

Koh Sdach is a small island that lies in the Gulf of Thailand. As yet virtually 'undiscovered' – you'll find barely a mention in most guidebooks – it is also little known by Cambodians, so those travellers who arrive here receive a genuine welcome. Even this part of mainland Cambodia is undeveloped, as it is divided from the rest of the country by the impenetrable jungle of the Cardamom Mountains.

The island's only settlement is clustered around the rickety wooden dock at which the boat between Sihanoukville and Koh Kong, the entry to Thailand, drops off goods and passengers. Prior to the Pol Pot regime, only seven families lived here, but the village grew after liberation in 1979, and now a mixture of Khmers, Vietnamese and a few Thais live here.

About 70 per cent of the working population are fishermen, but the island seems to be run by a Thai, who owns the two other existing industries here, an ice plant and a sawmill, as well as shops and a guesthouse. The buildings are mainly wooden, some on stilts over the water, and there are shops, pool parlours and little restaurants that turn into video houses at night. Footpaths meander between coconut palms and banana plantations, and on the far side of the hill that overlooks the town, the beaches are sandy and deserted, backed by lush, flowering vegetation, and trees laden with colourful tropical fruits. If you are happy to interact almost entirely with the local population, try to visit soon – the government plans to make a marine reserve and resort here and this is the sort of place that could easily be turned into Cambodia's answer to Thailand's Ko Samet.

Koh Russey

In the Gulf of Thailand, to the south of Sihanoukville, lies a group of islands known as the Ream Group. Most of them are barely inhabited – just a fishing family or two, living in picturesque poverty, in sun-faded, rickety wooden huts on stilts over the water. These stereotypical tropical islands, are the type that made Thailand into a major player on the tourism stage. Koh Russey, or Bamboo Island, is an exception – until a few years ago the island was the site of a small naval base, but now it has been opened up and several bungalow operations have started.

Tourism may be in its infancy here, but for some this is just the moment to come – the aura of undeveloped remoteness, combined with a very few, charming beach bungalows, with small attached restaurant/bars in which to drink sugar cane juice and eat delicious barbecued seafood. There is very little to do here except relax and enjoy yourself. The island is ringed with pale beige, sandy beaches, lapped by slow, turquoise waves, flanked by tall, leaning palms and notable for the lack of other people. Here you can walk, picking up seashells as you go, keeping an eye open for sea eagles and dolphins. Snorkel the coral reefs in secret coves, but only if you've brought your own gear – there's nowhere to rent it.

Narrow shady paths weave through the jungle-clad interior, leading to even more empty beaches on the other side. Hibiscus, bougainvillea, and great stands of bamboo abound. Take a boat and visit some of the other islands nearby. In the evening you might have light from a generator, but sitting round a fire on the beach, listening to the cicadas and the sound of the sea, it seems like heaven on earth.

POPULATION:
50 (estimate)
WHEN TO GO:
Any time, but between November and February the sea is more difficult to navigate.
HOW TO GET THERE:
By boat from Sihanoukville or Ream National Park.
HIGHLIGHTS:
The Russian guns, still in place on Koh Russey.
Ream National Park on the mainland.
Sihanoukville city.
YOU SHOULD KNOW:
Take everything with you – mosquito repellant, sunscreen, etc – you won't be able to buy it here.

Koh Rong

POPULATION:
50 (estimate)
WHEN TO GO:
Anytime, but the sea is more difficult
to navigate between November and
February.
HOW TO GET THERE:
By boat from Sihanoukville or
Koh Sdach.
HIGHLIGHTS:
Koh Rong Samloen, with its beautiful
beaches and heart-shaped bay.
A boat trip around the island.
Ream National Park on the mainland.

The Kampong Som Islands are another small group lying off Sihanoukville on the Cambodian coast, and Koh Rong, 44 km (27.5 mi) out to sea, is not only the largest of these, but also the second largest of Cambodia's islands. It does see a handful of visitors, mainly day-trippers from the mainland, but occasionally somebody stays and camps on one of the pristine beaches. This happy state of affairs is going to change over the next few years, as plans are afoot to turn both Koh Rong and its neighbouring island into major resorts.

In the meantime, this is pure Robinson Crusoe territory. Shaped like a dumbbell, the narrow 'waist' is flat, but both ends are mountainous and covered in thick, impenetrable jungle. On the southwest of the island is one of the world's most staggeringly beautiful beaches. Some 8 km (5 mi) of almost painfully bright

white sand curves gently into the distance, sand so fine that it lies in drifts and crunches underfoot, and fresh water streams down from the steeply forested hills. At one end is a fishing village, where basic supplies can be bought and a small, wooden temple stands on the southwestern point. The first set of beach bungalows for visitors are going up near here.

The abundance of fresh water feeds several mangrove forests around the coastline, but take a boat and you will find other empty coves and beaches to explore. Apart from the fantastic swimming and snorkelling, there are a couple of dive sites nearby – trips to these can be arranged on the mainland. If you are camping, come with friends if you like being sociable. Alternatively you can lie on the sand, looking up at the spectacular night sky, and muse on our wonderful world.

YOU SHOULD KNOW:
Don't attempt to venture inland – not only does illegal logging take place, but the jungle is home to cobras and other poisonous snakes. There are unfriendly rottweilers at the fishing village, but the villagers themselves are perfectly friendly.

One of Koh Rong's staggeringly beautiful beaches

411

Si Phan Don

POPULATION:
1,800 (estimate)
WHEN TO GO:
November to February
HOW TO GET THERE:
By air to Pakse, then by road, or by
boat down river from Pakse or
Champasak, or overland
from Cambodia.
HIGHLIGHTS:
Don Khon's boat racing festival, each
December.
Tat Somphamit rapids off Don Khon.
Kon Phapheng waterfall.
Taking a boat trip around the islands
and seeing if you can spot an
Irrawaddy dolphin.
YOU SHOULD KNOW:
Your best chance to see one of the
white Irrawaddy dolphins is in
April/May, but they are extremely
rare now; in fact they may not be
there at all any more. If you see one,
you should report it.

Si Phan Don

Deep down in the far south of Laos, the Mekong River fans out to a maximum width of 14 km (9 mi), within which area is the archipelago of rocks, sandbars, islets and islands known as Si Phan Don, or Four Thousand Islands.

Three of the islands not only have a permanent population but also a trickle of tourists. Though it remains a largely unspoilt and unchanged part of Laos, the border crossing with Cambodia will doubtless bring more and more visitors this way, and other islands will become available to stay on. The Mekong is all-important of course, both as the main source of protein, fish, and because its silt-rich waters fertilize the land.

Don Khon is the largest and most developed of the three, with two main villages and several small settlements clinging to the riverbanks, all connected by a coastal road. The interior of the island is agricultural, mainly rice paddies, but it is also home to several ancient Buddhist temples, dating back to around the 7th century. The most interesting of these is probably Wat Phou Khao Kaew, with its carved wooden Burmese sculptures and lovely, gently disintegrating brick stupa. Don Khon and Don Det are joined by a bridge, and are small enough to explore on foot. The former has

more genuine village life to enjoy while the latter is becoming a favourite haunt of the backpacking fraternity.

Scenically, these are all utterly delicious islands, picture postcard perfect. Sugar and coconut palm fronds shade the paths; once in a while you'll stumble upon a picturesque, down-at-heel, old French colonial villa, garlanded with plumeria trees and you might see a canoe carrying saffron-robed monks, umbrellas raised against the sun. Swim in the river, splash in the waterfalls, stay in simple but charming guesthouses, and recharge your batteries before moving on.

Whale Island

At the point where Vietnam bulges furthest east into the aquamarine South China Sea, the Hon Gom peninsula of virgin sand dunes and wild grasses curls round Van Phong Bay. Between April and July, the ocean currents make it a natural trap for huge masses of krill and plankton, and an invitation to migrating sperm and blue whales, and whale sharks, to pause and feed. Whale Island, in the middle, is the best place from which to see them.

Most of the time, Whale Island is an ordinary tropical paradise. Uninhabited until 1997, it still has no cars or motorbikes, ordinary mobile phones don't work, and the only buildings are the 23 traditional bungalows set into the dense foliage between the palm trees fringing the perfect beach. The facilities are basic, but visitors come here in the hope of merging seamlessly with the natural, marine world all around.

It's perfect for children, hopeless romantics, and experienced divers. Snorkelling and diving from the beach opens the door on an amazing marine landscape: the corals begin less than 30 m (100 ft) from the bungalows, and are heavily populated by seahorses, morays, frogfish, devil, stone, pipe and leaf scorpionfish among many others in the exceptionally clear waters. In fact Van Phong Bay is so protected that diving is possible from January to October, and from Whale Island the dive sites can be really spectacular. Hon Trau Nam (Three Kings) is named for three rock pinnacles that break the surface of the sea. At a depth of 20 to 35 m (70 to 120 ft) you discover a fantasy of yellow, white and purple soft corals and gorgonians, camouflage for shoals of outrageously patterned fish.

Or you can stroll, swim, or laze in a hammock watching parrots and fish eagles – until the day's catch is ready to eat as the sun sets in glory.

POPULATION:
Uninhabited (apart from resort staff)
WHEN TO GO:
January to October
HOW TO GET THERE:
By car/mini bus, from Nha Trang airport or rail station, to Vangia wharf at Dam Mon; then by boat to Whale Island.
HIGHLIGHTS:
White Rock dive site – sheer walls drop 40 m (135 ft) from the surface, with several massive pinnacles of soft corals and nudibranchs. The bottom is covered in gorgonians and black coral trees, and black rays rest on the open sandy patches.
The rare fire urchin shrimps (among other unusual invertebrates and fish species) at the 18 m (50 ft) level of Bai Su dive site – and at the upper level (up to 10 m, 34 ft), a pure coral garden of many hard and soft species is ideal for snorkelling.
Birdwatching.
The amazing sunsets.

Cat Ba, Ha Long Bay

POPULATION:
13,500 (2007)
WHEN TO GO:
Year-round
HOW TO GET THERE:
By bus/car from Hanoi or Haiphong to
Ha Long City, then by water-taxi or
tour boat to Cat Ba town.
HIGHLIGHTS:
Getting there – wind and sea have
carved Ha Long Bay's karst stacks into
fantastic shapes, evoked by names
like Kissing Rocks, Wallowing Buffalo,
and Fighting Cock.
Exploring the tunnels and grottoes of
Khe Sau and Gia Luan cave systems.
The floating village of Cua Van – a
fishing community of over 700 people
in 176 floating households, including
schools and shops.
Contemplating the visual haiku of a
red-sailed junk in the deep blue of Lan
Ha Bay.
Hiring a small boat to swim in any of
the deserted sandy coves and marine
grottoes of Cat Ba and its immediate
islets.
YOU SHOULD KNOW:
In 1288 General Tran Hung Dao
prevented a Mongol invasion by
placing steel-tipped wooden stakes at
high tide in the nearby Bach Dang
River, and sinking the Mongol Dubhai
Khan's fleet.

*Ha Long Bay translates as 'Bay
of the Descending Dragon'.*

Ha Long Bay, 170 km (103 mi) from Hanoi, blends earth, sea and sky into one of the world's most iconic beauty spots. Cat Ba, the biggest of a mini archipelago of 366 islands, typifies the spectacular rock relief and bizarre rock formations of the Ha Long World Natural Heritage Reserve: 2,000 large and small islands with cliffs towering a sheer 50-100 m (170-340 ft) from the shallow sea.

Cat Ba's mountainous interior is covered by tropical moist limestone forest, but its spectacular scenery also includes coral terraces, sandy beaches, freshwater wetlands, tidal flats, mangrove forests and willow swamp. Archaeological evidence shows farmers and fishermen have lived here for 6,000 years, but have only recently discovered that the island's dramatic biodiversity is itself a major source of income. Cat Ba's 1986 designation as a UNESCO Man and Biosphere Reserve – the first in Vietnam to include both terrestrial and marine ecosystems – includes them as well as the many rare species of plant, mammal and bird for which it is a refuge.

Cat Ba is an immensely popular destination for short breaks, but most visitors remain near the hotels and bars lining Cat Ba town's waterfront strip, the lively beaches of Cat Co and Cat Dua, or the floating hotel boats moored in Cai Beo Bay. The wooded limestone hills beyond, riddled with jungle caves and stalactite-filled grottoes, and dozens of deserted coves, gateways to a marine wonder-world, promise much greater mystery and adventure. Besides the golden-headed or Cat Ba langur, for which the island is the last sanctuary on earth, you might see the rhesus macacque, the southern serow, leopard cat, oriental giant squirrel, sea-eagle and massed formations of butterflies. And every time you raise your eyes, you can gaze at the marvel of Ha Long Bay, a natural sculpture on a gigantic scale.

Phu Quoc

Phu Quoc is a showcase of the complex forces challenging Vietnam's most precious, pristine environments. Despite being Vietnam's biggest island, its proximity to Cambodia, only 15 km (9 mi) away, has restricted almost all development of its wild beauty. There's still a military presence, but its beaches and mountain forests are completely unspoiled. Phu Quoc is shaped like a long teardrop, and lies deep in the Gulf of Thailand. Though most of it, and its offshore waters, is protected as a National Park, its remoteness and tranquillity, and above all its long strands of perfect beach have now attracted sufficient attention to interest big money developers.

There is very little infrastructure for visitors, even in the main towns. Duong Dong, halfway up the western coast, is a pleasant, unremarkable seaport with several 'nuoc mam' (fish sauce) factories (and Dinh Cau, a temple to the Whale God, full of skeletons of whales and other marine mammals used by cult devotees). An Thoi, a fishing town in the south, is noisier and fishier. Between are beaches like Bai Kem (Ice Cream Beach), a stretch of dazzling white coral sand comparable with the Seychelles, or the coconut palm-fringed infinity of Long Beach, on the west coast and the only place in Vietnam you can see the sun set on an ocean horizon. Inland you can follow the paths through pepper and cashew plantations until the dense rainforest closes in. Along the east coast, it's so thick that it's difficult to reach the empty beaches. The islanders want to open it all up, with a target of two million visitors by 2020. They have discontinued using dynamite for fishing, but so far don't agree that wholesale tourism could be equally damaging to what still is, ecologically and economically, a priceless virgin slice of Vietnam.

POPULATION:
70,000 (2007)
WHEN TO GO:
November to May (the daily short, intense showers from June to October are more refreshing than irritating)
HOW TO GET THERE:
By air, from Ho Chi Minh City or Rach Gia, to Duong Dong; by hydrofoil from Rach Gia to An Thoi, or by cruise ship to Duong Dong.
HIGHLIGHTS:
Diving at Turtle Island off the NW coast – one of Vietnam's best dive sites.
The otherworldly atmosphere of Ganh Dau, the unspoiled fishing village on the NE coast.
The natural sounds and sights of the beautiful Suoi Tranh waterfall on the Da Ban River, deep in the emerald forest.
The iridescence of local pearls grown at the pearl farms – they used to be gathered from the Phu Quoc sea-bed.
Snorkelling/diving on the coral reefs around the islets grouped at Phu Quoc's southern tip.
The tropical flavour of the pastoral idyll of Xa Cua Can – all rivers, flowered green banks and stands of trees.
YOU SHOULD KNOW:
Phu Quoc fish sauce is particularly esteemed for its smell, which comes from the small, protein-rich fish called ca com. The island produces six million litres of fish sauce each year.

Fishing boats on Phu Quoc

An aerial view of Con Dao

Con Dao

POPULATION:
5,000 (2007 estimate)
WHEN TO GO:
Con Dao's climate is governed by the convergence of warm and cool ocean currents. Frequent, violent squalls hit the archipelago's western side from June to September, then reverse to hit the eastern side from October to December. Come between March and early June when the sea is at its most calm.
HOW TO GET THERE:
By air from Ho Chi Minh City or by boat from Vung Tau, to Con Son.
HIGHLIGHTS:
The paper weapons and costumes made as props for prison inmates' New Year 'celebrations', and other artefacts and memorabilia on the guided tour of the prison complex.
Dam Trau, a beautiful, tranquil beach shaded by evergreen trees.
Tropical almond trees swaying in a cool sea breeze.
Dolphins jumping and playing round the boat when you visit Con Dao's smaller islands.
YOU SHOULD KNOW:
When people describe Con Dao's exotic fruits as 'abundant', don't be misled. Apart from bananas and coconuts, everything genuinely edible comes from the mainland.

The Con Dao Archipelago lies 180 km (110 mi) south of Vung Tau, exposed in the South China Sea. Its isolation makes it unsurprising that Con Son, its main island, was a penal colony until 1975. The Portuguese called it Poulo Condor in 1702, and it was under that name that it became notorious as a colonial French prison, from 1861 until the South Vietnamese took it over in 1954. Conditions became so brutal that tiny punishment cells were known globally as 'tiger cages', shaming the USA and its puppet South Vietnamese administration, when they were revealed after reunification in 1975. Today, in what used to be the French Governor's residence, the room housing illustrations of the inhuman torture meted out is labelled 'Hell On Earth'. The small town that has developed round the remains of the penal colony is friendly and attractive – but it's easy to see the poignant distinction between the administrators' comfort and the inmates' squalor.

With potential infrastructure already in place, major tourist development is inevitable unless Con Dao as a whole is elevated from its present National Park to full-blooded UNESCO World Heritage status. The dense forest cover – especially the humid forest growing above 500 m (1,700 ft) – is pristine. Over 1,000 hectares (2,471 acres) of Con Dao's living coral reefs survive in shallow waters, recovering from decades of French harvesting (for lime), and subsequent damage by fishermen using underwater explosives. The terrestrial and marine biodiversity is colossal: Con Dao's habitats attract hawksbill and green turtles, and dugong, among 1,300 species of sea animals. Seagrass meadow and mangrove ecosystems provide nursery space for the 300,000 baby turtles released in a decade. Nature is back in flourishing abundance, gradually obliterating the traces of human suffering that have, in the end, created the opportunity for the rest of us to celebrate.

Cu Lao Cham

In their haste to get from north to south Vietnam, or vice-versa, most people pass by the little archipelago of the Cham Islands Marine Park. Cu Lao, often called Cham Island, is the biggest of seven islands lying 15 km (9 mi) off the ancient trading port of Hoi An, with which it shares considerable history. Cu Lao is where the Indonesian Cham people first came to trade in the 4th century, and it became one of the Champa kingdom's principal ports until Hoi An took over in the 15th century. The significance of both lasted to the 20th century, when the Thu Bon River silted up, and trade moved from Hoi An to Tourane (now Da Nang). Seventeenth century pagodas in its two villages, small temples and monuments, and the rice terrace systems themselves, hidden in the dense forest, recall Cu Lao's historic importance. Now it's better known for its ecological purity, and as one of Vietnam's best reef dive sites.

Cu Lao is 7 km (5 mi) long and 1.5 km (1 mi) wide, with a 517m (1,750 ft) mountain in its centre. Tropical forest covers everything; and the seven white beaches on its western side are empty and untouched. Only on Bai Chong are there a few very friendly fishing families who are happy to offer rudimentary but stunning food and drink. In April monkeys come here to gorge on newly-ripe durian fruits and wild pineapples; freshwater streams run from the coconut palms across the sand; and the parrot, clown, angel, lion, damsel and pipefish, hollyqueen sweetlips, barracudas, moray eels, pink jellyfish and occasional dugong among the lustrous corals offshore complete the picture of paradise. Other reefs are even more spectacular, and there are several known Japanese, Portuguese and US wrecks still waiting to be located.

POPULATION:
3,000 (2007)
WHEN TO GO:
Come from the beginning of March to August, when the water visibility is likely to be much better.
HOW TO GET THERE:
By air to Da Nang, then by car/taxi to Hoi An, then by water-taxi or speedboat from Hoi An (boats wait at the waterside by the market place) to Cu Lao. Da Nang and Hoi An are also served by the Reunification Train and long-haul bus.
HIGHLIGHTS:
The swifts' nests clinging to the high cliffs – a rare chance to see the origin of the delicious bird's nest soup.
The courtly titillation of naming beauty spots, like Suoi Tinh (Love Stream), Hon Chong (Piled-Up Rocks), Suoi Ong (The Gentleman's Stream) and Hang Ba (The Lady's Cave).
Talking to the monks, who practise traditional medicine based on local plants, at the 1753 Hai Tang Pagoda on the western hillside of Hon Lao.
The Rang Manh Pinnacles, a superb series of coral canyons, arches and caves filled with diffused sunlight, each section and depth attracting different groups of species; the range of projecting pinnacles prevents damage to the luxuriant flora and fauna from nets or fishing lines.
The artistic atmosphere of Hoi An, almost car-free, full of brightly-coloured wooden buildings reflecting 300 years of Portuguese, Dutch, Japanese, French and Chinese influences, and an oasis of quiet, intelligent café life.
YOU SHOULD KNOW:
With just one road connecting its only two villages, Bai Lang and Bai Huong, Cu Lao Cham is a fragile gem of authentic history and impeccable ecology.

*One of Cu Lao Cham's
untouched beaches*

Palawan Island

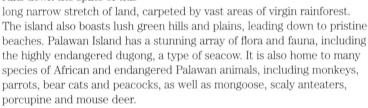

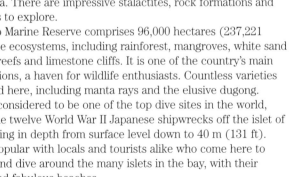

POPULATION:
737,000 (2000)
WHEN TO GO:
March to June
HOW TO GET THERE:
Fly from Manila to Puerto Princesa, or take a ferry which will take about 20 hours.
HIGHLIGHTS:
Tabon Caves – a series of chambers where anthropologists discovered the remains of 22,000-year-old Tabon Man, with various tools and other artefacts. The caves are located at Lipuua Point, Quezon.
Ursula Island Game Refuge and Bird Sanctuary – a haven for birds at Bataraza. Arrive here two hours before sunset, to see them congregate and roost for the night.
Coron Reefs, Northern Palawan – the seven enchanting lakes are surrounded by craggy limestone cliffs and attract hundreds of nature lovers.
Tabon Museum – Devoted to Palawan pre-history, the museum displays artefacts from the Tabon Caves, and gives information on the different tribes of Palawan.
Palawan Museum in Puerto Princesa – this interesting museum showcases the history, culture, music and crafts of Palawan.
The Taytay Fort – built in 1667 under the Augustinian Recollect Fathers, this historic fort was first used as a military station. The fort's small chapel and cannon are still intact.
YOU SHOULD KNOW:
Around 12 hours by boat from Puerto Princesa are the Tubbattaha Reefs, a UNESCO World Heritage Site and a wonderful place to dive.

The beautiful Bascuit Bay

In the northern Phillipines, between the South China Sea and the Sulu Sea, lies Palawan Island, blessed with immense natural beauty and plentiful marine life. With nearly 2,000 km (1,243 mi) of irregular coastline dotted with 1,780 islets, rocky coves, protected coral reefs and white sandy beaches, the island is renowned for having one of the most beautiful seascapes in the world.

A chain of mountains runs down the spine of this long narrow stretch of land, carpeted by vast areas of virgin rainforest. The island also boasts lush green hills and plains, leading down to pristine beaches. Palawan Island has a stunning array of flora and fauna, including the highly endangered dugong, a type of seacow. It is also home to many species of African and endangered Palawan animals, including monkeys, parrots, bear cats and peacocks, as well as mongoose, scaly anteaters, porcupine and mouse deer.

Palawan Island is full of natural wonders. Puerto-Princesa Subterranean River offers 8.2 km (5 mi) of navigable underground river, believed to be the longest in the world. The river winds through a deep cavern under rugged limestone and marble cliffs, and through an underground lagoon with crystalline waters before emptying out in to the South China Sea. There are impressive stalactites, rock formations and domed theatres to explore.

The El Nido Marine Reserve comprises 96,000 hectares (237,221 acres) of diverse ecosystems, including rainforest, mangroves, white sand beaches, coral reefs and limestone cliffs. It is one of the country's main tourist destinations, a haven for wildlife enthusiasts. Countless varieties of fish are found here, including manta rays and the elusive dugong.

Palawan is considered to be one of the top dive sites in the world, partly due to the twelve World War II Japanese shipwrecks off the islet of Busuanga, ranging in depth from surface level down to 40 m (131 ft). Honda Bay is popular with locals and tourists alike who come here to snorkel, swim and dive around the many islets in the bay, with their shallow reefs and fabulous beaches.

Luzon Island

This is the largest island in the Philippines Archipelago, giving its name to one of the country's three island groups (the others being Visayas and Mindanao). Luzon itself is the world's 15th-largest island, with an area of 105,000 sq km (40,550 sq mi), and the fifth most populous. The country's capital, Manila, is located here, along with the largest city, Quezon, making Luzon the centre of political and economic influence in the Philippines.

The area was claimed by Spanish conquistadors in 1571, and the Philippines were only freed from Spain's harsh control after a revolution in the 1890s. Even that came at a price – the revolutionaries were assisted by the Americans, then at war with Spain, but the USA soon annexed the country after waging a short war that destroyed the First Philippine Republic. The United States did not grant independence to the island nation until 1946, after the Philippines had been the scene of bitter fighting in World War II.

Mountainous Luzon is home to the country's second-highest peak (Mount Pulag) and most famous volcano (Mayon). Another natural highlight (stand by for a tongue twister) is the world's largest lake on an island in a lake on an island – Crater Lake on Vulcano Island in Lake Taal on Luzon. This amazing feature was once a vast inlet of the sea. As a result, it has many saltwater species that have adapted to fresh water – there were even bull sharks until the locals eliminated them in the 1930s.

Luzon has the best infrastructure of the Philippines' main islands, facilitating exploration, but still offers a breathtaking contrast between the hustle and bustle of its modern cities, a stunning variety of scenery, spectacular coastline and a rural way of life that has hardly changed for centuries.

POPULATION:
39,500,000 (2000)
WHEN TO GO:
The climate is temperate, allowing year-round visiting, but April to June is the peak tourist season.
HOW TO GET THERE:
There are commercial flights into Luzon's international airports, including cheap flights from Hong Kong.
HIGHLIGHTS:
The mountain haven of Baguio, north of Manila, the island's refreshingly cool summer capital.
Splendid rice terraces at Banaue, dubbed 'the eighth wonder of the world' by locals.
Waterfalls and hot springs on the fertile plain surrounding Laguna de Bay, Southeast Asia's largest freshwater lake.
St Paul's Underground River National Park near Barangay Sabang, a remote wonder consisting of a subterranean river and maze of caverns – now a UNESCO World Heritage Site. Another World Heritage Site – the well-preserved Spanish colonial town of Vigan on the west coast.
YOU SHOULD KNOW:
Vulcan Point on Vulcano Island in Lake Taal is the world's smallest (and the Philippines' second most active) volcano.

The rice terraces of Banaue

Alaminos Hundred Island National Park

POPULATION:
Uninhabited
WHEN TO GO:
All year round, though the rainy season (June-October) can see heavy showers and be quite chilly. April and May are the busiest months with the best weather.
HOW TO GET THERE:
Alaminos City is served by public buses from Manila, Baguio, Dagupan, Subic, Tarlac and Zambales.
HIGHLIGHTS:
Snorkeling to see the giant clam and coral garden on Quezon.
Shell Island for...its amazing shells, especially after the rainy season.
A superb cave on Milagrosa – one of the best among many in the Park.
YOU SHOULD KNOW:
Carry cash – the majority of suppliers (for example, of boat hire) do not accept credit cards.

Actually, it should be 123-Island Park (high tide) or 124-Island Park (low tide), but who's counting? With a total land area of just 18.5 sq km (7 sq mi), most islands are no more than rocky outcrops (some tiny) covered with dense vegetation, though there are plenty of hidden coves and sandy beaches. They are scattered like jewels in the azure waters of the Lingayen Gulf off the northern coast of Luzon. The Hundred Island National Park is now under the jurisdiction of Alaminos City, six hours from Manila by bus.

Most visitors to the Park stay in Alaminos City and set off by boat from the nearby Lucap Wharf where various options are on offer, including boat rental and island-hopping day tours. These tend to feature the major islands of Quezon, Govenor's and Children's plus one other, but customized trips are easily arranged. For those who enjoy the simple life, there is basic overnight accommodation in huts, cottages and shelters on the three main islands (no electricity, public rest rooms only) and camping is permitted (tents can be rented locally). Those are the only islands with tourist facilities, though the authorities – whilst determined to maintain the park's fragile eco-system – do not impose restrictive access rules to the other islands.

There are activities like parasailing, snorkeling or kayaking within the park, but most people simply enjoy island hopping or banana boat tours that allow them to appreciate the natural beauty of these pristine islands...with not a single resort to be seen. The park provides encouraging testament to growing awareness that original and unspoiled places can ultimately be worth far more economically than tacky developments that destroy the very things that most attract visitors.

Over a hundred islands are scattered like jewels across the Alaminos Hundred Island National Park.

Mindanao Island

Islands, islands everywhere – hundreds of them in the Mindanao Island group, of which the largest by far is 'big daddy' Mindanao at 97,500 sq km (37,500 sq mi). Once the seat of the Sultanate of Sulu, a Muslim state founded in the 15th century, Mindanao remains the centre of Islam in the Philippines, though it is now the island's minority religion. Even so, the struggle to secure an independent Muslim state on the island has been taking place for centuries and continues to this day. The Autonomous Region in Muslim Mindanao (ARMM) is a special self-governing area where most of the Islamic population lives, consisting of the Sulu Archipelago and two provinces on the mainland.

Mindanao is at once the most southerly and easterly point in the Philippines. The island has a unique character that makes it seem very different from the rest of the Philippines, resulting from its Muslim heritage and the dramatic mix of ethnic groups. It is also a land of stark contrast between the modern and the traditional.

The thriving industrial centre that is Davao City certainly belongs to the 21st century, as do the many intensive agri-businesses producing commodities like pineapples and meat. But once away from centres of population in the largely unspoiled back country, adventurous visitors will find themselves in a nature-lovers' paradise and be fascinated by the timeless way of life. Rich flora and fauna, outstanding natural attractions, stunning coastline and islands, different ethnic communities with colourful festivals – all combine to make Mindanao a destination that is attracting a rapidly increasing number of tourists. There is more than enough of Mindanao to go round, but despite awareness of the importance of eco-tourism, some of the new facilities will seem intrusive to those who prefer things just the way they were.

POPULATION:
18,134,000 (2000)
WHEN TO GO:
Any time – there is no significant wet or dry season and the climate is pleasant all year round.
HOW TO GET THERE:
Fly in to the recently upgraded Davao City international airport, or take an island-hopping flight if Mindanao isn't your first destination in the Philippines.
HIGHLIGHTS:
Mount Apo, the country's highest mountain, an inactive volcano in a range containing waterfalls, rapids, steaming lakes, geysers, sulphur pillars and primeval trees.
The 17th century Spanish Fort del Pilar in Zambonga, said by many to be the most romantic city in the Philippines.
Rio Hondo and Taluksangay, villages where members of the Samal tribe still dwell in stilt houses – representatives of the many ethnic groups that still live a traditional way of life on Mindanao.
The impressive hydroelectric complex at Iligan City, driven by the Maria Cristina Falls.
Orchids – in the wild or at public gardens like Puentespina (Davao City) or Yuhico (Greenhills).
YOU SHOULD KNOW:
Davao City is the world's largest by area, at the last count sprawling out over 2,450 sq km (940 sq mi)...and still growing.

A view from Mindanao Island

Mount Hibok-Hibok overlooks the beach.

Camiguin Island

POPULATION:
74,000 (2000)
WHEN TO GO:
Any time of year (the island is rarely visited by typhoons). April to June is the prime period, November to January the coolest.
HOW TO GET THERE:
Limited trips available from Cebu by air and sea. Or fly to Cagayan de Oro City, take a bus to Balingoan and boat to the island.
HIGHLIGHTS:
Binangawan Falls in Sagay – an unspoiled series of cascades into a single pool.
The Sunken Cemetery (scuba gear required) – immersed beneath the sea after the volcanic eruption of 1871, marked by a large cross.
Wonderfully elegant ancestral homes full of character that may be seen all over the island.
Old churches – Santo Rosario in Sagay (built 1882), the ruined San Roque in Barangay Bonbon and the Miracle Church in Baylao that saved many lives during a volcanic eruption.
Tangun Hot Spring at Naasag – an unusual natural seashore pool that is hot at low tide, changing to cool as the tide comes in.
YOU SHOULD KNOW:
If this is for you, be careful when you book – there is another Camiguin Island in the Philippines, part of the Babuyan Islands north of Luzon.

The independently minded Camiguin islanders have always fought their corner – unsuccessfully. The Spanish established a settlement in the early 1600s, the Americans invaded in 1901 and proved that bullets were better than *bolos* and spears and the Japanese ruthlessly crushed guerrilla activities in World War II. There was, however, a happy ending in 1946 when the Philippines gained independence.

The pear-shaped island is not large – 230 sq km (90 sq mi) – and is evidently of volcanic origin, as its nickname 'The Island Born of Fire' confirms. There are several large peaks, plus numerous domes and cones. Mount Hibok-Hibok, the largest, is still active, last erupting in 1953. It has hot springs, crater lakes and Taguines Lagoon, a volcanic maar. Hibok-Hibok is a popular destination for hikers, though a permit is required.

This is an island of contrasts, with traditional coastal villages, coconut plantations, lush forests, hot and cold springs, waterfalls, dramatic volcanic landscapes, abundant marine life and pristine beaches. Indeed, Camiguin has one of the world's finest beaches, as voted for by travel journalists – White Island Beach, a bleached sandbar in the turquoise Bohol Sea reached by boat, with great views of Mounts Vulcan and Hibok-Hibok.

Despite national efforts to encourage only sustainable eco-tourism, Camiguin's experience suggests this isn't easy. The newly discovered Camiguin hanging parrot, a handsome green, blue and red bird endemic to this island only, is already under threat as its habitat is eroded by increased economic activity and visitor-friendly development. And the rural tranquility and slow pace of life that makes this enchanted island so appealing is hardly helped by its designation as one of the 'Top 25 Tourist Destinations' in the Philippines.

Cebu Island

This is the main island of the Visayas group in the Central Philippines. It is a long, narrow sliver in the middle of the group, stretching for 225 km (140 mi) from north to south with an area of 4,500 sq km (1,750 sq mi). The capital, Cebu City, is half way down the east coast at the island's widest point. Its deep-water harbour was an important trading centre before the first Spanish settlement in the Philippines was established there in 1565. As a result, Cebu City has the country's first and smallest fort (Fort San Pedro), oldest church (Basilica of Santa Niño), oldest street (Colon) and oldest school (San Carlos). Its historical importance is confirmed by the fact that it was even incorporated as a city before Manila.

Cebu City has developed into an international container port that also acts as a hub for most of the country's domestic shipping, whilst also serving as a major commercial centre for island industries such as agriculture, fishing, copper mining, shipbuilding, steel and cement. Despite this intense industrial activity and the well-developed infrastructure that goes with it, Cebu is still an island that can delight the visitor. It has a rugged mountainous spine separating east and west coasts, rolling hills, limestone plateaux and coastal plains. There are excellent beaches and numerous coral atolls, with many first-class resorts. Principal leisure activities are diving, fishing, parasailing, boating, hiking and mountain biking. Cebu is the diving capital of the Philippines.

Over 150 islands surround Cebu, so it not only has a lot to offer in its own right but also serves as a popular base for day trips to offshore islands, or a jumping-off point for a longer stay.

POPULATION:
3,350,000 (2000)
WHEN TO GO:
Cebu is warm all year round, though the temperature is hottest in the dry season (March to May).
HOW TO GET THERE:
By air direct to Cebu's Mactan international airport, domestic flight from Manila or by sea on a choice of inter-island ferry services.
HIGHLIGHTS:
The Magellan Cross, a newer cross containing remains of the cross planted by the great Portuguese explorer Ferdinand Magellan when he reached the island in 1521 – see it in a small building with a richly painted ceiling in front of Cebu city hall.
Kawasan Falls at Matutinao near the southern town of Badian – the best waterfalls on the island, great for swimming and rafting.
Carcar, a town just south of Cebu with many preserved Castilian houses, gardens and churches.
The National Museum in Fort San Pedro, Cebu, providing insight into the island's colonial past.
A drive along the Cebu Transcentral highway for cool air and sensational mountain views.
YOU SHOULD KNOW:
Ferdinand Magellan was killed soon after arriving here, at the Battle of Mactan, fighting with the Spanish against local Visayan chief Lapu-Lapu.

Samal Island

POPULATION:
83,000 (2000)
WHEN TO GO:
The best months to visit are
November to May, especially if
intending to dive.
HOW TO GET THERE:
By vehicle ferry or small boat – any
number to choose from along the
Gulf shore or Santa Ana Pier in
Davao.
HIGHLIGHTS:
The Paradise Island resort, complete
with palms, mangroves and a small
zoo featuring island birds, turtles,
snakes, monkeys and deer.
Hagimit Falls – a series of low-drop
falls above beautiful pools in a forest
setting close to Peñaplata.
A beach-hopping, round-the-island
tour by pumpboat, lasting around
four hours (depending on stops).
Vanishing Island, a spit of mangrove-
covered land that is submerged at
high tide.
Pindawon and Aundanao marine
sanctuaries on the east coast, where
there is every chance of seeing
turtles.
YOU SHOULD KNOW:
Samal's renowned bat cave houses
the world's largest colony of
Geoffroy's rousette fruit bats (all 1.8
million of them).

The island is now known as the Island Garden City of Samal (aka IGaCOS), officially a third-class city. Don't be fooled – this is a delightful holiday destination for those who love a white-sand, blue-sea beach holiday, though it is situated in Davao Gulf within sight of the city of the same name. There are many resorts packed into the island's 300 sq km (115 sq mi) area, but the idea of eco-tourism is taken seriously in the Philippines and considerable effort has gone into ensuring that such facilities don't destroy the island's essential character. For those who like to get away from it all, there are plenty of hiking and biking trails in the forested interior, but you need to be fit as many of them are quite steep.

One of Samal's principal attractions is the wonderful variety of marine habitats and sea life. There is a profusion of small, colourful fish, occasional dolphins and sharks, turtles, a variety of coral reefs, underwater caves and dramatic rock formations. This water wonderland attracts both snorkelers and divers, with instant tuition available for beginners, though caution is advised as currents can be treacherous. Kayaking and (more intrusively) jet skiing are also popular activities.

The Philippines have more to offer than any one person could see in two lifetimes, but the resorts of Samal Island are typical of low-impact tourist developments found along many parts of the country's extensive shoreline – and they are exactly what the majority of visitors come for. If that's your idea of heaven too, Samal could be perfect!

Boracay Island

A typical tropical paradise in the Central Philippines, Boracay is just off the northwestern corner of the large island of Panay in the Visayas group. It rates as one of the country's top tourist destinations, but was a late starter – until the 1970s only the most clued-up of backpackers even knew the place existed.

The island is some 7 km (4 mi) long and extends to an area of some 10 sq km (4 sq mi). The reasons for coming are simple – sand and sea. The long main beach is on the west coast – and White Beach doesn't misrepresent itself. The sand is dazzling and the beach is sheltered from the prevailing wind in high season. This is the place for lazy loafing, with numerous beachfront facilities to cater for après-swim. Bulabog Beach on the east side is more athletically orientated, with kiteboarding and windsurfing on the menu. There are several other beaches for those who want to be different.

There are two distinct seasons on Boracay Island – Habagat and Amihan. They are associated respectively with, and vary in duration depending on the whims of, the global La Niña and El Niño weather patterns. Habagat (generally June to September) is hot and muggy with frequent heavy rain and unpredictable tropical storms. Amihan (usually October to May) sees little rainfall and moderate temperatures, with only the very occasional storm. The latter is very definitely high season.

Make no mistake – with nearly 400 beach resorts and the associated eating and drinking places, Boracay is an out-and-out tourist haven. But if you want to be marooned on a desert island for a week, 21st-century style, they don't come much better than this.

POPULATION:
12,000 (2000)
WHEN TO GO:
Amihan season (October to May) – more expensive, but worth it.
HOW TO GET THERE:
By internal fight to Godofredo P. Ramos Airport in nearby Caticlan, then boat from Caticlan Jetty to Cagban Beach on Boracay.
HIGHLIGHTS:
Traditional dragon-boat races featuring teams from all over the Philippines, held annually in April or May.
A self-sail tour of island waters in a hired *paraw* (canoe with two outriggers), or motorized *banca*.
Pitch and putt – actually a leisurely round on the world-class 18-hole par-72 course designed by top Aussie golfer Graham Marsh.
YOU SHOULD KNOW:
This isn't the ideal place to find peace and quiet – restaurants, clubs, bars and pubs sometimes keep going all night long.

One of the many beautiful beaches on Boracay

Sunrise over the Chocolate Hills

Bohol Island

POPULATION:
1,137,000 (2000)
WHEN TO GO:
Take your pick – November to April is mild, May to July hot and humid, August to October mild but rainy.
HOW TO GET THERE:
By sea to the Tagbilaran City Tourist Pier from Cebu, Manila and various other islands. By air to the recently enlarged city airport.
HIGHLIGHTS:
Antequera's beautiful Mag-Aso Falls – Mag-Aso translates as 'smoke' for reasons that will become apparent upon arrival.
Spelunking – not for everyone, but there are over 100 caves in the eastern part of the island to delight the subterranean adventurer.
A fabulous cruise up the Loboc River from the sea to its source in the centre of the island.
Rajah Sikatuna National Park near Bilar, the largest remaining natural forest on the island.
The tarzier, a delightful bug-eyed creature said to be the world's smallest primate – shy in the wild, but often seen in captivity.
YOU SHOULD KNOW:
During the American-Philippines War of 1901, US troops burned up to 20 villages on Bohol as a punishment for local resistance.

In common with the rest of the Philippines, Bohol came under Spanish influence in the 16th century. The island saw the conclusion of an historic treaty of friendship between the locals and Spain in 1565, when native chieftain Datu Sikatanu made a blood pact with the Spanish conquistador Miguel López de Legazpi. The event is celebrated to this day at the annual Sandugo Festival, and evidence of Bohol's colonial past is everywhere.

This oval-shaped island province lies to the southeast of Cebu Island and due north from Mindanao Island. Bohol is the 10th-largest island in the Philippines, with an area of 3,300 sq km (1,275 sq mi) and a coastline that is 260 km (160 mi) in length. It has gently rolling terrain and a mountainous interior with a central plateau.

One must see are the famous Chocolate Hills near Carmen, described as 'The Jewel of the Philippines'. That description may have been thought up by an astute tourist chief, but this certainly is an amazing natural wonder – some 1,200 uniform cone-shaped limestone hills. They are grass-covered and turn brown in summer, which is where the chocolate comes in. There is a good road system on the island, giving access to both the interior and coastal villages.

The capital city Tagbilaran is located on the south coast, popular with those who like beach holidays on sand that's whiter than white. Bohol is surrounded by 70 smaller islands. Many of these can easily be reached from the mainland, and some offer unusual experiences like whale and dolphin watching. This activity is conducted by former fishermen who now serve as 'stewards of the sea', showing how eagerly the concept of eco-tourism is being embraced in the Philippines.

Panglao Island

Located in the central Visayas Island group, just off the southwestern corner of Bohol Island, this is one of the top visitor attractions in the Philippines. Panglao Island is divided into two municipalities – Dauis town (nearest the mainland) and Panglao town. There are numerous tourist resorts, many clustered around the world-famous Alona Beach. Other notable beaches are Doljo (fronting interesting coral reefs) and Momo.

This small island is tourism in the Philippines personified. There are literally hundreds of assorted resorts along the sandy beaches, with investment money pouring in and many more under construction. There's even talk of a new international airport to make the going easier still. Apart from the obvious attractions of sand and sea, the night-life consists of good food and cold drinks, in the amiable company of fellow visitors and friendly locals.

However, with marine biodiversity said to exceed that of Japan and the Mediterranean Sea put together, Panglao does have one claim to fame that sets it apart. The island is a world-renowned diving location, so many visitors bring flippers and snorkels, or aim to do (or try) some diving.

Scuba dive sites are everywhere, best explored with the help of a local dive master who will know the best places and steer clear of dangerous currents. Apart from sensational corals thronged with small tropical fish, the main sights are hammerhead sharks, massive schools of jackfish and barracudas – even whale sharks in season.

In late August, the island fiesta – Hudyaka sa Panglao – takes place in the grounds of Panglao's San Agustin Church. The local *barangays* compete fiercely for top honours, serving as a reminder of the important place that music and dance have in the culture of the Philippines.

POPULATION:
48,000 (2000)
WHEN TO GO:
The temperate climate encourages any-time visiting.
HOW TO GET THERE:
Manila to Tagbilaran City on the main island of Bohol by air or fast ferry, from there by bridge or causeway to Panglao Island.
HIGHLIGHTS:
Out Lady of Assumption Church at Dauis, built by the Spaniards. It has attractive wall paintings and a holy well said to cure all ills.
Hinagdanan Cave in Bingag, with a passage leading down to a natural swimming pool.
An exploration of the interior on a (cheaply!) rented scooter – there's more to this delightful island than sand and sea.
Panglao Market, a tin-roofed area used by the locals, with all sorts of goodies on offer.
YOU SHOULD KNOW:
If you're considering a maiden dive, be aware that you're not allowed to drink alcohol in the previous 24 hours.

Fishing boats moored off Panglao Island

Borneo

POPULATION:
The population has jumped from
9 million in 1990 to 16 million in 2000.
WHEN TO GO:
It is always rainy and humid in
Borneo, but May to September is the
best time to go.
HOW TO GET THERE:
It is possible to fly to all three parts
of the island from Malaysia,
Singapore and Indonesia, and ferries
run from Java and Sulawesi.
HIGHLIGHTS:
Gunung Palung National Park.
Tanjung Puting National Park.
Trek through Pegunungan Meratus
primary forest.
Chill out, dive and snorkel the
glorious marine reserve at tiny,
unspoiled Derawan Island.
YOU SHOULD KNOW:
Since 1971, Dr Birute Galdikas has
run the orangutan rescue centre,
Camp Leakey. Her research is
essential to the fight to save the
species from extinction. There are
other research camps here too that
one can visit, as well as a
reforestation camp, where rangers
are replanting hardwood saplings in
an attempt to replace trees lost to
logging and forest fires.

The name 'Borneo' conjures up visions of a vast, unknown territory, shrouded in mystery and cloaked in deep, dense, dark rainforest sheltering fearsome tribesmen decked out in feathers and warpaint. Thirty years ago, this would have been largely correct, but Borneo has changed.

Borneo's largest part by far is Indonesian Kalimantan, but it also includes Sarawak and Sabah, (East Malaysia), and Brunei, a small, independent country on the northwest coast. Brunei is wealthy, thanks to crude oil and natural gas. East Malaysia has similar resources as well as logging, palm oil production and some tourism. Kalimantan has it all - oil, gas, minerals, gold, diamonds, timber and palm oil, but its Dayaks, various tribal peoples, are desperate. Their culture is being devastated by deforestation, and their future looks bleak.

Borneo is blessed with natural wonders. Mount Kinabalu, at 4095 m (13,435 ft) is its highest mountain, and there are wonderful National Parks and World Heritage Sites. Hundreds of rivers traverse Borneo and there are extensive, extraordinary cave systems.

The rainforest contains extremely high endemism. Since 1996, 513 new plants and animals have been discovered here. Local shamans have introduced scientists to medicinal plants that are now used in western medicines. However, with unprecedented logging laying waste to the rainforest, the endless palm oil plantations and the arrival of thousands of transmigrants from Java and Madura, who also need land, all this could vanish.

Come to Borneo as soon as you can – in a few more years it may be damaged beyond repair. Meet some of the Dayak tribes living in longhouses on the riverbanks. Gaze in awe at some of the world's last, luxuriant primary rainforest. Take a motorized canoe through Tanjung Puting National Park, seeing and hearing chattering macaques, perhaps spotting the beautiful Giant Bornean butterfly flitting past, and watching the fireflies light up the night.

A river runs through the lowland rainforest of the Danum Valley.

The crystal clear waters around the Maluku Islands provide great snorkelling opportunities.

The Islands of Maluku

The Islands of Maluku, formerly known as the Moluccas, are a group of islands that lie between Sulawesi and Papua, with Ambon at their heart. Stretched out from north to south across 1,000 km (625 mi) of water, Ambon is the gateway to the fabulous Spice Islands.

Until the 16th century these islands were the sole source of nutmeg and cloves, which were in great demand in India, Arabia and China, and which finally attracted explorers from Europe, thus beginning the colonization of the region. Ruled by sultanates until 1512, the Portuguese and the Dutch struggled over the islands for decades, but by 1660 the Dutch had won a monopoly for the trade, making themselves a fortune over the following century. In 1797 the British briefly occupied Maluku, and brought about its downfall by taking away precious seedlings to plant in other tropical British colonies. Within a generation, Maluku sank into the obscurity from which it is just emerging today.

Ambon's tropical flowers, shrubs, bamboo, fruit trees and weeds grow so fast you can almost see it happen. It's a beautiful island, with rolling hills, gentle mountains and beaches, lined with waving palms giving on to limpid, aquamarine seas. Kota Ambon, the region's capital, lost much of its colonial architecture during World War II, but it is gloriously situated on a perfect bay, hills rising behind it.

As befits its status, Kota Ambon is a busy, commercial city, though still small and undemanding in comparison to many. You can easily escape and explore the rest of the island peacefully – take a short 'live aboard' diving trip from popular Namalatu Beach, see the splendid 17th century Dutch fort at Hila on the north coast, or sit on the empty beach at Honimua and plan trips to some of the other remote islands in the area.

POPULATION:
368,000 (2007)
WHEN TO GO:
November to March
HOW TO GET THERE:
By air from Java, or by sea from Java, Sulawesi or Papua.
HIGHLIGHTS:
The sacred eel pool at Waai.
The market at Paso.
The Siwa Lima Museum in Kota Ambon.
Exploring the National Park of Pombo Island and snorkelling in its waters.
YOU SHOULD KNOW:
From 1999 to 2002 there was some serious inter-communal violence in Ambon and several other islands. The population is fairly equally divided between Christians in the south and Muslims in the north. Today, however, the troubles seem to be over and both the economy and tourism are on the rise.

Banda Islands

The Bandas are a remote archipelago of ten tiny, enchanting islands lying in the Banda Sea, well to the south east of Ambon. These specks in the ocean were the greatest source of the best quality nutmeg and mace in the world, which not only brought them wealth and fame but also terrible misery and punishment at the hands of their Dutch oppressors. Today the Bandas are becoming revitalized, for the first time since the early 1800s, by a nascent tourist industry, which it is hoped will ensure both a stable economy and prevent further depopulation of the islands.

The main island is Banda Neira, and its capital shares the same name. Bandaneira was historically the administrative centre, and the ruling Dutch administrators seem to have vied with each other by building bigger and better villas. Fortunately many of these have

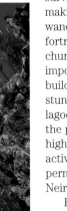

survived more or less intact, making the town a delight to wander around. There are fortresses to visit as well as churches and several important colonial era buildings. The town is stunningly located on a lagoon, opposite which rises the perfect, 666-m (2,198-ft) high cone of Gunung Api, an active volcano which is a permanent threat to Banda Neira's inhabitants.

Banda Besar is the largest island in the group, and produced the best and largest quantity of nutmeg of them all. Banda Besar and the other islands all have beaches, diving and snorkelling to die for – this is their strength. Ai and Hatta both have superb underwater drop-offs, with marvellous corals and fish. Run has impressive dive sites, and Neilaka, which you can walk around in just a few minutes, is the epitome of a perfect tropical island, surrounded by pristine, deserted, white sand beaches.

POPULATION:
15,000 (2001)
WHEN TO GO:
October to March
HOW TO GET THERE:
By air from Ambon or Seram, or by sea from Ambon, Sulawesi, Kei Islands, Papua, Timor and Java.
HIGHLIGHTS:
The 17th century forts, Benteng Nassau and Benteng Belgica in Bandaneira.
Bandaneira's museum in Rumah Budaya.
Climbing Gunung Api at sunrise for stupendous views.
The December boat races at Pulau Ai.
The Groot Waling plantation house and estate on Banda Besar.
YOU SHOULD KNOW:
In 1667 Britain offered to give back New Netherland, which included Manhattan Island, to the Dutch in exchange for sugar factories in Surinam. Declining this offer, the Dutch actually forced Britain to give up Pulau Run, thus achieving a nutmeg monopoly. After recapturing New Netherland in 1673, the Dutch were finally forced to cede it back to Britain, this time forever. In retrospect, the Dutch made a serious error…

A lionfish swims through the stunning reef.

Nusa Lembongan

POPULATION:
55,000 (2006)
WHEN TO GO:
Anytime, but it is driest from May
to September.
HOW TO GET THERE:
By sea from Bali.
HIGHLIGHTS:
The Goa Karangsari caves on
Nusa Penida.
The waterfall at Batukandik,
Nusa Penida.
The spooky temple of Pura Dalem
Penetaran Ped, Nusa Penida.
Mushroom Bay, Nusa Lembongan.
The dive sites of Blue Corner, Jackfish
Point and Ceningan Point around
Lembongan and Ceningan.

Just off the coast of south east Bali, in the Lombok Strait, lie Nusa Lembongan, Nusa Penida and the tiny Nusa Ceningan. Of these, Nusa Lembongan is generally the island of choice. Easy to cycle or walk around as it is only 4 km (2.5 mi) by 2 km (1.25 mi), Lembongan is a charming, relaxed and peaceful place – ideal for a few days R & R. There are no cars, and few motorcycles here and, apart from income derived from tourism, most of the inhabitants make their living from fishing and seaweed cultivation.

Circled by white sand beaches, Lembongan has attracted backpackers for years. Today however, the island has been 'discovered' and more upmarket facilities are beginning to appear. Lembongan has two villages, and a number of beautiful little bays and beaches. The north shore has good surfing, and there are still plenty of healthy coral reefs for snorkellers to enjoy.

Across a narrow suspension bridge at the south east of the island is Nusa Ceningan. This hilly little place has no roads, just tracks, and lovely views. There is only one village here, but lots of seaweed farming, and at low tide the frames in the lagoon are interesting to visit.

Nusa Penida is an arid, harshly beautiful, limestone island, with a hilly interior. Much less touristy, possibly due to the Balinese belief that it is cursed, it's an interesting place to visit. In the south, steep limestone cliffs drop directly into the sea, while the north coast has sandy beaches.

The big attraction of all three islands is their dive sites, and several dive operators have set up shop here, offering dives that range from shallow and easy, to serious drift dives. Diving off these shores you will probably see several large marine creatures, including sharks, turtles and sometimes sunfish.

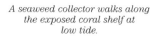

*A seaweed collector walks along
the exposed coral shelf at
low tide.*

Bali

Bali, the magical island of the gods, lives up to and beyond its reputation. Just 153 km (95 mi) wide and 112 km (69 mi) long, it is small enough to be driven around within a day. This is Indonesia's Hindu island, though like the other islands, animism exists beneath the surface, where art and beauty reign supreme. Three sacred volcanoes dominate the range straddling the north and east, providing bounteous soil – local people say that if you put a bare stick in the earth, it will take root.

When Java's Islamic empire arose in the 16th century, the vanquished Hindus fled to Bali, reinforcing its culture but making an enemy. Over time Bali has been invaded by Java, Lombok, the Netherlands and Japan. In the 1960s thousands died when Mount Agung erupted, and 100,000 more were killed in retaliation for an unsuccessful communist coup against the government in Java. In 2002 and 2005, terrorist bombs killed and injured hundreds of both tourists and locals, but despite these tragedies Bali always recovers.

Beauty touches every aspect of daily life. The island is bursting with artists, wood carvers, musicians and dancers, with Ubud, in central Bali, the artistic heartland, having been home to many European artists since the 1920s. Tourism took off in the 1970s, but is contained in particular areas, leaving much of the island undisturbed. Here you can see classic scenes of brilliant green, terraced rice paddies, stone temples intricately carved with fabulous creatures, and gamelan orchestras accompanying gorgeously costumed dancers performing the Ramayana in the moonlight.

You can climb volcanoes, swim with dolphins, walk along near empty beaches, admire exquisite offerings to the gods and watch colourful religious processions. Currently tourism is down, but Bali and its people are enchanting and completely irresistible.

Terraced rice paddies with Mount Agung in the background

POPULATION:
3.2 million (2006)
WHEN TO GO:
Anytime, but the driest season is from May to September.
HOW TO GET THERE:
International or domestic flights to Denpasar or ferry from other Indonesian islands.
HIGHLIGHTS:
The beaches and beach life around the island.
The galleries and performance art in Ubud.
Tanah Lot, Bali's most picturesque temple.
Trekking round Tirta Gangga and the water palace.
Shopping – you will be sorely tempted.
The Kecak (Monkey)
Dance at sunset in Ulu Watu temple.
YOU SHOULD KNOW:
Negara, in south-west Bali, is famous for its bull races. Water buffalo, pulling small, decorative chariots and carrying elegantly dressed riders, dash hell for leather down the beach in front of a large, hugely appreciative audience.

The coast near Labuhanbajo

Flores

Flores gained its name from the Portuguese, who named it Cabo das Flores, Cape of Flowers. It is a long, narrow island, lying to the east of Komodo and the Rinca Islands and stretching some 350 km (218 mi) from end to end, though only 70 km (44 mi) at its widest. A volcanic chain rises along its length like the jagged spikes on the back of a stegosaurus – this is a landscape of green mountains and steep sided valleys, rushing rivers, savannah, beaches and coral gardens.

Prior to the 16th century, Flores was animist, trading sandalwood, cinnamon and fabric with passing mariners. Sandalwood brought the Portuguese and Catholicism soon took root, leading eventually to Muslim invasions to halt the spread of Christianity. In 1859 the Dutch took over, but spent nearly 50 years gaining full control, and departing when Indonesia achieved independence. Today Flores is 90 per cent Catholic, though traditional beliefs are held as well.

In 2003 archaeologists discovered the skeleton of a tiny adult human, a mere 1 m (3.3 ft) high and since then several more have been found. *Homo floresiensis*, nicknamed Hobbit, lived only 12,000 years ago, and scientists are still arguing about his precise classification.

This lovely island receives far fewer visitors than the more popular Indonesian islands, but it contains some spectacular natural wonders, in particular the crater lakes at Keli Mutu. Here three lakes at the volcano's summit, separated only by low, rocky ridges display astonishingly different, vivid colours. These change on a regular basis, from turquoise, chocolate brown and dark green through maroon, pale green and café au lait, caused by dissolving minerals in the waters. This is a sacred place, to which the souls of the departed go, and it is impossible not to find it deeply impressive.

POPULATION:
1.8 million (2006)
WHEN TO GO:
April to September
HOW TO GET THERE:
By air from Bali or West Timor, or by ferry.
HIGHLIGHTS:
The Manggarai hill people's penti ceremony, held in August.
Bajawa and the Ngada people and their culture.
The ikat weaving villages of Nggela and Wolojita.
Diving, snorkelling and relaxing at Ahuwair and Waiterang beaches.
The cathedral at Larantuka and the Good Friday and Easter Sunday ceremonies.
YOU SHOULD KNOW:
The area around the fishing village of Riung is the only place to see Komodo dragons outside Komodo and the Rinca Islands.

Gili Islands

Lying in pristine waters off the north western coast of Lombok are three idyllic tropical islands, the Gilis. Fringed with golden, sandy beaches, and ringed with coral reefs that teem with a myriad of fish, the Gilis make a wonderful getaway if you need a break from Bali's cultural wonders, or have exhausted yourself by trekking up Lombok's Mount Rinjani. Come here for the quiet life – there is little traffic, and nothing to do except swim, snorkel, or lie in your hammock with a good book.

Gili Air, the closest to Lombok, is flat and rural. The government has helped the local population by donating coconut and mango saplings to keep the island green and attractive. The coastal path that encircles Gili Air can be walked in about an hour. The atmosphere here is relaxed, although in the high season things can get pretty busy.

Gili Meno, in the middle, is the smallest, quietest and least developed of the three, though it is thought to have the best beaches. To the northwest there is a lake, watch out for mosquitoes, though during the dry season it is used for salt production. Inland are many coconut plantations and few homes: the population here is tiny.

Gili Trawangan is the largest Gili, and a serious party island. Many tourists come here, not only backpackers and gap-year youth but also trendy Singaporeans and Indonesians too, and this is reflected in the number of facilities.

What is great about the Gilis is hopping from one to another, thus quickly discovering where you want to stay, which could be quite different from where you want to swim. Diving and snorkelling is terrific wherever you go, and care is being taken of the reefs themselves. On a clear day, fabulous views can be had across the water to Mount Rinjani, and the sunsets are legendary.

POPULATION:
Gili Air: 1,800; Gili Meno: 300; Gili Trawangan: 1,800 (2004)
WHEN TO GO:
April to September
HOW TO GET THERE:
By ferry or speedboat from Lombok or Bali.
HIGHLIGHTS:
The Taman Burung Bird Park on Gili Meno.
A snorkelling trip in a glass bottomed boat.
Seeing the islands from a horse and trap.
Learn to scuba dive and enjoy some of the Gilis' excellent dive sites.
YOU SHOULD KNOW:
Don't forget that people here are Muslim, and can be deeply offended by the sight of too much flesh.

A woman collects shellfish on Gili Air.

Ternate, Tidore and Halmahera

POPULATION:
Halmahera 162,728 (1995); Ternate 56,000 (1980); Tidore 40,000 (2000 estimate)

HOW TO GET THERE:
Flights from Java, Sulawesi and Ambon to the main airport in Ternate or by sea from Sulawesi, Papua and Ambon. Travel between the islands by boat.

WHEN TO GO:
November to March

HIGHLIGHTS:
The Sultan's Mosque and the Sultan's Palace and Museum in Ternate town. The Afo clove tree on Mt Gamalama, said to be over 400 years old, and the mother of all clove trees in existence today.
Morotai Island, off north eastern Halmahera, site of an important victory by the Allies over the Japanese during World War II. In 1973, Private Nakamura emerged from the rainforest here, to surrender. He was unaware that the war had been over for almost 30 years.

YOU SHOULD KNOW:
Halmahera now has two gold mines and a copper and cobalt mine in active production.

Ternate, Tidore and Halmahera lie in the Molucca Sea between north east Sulawesi and north west Papua, in a thread of other small, volcanic islands with little or no population. Halmahera is the largest island of Maluku, and is reminiscent of Sulawesi in shape. Ternate and Tidore lie to its west, and are small and circular, boasting larger populations than Halmahera despite the latter's size.

Ternate and Tidore are, historically speaking, enemies, and both have a violent past. They were clove islands, ruled by wealthy and powerful Islamic sultans. In the early 1500s the Portuguese settled in Ternate, and the Spanish were quickly invited to Tidore. By the beginning of the following century, the Dutch took control, building the fort of Oranje on Ternate, and continued to play politics with other interested European powers and to foment trouble between the various sultans.

Pulau Ternate is really just a volcanic cone. Rising to a height of 1,721 m (5,679 ft), Gunung Api Gamalama had its last major eruption in 1840, destroying virtually everything on the island. Small eruptions occurred during the 1980s and 1990s, but currently it is not considered a danger. Ternate town is the administrative centre for the north Maluku region, and there are several interesting buildings to visit here.

Tidore is a much calmer, quieter island, with a local language that is still spoken. Dominated by its own volcano, Gunung Kiematubu, much of it is steeply and lushly forested. The remains of a Spanish fort can be seen in the sleepy main town, Soasio, and there are two smaller islands off the coast, Maitara and Mare, to visit.

Halmahera is mountainous, with several volcanoes and very few roads. The main town, Tobelo, is on the north east coast, and there are various uninhabited, picturesque islands just off-shore upon which you can play Robinson Crusoe to your heart's content.

Gunung Api Gamalama volcano

Nias

Nias, the largest island off the west coast of Sumatra, is roughly 100 km (60 mi) long and 50 km (30 mi) wide, and is the home to a most unusual and ancient megalithic stone culture. The Niha people are farmers, growing many different crops, as well as rice. In the past they were ferocious warriors; fighting between different villages was commonplace, and head hunting was rife long after most other tribal people had stopped the practice.

The Niha divided themselves into three castes – aristocrats, commoners and slaves, who were traded, and until the early 1800s they had virtually no contact with the wider world other than via this trade. Nias itself divides into three parts – southern, central and northern – each having their own style, and the traditional villages are unique, often built defensively on high ground approached by stone steps and enclosed by a stone wall.

In the south, the houses are built along either side of a long courtyard. Made of teak and bamboo, their steep thatched roofs are constructed without nails, each beam slotting into the next. The Niha's wood carving skills are highly regarded throughout South-East Asia. Stone benches, occasionally with human skulls beneath them, and bathing pools, carvings and standing stones can readily be seen, as can the ancient ritual of stone jumping – now practised for important guests and tourists – where young men leap over stone columns some 2 m (6 ft 6 in) high, feet first.

This megalithic culture is not the only attraction here – another is the waves. Internationally famous amongst the surfing fraternity, they attract as many surfers to the south as visitors to the island as a whole. Nias is suffering from the after effects of natural disasters. Travelling is tough and people are needy, but the island is extraordinary and won't disappoint you.

POPULATION:
650,000 (2006)
WHEN TO GO:
June to October
HOW TO GET THERE:
By air or ferry from Sumatra.
HIGHLIGHTS:
The stone carvings and standing stones around Gomo.
The Chieftain's house at Hilinawalo Mazingo.
Stone jumping and war dances at Bawomataluo.
The architecture in Hilismaetano.
Surfing.
YOU SHOULD KNOW:
The surf break at Pantai Sorake is reputed to be the best right-hander in the world – even better since the height of the reef was raised by the 2005 earthquake. Take precautions against malaria and cholera.

Stone carvings on Nias

Samosir Island

POPULATION:
120,000 (2000)
WHEN TO GO:
June to September
HOW TO GET THERE:
By road over the bridge, or by ferry
from Parapat.
HIGHLIGHTS:
Batak Museum – in the village of
Simanindo, the museum sheds light
on the Batak way of life with displays
of handicrafts and traditional puppets
used in ceremonies and dances.
There are also displays of traditional
dance performed daily.
Batak handicrafts and musical
instruments – these are on sale in
many of the villages on the island.
The hot springs on the mainland just
over the bridge from Pangururan.
Tomok – in the village can be found
impressive stone sarcophagi and
other artefacts from the reign of
King Sidabutar.
Ambarita – see the traditional Batak
houses, and King Siallagan's
execution block.
YOU SHOULD KNOW:
Samosir is also known as 'Island of
the Dead'.

A typical home of the Toba Batak

The largest island within an island, and the fourth largest lake island in the world, Samosir is around 630 sq km (243 sq mi) and sits in Lake Toba in the north of Sumatra. The lake and island were formed after the eruption of a supervolcano around 75, 000 years ago, which is believed to have been severe enough to cause climatic change. Probably the largest and deepest caldera lake in the world, Lake Toba sits high amid treeless mountains. The island of Samosir was originally connected to the surrounding caldera wall by a small isthmus, which was cut through to allow ships to pass.

The eastern side of the island rises steeply towards a central plateau with an altitude of 780 m (2,559 ft), and the land gradually descends towards the southern and western coasts, which are scattered with small villages. The Samosir plateau consists mainly of rock, some scattered forests and swamps and a small lake. From Pangururan on the western side, a bridge connects the island with mainland Sumatra.

The island is best known as the home of the Toba Batak people, an ethnic group whose heartland centres around the lake. Toba Batak are known traditionally for their weaving, wood carving and particularly their ornate stone tombs, many of which can be seen on Samosir. Their burial and marriage traditions are very rich and complex, and in the past they had a reputation for being fierce warriors.

In the village of Tomok, under the sacred Hariara tree, you can see the 200-year-old royal stone sarcophagus of King Sidabutar's clan. Although they resemble coffins, the sarcophagi normally contain the collected skulls of an entire family. Stone sarcophagi have been found in 26 villages around the island.

The island's traditional wooden houses are interesting and may be decorated with clan symbols. In Tomok there are some good examples, as well as at Ambarita, where there are rows of traditional Batak houses. There are also artefacts dating from King Siallagan's reign here, including stone chairs and the execution block. The small museum offers a luridly graphic description of past executions.

The island has some nice sandy beaches, particularly around Ambarita. Or if you prefer your water hot, head over the bridge from Pangururan to the thermal springs on the mainland just 3 km (1.86 mi) away. There are several swimming pools to enjoy, or climb up the hill to where the springs emerge from the ground.

Riau Islands

Between Sumatra's swampy east coast, Singapore and the South China Sea lie the Riau Islands – some 3,000 of them altogether. Many are nameless, hundreds are uninhabited, and so far just a very few are being transformed under an economic development plan devised between Sumatra and Singapore.

Bintan Island

The history of the Riau Islands is interesting. Situated in a strategically important position on the shortest sea route between China and India, they were ruled by various Malaysian sultans, who were dominated first by the Portuguese and then the Dutch. The last sultanate of Riau was established on the now neglected Lingga Island, and it was the British who were responsible for the islands becoming part of Indonesia rather than Malaysia.

Bintan Island is the islands' administrative centre, the largest island of the archipelago and a major weekend getaway for Singaporeans. While its north shore consists of upmarket Singaporean resort hotels and golf courses, the east coast is much less organized; though the beaches are not as good, they provide fine swimming, and there are a few deserted offshore islands that are worth a visit. Apart from the beaches there are several places of interest to see here, and even a small mountain, Bintan Besar, to climb.

Batam Island is very different. The transport hub for the region, it has become an overspill for Singaporean industry. There is a wealth of factories and production plants on the island, and virtually everyone working here comes from somewhere else. There are resorts and golf courses, but most of their clients are businessmen and corporate visitors.

Should you want a quick break from either Singapore or Pekanbaru, Penuba Island might be the place for you. It has some beautiful beaches, is undeveloped and is perfect for relaxing and doing very little.

POPULATION:
Batam 714,000 (2006)
WHEN TO GO:
March to September
HOW TO GET THERE:
By sea to Batam or Bintan from Singapore or Sumatra.
HIGHLIGHTS:
Penyengat Island, across the harbour from Tanjung Pinang, Bintan's main port town, once the capital of the Riau rajahs.
The Chinese temple in Senggarang, Bintan. Trikora Beach, Bintan.
The ruins of the last Rajah's palace, and royal tombs on Lingga.
YOU SHOULD KNOW:
The first book of Malay grammar was published on Penyengat Island in 1857, and classical Malay is still spoken on the island.

Seram

POPULATION:
247,375 (1993)
WHEN TO GO:
November to March
HOW TO GET THERE:
By air or sea from Ambon.
HIGHLIGHTS:
Snorkel the coral gardens off shore from Sawai.
Look out for some of the island's huge butterflies, in particular the spectacular Blue Mountain Swallowtail (*Papilio Ulysses*), with its 11.4 cm (4.5 in) wingspan.
YOU SHOULD KNOW:
An earthquake of 6.7 on the Richter scale was recorded on Seram in March 2006.

The mysterious island of Seram lies to the north east of Ambon. A wild, mountainous place, rich with rainforest and wildlife, in particular fabulous, colourful birds and some 2,000 species of butterflies and moths, Seram is replete with myths and legends. One of Maluku's largest and least known islands, it is held in awe by the Ambonese, who believe that all life originated here.

Seram is home to numerous indigenous peoples, largely still living their traditional ways of life. Some 75 per cent of the population are animists, and one remote tribe, the Nuaulu, were still head hunting in the 1940s. This is a difficult island to get around, with few roads. Instead, people hop on boats to take them from village to village up and down the coast. Masohi is the island's main town, but most people come here to take guided treks into Manusela National Park, or to visit the dramatically beautiful Teluk Sawai Bay.

Sadly, the Indonesian government have leased logging concessions on Seram, one consequence of which is the loss of

birdlife. In the national park, however, the forest is alive with screaming cockatoos and multi-coloured parrots. At Saleman, on Teluk Sawai Bay, great flocks of Lusiala birds, believed to be carrying the souls of their human ancestors, fly from a cave at dusk. Seram is also home to the salmon crested cockatoo, endemic to only four places in Indonesia, but there are other endemic species too – honeyeaters, lories and white-eyes for example. Mount Binaiya at 3,019 m (10,000 ft) is the island's highest peak, and the fabulous, rushing rivers and plunging waterfalls combined with exotic peoples and wonderful wildlife make Seram an adventure not to be undertaken lightly.

The spectacular Blue Mountain Swallowtail butterfly

Siberut

The largest island of the Mentawai group, Siberut is believed to have broken off from Sumatra some 500,000 years ago. Hence the indigenous people remained isolated and evolved their own culture. Siberut's flora and fauna is also unique, and therefore it was listed as a UNESCO Man and Biosphere Reserve in 1981. Additionally a large part of the island is a National Park, as extra protection against predatory loggers.

Until missionaries arrived in the early 1900s, Mentawaians were hunter/gatherers, highly skilled at boat building. They looked exotic: the Sakkudei, for example, wore bark loin cloths or skirts, red rattan bands, beads, tattoos, and filed their teeth to points. Today these customs have largely died out, but many cling to their old beliefs despite the missionaries' best efforts.

Mentawaians live mainly in riverside villages, with a communal longhouse in which to make important decisions. Houses contain several families and there are separate buildings for unmarried men and widows. Some cultivation occurs and hunting (with bows and poisoned arrows) and fishing are important social activities.

The flora and fauna here are extraordinary – 60 per cent of the mammals are endemic, including the Kloss gibbon, one of the 25 most endangered animals. As there are no facilities in the interior, most visitors arrive as part of a group, with local hosts organized in advance. The coast, however, is another story. Highly thought of by the surfing fraternity, small resorts have begun popping up on the best beaches.

Hilly, startlingly green and always humid, luxuriant plant life still smothers large parts of Siberut. As one travels by river, not road, seeing rainforest in every direction and hearing the calls of birds and monkeys rather than the rumble of traffic, it's hard to believe that the city of Padang is a mere 100 km (60 mi) away. Siberut is another world.

POPULATION:
35,000 (2005)
WHEN TO GO:
It is always rainy here, but the driest month is May. The highest rainfall occurs from September to December.
HOW TO GET THERE:
By sea from Sumatra.
HIGHLIGHTS:
Trekking in the interior.
Surfing between April and October.
YOU SHOULD KNOW:
Beware of chloroquine-resistant malaria. Take things with which to barter, and gifts for your village hosts.

Mentawai men in a dugout canoe set out down the Rereiket River.

Sulawesi

POPULATION:
15,500,000 (2006)
WHEN TO GO:
Almost always wet, the driest months are probably July and August.
HOW TO GET THERE:
By international or internal flight to Makassar, Manado or Pula, or by ferry.
HIGHLIGHTS:
Tana Beru – watch Bugis schooners being fashioned by hand.
Lore Lindu National Park, a UNESCO Man and Biosphere Reserve.
Ancient megalithic stone statues in the Napu, Besoa and Bada valleys.
Diving and snorkelling in Tukang Besi National Marine Park.
Chill out in the glorious Togean Islands.
Sungguminasa's Ballompoa Museum.
YOU SHOULD KNOW:
Sulawesi's complicated coastline is longer than that of the whole of continental USA.

Sulawesi lies to the east of Borneo. It's a bizarrely shaped island – the four 'arms' radiating from its mountainous centre make it look like some weird sea creature. Marginally smaller than Britain, nowhere in Sulawesi is more than 100 km (60 mi) from the ocean. Many different ethnic groups and cultures survive here, the most famous of which are the Toraja and the Bugis. The latter are a proud, seafaring people, whose elegant schooners still ply their trade around Indonesia's waters.

Most visitors to the island go to see the extraordinary Torajan people, who live in the fertile valleys of the mountains in the north of South Sulawesi. Their culture is fascinating – living in large, traditionally built family houses with high roofs that rear up at both ends, resembling either the ships in which their ancestors arrived here, or buffalo horns, depending on who you ask.

Buffaloes are essential to the Toraja, a sign of wealth and status and a necessary sacrificial animal in many ceremonies, particularly the Torajans' elaborate funeral rituals. The dead often remain in the house for months or years before the funeral festivities occur, a process lasting several days, involving the slaughter of many animals, with parades, dances and feasting. The dead and their valuables are placed in tombs carved into sheer limestone cliffs, closed with a wooden door and, if they were highly respected, a life sized wooden effigy, dressed appropriately, is placed on a gallery carved into the cliff face.

Sulawesi's largely upland landscape is dramatically spectacular. Its isolation has produced vast numbers of endemic species – some two thirds of its mammals and a quarter of its birds, reptiles and insects. Sadly, this incredible fauna is threatened by habitat loss. Whilst visiting Toraja-land is a unique experience, all the rest of the island deserves your attention as well.

A traditional Torajan house

Sumatra

The island of Sumatra is the sixth largest in the world, stretching almost 2,000 km (1,250 mi) from north to south. To the west, the Bukit Barisan Mountains run almost the entire length of the island, rising from a narrow coastal strip. The highest of the 93 volcanic peaks, 15 of which are still active, is Mount Kerinci, at 3,805 m (12,556 ft). To the east, mountains slope down to swamps and marshes, cut by seething, silt-laden rivers.

Islam reached Sumatra in the 14th century, by which time several fabulous empires had come and gone, and Europeans were ogling the island's natural wealth. Several powers vied for it, with the Dutch emerging victorious in 1824. Sumatrans, however, were not subdued, and they continued fighting until independence in 1949. The Acehnese people still cause headaches for the current Indonesian government.

This is a wild and glorious island. Mainly covered with dense jungle, it contains some of the world's greatest biodiversity. Endemic species such as the Sumatran tiger and the two-horned rhino still survive here, as do orang-utans. Here, too, are both the world's largest and tallest flowers. The island encompasses many different ethnic groups, languages and cultures such as the matrilineal Minangkabau of West Sumatra, the Christian Bataks around gorgeous Lake Toba, and the fiercely Muslim Acehnese.

Sumatra is an adventure. Now largely forgotten by tourists, it can be hard work – the roads are dreadful and the transport worse – but the landscape is fabulous and the traditional architecture, such as the Minankabau longhouses with their buffalo-horn style roofs, breathtaking.

A string of natural disasters has hit Sumatra in the recent past, drastically curtailing tourism, but if you want to explore off the beaten track, amidst fabulous natural wonders, meeting people who will welcome your arrival with open arms, Sumatra is the place for you.

POPULATION:
40,000,000 (2005)
WHEN TO GO:
Always hot and always wet, the driest months are June and July.
HOW TO GET THERE:
By international flights to Medan, domestic flight, or ferry from Malaysia, Singapore or other Indonesian islands.
HIGHLIGHTS:
The orang-utan rehabilitation centre in Bukit Lawang.
Lake Toba for Batak culture.
Climbing the Sibayak volcano.
Trekking in Kerinci Seblat National Park.
The Hindu-Buddhist temple complex at Muara Jambi.
YOU SHOULD KNOW:
The famous World War 1 French spy, Mata Hari, lived in Sumatra for some years. In the Bahasa Indonesian language 'mata hari', literally 'the eye of the day' means 'the sun'.

A Minankabau rice barn, with traditional buffalo-horn style roofs

Sumba

POPULATION:
540,000 (2007)
WHEN TO GO:
April to December
HOW TO GET THERE:
By air from Bali or West Timor, or by ferry.
HIGHLIGHTS:
The Resi Moni megalith, one of the largest on Sumba.
The Purunga Ta Kadonga ceremony at Lai Tarung.
Sodan village and its annual October New Year ceremony.
Ikat weaving at Ngallu and Kaliuda.
Waikabubak and the villages of Anakalang district.
The white sand beach of Pantai Marosi.
YOU SHOULD KNOW:
Betel nut, or *sirih pinang* is widely chewed on Sumba, and it is offered to visitors as a welcoming gesture. It is impolite to refuse it, but if you can't face chewing it, put it away as though to enjoy later.

To the south of Komodo and Flores is the island of Sumba, the arid backwater of the Nusa Tenggara. Some 300 km (180 mi) long and 80 km (50 mi) wide, west Sumba is fairly isolated, but because it receives more rain and is more fertile it is home to 65 per cent of the population. This is a land of low, undulating hills, cassava and maize crops and open grasslands grazed by cattle, buffalo and horses.

Most of the religious influences that affected other islands passed Sumba by, and until Dutch rule in the early 1900s, it was never colonized by outsiders. Instead it was formed of various separate, warring kingdoms. Besides Bahasa Indonesia there are nine other languages spoken on Sumba, eight of which are used in the west, whilst the ninth is exclusive to the east.

Historically known for its horses, slaves and sandalwood, Sumba is now famous for its extraordinary annual Pasola festivals. Held after the full moon in February and March, these are ritual battles between spear-carrying, bareback, tribal horsemen. Although the spears are blunted, this tradition reflects those early kingdoms, and occasionally genuine fighting and deaths occur. The start of the Pasolas is determined by the arrival of thousands of seaworms on the shoreline. Fulfilling their reproductive cycle, the worms are thought to predict the abundance of the coming harvest.

Geographically very different from the west, east Sumba is a barren, rocky place. The 250,000 inhabitants live, for the most part, near the coast, and are renowned for their ikat weaving. The motifs used are often animals such as horses, crocodiles and cockatoos, each deeply symbolic. Despite being largely Protestant, animism is still strongly rooted here.

This island is off the tourist trail, but those who visit will find fascinating traditional villages, extraordinary megalithic tombs, exotic tribespeople and remarkable death ceremonies.

A rider battles it out in a traditional Pasola festival.

Sumbawa

Sumbawa, which lies to the east of Lombok, is larger than Bali and Lombok put together. It is a poor, rugged island, which, thanks to an enormous gold and copper mining project that has recently begun operations, may well become more developed and much wealthier in future. Meanwhile, most of the inhabitants are farmers or fishermen, while some breed and export the island's tough little horses.

Sumbawa naturally divides into two parts, west and east, separated by the Tambora volcano. In 1815 Gunung Tambora erupted, killing thousands and reducing the peak from 4,200 m (13,900 ft) to the 2,850 m (9,400 ft) it is today. The western Sumbawans lean towards Lombok in both looks and language, whilst the easterners lean towards Flores. Everyone, however, is strongly Muslim, and has been since the early 1600s, although traditional animism still plays its part.

The island's attractions are mainly natural: the volcano can be climbed, although it is a hard, two-day trek to the top. Once there, on a clear day, the views are spectacular, and the caldera, which is some 6 km (3.7 mi) wide, contains a two-coloured lake. Most of the visitors to the island, however, come for the world-class surfing at Hu'u and Lakey Beach, which is at its best between June and August.

The island's main town, Sumbawa Besar, is small, dusty and provincial – easy to explore on foot or by horse and cart. People are friendly and hospitable and it makes a good base from which to visit nearby Poto, where the songket (silver or gold threads woven into cloth) sarongs are highly thought of. Also within visiting distance are some fascinating megalithic, carved tombs, believed to be 2,000 years old. Sumbawa may be a fairly low-key island, but it is well worth a few days of your time.

Most of Sumbawa's visitors come for the world-class surfing.

POPULATION:
1,000,000 (2007)
WHEN TO GO:
May to October
HOW TO GET THERE:
By air to Sumbawa Besar or to Bima from Bali, Sumba or Flores. By ferry from many other Indonesian islands.
HIGHLIGHTS:
The wooden Sultan's Palace and the Art Deco Yellow House in Sumbawa Besar.
Surfing at Maluk and Sekongkang.
A trip to Pulao Moyo, an island nature reserve surrounded by excellent coral reefs.
Hire a horse to trek through the forest near Tegel.
Horse racing on a Sunday at the Desa Panda stadium near Bima.
The museum in the Sultan's Palace in Bima.
YOU SHOULD KNOW:
Don't dress skimpily unless you're at the beach – this is a strongly Muslim island and you will cause unnecessary offence.

Java

POPULATION:
120,000,000 (2006)
WHEN TO GO:
May to September
HOW TO GET THERE:
International flight to Jakarta,
domestic flight or ferry from
Malaysia, Singapore and the other
Indonesian islands.
HIGHLIGHTS:
Jakarta's Sunda Kelapa harbour, with
its superb traditional schooners.
Ujung Kulong National Park.
The Waicak festival in May at
Borobudur.
The Ramayana, danced at full moon
at Prambanan.
The Dieng Plateau and its temples.
The hill towns of Malang and Tretes.
YOU SHOULD KNOW:
Some of the best and most
expensive coffee in the world comes
from Java. Kopi Luwak comes from
coffee berries that have been
previously digested by palm civets, a
type of wild cat.

Indonesia's heartland, Java, has twice the population of Britain in roughly half the area, and is naturally the political and economic hub of Indonesia. Jakarta, the capital, is a city of at least 15 million, where extremes of wealth and poverty sit awkwardly side by side. There are several other large cities, but once outside them, one is unaware of the crowded nature of the island. Some 50 per cent of the population are farmers, tending land which is fantastically fertile, thanks to the residue from the active volcanoes that form the island's spine.

Java Man proves that history here reaches back for a million years. Wonderful Buddhist and Hindu temples, particularly Borobudur and Prambanan, built in the 8th and 9th centuries show cultural depths rarely achieved elsewhere, although the island's golden age came during the 16th century. The three main ethnic groups are the Javanese, Sundanese and Madurese, each speaking their own language, the Javanese being the main group, famous for all things artistic.

Java is beautiful; the landscape soars and swoops, crops growing at every level. Fruit such as apples and strawberries grow around the hill towns, while rice, tobacco, tea, coffee, vegetables and spices seem to grow everywhere else.

This is a fascinating island, where performance arts such as *wayang kulit* – shadow puppet plays – and traditional dance can be seen in tiny villages or a Sultan's palace, and artists and galleries abound. Whether you climb Mount Bromo to stand by the smoking crater as the sun rises, swim or surf in the crashing Indian Ocean on the southern coast, learn batik-making, cookery or massage in vibrant university towns such as Solo or Yogyakarta, or exchange laughter and ideas with students over several 'Bintang' beers, amidst clouds of pungent clove cigarette smoke, Java's exotic, ancient culture is show-stopping.

The smoking crater of Mount Bromo in Bromo Tengger Semeru National Park

Komodo

Part of the Lesser Sunda chain and lying between the neighbouring islands of Sumbawa to the west and Flores to the east, Komodo is one of the many islands which make up the Republic of Indonesia. The inhabitants of this barren volcanic land are descendants of former convicts who were exiled to the island and who have mixed themselves with the Bugis from nearby Sulawesi. However, the island is most famous not for its heritage of convicts, but for the unique fauna which inhabit it. The Komodo dragon, the world's largest living lizard, takes its name from the island. A type of monitor lizard, the dragon inhabits Komodo and some of the smaller surrounding islands, attracting thousands of tourists every year.

A Komodo dragon

The lizards are active during the morning and late afternoon, but burrow into dry stream beds during the heat of the day to keep cool. Guided tours take visitors to see the lizards and this is a good bet if you want to guarantee spotting one. They can grow up to 3 m (10 ft) in length and, despite their short legs, they can run as fast as a dog. Visitors are advised not to wear red and to keep an eye out for their footprints while visiting the island as they can bite. They can also swim from island to island so even the sea is not necessarily a safe place.

Komodo dragons were only discovered by Western scientists in 1910 when a Dutch officer, Van Steyn van Hensbroek, heard rumours of giant crocodiles and went to investigate. Today their range has contracted due to human activities, and they are listed as vulnerable by the World Conservation Union.

The Komodo National Park was set up in 1980 to protect the Komodo dragon, and the area is also now on the UNESCO World Heritage list. The national park includes the three large islands of Komodo, Rinca and Padar, as well as numerous smaller ones. Later it was dedicated to protecting other species as the three islands have a high marine biodiversity, including whale sharks, ocean sunfish, manta rays, eagle rays, pygmy seahorses, false pipefish, clown frogfish, nudibranchs, blue-ringed octopus, sponges, tunicates, and coral. The coral reefs, seamounts, seagrass beds and mangroves make the islands a popular place for diving.

POPULATION:
2,000 (2005)
WHEN TO GO:
April to October
HOW TO GET THERE:
By air to Labuanbajo from Bali, then by boat.
HIGHLIGHTS:
The Komodo dragons – consider joining a guided tour to get a good look at these prehistoric beasts.
YOU SHOULD KNOW:
All visitors to the Komodo National Park now have to pay a contribution to protect wildlife in the park, help support local communities and promote ecotourism.

Krakatau

Anak Krakatau still smoulders on!

POPULATION:
Uninhabited
WHEN TO GO:
April to June and September to October
HOW TO GET THERE:
Join a guided tour, or charter the best, most seaworthy boat you can find.
HIGHLIGHTS:
If you are in west Java to visit Krakatau, make time for a trip to the UNESCO World Heritage Site of Ujung Kulon National Park, home to several rare and endangered mammals.
YOU SHOULD KNOW:
Although the Krakatau explosion is a world famous event, the eruption of Sumbawa Island's Gunung Tambora was roughly equivalent. Tens of thousands were killed, and the island was devastated when the volcano exploded, losing 1,350 m (4,500 ft) of its height, and causing 1815 to be known globally as 'the year without a summer'.

The volcano of Krakatau is probably the most famous in the world. It lies between Sumatra and western Java, quite the reverse of the famous film entitled *Krakatoa, East of Java*. Krakatau earned its notoriety in 1883, when it erupted so violently that it almost completely disintegrated. Great columns of ash rose from the explosion to a height of 80 km (50 mi), which triggered a tsunami that crashed across the nearby Sumatran and Javan shorelines, wiping out over 160 villages and killing some 36,000 people. The noise of the explosion is thought to have been the loudest ever recorded, and the waves' passage was even measurable in the English Channel.

Most noticeable of all were the ash clouds, which travelled around the world for three years, causing extraordinarily vivid, colourful sunsets. It is thought that the background to Edvard Munch's famous painting, 'The Scream', was painted from the sunsets at that time.

In 1928, Anak Krakatau, or 'Child of Krakatau', made its appearance, and has been growing steadily ever since. This is an active, volatile 'child', and as you pass by on the night ferry, rivulets of molten lava are sometimes visible on its flanks. Anak Krakatau lies amongst several other small islands. At its birth, no life existed here, but today, some 80 years later, vegetation has returned, as have snakes, rats, insects, bats and birds.

It is possible to visit and trek on Anak Krakatau with a guided tour, though you cannot go to the caldera as it is potentially dangerous. A trip like this also enables you to visit some of the neighbouring islands, and to snorkel or dive nearby. Underwater, life is thriving – the thermal springs bring abundant plants as well as fish. A visit to Krakatau is truly a once-in-a-lifetime experience.

Lombok

The string of islands lying to the east of Bali are known collectively as Nusa Tenggara, and of them, Lombok is the main destination. Roughly 80 km (50 mi) from north to south, and about the same from east to west, Lombok's landscape is dominated by its northern mountains, their slopes covered in protected forest, from which rises Mount Rinjani, the second highest volcano in Indonesia. The western side is green and lush, but the east and south of the island are noticeably drier and less populated.

Indigenous Sasak people make up 90 per cent of the population, alongside Balinese and others. Sasaks have their own language and culture and although the predominant religion is Islam, they also have their own religion, Wektu Telu, a mixture of Islam, Hindu and animist beliefs. Invasions during the early 1600s led to Lombok being in Balinese hands by 1750, and under Dutch control from the late 1800s until independence. Like Bali, the island suffered massacres after the attempted coup in Java, and in the 1960s and 70s suffered famine conditions. Tourism began in the 1980s but has suffered with the rest of the country. Today there are high hopes for tourism potential in the future.

Lombok has something for everyone: landscapes as lush as Bali, empty white sand beaches, good snorkelling and surfing, hot springs, waterfalls, palaces, temples, and trekking on mighty Rinjani. You can watch traditional dances and ceremonies that follow the seasons, and listen to a remarkable musical style in which voices imitate the sounds of the Gamelan orchestra. There are also unique Sasak contests – Peresehan involves two men fighting with staves and shields, and Lanca, where men fight with their knees. Much less crowded than the better-known islands, Lombok is a great place for a getaway.

POPULATION:
3,100,000 (2007)
WHEN TO GO:
April to September is the driest time.
HOW TO GET THERE:
By air from Kuala Lumpur, Singapore, Java, Bali or Sumbawa, or by ferry between the islands.
HIGHLIGHTS:
The temple of Pura Meru.
The temple compound of Pura Lingsar.
The pottery making villages of Banyumulek and Penujak.
The craft villages south of Tetebatu.
The Sasak Nyale festival, held on the beach at Kuta in February/March.
The Mayura Water Palace and gardens.
YOU SHOULD KNOW:
The Wallace Line, imagined by naturalist Sir Alfred Wallace in the 1800s, separates Bali and Borneo from Lombok and Sulawesi. Theoretically Eurasian plants and animals exist on the western side while Australian species live on the east. In fact, this is a transition area between the two.

Clouds drift over the crater rim of Mount Rinjani.

Madura

POPULATION:
3,300,000 million (2006)
WHEN TO GO:
May to October
HOW TO GET THERE:
Ferry from Surabaya, Java.
HIGHLIGHTS:
The bull racing championship finals in Pamekasan, held every September/October.
The tombs of the royal family at Asta Tinggi, outside Sumenep.
The tombs of the Cakraningrat royal family at Air Mata, near Arosbaya.
Tanjungbumi village – for Madurese batik.
YOU SHOULD KNOW:
Before a big race, the bulls are given honey and herbs and up to 50 raw eggs per day to eat. Music is played to them, and they are given massages. Just before they race, they are given the local firewater, arak, to drink.

Separated from Surabaya in northwest Java by a 3 km (1.8 mi) channel of water, the island of Madura is a world of its own. Little visited either by tourists from overseas or Java itself, except from late August to October, the islanders are proud of their heritage and their reputation as a warrior people.

Madura is some 160 km (100 mi) long and 35 km (22 mi) wide. The south is well-cultivated and lined with shallow beaches, the interior mainly rock and sand, whilst such hills as there are to the north culminate in steep cliffs, with breakers relentlessly pounding on the shore below.

Most Madurese are farmers, fishermen, salt producers or cattle breeders. Cattle are extremely important, not only to the economy but also because of the famous bull races that take place each year. This exciting and colourful sport involves pairs of the finest bulls harnessed to a small sled upon which stands the 'jockey'. The bulls, lovingly nurtured for these events, are decked out in finery and, to the accompaniment of gamelan orchestras and cheering spectators, race down a course of some 120 m (396 ft).

A decent road links the three main towns on the island. Bangkalan, in the west, is the main base from which to go bull racing, Pamekasan is the sleepy capital in central Madura, with Sumenep, in the east, the most attractive of the three. Sumenep's sights are all closely situated around a large, central square, where there is a splendid 18th century mosque, and a *kraton*, a Javanese royal palace. Here you can visit some of the rooms, which contain a curious collection of weapons, ceramics and other assorted items. Beside it is a small, enclosed water garden – *taman sari* – with a clear pool full of fish.

Water buffaloes race at Pamekasan.

Rote

Rote, or Roti Island, is Indonesia's southern-most inhabited island and the southernmost point of Eurasia. Even if it were not both remote and beautiful, those facts alone would give it a certain romantic appeal. As it is, Rote, one fifth of the size of Bali, is full of hills and valleys, cultivated terraces, acacia palms, savannah and forested areas, and its exotic people belong to some 18 different ethnic groups. Rote lies off the southwestern tip of West Timor and, because it is so arid, relies on the extremely useful, drought-resistant Lontar palm to fuel its economy.

In the late 17th century, the ruling Dutch took many slaves from Rote, but as the Rotenese adopted Christianity – today 90 per cent of the islanders are Christians – they were rewarded with an educational system that grew and prospered, turning out many administrators and nationalist leaders. Rotenese men are known throughout the archipelago for their debating skill, although today's standards of education and health are both falling behind the Indonesian average.

The Lontar palm leaf can be made into shoes, bags and the traditional wide-banded hat, with its unusual frontal spike. It provides roofing and interior walls and is also turned into a unique, stringed instrument, the sasando. The wood is made into furniture and planks, and the sap into a nutritious fresh drink that, if left to ferment, makes alcoholic palm wine. Distilled, it becomes the local firewater. Crafts are practised, too – silver jewellery making and ikat weaving.

Rote has some interesting local architecture, boasting carved and thatched roofs, but is best known for its empty, white beaches, translucent waters, surfing, diving and snorkelling in a superbly lush marine environment, complete with spectacular underwater caverns.

POPULATION:
100,000 (2001)
WHEN TO GO:
April to November
HOW TO GET THERE:
By plane or ferry from West Timor.
HIGHLIGHTS:
The island's capital, Ba'a.
The Saturday market at Papela.
Nemberala Beach, with its famous 'left break' surf – best from June to October.
N'dana Island, a tiny, uninhabited nature reserve, with turtle nesting sites.
Ndao Island, and its renowned gold- and silversmiths.
YOU SHOULD KNOW:
There is a red lake on N'dana Island, which is said to be stained with the blood of the inhabitants who were all massacred in an act of vengeance during the 17th century.

Fishing boats at low tide on Rote Island

Weh

Lying a mere 350 m (1,150 ft) off northern Sumatra is the tiny, volcanic island of Weh, surrounded by the Andaman Sea. Weh is the northernmost point of Indonesia's archipelago, and was formed during the Pleistocene age by an eruption that separated it from the mainland. The highest point is a fumarolic volcano reaching 617 m (2,024 ft) in height, but there is also a volcanic cone in the rainforest, three boiling mud fields, hot springs and underwater fumaroles. During the 2004 tsunami Weh received some damage. However, thousands of replacement mangrove seedlings have since been planted, houses rebuilt and the island has recovered.

Sabang harbour, which is both deep and sheltered, was used as a re-fuelling station, first for Dutch naval steamships in the 1880s, and later for merchant vessels. It was a Free Port for a time, though the government withdrew that status during the 1980s, since when both the economy and the population have declined. Today the island's economy is based upon cloves, coconuts, fishing, rattan furniture production and a little tourism.

For those who make the trip, Weh is charming. Scenically lovely, with hills, rocks, caves and secluded beaches, its significant ecosystem has been recognized with a nature reserve, covering both sea and land. The spectacular coral gardens have suffered somewhat, but there are still magnificent underwater walls and canyons to explore, and a multitude of both small, colourful reef fish and large species such as lion fish, manta rays, sharks and turtles. During the winter monsoon, whale sharks can be seen. In 2004 a megamouth shark was found here, thought to be only the twenty-first sighting since 1976.

Weh is a tranquil spot, as yet undeveloped. The locals don't see many foreigners, just a few NGOs from Aceh, and the occasional intrepid diver – simplicity and natural beauty are its strengths.

A giant sea fan in the spectacular coral gardens that surround the island of Weh.

POPULATION:
25,000 (2007)
WHEN TO GO:
It can always rain on Weh, but the wettest months are from November to February
HOW TO GET THERE:
By ferry from Uleh-leh in north Sumatra.
HIGHLIGHTS:
The fresh-water lake near Sabang.
The diving and snorkelling around the island.
The Iboih Forest Nature Reserve.
The Sea Garden coral reefs.
YOU SHOULD KNOW:
Northern Sumatra is very strongly Muslim, so be careful not to offend people by dressing or behaving inappropriately.

Timor

The island of Timor lies to the east of Sumba, and north west of Australia. Like its neighbours, it is an arid place, with a mountain range stretching right across it, from end to end. Timor is divided into West Timor, which is part of Indonesia, and the independent state of East Timor. Divided for centuries, the Portuguese began colonization during the early 16th century, but Timor, which was rich with valuable sandalwood trees, was also desirable to the Dutch. After years of conflict, the Portuguese were relegated to the eastern part of the island.

West Timor became Indonesian when that country gained independence in 1945, whilst East Timor remained Portuguese until 1975. Years of civil war, and brutal annexation by Indonesia followed, but in 1999 East Timor became independent, though sadly there are still serious internal problems.

West Timor is a good jumping off point for the eastern Indonesian islands. Kupang, a busy, noisy city, is the capital of East Nusa Tenggara province. Beyond it, starkly beautiful, rugged countryside sweeps away, sprinkled with traditional villages of neat, beehive shaped, grass and bamboo huts. While West Timor is, of course, Muslim, East Timor is about 90 per cent Christian, mainly Catholic, and churches, some well worth visiting, can be found across the whole island. Naturally, however, pockets of animism still occur here.

Timor is ringed with unspoiled beaches, most of which are completely undeveloped. In the hills, maize, sweet potatoes and coffee are grown, while rubber, coconuts, tobacco and rice grow nearer the coast. The island has lots of potential: in time, East Timor will enjoy the financial benefits of having off-shore oil and gas fields, which are being developed with Australia and which are needed to rebuild infrastructure and other war damage. Meanwhile, West Timor will no doubt see tourism increasing, now that hostilities are over.

Timor is ringed with unspoiled beaches.

POPULATION:
2,220,000 (2002)
WHEN TO GO:
The driest months are from May to November.
HOW TO GET THERE:
By air from Indonesia and Australia, or by sea from Indonesia.
HIGHLIGHTS:
Bird watching trips around the island.
The Tuesday market in Oinlasi, W. Timor.
The animist village of Boti, W. Timor.
The ikat weaving village of Temkassi, W. Timor.
YOU SHOULD KNOW:
In 1789 Captain William Bligh reached Timor after having been cast adrift from his ship, HMS *Bounty*, by mutineers. He self-navigated an extraordinary 6,701 km (3,618 miles) from near Tahiti to Timor in 47 days, losing only one seaman of the 18 who were with him.

New Guinea

POPULATION:
7,100,000 (2007)
WHEN TO GO:
New Guinea is always wet and
humid, but the driest months are
from June to September.
HOW TO GET THERE:
To Papua: by air from Java or
Sulawesi, or by boat.
To PNG: Fly from Australia.
HIGHLIGHTS:
Explore Biak Island and swim and
dive from its white sand beaches.
Hike around or cruise Lake Sentani
on a longboat.
Visit Wasur National Park.
Trek The Kokoda Trail, scene of
Australia's hard-fought victory over
the Japanese in WWII.
Visit the Huli tribe in the Tari Valley.
YOU SHOULD KNOW:
Thousands of endemic species of
flora and fauna exisit in New Guinea,
including thousands as yet unknown
to the West. Of 284 species of
mammal, including tree kangaroos
and wallabies, 195 are endemic. Of
578 species of breeding bird,
including most Birds of Paradise, 324
are endemic. There are 200,000
species of insect, 400 amphibians,
455 butterflies and 1,200 species of
fish. New Guinea is home to 75% of
the world's coral.

New Guinea is the world's second largest island, and is also one of
the world's last, vast and remote wildernesses. With a complex
political history, this great island is divided. The western half, is now
known as Papua, a region of Indonesia, while the eastern half, Papua
New Guinea or PNG, has been an independent country since 1975.

New Guinea is part of the Pacific Ring of Fire, and endures
sporadic volcanic eruptions, earthquakes and occasional tsunamis. A
mountain range rises across the length of New Guinea and deep
rainforest is all enveloping. The island contains an astonishing
wealth of natural features, some protected by National Parks and
UNESCO Man and Biosphere Reserves, but huge swathes of it are
unmapped and virtually unreachable. The main towns of both
countries are, naturally, on the coast, but there is little in the way of
roads or infrastructure. Travel is mainly by boat – rivers criss-cross
the whole region – on foot, or by plane

New Guinea is inhabited by about 1,000 different tribes,
speaking a similar number of languages. Tourists are few, mainly
visiting the extraordinary Dani culture, in Papua's beautiful Baliem
Valley. Despite being nominally Christians, the Dani live traditionally.
Men wear penis sheaths, women wear short skirts, made of orchid
fibres, worn beneath the buttocks. This high valley, surrounded by
mountain peaks, is a vision of incredibly fertile cultivated fields. The
Baliem River provides fish, and pigs are essential, being eaten at
every ceremony.

In PNG the major attraction is the tribal hunter/gatherers who
live along the banks of the
island's longest river, the Sepik.
This culture is intrinsically
entwined with crocodiles, and
the men's extensive scarification
reflects the animal's scales.
Living in communal longhouses,
Sepik River people are famous
for their wood-carvings. Varying
in style from village to village,
many of these find their way into
the great museums of the world.

*Huli warriors taking part in
a 'sing sing' feast.*

New Britain

New Britain is the largest island in Papua New Guinea's eastern Bismark Archipelago – in fact, it is the 38th largest island in the world. Mountainous and volcanic, much of the island is covered with a lush tangle of rainforest, the high rainfall feeding several large rivers.

In 1700, William Dampier, the first European visitor, named the island. In 1884 New Britain became part of German New Guinea but in 1914 the Australians took the island from Germany, and it remained Australian, apart from being conquered by Japan in WWII, until New Guinea's independence in 1975. Today, while East New Britain is a tourist destination, West New Britain is largely untouched and undiscovered.

Today's capital, Kokopo, superceded Rabaul in 1994, when a huge eruption destroyed most of the town, covering it with ash and lava. Prior warning enabled all the inhabitants to escape with their lives. The economy here is mixed – palm oil, copra, cotton, coffee and rubber plantations are extensive, while copper, coal and gold are mined. Unfortunately the interior and some of the south coast is now being logged.

The people and cultures that exist here are fascinating. The Kove people in the west were documented for *National Geographic* magazine in the 1960s, and within Papua New Guinea they are known for their practice of superincision of the penis. In the east there are several tribal groups who are matrilineal, and who use threaded shells as currency, not only for dowries and ceremonies but also for buying land and food.

This is a gorgeous island, flowers and plants thrive on the rich, volcanic soil, and scrumptious fruit and vegetables abound. Apart from the fabulous diving and snorkelling there are other attractions such as hot springs and caves, and above all, charming friendly people who are pleased to meet you.

Ulauan volcano

POPULATION:
404,873 (2000)
WHEN TO GO:
It's always hot and wet, but probably receives most rain between December and March.
HOW TO GET THERE:
By air to Tokua from Papua New Guinea.
HIGHLIGHTS:
Bitapaka War Cemetery – a moving memorial to the fallen, maintained by the Commonwealth War Graves Commission.
The Japanese War Tunnels.
Night diving the Cathedral, at Kimbe Bay.
Kokopo market.
YOU SHOULD KNOW:
A French caving team believes that not only is the Muruk cave system in West New Britain the deepest recorded in the southern hemisphere, but also that there is a canyon 1,200 m (3,960 ft) below the cave's entrance.

New Ireland

With the Bismark Sea to the southwest and the Pacific Ocean to the northeast, New Ireland is some 320 km (200 mi) long but never much more than 10 km (6 mi) wide. This narrow island contains a range of sharp, rugged mountains – the highest, Mount Lambel, rises to 2,150 m (7,054 ft) – and dense rainforest.

Thought to have been inhabited for 30,000 years, it was not until 1900 that Franz Boluminski, the German administrator for the region, arrived. Until then New Ireland's people were known as ferocious cannibals who cheerfully slaughtered foreign sailors arriving on their shores. Boluminski set up highly successful copra plantations, building a long road of coral in order to utilize the good harbour at Kavieng, the island's capital. After the Japanese invasion of WWII, New Ireland was ceded to Australia, and is now part of Papua New Guinea.

The Melanesian islanders have three distinct cultures, and 22 languages between them. Unique are their splendidly carved Malagan funerary figures, many of which have found their way into European museums. Sculptors can still be found in a couple of villages, but sadly this seems to be a dying art. Shark calling is another tradition. Some islanders can 'call' sharks, which come to the caller's boat where they are speared.

Kavieng is a pleasant town, the road around the bay shaded by beautiful, old trees. While large ships still come for copra and oil, tourists come as well, to enjoy this 'typical Somerset Maugham south-sea-island port', as it has been described. Diving here is exciting – wrecks lie scattered over the seabed, even in the harbour itself. Hire a canoe and paddle out to the islets in the bay, or visit Karu Bay to see where sea turtles come to lay their eggs.

POPULATION:
10,600 (2000)
WHEN TO GO:
The south is always hot and quite wet, while the centre and north is always hot and have a dry season between May and October.
HOW TO GET THERE:
Fly from Port Moresby, Lae or Rabaul, or boat from Rabaul.
HIGHLIGHTS:
The Luka Barok festival held each June/July.
The Malangan Show and Independence Day Festival, held during four days each September.
The Tabar Islands, with their wood carvers and shark callers.
Lihir Island – said to have the second largest gold deposit in the world.
YOU SHOULD KNOW:
During the 1870s and 80s, the Marquis de Raye sold hundreds of hectares of land at Cape Breton, which he described as a thriving settlement, to gullible settlers who were left in the jungle with just 3 weeks' food and little else. Most people died before they could be rescued, and the Marquis ended his days in an asylum in France.

A striking blue starfish on the coral reef

Samarai and Kwato

Lying just 5 km (3 mi) off the south-eastern tip of Papua New Guinea, is the tiny, pretty island of Samarai. Once the bustling administrative centre and port town for Papua, today, a shadow of its former self, the current government has declared it a National Historical Heritage Island.

Discovered by Captain John Moresby in 1873, a mission station was established here five years later. By then a small trading post had been set up, and under British rule it had become a large, successful port. By 1927 Samarai had electricity and street lighting, and the European settlers lived here in fine style – so much so that it was named the 'Pearl of the Pacific'. During WWII, much of the infrastructure was destroyed by the Australians, fearful of a Japanese invasion, and although this never occurred, the Japanese did bomb what was left of the town.

Somewhat restored after the war, Samarai never really recovered, and the administrative centre was relocated to Alotau. Today, visitors to the island, which can be walked in about 30 minutes, can see the remnants of its colonial past, including a church, a school and several small shops as well as an almost surreal cricket oval which is still in use. The inhabitants live simply, mainly doing a little farming and fishing – there is no industry here, although there is talk of setting up a cultured pearl business.

The quiet, forested island of Kwato, just five minutes away, was once a boat-building centre. Settled by a missionary, Charles Able and his family in 1891, the open walled church, built from Scottish limestone and with fine views over Samarai and the China Strait, is still active, and the boat- and house-building tradition lives on.

POPULATION:
Unknown
WHEN TO GO:
October to December
HOW TO GET THERE:
By air from Port Moresby to Alotau and by boat from Alotau, or as part of a cruise.
HIGHLIGHTS:
The Memorial Hall and the District Commissioner's residence on Samarai. Exploring the islands of Milne Bay. Diving around the undisturbed coral atolls and island reef systems. Attending a church service, after taking advice on which has the best choir.
YOU SHOULD KNOW:
The wreckage in Samarai's harbour not only shelters a wide variety of fish but also unusual encrusting corals, including the second of only two colonies of *Acanthastrea minuta* ever to have been recorded. These waters are also home to a rare – possibly endemic – Black velvet angelfish, with a pale head rather than the normal pale back.

Milne Bay on Samarai Island

Bougainville Island

POPULATION:
175,165 (2000)
HOW TO GET THERE:
By air from Port Moresby to Nissan Island, to the north of Buka, then by sea, or by sea from the Solomons.
WHEN TO GO:
At any time – it is always hot, wet and humid.
HIGHLIGHTS:
The wreck of the famous World War II Japanese Admiral Yamamoto's plane. Kangu Beach, at Buin, Bougainville. Organize a boat trip to the Shortland Islands. Only 20 minutes away, the islanders cross the border every Saturday to sell their fish at Buin market.
YOU SHOULD KNOW:
The Upe, a traditional hat and the symbol of Bougainville, is still worn by young men in the west of the island. The island was a major battle ground between US and Japanese forces during World War II, and war relics including live ammunition and bombs still lie in the jungle.

Bougainville Island lies to the east of New Britain and is, geographically, the largest of the Solomon Islands. At 120 km (75 mi) long and 65-95 km (40-60 mi) wide, its spine is formed of two mountain ranges running from north to south, including seven volcanoes, some of which are active. The mountains slope down to plains and coastal lowlands that include both mangrove and freshwater swamp forests, as well as untouched rainforest.

Bougainville is an autonomous region of Papua New Guinea, with its own government and parliament on Buka Island, from which it is separated by a narrow, 100 m (330 ft) stretch of water, the Buka Passage. In the next few years Bougainville is expected to become independent.

Bougainvilleans are remarkable people – friendly and hospitable, they are also extremely strong minded and determined, as recent history shows. During the 1970s, the infamous Rio Tinto mining company set up shop here to exploit the island's vast copper and gold reserves. The resulting pollution, ecological destruction and totally unreasonable distribution of profits exploded into a lengthy guerrilla war.

The mine was forced to close in 1989, but PNG, with the help of Australia and mercenaries from Sandline International, attempted to quash the rebellion, killing 10 per cent of the population and destroying the island's infrastructure. Failing again, PNG blockaded Bougainville for six years, obliging everyone to return to self-sufficiency and bush medicine. The last Australian military personnel withdrew in 2003, and today the islanders are busy rebuilding houses, townships and the economy.

Fringed with reefs, Bougainville is a lovely island, full of natural resources. Hiding within the lush tangle of rainforest are one of the world's largest caves, spectacular waterfalls and hot springs. Its rivers are rich with fish, as is the sea, and coconut and copra are being replanted. The gorgeous Tonolei Harbour is one of the only tuna breeding grounds in the world.

The active volcano Mount Bagana on Bougainville

Manus

Remote Manus Island, part of Papua New Guinea's Manus province, and the largest of the Admiralty Islands, lies 320 km (200 mi) north of Papua New Guinea, and just south of the Equator. Mountainous and cloaked in rain forest, the highest point is Mount Dremsel, at 718 m (2,356 ft). The wild and rugged terrain means that only the eastern end of the island, and some small areas on the coast, are suitable for cultivating the taro, yams, sago and fruit that are grown.

Inhabited for some 40,000 years, close contact with Americans who built a huge naval base at Lombrun after defeating the Japanese invaders in 1944 left a heritage of cargo cults on the island after their departure. Otherwise the local culture of clans, several of which would form a village, believe they have ancestral spirit protection, though the spirits are not gods. Christianity is a recent phenomenon.

The flora and fauna here reflect the isolated position of the Admiralty Islands, and there are six species of endemic birds, three of which are considered vulnerable, and two endemic mammals, the Admiralty Islands cuscus and the Mosaic tailed rat. Otherwise the forest animals include bandicoot, possum and wild pig, and high up in the tree canopy many different species of bird chatter and fly, and brightly coloured orchids cling to the branches, their roots taking sustenance from the air. As the inaccessible trees here become more interesting to loggers, the habitat of the endangered, brilliant green Manus Island tree snail is gradually disappearing.

Most of the population live around the coast, although in the more fertile east there are many inland settlements too. The island's traditional dances are unique. Slit drums – garamuts – with different sizes and tones, produce fast, rhythmic beats while people with bright body paint perform energetic, wild dances.

Children play on one of the many beautiful beaches on Manus Island.

POPULATION:
33,000 (2004)
WHEN TO GO:
Any time, but August and September are probably the driest months.
HOW TO GET THERE:
By air to Momote airport on the neighbouring island of Los Negros, which is connected to Manus by a bridge.
HIGHLIGHTS:
The remote and beautiful west coast, accessible only by boat.
Lorengau, the main town.
Diving around the Admiralty Islands is some of the best in the world, with visibility of 100 m (330 ft) or more.
Take a boat trip in Kali Bay to look for dugong and turtles.
Visit Seleheu Island, close to Kali Bay, and used for gardening by the inhabitants of the adjacent Nihon Island.
YOU SHOULD KNOW:
Throughout Manus, hundreds of tales are told about mythical heroes known as Pokops. Supposedly based on the mountain-tops, these heroes were all men, had no ancestors and left no children – an anthropologically interesting concept.

POPULATION:
12,000 (2003)
WHEN TO GO:
April to November
HOW TO GET THERE:
By air from Port Moresby.
HIGHLIGHTS:
Sit on a deserted beach at night,
with local friends, and watch for sea
turtles coming to lay their eggs.
Watch local artisans carve walking
sticks, huge bowls and figures –
these are possibly the best carvers
in PNG.
Swim and snorkel beautiful reefs in
the impossibly blue sea.
Explore freshwater holes, limestone
caves, hot springs, mudpools
and geysers.
YOU SHOULD KNOW:
The Trobriand Kiss is described thus:
couples lie together on a mat,
hugging, then tear out handfuls of
each other's hair and nibble off each
other's eyelashes. It's considered
really cool to have short eyelashes!
A note of warning, though, it is not
considered appropriate for foreigners
to form liaisons with the locals.

Trobriand Islands

Otherwise known as the 'islands of love', the Trobriands are a remote
group of low lying coral islands to the north east of Papua New
Guinea. There are four main islands, Kiriwina, Kaileuna, Vakuta and
Kitava, as well as several islets, most of which are fringed with utterly
pristine reefs.

Not much is known about their early history, but the Trobriands
were 'discovered' by a French ship in 1793 and named after its first
lieutenant. In the early part of the 20th century the culture, curiously
more closely linked to Polynesia than to Melanesia, was studied at
length by the anthropologist Bronislaw Malinowski.

Malinowski was fascinated by the islanders' matriarchal society,
their yam culture and gift exchange systems, but he was utterly
seduced by their colourful sexual behaviour, hence the islands'
nickname. Sexual experimentation begins in childhood, and by the time
adolescence is reached, a fully active sexual life is encouraged, with
multiple partners. During this period the lucky adolescents live a life

*The yam feast in
Yalumugwa village*

460

devoted to pleasure; working duties and taboos are not yet binding. Eventually young couples begin to cohabit, a situation that can be withdrawn from without repercussion or, alternatively, made permanent through marriage.

The islands are fertile, and the economy based on yam growing – people take huge pride in their yam gardens, even having yam growing competitions. More exciting for the visitor are the fabulous fish and shellfish that are available – imagine swimming on the reef on a moonless night, watching the local youth dive for crayfish which will be cooked on the beach and eaten with a splash of lime juice – sublime.

The flora and fauna here is also unusual, and endemism is high. The Trobriands are covered in lowland rainforest, and the birds are fabulous – you might just see two endemic species of bird of paradise – appropriate really, since these islands remain little, lost specks of heaven.

Umboi Island

Umboi Island lies between mainland Papua New Guinea and the western tip of New Britain and, at 50 km (31 mi) long, it is the largest of the islands just off New Guinea's northern coast. Formed of several volcanoes, some of which have satellite cones on their flanks, its highest point rises to 1,548 m (5,100 ft). To the north-east it is cut by a large, deep caldera. Breached by the sea, this contains three cones, each with a summit crater lake. However there is no history of eruptions on the island.

Despite its remote location, steamy, mountainous and jungle-clad terrain, missionary activity has led to schools and churches being built, not only in the coastal villages, but also deep in the interior, and some English is spoken. However, Umboi is best known as the home of the ropen, a large, nocturnal creature, said to closely resemble a pterosaur.

Since 1994, American researchers have been exploring the island in an attempt to discover more about the ropen. Hundreds of eyewitnesses describe this creature as having a large wingspan, a long tailed, scaly body and a crocodile-like mouthful of teeth. Some mention a crested head and a flange on the tail. Hunting for fish at night, the ropen is bio-luminescent, apparently glowing for short bursts, attracting fish towards the light.

As yet, no-one has managed to photograph the ropen, which has also been seen on the Papua New Guinea mainland. Lending some credence to this tale are indigenous carvings on display in Port Moresby showing a shaman sitting beneath a lizard like creature with a long neck, scaly wings and a beak. Though there is some doubt about the existence of the ropen, what is certain is that Umboi is home to no less than eight species of fruit bat – all of which are very large.

POPULATION:
4,500 (1997 estimate)
WHEN TO GO:
April to November, although Umboi Island is always hot and wet.
HOW TO GET THERE:
By boat from PNG.
HIGHLIGHTS:
Exploring the island and attempting to become the first person to film or even capture the ropen.
YOU SHOULD KNOW:
Umboi is also one of only two places where Matschie's tree kangaroos are found. Nut brown in colour, with a golden tail and lower limbs, they can hop, but their limbs are slightly shortened to enable them to climb trees successfully.

461

Hainan

POPULATION:
8,200,000 (2004)
WHEN TO GO:
Year-round
HOW TO GET THERE:
By air, from mainland China, Hong Kong, Singapore or Japan, to Haikou (N) or Sanya (S); by train and rail-ferry, from Guangzhou in Guangdong, to Haikou; by boat, from several Chinese ports, to Haikou or Sanya.
HIGHLIGHTS:
The stone forest and coastal scenery of Tianyahaijiao ('the end of sky and the corner of the sea'), where exiles from ancient China's feudal dynasties bewailed their isolation. The Hainan-China Nationality Village, near the 'Jadeite City' of Tong Zha at the southern foot of Five-Fingered Mountain – a collection of ethnic villages from all over southern China in their original folkloric style, with appropriate music, song and dance.
The cliffs, beaches, reefs and islands of Yalong Wan (Crescent Dragon Bay). Its beauty and ethnic cultural interest is threatened by development plans for conference facilities and the most intrusive forms of tourist attractions on the 7 km (4.5 mi) beach.
The Hainan gibbons, one of the world's most endangered primates, at Bawangling Reserve.
The hot springs at Guantang, typical of several around Hainan.
The five large cannon at Xiuying Fort Barbette, built in 1891 to defend China's SE corner during the Sino-French War.

Hainan is China's Hawaii. It's on the same latitude, with a highly developed agricultural economy, roads and infrastructure. It's China's smallest province, separated by a 1.5 km (1 mi) strait from Guangdong, and nestled between the Gulf of Tonkin and the South China Sea. Like Hawaii, its indigenous culture has been fairly swamped by history, and though it's heavily populated, it's not heavily industrialized. It has the beaches, hills, forests, wildlife, and recreational roster essential to a major holiday destination – and it's already popular among newly mobile Chinese. For international visitors, it's this Chinese accent on otherwise familiar activities that makes Hainan really special: China's new Space Launch Centre is being built there not far from temples and halls from the Tang (618-907) and Song (960-1279) dynasties, which are to be included in the accompanying Space theme park.

In the central highlands, the descendants of the Li, Miao and Han wear tribal dress in the villages, and ancient Chinese poetry (engraved on roadside rocks!) proclaims the beauty of the waterfalls, gorges, lush forests with chattering monkeys – and the same coconut, banana, pepper and fruit fields you can see, if on a different scale. This is where to join in the song and dance of the annual Water-Splashing Festival, and to eat – or drink? – fried milk.

Sanya, Hainan's second city in the south, is the centre of beach life, and focal point of all tourism. Xiao Dongtian, to the west at Yazhou Bay, is exceptionally pretty, with beauty spots called 'Large Celestial Peaches', 'Celestial Toad Looking up to Moon' and 'Copulating Frogs' alongside regular beach and countryside facilities. It's typical of Hainan's attempt to tap into international tourism without obscuring the real business of respecting ancestors, history and the myths and legends that bind them to the living world. So far, it's a little weird, but very successful.

Hainan is China's tropical island holiday destination.

Hong Kong

Hong Kong encompasses a collection of 262 islands and peninsulas in the South China Sea. Hong Kong Island is the second largest and the most populated of the islands, and it is here that much of the city lies. The name Hong Kong means 'fragrant harbour' and comes from the area of Hong Kong Island where fragrant wood products and incense were once traded.

In January 1841, Hong Kong became a British colony after the defeat of the Chinese Qing Dynasty in the First Opium War. In July 1997, Hong Kong reverted back to Chinese rule, becoming a Special Administrative Region (SAR) of the People's Republic of China. Today, under the slogan 'One Country, Two Systems', Hong Kong remains a capitalist economy without the restrictions that apply in the rest of China, such as news censorship and foreign exchange controls. On paper, Hong Kong enjoys a high degree of autonomy, but Beijing still exerts much influence, which is unwelcome to many living in the city.

Hong Kong Island was the site of the original British settlement. Today the north of the island is densely populated and most of Hong Kong's skyscrapers are found here, along with the main business and commercial centres, government offices, hotels and restaurants. The south of the island is less developed, with leafy residential areas, pretty bays and some lovely beaches.

Hong Kong is a thoroughly modern international city, famed for its 24-hour lifestyle, shopping, bright lights and skyscrapers, but scratch the surface and you will find a tremendous variety of different sights and sounds, from the street markets of Mong Kok, food stalls selling chickens' feet, the bars and restaurants of Lan Kwai Fong and the beaches in Stanley and Repulse Bay. This vibrant and busy city, with its fusion of East and West, offers a wealth of experiences.

Hong Kong is a great place for shopping, especially for goods made in China, such as electronics, shoes, jewellery, expensive brand-name goods and Chinese antiques. The upmarket areas such as Central and Causeway Bay are among the best in the world. There are also a lot of fascinating street markets selling food, clothes, bags and electronic goods. For a colourful and interesting slice of local life, visit the flower market, bird market, jade market or goldfish market. Don't miss the view from Victoria Peak across the skyline, or the lovely Ocean Park, a great place for people-watching.

POPULATION:
6,980,412 (2007)
WHEN TO GO:
March to April, or September to November
HOW TO GET THERE:
Fly to Hong Kong international airport
HIGHLIGHTS:
The Spring Lantern Festival.
A trip across the harbour, either by day or by night on the famous Star Ferry.
The food – Hong Kong has some of the best restaurants in the world, serving a wide range of different cuisines. But don't forget to try some of the wonderful snacks on offer from street vendors.
The street markets, particularly those in Mong Kok.
YOU SHOULD KNOW:
Many of the shops and restaurants close around the Chinese New Year.

Hong Kong's fabulous skyline as seen from Kowloon

A traditional Chinese temple set in beautiful gardens.

POPULATION:
560,000 (2004)
WHEN TO GO:
Come for the penguin swimming contest in winter, cherry blossom festival in spring, midsummer night's beach festival, or the festival of horses in autumn when the maples turn brilliant reds and yellows.
HOW TO GET THERE:
By air to Jeju's international airport or by boat, from ports all round the South Korean mainland, to Jeju Port.
HIGHLIGHTS:
Watching the *haenyo* ('sea women'), Jeju's iconic free-divers for abalone and conch, in action. The women – archetypes of Jeju's culture of matriarchy – pass their skills down the generations.
Chonjiyon waterfall, near Seogwipo: the cascades plummet 22m (73 ft) into a basin known as 'Pond of the Heavens' Emperor' among dense subtropical foliage.
Elvis Teddy, Mona Lisa Teddy and the whole of the Last Supper in Teddy Bears at the Teddy Bear Museum.
Loveland – a sexually explicit open-air theme park full of graphic, hands-on exhibits and working models designed to inspire and perhaps instruct bashful but willing newlyweds.
YOU SHOULD KNOW:
Jeju was an independent country called Tamna until 662, and though it has been governed by several powers since then, its isolation has helped it preserve a unique culture incorporating a form of shamanism. You feel it everywhere as an underlying current.

Jeju

Jeju/Cheju is a volcanic island, 73 km (46 mi) long, and 41 km (25 mi) wide, some 60 km (40 mi) southwest of the Korean peninsula. It is a lush, semi-tropical oval with Korea's highest mountain, 1,950 m (6,300 ft) Hallasan, at its centre – and it gets 4 million visitors each year. Most of them are Korean newlyweds: 60 per cent of Korean weddings are followed by a honeymoon on the 'Emerald Island of Asia', or 'Love Island'.

Jeju's cultural and ecological attractions make it a massive tourist magnet in any circumstances. For Korean couples, many of whom don't even meet each other before their wedding, the sheer variety of beautiful, romantic and interesting places to go and things to do gives them a chance to face down their shyness and discover each other. Being Korea, these opportunities are not so much organized as regimented. Everything in Jeju is geared to whisking honeymooners at speed through as many different photo opportunities as possible to fill their official wedding albums. Other visitors can tag along, or muddle through.

Much of the Jeju pleasure production line is seasonal. In spring forsythia turns the island yellow, and cherry blossoms, pineapples, bananas and tangerines are everywhere. By May Hallasan's crater lake reflects a sea of azaleas. Couples explore ancient lava columns and catacombs like the Manjanggul, the longest lava tube on earth at 13 km (8.4 mi) and part of a UNESCO World Biosphere Reserve; or pose at one of the scores of scenic waterfalls in the green countryside and forests. Jeju is awash with a sense of mystery and old legends, and everywhere you see *dol hareubangs* ('stone grandfathers'), cult phallic figures carved from basalt. But the real mystery is when honeymooners get any time to themselves.

Ogasawara Islands

Administratively part of the Tokyo Prefecture, despite lying 1,000km (600 mi) south of the city, the Ogasawara Islands are scattered over the Pacific Ocean south of the Izu Islands. The 30 islands in the group are arranged in three distinct blocks. The Ogasawara Archipelago consists of Muko-jima Island, Chichi-jima Island and Haha-jima Island. The Iwo Islands (Volcano Islands) form the second blocks, while Nishi-no-shima Island, Minani-tori-shima Island, and Oki-no-shima Island belong to the last block. The whole area falls within the Ogasawara National Park.

The islands were claimed by the Japanese in the 14th or 15th century, but in 1827 a British warship came across the uninhabited islands and claimed possession until 1876 when they were handed back to Japan. During World War II, most of the inhabitants were evacuated to the mainland, and a Japanese military base was established there. The Battle of Iwo-jima, one of the fiercest battles of the war, was fought here in 1945. The islands were taken by the US Navy, who allowed the inhabitants of Western descent to return. The islands were given back to Japan in 1968, and the Japanese evacuees were finally allowed home. Nowadays, nearly all of the inhabitants, including those of Western ancestry, are Japanese citizens.

The islands are the highest points of an ancient underwater volcano, so sheer cliffs of up to 100 m (328 ft) characterize their magnificent coastlines. The islands are fringed with beautiful coral reefs, and many have lovely beaches. The highest peak is on South Iwo-jima, at 916 m (3,005 ft).

As the Ogasawara Islands have always been remote and have never been part of a continent, much of the flora and fauna is unique, with species varying between islands as they do in the Galapagos. For this reason, the islands are being considered by UNESCO to be added to the World Heritage List. Unspoilt and unpolluted, the waters surrounding the Ogasawara Archipelago are part of the Ogasawara Sea Park, and diving and snorkelling are very popular here as the visibiltity is very good and there are plentiful coral reefs and colourful tropical fish.

This is also a great place for whale watching – sperm whales can be spotted all year, while humpback whales and their calves are around from February to April. Many different types of dolphin inhabit the waters too, and it is sometimes possible to swim with bottlenose and spinner dolphins.

POPULATION:
2,300 (2005)
WHEN TO GO:
Any time of year.
HOW TO GET THERE:
By ship from Tokyo to Chichi-jima. The ship leaves once a week and the journey takes 25 hours.
HIGHLIGHTS:
Swimming with dolphins – both bottleose and spinner dolphins can be found in the clear waters around the islands.
Whale watching – see sperm whales and humpback whales in their natural habitat. An organized tour will lead you to where the whales are most plentiful and increase your chances of seeing them.
Snorkelling and diving among the coral reefs. Marine life is plentiful, and this is where the first-ever filming of a giant squid took place in 2004. At around 8 m (25 ft) long, these creatures are, luckily, only to be found deep in the ocean.
YOU SHOULD KNOW:
In English, the islands are called the Bonin Islands.

A whale's giant tailfin breaks through the waves.

Rebun and Rishiri Islands

POPULATION:
Rebun 3,400; Rishiri 6,200 (2005)
WHEN TO GO:
June to August when the wild
flowers are in bloom.
HOW TO GET THERE:
Travel by air or ferry from Wakkanai
to Rebun and Rishiri.
HIGHLIGHTS:
The Hachi-jikan hiking trail – the trail
runs down the whole of the west
coast of Rebun, from Sukoton Misaki
in the north, through woods and
across flower-filled meadows, to
Motochi in the south.
Rishirifuji Onsen – a hot spring with
indoor and outdoor baths in the
town of Oshidomari on Rishiri.
Otatomari Pond – a beautiful pond in
the south of Rishiri Island. The views
of Mount Rishiri reflected in the still
water are fantastic.
Garota Beach – a sandy beach on the
western coast of Rebun, popular with
wind surfers. The section of hiking
trail between Cape Sukoton and
Garota Beach on the island of Rebun.
YOU SHOULD KNOW:
The islands are known as Rishirito
and Rebunto in Japanese.

In the far north of Japan off the north-west coast of the island of Hokkaido, lie two smaller islands famed for their natural beauty, abundant wild flowers and hiking trails. The islands of Rebun and Rishiri form part of a national park, along with the island of Sarobetsu and part of Hokkaido.

Rishiri Island is dominated by Mount Rishiri a 1,721-m (4,170-ft) dormant volcano. Most visitors come here to climb the volcano, an arduous but enjoyable hike which takes about 12 hours. There is a small shrine at the summit, and the views of the neighbouring islands are fantastic. There are many other hiking routes on the island from which you can appreciate the wonderful scenery, including a lovely three-hour trail from the lake at Himenuma, crossing the lower slopes of two smaller peaks.

Another way to take in the scenery is to explore by bicycle. A 20-km cycle track follows the northern coast of Rishiri from Hime Pond to Kutsugata, a lovely route offering stunning views of the volcano. Bicycles can be hired or borrowed from your hotel.

The coast of Rishiri is peppered with small fishing villages and the island is famous for its sea urchins (*uni*) and konbu seaweed. Near the port of Oshidomari, Rishiri's largest town, is the picturesque headland of Cape Peshi. There is a walking trail to the top of the headland, from which there are stunning views of Oshidomari and Mount Rishiri.

In contrast, Rebun is a low-lying island. It is most famous for its rich flora, particularly its alpine flowers, some of which are not found anywhere else in the world. The flowers bloom between June and August, so this is a good time to visit. Look out particularly for the Rebun Usuyukiso, rather like an Edelweiss. It is one of several protected, rare plants found on the island and can be seen in the Rebun Usuyukiso Area, a place

with a relatively high number of them.

With its breathtaking scenery and views of nearby Rishiri, the island of Rebun is best enjoyed from a network of hiking trails. Among the highlights is Cape Gorota, a beautiful cape in the northern part of the island. Motochi, an area in the south-west of the island, is characterized by its scenic, sheer coastline and rocks which are said to resemble a cat's head. There is a small village here with ryokan (traditional Japanese inns), which make a fascinating place to stay. Momoiwa (Peach Rock), a roundish hill, is nearby. The flowers here are stunning and the lovely views of Mount Rishiri can be enjoyed from the observation deck.

A view of Rishiri Island from Rebun Island

*Playtime on Japan's most
beautiful beach*

Hateruma Island

At the southern-most tip of Japan in the Pacific Ocean near the Tropic of Cancer lies the island of Hateruma (Hateruma-jima), part of the Yaeyama Island group. This enchanting coral island is clothed in banyan trees, Indian almonds, bamboo orchids and colourful hibiscus. There is a blissful feeling of remoteness in this beautiful rural backwater, with virtually no man-made noise, and the exotic scent of frangipani perfumes the air.

Tourism is virtually non-existent on Hateruma – there are no big hotels or coach parties – making this the perfect place to unwind. The island is best explored by bicycle, at a slow pace fitting the pace of life here. The empty roads lead to the endless reaches of sea and sky. There is just one village in the centre of the island, with most of the inhabitants involved in fishing, growing sugarcane or producing Awanami, a highly-prized alcoholic drink. Some of the wooden houses are plain and weathered, others are painted in pretty shades of green or blue, with traditional orange tiled roofs.

The clear blue waters around the island make this a good place for diving and snorkelling. There is plenty to explore, including coral reefs, rock arches and brilliantly colourful tropical fish. In the spring migratory fish, such as hammerhead sharks, can be seen. If you want to relax, the beach at Nishi, edged with pandanus trees, is thought by many to be the most beautiful beach in Japan.

Hateruma is also famous for its astronomical observatory, as this is the only place in Japan from where you can view the Southern Cross. Of the 88 constellations, 84 can be seen from here, and the clear skies and lack of light pollution make this a great place to view the night sky.

Iriomote

Only 20 km (12 mi) wide and 15 km (9 mi) long, Iriomote's infrastructure is limited to a single coastal road between its northern and eastern hamlets. 80 per cent of the island is protected by the state, and a third of it forms part of the Iriomote National Park, which includes Japan's biggest coral reef – the lagoon between Iriomote and its near neighbour, Ishigaki. Both islands belong to the Yaeyama group, the southern-most of the Ryokyu Islands.

Iriomote is covered by dense, subtropical jungle and mangrove swamps, threaded through and around a dozen peaks over 420 m (1,350 ft). Rainfall on their steep flanks feeds a network of streams and rivers – and you can explore the two longest, the Nakamagawa and the 17.5 km (11 mi) Urauchigawa, by guided boat or alone in a canoe. The island has seven kinds of mangrove, including what is said to be Japan's biggest and oldest, the Sakishimasuou tree.

A short walk from the Urauchi brings you first to the exquisite Mariyudo waterfall (the Gunkan-Iwa rock, by the slightly calmer waters 250 m (825 ft) downstream is known as 'the place where the gods sit'), and then to the Kampire, descending rapids so fast and turbulent they can create a spectacular veil of mist. Part of the thrill is that you are walking in the buffer zone of genuinely virgin territory: 30 sq km (12 sq mi) of Iriomote is closed to all forms of human intervention.

This is the only home of the Iriomote wildcat, one of the world's most endangered species. It looks deceptively cuddly, like a large house cat, but has the attitudes of the leopard, its nearest relative. It is the highlight of Iriomote's extraordinary ecology: visitors willing to reach such an isolated outpost find rare and pristine terrestrial and marine environments.

POPULATION:
2,251 (2006)
WHEN TO GO:
Year-round. Come for the Yamaneko Marathon in February, or the Festival of Shitsumatsuri in November.
HOW TO GET THERE:
By air, from Japan's main islands or Taiwan via Okinawa, to Ishigaki; then by boat, from Ishigaki Port to Funaura and Uehara.
HIGHLIGHTS:
Watching the Yamaneko (Iriomote) wildcat live on CCTV at the Iriomote Wildlife Centre.
Leaving at dawn, by canoe or kayak, to witness the life cycle of the Sagaribana trees lining the river channels. The Sagaribana flower gives off an intense, sweet smell, filling the air as it blossoms overnight, and drops into the water at dawn. The feathery pink and white blossoms are overpoweringly exotic en masse, and the subject of much Japanese poetry.
The Festival of Shitsumatsuri, a series of Yaeyama rituals to welcome the god Mayunganas, including speeches, mock duels, boat races, mass singing and frenetic dancing – all in traditional costumes, and exclusively on the beach.
The coastal flora and large sea bird colonies on the steep cliffs of Nakanougan Island, nearby. Only residents of the traditional Ryokyu community may land there.
YOU SHOULD KNOW:
The after-party of the Yamaneko Marathon starts with a free-for-all grab for two boatloads of sashimi, and ends in compulsory group dancing.

The exquisite Mariyudo waterfall

Taketomi

POPULATION:
361 (2006)
WHEN TO GO:
March to August, November and December (September to October is the typhoon season).
HOW TO GET THERE:
By air, from Okinawa or mainland Japan, to Ishigaki; by boat, from Taiwan or Nagoya, to/from Ishigaki; then by boat from Ishigaki to Taketomi.
HIGHLIGHTS:
The local language – everyone understands standard Japanese, but Taketomi speaks a dialect of the unique Yaeyama Islands language, itself derived from an Okinawan dialect; locally, Taketomi is pronounced 'Tedun'.
The indigenous ideographical writing system called *kaida*, once used on the island, but now confined to (precious) souvenir T-shirts.
The 'star-sand' (*hoshizuna*), made of the remains of tiny animals, which makes some beaches a beautiful pink.
Diving on the local reef – like everything, ultra-clear and unpolluted.
Snake soup and 'mimiga', a salad of pork ear, cucumber and vinegar.
YOU SHOULD KNOW:
Taketomi, like all the Yaeyama Islands, has *utaki,* which are holy places for venerating the gods, marked off with low stone walls and signs in Japanese. Please do not enter the enclosures.

The beautiful coastal scenery of Taketomi Island

The Yaeyama Islands are part of southwest Japan's Okinawa Prefecture, but they are so remote they are closer to Taiwan than to Okinawa Island, let alone the mainland. Taketomi is one of the smallest, a round, green jewel of 6.32 sq km (4 sq mi), and a 10-minute boat ride from Ishigaki Island. Long before you get there, you know you're going to visit a beautifully preserved, maintained, and lived in, traditional Ryukyu village – a kind of essence of Japan.

Nothing really prepares you for the actual time-travelling of arrival. The one small village consists entirely of the most ancient style of single-storied houses with red tile roofs, stone walls and *shiisaa*, the lion-maned talismanic carving placed at the door to ward off evil spirits. The lanes between the houses are of pure white sand, and lined by dry-stone walls with flowers and trees draped over the top. Everything is symbolic, and everything represents the classic style of Okinawa Prefecture. Certainly, there are rules to keep it this way – but the residents, all from families who have belonged there for centuries, wouldn't have it any other way.

Even so, Taketomi is part of the Iriomote National Park, along with its surrounding waters. Visitors can hire a bicycle to circle the place, but most take a ride in a bullock-drawn cart, or simply walk round the island's lovely beaches, where the swimming and snorkelling is wonderful. Some houses serve as *minshuku* – Japanese bed-and-breakfast lodgings like ryokan, where your room, bath and futon are all in the most authentic traditional manner. The truly amazing thing is that you never feel Taketomi is a living museum, because it isn't. It is completely true to itself, and local folk have no intention of letting visitors change that. It's one of Japan's true marvels.

Yaku Island

Yaku Island (Yakushima) is a small, nearly round volcanic island rising almost 2,000 m (6,562 ft) out of the Pacific off the southeast coast of Kyushu north of Okinawa. This is one of the wettest places in Japan, raining more than the half the days of the year, with an annual average of 4 to 10 m (13 to 32 ft). Because of its isolation, steep hills and valleys and uncompromising climate, the island has remained one of Japan's natural wonders.

The few visitors who come to the island each year are here to see the forests. Between 800 and 1,600 m (2,625 to 5,250 ft) above sea level is a band of coniferous forest containing the Yaku cedars, some of the world's oldest trees at about 3,500 years of age. The largest, known as Jomon Sugi, has a circumference of 16.4 m (54 ft) and it takes eight adults with their arms outstretched to encircle its trunk. The trees are considered to be sacred and all have names, including Meoto-Sugi, or Married Couple, two separate trees which have grown together over time. The best place to enjoy the forests and see the Yaku cedars is in the Shiratani Unsuikyo forest. This stunning forest, with its soft, thick carpet of moss is truly beautiful and contains several ancient cedars, including the magnificent 3,000-year-old Yayoi Sugi. The marked route leads you up steps and over boardwalks past glorious waterfalls.

Ancient trees aside, the island has immense natural beauty, with softly flowing rivers, waterfalls and stunning tropical gardens. There are deer here, and macaques, as well as several endangered bird species. It has the nesting sites of both green and loggerhead turtles, both of which are also endangered. The rocky coastline and beaches are often spectacular, and there are wild flowers and blossom everywhere.

The island is also known for its soft pink sunrises and glorious red sunsets over the ocean. White clouds form on the horizon, contrasting sharply with the blue sky, and soft mists and rain clouds envelope the verdant mountain peaks. Everywhere you look there is a photograph to be taken.

Moss covered trees along the Shiratani River

POPULATION:
6,947 (2005)
WHEN TO GO:
Any time of year.
HOW TO GET THERE:
By plane from Kagoshima, or by ferry from Kagoshima or Shimama.
HIGHLIGHTS:
Yaku-Sugi Museum at Anbo – the exhibits show the island's natural wonders and the history of the logging industry. You can also hug a section from a Yaku-Sugi. Yakushima Fruit Garden dating back to 1660 – see the hundreds of tropical fruit trees and plants, and taste the fruits in season, like papaya, mango, guava or starfruit. Shitogo Gajumaru-en Banyan Garden – this garden features 300-year-old Banyan trees and a variety of sub-tropical plants in a lovely park-like setting.
The island's waterfalls – there are several on the island, but the best is Ooko-no-taki. With a 90-m (295 ft) drop, this is one of Japan's most spectacular. You can scramble over the rocks and swim in the plunge pool if you want a closer look. Giant turtles – turtles come ashore to lay their eggs on several of the island's beaches, including Nagant-inaka-hama. This happens from May to August in the middle of the night.
Bathing in the seaside *onsen* (hot springs) – these can be found at Kaichuu and at Yudomari, just below the pretty village.
YOU SHOULD KNOW:
The island is on the World Heritage List.

Kume-Shima

Kume-Shima is just 102 km (63 mi) southwest of Okinawa's capital, Naha, and for mainland Japanese it is the ultimate domestic destination. It has beautiful beaches and excellent dive sites. Its green interior presents shifting landscapes of fields, exuberant flowers, and hillside slopes of elegant Fukugi trees with the sea always sparkling in the background.

In the Maju district, a particular and extensive group of 200 year-old Fukugi is especially esteemed – along with a 250 year-old Ryukyu pine that looks like a paradoxical giant bonsai, and is a designated National Treasure. With a diameter of 4.3 m (15 ft), 6 m (20 ft) high, and covering 250 sq m (800 sq ft), this magnificent pine is celebrated in Ryukyuan poetry as one of the sacred natural beings – like the yonic lava tube called 'miifugaa' at Kume's north tip, or the offshore phallic lava column called 'garasaa-yama' in the south – revered by its animistic culture. Beneath the meticulous service culture of its resorts, Kume is an outstanding exemplar of a tradition rooted in its history as part of a once independent Ryukyu kingdom.

Kume's triumph is to have incorporated its fundamental beliefs into its tourist economy. Visitors love the textiles called Tsumugi, made by a process kept alive since the 15th century and considered an 'Intangible Cultural Property'. They adore the island's version of Awamori liquor, made from local spring water, Thai rice and black malt yeast. Like certain places, these are associated with ancestors, and regarded with reverence. The respect extends to Kume's magnificent indigenous fireflies and superb marine ecology.

Lack of respect causes real resentment: the US has used the nearby islet of Torishima, a traditionally brilliant fishing ground, for fifty years of regular bombing practice, carelessly pounding it to gravel in a culture that holds care for natural things as the highest human responsibility.

Miyako

Roughly 300 km (180 mi) southwest of Okinawa, a low plateau sits above the translucent, turquoise sea. This is Miyako, centrepiece of a small archipelago of the same name, and of the coral reefs, raised from the seabed thousands of years ago. Miyako's fame in Japan's main islands is based on its gorgeous white sand beaches, its golf courses and its reef dive sites. Two long bridges unite Miyako with its seven satellite islands, making their coral reefs and wildlife easily accessible. The islanders are justly proud of their status as a mainstream tourist destination.

Most visitors remain oblivious to Miyako's indigenous culture, a variant developed from the ancient Ryukyu kingdom centred in Okinawa. Over 15,000 islanders speak Miyako, a Ryukyuan language – and four of its satellites have their own distinct dialect, even though they are so close.

There are 15 surviving Gusuku sites scattered round Miyako, shrines sacred to a history and way of life veiled to beach holidaymakers. During the year, each district conducts its own sacred rite. Shimajiri district's Pantu rite consists of three local men daubed in grass and mud, and carrying sticks and a grotesque face-mask. They represent gods, and chase people to smear them with mud. Being caught and muddied-up guarantees a year of protection by the deities. The Karimata district has its Uyagan rite, a form of harvest festival. In the sugarcane fields not yet claimed for new tourist facilities, these rites are the public face of Miyako's cultural soul, and like the island itself, they have a rare and profound beauty.

POPULATION:
55, 914 (2006)
WHEN TO GO:
Year-round
HOW TO GET THERE:
By air, from Naha (Okinawa), Haneda or Kansai, to Miyako.
HIGHLIGHTS:
Diving the Tori-ike reef off Shimoji Island.
Exploring the 2 km (1.3 mi) long and 140-200 m (450-620 ft) wide Higashi-hennazaki, the extreme eastern cape of Miyako, with a lighthouse at the end. Its 360° panorama as the sun rises guarantees a place in Japan's top 100 beauty spots.
The replica of German fairytale Marksburg Castle at the Ueno German Culture Village – an improbable theme park built in 1993, commemorating the 1873 rescue of German sailors from a shipwreck, a story told since 1937 in Japan's schoolbooks.

Rock formations on Jodogahama Beach

473

Shikoku

POPULATION:
4,500,000 (2006)
WHEN TO GO:
Come for Oshiro Matsui, the late
March/April cherry blossom festival of
the 300 Sakura trees in Matsuyama
Castle Park; or the dazzling fall foliage
displays at Kankakei in Kagawa, or
Iyakei in Tokushima, from October to
mid-December. The Awa Odori Festival
in Tokushima is in August.
HOW TO GET THERE:
By air, via Tokyo or Osaka, to the
Prefectural capitals of Takamatsu (N),
Matsuyama (W), Kochi (S) and
Tokushima (E); by train/bus/car, via the
three new bridges from Honshu; or –
much the most fun – by ferry from
Osaka's Nanko Port, to Matsuyama.
The overnight ferries are miniature
ocean liners, with panelled cabins and
baths to match.
HIGHLIGHTS:
The turrets and fortifications of
Matsuyama Castle (1627), including the
extraordinary 10 m (32 ft) stone gates,
all different, and with individual
histories of national significance, eight
of which are individually designated
'Japanese National Treasures'.
Watching a nocturnal performance of
Noh theatre by the flickering light of
bonfires, medieval-style, in the
restored Matsuyama Castle Ninomaru
Historical Garden.
The opulent merchant's mansion of
Kami-Haga House, and traditional wax
and candle-making at Uchiko, a
beautifully preserved 19th century
small town in Ehime.
Bathing at Japan's oldest hot spring,
Dogo Onsen, near Matsuyama – even
the no-frills 'Kami-no-Yu' ('Bath of the
Gods') gets you the huge, traditional
wooden Japanese buildings and
marble trimmings.
YOU SHOULD KNOW:
Kobo Daishi is the posthumous title
awarded to the scholar monk Kukai,
the 9th century polymath who created
the Kana syllabary, brought the tantric
teachings of esoteric Buddhism from
China, and developed them into the
Japanese Shingon sect.

*Cherry trees growing on
the mountainside on Shikoku.*

The smallest of Japan's four main islands, Shikoku has always been a backwater cut off from direct access to Honshu or Kyushu by the Inland Sea. Now, even after new bridges were supposed to integrate it culturally and economically with mainstream Japan, Shikoku remains isolated, and the loveliest and most bucolic region of the whole country. It helps that most of its population lives in the big cities along its north coast. The mountainous ridges running east-west concentrate both Shikoku's industry and its intensive agriculture: the wide, alluvial northeast produces two crops of rice and wheat each year, and is rich with citrus fruits, persimmons, peaches and grapes. A road map of the north also demonstrates the density of its express and freeway network, and the graphic distinction from the sparsely populated, deeply rural south. The south is the traditional Japan of fabulous mountain scenery, samurai castles, craft workshops, farming villages where oxen pull creaky wagons, and small terraces of vegetables or orange trees cut into the dense woods.

In Shikoku, ancient Japan is no ghost: each year 100,000 people complete the '88 Temple Pilgrimage', a rite originating around 1570-90 that requires followers of the 9th century Buddhist priest Kobo Daishi to visit his 88 special shrines over a 1,450 km (906 mi) route. In Uwajima in Shikoku's southwest corner, bullfighting is described as 'bovine sumo', because trainers, instead of killing the bulls, incite two immense and pampered creatures to push and barge each other out of a ring. Nearby, at Taga Jinja, a medieval Shinto shrine to fertility has developed into a full-blown, three-floor museum of sex and erotica – with no discernible loss of sanctity. Quirky, charming, and absolutely lovely, Shikoku keeps reminding you of the ancient soul behind Japan's façade of white-hot technological modernity.

Okinawa

Their English name means the chain of islands stretching from Kyushu to Taiwan, dividing the East China Sea from the Pacific Ocean, but in Japan, 'Ryukyu Islands' signifies only the southern half – Okinawa Prefecture. Okinawa is the largest island, still and always the capital of what was once an independent kingdom paying tribute to China from 1372 until a 1609 invasion by 2,500 Japanese samurai, and eventual (1879) annexation by the Japanese Meiji. Japan enforced its language, culture and identity on the islanders, but today, and especially in Okinawa, the indigenous Ryokyu culture (with at least seven distinct languages) is resurgent. Okinawans' desire for cultural separatism is in direct proportion to their poor treatment by Japan and the US since World War II, and is reinforced by their obvious geographical isolation, and their ecological and ethnic affinity to South East Asia.

Enduring evidence of Ryukyu tradition is in the breathtaking medieval castles and related buildings called Gusuku sites, which include hundreds of sacred groves called Utaki. The combination of ancestor-worship and animism underpins Okinawan culture: the castles are themselves sacred, and services are held within them. The best are UNESCO World Heritage Sites, cited for their modern relevance, not as historic ruins.

Although Okinawa's tourist credentials are first-class – beautiful beaches, subtropical forests full of wildlife and waterfalls, throbbing resort complexes, coral reefs and marine parks – what really catches your eye is the way of life in the canefields, orchards and vegetable gardens. Rural Okinawa is alive with myth and legend – you'll hear it in music and dance, and the hundreds of local country festivals. For visitors, the island feels like a lost world, fortuitously recovered from what, in more urban areas, looks like wholesale Americanization.

POPULATION:
1.3 million (2004 estimate)
WHEN TO GO:
Year-round
HOW TO GET THERE:
By air, from the Japanese main islands, Taiwan or Hong Kong, to Naha; then by train, bus or car around the island.
HIGHLIGHTS:
The World War II Peace Memorial at Mabuni, the Cornerstone of Peace, inscribed with the names of those who died in the battle for Okinawa in 1945, regardless of nationality.
Modern Ryukyu glassware – traditional Meiji-era skills developed a new style from melting down and re-using soft drink bottles discarded by US troops.
Hiking the dense forest trails between Kunigami and Higashi village areas in the north – from coastal mangroves up to rocky waterfalls, to the chorus of a parliament of birds.
Shuri Castle, overlooking Naha – one of the biggest Gusuku, and the only one to have been part of Ryukyu royal history from its medieval inception to its end in 1879.
Shikina-En Gardens, near Naha – a former residence of Ryukyu kings. Rebuilt in 1800 for the coronation of King Sho On.
Sefa Utaki, in Chinen village on the southern Pacific coast – huge rocks and trees shelter ceremonial altars in this most sacred Ryukyu site. The highest-ranking priestesses, the Kikoe Ogimi, were consecrated here, and it attracts many Agari Umai pilgrims.

Sea-bleaching traditional fabrics

OCEANIA

Pelsaert Island, one of the Houtman Abrolhos Islands

Houtman Abrolhos Islands

POPULATION:
Uninhabited, apart from temporary commercial fishermen.

WHEN TO GO:
Very changeable weather, and often windy. The best months for boating in particular are from February to June, and September to October. But still best to avoid the cyclone season from November to April – when most of the annual rain also falls.

HOW TO GET THERE:
Day trips by boat (with fishing and snorkelling) or scenic flights out of Geraldton on the mainland.

HIGHLIGHTS:
The Long Island Dive Trail – in the Wallabi Group of islands. A self guided tour in an area of outstanding marine life.
Diving on the wrecks (eg *Batavia*, 1629) in the Wallabi Group.
Wooded, Morley and Leo islands – blue lagoons and sandy beaches.

YOU SHOULD KNOW:
The islands are named after the Dutch Commander Frederick de Houtman who came across them in June 1619. 'Abrolhos' is thought to derive from the Portuguese expression *Abre os olhos* – 'Keep your eyes open' – certainly sound advice on these reefs.

It might seem careless to forget a chain of 122 coral islands about 60 km (37 mi) off the coast of Geraldton, Western Australia — but forgotten it is. This is the world's most southerly coral island formation, stretching across 100 km (62 mi) of ocean and bathed by the warm Leeuwin current where tropical and temperate waters meet. You can't stay on the archipelago itself, but to skim over in a seaplane or fish and dive among the coral reefs is magic.

The real beauty of these wild islands lies below the surface, where unique corals abound and colourful fish dart in and out of cover. The islands are also home to sea lion colonies and over 90 species of sea birds – not to mention golden orb spiders, carpet pythons, small Tammar wallabies and marine green turtles. The obvious beauty of the reefs masks a slightly darker side to their nature: they have sunk many a ship in their time. The Dutch East India Company's vessels, *Batavia* and *Zeewijk*, are probably the best known of the Abrolhos wrecks.

The 'Abrolhos', as they are know locally, guard their treasures jealously – the islands are highly protected and any industry is carefully monitored. In the past, the abundant bird droppings or 'guano' fuelled a fertilizer industry; now the waters around the Abrolhos are an important lobster-breeding site. During the lobster fishing season from March to June, licensed fishermen and their families take up camp on 22 designated islands. You may not be able to stay yourself, but to have the privilege of setting foot on these untouched islands is quite simply enough.

Barrow Island

Barrow Island is a life raft for Australia's rarest creatures. In many ways, it is a living record of how parts of mainland Australia might have looked prior to European occupation. Many animals here are now extinct elsewhere on the continent. This arid, antipodean 'Galapagos' lies in the Indian Ocean off the coast of northern West Australia – 56 km (36 mi) from the mainland and just 25 km long (15.5 mi). Not only is it rich in wildlife but also in that 'liquid gold' – oil.

Most of the human residents are male – a reflection of the island's somewhat schizophrenic nature. In 1954, geologists working for West Australian Petroleum realised the island's rich potential for oil fields. Today there are over 400 production wells here, but alongside this has recently come a greater understanding and empathy with the wild inhabitants. Amazingly, wells and wildlife seems to rub along pretty well – with no species having been lost in the 36 years of oil production. But battles still rage over its future.

Inland from white dunes and reefs, the limestone uplands are littered with tussocks of spinifex, a spiny leafed grass. Here live the somewhat bizarre nocturnal burrowing bettongs or 'rat kangaroos'. Holing up in underground burrows by day, these sociable animals forage at night, grunting and squealing as they feast on their favourite food, figs. Since European settlement, numbers elsewhere have dropped dramatically but here about 5,000 burrowing bettongs thrive – as long as no cats and dogs arrive.

At first this may not seem like an easy place to be, but it is a last refuge for Australia's weirdest and most wonderful wildlife, and for that it's a must-see.

POPULATION:
50 to 100 (2005 estimate)
WHEN TO GO:
November to February when the weather is fair. Avoid the cyclone season.
HOW TO GET THERE:
Flights to Barrow airport from the mainland.
HIGHLIGHTS:
Green turtles nesting and laying eggs along the West Coast – November to February.
The grand perentie – the world's second largest lizard, beaten only by the Komodo dragon.
YOU SHOULD KNOW:
Barrow is the largest of the Montebello Islands, which were the site of three British nuclear bomb tests in 1952 and 1956.

A green turtle returning to the sea at sunrise.

Montague Island

POPULATION:
Uninhabited
WHEN TO GO:
All year round for diving (but
February to June is the best time).
Whale watching from October
to November.
HOW TO GET THERE:
Official boat tours out of Narooma.
HIGHLIGHTS:
Swallowing succulent mud oysters.
Swimming with playful fur seals.
Southern right and humpback whales
migrating past.
Diving – one of the island's
best-kept secrets.
YOU SHOULD KNOW:
The island has a major weed
problem. Kikuyu was introduced in
the early 19th century to help feed
animals kept by the lighthouse
keepers and their families, and it got
out of control. It is now being cleared
as it can prevent penguins and
shearwaters from burrowing
or moving.

Just 9 km (6 mi) off Narooma on the south coast of New South Wales lies Montague Island, a sanctuary for little penguins and seals, and a delightful retreat for divers, fishermen and eco-tourists alike.

Barunguba or Montague Island as it is now know was once fertile Aboriginal hunting ground – sea-bird eggs and meat were there for the taking. But the task wasn't easy – legend has it that an estimated 150 Aboriginal people were drowned in the early 1800s when their bark canoes where swamped in a squall.

Surrounded by rich but sometimes tricky waters, construction of Montague's lighthouse, designed by James Barnet, commenced in 1878. This striking 21 m (69 ft) landmark was hewn from the island's own granite. Barnet was responsible for at least 15 major lightstations along the coast of New South Wales. The lighthouse keepers and their families are long gone – it was automated in 1986. But since its completion in 1881, visitors have landed here to climb the lighthouse and take in the wildlife.

The island and surrounding waters are teeming with life – migrating whales and dolphins, little penguins and fur seals, manta rays and sunfish. Fortunately for the penguins, the island has no foxes or feral cats, and breeding boxes have increased their number to around 12,000. After feeding at sea, these delightful creatures waddle ashore at dusk and can be watched from a platform near the island's jetty. Recently, lucky eco-tourists have been able to stay overnight in the heritage-listed lighthouse keeper's cottage, now restored in true Edwardian style. These visitors get the rare chance to stay on the island in return for a little work – maybe penguin monitoring, weed clearing or doing bird and whale counts. It seems to turn work into pleasure.

*The granite lighthouse on
Montague Island*

Norfolk Island

A tiny jewel set in the azure seas of the South Pacific, Norfolk Island is just 8 km (5 mi) long, and 1,600 km (994 mi) northeast of Sydney. It is the biggest of a cluster of three islands on the Norfolk Ridge, fringed by coral reefs and crowned by pristine rainforest and some of the world's tallest tree ferns.

On 10 October 1774, James Cook first landed on this diminutive island and named it in honour of the then Duchess of Norfolk. Convicts started to arrive 14 years later and over time it gained quite a reputation, becoming known as 'hell in the Pacific'. Then in 1856, descendants of the Bounty mutineers with their Tahitian wives and children sailed for five weeks from Pitcairn Island to settle on Norfolk Island. These new settlers brought with them a distinct culture and language, and many held mutineers' names such as Adams, Buffett, Christian and McCoy. From that day, Norfolk Island began its steady climb out of hell and into heaven.

Once sustained by agriculture and fishing, visitors now keep the island alive. But traditional culture remains deep-rooted – with dancing, singing and a unique cuisine. Banana dumplings, fried fish and Hihi pie, concocted with periwinkles, can be sampled at one of the fine restaurants scattered across the island.

The blue waters around Norfolk Island are teeming with fish, and there are countless fishing charters and scuba-diving trips out to the reef to explore this kaleidoscope underwater world. In the sheltered waters of Emily Bay, you can also indulge in some lazy swimming and snorkelling, and endless relaxation.

Norfolk Island is favoured by well-heeled Australians and New Zealanders, and a few millionaires have migrated to this tax-free haven. There are over 70 low-tax shops and many eager customers. Yet the island seems to balance the old and the new perfectly – honouring its Pitcairn people, its rich environment and its visitors.

Norfolk pine trees flank the shoreline.

POPULATION:
1,800 (2007)

WHEN TO GO:
Idyllic in December-January, with temperatures ranging from 12°C (54° F) at night to 19-21°C (66-70° F) in the day.

HOW TO GET THERE:
Regular flights from Sydney, Brisbane, Newcastle and Auckland – with an average 2 hours flying time.

HIGHLIGHTS:
Bounty Day – 8 June. When the islanders re-enact the landing of their ancestors on the island.

Kingston – built by convicts of the second penal colony, with many historic buildings.

Bushwalks through the National Park – to see some of the 40 plants unique to the island.

Lazing under the Norfolk Island Pines – up to 57 m (187 ft) tall.

A hot-stone massage with heated basalt stones from the nearby beach.

YOU SHOULD KNOW:
English is the main language here, but the islanders still talk to each other in 'Norfolk' – a mix of 18th century English and Polynesian. *Wataweih yorlye?* means 'How are you?'

The main beach seen from Point Lookout.

North Stradbroke Island

POPULATION:
3,200 (2005) – but greater during the holiday season.
WHEN TO GO:
June to October for humpback whale watching, and to avoid the summer crowds.
HOW TO GET THERE:
Thirty min vehicle ferry or water taxi from Cleveland (just 30 km (19 mi) south of Brisbane). There's also a fast catamaran service.
HIGHLIGHTS:
North Gorge Headlands walk – spectacular, surf-crashing walk around the Point Lookout cliffs.
A cooling swim in Blue Lake, Blue Lake National Park.
Tours of Amenity Point and the lakes in glass-bottomed canoes.
Sandboarding, scuba diving, surfing and sea kayaking.
YOU SHOULD KNOW:
Stradbroke Island's most famous local was Oodgeroo Noonuccal, formerly known as Kath Walker, the Aboriginal poet and native-rights campaigner. She was one of the prime movers who lead the 1997 agreement between the local government council and the aboriginal people of the area claiming rights over the island and parts of Moreton Bay.

Affectionately known as 'Straddie' by the locals, North Stradbroke Island is the textbook beach get-away. Just 30 km (19 mi) southeast of Brisbane and the Gold Coast, it languishes at the southern end of Moreton Bay. At 30 km (19 mi) long, it is one of the world's largest sand islands, boasting pristine beaches, rugged coastline and inland freshwater lakes.

It lost its native name of Minijerribah in 1827, when one Captain H. J. Rous, or Viscount Dunwich, commander of the HMS *Rainbow*, named the island after his father the Earl of Stradbroke, the main town after his own title and Rainbow Beach after his ship.

A cluster of three picturesque villages – Dunwich, Amity Point and Point Lookout – act as convivial bases for many visitors. Dunwich was once a penal colony and quarantine station, and, as is often the case, its cemetery is a telling record of the island's past. At Point Lookout, the aptly named Whale Rock is the perfect spot from which to scan the vast oceans in search of migrating humpback whales, dolphins and turtles.

In the 1960s, sand mining operations began to impact on the fragile island environment, but by the 1990s environmental issues came to the fore and half of the island became a national park. Mining is still very active on the island, but mainly away in the restricted southern end.

Point Lookout on the eastern surf side of the island is a natural draw. Spreading across Straddie's single rocky headland it overlooks a string of white beaches. The western side enjoys the calmer waters of the bay and is safer for families. The island is famous for its fishing – with the annual 'Straddie Classic' every August being one of Australia's richest and best-known fishing competitions.

Rottnest Island

Sitting on the edge of the Australian continental shelf near Perth in western Australia, Rottnest Island is just 11 km (6 mi) long and 4.5 km (2.7 mi) at its widest point. An iconic holiday destination for Perth residents, with 70 per cent of visitors coming for a day out, the entire island is run as a nature reserve and the surrounding waters as a marine park.

Known to local Aboriginal people as Wadjemup, the island is believed to be a place of spirits and is of significance to the Aboriginal communities. Artefacts have been found at a number of sites on Rottnest Island which are at least 6,500 years old, and possibly older, so there were indigenous people living here before sea levels rose and the island was separated from the mainland.

The first Europeans to discover the island were Dutch navigators who were searching for a shorter route from the Cape of Good Hope to Batavia in the 17th century. At that time the island was uninhabited. Samuel Volkerson was the first European to actually land on the island in 1658. William de Vlamingh visited in 1696 and named the island Rottnest after the abundance of quokkas (small marsupials) he saw, mistaking them for rats. Other Europeans soon followed, believing the island had potential for salt harvesting, farming and fishing. From 1839 for almost a century the island housed a penal colony for Aboriginal men and boys. When the colony closed, the leisure potential of the island was realized and tourism took off.

The island is best explored by bicycle as private cars are not allowed. The 24-km (15-mi) route around the coast runs through some of the most beautiful scenery, passing small, sandy beaches in secluded coves. The island has a total of 63 beaches and 20 bays, some of the finest in the world, and the turquoise water makes swimming here a must.

There are lovely reefs here, with twenty species of colourful corals and 360 species of fish, which can be explored by snorkelling, diving or a trip in a glass-bottomed boat. There are also a number of shipwrecks close to the shore, making diving here a popular pastime. Look out for humpback whales, green and loggerhead turtles, rays and bottlenose dolphins.

The secluded Mary Cove

POPULATION:
128 (2006)
WHEN TO GO:
November to February.
HOW TO GET THERE:
By air or sea from Perth or Fremantle.
HIGHLIGHTS:
The cycle trail – explore all 24 km (15 mi) of coastline by bicycle. You will need at least 2½ hours for a leisurely trip.
Quokkas – these cute marsupials are almost tame and will come cadging when you are having a picnic.
The Quokka Arms – this hotel was constructed between 1859 and 1864 as the Governor's summer residence. More recently, it is open to the public as a hotel and is a popular drinking spot.
Snorkelling above the reefs – there are marked trails with underwater plaques to point out what to look for.
YOU SHOULD KNOW:
The island is very busy during school holidays so check dates before you go.

Fraser Island

POPULATION:
1,378 (1996)
WHEN TO GO:
Anytime, but the whale watching
months are rightly busier (August to
October) so book ahead.
HOW TO GET THERE:
Flights from Brisbane to Harvey Bay,
then boat to the island.
Day trip – fast ferry from Urangan
Marina to Kingfisher Bay resort.
Or barge from Urangan Harbour for
more serious exploration by vehicle.
HIGHLIGHTS:
Lake Wabby – the deepest lake on
the island.
The coloured cliffs at the Cathedrals.
A walk to the top of Indian Head –
with sightings out to sea of dolphins,
whales and sharks.
The Champagne Pools – a cluster of
safe swimming pools just above the
surf line.
Whale watching – 1,500 humpback
whales visit Harvey Bay in August,
September and October en route
to Antarctic waters.
YOU SHOULD KNOW:
The island got its European name
from James and Eliza Fraser (the
captain of the *Stirling Castle*, and his
wife) who were shipwrecked on the
northwest coast in 1836. He died
here, and she would have too but for
the help of the Aborigines.

Ranked alongside Uluru and the Great Barrier Reef, Fraser Island is a World Heritage Site and much vaunted as one of Australia's great natural treasures. From the Queensland coast, it appears cloaked in lush, deep green forest. But for all its rainforests and lakes, Fraser Island is in fact the largest sand island in the world – 120 km (75 mi) by 15 km (9 mi) – with supposedly more sand than the Sahara Desert, and with dunes up to 224 m (735 ft) high. There is nowhere like it on earth.

The Buchulla tribe, who called the island K'gari, or 'Paradise', lived in harmony with their environment for thousands of years. Tragically, what they spent so many years creating the Europeans soon dismantled. Settlers woke up to the value of the timber and vast tracts of rainforest were cleared. Happily, in 1991, the island became part of the Great Sandy National Park and its future was secured.

The east coast forms the main highway, and other quieter tracks criss-cross the interior and pierce the island's wooded heart. Towering kauri pines and cycads encircle the blue and even 'tea'-tinted lakes. Lake turtles are a joy to encounter, and will sometimes pester you for bread. The west coast is given over to mangrove swamps and, with its more treacherous soft sand, is pretty inaccessible.

The authentic Fraser experience can only come with walking – and a three-day hike, with camping overnight, reveals the hidden depths of this paradise island.

Fraser Island is one of the few remaining strongholds for a pure race of wild dingoes. Sadly, in recent years these dingoes have gained something of a reputation, but some of the blame for their aggression seems to point back to tourism. Visitors are just asked never to feed them and admire them from afar – to be 'Dingo Smart'.

*Dunes and lush forest on
Fraser Island*

*The rocky beaches of
Kangaroo Island*

Kangaroo Island

Kangaroo in both name and nature, this large island just 13 km (8 mi) off the South Australian mainland has remained relatively untouched for thousands of years; and as such is an unblemished microcosm of the vast red continent. Towering cliffs protect the northern shores, giving way to more exposed sandy beaches in the south. Bushwalking is pretty compulsory, and trails meander across the national and conservation parks that cover a third of the island.

Wild koalas hug the trees and kangaroos hop down the streets. Isolated from the ravages of European diseases and introduced species that afflicted their near neighbours, the native animals and plants have flourished – echidnas, platypuses, possums and penguins are all on the wildlife fanatic's list.

In 1800, Captain Matthew Flinders was commissioned by the British Government to chart the southern coastline of Terra Australis in HMS *Investigator*. He first sighted this island in March 1802, came ashore and named it Kangaroo Island, after dining well on wild kangaroo meat. Just weeks later he spotted a French ship on the horizon, under the command of Nicholas Baudin. Despite their two countries being at war, the two men were civil, exchanging ideas and even vital supplies. Baudin went on to map the south and west coastlines, leaving many French names in his wake: Ravine des Casoars, D'Estress Bay and Cape de Couedic – now home to a colony of New Zealand fur seals.

Experienced divers may discover one of the 50 or so wrecks that litter this rocky coastline. Following the earliest recorded shipwreck in 1847, the first lighthouse in South Australia was built at Cape Willoughby, and stands to this day – 27 metres (89 ft) high and a healthy climb to the top. Ferries landing at Penneshaw on the eastern tip make it a hotspot for tourists, but it is easy enough to get away into the wilds and delight in this well-preserved refuge.

POPULATION:
4,500 (2003)
WHEN TO GO:
June through to August is fabulous. The countryside is lush and the wildlife active during the day: kangaroos are popping out of the pouch, koalas, Southern right whales are steaming by on migration, and the male echidnas are out looking for mates. September to November sees Kangaroo Island in full bloom, and eucalyptus oil in full production.
HOW TO GET THERE:
By regular ferries (45 mins) from Cape Jervis to Penneshaw. By air – from Adelaide (30 mins).
HIGHLIGHTS:
Flinders Chase National Park – incredible rock formations including Remarkable Rocks and Admiral's Arch.
Little penguins on parade around Kingscote and Penneshaw – as they head back from the water to their seaside burrows for the night.
Surfing or swimming at Vivonne Bay – Australia's top beach for clear, clean waters and privacy.
Emu Ridge Eucalyptus Distillery is the only commercial distillery of its type in South Australia, still employing 600 islanders.
YOU SHOULD KNOW:
Here you can taste honey from the only known pure strain of Ligurian bee in the world. Twelve hives were imported from Liguria, Italy in the 1880s and in splendid island isolation they have remained pure – untouched by other breeds of bees, and producing true nectar of the gods.

Melville and Bathurst

POPULATION:
2,500 (2007)
WHEN TO GO:
Tours available from May to October (the wet season is October to March).
HOW TO GET THERE:
Chartered planes/tours out of Darwin.
HIGHLIGHTS:
Early Catholic mission buildings. Morning tea with the Tiwi women. The Pukamani burial sites.
YOU SHOULD KNOW:
Football is a Tiwi passion. It was introduced in 1941 by the missionary John Pye. The Tiwi grand final (mainly barefoot) in April is a significant local event, and football here has the highest local participation rate of anywhere in Australia (35 per cent).

Just 80 km (50 mi) due north of Darwin, Melville and its intimate smaller neighbour Bathurst make up the Tiwi Islands, home of the Tiwi Aboriginal people. Most of these people now live on Bathurst having abandoned their hunter-gatherer lifestyle, but some return to their traditional lands on Melville for just a few weeks each year.

For thousands of years they had hardly any contact with their mainland neighbours, and are rightly proud of their unique land and culture. Today, these determined people have created their own success story; leading their own tours on the islands, and turning their talents to beautiful and highly valued art – crafting and selling bark painting, textiles and pottery.

The Tiwi people's presence on the islands is most clearly marked by their Pukumani wooden burial poles, erected around graves and carved and painted with symbolic figures. This decorative patterning extends to body painting for ceremonies, and has been practised for thousands of years. The traditional form of mark making was derived from the creation story, and the Tiwi people's positioning of line and dot is very distinctive.

Clear waters, empty beaches and lush forest are the trademarks of these big, flat islands. Eucalyptus forest gives way to bush, and the waters offshore are favoured by sharks and freshwater crocodiles cruising out from the mainland.

You need a permit to visit the islands – and it is almost essential to book a tour, which employs the Tiwi islanders and takes in the local craft workshops. Food gathering in the bush or offshore with the local people, and staying overnight in a bush camp, draws you even deeper into their ancient and forgotten culture.

Flinders Island

This remarkable 'mountain' in the sea is the main island of the Furneaux chain – 50 or so dots across the Bass Strait, stretching from Tasmania to Australia. These islands are all that remains of the land bridge that once fused Tasmania to the mainland.

In the late 1800s, George Bass and Matthew Flinders circumnavigated Tasmania and left their names indelibly on the map. Flinders was also the destination for the last surviving Tasmanian Aborigines. They were literally herded here under the supervision of Reverend George Augustus Robinson to 'save' them from extinction by civilizing them and converting them to Christianity. Isolated, hungry

and plagued by disease, they gradually died out, and a tiny chapel and cemetery at Wybalenna is all that remains.

On Flinders, rugged granite peaks give way to white crescent beaches and turquoise waters. Much of the land is now a natural reserve and Strezelecki National Park is a wonderful place, adored by hikers. From Settlement Point, you can gaze out over the vast mutton bird colony – where hundreds of thousands of birds scream in to their nests at dusk during the breeding season, from October to March.

On foot is the classic way to take in this island – six days from top to toe – or following one of the many shorter bushwalking trails. And to soothe those weary limbs, nothing compares with soaking in the tepid waters on one of the many fine beaches, interspersed with some gentle fishing off the rocks.

Trousers Point

POPULATION:
897 (2005)
WHEN TO GO:
Pleasant throughout the year, but January is the warmest with temperatures from 13-22° C (60-71° F), with cooling sea breezes.
HOW TO GET THERE:
Daily flights from Tasmania, also some flights from Victoria.
HIGHLIGHTS:
Trousers Point – an idyllic cove with swimming, camping and picnicking.
Settlement Point – for a short coastal walk with swimming, rock hopping and views.
Climbing to the top of Mount Strezelecki.
YOU SHOULD KNOW:
One of the more unusual pastimes here is fossicking for 'diamonds' – small fragments of topaz – on the beach and in the creek at Killiecrankie Bay.

Royal penguins out for a stroll on Macquarie Island

Macquarie Island

'Macca' rests at the ends of the earth. This remote wilderness is tucked away in the southeast corner of the Pacific, halfway between Australia and Antarctica. A tiny fragment of land, it is of huge significance on a world scale, yet was only discovered by accident by Frederick Hasselborough in 1810 while he was looking around for new sealing grounds.

Under Tasmania's wing, the only human inhabitants on this extraordinary wildlife sanctuary are from the Australian Antarctic Division, based on the north of the island. Over the centuries, scientists have been endlessly drawn to this unsung wonder of the natural world. On the animal front, the visitors are visually and audibly overwhelming. Each spring, around 3.5 million seabirds, mostly penguins, and 80,000 elephant seals pull themselves up on to the rocky shoreline to breed. There are penguins galore – rockhoppers, kings, royals and gentooes; and on occasion the fabulous sooty and wandering albatrosses. Rabbits are a less welcome sight and are literally eating away at this World Heritage Site. Their days may well be numbered.

You have to work extremely hard to get to this island, but the rewards for true lovers of wildlife and wilderness are unparalleled. It's a cold, inhospitable place at the best of times, but you don't come here for the weather.

Lord Howe Island

Unpolluted and untouched, Lord Howe Island is the ultimate eco-destination. Back in Victorian times, stories came to England of this 'gem of the sea', and to this day over two-thirds of the land is given over to a park reserve and only 400 people can visit at any one time. Often the animals outnumber the people.

There's only one road, and everyone tends to get around by bicycle, boat or on foot. Just 11 km (7 mi) long, this boomerang-shaped beauty is topped by the rainforest-clad Mount Gower and Mount Lidgbird and dips down into the cool Tasman Sea. Born of a volcanic eruption some seven million years ago, it has the southern-most coral reef in the world – safe haven for 500 species of fish and 90 species of corals.

Lord Howe Island was discovered in 1788 by Lieutenant Henry Lidgbird Ball of HMS *Supply*, while on his way from Botany Bay to Norfolk Island with convicts on board. Many government ships, whaling and trading vessels stopped here but a permanent settlement wasn't established until 1834, at an area now known as Old Settlement.

Nowadays, the locals are laidback and often barefoot, and set the tone for any visit. On the more popular northern end of the island, there are endless walks and lookouts, and ideal places for a picnic along Old Settlement Beach. Bushwalking apart, there are fabulous swimming, snorkelling and diving spots. This insanely beautiful island never appears crowded – and if it is, it's with exotic flora and fauna not human life.

POPULATION:
300 (2007)
WHEN TO GO:
Cheapest to get there out of season but it can be wetter and windier and some places may be closed. From September to April huge numbers of exotic seabirds nest here.
HOW TO GET THERE:
By air from Sydney or Brisbane.
HIGHLIGHTS:
Sooty terns on the accessible summit of Mount Eliza (from August to March).
Mist forests of Mount Gower in the south – strenuous guided walk of about 8 hours.
Ned's Beach – a daily fish feeding frenzy attracting reef and sharks.
Ball's Pyramid – dive trips around the world's tallest stack, rising from the sea 23 km (14 mi) to the southeast.
YOU SHOULD KNOW:
Some rare mushrooms on the island glow in the dark. These glowing mushrooms appear after heavy rain in the palm forests. If picked they glow for a number of days. The glow is so bright that you can read by it in the dark.

The twin peaks of Mounts Lidgbird and Gower

The Whitsunday Islands

POPULATION:
14,103 (2001)
WHEN TO GO:
Any time of year.
HOW TO GET THERE:
Fly to Hamilton Island direct, or to Proserpine on the mainland. Take a ferry from Shutehaven or Airlie Beach on the mainland.
HIGHLIGHTS:
Scenic flights over the Great Barrier Reef – these can most easily be arranged on Hamilton Island.
Whitehaven Beach – located on Whitsunday Island, this 7-km (4.3 mi) beach has brilliant white sand, so bring your sunglasses.
Aboriginal cave paintings – accessible by boat, the paintings can be found at Nara Inlet on Hook Island.
Migrating whales – if you visit the islands in July-September, look out for migrating whales as they make their way through the warm waters past the islands.
Hamilton Island Race Week – this yachting festival takes place in August each year. More than 150 yachts come from across Australia and New Zealand to compete in a week of races. On Whitehaven Day, the yachts descend on Whitehaven Beach and enjoy an enormous beach party.
YOU SHOULD KNOW:
The islands can get busy in the peak season.

A group of 74 islands lying off the coast of Queensland, Australia, between Townsville and Mackay, the Whitsunday Islands are part of the Great Barrier Reef and one of Australia's most popular destinations attracting over half a million visitors each year. These forested mountainous islands are surrounded by spectacular coral reefs, warm crystal-clear aquamarine waters and white sandy beaches. They were first discovered by Captain Cook in the 1770s on his fraught voyage to try to find an exit from the reef system without destroying his ship. He named the islands Whitsunday because he thought it was Whit Sunday on the day he discovered them, though it turned out he was wrong. The name, however, stuck.

Most of the islands are designated as national park, although some are privately owned. Apart from the bigger more developed islands, the majority are uninhabited, unspoiled wildernesses. There are small resorts on some of the islands, and camp sites on others if you really want to get away from it all.

Hamilton Island is the most developed and many visitors use it as a base from which to access the Great Barrier Reef. There are many other activities on offer from Hamilton, including sea kayaking, twilight sailing, game fishing, scenic flights over the Great Barrier Reef, diving, cuddling a koala, bushwalking and waterskiing. Despite its development, the island is still largely untouched and has some lovely beaches, coves and inlets.

Hook Island, the second largest of the islands, is another popular destination for tourists. It is best known for its colourful coral gardens, a great place for snorkelling and diving.

Whitsunday Island is the largest of the group and is best known among boating-types for Hill Inlet, the secure anchorage of Cid Harbour, the sheltered waterway of Gulnare Inlet, and the famous Whitehaven Beach, with its 7 km (4.3 mi) of pure white silica sand.

The stunning Whitehaven Beach

This stunning beach attracts lots of day-trippers from the mainland ports of Airlie Beach and Shute Harbour.

There is a bewildering variety of organized tours on offers, with sailing boat, catamaran and cruise trips to the islands and reefs, many to sites where visitors can snorkel in the reefs and watch the fish. Several companies also run trips in glass-bottomed boats or semi-submersibles. The islands are not only worth visiting for the marine life, however. Many have walking trails up to their peaks through lovely rainforest full of birdsong, and there are so many beaches you are bound to find one to yourself.

The rugged, volcanic coastline of Christmas Island

Christmas Island

David Attenborough once famously sat on the beach here, in the pitch dark, as millions of red land crabs scuttled over his legs and marched determinedly down to the sea. Christmas Island is a scientist's heaven, and for the rest of us a retreat from reality. In Australia's remote Indian Ocean Territories, it lies 360 km (224 mi) south of Jakarta and 2,300 km (1,429 mi) northwest of Perth. Its people are a blend of Chinese, Malay and European-Australian, and so is its food, language, religion and customs.

It took millions of years for the island to emerge from the depths, and it remains of immense scientific importance. For centuries, Christmas Island's isolation and rugged coasts were a natural barrier to settlement. On 25 December 1643, Captain William Mynors of the British East India Company's *Royal Mary* had sighted the island and given it its name. And yet no humans resided here until the late nineteenth century; leaving many unique animal species to evolve without human interference.

Sixty percent of the island is now protected, and harbours wildlife found nowhere else in the world. The famous red land crabs are dotted across the forest floor; pneumatic robber crabs scale the coconut trees and frigatebirds, noddies and boobies nest on the cliffs and in the forests. The coastline is rugged, but notched with tiny sheltered bays and sand and coral beaches seemingly purpose built for a swim.

POPULATION:
1,600 (2007)
WHEN TO GO:
Dry season – April to November.
November/December for the mammoth red land crab march.
HOW TO GET THERE:
Flights form Perth (via the Cocos Islands); and from Singapore and Jakarta.
HIGHLIGHTS:
Diving with whale sharks – October to April.
Cave dives.
Flying Fish Cove – swimming and snorkelling.
Walks through the rainforest.
Hugh's Waterfall.
The Blowholes – a series of rock formations that hiss and spurt water when it is forced through from the ocean swell.
YOU SHOULD KNOW:
This remote island unexpectedly hit the headlines in August 2001, when the Norwegian container ship *Tampa* with its cargo of rescued asylum seekers from Afghanistan was refused permission to land.

491

Hobart harbour

Tasmania

A world apart in every sense, Tasmania is Australia's only island state, and the very isolation that once made it an ideal location for penal settlements now helps preserve its natural riches. Tasmania would seem to have it all – from history and wilderness to friendly people and great food and wines.

Tasmania certainly seems to move at a much slower pace than the mainland – affording visitors the time and space to relax. Over 360 km (224 mi) long and 306 km (190 mi) wide, it's big enough to allow you to head for the hills on the back roads and escape everyday life. Along the way are magnificent peaks, old colonial settlements and empty beaches. It also purports to have some of the cleanest air in the world.

The first European to sight Tasmania was the Dutch navigator Abel Tasman in 1642, and from then on many explorers came this way, including James Cook and William Bligh. But the arrival of these men was bad news for the Tasmanian Aborigines. They lost their traditional hunting grounds and sometimes their lives, and were resettled to Flinders Island to be 'civilized'. Many Aboriginal sites are sacred, but on the cliffs around Woolnorth can be seen some of their unique art.

Corners of Tasmania are often likened to the green pastures of England but here there are also vast wildernesses: the west is wild and untamed, inland are glacial mountains and roaring rivers. For the less adventurous, there is the cosmopolitan capital Hobart – spread out over seven hills and with a waterfront location to match Sydney's. In the heart of the countryside lies sleepy old Richmond – with some of Australia's finest and most pristine colonial architecture it's now a Mecca for artists and artisans.

Tasmania appears to have been slightly overlooked. Yet this discreet island, roughly the size of Ireland, is both gentle and wild, charming and challenging.

POPULATION:
484,700 (2005)
WHEN TO GO:
October to March – when it's pleasantly warm and mild.
HOW TO GET THERE:
Flights from Melbourne and other mainland capitals. High speed ferries from Sydney and Melbourne.
HIGHLIGHTS:
The capital Hobart with its Salamanca market place.
Walking the rugged Overland Track through Cradale Mountain-Lake St Clair National Park.
Hiking through Freycinet National Park to Wineglass Bay.
White-water rafting on the wild Franklin River.
YOU SHOULD KNOW:
The tale of the Tasmania tiger – a striped carnivore that once roamed Tasmania – has two endings: one is that it was hunted to extinction by European settlers, while the other maintains that this large thylacine still leads a secretive life way out in Tasmania's great wilderness.

Torres Straits Islands

Dividing Australia from Papua New Guinea, the Torres Strait is one of the last frontiers on earth, and is sprinkled with stepping-stone islands. Of these islands, 17 are inhabited and Thursday Island is seen as the 'capital'. This tiny speck of an island, just visible from the Australian mainland, was once called the 'Sink of the Pacific', reflecting the sheer variety of people who have passed through since its pearling heydays – Aboriginal, Malay, Chinese, Japanese, Melanesian and Anglo. In this now lies its charm.

In the 19th century, Europeans quickly discovered the Strait's rich pearl beds and Thursday Island was once a thriving centre for pearl diving. For decades this was the only job on the island and many Japanese pearl divers tragically lost their lives here, and are buried in the local cemetery. Most died of compression sickness.

Many foreigners have influenced the islands' history. In the late 1800s the London Missionary Society landed on Darnley Island – and the advent of Christianity stabilized the community, but also led to the demise of traditional life. South Sea Island teachers also came, and brought with them a new dance culture and crops, and intermarried with the locals.

Access to the smaller more remote islands is limited, but a few are little gems. Badu is fringed by mangrove swamps and is the centre of the Straits burgeoning crayfish industry; and Saibai, just 16 km (10 mi) from the New Guinea mainland is the only place in Australia from which you can see another country. In many ways, Thursday Island is the easiest and most interesting island to visit, with its laid-back attitude and multicultural mix. Here the hotel clock has no hands – paying homage to the leisurely pace of life.

POPULATION:
8,089 (2001)
WHEN TO GO:
Avoid the monsoon season.
HOW TO GET THERE:
Ferry from mainland to Thursday Island. Access to other islands limited and more expensive.
Flights from Cairns to Thursday Island via Horn Island – a few minutes by water taxi from Thursday Island. Small airline operators service other islands
HIGHLIGHTS:
Thursday Island:
Coming of Light festivities on 1 July.
All Souls Quetta Memorial Church – built in 1893 in memory of the shipwreck of the *Quetta*, with 133 lives lost.
Aplin Road Cemetery – tiled islander tombs, and the Japanese area filled with hundreds of pearl divers graves.
Thursday's colonial-style Customs House.
Pearling Museum on nearby Horn Island.
YOU SHOULD KNOW:
In any one season in the annual (July) Island of Origin rugby league matches up to 25 players may be hospitalized, and there is sadly an occasional death.

Waier Island, part of the Murray Island group in the Torres Straits

The rich variety of fish found in the waters surrounding Mayor Island make this a popular dive location.

Mayor Island

POPULATION:
3 (2001)
WHEN TO GO:
October to May.
HOW TO GET THERE:
By boat from Whangamata or Tauranga.
HIGHLIGHTS:
The island offers great opportunities for off-shore activities, including big game fishing, diving and snorkelling, to appreciate the rich marine life here, including swordfish, marlin and mako sharks.
The hiking trails on the island allow good views of the crater, with its lakes and hot springs.
YOU SHOULD KNOW:
Strict quarantine measures are in place to protect the wildlife around the island, so you must contact the caretaker before landing here.

Located off the Bay of Plenty coast of New Zealand's North Island, Mayor Island is the top of a dormant shield volcano, rising 355 m (1,164 ft) above the waves and believed to have formed about 7,000 years ago. Known as Tuhua by the indigenous Maori, the island was named Mayor Island by Captain Cook, who first sighted it three days before Lord Mayor's Day in 1769. The sides of the volcano rise fairly steeply from the sea, and the majority of its interior is a vast crater. Hot springs abound, and there are two small crater lakes on the island, Green Lake and Black Lake, which were formed by eruptions 36,000 and 6,000 years ago.

The island is best known for its lava flows and domes, containing deposits of obsidian, a black volcanic glass created by the rapid cooling of silica-rich lava. The obsidian, *tuhua* in Maori, was prized by the Maori for making cutting and scraping tools and pieces from the island have been found throughout New Zealand and the Kermadec Islands.

The waters around the island are renowned for game fishing, with marlin, mako sharks and swordfish being plentiful here. The island and the waters close to its shores are protected as a small marine reserve, but diving, snorkelling, sailing and swimming are all encouraged here. The old game-fishing centre on Sou'East Bay is on a beautiful beach and the clear waters and rich variety of fish here make it the most popular destination for divers.

There are several hiking tracks on the island, so visitors can explore the native bush and see the birdlife. Because it is protected, the easiest way to get here is with a registered tour operator.

Stewart Island

In Maori legend, if North Island was once the great fish and South Island the canoe, then Stewart Island was its anchor. Due south of Invercargill, the Maori name for the third largest island in New Zealand is Rakiura or Glowing Skies. Gazing at a crimson sun setting over the horizon or the Aurora Australis (Southern Lights) sweeping over inky skies, this is the end of that quest for paradise.

This laidback and unspoilt wilderness reverberates with the sound of birdsong. Parakeets, tui, kaka, bellbirds and robins flutter overhead and sing their hearts out. Eighty-five percent of the island is protected, and it is unadulterated heaven for walkers and birders. Just offshore are albatrosses, blue penguins and petrels. Added to that, the coast is punctuated by endless sandy coves for a swim in the somewhat bracing waters.

Searching for New Zealand's national bird, the kiwi, is at its easiest here. The birds are large and pretty common around the beaches, even during the day. They are so short-sighted and slow they may even bump into bathers.

The only real settlement on the island is Oban. This lazy little fishing village nestles in Halfmoon Bay and has enough shops and cafés to keep the relaxed traveller content. Despite its 7,000 km (4,350 mi) coastline, Stewart Island only has 20 km (12 mi) of roads. Shrug off the cares of the world and relax Stewart-style.

POPULATION:
420 (2006)
WHEN TO GO:
The weather can swing dramatically in any given day, but December and January are warmest with temperatures averaging 16.5° C (62 °F).
HOW TO GET THERE:
Flights from Invercargill.
HIGHLIGHTS:
Walking the 29 km (18 mi) Rakiura Track (a circuit out of Oban) with camping and huts along the way.
Eating crayfish as fresh as it gets.
Swim at isolated Mason Bay – the water may be cold but kiwis abound.
Ulva Island – tiny island just offshore and heaving with wildlife, and plenty of trails.
Paterson Inlet for kayaking and walking.
YOU SHOULD KNOW:
Bring a torch if you are staying in Oban – there are no streetlights at night.

The Aurora Australis over Stewart Island

Mokoia Island

A sacred island in a lake, Mokoia is a green lava dome rising 180 m (590 ft) above the still waters of Lake Roturua in the heart of North Island. Stepping ashore, its deeply spiritual nature seems to reverberate through the air. This natural sanctuary for wildlife belongs to the Te Arawa people and was once know as Te Motu Tapu a Tinirau – the Sacred Island of Tinirau. Fertile and isolated for hundreds of years, it holds a unique *kumera* (sweet potato) plantation, which meant it was once hotly contested by warring tribes. It was once also a thriving village for Maori and missionaries, but is now stands quiet and alone.

Steeped in tradition, it is said that Mokoia was home to Tutanekai, a young warrior. It was to Mokoia that Hinemoa, the daughter of a famous chief, defying her family, swam some 2.5 km (1.5 mi) from the shores of Lake Roturua at night guided only by the sound of her true love's flute. So deep and rich is this story that the two main streets in Rotorua are named after this lovestruck couple.

The shores of Mokoia hold geothermal springs and Roturua is New Zealand's most dynamic thermal area – with geysers, hot springs and bubbling mud pools. The area is also the epicentre of Maori culture, with one-third of its residents being Maori. 'Sulphur City' as it is known is a much-favoured spot for tourists and backpackers; so, to find more spiritual solace, cruise out to the hidden island of Mokoia.

A view of Mokoia Island across Lake Rotorua

Chatham Islands

Head due south of Christchurch, way out into the South Pacific, and you'll stumble upon the ten Chatham Islands. As befits this remote, brooding location, there are rugged coastlines, towering cliffs and endless, empty beaches. Its Moriori name of Rekohu or 'Misty Sun' respects a peaceful past with people of Polynesian extraction. Sadly the last full-blooded Moriori, Tommy Solomon, died over 70 years ago. But slowly the descendants of these people are gaining recognition for their rights and values.

The Chathams are the first inhabited land in the world to greet the dawn – on 1 January 2000 the dawn was greeted here at 4.00 am (NZST) with major international celebrations linking all nations of the world.

Only Chatham Island and Pitt Island are inhabited, and the best way to get around the islands is to ask these locals. Around the shores live many rare birds – from black robins and magenta petrels to mollyhawks; and inland ancient Moriori tree and rock carvings survive. At Blind Man's Creek 40 million-year-old sharks' teeth can be found – but visitors are asked to leave them where they find them, for obvious reasons!

This is an unworldly place, offering enormous peace and solitude. There are no public roads, no flashy resorts and limited accommodation; and the fiercely independent yet welcoming locals take good care of their guests. From the moment you arrive you are placed under the wing of an island family.

Large colonies of fur seals can be found in the Chatham Islands.

POPULATION:
770 (2006)
WHEN TO GO:
Best to visit from September to March, with temperatures of 15-24° C (59-75° F) – but these are also the busiest times. All visitors must have confirmed accommodation before arriving. In summer the hotel and lodge are often filled by tours so book as far ahead as possible.
HOW TO GET THERE:
Direct flights from Wellington, Christchurch and Auckland.
HIGHLIGHTS:
Early Moriori settlement sites and middens.
Memorial to Tommy Solomon, the last full-blooded Moriori.
Crayfishing off the beach, and wonderful seafood to savour.
Fishing and diving tours.
Fur seal colony near Kaingaroa, Chatham Island.
YOU SHOULD KNOW:
The international date line lies to the east of the Chathams, even though the islands lie east of 180° longitude. Consequently, the Chatham Islands observe their own time, 45 minutes ahead of New Zealand time.

Sub-Antarctic Islands

With a past lost in sealing and shipwrecks, New Zealand's Sub-Antarctic Islands (Snares, Bounty, Campbell, Antipodes and Aucklands) have finally found their true vocation as wondrous, wild nature reserves and biodiversity 'hot spots'. Home to half the world's seabirds, they also offer fabulous breeding grounds for the 'giants' of the natural world – elephant seals, crested penguins and wandering albatrosses.

Many of the islands are rightly out of bounds, but some can be landed on with a permit. Landing on Campbell Island is a treat – to make acquaintance with over 7,500 pairs of southern royal albatrosses and the rare Campbell Island teal. One out-of-bounds group is the magical Antipodes Islands that got their name from their position at latitude 180° – exactly opposite 0° at Greenwich, England. Bobbing offshore you may catch a glimpse of the endemic Antipodes Island parakeet or the huge albatrosses nesting in the short grass. On the Bounty Islands there are literally thousands of penguins and mollyhawks –– definitely no room for humans.

The Auckland Islands were plagued by shipwrecks in the 1800s, and settlement here failed miserably when the introduced cattle had to be destroyed. So now the land is given over to wildlife. On the wondrously named Disappointment Island there are over 60,000 white-capped mollyhawks and more. But the plant life of these islands should not be forgotten. Sir Joseph Hooker, botanist aboard Sir James Clark Ross's 1840 Antarctic expedition wrote of 'a flora display second to none outside the tropics'. He was to become the curator of Kew Gardens.

The Sub-Antarctics are not for the faint-hearted. Arrive armed with a sense of adventure and a love of the wilder side of life and you will leave all the wiser.

POPULATION:
Uninhabited
WHEN TO GO:
November to January
HOW TO GET THERE:
Most easily on ecotourism boat trips out of Manpouri.
HIGHLIGHTS:
Birds... a day ashore on Enderby (Auckland Islands) – to see flightless teal, snipe and yellow-eyed penguins.
Auckland Island – southern royal albatrosses among the flowering mega herbs.
Early morning on Snares Island with six million sooty shearwaters.
YOU SHOULD KNOW:
If you are very lucky you might just hitch a lift to the islands on board a scientific boat expedition as a 'casual explorer'. But there is often a long waiting list.

Surf surging through the kelp on Snares Island.

The Bay of Islands

Close to the northern tip of New Zealand, 60 km (40 mi) north-west of Whangarei, is one of the most popular fishing, sailing and diving destinations in the country. The clear blue waters of the Bay of Islands boast a rich variety of marine life, and are dotted with 144 small islands which together make a picture-postcard scene. The warm equatorial waters give the bay a mild climate which is pleasant all year round.

The Bay of Islands was the first part of New Zealand to be settled by Europeans. British explorer Captain Cook gave the bay its modern name when he stopped here in 1769 on his round-the-world voyage. He put down his anchor at Motoroahia (Roberton Island) where he met the local Maori tribes and began trading on (largely) friendly terms. This is also the place where 500 Maori chiefs and representatives of Queen Victoria signed the Waitangi Treaty in 1840. The treaty made New Zealand a British colony, but gave Maoris the rights of British citizens and the right to own their own lands and other property. The treaty has caused much controversy since it was signed, partly because there were differences between the Maori and British translations. You can find out more at the Waitangi Treaty Grounds, a half-hour stroll along the beach from Paihia.

The best way to enjoy the islands and their abundant wildlife is by boat, whether it is a kayak, yacht or cruiser. Dolphin and whale sightings are very common here. It is even possible to swim with dolphins on a licensed tour.

Jacques Cousteau described the diving around Poor Knights Islands as among the very best in the world, with an abundance of marine wildlife including manta rays and killer whales. There are more than a hundred dive sites in the bay, with coral reefs, rocky coastlines and ship wrecks to explore, including the wreck of the Greenpeace ship, *Rainbow Warrior*, sunk here by the French secret services in 1985. The bay is also famous for its fishing, with good populations of marlin, kingfish and snapper.

POPULATION:
149,600 (2006)
WHEN TO GO:
Any time of year.
HOW TO GET THERE:
By road or rail from Auckland to Russell or by air to Kerikiri then by road.
HIGHLIGHTS:
Swimming with the dolphins.
Whale-watching boat trips.
Watching penguins and gannets.
YOU SHOULD KNOW:
There are strict rules about how closely boats can approach whales and dolphins.

Urupukapuka Island in the Bay of Islands

Espiritu Santo Island

POPULATION:
31,000 (2007 estimate)
WHEN TO GO:
The temperate climate doesn't vary much, though November to February is the hottest, most humid time.
HOW TO GET THERE:
By light aircraft from Port Vila or direct Air Vanuatu flights from Australia (Sydney).
HIGHLIGHTS:
Informative tours for those who want to explore the island's delights with the help of knowledgeable guides.
Luganville market – for a wealth of colourful island produce (and characters).
For divers only – Million Dollar Point, where US forces dumped everything from aircraft to military vehicles into the sea after World War II; the wrecks of the SS *President Coolidge* and USS *Tucker*, both victims of 'friendly fire' (US-laid mines).
Big Bay National Park in the north of the island, a beautifully preserved and completely unspoiled area.
Guided trekking – magical jungle exploration in a small party with an experienced local leader.
YOU SHOULD KNOW:
Take what you need – only the most basic of necessities can be bought on the island.

With an area of 3,950 sq km (1,525 sq mi), this is the largest island in the Republic of Vanuatu, formerly known as the New Hebrides. Vanuatu consists of 83 islands in Melanesia, until recently an isolated part of the western Pacific visited only by the most intrepid of travellers. Now times are changing, but happily for those who like their tropical and sub-tropical islands unspoiled, not that fast.

Espiritu Santo (from the Spanish 'Holy Spirit') is often referred to simply as Santo. The main town and provincial capital is Luganville, the second largest settlement in Vanuatu. The name reflects the fact that the islands were once governed jointly by the British and French, with the latter rather more influential. However, it was the Americans who had bases on Espiritu Santo in World War II, and there are plenty of decaying reminders of their stay. The town has an excellent harbour that is an important centre of the trade in commodities like copra (dried coconut meat) and cacao. It has modernized to the extent that broadband internet access is available, and there are now plenty of buses and taxis to help visitors get around locally.

From Luganville, there are roads to the north and west, but they don't stray far from the coast, leaving the bulk of the island remote and inaccessible. It has a rocky spine, with Mount Tabwemasana rising to around 1,900 m (6,200 ft) – the highest point in Vanuatu. Cruise ships often visit Luganville, and the island is a popular destination with divers who like to get away from the underwater crowd to explore freshwater caves and extensive coral reefs. There are excellent beaches, like the aptly named Champagne Beach (sparkling water and pink sand). The number of annual visitors is still small, but that is changing – get there ahead of the crowd!

Champagne Beach

Tanna Island

In parts of this island, it seems that time has stood still for a thousand years – many villagers still wear traditional costume (which is pretty skimpy), follow the customs of their ancestors and shun all the trappings of modern life. Tanna is a small but interesting island in Vanuatu. Captain James Cook was the first European to arrive, in 1774, attracted by a glowing volcano in the night. Cook was followed by traders and missionaries, but the latter had little success in weaning the islanders off their old beliefs, and in the 19th century some were sadly cannibalized. Even today, outsiders are only welcome in rural villages if travelling with a local guide.

That notwithstanding, Tanna is trying to encourage tourism to supplement the traditional farming and fishing activities. There are a limited number of low-key resorts and bungalow accommodation on the west and east coasts, with wild trekking a major activity in the south around the island's highest mountain, Tukosmera, and nearby Mount Melen. There are one or two inland lodges behind Mount Yasur, on the northwest coast, said to be the world's most accessible active volcano. It is near Sulphur Bay and one-day volcano tours are the most common tourist activity, but the island merits a longer stay.

Tanna has the beautiful white beaches and tropical vegetation of many Pacific islands, but retains an atmosphere that will delight the traveller who dislikes wholesale modern development. There are still places in the world that still allow adventurous travellers to feel that they've discovered the idyllic back of beyond, but are not too difficult to reach. This is one of them.

POPULATION:
20,000 (2007 estimate)
WHEN TO GO:
The climate is at its best between March and October.
HOW TO GET THERE:
By Air Vanuatu from Port Vila on the island of Efate to White Grass airport on Tanna's east coast. On from there by public transport (usually a pickup truck).
HIGHLIGHTS:
Old-fashioned Port Resolution, founded by Captain Cook and named after his ship, HMS *Resolution*. Friday evening meetings of the John Frums cargo cult, that still believes that gods in the USA are responsible for the miraculous appearance of modern goodies such as radios and fridges (visitors genuinely welcome).
YOU SHOULD KNOW:
There is a cargo cult on Tanna that worships...Prince Philip, Queen Elizabeth II's husband.

Mount Yasur, the world's most accessible active volcano

Lake Te Nggano, home to a rich variety of bird life

Rennell Island

POPULATION:
1,500 (2007 estimate)
WHEN TO GO:
Beware of cyclones – the best chance of avoiding an inside-out golf umbrella is between May and October.
HOW TO GET THERE:
Solomon Airlines has five weekly flights to Rennell from Afutara Airport.
HIGHLIGHTS:
A visit to the ancient burial places, caves and temples of the legendary Hiti people.
The abundant and varied bird life on Lake Te Nggano.
Attending a *hetaki* bout – it's the island's traditional form of wrestling.
Visiting one of the villages that specializes in traditional wood carving of extraordinary quality.
YOU SHOULD KNOW:
Eight US Navy Catalina flying boats were scuttled in Lake Te Nggano at the end of World War II, after both Japanese and American forces had been based there.

How about a trip to the world's largest raised coral atoll? That'll be Rennell Island, traditionally known as Mu Nggava, the southern-most of the Solomon Islands in the western Pacific. It is 80 km (50 mi) long and 40 km (25 mi) wide with an area of 630 sq km (245 sq mi), sparsely populated and largely covered with tropical forest. The island is surrounded by high cliffs, has no beaches and boasts the Pacific Ocean's largest freshwater lake – brackish Lake Te Nggano. There are no rivers or streams, so islanders rely on wells and rainwater tanks.

The inhabitants – who live in closely-knit clans – operate a subsistence economy involving horticulture, fishing, hunting and gathering, with coconuts, yams, taro and bananas being important staples. The profession of *mataisau* (carpenter and expert wood carver) is highly respected.

This is not a casual holiday destination for conventional tourists. Facilities are primitive and those wishing to see this remote place are advised to join an organized group. There are various specialized tours like birdwatching, scuba diving (by boat) and World War II battlefield tours (there was a naval battle off the island in 1943), whilst some basic guest-houses do cater for the bold solo artist – find them near Tingoa airfield or around the lake.

East Rennell (paradoxically the southern third of the island) is a UNESCO World Heritage Site, listed for its importance as a stepping-stone in the migration and evolution of species in the western Pacific. It is not protected by national legislation and – as with many of the Solomon Islands – logging is an ever-present threat.

Guadalcanal Island

In 1942 and 1943, Guadalcanal Island in the southern Solomons was the scene of the first major Allied assault on the Japanese Empire. The intense campaign raged for six months and involved three major land battles, five naval battles and daily air combat, as the Japanese strove to recapture their strategically vital airfield on Guadalcanal. The Allied victory marked a turning point in the Pacific theatre, with defence moving to successful offence. However, violence didn't altogether cease after World War II. There was a civil war at the end of the 20th century when the local people rose against immigrants from neighbouring Malaita, a conflict not resolved until 2003.

The island is large – at 5,330 sq km (2,050 sq mi) and it contains the national capital of the Solomon Islands, Honiara. This is on the north coast, home to the majority of the population and much of which is fringed by sandy beaches and steeply sloping raised coral reefs. The mountainous interior is mainly jungle, and the south coast is subject to such heavy rainfall that it is known as 'The Weather Coast'. There is a road along the north coast, but those hardy enough to head south must go by boat or helicopter.

This is not a well-developed tourist destination, but a great many visitors do arrive. They are drawn mainly by the wealth of World War II relics on land and sea – the latter contributing to the attraction of Guadalcanal as a top dive location. Other activities include sailing, sea kayaking and inland canoeing, cave exploration, bird and wildlife watching, cycling and hiking. There is a variety of accommodation available, from luxury hotels to budget lodges, and there are cars to be hired. Positively cosmopolitan by Solomon Islands' standards!

POPULATION:
73,000 (2007)
WHEN TO GO:
Avoid the (very) wet season
(November to May).
HOW TO GET THERE:
Fly in to Honiara International Airport
– formerly Henderson Field, which
that World War II battle was all about.
HIGHLIGHTS:
The National Museum in Honiara,
containing historical artefacts and
traditional handicrafts.
Guided tours of World War II battle
sites, and a visit to the Vilu
War Museum.
Spectacular Mataniko Falls, which
pour over the mouth of a cave with
resident bats and swallows.
The giant clam farm west of Honiara
– yes, they really are huge.
Local handicrafts (and war
souvenirs!) on sale at Betikama High
School, outside Honiara.
YOU SHOULD KNOW:
Guadalcanal is infested with
mosquitoes and malaria is endemic.

*The World War II memorial
on Guadalcanal*

New Caledonia

POPULATION:
240,000 (2007 estimate)
WHEN TO GO:
The best time for island activities and good weather is mid-May to November. December to March is hotter, wetter and hurricane-prone.
HOW TO GET THERE:
Fly to Nouméa from Paris, New Zealand, Australia, Japan, USA and via various other Pacific islands, notably Nada in Fiji.
HIGHLIGHTS:
A national symbol – the extraordinary flightless kagu, an endangered greyish-white bird with red legs and bill endemic to the island.
A day trip to the picture-postcard-perfect L'Ile-des-Pins off the southern tip of the island, by air or high-speed catamaran.
The stunning modern Jean-Marie Tjibaou Cultural Centre in Nouméa, designed by Renzo Piano.
Hienghène on the east coast – a place of extraordinary natural beauty where mountains plunge dramatically into the sea.
YOU SHOULD KNOW:
The New Caledonia Barrier Reef surrounding Grand Terre is the world's second longest, after Australia's Great Barrier Reef.

This is a French overseas territory, like other islands in various exotic locations around the globe. New Caledonia lies on the Tropic of Capricorn in Melanesia, and the main island (Grand Terre) is bundled up with the Loyalty Islands, 100 km (60 mi) to the west. It is 350 km (217 mi) long and 70 km (44 mi) across at the widest point. The island's shores are lapped by the Coral Sea and South Pacific Ocean. New Caledonia is a mountainous island, rising massively to Mount Panié at 1,630 m (5,340 ft). Seasonal rainfall on the higher, eastern side is double that of the west coast, which lies in a 'rain shadow' cast by the central spine of mountains. The east coast is lush and tropical, the west coast a more temperate zone.

Unlike many Pacific islands of relatively recent volcanic origin, New Caledonia is a fragment of the long-lost Gondwana continent that once also included New Zealand and Australia. The island had therefore preserved a fascinating biological heritage for tens of millions of years, though in a parable for our times this has been badly degraded in less than a century by extensive open-cast nickel mining and logging. The surrounding sea, however, is well protected, with the world's largest lagoon complex containing a stunning variety of marine life.

New Caledonia has a great deal to offer the visitor, and this tropical island is a popular destination, with an endless variety of landscapes and everything from beautiful white sand beaches lapped by emerald-green sea to cool mountain retreats – even fine French restaurants and lively night life in the rather glamorous capital, Nouméa.

The Gossanah tribal team playing cricket, a popular sport among the women of the indigenous Melanesian Kanak community.

Viti Levu Island

Welcome to Fiji's largest island, at a chunky 145 km (90 mi) by 105 km (65 mi). Viti Levu is divided in half geographically and climatically by a rugged north-south mountain range peaking at Mount Victoria, also known as Tomanivi. To the east – heavy rainfall and a strong dairy industry. To the west – drier climate and sugar cane production. Other industries include gold mining, light manufacturing and – of rapidly increasing importance – tourism. The island is a major hub of air and sea communications in the southwest Pacific.

Fiji is renowned for its colourful coral and the clear waters around Vitu Levu are perfect for snorkelling.

The Republic of Fiji's vibrant capital city, Suva, is here, along with some three-quarters of the nation's population. There is a good route around the island's perimeter, connecting Suva with the coastal towns of Sigatoka, Rakiraki, Nausori, Nadi, Lautoka and Ba. Most visitors arrive at Nadi International Airport on the dusty west coast, which serves as a good starting point for those who take the island driving tour. This involves a leisurely two- or three-day circumnavigation on the island's only paved roads – Queen's Road along the southern coast from Suva to Lautoka, and King's Road along the north shore from Lautoka back to Suva.

It is an excellent way to see the island, stopping frequently to explore intriguing tracks into the interior or down to the sea, and chatting with the famously friendly locals. King's Road is in poorer shape, is longer and not much travelled by tourists, passing through country that is less developed than the south. For those who prefer a classic Pacific beach holiday, there are numerous attractive resorts, both on the mainland and offshore islands.

Best of all, it doesn't have to stop there – Viti Levu is the gateway to the Fiji Archipelago's thousands of islands, at least 100 of which are inhabited and are waiting for visitors with open arms!

POPULATION:
435,000 (2007 estimate)

WHEN TO GO:
The temperature is pretty even (and hot) all year round, with the driest months being April, May and June, followed closely by October.

HOW TO GET THERE:
By air from almost anywhere – long or short haul, or a mixture of both.

HIGHLIGHTS:
The Sigatora Valley, Sand Dunes and the excellent beach at the mouth of the Sigatora River.
Kula Eco Park in the southern Coral Coast area, an excellent facility dedicated to the preservation of Fiji's flora and fauna.
Seeing it all in 25 minutes, by taking the helicopter tour offered by Island Hoppers out of Nadi.

YOU SHOULD KNOW:
The Garden of the Sleeping Giant at Lautoka is an impressive tropical garden rich in orchids that once belonged to Perry Mason – TV star Raymond Burr.

The village of Savusavu

Vanua Levu Island

POPULATION:
130,000 (2007 estimate)
WHEN TO GO:
Any time, though some prefer to miss high summer (January and February) which – although only a few degrees above average – seems hotter because of high humidity.
HOW TO GET THERE:
By helicopter or light aircraft from Viti Levu, to either Labasa or Savusavu. Also by local ferry from Viti Levu.
HIGHLIGHTS:
Treat yourself to a local speciality – a souvenir black pearl raised from local waters or a piece of jewellery containing the black beauties.
Saturday night at a classic South Seas haunt – the Planters Club in Savusavu, which is as good as Vanua Levu's nightlife gets. Guests welcome.
The Waisali Rainforest Reserve, complete with cooling waterfall.
Spectacular windsurfing in the fabulous setting of Savusavu Bay.
YOU SHOULD KNOW:
In 1789, the infamous Captain William Bligh called here on his way to Timor, after being cast adrift by the mutinous crew of HMS *Bounty*.

Formerly Sandalwood Island, this wedge-shaped island is Fiji's second largest, measuring 180 km (110 mi) in length and up to 50 km (31 mi) across. Cape Udu at its northeastern tip is the northernmost point in Fiji. A long peninsula sticks out from the southeastern portion of Vanua Levu, and the island is divided horizontally by a craggy mountain range capped by the twin peaks of Nasorolevu and Dikeva. The south of the island is the wetter half, with the dryer north supporting major sugarcane plantations.

In the north, three rivers form the delta where the island's largest town, Labasa, is located. This is the workaday centre of the sugar industry. In the south, the main settlement is Savusavu, beloved by the relatively small number of tourists who get to the island for its diving, kayaking and a stunning bay that is home to an active yachting community. There is an ill-maintained basic road system with few paved roads.

Although Savusavu is the place most visitors head for, it has rustic storefronts and many ramshackle buildings. Efforts are being made to spruce the town up, to encourage more tourists and cater for wealthy incomers who are buying ocean-front plots for serious money and building holiday homes. As a pointer to future development, a large new marina has been constructed and the process of 'tourist gentrification' will doubtless continue apace.

But for now, Vanua Levu has plenty of original character, and offers an ideal opportunity to study local culture and traditions before they are overwhelmed by tourism. That said, there are plenty of fine resorts in superb settings around the island for those who prefer to pursue the perfect suntan (though sadly there are few beaches to lie on).

Beqa Island

This tiny island extends to just 36 sq km (14 sq mi) and is some 10 km (6 mi) south of Navua off Viti Levu, Fiji's main island. There are nine coastal villages on Beqa, with some agriculture and fishing, but tourism is the main economic activity. The island rises steeply to a volcanic point. The villagers live in extended clans and trade fish and produce for essentials at mainland markets in Navua and Suva. There are several resorts on the island, including Beqa Lagoon, Lalati, Kula Bay and the exclusive Royal Davui on its own islet. More are planned, which may slightly dilute the get-away-from-it-all rationale of this exquisite place. As yet there are no roads and all transport is by boat.

The Shark Reef Marine Reserve on the fringes of Beqa Lagoon has been created to study the resident shark population and thus contribute to the long-term worldwide conservation of sharks. Up to eight species are to be found in the reserve at any one time, and those with the necessary diving skills and nerves of steel can get to meet them, with the help of experienced professional guides. Wreck diving is also popular and there are amazing reefs to explore.

Indeed, Beqa Lagoon is the island's crowning glory, with a fringing reef around the island extending into a barrier reef that together are nearly 70 km (43 mi) long, with the latter enclosing a deep lagoon with an area of just under 400 sq km (155 sq mi). The reefs are made up of colourful corals that have been developing for centuries.

POPULATION:
2,100 (2007 estimate)
WHEN TO GO:
All year round – the island is generally hot and humid, often with tropical storms, especially between December and April.
HOW TO GET THERE:
By boat from mainland Viti Levu.
HIGHLIGHTS:
Try and see the local tradition of sacred firewalking in action, especially in the villages of Rukua and Daku-I-Beqa.
Climbing to the virgin rain forest and finding one of the island's many cooling waterfalls.
World-famous dive sites like Side Streets, Golden Arches and Caesar's Rocks.
YOU SHOULD KNOW:
The correct pronunciation of Beqa is not 'becca' but 'mbenga'.

Sacred firewalking is a local tradition on Beqa.

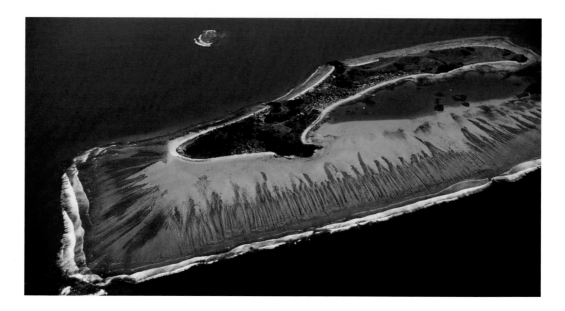

An aerial view of the fabulous beaches of the Mamanuca

Mamanuca Islands

POPULATION:
2,100 (2007 estimate)
WHEN TO GO:
All year round – the weather is sunny, the seas calm and the breezes cooling.
HOW TO GET THERE:
By air to Nadi International Airport. Onward transfer by light aircraft, helicopter or boat to the island of your choice.
HIGHLIGHTS:
A trip around the islands in an old-fashioned South Sea schooner.
A self-drive/sail boat trip on a craft hired from the Musket Cove marina. Game fishing or scuba diving along the renowned Malolo Reef.
YOU SHOULD KNOW:
Despite the large number of tourists in the Mamanucas, the island of Modriki was chosen as the setting for the miles-from-anywhere Tom Hanks film *Castaway*.

This archipelago is scattered off Nadi Bay on Viti Levu's west coast. There are about 20 islands, but be careful which one you choose – some are completely covered at high tide. The Mamanuca Islands are a serious visitor attraction, offering tiny coral islets to explore and numerous beach resorts to suit every pocket, plus all the watersports and diving activities for which Fiji is famous. Most resorts offer complementary kayaks, hobby cats and reef snorkelling trips.

These are not the most beautiful islands you will ever see, but the beaches are fabulous and the water is inviting. The resort islands are Malolo, Beachcomber, Mana, Malolo Lailai, Monu, Monuriki, Navini, Tavarua, Tavua, Tokoriki and (especially for Robert Louis Stevenson fans) Treasure Island. The inner Mamanucas consist of small, flat coral isles. The middle islands are the largest and offer gentle hills with paths to summits that offer stunning views over the archipelago, and the opportunity to find less crowded beaches. The outer islands are more rugged, with isolated bays and interesting volcanic rock formations. They have traditional fishing villages and – at 90 minutes from the mainland by fast catamaran – those outer islands are the destination of choice for people trying to get far from the madding crowd.

You will pay a premium to holiday on the Mamanuca Islands, but at many resorts you will share your island with more than enough people. However, as soon as you've settled comfortably into your space on the beach lots of day-trippers may suddenly invade from the mainland – a budget treat for them and a pain for you. And if it's traditional Fijian culture you're looking for, you won't find it here.

Yasawa Islands

Fiji's Yasawa Islands extend majestically to the north of the Mamanucas, and are much less commercially orientated than their southern cousins. The Yasawas form a thin broken line, consisting of 16 larger islands and dozens of smaller ones, stretching for 80 km (50 mi) from a point just off Kautoka on the northwestern coast of Viti Levu. Their scenic appeal is tremendous, with impressive panoramas and stunning beach vistas, whilst unchanging fishing villages provide an opportunity to observe the traditional way of life. These sun-drenched volcanic islands have fabulous beaches and clear lagoons, basic rest houses for backpackers, exclusive resorts for the well-heeled and plenty in between. It all adds up to the South Pacific at its most typical, so it's no accident that both versions of *The Blue Lagoon* were shot on location here.

Though the islands have been a popular cruise destination from the 1950s, land-based tourism was forbidden by the Fiji government until 1987. Since then, the popularity of the islands has been growing as they moved from back-packer heaven ('find a fishing boat to take you') towards mainstream tourism (from 2002, following the introduction of a catamaran service). New development is inevitable, but the wonderful island scenery has not been compromised thus far and there is more than enough coastline to go around. Resorts tend to be fairly isolated, most island villages are without electricity or running water and there is little public infrastructure. Indeed, the absence of sufficient fresh water to support a resort is a bar to development on some islands.

Many of the resorts are owned and operated by friendly islanders, retaining a rustic charm that combines with majestic scenery to ensure that visitors to the Yasawas feel they have indeed discovered the 'real' South Pacific.

POPULATION:
6,000 (2007 estimate)
WHEN TO GO:
There is no preferred special season – hot and dry conditions predominate, with cool nights.
HOW TO GET THERE:
From Lautoka by fast catamaran (2-4 hours) or seaplane (20 minutes). Arrange it all upon arrival at Nadi International Airport.
HIGHLIGHTS:
Sunrise (or sunset, for late risers) viewed from the top of Wayalailai Island.
A Sunday church service in one of the island villages for beautifully harmonious singing.
Overnight cruises to the Yasawas – visiting traditional villages, empty beaches and anchoring in remote lagoons. Lasting three to seven nights.
For those looking to treat themselves – the real Blue Lagoon, at the hugely expensive Turtle Island Resort on the privately owned island of Nanuya Levu, as patronized by the stars.
YOU SHOULD KNOW:
For those who want to explore the islands at leisure, a Yasawa Travel Pass gives unlimited return transfers on the fast catamaran *Yasawa Flyer*.

A beautiful beach on Matacawa Levu Island

Lau Islands

POPULATION:
15,000 (2007 estimate)
WHEN TO GO:
Unless you like singing in the rain, make it the cooler, drier months from April to October.
HOW TO GET THERE:
Stand by for a true flashback in modern tourist terms – the only way is to catch one of the cargo boats that sporadically serve the Lau Islands from Suva, then island-hop by fishing boat.
HIGHLIGHTS:
Wonderful wood-carvings and striking masi painting (on cloth made from the paper of the mulberry tree) produced by the locals.

The relatively accessible Yasawa Islands may seem like the real thing, but to discover the true South Pacific of yesteryear it is necessary to mount an expedition to the Lau Islands. This cluster of one hundred or more islands and islets makes up Fiji's remote Eastern Archipelago. Around 30 are inhabited – by villagers who remain entirely traditional. To the south are low coral isles and to the north high volcanic islands, making for a wonderful variety of scenery. They are notable for producing a disproportionate number of people who have become prominent in the country's business and political life, including prime ministers and a president.

This is the place where Melanesian Fiji comes closest to Polynesian Tonga, acting as a mixing point for the two cultures. Tongan influence is apparent in names, language, food and buildings – Lauan houses tend to be rounded in Tongan fashion rather than square in Fijian style. The island of Lakeba in the south is a traditional meeting place, and one of the few islands where the intrepid traveller will find guest-houses.

Some of Fiji's most pristine dive sites – best to bring your own boat (and live on it).
The caves – Qara Bulu on Lakeba (once a prison) and the large sea cave on Vanau Balavu (used by people over a thousand years ago).
YOU SHOULD KNOW:
Anyone for cricket? Unlike the rest of Fiji (rugby mad, soccer crazy), the Lau islanders prefer cricket, and supply almost all the national team's players.

Another is Kaimbu, a private resort island. Accommodation may also be found on Vanua Balavu, the archipelago's second-largest island and biggest in the northern group. It has an extensive reef system, steep undercut cliffs, hot springs and the Yanuyanu Island Resort built to advance tourist development in this hitherto 'undiscovered' archipelago (though a permit to visit must be obtained from the Ministry of Foreign Affairs in Suvu!). There is also an airfield and a small copra port on the island.

For those of adventurous bent who don't rely on advanced booking, the Lau Islands can deliver the trip of a lifetime. Catch it while you can – it's only a matter of time before the modern world arrives.

Taveuni Island

Fiji's third-largest island is shaped like a fat cigar. Taveuni lies just to the east of Vanua Levu, extending to around 42 km (26 mi) by 10 km (6 mi). It is the top of a shield volcano, dotted with volcanic cones that include Des Vœux Peak and Uluigalau, the country's second-highest peak at 1,195 m (3,920 ft). The island is divided by a volcanic spine, with verdant forests spilling down the sides. As with many Fijian islands the western end, sheltered by mountains from the trade winds, is drier than the rain-soaked eastern end.

Tourism is not yet a massive contributor to the local economy, which relies on copra production and speciality crops like tropical fruits, vanilla and kava. But there are a number of small resorts and guest-houses on the island, with more planned. Visitor numbers are set to rise dramatically, but for the moment Taveuni remains pleasantly uncrowded.

That's rather surprising as Taveuni has some great attractions. The climate is hot and humid, though not unbearably so, and the place retains much of its original natural character, having been subject to less land clearance than many Fijian islands. Indeed, it is known as 'The Garden Island' after the profusion of flowers and tropical plants found here. Some of the most famous dive sites in Fiji are around Taveuni, including Rainbow Reef and the extraordinary Great White Wall, a luminescent tunnel surrounded by glowing coral. The island has Fiji's most famous waterfall, Bouma Falls in the delightful Bouma National Heritage Park. There is also the spectacular Lake Tagimacuia in a volcanic crater at a height of 800 m (2,625 ft), where the eponymous red-and-white tagimacuia flower grows.

If unspoiled tropical islands are your idea of bliss, they truly don't come much better than this.

POPULATION:
9,500 (2007 estimate)
WHEN TO GO:
Any time, but take an umbrella – this is one of the wettest places in Fiji, with up to 2,600 mm (102 in) of rain each year. The driest months are April to October.
HOW TO GET THERE:
Fly in from Suvu or Nadi to Taveuni Airport in the northern part of the island.
HIGHLIGHTS:
Two sanctuaries designed to protect the island's flora and fauna – Taveuni Forest Preserve in the centre of the island and Ravilevu Nature Preserve on the east coast.
Birdlife – the mongoose was never introduced here so many birds that are no longer found on the other islands thrive (as does the magpie, introduced to destroy coconut pests).
The Vunivasa Tour – a visit to the archaeological site of a fortified Fijian village, followed by a waterfall visit that culminates in a toe-curling 'flight' in an airborne chair.
Wairiki Mission, a fine example of British colonial Romanesque architecture, overlooking the sea where Taveuni warriors once repulsed Tongan invaders.
YOU SHOULD KNOW:
The international dateline (180th Meridian) passes right through the island, so you can literally have one foot in today and one foot in yesterday – but it has been notionally 'moved' so the island can pretend to operate on the same day.

Sunset on Taveuni Island

Girls in a ceremonial dance on Rotuma Island

Rotuma Island

POPULATION:
2,800 (2007 estimate)
WHEN TO GO:
The rainy season is best avoided, so make it April to October. Even then the humidity may come as a shock, though cool sea breezes can dilute the impact.
HOW TO GET THERE:
Fly in to the airstrip on the north shore on Air Fiji's weekly flight from Suva.
HIGHLIGHTS:
The remarkable islet of Haf'lius (Split Island), with a fissure down the centre that's large enough to take a boat through.
Mount Suelhof – at 256 m (840 ft) it's a splendid vantage point for those willing to undertake the necessary hike.
A variety of old churches that serve as a reminder of the island's colonial past (in which Christian missionaries loomed large, and largely succeeded in converting the islanders).
The many traditional ceremonies, including the installation of chiefs (there are lots of those), religious occasions, weddings and funerals.
YOU SHOULD KNOW:
The first European sighting of Rotuma was by Captain Edward Edwards of HMS *Pandora*, who landed here in 1791 looking for Fletcher Christian and the mutinous crew of the *Bounty* (bad luck, wrong island).

Roughly 470 km (290 mi) north of Fiji, this small group – Rotuma Island plus four offshore islets – is a Fijian dependency and home to the unique race known as Rotumans. Actually, Rotuma isn't the home it once was – economic hardship has caused roughly four-fifths of the indigenous population (of under 15,000 in total) to migrate to the main Fijian islands. Rotumans more closely resemble Polynesians (physically and culturally) than Fiji's Melanesians, and those who remain live in coastal villages. Dependency status allows the island more political autonomy than other parts of Fiji, with the Ahau-based Council of Rotuma making key local decisions in conjunction with a government office.

It is possible to visit this isolated island, though the Rotumans voted against opening the place up to tourism as recently as 1985. Even now, the door is barely ajar, with visits strictly rationed by Rotuman elders who are determined that their island paradise will not be spoiled by the intrusive demands of mass tourism. The people are gracious, but expect visitors to respect their customs and be modest in behaviour and dress.

There are no hotels or resorts on Rotuma, though simple accommodation can be arranged. The determined voyager will find a rugged volcanic island with many small cones that is covered in lush vegetation, measuring 13 km (8 mi) by 4 km (2.5 mi). It has a large reef, spectacular coral, abundant sea life (including dolphins and turtles) and some of the most beautiful and untouched beaches in all Fiji. Give it a serious go – the rewards will more than repay the effort, and you'll be one of the tiny minority who've ever been privileged to visit this very special island.

Matareva Point on Upolu Island

Upolu

The most heavily populated of Samoa's islands is Upolu, a massive shield volcano that is 75 km (47 mi) long. The Samoans believe their islands were the cradle of Polynesian civilization, and Upolu is certainly the sort of place that would arrive from central casting if the director called for an unspoiled Pacific Island where real people live real lives. The interior is rugged, tropical and lush, with rushing rivers and spectacular waterfalls. The exquisite palm-fringed beaches with protective reefs are often totally secluded and mostly deserted. There are no big tourist hotels or over-developed resorts and the focus of the islanders is on extended family, tradition and culture. It is a point of honour that *fa'a Samoa* (the Samoan way) should continue to flourish. As a result, the whole atmosphere is wonderfully relaxed.

Samoa's capital Apia is here – a town of old colonial buildings, a harbour that screams 'South Seas schooner', giant pulu trees and shabby charm. This is the only place on Upolu where there are shops, markets, hotels, restaurants, banks and international communications. Maketi Fou is the vibrant main market, a centre of town life that offers an amazing range of fresh produce and seems to be busy 24/6 (the Samoans are very religious and everything closes on Sunday). There is a flea market in the market building on Beach Road that sells clothing, food and handicrafts.

Outside Apia, visitors should look for the traditional thatched huts, here called *fales*, which are scattered along the coast – usually owned and operated by locals to generate a little collective income for the village. This is an inexpensive way to see the island, and Samoa is actually one of the most affordable destinations in the Pacific.

POPULATION:
113,000 (2007 estimate)
WHEN TO GO:
No special season – Samoa is hot and humid all year round, though cooling trade winds blow from May to October.
HOW TO GET THERE:
Fly in to Faleolo International Airport on the western end of the island.
HIGHLIGHTS:
Vailma, the Robert Louis Stevenson Museum – former home of the *Treasure Island* author who died there in 1894 and is buried with his wife on the summit of Mount Vaea, overlooking Apia.
The Independence celebrations during the first week in June, culminating in the fautasi race when great longboat canoes with dozens of crewmen battle for supremacy.
Uafato Conservation Reserve – natural tropical forest with thriving bird life.
Togitogiga waterfall – several small falls running into the perfect plunge pool.
YOU SHOULD KNOW:
Land in Samoa is family-owned, so don't be offended if you find a wonderfully secluded beach, only for a local to appear and request a small payment for the privilege of using it.

Afu Aau Waterfall is set in virgin rainforest on Savaii.

Savaii

POPULATION:
45,000 (2007 estimate)
WHEN TO GO:
Any time of year – even in the rainy season (November to April) there are plenty of sunny days. There are occasional hurricanes between December and March.
HOW TO GET THERE:
A local flight from Apia on Upolu, or by ferry (fast or slow) from Mulifanua in western Upolu.
HIGHLIGHTS:
Falealupo Rainforest Preserve, offering canopy walkways.
The Alofaaga Blowholes, near the village of Taga.
Lava landscape at Sale'aula.
Strolling round the picturesque little town of Asau, before trying to spot the bay's numerous turtles.
Pulemelei Mound, Polynesia's largest archaeological site – the grand pyramid is 60 m (200 ft) long and 15 m (50 ft) high.
YOU SHOULD KNOW:
Samoa's proximity to the international dateline means it is the last place on earth to see the sun set. Watch it from Falealupo on Savaii, one of the world's most westerly villages.

This is the larger of Samoa's two main islands, but Savaii has fewer people than Upolu and is even less well developed. This is another volcanic shield island, and remains active (last eruption – 1911, lasting for four years). The island has a gently sloping profile, rising to a height of 1,860 m (6,100 ft) at Mount Silisili, and the evidence of lava flow is everywhere, often giving the landscape a dramatic quality. This really is the South Sea island that tourism forgot, with hardly any visitor-orientated development. But there is some basic accommodation, and an occasional low-key resort to be found by the determined traveller, whose reward will be some spectacular scenery and a close encounter with laid-back living, Polynesian style.

Salelologa on the island's southeastern corner has the airport, wharf and a colourful market. Otherwise it's pretty much a workaday place with little to attract the visitor. It's another matter south of town, where the Tafua Peninsula has a huge accessible crater and wonderful views of the wild coastline, which can be followed by a trip to the peninsula's lovely Aganoa Beach. Actually 'accessible' is a significant word in a Savaii context. There are irregular buses and a few expensive taxis, so the best plan is to hire a car and explore at leisure. Even then, the road system leaves a lot to be desired, but a circumnavigation of Savaii on the coast road will deliver some wonderful surprises – unspoiled traditional villages, huge churches, amazing lava formations, beautiful beaches and shimmering lagoons.

Tutuila

American Samoa is an unincorporated territory of the USA in the South Pacific, and Tutuila is its largest island with most of the population. The island is 30 km (18 mi) long and 10 km (6 mi) across at the widest point. The mountainous backbone culminates in Mount Matafao at 653 m (2,142 ft).

Tutuila is notable for the large natural Pago Pago harbour upon which is located the village of Pago Pago and the tuna canneries which are the island's principal economic activity. Pago Pago International Airport, on the other hand, is further down the coast between Tafuna and Fagatogo. Mount Alava overlooks the harbour from the north and a hike to the summit is rewarded with panoramic views of rugged coastline and virgin forest. There are few beaches and much of the north coast is inaccessible.

Fagatogo, Tutuila's capital and commercial centre, is also on Pago Pago Harbour, as is Utulei where government bureaucracy is concentrated. Most American Samoans (who are US nationals but not US citizens) live in villages along the south coast, serviced by regular buses from Fagatogo market. This is undoubtedly a South Pacific island, but American influence is pronounced and there are some messy corners. Tourism is not a major activity, though there are a number of motels, hotels and guesthouses around the harbour and west of Tafuna. Visitors come mainly for the wild scenery.

The National Park of American Samoa is on Tutuila and two neighbouring islands – Ofu and Ta'u. It includes coral reefs and some of the best coastal rainforest in the Pacific, with snorkelling, scuba diving and hiking permitted. There are many archaeological sites on the island, which is one of several (including nearby Ta'u) that lay claim to the title 'cradle of Polynesian civilization'.

POPULATION:
56,000 (2000)
WHEN TO GO:
To be different, try the rainy season between November and April, to see Tutuila's rainforest at its very best (the mornings are usually sunny, but beware mosquitoes!).
HOW TO GET THERE:
Fly to Apia on Western Samoa and from there to Tutuila by Polynesian Airlines or Samoa Air.
HIGHLIGHTS:
Leone village in the west, where large churches bear witness to zealous missionary activity during the 19th century.
A trip to Aunu'u Island National Landmark off the southeast corner of Tutuila, to see the unusual Red Lake.
The scenic south coast road from the airport via Cape Taputapu to the end of the line, Fagamalo village.
Picturesque Alega Beach, with its famous Tisa's Barefoot Bar.
YOU SHOULD KNOW:
Most beaches are village owned and both scanty dress and Sunday swimming are banned.

A church in the village of Afono

Manu'a Islands

POPULATION:
1,400 (2000)
WHEN TO GO:
Warm and wet (November to April) or
warm and dry (May to October).
HOW TO GET THERE:
Via an internal flight from Pago Pago
International Airport.
HIGHLIGHTS:
South Ofu Beach, for one of the most
stunning panoramas of beach, sea
and mountains in the entire
Pacific Ocean.
An adventurous trek to the huge
Judds Crater, a six-hour hike from
Ta'u village.
Some of the world's tallest sea cliffs
on the south coast of Ta'u.
YOU SHOULD KNOW:
Visitors are advised to bring their
own necessities (including food), as
supplies are not generally on sale in
the Manu'a Islands.

Apart from the 'mainland' of Tutuila, American Samoa extends to Rose Atoll, Swains Island and the Manu'a Islands. The latter group consists of adjacent high volcanic islands – Ta'u, Ofu and Olosega – located 110 km (70 mi) east of Tutuila.

Ta'u is the largest of the three, and the most easterly volcanic island in Samoa. It has American Samoa's high point in Lata Mountain, rising to 966 m (3,170 ft), the group's main airport at Fiti'uta and a boat harbour at Faleasao. A road connects the small villages on the northern shore. The south of the island and its reefs are part of the National Park of American Samoa, which includes the sacred site of Saua – another contender for 'birthplace of the Polynesian people'. Unusually, the park is not owned by the US government, but leased from the islanders. There is no tourist infrastructure, though accommodation can be found in the sleepy villages.

Nearfby Ofu and Olosega are tropical Siamese twins. They are saw-tooth volcanic remains separated only by the narrow strait of Asaga, and effectively joined by a coral reef. Until recently, it was possible to wade from one island to the other at low tide, but now there is a bridge. Ofu Island has a small airport and boat harbour, together with one village, also Ofu, and a visitor lodge. The National Park extends to this most beautiful of islands, protecting a pristine southern coastline and rainforest. The park is being extended to Olosega, where the small population lives in Olosega village, after a second village (Sili) was destroyed by a hurricane.

There are many places that claim to offer serious travellers the opportunity to discover the 'real' South Pacific, untainted by commercialism – but these islands aren't kidding.

*The stunning panorama of
South Ofu Beach*

Tongatapu

Spectacular blow-holes near the village of Houma

Captain Cook named Tonga 'The Friendly Islands' after arriving during a feast and finding natives who appeared welcoming. In fact, it is said that the chiefs wanted to kill him but couldn't agree on a plan. Tongatapu is Tonga's main island, and the location of the former British protectorate's capital, Nuku'alofa. The second city of Mu'a is also here, along with most of the commercial activity and the grandiose official residence of the king.

Nuku'alofa is full of Victorian buildings, churches, old graveyards, bustling markets (don't miss excellent local arts and crafts upstairs at Talamahu Market) and a classic Pacific waterfront. Most of the island's hotels are here, too, though this is very much a shabby working town that doesn't give excessive thought to pleasing tourists – a comment that might justifiably be applied to the island as a whole.

Indeed, most visitors make Tongatapu a stepping stone to the offshore coral islands of Fafa, Atata and Pangaimotu, which offer excellent beach holidays. Along with a number of other islands in the main lagoon off Nuku'alofa, they are very like the ever-popular Manamuca Islands in Fiji, but without the same tourist pressure.

But for all that Tongatapu itself is no resort island, it will reward the curious traveller with its interesting combination of history and natural beauty. Though much of this largely flat island is covered in plantations, the eastern end is relatively undeveloped, with deserted sandy beaches, coves and caves. There is also a wealth of monuments testifying to the island's long history and cultural traditions. The south coast is wild, with dramatic coastal scenery and high cliffs punctuated with sandy coves, well worth the effort needed to get there in a hire car that will have seen much better days.

POPULATION:
71,000 (2007 estimate)
WHEN TO GO:
Any time – the tropical climate is even all year round and Tongatapu is milder than Fiji or Samoa, with less rainfall.
HOW TO GET THERE:
Various international carriers serve the airport at Fu'amotu.
HIGHLIGHTS:
Tongan culture at its best (dancing and food, among other things!) – find it all at the Tongan National Centre just south of Nuku'alofa.
The ancient langi pyramids (royal burial tombs) near Mu'a, once the ancient capital of Tonga.
A flying fox preserve in the western district of Kolovai for close-up contact with the world's largest bats (there are plenty, as only the king is allowed to hunt them).
The 13th century stone trilithon, which is known as Ha'amonga 'a Maui, in the north of the island,.
Spectacular blow-holes near the village of Houma.
YOU SHOULD KNOW:
There have been recent pro-democracy riots in Nuku'alofa (accompanied by arson and several deaths) as younger Tongans protested at the country's rule by a feudal absolute monarchy.

Niue

POPULATION:
1,700 (2007 estimate)
WHEN TO GO:
To dodge the sometimes intense rainy season, avoid the summer months (November to April).
HOW TO GET THERE:
There's one flight a week from New Zealand.
HIGHLIGHTS:
Whale watching, or swimming with them – it's a proud boast that the whales often outnumber the tourists! Game fishing in deep water right off the island.
The Huvalu Forest Conservation Area near Hakupu village, with a wonderful variety of flora and fauna.
Matapu Chasm – a swimming and snorkelling pool enclosed by cliffs, protected from sea currents.
Caves – lots of them, ripe for exploration, including Talava Arches, Palaha Cave and Liku Sea Track and Cave.
YOU SHOULD KNOW:
Perhaps sadly, as a result of sustained migration there are many more Niue Islanders living in New Zealand than on their native island.

One of the world's largest coral islands is shaped rather like a human head, complete with pointed nose and chin. That still doesn't make it all that big – Niue has an area of only 270 sq km (105 sq mi). This tropical island is located in the South Pacific, within a triangle formed by the Cook Islands, Samoa and Tonga, and is nicknamed the 'Rock of Polynesia' or (by islanders) simply 'The Rock', because it is ringed by cliffs surrounding a central plateau. The coast is honeycombed with limestone caves. Niue is surrounded by a coral reef, which is only broken in one place – on the west coast near the capital, Alofi.

Niue was named 'Savage Island' by Captain Cook in 1774, when legend has it that the inhabitants not only refused to allow him to land, but also appeared to have blood-stained teeth (actually caused by eating red bananas). They remained resistant to the outside world until an islander who had been trained as a missionary introduced Christianity in the mid-19th century. Britain was the colonial power, but Niue is now a self-governing protectorate of New Zealand.

The economy has only recently started developing (slowly) from virtual subsistence level and dependence on New Zealand aid, with a newly liberated private sector and activities like mineral exploration, fishing and tourism earmarked for growth. With regard to the latter, there is very little accommodation on this friendly island, so a visit is almost like being welcomed into the family. Niue is a place where rainforest and an amazing shoreline go hand in hand, and it really is true to say that the visitor can experience unspoiled Polynesia, just the way it used to be. And that's without a white-sand beach to be seen!

Coral reef surrounding Niue Island

Tuvalu Islands

This Polynesian island nation was formerly the Ellis Islands, part of the British Gilbert and Ellis Islands protectorate, and consists of three reef islands and six atolls. With a total land mass of just 26 sq km (10 sq mi) Tuvalu is one of the smallest independent countries in the world – and that tiny area is spread in a ragged line across some 1,500 km (930 mi) of the Central Pacific. Its nearest neighbours are Kiribati (formerly the Gilbert Islands), Samoa and Fiji.

The islands are Nanumanga, Niulakita and Niutao. The atolls are Funafuti (the capital and only relatively easy destination), Nanumea, Nui, Nukufetau, Nukulaelae and Vasafua. The atolls all have associated islets. Tuvalu has no natural resources and very little gainful economic activity, being kept afloat by international aid. Actually, keeping afloat may be a problem, as Tuvalu's highest point is just 5 m (16 ft) above sea level, so global warming could have catastrophic consequences.

Because of their remote location and scattered character, tourism has yet to become a significant part of life in Tuvalu. A serious shortage of drinking water means that there is not much likelihood of that changing, though the islands have all the attributes necessary to provide the typical South Seas vacation – coral reefs, white beaches, palm-fringed lagoons and friendly people. The upside is that determined visitors who do manage to reach Tuvalu find a few delightful guest-houses and lodges in an unspoiled corner of the Pacific that is ideal for R&R (that's rest and relaxation rather than rest and recreation). And the distinctive Polynesian culture is upheld by the island people, who maintain traditional social organization, arts and crafts, architecture, music and dance. And they mostly speak English.

POPULATION:
12,000 (2007 estimate)
WHEN TO GO:
Whenever – the pleasant tropical climate is consistent all year round. Rainfall is unpredictable, but is generally more prevalent between November and April.
HOW TO GET THERE:
Air Fiji flies in from Suvu to Funafuti twice a week, and the supply ships *Nivaga II* and *Manu Folau* make the same trip (rather more slowly) four times a year.
HIGHLIGHTS:
Funafuti Conservation area on the western side of the atoll, including lagoon, reef, channel, ocean and island habitats, rich in flora, fauna and marine life.
An old World War II American airbase on Nanumea, complete with the remains of abandoned aircraft, and there's also a wrecked landing craft on the reef.
Traditional dancing – performed on special occasions and to celebrate Christian holidays.
YOU SHOULD KNOW:
Tuvalu recently became the 189th member state of the United Nations.

An aerial view of Funafuti

Pitcairn Island

POPULATION:
50 (2007 estimate)
WHEN TO GO:
Whenever you can get there –
weather-wise the climate is hot and
humid, with occasional typhoons in
summer (November to March).
HOW TO GET THERE:
Cruise ships (including dedicated
Pitcairn cruises) visit, as do private
yachts and occasional cargo ships. A
licence is required to stay on Pitcairn
for any length of time.
HIGHLIGHTS:
HMS *Bounty*'s anchor, on display in
the town square.
Down Rope, a cliff with Polynesian
petroglyphs, showing that the
mutineers weren't the first
inhabitants of this isolated place.
A quick return visit to the modern
world – take a laptop and enjoy free
wireless internet access via satellite.
The grave of John Adams – the only
marked grave of a mutineer.
YOU SHOULD KNOW:
Actually, the determined Captain
Edwards nearly did find Fletcher
Christian and his men – in 1791 he
got as close as Ducie Island (which
he named), just 540 km (335 mi) east
of Pitcairn.

It's no wonder that HMS *Pandora* under Captain Edward Edwards didn't find all the Bounty mutineers – despite catching most of them on Tahiti. In 1789 the rest, under ringleader Fletcher Christian, had hidden on one of the remotest islands in the Pacific, Pitcairn, and literally burnt their boat (the remains may still be seen in Bounty Bay). It ended badly; with mutineers and six Tahitian men they took with them killing each other. In 1808 when the American ship *Topaz* visited, only one mutineer (Alexander Smith, alias John Adams) was still alive.

This British Overseas Territory is officially the Pitcairn, Henderson, Ducie and Oeno Islands. The last three are uninhabited coral atolls scattered round the South Pacific some distance from Pitcairn – Henderson Island having the distinction of being a UNESCO World Heritage Site because of its bird life (including four species found only on Henderson).

Pitcairn is a volcanic peak jutting out of the ocean to a height of 337 m (1,100 ft) and is tiny – just 5 sq km (2 sq mi). It is a green, steep-sided island with cliffs that fall into the sea. Bounty Bay (in reality no more than a cove) is the only landing place, and then only for longboats that fetch visitors from boats anchored off shore. It is connected by the newly paved Hill of Difficulty to Adamstown, the settlement, where the few islanders live largely self-sufficient lives.

Every year, Bounty Day (23 January) is celebrated with a community feast and the ceremonial burning of a model *Bounty*. There's no getting away from it – Pitcairn and memories of the infamous mutiny will be inextricably linked for ever and a day. And if you do manage to visit this extraordinary place, you will have the travel experience of a lifetime to remember.

Commemorative plaque for HMS Bounty

Aitutaki

North of Rarotonga, the beautiful island of Aitutaki is the second most populous of the Cook Islands, a group of 15 lovely islands in the South Pacific. This coral atoll boasts low rolling hills, banana plantations and coconut groves. This is an archetypal desert island and a wonderful place to unwind, with palm-fringed white sandy beaches, magnificent clear sea and a relaxed pace of life. Aitutaki has a main island and a string of small islets (including Mangere, Akaiami, and Tekopua), all surrounded by a barrier reef, thus creating the spectacular turquoise lagoon that makes it such a perfect place for swimming, snorkelling and scuba diving. Although it is the second most visited of the Cook Islands, Aitutaki is still unspoiled.

Polynesians probably first settled here around AD 900. The first European contact was with Captain Bligh and the crew of HMS *Bounty* who arrived on the island in 1789, just before the infamous mutiny. Hire a bicycle, scooter or car to explore this stunning island, taking a relaxed tour of the beaches and plantations. The highest peak, Maunga Pu, offers great views over the whole island.

A 20-minute boat ride will take you to Akaiami, one of the smaller islets at the far end of the lagoon. This remote and tranquil islet is surrounded by pristine turquoise lagoon and coral reef. The one inhabitant here owns the island and runs a small lodge.

One-Foot Island is probably the biggest tourist attraction and another must-see. Along with the blue lagoons and flawless white beach, there is a post office, one of the most remote in the world.

Several operators offer tours of the lagoon by boat, and if you haven't seen enough marine life, visit the Ministry of Marine Resources to learn about the sea life in the lagoon, and see baby sea turtles and giant clams. The lagoon also offers great scuba diving and fishing, both game fishing and fly fishing.

Aitutaki is the archetypal desert island.

POPULATION:
2,194 (2006)
WHEN TO GO:
April to November
HOW TO GET THERE:
Fly from Auckland via Rarotonga
HIGHLIGHTS:
The church in Arutanga – the oldest church in the islands, this was built by two teachers from the London Missionary Society in the 1820s. Aitutaki was the first of the Cook Islands to accept Christianity.
A lagoon cruise to the islets of Akaiami and Tapuatae (One-Foot Island) – explore the perfect white sand beaches and spot marine life on the way.
Flyfishing for the fighting bonefish.
Ika mata – a local dish of marinated raw tuna with coconut sauce.
Aitutaki's dancers, who are famous throughout the Cook Islands – attend an 'Island Night' to see a dancing show and experience the local cuisine.
YOU SHOULD KNOW:
If you hire a car, you will need to buy a local driving licence from the police station at Arutanga

Aroa Beach

Rarotonga

The island's name means 'down south' and as the largest and most populated of the Cook Islands, it is the jumping off point for exploring the rest of the Cook Islands. At just 671 sq km (259 sq mi), Rarotonga is one of the most beautiful of the Cook Islands, and often referred to as the 'Jewel of the Pacific' and it's easy to see why.

Long palm fringed beaches and coral-filled seas make this island paradise an idyllic haven for travellers. Along the coastline, the lagoon is an ideal place for snorkeling and getting close to the wildlife in the water. The climate is equable and rarely ventures outside the margins of 18 °C to 29 °C (64 °F to 84 °F) . The interior is a volcanic mountainous region which is virtually uninhabited. The summit is called Te Rua Manga (The Needle), aptly named for its jagged peaks. It has dense jungle and a cloud forest beginning at 400 m (1,300 ft) above sea level, abundant in rare indigenous species of plants. The Cook Islands Natural Heritage Project was set up to educate people about the need for conservation and actively promotes eco-tourism.

In 1997 Japanese archaeologists found an undiscovered sacred site on Motu Tapu, an islet in the lagoon at Ngatangiia. This dated human life on Rarotonga to about 5,000 years ago. Statues of Tangaroa, the god of fertility, are still dotted around the island. The Polynesian dancing here is considered to be some of the best in Polynesia, and was described by a nineteenth century missionary as, 'positively obscene'.

Land tends to belong to families and is rarely sold and derelict houses pepper the island as without ownership of the land as well, they are un-saleable. There is much nineteenth century architecture to be seen, leftover from when the missionaries arrived on the island and one of note, is the Cook Island Christian Church. There are many of these scattered over the Cook Islands and this one has an interesting graveyard and pretty exterior.

POPULATION:
18,000 (2006)
WHEN TO GO:
The weeklong Te Maeva Nui Festival takes place annually at the end of July, and is worth a visit for this vibrant expression of Polynesian culture.
DON'T MISS:
The spectacular diving.
YOU SHOULD KNOW:
In areas of the lagoon marked by boundary poles, taking any fish, coral or shells is strictly prohibited.

Manihiki

Populated since 1500 AD and 'discovered' in 1832 by the American ship *Good Hope*, Captain Patrickson originally named Manihiki, Humphrey Island. This flat island paradise rises only a few metres above sea level and sits on top of an underwater mountain which stands 4,000 m (13,000 ft) above the ocean floor. This triangular coral atoll is 1054 km (655 mi) north-northwest of Rarotonga, which is its centre for administration.

The inhabitants of Manihiki had a close relationship with their sister island, Rakahanga. The inhabitants of both islands travelled between the two on wooden boats and canoes in search of food. This often resulted in death due to the distance between each island and the fact that it was impossible to see either at the mid-way point. The missionaries that arrived in the nineteenth century discouraged this practice, and their arrival heralded the end of native gods on the island. By 1852 Christianity was accepted and is still the religion of the islanders. An oral heritage survives though, and this makes the island rich in Polynesian culture.

The island is made up of a string of coconut palm covered islets and is shaped around the rim of a lagoon, 4km (2.5 mi) across. The lagoon is home to the black pearl, and most of the islanders are involved in farming the black-lip pearl oyster; the Cook Islands' most important export. A survey carried out for the Ministry of Marine Resources in 2000 recorded 111 pearl farms covering 7 km sq (4 mi sq).

POPULATION:
1,000 (2004)
WHEN TO GO:
The hurricane season is from November to April so it's best to avoid this period.
DON'T MISS:
A multitude of different types of coral and fish makes for spectacular diving in the region.
YOU SHOULD KNOW:
You will need to get a diving permit from the village of Tauhunu.

Islanders roast coconut crabs on a bed of hot stones.

Bora Bora

POPULATION:
7,250 (2002)
WHEN TO GO:
There isn't a bad time to go, but the high season is July to October.
HOW TO GET THERE:
By Air Tahiti to Motu Mute airport on the reef, which also accepts some direct international flights.
HIGHLIGHTS:
An excursion into the hills by 4 wheel drive vehicle to see the interior – don't miss the impressive World War II guns.
For daring sub-aquatic types, an expedition to feed sharks and manta rays in the lagoon.
Nightly sunset sailing trips that let you experience spectacular Pacific sunsets from the water.
Black pearl jewellery hand-crafted by locals.
YOU SHOULD KNOW:
There was an American supply base here in World War II, and many US personnel liked the place so much they stayed behind – until some were forcibly removed by the military following complaints from their families back home.

Welcome to French Polynesia, and one of the Pacific's most desirable destinations – or even, as the island's website proclaims with typical Gallic understatement, 'the most beautiful island in the world'. Even if that's going a bit far, this is certainly a romantic faraway place that attracts lots of people, and to be sure everyone gets the point there's plenty of the grass-skirt dancing that has become a Polynesian trademark.

Bora Bora is in the Leeward Islands, 230 km (140 mi) northwest of Tahiti, and now depends on visitors for its economic wellbeing. The only other commercial activities are fishing and harvesting coconuts, so the advent of tourism has given the island a huge fillip. The locals speak French and Tahitian, but most have a good grasp of English. The island is surrounded by a barrier reef that encloses the bluest of lagoons, and the land rises from white beaches through lush jungle-covered slopes to the dual peaks of an extinct volcano – Mounts Pahia and Otemanu. The main settlement of Vaitape is on the west coast, opposite the entrance to the lagoon.

The Hotel Bora Bora pioneered the use of palm-thatched tourist accommodation built out over the water on stilts, and this is now a standard feature of most resorts. Despite a deliberately rustic appearance, these are spacious, luxurious and priced accordingly. There are a number of high-end resorts on palm-fringed *motu* (islets) around the lagoon, and cheaper lodgings on shore.

There is one bus that shuttles back and forth around half the island, but exploring is best done by bicycle or on foot. The lagoon offers the usual activities – scuba diving, snorkeling, windsurfing, kitesurfing, water skiing and jetskiing – but in truth the key words on beautiful Bora Bora are 'relax' and 'enjoy'.

The brilliant blue lagoon of Bora Bora

Tahiti

This is the largest of the Windward Islands in French Polynesia, some 45 km (28 mi) long with an area of 1,050 sq km (405 sq mi). Tahiti's inhabitants are French citizens but enjoy considerable autonomy. The island consists of two oval portions, one large (Tahiti Nui) and one small (Tahiti Iti), connected by an isthmus. The capital, Papeete, is on heavily populated Tahiti Nui, which has quite good infrastructure, with *Le Truk* public buses offering an excellent and affordable way of getting around. But Tahiti Iti is less well developed, with its remote southeastern half accessible only by boat or on jungle-booted feet. Much of the island is covered in lush rainforest and the heavy scent of tropical flowers is everywhere. The national flower is the Tiare, a gardenia that forms the basis of traditional lei necklaces.

Although many visitors stop only long enough to catch onward flights to the popular islands of Bora Bora and Moorea, Tahiti itself has a lot to offer. The very name is enough to conjure up thoughts of an earthly paradise with a delightful climate, where palm-fringed beaches are lapped by aquamarine sea and handsome islanders extend the warmest of welcomes. It's all true!

Start at Papeete, a fascinating metropolis with a colourful morning market and bustling waterfront. But Tahiti is really an outdoor destination. It offers a wide choice of places to stay, from high-end beachfront resorts to hotels, motels, backpacker hostels and campsites. For those who want more from a holiday than sun, sea and sand, Tahiti offers endless possibilities – diving, snorkelling, wind surfing, sailing, game fishing, reef watching in glass-bottomed boats, horse riding, trekking, 4x4 expeditions into the interior... whatever takes your fancy, this magical 'Island of Love' will surely oblige.

A Tahitian dance festival in Papeete

POPULATION:
170,000 (2002)

WHEN TO GO:
It's warm all year round, but very wet, humid and stormy between November and April. If that doesn't appeal, be prepared to pay premium prices from May to October.

HOW TO GET THERE:
Fly in to Faa'a Airport, served by several international carriers.

HIGHLIGHTS:
Papeete's two-week Heiva Festival in July, celebrating the rather odd combination of Polynesian culture and Bastille Day (book your trip early if you want to be there).
For those with time and money to spare – a cruise to the distant Marquesas Islands on the passenger-carrying freighter *Aranui*.
The three Faarumai waterfalls – one of them is among the highest in French Polynesia.
Tahiti's longest bridge, crossing its longest river, at the end of its largest valley, by one if its largest rural villages – all called Papenoo.

YOU SHOULD KNOW:
The great but penniless Post-Impressionist French painter Paul Gauguin relocated to Tahiti in the 1890s and painted many Polynesian subjects. There is a small Gauguin museum on the island.

The lagoon at sunset

Moorea

This is definitely a case of high society – Moorea is a soaring island formed by volcanic action in French Polynesia's Society Islands (so named by Captain Cook). The island is 19 km (12 mi) to the east of Tahiti, and shaped like an inverted triangle with two deep bays nibbled out of the north coast. It isn't huge at 135 sq km (52 sq mi), but large enough to absorb the many tourists in reasonable comfort. There are three main settlements – Teavaro, Papetoai and Afareaitu, plus numerous resorts including those with the inevitable stilt houses extending into the lagoon.

This is the destination of choice for thousands of honeymooners each year, so be prepared to mingle with lots of love-struck fellow travellers. It's not hard to understand the romantic appeal. From the first glimpse of Moorea, rising steeply out of the ocean to eight impressive mountain ridges, it is apparent that this is a beautiful place with stunning scenery. Upon closer inspection, that initial impression is confirmed. The island is clad in lush vegetation, surrounded by a barrier reef sheltering a fabulous lagoon and is everything that a perfect tropical island should be. Indeed, there is a hilltop lookout between majestic Mount Tohivea and shark-toothed Mount Rotui, where the view down to the twin inlets of Cooks Bay and Opunohu Bay takes the breath away – it's so good that local tradition insists it was once reserved for the gods alone.

Of course Moorea offers all the usual holiday distractions for those who want to take advantage of them – watersports, sailing, fishing, tours on land and sea, adventure activities, hiking, biking, shopping and nightlife. But in truth, many visitors would honestly say that simply being here is enough.

Maupiti

Way out west in French Polynesia's Leeward Islands you come to the volcanic high island of Maupiti, a green postage stamp in the vast ocean with a surface area of just 11 sq km (4 sq mi), surrounded by long motu (islets) that enclose an immense shallow lagoon with just one access point for boats. Traditionally, Maupiti has strong cultural links with Bora Bora, 40 km (25 mi) to the east, and is sometimes described as 'Bora Bora's beautiful little cousin'.

If you really want a get-away-from-it-all holiday, this is the place for you. There are no resorts and no organized tours – just a few simple guest-houses and rooms to rent in family homes. Remember to take cash, because there's no way of getting any unless the bank is open (which is an infrequent occurrence). The pace of life here is slow and peaceful, ensuring that the only viable options are to relax, relax, relax.

It takes but two hours to stroll around the island, enjoying dramatic scenery (Mount Hotu Paraoa plunges straight into the sea at the island's southern tip) and wonderful sandy beaches (notably Tereia Beach at the western point). The main settlements of Farauru and Vaiea are on the eastern side. A three-hour hike takes you to the top of the central peak of Mount Teurafaatui, and the reward is a sensational panorama over the lagoon to Bora Bora and (on a clear day) Raiatea and Tahaa.

Maupiti is a genuine South Sea island paradise.

POPULATION:
1,200 (2002)
WHEN TO GO:
Any time – this is a magical island for all seasons, even more spectacular in the summer rainy season (December to April) when clouds and sudden storms enhance the drama.
HOW TO GET THERE:
By twice-weekly boat from Bora Bora (the *Maupiti Express*) or thrice weekly by air from Tahiti via Raiatea or Bora Bora.
HIGHLIGHTS:
The tiny islet of Motu Paeao on the north side of Maupiti, where archaeologists found graves and artefacts from the earliest period of Polynesian civilization.
Snorkelling around Onoiau Pass – the only boat access to the island.
Interesting petroglyphs carved into rock at the northern end of the island.
YOU SHOULD KNOW:
After tourism, Maupiti's chief economic activity is growing *noni* (Indian or beach mulberry), but don't be tempted to scrump one – an alternative name is 'vomit fruit'.

An aerial view of the volcanic island of Maupiti

Rangiroa

POPULATION:
3,400 (2007)
WHEN TO GO:
June to October.
HOW TO GET THERE:
Fly from Tahiti or Bora Bora.
HIGHLIGHTS:
The bird sanctuary on Motu Paio.
Take a lagoon cruise in a glass-
bottomed boat to see the wonderful
corals, sea fans and multitudinous
fish species.
The Pink Sands – at the far south-
west of the atoll, the sands are a
lovely shade of pink, a beautiful
contrast to the turquoise lagoon and
blue sky.
The Island of the Reef – here raised
coral formations create a dazzling
tidepool environment.
Shooting the pass of Tiputa – here
hundreds of fish, sharks and moray
eels swim around you, swept along
by the strong currents. You may even
spot a rare black and white dolphin.
YOU SHOULD KNOW:
The numerous reef sharks in the
lagoon will come up to investigate
but they are nosy rather
than aggressive.

Rangiroa is a stunning archipelago of 78 low islands spread over several hundred kilometres of the eastern Pacific around 200 km north of Tahiti. This is the second largest atoll in the world, the coral-encrusted rim of an ancient submerged volcano encircling an enormous shallow inland sea with more than 240 islets or *motu*. The *motu* are separated by at least 100 shallow channels and three passes, two of which are big enough for ships to enter the lagoon.

The lagoon waters are sparklingly clear, and vary in colour from jade-green to purple, a real surprise for first-time visitors. The marine life here is truly astonishing, with over 400 varieties of rainbow-hued fish glinting in the iridescent waters among the brightly coloured hard and soft corals, and the gently waving sea fans. The lagoon is understandably famous for its unsurpassed snorkelling and scuba diving, while outside the reefs there are amazing numbers of eagle rays, sharks, barracuda and tuna along the walls of the drop-offs.

The main villages in the archipelago are Avatoru and Tiputa, which offer the visitor a unique look at the South Pacific lifestyle, with their coral churches, craft centres, restaurants and tiny shops. Tiputa is situated at the eastern end. Its picturesque houses are ringed with bleached coral and flowering hedges, and nearby is the bird sanctuary on Motu Paio, well worth a visit.

There were more settlements on Rangiroa during the 14th and 15th centuries, and the remains of these can still be seen today, including cultivation pits and coral temples. To protect themselves from the aggressive Parata warriors from the atoll of Anaa, the Rangiroa inhabitants took refuge on the southwest side of the atoll. The village they created there was destroyed by a natural disaster, probably a tsunami, in 1560 and the entire population disappeared.

The Blue Lagoon at Taeo'o, an hour's boat ride from the village of Avatoru, is a natural pool of aquamarine water on the edge of the reef, and probably one of the most idyllic places in the world. This is like a gigantic natural aquarium with wonderful colourful corals and numerous reef sharks. The surrounding *motu* are home to rare birds, including the Vini ultramarine parakeet.

The blue lagoon and one of the many motu

The Marquesa Islands

Hiva Hoa Island

Further from a continental landmass than any other islands on earth, the Marquesas lie in the Pacific Ocean about 1,400 km (870 mi) north-east of Tahiti. Due to their remoteness, these lush and rugged islands are almost entirely unspoiled. The wild, steep cliffs and valleys lead up to high central ridges, and sharp volcanic pinnacles pierce the skyline. This uncompromising landscape is, however, softened by the wonderful rampant vegetation, including colourful bougainvillea, orchids, lilies, ginger and jasmine. The wildlife is extraordinarily rich and varied, with 80 per cent of birds, half the native plants and insects, and many of the numerous marine species unique to the Marquesas.

The administrative capital of the southern group, Hiva Oa is perhaps the best known of the Marquesas. Paul Gauguin spent the last years of his life here and some of his paintings are on display in the museum. There are many archaeological sites on Hiva Oa, including characterful and fascinating rock carvings and tombs. Separated from Hiva Oa by a narrow channel only a few kilometres wide, Tahuata is the smallest inhabited island of the Marquesas. The first Europeans disembarked on the white sand here in 1595, but still today there are few visitors to this paradise.

The most populated island of the Marquesas, Ua Pou is said to be both young and old as its rocks and geographical features were formed in two different volcanic periods. The largest settlement is Hakahau, the centre of which is its Catholic church built from wood and stone.

At the far south of the island group, Fatu Iva is the most isolated and possibly the most beautiful island. There are around 500 inhabitants living in the valleys here, and they rely on small cargo ships to bring provisions. This makes it a relaxing place to explore, miles from the modern world. The inhabitants specialize in the making of tapa, a beaten bark cloth used for drawing on.

Ua Huka, in the northern Marquesas, is less fertile than its neighbouring islands and the vast tracts of scrubby land are grazed by wild goats and horses. The island's inhabitants live mainly on the south coast, in the villages of Vaipaee, Hane and Hokatu, each of which boasts a handicrafts centre. Also worth a visit are the arboretum and two interesting museums on the island.

Wherever in the Marquesas you choose to visit, you will discover an island paradise rich in both wildlife and cultural treasures.

POPULATION:
8,632 (2007)
WHEN TO GO:
April to May, or September to October.
HOW TO GET THERE:
Fly from Papeete or Rangiroa to Nuku Hiva, or take a cruise ship or freighter from Papeete, calling at all six of the inhabited Marquesas.
HIGHLIGHTS:
Surfing – the size and quality of the ocean waves make these islands a hot spot for surfing. Relax on the beautiful deserted white sand beaches to get your breath back. The archeological remains – Oipona, on the island of Hiva Oa, is one of the most impressive sites presided over by a 7-foot stone tiki (statue) called Takaii, two large paepae (stone platforms), eighteen stone sculptures and two carved boulders. Another important site is the Taaoa Valley.
YOU SHOULD KNOW:
The islands are busiest in July and August, so book accommodation in advance for these months.

*A church service
on Tubuai*

Austral Islands

POPULATION:
6,700 (2002)
WHEN TO GO:
Any time – the islands enjoy a cooler
climate than Tahiti, but the warmest
season (November to February) is
also the wettest.
HOW TO GET THERE:
There are three flights a week from
Tahiti to Rurutu, Tubuai and Raivavae.
Or spend a couple of days on the
ocean – the supply ship *Tuhaa Pae II*
sails three times a month from Tahiti
(but only visits distant Rapa every six
weeks).
HIGHLIGHTS:
The aamoraa ofai ceremony on
Rurutu each January and July, when
youngsters from different villages
prove themselves by lifting heavy
stones – followed by exuberant
dancing and feasting.
Old hilltop fortresses (*pas*) and
religious gathering places (*maraes*)
on Rapa Island.
Close-up whale watching from the
cliffs of Rurutu between July
and November.
Elaborate hats, mats and bags woven
by islanders from pandanus and
coconut leaves. Also traditional wood
and stone carvings.
YOU SHOULD KNOW:
Canoes in the Austral Islands are the
only ones in Polynesia with
outriggers on the right-hand side.

At the southern extremity of French Polynesia's far-flung island collective, spread across some 1,280 km (800 mi) of ocean and straddling the Tropic of Capricorn, lie the Austral Islands. There are two distinct volcanic archipelagos. The Tubuai Islands consist of Iles Maria, Rimatara, Rurutu, Tubuai and Raivavae. The Bass Islands are Rapa and Marotiri, plus various uninhabited islets. Their combined land area is a mere 300 sq km (115 sq mi).

The remote Australs are largely self-sufficient and definitely not the place for those who like creature comforts. There are no resorts, and only four islands (Rurutu, Tubuai, Raivavae and Rapa) offer accommodation in small guest-houses and family pensions. These rather bare volcanic high islands are not even the prettiest in the South Pacific, though in truth some (notably Tubuai and Raivavae) have reefs and lagoons that are the equal of any in Polynesia. But those seeking a classic resort holiday must look elsewhere, because the Australs offer something completely different.

It's almost like stepping into a time machine and travelling backwards into the Polynesia discovered by Europeans centuries ago. The inhabitants live simply in villages where the houses and churches are often constructed in coral limestone. They catch fish, grow coffee, arrowroot, tobacco and coconuts, unworried by the cares of the modern world. Very religious, they have preserved the old rituals, celebrations, dance and polyphonic singing, giving the Australs an authenticity and traditional quality of life that can hardly fail to impress the adventurous traveller, who will be warmly welcomed to share (and respect) it. That's the reason for coming, and there couldn't be a better one.

Maui

Maui is the second largest of the islands in the Hawaiian Island chain, standing at 1,883 sq km (727 sq mi), and is also known as 'The Valley Isle'. Formed by six volcanoes, the islands of Maui, Lanai, Kahoolawe and Molokai were originally known as Maui Nui and were one landmass, which has since been separated by rising sea levels.

The shallow waters created by these sunken valleys provide excellent shelter to breeding humpback whales that can often been seen from the shore with their calves. The warm shallow waters are also host to huge numbers of fish and expanses of coral, making this a snorkelers' paradise.

The historic whaling village of Lahainha, on the west of the island, is a must-see. Steeped in history, the town was the home of King Kamehameha I, and later made the capital in 1790. It was also home to missionaries from 1824 who brought with them their religion and education for the masses but also measles and small pox. Today it is a bustling tourist town with a multitude of shops selling souvenirs and sea cruises. Ride the Lahainha Kaanapali Railroad, often referred to as Sugar Cane Train the only train in the whole of Hawaii, between Lahainha and Kaanapali for a different view of the island.

Haleakala National Park, famous for its endangered silversword plant, protects 122 sq km (47 sq mi) of land from the peaks of Haleakala, down to sea level along the Kipahulu coast. You'll need to purchase a pass on arrival at the park, but it is well worth it. For a swim, head down to the southeast part of the island to visit the Ohe'o Gulch, or Seven Sacred Pools. This stunning series of waterfalls and plunge pools progresses for four miles down to sea level and is often busy by the afternoon, so get there early.

POPULATION:
118,000 (2002)
WHEN TO GO:
Arrive between December and April and witness the majestic humpback whales breeding season.
DON'T MISS:
An authentic evening at a *luau* with traditional dancing and food.
YOU SHOULD KNOW:
Maui was voted 'the best island in the world' by independent travel magazine, *Condé Nast Traveller*.

Lava, palm trees and waterfalls blend in perfect harmony at the Seven Sacred Pools of Haleakala National Park.

Kauai

POPULATION:
58,303 (2000)
WHEN TO GO:
January, or September to November.
HOW TO GET THERE:
Fly from Honolulu, California
or Arizona.
HIGHLIGHTS:
The beaches around Poipu, near the
southern tip of the island, are perfect
for snorkelling and diving.
The Huleia National Wildlife Refuge –
for native wild birds and animals.
Wailua Falls – this 60 m (173 ft)
waterfall has three spouts of water. In
ancient times, Hawaiian men would
jump from the top of the falls to prove
their manhood.
The Na Pali coast – the scenery is
spectacular here and the best way to
explore is by hiring a 4 wheel drive.
Alternatively, book a helicopter ride
over the coast for a view from above.
The Kauai Museum – located in the
old part of Lihue, it features the
history, geography and culture of
the island.
YOU SHOULD KNOW:
Large parts of *Jurrassic Park, Fantasy
Island, Raiders of the Lost Ark*, the
original *King Kong* and *6 Days and 7
Nights* were filmed here.

*A beach on the spectacular
Na Pali coast*

Kauai is the northernmost of Hawaii's major islands which make up a volcanic archipelago in the Central Pacific. Known as 'the Garden Island', it is covered by tropical lush greenery due to its abundant rainfall. Because it is the oldest of the islands, formed more than six million years ago, it has been changed the most by erosion which has created some spectacular natural wonders such as Waimea Canyon and the Na Pali Coast. The island is less developed and more laid back than some of the other Hawaiian islands. This makes it popular with visitors and Hawaiians alike. It is also home to more white sandy beaches than any other major island in Hawaii..

The north and east coasts of Kauai are on the windward side of the island, where the winds blow onto the shore and deposit the most rain. These are the most lush and tropical sides of the island. By contrast, the south and west sides are sunnier and drier.

West Kauai is littered with spectacular natural wonders. Waimea Canyon, which has been likened to the Grand Canyon, is the main draw. At over 16 km (10 mi) long and an awe-inspiring 1,098 m (3,600 ft) deep, it is enormous. Carved over hundreds of thousands of years by runoff from Mount Waialeale, the canyon shows millions of years of geological history. The colours of its rocks rival that of its Arizona counterpart, except that Waimea Canyon also has touches of green. Also on the western side of the island is Kalalau Valley. Don't miss the views into the valley at sunset when the walls reflect beautiful shades of pink, orange, red and grey.

On the sunny south side of the island is the National Tropical Botanical Garden, home to a wide collection of colourful tropical plants. Nearby is Spouting Horn, named after the howling geyser effect created when water rushes into a series of natural lava tubes.

In the north is Hanalei Bay, a spectacular crescent of sandy beach at the foot of a sheer cliff. The town has good restaurants and shops, making this a great place for chilling out on the beach. Further west, the Na Pali coast is known for its lush valleys, enormous jagged cliffs towering above the ocean, lava tubes and caves, and its unspoilt, pristine beaches. The Na Pali coast State Park was formed to protect the Kalalau Valley, where overgrown gorges drop dramatically into the sea 1,219 m (4,000 ft) below. The park is a wonderful place for hiking or kayaking, and a helicopter ride over the awe-inspiring scenery is a truly memorable experience.

Kiritimati Island

Feel like a trip to London and Paris? You'll find both on Kiritimati in mid-Pacific, also known as Christmas Island (Captain Cook arrived on 24 December 1777, in 'naming' mood). The world's largest coral atoll extends to a substantial 640 sq km (247 sq mi) and makes up 70 per cent of the land area in the scattered island republic of Kiribati. Its villages are London, Tabwakea, Banana, Poland and Paris (now sadly in ruins). And no, you don't have to take a Geiger counter – the radiation from Britain's 1950s H-bomb tests on Maiden Island, 320 km (200 mi) south of Kiritimati, has long dissipated on the four winds.

Many place names on Kiritimati date from the tenure of Emmanuel Rougier, a French priest who leased the island between the two World Wars, planting nearly a million coconut trees as his contribution to the islanders' future. London is the main village and has a modern port facility handling exports like coconuts, copra, seaweed and tropical saltwater aquarium fish. There is little tourism, because the island is a long way from anywhere and – despite some good beaches and a splendid lagoon – doesn't have much to offer that's worth going that far for, other than sport fishing and the opportunity to observe millions of nesting seabirds.

There is a hotel, but most of the Micronesian inhabitants live without electricity, running water or sanitation. This is one of the most primitive places on earth, but the people are very friendly and live a traditional community life, sheltered by thatched huts skilfully constructed from coconut palms and pandanus trees, subsisting on coconut products and the fruits of the sea.

POPULATION:
5,000 (2005)
WHEN TO GO:
Any time, as there is no rainy season (indeed little rain at all). Avoid El Niño periods if you're a bird watcher – the birds vanish.
HOW TO GET THERE:
The weekly Aloha Airline flight from Honolulu to Cassidy International Airport (a three-and-a-half hour flight). Cruise ships visit frequently.
HIGHLIGHTS:
A lung-bursting climb to see the panoramic view from the island's highest point, La colline de Joe (Joe's Hill), at a dizzying 12m (40 ft) above sea level.
Fly fishing in the lagoon for that most prized of quarry species – bonefish.
Colourful cultural presentations to visitors from cruise ships on the main wharf at London – or uninhibited singing and dancing that takes place with the slimmest excuse.
The renowned Cook Islet Bird Sanctuary at the entrance to the enclosed lagoon.
YOU SHOULD KNOW:
This is the first inhabited place on earth to see in each New Year.

The world's largest coral atoll

533

One of Tarawa's beautiful islets

Tarawa Island

This Micronesian atoll in the central Pacific used to be the capital of the British Gilbert and Ellis Islands, now fulfilling the same role for the Republic of Kiribati, an island nation of 33 atolls spread over 3,500,000 sq km (1,350,000 sq km) of otherwise empty sea. Kiribati extends north and south of the Equator, also east and west of the International Date Line.

Tarawa consists of a reef shaped like a rough triangle enclosing a lagoon, the eastern side of which is submerged and the remainder is made up of 24 thin islets, not all of which are connected. The largest is South Tarawa, extending along most of the lagoon's south side. Tarawa supports many more people than the basic way of life generally practised by the Kiribatis should allow, even though some have been relocated to other islands to ease the pressure. The majority are concentrated on South Tarawa, which only has an area of 16 sq km (6 sq mi). Despite an influx of foreign aid, this has led to problems of overcrowding, unemployment and poor health.

However, that does mean that many of Tarawa's other islets are uncrowded (some are unihabited) and these typical tropical treasures may be explored by boat. However, whilst accommodation is available (from a luxury hotel down to basic guest-houses), this is not a tourist destination. That doesn't mean it isn't interesting, if only because it demonstrates what real life can be like for tens of thousand of Pacific islanders where the magic wand of tourism has yet to wave.

One of the bloodiest battles in World War II's Pacific Theatre took place on Tarawa in 1943, when US marines landed and were met by 4,500 well-prepared Japanese defenders, who fought almost to the last man.

POPULATION:
29,500 (2007 estimate)
WHEN TO GO:
To avoid the heaviest rains, visiting in May to October is recommended.
HOW TO GET THERE:
Fly Air Nauru from Australia to Bonriki International Airport on South Tarawa.
HIGHLIGHTS:
Numerous World War II relics dating from the Japanese occupation.
Canoe racing in the lagoon off South Tarawata.
Ambo Islet, with its beautiful beach and the famous Ambo Lagoon Club.
The good diving and snorkelling in the lagoon and all around the eastern islets.
YOU SHOULD KNOW:
Visitors to Kiribati require a visa.

Chuuk Islands

This island group is a quarter of the Federated States of Micronesia, and the FSM's most populous state. It consists of more than 40 islands, some 15 of which are inside the main lagoon. There are five sets of outer islands – the Upper and Lower Mortlocks to the south, the Western Islands, the Hall Islands and Nomwin Atoll to the north. The outer islands need be of little concern to the visitor, as they can be reached only with great difficulty and have no tourist facilities.

The lagoon islands are another matter. Chuuk (sometimes called Truk) Lagoon has a diameter of 80 km (50 mi), and is up to 90 m (300 ft) deep. Reef diving alone would be rewarding, but the lagoon's true surprise is the 'Graveyard of the Pacific' – hundreds of wrecks including submarines, warships, freighters and planes that have lain undisturbed on the seabed since a fierce battle between the Japanese Imperial Fleet and American carrier planes in 1944. Over time, these have become an amazing underwater museum, where wrecks have become breathtaking coral gardens that provide a happy hunting ground for hundreds of exotic marine fish and animals. The phrase 'divers' heaven' is frequently used, and fully justified.

Life on the lagoon islands hasn't changed much for centuries. Weno is the main island, and has the airport, whilst other significant islands are Tonoas, Fefen, Uman and Udot. Through a combination of circumstances – extreme distance from anywhere and tourism centred on diving, whose participants are more interested in action than luxury accommodation – the islands have remained remarkably unspoiled, with islanders living peacefully on the fruits of nature and their own husbandry. The result, for those willing to make the not inconsiderable effort needed to get there, is enchanting.

POPULATION:
53,000 (2004)
WHEN TO GO:
The best time to visit is January to March, when there is generally little rainfall.
HOW TO GET THERE:
Fly from Hawaii on the island-hopper, or go via Guam.
HIGHLIGHTS:
Warrior masks and busts carved by islanders, who also make a selection of beautifully woven traditional goods.
Sapuk Lighthouse, built by the Japanese in the 1930s, with a superb view of the strategic northeast reef passage. Also marvel at the huge World War II guns nearby.
An incomparable panorama of the Chuuk Islands from Tonachau Mountain atop Weno, legendary home of the god Souwoniras and his divine son.
Tonata guns and caves, as a fine example of the many fortifications dating from World War II when Chuuk was a major Japanese base.
Nemwes and Fouman Rocks on Udot Island, symbolic sites that recall ancient rivalries between Chuuk and the Yap Islands.
YOU SHOULD KNOW:
The local courtship ritual involves unique tokens known as 'Chuukese Love Sticks' (don't ask).

The waters around Chuuk are often described as a diver's heaven.

Pohnpei

POPULATION:
35,000 (2007 estimate)
WHEN TO GO:
The (very) rainy season (July to October) is best avoided – otherwise the warm, tropical climate doesn't vary much.
HOW TO GET THERE:
By air, at considerable expense, flying Continental Micronesia from Guam. Or island-hop from Hawaii.
HIGHLIGHTS:
Nan Madol on Temwen Island, off Pohnpei's eastern shore, sometimes called the "Venice of the Pacific" – a network of canals and artificial islands covered in imposing stone ruins that date back to the 12th and 13th centuries.
The impressive Liduduhniap Twin Waterfalls on the Nanpil River, near Kolonia.
Kolonia's Spanish Wall, built in 1899 as part of Fort Alphonso XII, and the nearby Catholic Mission Bell Tower, all that remains of a church demolished by the Japanese in World War II.
A glass (one should be enough) of numbing sakau, a local drink made from pepper root used in traditional ceremonies and now sold in most bars.
YOU SHOULD KNOW:
Waterproof clothing is de rigueur – Pohnpei is one of the wettest places on earth with annual rainfall of 1,000 cm (400 in).

The ruins of Nan Madol

Micronesia's Federated States of Micronesia (FSM) consists of some 600 small islands spread across nearly 2,900,000 sq km (1,100,000 sq mi) of the Western Pacific just above the Equator. For all that, the FSM can only muster around 700 sq km (270 sq mi) of terra firma. The four states are Pohnpei, Chuuk, Kosrae and Yap. Each consists of one or more main high volcanic islands, with all but Kosrae including numerous outlying atolls.

Pohnpei is the FSM's largest island, with a circumference of 130 km (80 mi). It hosts a mixed population – as home to the national government, it has attracted employees from other states to join a hotch-potch of different Pacific islanders, Japanese, Americans, Australians and Europeans who have settled over the years. In addition to Pohnpei itself, whose reef encloses 25 islets and has eight atolls, the state consists of another 137 widely scattered atolls. Kolonia on the north coast is the island's commercial centre and capital.

Most of Pohnpei's shoreline is covered in mangrove swamps, but artificial beaches have been created on the mainland and reef atolls have excellent natural beaches. The island is rich in unspoiled coral reefs that delight divers and snorkelers, whilst a reef aperture known as Palikir Pass has acquired a well-deserved reputation as a surfing hotspot. Rugged mountain terrain and luxuriant rain forest cover the interior of the island, rising to the high point of Mount Nahnu Laud 788 m (2,585 ft). There are some fine nature trails and trekking opportunities, with numerous rushing streams, waterfalls and cooling plunge pools to enjoy along the way.

This is an island where tourists are welcomed by friendly people, that retains much original character simply because it has not yet become a well-known international resort destination. Enjoy!

Kosrae

This is said to be Micronesia's most remote destination and, unlike the other three Federated States of Micronesia, Kosrae has no outlying atolls. It is a high volcanic island extending to some 110 sq km (42 sq mi) in area with steep contours and dense vegetation that have prevented development. The island is sometimes called 'the sleeping lady' because it appears to have the female form when viewed from the sea. It is surrounded by coral reefs that are carefully protected against damage. More than 170 species of hard coral have been identified, plus ten soft corals, and the reefs and lagoons are home to over 250 different types of fish and marine animal. The Utwe-Walung Marine Park preserves untouched forest and mangrove ecosystems.

The island government is the main employer, and though the inhabitants continue to rely on traditional farming and fishing for subsistence, imported goods now meet their wider needs. They used to live in family groups surrounding a communal cookhouse, but this practice is in decline. For all that the 21st century has crept in, the islanders still delight in traditional singing, chanting, weaving, woodcarving, canoe building and house construction. They are extremely devout and welcome visitors warmly.

There are a few small resorts, but you won't be sharing the beauties of Kosrae with many others – this is the island that mass tourism has yet to discover. The visitors who do make it are inevitably captivated, and some do no more than unwind from the hectic pace of the modern world – sunbathing, snorkelling, meeting islanders and eating wholesome food. Others dive on the reefs and wrecks, or trek into the lush interior and discover the island's rich archaeological heritage. Whatever their preference, not one is disappointed by this wondrous tropical island.

Mangrove swamps and hanging tree ferns on Kosrae

POPULATION:
7,700 (2007 estimate)
WHEN TO GO:
December to April is the best time, July to October the wettest.
HOW TO GET THERE:
It's best to travel via Guam from whence (if you want to 'do' all four of the FSM's states) a 'Visit Micronesia' pass is available. Or go the other way on Continental's island-hopper flights from Hawaii.
HIGHLIGHTS:
The extended hike to the top of majestic Mount Finkol.
The remains of two 19th century whalers, *Henrietta* and *Waverly* – the former was burned in Okat Harbour as reprisal after crew members molested local women.
Exploring atmospheric mangrove swamps by canoe.
Spotting bottleneck dolphins and the occasional whale.
YOU SHOULD KNOW:
The last buccaneer, the American William 'Bully' Haynes, was shipwrecked here in 1874 – and is said to have buried his treasure here – it has never been found...

Babeldaob Island

POPULATION:
4,500 (2007 estimate)
WHEN TO GO:
At any time, though the monsoon season (June to October) does see intense rainfall almost every day.
HOW TO GET THERE:
Various international carriers fly in to Koror-Babeldaob Airport, often via Guam.
HIGHLIGHTS:
Paluan storyboards – traditional wood carvings depicting local myths and legends.
The bai (men's meeting house) in Airai, said to be the world's oldest.
Lake Ngardok near Melekeok, the largest natural freshwater lake in Micronesia – and home to crocodiles.
The many mysterious stone monoliths around Ngarchelong Province, in the north of the island.
The scenic Taki Falls at Ngardmau on the west coast.
YOU SHOULD KNOW:
Palauans have traditionally operated a matrilineal society where titles, land and property pass through the female line to eldest daughters.

This is the largest island in the Micronesian Republic of Palau, one of the world's youngest and smallest nations (independent only since 1994). Unlike many far-flung Pacific nations, Paulau's islands are well grouped, some 800 km (500 mi) east of the Philippines. Palau is mostly flat, but Babeldaob (also known as Babelthuap) is mountainous and contains the country's highest point, Mount Ngerchelchuus 242 m (794 ft) tall. It also has over two-thirds of the country's land mass and the main airport is there.

For many years, Babeldaob played second fiddle to its immediate neighbour, the urbanized Koror Island. But the recent construction of a bridge connecting the two (replacing one that collapsed) and a new highway that rings Babeldaob has altered the relationship. The new capital, Melekeok, is on Babeldaob and the island has been opened up for rapid economic exploitation and the promotion of tourism. This major infrastructure project has been controversial, as it will degrade the ecology of an environmental treasure – the Ngermeskang River (Micronesia's largest), its estuary and Ngaremeduu Bay. The designation of a large conservation area may not be enough to limit damage, but therein lies the dilemma of many small, poverty-stricken Pacific nations – an unspoiled environment and poverty, or development and improved living standards?

The decision has been made here, for better or worse, with an influx of middle-class professionals from Koror who are building commuter homes, and farmers who are clearing forest and mangrove swamps to plant cash crops. Despite existing tourist facilities, it's still possible to see the islanders living as they always have, by gathering food and fishing, and experience an island that still has extraordinary natural beauty. But hurry – it won't be long before Babeldaob changes almost beyond recognition.

Many mysterious stone monoliths can be found in the north of the island.

Ngercheu Island

Palau is a nation that really does live up to the description 'tropical paradise'. This archipelago consists of 343 islands where major ocean currents of the Pacific and Philippines Sea meet and mingle, creating a wonderful maze of small islands, incredible underwater features and a colourful variety of marine life. This has ensured that Palau, whilst no over-developed Pacific tourist trap, has become one of the world's top destinations for diving and snorkelling.

The famous Rock Islands are a collection of rounded, foliage-covered islets that seem to float above the water, an illusion caused by the fact that they have been undercut by the sea's action over millennia. They are occupied by birds, bats, monkeys and saltwater crocodiles. Ngercheu is right in the middle of the 'Rocks', some 25 km (15 mi) south of Palau's most populous island, Koror. It is a tiny uninhabited island that was developed as the Carp Island Resort, and Ngercheu is now often referred to as Carp Island. It offers panoramic views of the Rock Islands, white sandy beaches and proximity to world-famous dive sites to lure visitors, who stay in the simple accommodation or visit for the day from Koror's more developed tourist facilities. The 'resort' consists of a large central building ringed by thatched cottages and bungalows, and is mainly occupied by those who come not for a luxury beach holiday, but for tempting diving opportunities.

These include named wonders like Manta Ray Point, New Drop-Off, Big Drop-Off, Peleliu Wall (the deepest reef structure in Palau), Blue Hole and Blue Corner – a wonderland of multi-coloured coral, teeming tropical fish, turtles and reef sharks. But divers do require a permit and must be certified.

POPULATION:
Uninhabited
WHEN TO GO:
Any time – the weather matters not to divers. Even the rainy season from June to October generally sees a mixture of sunshine and showers.
HOW TO GET THERE:
By boat from Koror.
HIGHLIGHTS:
For divers – the Ngemelis Wall, considered by many to be the world's finest dive site.
A fascinating variety of bird life. Spectacular sunrises and sunsets over the Rock Islands.
YOU SHOULD KNOW:
The local saltwater crocodiles are not as large or fearsome as their Australian brethren, with only one attack on a human ever reported.

The fantastic formations of the Rock Islands

COUNTRIES